Progress in IS

For further volumes:
http://www.springer.com/series/10440

Karl E. Kurbel

Enterprise Resource Planning and Supply Chain Management

Functions, Business Processes and Software for Manufacturing Companies

Springer

Karl E. Kurbel
European University Viadrina
Faculty of Business Administration and Economics
Chair of Business Informatics
Frankfurt (Oder)
Germany

DOI 10.1007/978-3-642-31573-2
Springer Heidelberg New York Dordrecht London

Printed on acid-free paper

Springer is part of Springer Science+Business Media (www.springer.com/mycopy)

Preface

This book is about running modern industrial enterprises with the help of computer-based information systems.

Enterprise resource planning (*ERP*) is the core of business information processing. In most companies, an ERP system is the backbone of the information systems landscape. All major business processes are handled with the help of this system, and most business transactions are recorded in the ERP system.

Supply chain management (*SCM*) looks beyond the company's borders, taking into account that companies are increasingly concentrating on their core competencies, leaving other activities to partners who have more expertise. With the growing dependency on the partners, effective supply chains have become as important for a company's success as efficient in-house business processes.

This book is organized as follows: Chap. 1 introduces the general topic, including concepts of business processes and important planning and control tasks of an industrial enterprise. Chapters 2 and 3 discuss the major stages in the evolution of enterprise resource planning: material requirements planning (MRP) and manufacturing resource planning (MRP II). While MRP just focuses on the planning of end-product demand and material requirements to satisfy this demand, MRP II deals with the temporal side of production: scheduling manufacturing orders while taking the production capacities into account.

Essential concepts of enterprise resource planning and core business processes supported by ERP systems—such as procurement, order fulfillment, and production—are discussed in Chap. 4. The notation of event-driven process chains (EPCs) is used to illustrate the process flow. While Chap. 4 explains enterprise resource planning and ERP systems in general, Chap. 5 shows how the general concepts are implemented with the help of a particular ERP system—SAP ERP.

This system is widely disseminated across the world. Its vendor, SAP AG, is the world-market leader in enterprise resource planning software. Screenshots exemplifying major steps of the core business processes were taken from our SAP ERP installation and included in the chapter. In this way, the reader can understand how the business processes are actually carried out "in the real world."

Chapter 6 discusses the ERP implementation process. Since an ERP system is "standard software," made for a wide spectrum of businesses, the main challenge here is to adapt the "standard" to the individual company's needs. While the problem statement sounds simple, the solution is extremely complex, requiring companies to spend years in the preparation and implementation.

Chapter 7 highlights the IT environment of enterprise resource planning in the factory: manufacturing execution systems (MES), complementing enterprise resource planning with planning and controlling functionality for the shop floor, and engineering information systems. The latter ones, in particular the so-called *CAx systems* (computer-aided design, computer-aided manufacturing, etc.), are outlined because they have important interfaces with enterprise resource planning.

Chapters 8, 9, and 10 are dedicated to *supply chain management*. Chapter 8 introduces the motivation for SCM and the main issues of coordination and cooperation. A common modeling technique for intercompany business processes, the SCOR model (supply chain operations reference model), is presented, and major tasks of supply chain management on the strategic, planning, and execution levels are discussed.

Chapter 9 is about SCM data structures and advanced planning approaches. Supply chain management requires additional data structures, beyond those known from enterprise resource planning. *APS* (*advanced planning and scheduling*) solutions to typical SCM planning problems are explained. Due to today's powerful computers, APS methods such as linear optimization are increasingly found in SCM systems.

In Chap. 10, a practical solution supporting supply chain management, SAP SCM, is outlined. The core of this system is the so-called *advanced planner and optimizer* (*APO*). As the name suggests, this module provides advanced planning functionality, including optimization. A number of screenshots from SAP SCM have been included that illustrate selected problems and solutions computed by the APO.

Finally, Chapter 11 outlines current and future trends that are expected to have an impact on future ERP and SCM systems, such as software-as-a-service (SaaS), cloud computing, and ERP on demand. Another major impact will probably come from the so-called Internet of Things (IoT), based on RFID (radio frequency identification). RFID applications are already influencing not only business operations but also our private lives.

This book is not only the author's achievement but has been made possible through the work of other people. I am particularly thankful to Elvira Fleischer for creating most of the figures; Olga Stawnicza for carrying out many business transactions in our SAP University Alliances installation of SAP ERP and SAP SCM, to create the screenshots included in this book; Dr. Anke Gericke for contributing several screenshots from the BOC Technologies' ADONIS and ADOlog suites; Prof. Dr. Markus Nüttgens for his comments on my event-driven process chains; Dr. Michael Muschiol for his help regarding engineering information systems; and Sarah Van Horne for proofreading, revising, and improving my manuscript.

Finally, I want to thank my wife Kirti for her understanding and support over the 2 years—including many weekends filled with work—that it took to complete the book.

Karl E. Kurbel

Contents

1 Business Information Systems

The basic questions we will answer in this book are as follows: What are the core information systems a business firm needs today, what do these systems do, and how can they be used effectively?

Information systems are the foundation of doing business today, implying that most business firms would not be able to operate without their information systems (Kurbel 2008, p. 3). Although we will be focusing on the manufacturing industry, many of the fundamental principles, methods, and technologies discussed in this book are applicable to other types of organization as well. Enterprise resource planning, in particular, is a very comprehensive approach supporting all kinds of business processes. It covers not only the needs of the manufacturing industry, but also the needs of most other industries, including the financial sector and other service companies.

Most tasks in today's business organizations are supported by software systems. The preferred term for these systems in academia is *information system (IS)*. Practitioners more commonly speak of business software, application software (application system, application package), or just application.

A general definition of the term information system is as follows (Kurbel 2008, p. 4): An *information system (IS)* is a computer-based system that processes inputted information or data, stores information, retrieves information, and produces new information to solve its task automatically or to support human beings in the operation, control, and decision making of an organization.

1.1 The Evolution of ERP and SCM

The roots of enterprise resource planning (ERP) and supply chain management (SCM) go back to the 1960s when computers were first used for solving business problems. To promote the sales of their hardware, the big computer manufacturers would develop application software in addition to the computer hardware.

For production companies, computer vendors offered software for *material requirements planning (MRP)*—so-called MRP systems or MRP packages. MRP systems were rather sophisticated compared to other types of business software available at the time. Most of this software exhibited only simple processing logic, merely transforming input data into output data. In MRP, both the planning problems and the data structures were far more complex.

The core of MRP was planning the material requirements that corresponded to a given production program. The fundamental questions in MRP were as follows: (1) Which materials and which quantities of these materials (= *secondary*

K.E. Kurbel, *Enterprise Resource Planning and Supply Chain Management*,
Progress in IS, DOI 10.1007/978-3-642-31573-2_1, © Springer-Verlag Berlin Heidelberg 2013

or *derived requirements*) are needed to produce a given production program (= *primary requirements*)? (2) How can the material requirements be fulfilled?

Notwithstanding the simple nature of these questions, answering them required a great deal of computation and the consideration of many details. This is mainly due to the complex structure of industrial products and the large number of items contained in real-world bills of materials. Manufacturing companies benefited from MRP systems because the computational effort to calculate reasonable secondary requirements was substantially reduced.

However, good material planning is not the same as good production planning. It is a necessary but not a sufficient condition for a good production plan—not even for a feasible one. Although MRP is about planning the quantities of the materials needed, implicit assumptions are made regarding the production dates. Producing the planned quantities of all materials within the given time period is only possible if the production capacities are available exactly at the times when they are needed. This means, for example, that the right machines must be available whenever production orders request them. Since machine loading and scheduling of production orders are not considered during material requirements planning, it is highly unlikely that capacities will be available at the time that they are needed.

The next steps in the evolution lead from MRP to *closed loop MRP* and *MRP II*, explicitly including capacity requirements planning and scheduling of production orders into the planning approach. MRP II, according to its founder Oliver Wight, is an abbreviation of *manufacturing resource planning* (no longer of material requirements planning), indicating that all necessary resources have to be considered in the planning, not only the materials. Following Wight, MRP II is a "... comprehensive market and resource oriented planning of the sales, production and stock levels, which begins at the executive level" (Wight 1984, pp. 53–54).

Information systems for MRP II, so-called *MRP II* systems, were widely disseminated. In most manufacturing companies, an MRP II system became the firm's core information system, supporting not only the planning and controlling of materials, capacities, and production orders but also other business areas such as procurement, cost calculation, sales, and production data acquisition.

However, the fundamental idea of MRP II, that is, to include *all* resources that are relevant for the success of a company in the planning, was not really implemented. There are more business areas than those directly related with production that contribute to the company's success.

Enterprise resource planning (ERP) as the next step in the evolution closed this gap and also took into account that there are other industries besides manufacturing. These industries also need powerful information systems to be able to do their business effectively. ERP systems are cross industry systems supporting all major business processes within a wide range of company types. They include MRP II functionality (for manufacturing firms) and general business functionality such as accounting, controlling, financial planning, and human resources for all types of businesses.

The term "enterprise resource planning" was coined in the 1990s by vendors of business software such as SAP, PeopleSoft, Baan, and others. It was obviously an allusion or follow-up to "manufacturing resource planning," indicating that all resources of an enterprise, not only those needed for manufacturing, are covered by the approach.

With the emergence of ERP systems, the former MRP II systems "disappeared." Some of them were simply renamed (from MRP II to ERP); others became parts of larger ERP systems. Nowadays, an ERP system constitutes the information system backbone of most organizations across all industries.

Although enterprise resource planning is a very comprehensive approach, it has its limits. More and more companies today are concentrating on their core competencies, leaving other activities to partners who have more expertise. In the manufacturing industry, this means that a company does not produce all intermediate goods in-house, but obtains them from suppliers. The suppliers do the same, that is, they buy parts and assemblies from their suppliers. In this way, the in-house production depth is significantly reduced, but the company's dependence on the supply chains is increased. Nowadays, effective supply chains have become at least as important for a company's success as efficient in-house business processes.

This shift of focus from optimizing internal processes to improving intercompany processes gave rise to the field of *supply chain management (SCM),* both in research and in practice. Supply chain management stresses the collaboration between partners in a supply chain, including intensive information exchange and harmonization of the partners' respective procurement, production, and distribution plans.

Information systems supporting supply chain management *(SCM systems)* were developed both by ERP vendors and by software companies specialized in logistics. The former either extended their ERP systems with additional SCM functionality or developed new SCM systems that collaborate with their ERP systems. Software companies developed dedicated SCM systems and in addition provided interfaces to common ERP systems. The reason for this is that SCM without ERP is hardly possible.

A trend that could be observed in the past was that some specialized SCM vendors were acquired by large ERP vendors. In this way, the ERP vendors are now able to offer supply chain management as a part of their business software portfolio.

Planning in supply chain management looks beyond the limits of the individual company, extending to the entire supply chain (or supply network). Procurement, production, and distribution are planned both within the company and across the companies involved in the supply chains. In this way, a company further down a supply chain will be able to consider the impact of a capacity bottleneck occurring with one of the partners further up the chain in their own procurement, production, and distribution planning.

A large number of mathematical models and methods including heuristic approaches have been proposed for optimization problems in MRP, MRP II, and later in SCM. While the early optimization models could not be solved with the computers of the time when problems of real-world dimensions were considered, optimization has become feasible in the meantime. This is due to the fact that powerful information technology and advanced mathematical and heuristic methods are available today. These approaches are often summarized under the name *APS (advanced planning and scheduling).*

1.2 Business Application Software

In the beginning of business computing, most application systems were designed to solve a specific problem or support a particular function, such as material requirements planning, payroll, or financial accounting. These systems were stand-alone systems, developed only to solve or support the task at hand. The "islands" were not connected with one another.

A typical enterprise today uses a large number of information systems. These systems tend to be integrated so that they can work together. All major business processes are represented and executed with the help of information systems.

Fewer and fewer companies use systems that they developed themselves. Instead, they work with *standard software*, customized and extended to their needs. The term standard software, also called standard or application package, denotes a software system that was developed with the aim of being used by many organizations. Standard software exists for many problem areas: enterprise resource planning, supply chain management, office work, database management, etc. In the business field, the term *business software* is also used.

A typical configuration of business software in a manufacturing company comprises at least three large systems as shown in Fig. 1.1: an enterprise resource planning system, a supply chain management system, and a customer relationship management (CRM) system. All are built on top of one or more database management systems (DBMS)—ideally using the same logically integrated database.

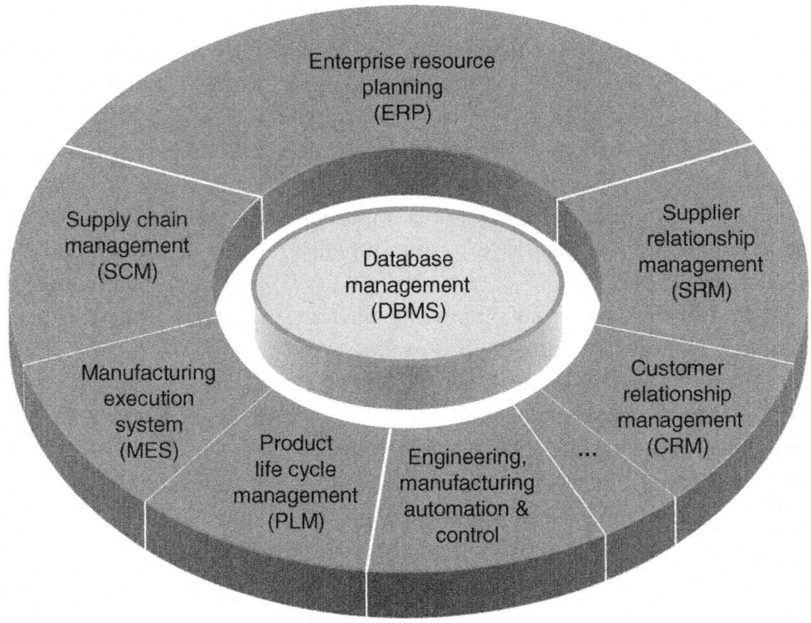

Fig. 1.1 Core application systems of a manufacturing company

The ERP, SCM, and CRM systems are usually standard software that has been customized according to the requirements of the individual organization. Nowadays, these three types of systems tend to be integrated: An SCM module, for example, will have access to information available in the ERP system directly or through a common database.

Since ERP and SCM are the main topics of this book, they will be explained in more detail later. At this point, only the other core application systems shown in Fig. 1.1 are briefly described.

Customer Relationship Management Customer relationship management (CRM) is an integrated approach to identifying, acquiring, and retaining customers. The following discussion of CRM is adopted from (Kurbel 2008, pp. 13–15).

Some authors consider good customer relations the most valuable asset of a business firm. While marketing and management have always placed high importance on customer relationships, business information systems have not supported this view until the late 1990s. Previously, valuable customer information was distributed and maintained in various information systems—in the ERP system, in e-commerce, call center, customer-service systems, and more.

The need to place the focus on customer relationships emerged when marketing, sales, and service departments developed new channels beyond traditional ones such as retail stores and field sales: websites (electronic shops), e-mail ordering, call centers, mobile commerce, push services, etc. As the number of sources of customer information increased, redundancies and inconsistencies in the databases also grew. It became increasingly difficult to find, maintain, and update customer information efficiently and consistently.

Analyzing customer data for marketing in a unified way, in order to generate more value for the firm, was not possible. By enabling organizations to manage and coordinate customer interactions across multiple channels, departments, lines of business, and geographical regions, CRM helps organizations increase the value of every customer interaction and improve corporate performance.

A *CRM system* is an information system that is used to plan, schedule, and control the presales and postsales activities in an organization (Finnegan and Willcocks 2007, p. 4). The goal

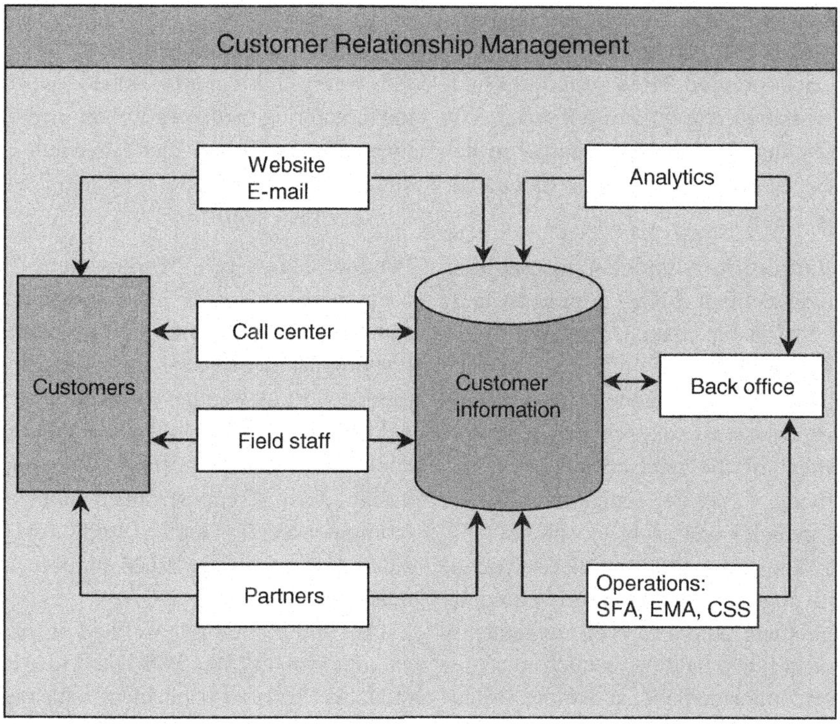

Fig. 1.2 Sources and uses of customer information (Source: Siebel Systems, Inc. (now: Oracle Corp.))

of CRM is to improve long-term growth and profitability through a better understanding of customer behavior. CRM includes all aspects of dealing with current and prospective customers: call center, sales force, marketing, technical support, field service, etc. All customer information from these sources is collected and maintained in a central database as illustrated in Fig. 1.2. This means that the marketing, sales, and service departments access the same information.

A typical "back office" system that the CRM system is connected with is the company's ERP system. CRM systems are sometimes called "front office" systems because they are the interface with the customer.

CRM systems are composed of operational and analytical parts. *Operational CRM* primarily includes support for:

- SFA (sales force automation—e.g., contact/prospect information, product configuration, sales quotes, sales forecasting etc.)
- EMA (enterprise marketing automation—e.g., capturing prospect and customer data, qualifying leads for targeted marketing, scheduling, and tracking direct marketing)
- CSS (customer service and support—e.g., call centers, help desks, customer support staff; web-based self-service capabilities etc.)

Analytical CRM consolidates the data from operational CRM and uses analytical techniques to examine customer behavior; identify buying patterns; create segments for targeted marketing; identify opportunities for cross selling, up-selling, and bundling; and separate profitable and unprofitable customers. This is done with business intelligence techniques such as OLAP (online analytical processing) and data mining, based on a data warehouse (Howson 2008).

In addition to operational and analytical customer relationship management, many CRM systems include components for ERM (employee relationship management) and PRM (partner relationship management). This is due to the fact that employee performance and partner (e.g., dealer) performance are closely related with customer relationships.

CRM and various parts of enterprise resource planning are very tightly connected. That is why ERP vendors also provide CRM systems, which interoperate with their respective ERP systems. It is not surprising that the long-time market leader in CRM, Siebel Systems, was bought by Oracle, a leading ERP vendor.

Supplier Relationship Management Supplier relationship management (SRM) is an equivalent to customer relationship management but in the direction of the company's suppliers.

As in CRM, different channels for procurement exist. SRM systems support administration and management of the relationships with the suppliers in many ways. The functionality of an SRM system includes analyzing existing suppliers; assessing future suppliers, supplier selection, and framework contracts; and monitoring compliance of procurement activities with agreements, requests for quotations, bidding, catalog management, document management, and more. Many SRM systems also support procurement processes, but this is usually the domain of ERP systems.

SRM systems assist supplier relationship management by partly or completely automating the respective tasks, including the collaboration between the firm and its suppliers. Providing technological means such as a supplier portal, SRM systems help to accelerate the exchange of documents (e.g., quotations, orders, and invoices) and of information in general, making the collaboration more effective.

Manufacturing Execution Systems Manufacturing execution systems (MES) support planning and control tasks that are not sufficiently covered by enterprise resource planning and supply chain management systems. A typical MES has three main components:

- *Shop-floor control (SFC)*—covering a rather short period with a granularity of days, hours, or even minutes
- *Quality assurance (QA)*—supporting quality control based on inspection plans, legal regulations, tracking of production batches, etc.
- *Production* and *machine data acquisition (PDA/MDA)*—obtaining and providing feedback regarding the actual state of manufacturing

These components were available as separate application programs before. At the beginning of the twenty-first century, vendors specializing in manufacturing software combined them into integrated systems and invented the name "manufacturing execution system." MES will be discussed in Chap. 7.

Product Life Cycle Management Product life cycle management (PLM) is an approach to manage products and production processes from the first product idea through the entire life cycle of the products. PLM was developed in the engineering field based on technological data and engineering application systems such as CAD (computer-aided design), CAE (computer-aided engineering), CAP (computer-aided planning), and CAM (computer-aided manufacturing). PLM supports all product-related processes.

An important part of PLM is *product data management (PDM)*. PDM has close connections (and overlaps) with business data management. Both ERP and PDM systems store and maintain product data (e.g., bills of materials and product master data).

Product life cycle management (PLM) can be defined as an approach that "... encompasses all aspects of a product from early requirements, through design, into production and service, and finally recovery and disposal" (Active Sensing 2009). PLM software "... serves as a central hub for product data, with associated software systems (CAD, ERP, CRM, SCM) obtaining their product-related information from the PLM system and, in some cases such as CAD, creating information for management within the PLM repository" (Active Sensing 2009).

The overall goal of PLM is to support all stages of the product life cycle through a unified approach, based on consistent models, methods, and tools.

Engineering, Manufacturing Automation, and Control Under the term *engineering application systems*, we summarize systems supporting engineering tasks, including product design (CAD/CAE), work planning (CAP), and manufacturing (CAM). These systems together are often referred to as *CAx systems*.

Systems for *manufacturing automation and control* help to partly or completely automate manufacturing processes. They include CNC (computerized numerical control), flexible manufacturing systems, automated guided vehicle systems, robot control, and more.

Engineering and automation systems are beyond the scope of this book. However, their data and processes have many interfaces with business application systems such as ERP and SCM. Therefore, they will be briefly outlined in Sect. 7.2.

Database Management MRP systems and other early business information systems stored their data in program-related data files. Some quite sophisticated forms of file organization came into existence. With the amount of data growing rapidly, *database management systems (DBMS)* eventually substituted the program-related data organization. Nowadays, all nontrivial business information systems store their data in databases. The following summary is based on (Kurbel 2008, pp. 15–17).

Since the roots of database management systems go back to the 1960s and 1970s, it is not surprising that today's systems have reached a high level of maturity. The functionality of a modern DBMS comprises a lot more than just storing and retrieving data. For example, database schemata can be generated automatically from models. Visual tools for semantic data modeling, creating graphical user interfaces and querying the database as well as workflow management, and much more are provided. In fact, Oracle's core ERP functionality is largely based on tools that use Oracle's database management system. This is not surprising as Oracle Corp. is one of the world's largest DBMS vendors.

A *database management system (DBMS)* is an information system that handles the organization, storage, retrieval, security, and integrity of data in a database. It accepts requests from programs or from end users, processes these requests, and returns a response, e.g., by transferring the requested data.

Most of today's database management systems are relational systems (RDBMSs). With the emergence of object-oriented analysis, design, and programming, RDBMSs were extended to accommodate not only data records but also objects, thus realizing object persistence. Notwithstanding the existence of dedicated object-oriented DBMSs, the majority of business information systems use relational database management systems.

There are many relational database management systems on the market. Oracle (Oracle Database), IBM (DB2), Microsoft (SQL Server), and SAP/Sybase (Adaptive Server Enterprise) have the largest market shares. MySQL and PostgreSQL are popular open-source products. A widely used DBMS for end users, not for large professional business systems, is Microsoft Access.

A major achievement of more than four decades of business information processing was the decoupling of application systems and database management systems. Earlier, the programs of an MRP II or ERP system referenced the DBMS directly. Since each vendor's DBMS implementation had its own extensions and modifications, the application system and the database management system were tightly coupled. Portability of a database—and thus of an entire ERP system—was a difficult, sometimes an impossible task.

Nowadays, an RDBMS supports common interfaces through standard access methods. Programs now invoke operations provided by the interfacing technology instead of directly accessing the database management system. Portability has significantly improved in this way. Standard technologies and access methods include:

- ODBC (open database connectivity)—providing access to databases on a network for Windows programs
- JDBC (Java database connectivity)—allowing Java programs to access a relational database via the SQL language
- JDO (Java data objects)—allowing Java programs to write and read program objects directly to/from any kind of datastore, including relational and object databases, XML, flat files, and others

- Java EE/EJB (Java Enterprise Edition/Enterprise JavaBeans)—giving higher-level access to a database than JDBC, using EJB entity beans
- XML (Extensible Markup Language)—enabling and providing standard access methods for navigation and queries in XML. Data are extracted from a database and put into XML documents and vice versa

Figure 1.1 suggests that there is only one DBMS in the center. This is, however, a rather idealistic scenario, implying that all application systems are using the same database and thus always are in the same consistent state regarding their data.

In practice, this is rarely the case. Many application systems use their own databases, administered by heterogeneous database management systems. This is often what happens when the application software comes from different vendors. In such a case, data integration mechanisms have to be put in place in order to create a logically integrated view of the data on a higher abstraction level. Data integration is a complex field of study that has been intensively investigated in database research.

Provided that the integration efforts have been successful, the logical situation is in fact the same as in Fig. 1.1. Diverse application systems can then access just one virtual database, even though this virtual database is built upon a number of heterogeneous DBMSs administering the real databases.

1.3 Business Processes

Most business work is nowadays planned and executed in the form of business processes. Hammer and Champy stimulated process-oriented thinking with their seminal book on *business process reengineering (BPR)* in 1993 (Hammer and Champy 1993). Since that time, most organizations have changed their business approaches from function oriented toward process oriented.

1.3.1 Processes Versus Functions

The conventional approach to structuring business work and also business organizations was based on *business functions* such as procurement, inventory management, accounting, marketing, and production. Even today, most companies have departments with these or similar names.

On the other hand, most companies have realized that they need to organize their business along the processes they perform. One insight promoted by Hammer, Champy, Davenport, and other authors was that successful companies are process oriented (Hammer and Champy 1993; Davenport 1993). Based on this finding, these authors proposed a complete reorientation and reengineering of the company.

Business process-oriented thinking was not completely new. To our knowledge, one of the first authors to introduce business processes was August-Wilhelm Scheer (1985). He also proposed a modeling technique for business processes that later became known under the name *event-driven process chains (EPCs)*.

Hammer and Champy defined *business process reengineering (BPR)* as "... the fundamental rethinking and radical redesign of business processes to achieve dramatic improvements in critical contemporary measures of performance, such as cost, quality, service, and speed" (Hammer and Champy 1993, p. 32).

The proposed reorientation went far beyond improvements of existing structures, asking for a complete redesign of the company based on business processes. This radical rethinking showed in the title of an early publication on BPR: "Reengineering work—don't automate, obliterate" (Hammer 1990).

Although in practice the majority of organizations did not completely reinvent themselves according to BPR, they adopted the fundamental idea of organizing work along business processes. Nowadays, process orientation is the dominating paradigm both in practice and in business informatics research.

1.3.2 Basic Concepts of Business Processes

Many notions and definitions of the term business process exist. Often the term is used in a very general sense. Hammer and Champy

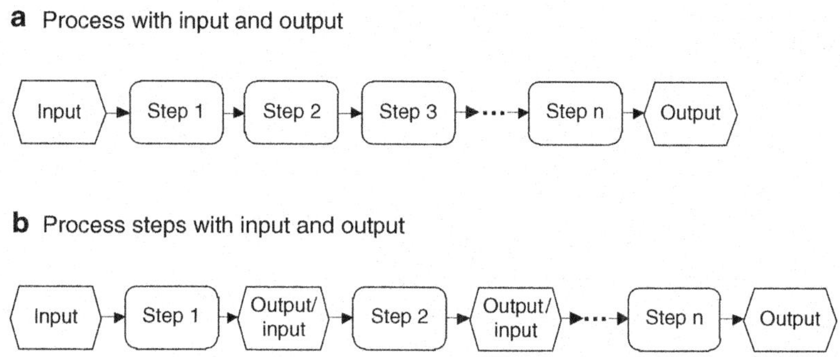

Fig. 1.3 Schematic view of a business process

described a business process as a set of activities that have one or more inputs, creating an output that has value for the customer (Hammer and Champy 1993, p. 35).

Starting from this description, we define the term business process as follows: A *business process* consists of a sequence of steps (process steps, activities), which are executed sequentially or parallel. Each step has a defined input and produces a defined output. Processes may initiate other processes—either subprocesses refining the main process or independent processes. The result of a process is an output that is of value to the company.

The reason why the result of the process is described rather vaguely in the definition is because many different kinds of processes exist. Some are internal processes, while others include external partners, such as customers and suppliers. In a sales process, for example, the value to the company is a happy customer who received their goods on time and is willing to do more business with the company in the future. In a manufacturing process, the value is that the lead times of the released production orders are as short as possible, and scrap ratios are minimized.

Business processes can be described in different languages and graphical notations, for example, BPMN (business process model and notation) (OMG 2011a), EPCs (event-driven process chains) (Mendling 2007, pp. 36–100), YAWL (yet another workflow language) (Russell and ter Hofstede 2009), and activity diagrams in UML (unified modeling language) (Ambler 2009). Many authors also use informal graphical notations.

Figure 1.3 shows a generic business process. In part a of the figure, only the input and the output of the entire process are shown. In part b, the input and the output of each activity are also depicted. The output of one process step serves as input for the next step.

It should be noted that the process scheme shown in the figure is oversimplified. In more realistic cases, any process step can have several inputs and can produce several outputs. The outputs will be used not only in the next process step but also in other steps and processes. In addition, the figure suggests that processes are sequential, which is usually not the case. Many processes have branches that are dependent on conditions and are refined by subprocesses. This will be shown later.

1.3.3 Graphical Notations

Throughout this book, we will mostly use the notation of *event-driven process chains (EPCs)*. The fundamental concepts of an event-driven process chain, which are employed to create a model of the process, are events and functions.

An *event* is a state of the model that is either established as the result of a function or has to be in place so that a function can be executed (Mendling 2007, p. 37). A *function* effectuates a transition from one state to another. In user terminology, functions are also named *activities* or *process steps*. EPCs generally start with an event (starting condition) and end with an event (result of the process).

Figure 1.4 gives an example of a business process (procurement) using the EPC notation. The process is initiated when someone detects a

Fig. 1.4 A simple procurement process in EPC notation

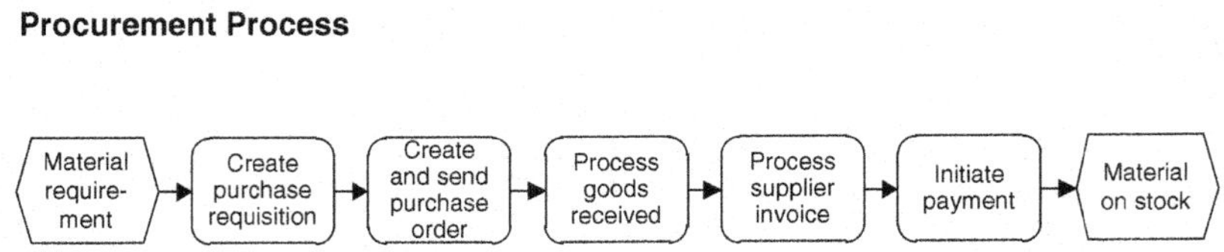

material requirement. The employee responsible for this material creates an internal procurement order. The purchasing department processes this order and perhaps other orders for the same material coming from other departments, combining them into a purchase order that will be sent to the material supplier. After the material has been delivered, incoming goods activities such as quality control are carried out. Then the supplier's invoice is checked, booked, and paid. The result of the process is a positive inventory of this material.

Another common modeling technique is *BPMN (business process model and notation)* (OMG 2011a). BPMN uses similar symbols as EPCs, including events, tasks, and gateways (logical connectors). In contrast to the EPC model, events are only modeled to indicate the start and end of the process and when they provide a notification (message) so that the process can continue.

Figure 1.5 shows the same procurement process as above, with minor extensions, now in BPMN.

Creating process models on paper can be a cumbersome chore, involving plenty of cutting and pasting. Automated tools allow the user to create electronic models instead of paper models. The more advanced a tool is, the more semantic support is available to the user. While simple drawing tools (e.g., MS Visio) provide little more than just the necessary symbols, professional modeling toolsets are also capable of giving semantic support.

A common toolset providing, among many other things, event-driven process chains is the *ARIS platform*, nowadays offered by Software AG, Darmstadt (Germany) (Software AG 2012).

BPMN modeling is supported by various tools. The model shown in Fig. 1.5 was created with *ADONIS*, a business process modeling toolset offered by BOC Information Technologies Consulting AG, Vienna (Austria) (BOC 2012b). In Sect. 4.3.7, another model created with this toolset will be presented.

The process used above as an example, *procurement,* is one of the typical business processes found in any company and industry. Another important process is *order fulfillment.* It covers all steps, starting with a customer inquiry and continuing with quotation, all the way to the delivery of the product and invoicing the customer. *Production* is the core process of any manufacturing company. All three processes, procurement, order fulfillment, and production, will be explained in more detail in Chaps. 4 and 5.

1.4 Production Planning and Control

Production planning and control has a long history, both in research and in industry. In *operations research (OR)*, production planning problems have been investigated since the 1950s. The first business application systems beyond simple accounting and payroll software in the 1960s were MRP systems. Later, MRP II systems supported not only manufacturing-related tasks but also included more and more business functionality, such as cost calculation, procurement, dispatching, and human resources management.

Despite several decades of research and development, many of the planning problems have not been completely solved. This is due to the fact that some of the problems are just too difficult. On the other hand, new challenges and new opportunities have emerged as a result of technological advances, increased personal mobility, and the extended scope of doing business in today's world. Altogether, many problems have yet to be solved.

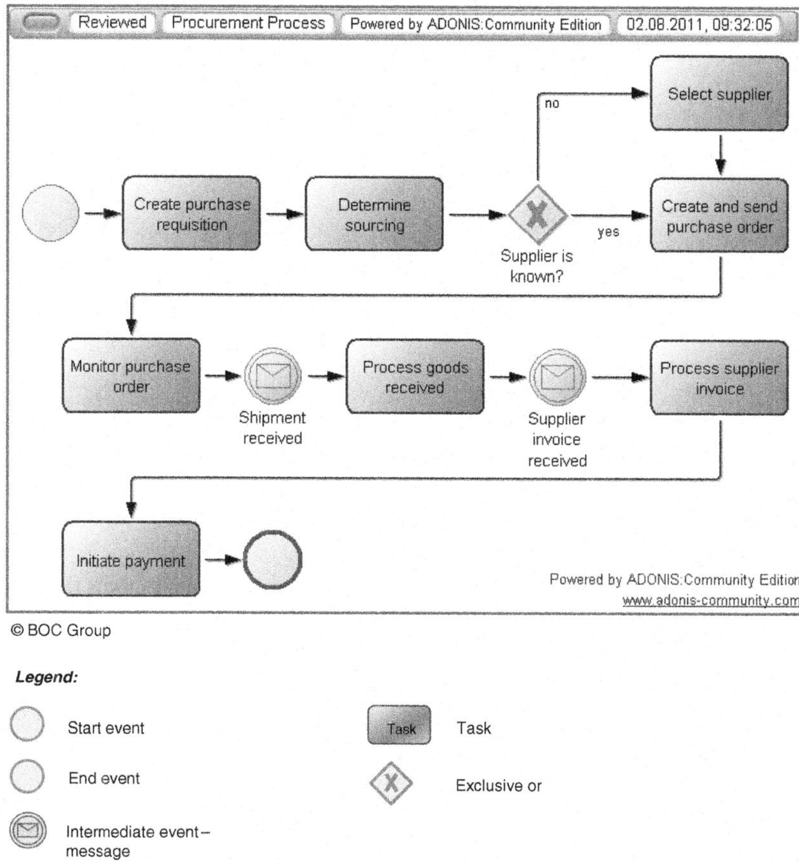

Fig. 1.5 A simple procurement process in BPMN

1.4.1 Tasks of Production Planning and Control

The term production planning and control summarizes a wide range of decision problems. Some decisions have very long-term consequences (such as the company's locations and product program), while others have midrange consequences (such as the manufacturing capacities) or affect very short-term time periods (such as job sequences).

A common approach is to assign the different types of problems to different planning levels: a strategic level and an operative level. On the strategic level, fundamental decisions with long-term consequences are made. On the operative level, where the overall manufacturing conditions are given, decisions are made about the product quantities and the manufacturing process.

The term production planning and control usually refers to operative planning and control. On this level, the tasks of *production planning* are to determine:

- Which quantities of which end products are to be produced within the planning period (master production planning)?
- Which quantities of raw and intermediate products are needed to produce the end products (secondary requirements planning)?
- How customer orders should be processed in order to satisfy the customer's requirements as closely as possible (order fulfillment planning)?
- Which quantities of end, intermediary, or raw products should be combined into one production lot or one order quantity, respectively (lot-size planning, order-quantity planning)?
- At which times should the manufacturing of production orders take place at the various work places and machines and when should purchase orders for supplied products be issued (scheduling)?

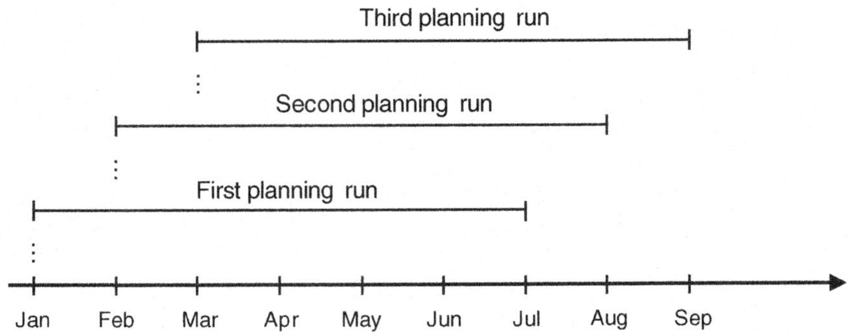

Fig. 1.6 Rolling planning principle

- How should the needed and the available capacities be balanced (capacity planning)?

Production control includes measures to be taken when discrepancies to the planned data are detected during the production process.

It is important to note that the above areas of production planning have rather different time horizons. Master production planning on the end-product level, for example, may extend to 1 or 2 years, whereas scheduling and detailed capacity planning cover only a few days.

Historically, the term production planning and control used to refer to planning and control within a single enterprise. This was not a problem as long as most of the production took place inside the company. Nowadays, with decreasing production depth, most companies buy more goods than they produce and increasingly depend on their suppliers. These dependencies gave rise to the discipline of *supply chain management*, as mentioned earlier in this chapter. Even an optimal in-house production plan is of no use if materials ordered from suppliers are not delivered on time because of a bottleneck at a supplier's end.

This is why many problems of production planning and control have been reconsidered in supply chain management. Solutions are now developed which take intercompany relationships into account. For example, instead of optimization within a company, optimization is pursued across the entire supply chain. Some of these problems will be discussed in Chap. 9.

Planning Principles When and how often are plans created? The answer to this question depends on the scope of the planning and the planning horizon. For example, planning the production program (end products) extends to months or years, material requirements planning to months, capacity requirements planning to weeks, and shop floor control to days.

This does not mean, however, that a plan established for a certain period of time will remain untouched until this period is over. For example, a material requirements plan covering the months from January to June will not be carried out until the last day of June but may be adapted over the course of time. This can happen in several ways:

- Rolling planning versus event-oriented planning
- New planning versus net-change planning

Rolling means that a new plan is created after some time, for example, after 1 month. The basic idea is shown in Fig. 1.6. The new plan now extends from February to July. One month later, another new plan is established, covering March to August.

Event-oriented means that unlike rolling planning, new plans are not created at fixed intervals but whenever important events occur. Such an event could be, for example, a large customer order arriving, a critical supplier going out of business, or a bottleneck machine breaking down. Event-oriented planning is often used in such a way that it extends period-oriented rolling planning to cope with new situations that cannot wait until the next planning run is scheduled.

One question still remains open in either approach: What happens to the previous plan when a new one is established? Will the new plan be made *from scratch*, meaning that the old plan is ignored and all earlier decisions are discarded?

Another possibility is that only new information will be considered that was not available when the earlier plan was set up (i.e., assumptions and parameters that have changed compared to the time of the last planning). This is sometimes called *net-change planning*, meaning that only changes are taken into account, leaving unchanged matters as they were originally planned.

1.4.2 Production Planning Goals

Production planning is a part of business planning. Therefore, the goals pursued in production planning have to match the overall goals of the enterprise. Entrepreneurs and external stakeholders often measure the success of a company in terms of the return they get for the money they invest:

$$\begin{aligned}&\text{Return on capital employed}\\&\quad = (\text{revenue} - \text{expenses})/\text{capital}\end{aligned}$$

The numerator of the quotient on the right is computed for a certain period, for example, 1 year.

In order to reach a good return on the capital employed, the company's management will take appropriate measures in accordance with the *economic principle*. The economic principle is one of the fundamental principles for entrepreneurial action, at least in theory. It states that the profitability, i.e., the quotient of the performance (output) and the required cost for this performance (input), should be as high as possible:

$$\text{Profitability} = \text{performance}/\text{cost}$$

This rule is operational if the performance and the cost can be measured in monetary units for a defined period of time.

Within the scope of production planning, it is primarily the cost that can be influenced. The performance mostly depends on factors that are outside production planning. For example, both the product quantities and the sales prices are influenced by marketing, sales planning, acquisition of new customers, etc.

For this reason, production planning focuses on the denominator of the profitability equation, i.e., the cost. Derived from the economic principle, the overall goal of production planning is to make decisions so that a given performance is achieved with minimal cost.

For operative production planning, a number of cost categories are already given, for example, the salaries of the employees. Other costs can be influenced by planning decisions (decision-relevant costs). These costs include:

- Preparing the production facilities (setup cost)
- Idle production facilities (idle cost)
- Storing raw, intermediate, and end products (inventory cost)
- Exceeding delivery dates (contractual penalty, loss of goodwill, etc.)
- Avoiding deadline violations (overtime cost, cost for additional shifts)

Planning and controlling based on cost is often difficult because complete and up-to-date cost data are not available. Therefore, it is common to pursue *substitute goals*, which are presumed to have a direct or indirect impact on the cost.

Substitute goals can be time goals or quantity goals. *Time goals* include the following:

- Minimizing order lead times
- Minimizing order wait times
- Maximizing utilization of production capacities
- Minimizing idle times of production capacities
- Minimizing deadline violations

Quantity goals within production planning focus on the inventory levels because the inventory can be influenced through decisions made in production planning. Other variables such as the total end-product quantities to be produced are already predetermined by sales planning. Quantity goals include:

- Minimizing inventory of raw, intermediate, and end products; products in transport and quality control; etc.
- Minimizing stockouts (i.e., shortage of material)

Obviously, these goals are not independent from each other. For example, minimizing the inventory of intermediate goods may cause stockouts and disrupt manufacturing processes. As a consequence, orders will not be processed, lead times will increase, machines will be idle, and delivery dates will be exceeded. On the other hand, maximizing the utilization of production capacities may require higher inventory levels, thus increasing inventory costs.

Goal Priorities Up to the 1960s, when the markets were dominated by the *sellers*, many companies engaged in mass and large-series production. Their main goal was to maximize capacity utilization. Other goals such as short lead times, low inventory levels, and meeting deadlines were less important.

As saturation of the market and competition increased, the power of the *buyer* rose. Companies were forced to pay more attention to their customers and the customers' individual wishes, leading to product diversification. Planning now included a much larger number of products and variants. Customers wanted their products on time and as fast as possible.

Taking the shift of priorities into account, the importance of the production planning goals also changed. Instead of maximum capacity utilization, other issues such as short-order lead times, meeting deadlines and keeping inventory levels low became critical for success. Small inventory increases the flexibility of the company, allowing for faster adaptation to changing market demand.

The *lead times* are a critical factor in the system of goals. Unfortunately, it is often the case that planned lead times and actual lead times significantly diverge, causing to miss their deadlines production orders. At the same time, as the lead times are longer, inventory levels also rise, thus increasing the inventory cost and finally the product cost.

"Just-in-Time" Principle An approach to reducing long lead times and high inventory levels was discussed under the term "just in time" in the 1980s. The just-in-time principle has two basic forms: just-in-time production and just-in-time delivery.

Just-in-time production means that all requirements regarding end products and inter mediate products are manufactured as late as possible. This implies, among other things, that intermediate products are not made to stock but only when there is immediate demand from the next manufacturing level. A well-known implementation of the just-in-time principle is *Kanban* production (see Sect. 2.3.1).

Just-in-time delivery means that the flow of material is organized in such a way that all materials reach their destination just before, or exactly when, they are needed in the manufacturing process. Suppliers, in particular, must deliver their goods exactly when the customer requests them. For the supplier, this means that they have to make provisions so that deliveries can be shipped to the customer just in time. For example, the supplier will need to build up additional inventory and perhaps propagate the just-in-time requirement to their own suppliers.

Just-in-time delivery entails for the customer minimum inventory levels, resulting in low capital tie-up and low inventory cost. On the other hand, the risk of stockouts and disruptions to the manufacturing process grows because buffers in the form of stock are no longer available.

With the just-in-time approach, *intercompany logistics* and transportation have become of paramount importance. Critics put forth that inventory is now being kept on the highways. The number and the volume of transport activities have significantly increased, resulting in elevated traffic on our roads and damage to the environment.

Globalization and Cost Pressure Access to worldwide markets and global competition has increased the cost pressure on the manufacturing industry. Since the beginning of the 1990s, companies have tried to reduce their production cost through various measures, including:

- Procurement of raw materials and intermediate products on the world market ("global sourcing")
- Outsourcing parts of their production to other countries, in particular to countries that have lower cost levels
- Reducing procurement cost by exerting pressure on the suppliers whenever the market allows them to do so
- Reducing labor cost by negotiating or renegotiating collective wage agreements
- Giving work to other manufacturers (subcontracting)

1.4.3 Benefits and Shortcomings of Production Planning

Many authors have studied the benefits of systematic production planning and in particular of automated solutions to the underlying problems. These benefits often serve as arguments when a company considers implementing an MRP II or ERP system. Typical benefits include the following (Matsui and Sato 2002, p. 195):

- Reduction in manufacturing cost
- Decrease in inventories
- Overall lead-time reduction
- Improvement in on-time deliveries
- Increased product-mix flexibility
- Increased production-volume flexibility
- Reduced new product introduction time
- Improved customer service
- Increased level of cooperation with customers and suppliers
- Improved product differentiation
- Improved product quality

These benefits are achieved due to intrinsic causalities. Improvements in one planning area positively impact other planning areas. For example, higher precision in material requirements planning leads to fewer bottlenecks, better balanced machine loads, higher capacity utilization, and thus more quantitative production output. Likewise, inventory levels will be reduced, implying less capital tied up in current assets, and as a result, lower capital cost.

Another example is integrating material requirements planning with capacity requirements planning. Positive effects are shorter order lead times (because unnecessary waiting times can be avoided), less working inventory (and consequently less capital cost), fewer deadline violations, and thus increased customer satisfaction.

In addition to these improvements, many companies benefit from *business process reengineering* (cf. Sect. 1.3) during or before the implementation process. The decision to implement a new system often stimulates a critical examination of the company's business processes and a rethinking of how the work should be done. Furthermore, ERP vendors and consultants recommend best industry practices, which may also require the company to adapt their processes.

Shortcomings of conventional production planning arise from two major problems:

1. Planning the materials (quantities) to be produced and planning the manufacturing dates and capacity loads are done in *separate steps*—material requirements planning, lead-time scheduling, and capacity requirements planning. Therefore, it is not guaranteed that the planned materials can be produced by the dates they are needed. This in turn means that input materials have to wait longer in the warehouse, increasing the inventory cost, and that order deadlines are missed, causing disruptions to the manufacturing process and adversely affecting customer satisfaction.
2. The plans created in the planning steps are *not up to date*, meaning that the actual manufacturing situation does not correspond to the planned situation. The reasons for this discrepancy are manifold, including: assumptions made in the planning were wrong, unforeseen problems occur (e.g., machine breakdown, material from supplier is missing, or machine operator gets sick), and actual data to update the plan are not available because production data acquisition (PDA, cf. Sect. 7.1.2) is not integrated with the planning system.

Management Science It is worth mentioning that many of the conventional production planning problems have been investigated in management science. A large number of optimization models were developed, covering mainly four types of problems:

1. *Planning the quantities*, e.g., computing optimal lot sizes for production ("economic lot size") and optimal order quantities for procurement ("economic order quantity")
2. *Sequencing*, i.e., planning the sequences in which production orders should be processed on the company's machines and other assets

3. *Scheduling,* i.e., planning the dates when the in-house production orders should be performed and the procurement orders should be triggered
4. *Assignment* problems, e.g., which resources (workers, machines, tools, etc.) should be assigned to which orders

Many of the planning models covered just one type of problem, for example, lot sizing, sequencing, or scheduling. Had these models been applied in practice, the different types of problems would have been solved one after the other (successively).

On the other hand, the above-mentioned shortcomings of dealing with isolated subproblems were obvious to the researchers just as they were obvious to practitioners. Therefore, a great deal of research effort has been spent on approaches integrating the subproblems into more comprehensive *total models* and computing the total solution simultaneously.

One immediate advantage of *simultaneous planning* is that interdependencies between the planning areas (e.g., between quantity planning and scheduling) are taken into account within the model. In this way, unfeasible material plans can be avoided.

The main disadvantage of simultaneous planning is the model size. Considering several planning areas at the same time leads to mixed-integer models with millions of variables. At the time most models were developed, computing power was far from sufficient to calculate a solution to a nontrivial problem within a reasonable time or at all.

Computability was a problem not only for total models but for partial models as well. The state-of-the-art of computing prevented most optimization models to be implemented in practice under realistic circumstances. However, the computing power has substantially increased since then. This has lead to a revival of mathematical models and optimization approaches, in particular within the field of supply chain management. These approaches are nowadays summarized under the term *advanced planning and scheduling (APS).*

1.5 Coping with Mass Data

Business information systems are *data oriented.* Such systems store, process, and create large amounts of data. This is true for practically all types of business software, supporting a wide range of tasks—from manufacturing and logistics all the way to accounting and human resources management.

Data management was an important issue in MRP and MRP II and continues to be in ERP and SCM. This is due to the fact that the volume of the data these systems rely on is extremely large and the interrelationships between the data are rather complex.

Scheer gave an often-cited example of the data volume that is typical for a medium-sized manufacturing company (Scheer 1976, p. 19):

- 40,000 parts, among these 100 end products and 10,000 parts manufactured in-house
- 280,000 product structure records for the bills of materials
- 20,000 routings
- 100,000 operations
- 200,000 assignments of operating facilities to operations
- 150 groups of operating facilities
- 750 individual operating facilities

Altogether, 640,900 data records have to be stored and maintained.

In this example, 40,000 records are *material master records.* Other practical examples illustrating the numbers of material master records in various industries were collected by Dittrich and coauthors (2009a, p. 2). Figure 1.7 shows these numbers.

Not only the number of data records but also the size of an individual record can be substantial. A material master record of 100 or more data fields is common.

While the early MRP and MRP II systems had their own data organization, today's ERP systems employ *database management systems* to maintain their data. Since ERP databases contain more than just production-related data, they are usually very large.

Fig. 1.7 Material master records in various industries

Organization	Industry	No. of material master records
University Hospital Erlangen	Health care	31,000
Esselte Leitz GmbH & Co. KG	Office supplies	40,000
Festo AG & Co. KG	Automation	175,000
Machine Works Reinhausen GmbH	Switchgear engineering	280,000
Robert Bosch GmbH	Electrics	350,000

2 MRP: Material Requirements Planning

The first application systems for manufacturing companies in the 1960s were systems for *material requirements planning (MRP)*. Even though the roots of MRP are fairly old, most of the MRP functionality is still available in today's ERP systems. In this chapter, the master data for MRP are described, followed by an explanation of the main functional areas supported by MRP.

Some of the vendors of MRP systems were computer manufacturers such as IBM, Honeywell Bull, Digital Equipment, and Siemens. These companies tried to penetrate the business sector with computers, which they would otherwise only be able to sell to military and scientific institutions. A well-known MRP system dating back to 1968 was IBM's *PICS (Production Information and Control System),* later extended to *COPICS (Communication-Oriented Production Information and Control System).*

Systems like PICS primarily supported material requirements planning and inventory control for manufacturing companies doing business in the US market. This is worth mentioning because many assumptions underlying conventional MRP systems are derived from the circumstances particular to this market in the 1960s and 1970s. The market was a sellers' market. Most manufacturing companies produced large quantities of identical goods in batch production, stored these goods in a warehouse, sold them to customers as long as they could satisfy the demand, and then produced another large batch. Other companies continuously produced the goods in mass production and sold them to the customers.

In business terms, this means that the framework for production planning, and in particular for material requirements planning, was characterized by:

- A standard production program (on the product group or individual product level)
- Well-defined product structures
- Uniform or otherwise known demand curves
- Mass or large-series production

It is also worth noting that these characteristics are no longer typical of today's market and manufacturing environment, nor have they been for smaller economies outside North America. In the USA, the customer did not play any significant role in the production planning of the 1960s and 1970s. However, the situation has dramatically changed since then. Today, it is the customer who influences many aspects of material requirements and manufacturing resource planning. In the Sects. 2.2 and 2.3, some implications of customer orientation on material requirements planning will be discussed.

The main task of a conventional MRP system is to support the planning of material requirements on all manufacturing levels, starting with the production program for end products and including inventory management and procurement. However, most dedicated MRP systems

K.E. Kurbel, *Enterprise Resource Planning and Supply Chain Management*,
Progress in IS, DOI 10.1007/978-3-642-31573-2_2, © Springer-Verlag Berlin Heidelberg 2013

have ceased to exist. They eventually evolved into MRP II systems and later into ERP systems where the core MRP functionality is still available.

2.1 Master Data for MRP

The data structures used in business information systems can be divided into two categories: master data and transaction data. *Master data* are data that exist independent of specific orders (customer, production, purchase, transport orders, etc.). Master data constitute the frame in which the planning and controlling of orders takes place.

Transaction data are created during business operations, for example, when a customer places an order, procurement initiates a purchase from a supplier, production planning releases a production order, or dispatching prepares a shipment to the customer.

Master data are the foundation of any business information system. Without reliable and robust master data, planning and controlling of an enterprise are not possible. Henning Kagermann, the former CEO of SAP, and Hubert Österle, a professor of business informatics at the University of Sankt Gallen, stressed the importance of *master data management* in their book on modern business concepts:

"Master data identify and describe all the important business objects, for example business partners, employees, articles, bills of materials, equipment and accounts. Since all business activities such as quotes, orders, postings, payment receipts and transport orders refer to the master data, these data are the basis of any coordination effort. However, the high expenditures for the construction and maintenance of the master data exhibit their benefits only indirectly – via the processes that use the data. Therefore master data projects have a much lower priority than they should have. Master data management needs support from the management and endurance. New tools for master data management can noticeably reduce the effort for the cleaning up and maintaining of master data" (Kagermann and Österle 2006, pp. 231–232, author's translation).

The most important master data for production planning and control are data concerning:

- Parts
- Product structures
- Operations
- Routings
- Operating facilities or work centers
- Manufacturing structures

These as well as other types of master data will be discussed in more detail below. *Entity-relationship diagrams* will at times be used for the purpose of illustration. The notation of these diagrams is explained in Appendix A.1.

2.1.1 Parts and Product Structures

Part master data play a central role in every manufacturing application system. The generic term "part" comprises assemblies, component parts, raw materials, end products, and more. It refers to all parts of the end product, including the end product itself and all other components needed to produce the end product. In addition to "part," the terms "material," "article," and "product" are also in use. In SAP ERP, for example, the parts are called materials.

Considering the number of parts and the number of attributes, part master data are usually quite substantial. Important attributes (or fields) of part master data include the following:

- Part number
- Variant code
- Part name
- Part description
- Part type (e.g., finished product, assembly, and additional material)
- Measuring unit (e.g., piece, kg, and m)
- Form identification
- Drawing number
- Basic material
- Planning type (e.g., in-house production and consumption-driven MRP)
- Replenishment time
- Scrap factor for quantity-dependent scrap
- Scrap factor for setup-dependent scrap
- Date from which the master record is valid
- Date up to which the master record is valid
- Date of the last modification

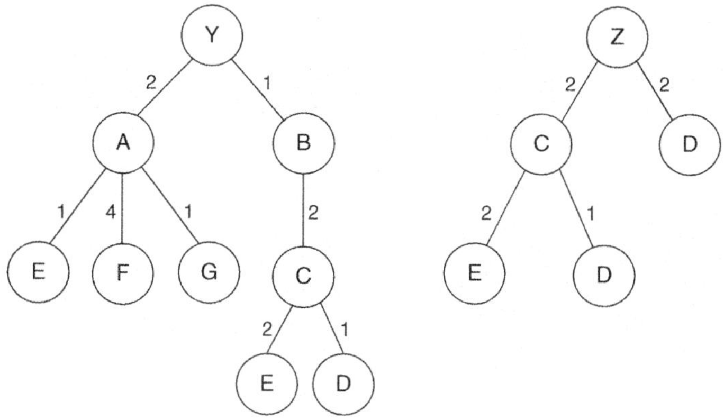

Fig. 2.1 Product structure trees ("consists of")

- Date of the first creation
- Person in charge

Often, many more attributes are used to describe parts. For example, the part master data managed by SAP ERP (called material master data) exhibit more than 400 attributes. The number of attributes and the degree to which the attributes are differentiated depend on, among other things, which business areas are covered by the ERP solution, whether or not related application systems (e.g., CAD for construction, CAM for manufacturing, and SCM for delivery) are available, and whether or not interfaces for these systems exist.

The various attributes are sometimes categorized in data groups such as:

- Identification data (part number, etc.)
- Classification data (technical classification)
- Design data (measurements, etc.)
- Planning data (procurement type, lot size, etc.)
- Demand data (accumulated demand, etc.)
- Inventory data (warehouse stock, etc.)
- Distribution data (selling price, etc.)
- Procurement data (buying price, etc.)
- Manufacturing data (throughput time, etc.)
- Costing data (machine cost, inventory cost, etc.)

In SAP ERP, for example, attributes are divided into 28 categories called "views" (because they reflect the user's "view" of the data, i.e., the various forms in which the data is presented to the user).

Not all fields shown in a part master-data form are necessarily attributes of a database table with the name "part." In fact, many of the shown values are just calculated or taken from other tables. For example, the warehouse stock as it appears in a part master-data form is, as a rule, retrieved and aggregated from several database tables, which are maintained for different inventory locations.

Product Structures Product structures show what parts make up a product. This composition is often depicted as a tree. The edges of the tree represent either "consists of" or "goes into" relationships, depending on the perspective. Figure 2.1 shows two simplified product structure trees for the end products Y and Z. The numbers on the edges are quantity coefficients. Y consists of two units of A and one unit of B. Conversely, A and B go into Y with 2 and 1 units, respectively.

Reversing the perspective, so that the leaves of one or more product structure trees become the roots and the end products are the leaves ("goes into" relationship), creates trees like those in Fig. 2.2. The figure directly shows where a given part is needed. For example, part E goes directly into part A with one unit and into part C with two units, as well as indirectly into parts Z, B, and twice (through parts A and B) into part Y.

The two different perspectives can be combined into a so-called *Gozinto graph*. The name "Gozinto" is supposedly derived from the words "goes into." A Gozinto graph allows for network structures that avoid redundant branches and nodes. For example, in Fig. 2.1, part C is shown twice, and part D is shown three times. In a Gozinto graph, as in Fig. 2.3, parts C and D

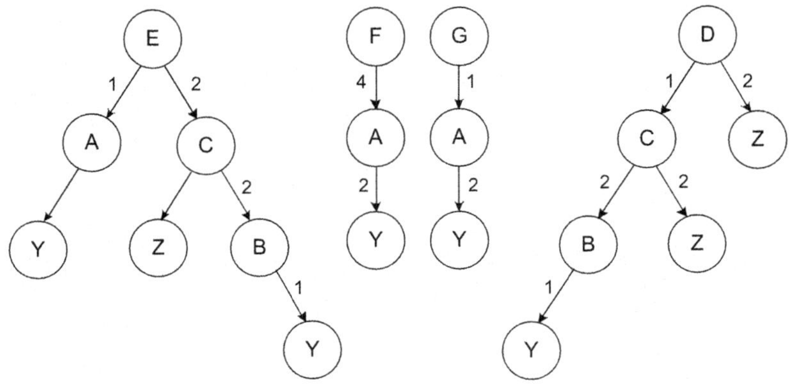

Fig. 2.2 Reversed product structure trees ("goes into")

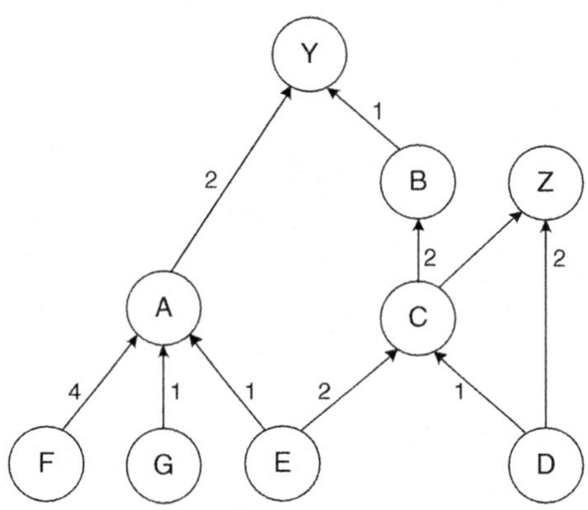

Fig. 2.3 Product structure as a Gozinto graph

appear only once. D goes into C and Z, and C goes into B and Z.

A product structure, like any other higher-order tree, can be transformed into a binary tree, as long as the information on the edges is preserved. Fig. 2.4 shows this transformation for the product structures Y and Z. In comparison to the original tree, the following changes should be noted:

- The edges of the tree now have a different meaning. An edge that leads to the *left* child of a node indicates the first part of the next level that goes directly into the parent node.
- An edge that leads to the *right* child of a node indicates the next part on the same level that goes directly into the same parent node as its predecessor.
- The information on the original edges must be preserved during the transformation. This means that the quantity coefficients, and possibly more information, have to be stored elsewhere because the original edges no longer exist. In the figure, the edges of the original product structure trees are drawn with dotted lines.

A binary tree such as the one shown in Fig. 2.4 is a symbolic representation of a single-level bill of materials (BOM). Bills of materials are discussed below.

Product structures ultimately express *relationships between parts*. Using entity-relationship terminology, a product structure can be regarded as a relationship connecting objects of the same entity type with each other.

Figure 2.5 shows this situation with the help of a "structure" relationship type, which can be interpreted both as a "consists of" and a "goes into" relationship. The cardinalities indicate that a part can consist of any number of other parts but also of no other parts (e.g., a raw material or an externally procured part). Conversely, it is possible for a part to go into any number of other parts or into no other part (e.g., an end product).

Out of the large number of part and product structure attributes, only the "part-id" and the "quantity" are shown in the diagram. The part-id attribute is important because it can be used to uniquely identify a particular structure relationship (i.e., one edge of a product structure tree).

At first glance, Fig. 2.5 seems to express only the relationships between parts involving two

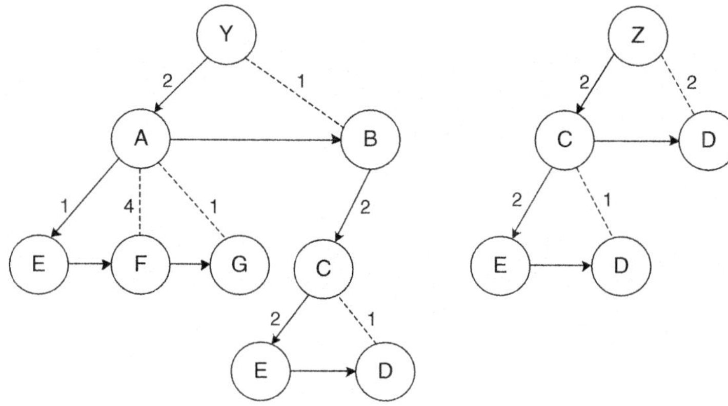

Fig. 2.4 Product structure, transformed into a binary tree

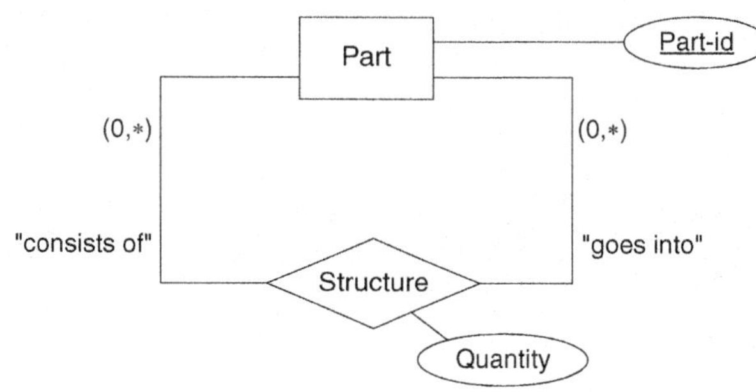

Fig. 2.5 Product structure as a relationship type in an ER diagram

levels and not the multilevel structures that were shown in the earlier figures. However, multilevel structures can be easily generated through appropriate database queries. For this purpose, the part-ids of related subordinate and superordinate parts are employed to link single-level structures into a multilevel structure.

The ER model of Fig. 2.5 can be mapped to a relational database with the help of two tables, "part" and "structure." In relational notation (see Appendix A.2), these two tables are defined as follows:

Part (<u>part-id</u>, part name, part type, unit of measurement...)

Structure (<u>upper-part-id</u>, <u>lower-part-id</u>, quantity, valid-from...)

The "structure" table has a composite key, indicating the two part entities to be linked. Graphically speaking, the "upper-part-id" attribute identifies the parent node in the product structure, while the "lower-part-id" identifies the child node.

Figure 2.6 exemplifies a product structure tree of an electric motor with part number "E10." Figure 2.7, which is based on this product structure, exhibits two tables—one with the parts and the other with the relationships between parts—according to the E10 product structure.

The part table shows, along with the part number ("part-id"), three additional attributes. The "part type" attribute has values that are abbreviations of in-house production (I), external procurement (E), end product (P), assembly (A), raw material (R), consumables (C), etc. For example, ER stands for external procurement/raw material.

In the "structure" table, the first line uniquely identifies the edge between the end product "electric motor" (upper-part-id "E10") and the assembly "complete casing" (lower-part-id "901"). The most important attribute of the structure relationship, in addition to the keys, is the quantity.

A number of other attributes may also appear in a "structure" table. Just as with the part master data, the type and number of attributes are dependent upon the level of detail and the application environment. Typical fields of a structure table include:

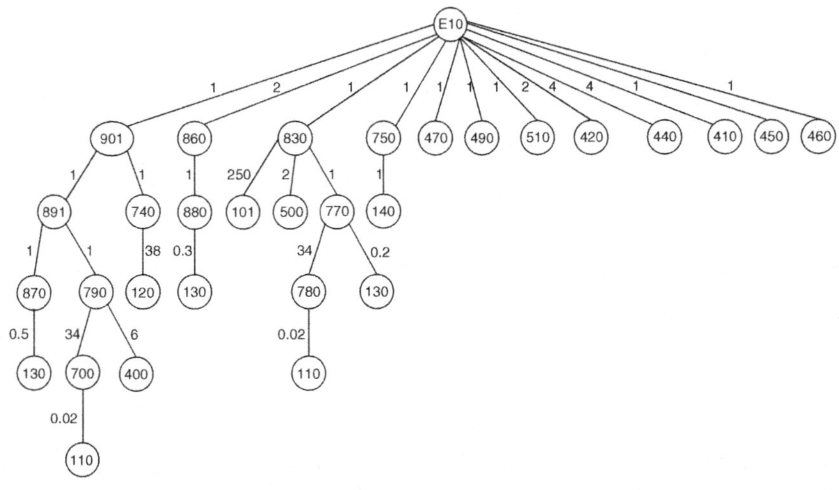

Fig. 2.6 Product structure of an electric motor

Part				
Part-id	Part name	Part type	Unit	...
E10	Electric motor	IP	pc	
901	Case (complete)	IA	pc	
891	Case with laminations	II	pc	
880	Bearing cap (aluminum)	II	pc	
870	Housing block (aluminum)	II	pc	
860	Bearing cap with breakout	IA	pc	
830	Arbor (complete)	IA	pc	
790	Plate packet (complete)	IA	pc	
780	Muller plate	II	pc	
770	Base plate 30×40 cm	IA	pc	
750	Muller plate packet (complete)	IA	pc	
740	Stator winding	II	pc	
700	Stator plate muller	II	pc	
510	Junction plate box cap	EA	pc	
500	Roller bearing	EA	pc	
490	Junction plate 3-pin	EA	pc	
470	Nut M 4	EC	pc	
460	Rigid coupling ∅ 14 mm	EA	pc	
450	Capacitor 16 µF	EA	pc	
440	Hex nut M 4×200	EC	pc	
420	Hex nut M 4×10	EC	pc	
410	Hex nut M 8×30	EC	pc	
400	Rivet 4×150 mm	EC	pc	
140	Sheet metal board St 37	ER	pc	
130	Aluminum bar	ER	kg	
120	Copper wire ∅ 0.5 mm	EC	m	
110	Electrical sheet coil 200 mm	EC	m	
101	Round bar 37×30 mm	ER	pc	

Structure			
Upper part-id	Lower-part-id	Quantity	...
E10	901	1	
E10	860	2	
E10	830	1	
E10	750	1	
E10	510	1	
E10	490	1	
E10	470	1	
E10	460	1	
E10	450	1	
E10	440	4	
E10	420	2	
E10	410	4	
901	891	1	
901	740	1	
891	870	1	
891	790	1	
880	130	0.3	
870	130	0.5	
860	880	1	
830	770	1	
830	500	2	
830	101	250	
790	700	34	
790	400	6	
780	110	0.02	
770	780	34	
770	130	0.2	
750	140	1	
740	120	38	
700	110	0.02	

Fig. 2.7 Database tables "part" and "structure" (electric motor)

- Upper-part-id
- Lower-part-id
- Variant code
- Quantity coefficient
- Structure type (e.g., is the quantity coefficient dependent on the quantity of the upper part?)
- Scrap factor for structure-dependent scrap
- Date from which the master record is valid

- Date to which the master record is valid
- Date of the last modification
- Date of the first creation
- Person in charge

Important uses of product structures include (1) compiling bills of materials and where-used lists and (2) determining dependent requirements for material planning.

Dependent material requirements, that is, the quantities of lower-level parts needed to produce the planned end products (or other higher-level parts), are calculated with the help of the quantity coefficients, which are stored in the "quantity" column of the "structure" table. Sect. 2.3.2 will discuss the calculation process in more detail.

Bills of Materials A bill of materials (BOM) represents a product structure together with essential information about the nodes (i.e., part master data) in the form of a list. Each row shows one subordinate part. The parts are described by part number, part name, quantity needed for the upper part, etc. In this way, a bill of materials describes the composition of an end product or an intermediate product (assembly).

Bills of materials are especially relevant in *discrete manufacturing*, that is, in manufacturing processes in which the quantities are mostly measured in discrete units (pieces). This is typically the case when assembly plays a dominant role, for example, in the production of machines, bicycles, or furniture.

The opposite of discrete manufacturing is *continuous manufacturing*, which occurs particularly in the chemical and pharmaceutical industry. There, the equivalent of a bill of materials is a *formulation*. The main difference between a bill of materials and a formulation is that the quantities are measured in continuous units (kilogram, ton, liter, etc.) and that the product structure graphs are not necessarily trees but may contain cycles. A cycle means that in order to manufacture a product, the product itself is needed.

In this book, we will focus on discrete manufacturing using bills of materials, although a number of similar problems also occur in continuous manufacturing.

Bills of materials are employed for various purposes: requirements planning, assembly, computer-aided design, etc. The content, structure, and format of a bill of materials depend on the intended use. Hence, a number of labels exist, for example, planning BOM, assembly BOM, manufacturing BOM etc.

Different types of bills of materials exhibit different structures, depending on how much structural information is mapped to the bill. Relating to this, three types can be determined:

1. *Single-level bills of materials* are used to define the immediate components of a higher-level part, that is, what lower-level parts go *directly* into the higher-level part. A single-level bill of materials typically shows the assemblies (plus other parts) an end product is made of. However, it can be used for any part, depicting the next-level decomposition of the part.

   Figure 2.8 gives an example using the electric motor with part number E10 (cf. Fig. 2.6). A bill like this is easily created from the tables "part" and "structure" in Fig. 2.7 with the help of a simple database query. It should be noted that the rows of this bill of materials correspond to the level 2 nodes of a binary tree created as the one in Fig. 2.4.
2. *Multilevel bills of materials*, unlike single-level, expand the higher-level part down *all* levels of the product structure. This type of bill displays the entire product structure tree in the form of a list. The upper-part/lower-part relationships are indicated with level numbers.

   Figure 2.9 shows the product structure of the electric motor E10 as a multilevel bill of materials. (Such a list can be created from the "part" and "structure" tables using nested database queries.)
3. *Summarized bills of materials* indicate all parts that go into a product, but do not reflect the structure of the product. This means that the tree is "compressed" into one level. When

Fig. 2.8 Single-level BOM for electric motor E10

Single-level Bill of Materials			**Page 1**	
Part: Electric motor, part-id: E10				
Part-id	Part name	Unit	Quantity	…
901	Case (complete)	pc	1	
860	Bearing cap with breakout	pc	2	
830	Arbor (complete)	pc	1	
750	Base plate 30×40 cm	pc	1	
510	Junction plate box cap	pc	1	
490	Junction plate 3-pin	pc	1	
470	Nut M 4	pc	1	
460	Rigid coupling ∅ 14 mm	pc	1	
450	Capacitor16 µF	pc	1	
440	Hex nut M 4×200	pc	4	
420	Hex nut M 4×10	pc	2	
410	Hex nut M 8×30	pc	4	

Fig. 2.9 Multilevel BOM for electric motor E10

Multi-level Bill of Materials				**Page 1**	
Part: Electric motor, Part-id: E10					
Level	Part-id	Part name	Unit	Quantity	…
1	901	Case (complete)	pc	1	
. 2	891	Case with laminations	pc	1	
. . 3	870	Housing block (aluminum)	pc	1	
. . . 4	130	Aluminum bar	kg	0.5	
. . 3	790	Plate packet (complete)	pc	1	
. . . 4	700	Stator plate muller	pc	34	
. . . . 5	110	Electrical sheet coil 200 mm	m	0.02	
. . . 4	400	Rivet 4x150 mm	pc	6	
. 2	740	Stator winding	pc	1	
. . 3	120	Copper wire ∅ 0.5 mm	m	38	
1	830	Arbor (complete)	pc	1	
. 2	770	Muller plate packet (complete)	pc	1	
. . 3	780	Muller plate	pc	34	
. . . 4	110	Electrical sheet coil 200 mm	m	0.02	
. . 3	130	Aluminum bar	kg	0.2	
. 2	500	Roller bearing	pc	2	
. 2	101	Round bar 37x30 mm	pc	250	
1	860	Bearing cap with breakout	pc	2	
. 2	880	Bearing cap (aluminum)	pc	1	
. . 3	130	Aluminum bar	kg	0.3	
1	750	Base plate 30x40 cm	pc	1	
. 2	140	Sheet metal board St 37	pc	1	
1	510	Junction plate box cap	pc	1	
1	490	Junction plate 3-pin	pc	1	
1	470	Nut M 4	pc	1	
1	460	Rigid coupling ∅ 14 mm	pc	1	
1	450	Capacitor 16 µF	pc	1	
1	440	Hex nut M 4×200	pc	4	
1	420	Hex nut M 4×10	pc	2	
1	410	Hex nut M 8×30	pc	4	

Fig. 2.10 Summarized BOM for electric motor E10

Summarized Bill of Materials				**Page 1**
Part: Electric motor, Part-id: E10				
Part-id	Part name	Unit	Quantity	...
901	Case (complete)	pc	1	
891	Case with laminations	pc	1	
880	Bearing cap (aluminum)	pc	2	
870	Housing block (aluminum)	pc	1	
860	Bearing cap with breakout	pc	2	
830	Arbor (complete)	pc	1	
790	Plate packet (complete)	pc	1	
780	Muller plate	pc	34	
770	Muller plate packet (complete)	pc	1	
750	Base plate 30×40 cm	pc	1	
740	Stator winding	pc	1	
700	Stator plate muller	pc	34	
510	Junction plate box cap	pc	1	
500	Roller bearing	pc	2	
490	Junction plate 3-pin	pc	1	
470	Nut M 4	pc	1	
460	Rigid coupling ∅ 14 mm	pc	1	
450	Capacitor 16 μF	pc	1	
440	Hex nut M 4×200	pc	4	
420	Hex nut M 4×10	pc	2	
410	Hex nut M 8×30	pc	4	
400	Rivet 4×150 mm	pc	6	
140	Sheet metal board St 37	pc	1	
130	Aluminum bar	kg	1.3	
120	Copper wire ∅ 0.5 mm	m	38	
110	Electrical sheet coil 200 mm	m	1.36	
101	Round bar 37×30 mm	pc	250	

a part appears more than once in the product structure, its quantities are added. Consequently, the bill shows only the total quantity needed for one unit of the top part (e.g., the end product). Figure 2.10 illustrates this, again using the electric motor example.

The part numbers 880, 130, and 110 are examples showing how several quantities are summarized into one. Because one piece of 880 (bearing cap) is needed for one 860 (bearing cap with breakout) and two pieces of 860 are needed for one E10 (electric motor), the result is that two pieces of 880 are needed for one E10.

How many units of 130 (aluminum bar) are needed for one electric motor E10 can be calculated by multiplying the quantity coefficients on the edges

870–130 (0.5)	and	880–130 (0.3)	and	770–130 (0.2)
891–870 (1)		860–880 (1)		830–770 (1)
901–891 (1)		E10–860 (2)		E10–830 (1)
E10–901 (1)				

and adding up the products

$0.5 \times 1 \times 1 \times 1 + 0.3 \times 1 \times 2 + 0.2 \times 1 \times 1$ to 1.3 kg. (This total is shown in the fourth to the last line in the summarized bill of materials in Fig. 2.10).

Where-Used Lists While bills of materials reflect "consists of" relationships between parts,

Fig. 2.11 Multilevel where-used list

Multilevel Where-used List					Page 1
Part: Aluminum bar, Part-id: 130					
Level	Part-id	Part name	Unit	Quantity	...
1	870	Housing block (aluminum)	kg	0.5	
. 2	891	Case with laminations	pc	1	
. . 3	901	Case (complete)	pc	1	
. . . 4	E10	Electric motor	pc	1	
1	880	Bearing cap (aluminum)	kg	0.3	
. 2	860	Bearing cap with breakout	pc	1	
. . 3	E10	Electric motor	pc	2	
1	770	Muller plate packet (complete)	kg	0.2	
. 2	830	Arbor (complete)	pc	1	
. . 3	E10	Electric motor	pc	1	

Fig. 2.12 Summarized where-used list

Summarized Where-used List				Page 1
Part: Aluminum bar, Part-id: 130				
Part-id	Part name	Unit	Quantity	...
770	Muller plate (complete)	kg	0.2	
830	Arbor (complete)	kg	0.2	
860	Bearing cap with breakout	kg	0.3	
870	Housing block (aluminum)	kg	0.5	
880	Bearing cap (aluminum)	kg	0.3	
891	Case with laminations	kg	0.5	
901	Case (complete)	kg	0.5	
E10	Electric motor	kg	1.3	

where-used lists (part-usage lists) represent "goes into" relationships. Let us take another look at Fig. 2.2. This figure shows that reverse product structure trees can be constructed based on the "goes into" relationships.

As for bills of materials, different types of where-used lists can be identified, according to the degree to which the multilevel structure of the trees is reflected:

- *Single-level where-used lists* comprise all parts into which the given part goes directly. For example, the list for part 130 (aluminum bar, cf. Fig. 2.6) would display parts 870 (with 0.5 units), 880 (with 0.3 units), and 770 (with 0.2 units).
- *Multilevel where-used lists* show all parts into which the given part goes directly or indirectly (through other parts). The hierarchical structure of the tree is preserved and is expressed with level numbers. Figure 2.11 illustrates the basic idea using part 130 as an example.
- *Summarized where-used lists* include all parts of the "goes into" tree, but the tree is compressed to one level, as in a summarized bill of materials. This means that the quantities are added up. The where-used list that corresponds to Fig. 2.11 is shown in Fig. 2.12.

2.1.2 Product Variants

The term *product variant* is used to describe parts, especially end products, that differ from a basic model. Nowadays, many products are available in multiple versions. This means that the products are not 100 % identical, but vary in some features.

Automobiles are an obvious example of a product produced in variants. They are based on a certain model but are available with a variety of options. Different engines, transmissions, seats, colors, wheels, with or without fog lamps, cruise control, tow bar, navigation system, etc. are just some of the many options the customer can choose from.

Because of the emphasis on the customer, variant production has become very popular in many industries. This is true both for the consumer market (e.g., automobiles, furniture, and clothing) and the market for investment goods (e. g., machinery). Since customer orientation is an important success factor, companies attempt to serve the individual wishes of their customers as well as possible. Product variants are one means to take individual requirements into account.

The number of possible variants of an end product can be very large. An automobile, for example, can easily have hundreds of thousands or even millions of variants, because there are many ways to combine the customizable features. Assemblies and intermediate parts may also come in many different variants. For example, the cable harness that connects the electric and electronic parts of a VW Passat has approximately 1,000 variants. In other cases, there are only a few possible variants. An electric motor, for example, may be available with 40, 60, or 80 W.

In practice and in the literature, variants are divided into several categories, including structure, quantity, mandatory, optional, and internal variants:

- A *structure variant* is when several different versions of a part are possible and one of these versions goes into the end product (e.g., a 110-, 140-, or 180-hp engine) or when a subpart is optional (e.g., a tow bar).
- A *quantity variant* is when different quantities of one part can be built into the end product (e.g., two or four loudspeakers).
- A *mandatory variant* is when several different versions of a part are possible, one of which *must* go into the end product (e.g., either a 110-, 140-, or 180-hp engine).
- An *optional variant* is when a part can be *added* to the basic model of a product (e.g., fog lights and mobile phone mounting).
- An *internal variant* is a variant that is only relevant in-house and does not have an explicit effect on the end product (e.g., batteries from different manufacturers built into the vehicles, depending on internal procurement and inventory policies).

The terms obviously overlap. Mandatory variants are structure variants. Optional variants are structure (additional tow bar) or quantity (additional loudspeakers) variants. Internal variants are usually structure variants but are not apparent to the client. In practice, structure and quantity variants often appear together.

There are different ways to represent variant product structures: static and dynamic. *Static* means that all possible versions of the product are defined and stored in the database. Each variant is an entity in the master data and can be retrieved from the database when needed. When a product has only a few variants (i.e., not too many combinations of variant features), the variants are usually stored statically in the database.

Dynamic variants, on the other hand, are only created when they are explicitly requested, for example, when a customer orders that particular combinations of features. When there are many possible combinations, dynamic creation of variants is preferred.

Static variants are stored in a conventional way, that is, in database tables such as "part" and "structure." The part master records will indicate whether a part has variants or not. In the "structure" table, the variants are basically treated as if they were separate parts.

As an example, consider the Figs. 2.13 and 2.14. The end product X comes in two variants, X1 and X2. They differ in that X1 needs an assembly A1, whereas X2 needs A2. A1 is similar to A2 but uses a part E1, whereas A2 uses E2. Consequently, the "structure" table shown in Fig. 2.15 has rows connecting "upper parts" and "lower parts" as follows:

X1–A1	X2–A2
X1–B	X2–B
X1–C	X2–C
A1–E1	A2–E2
A1–D	A2–D

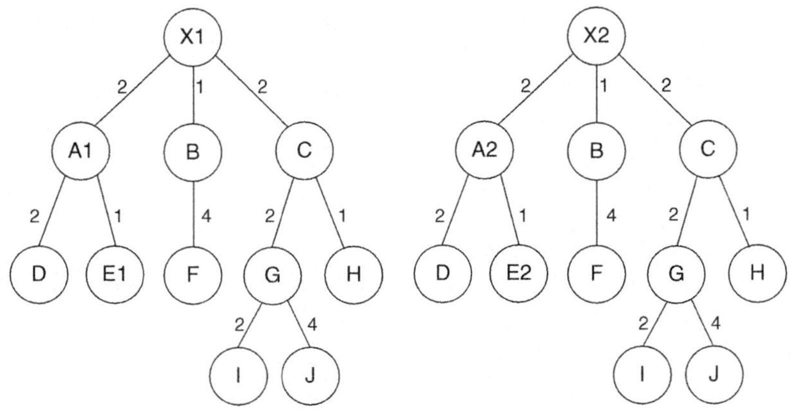

Fig. 2.13 Product structure trees of variants X1 and X2

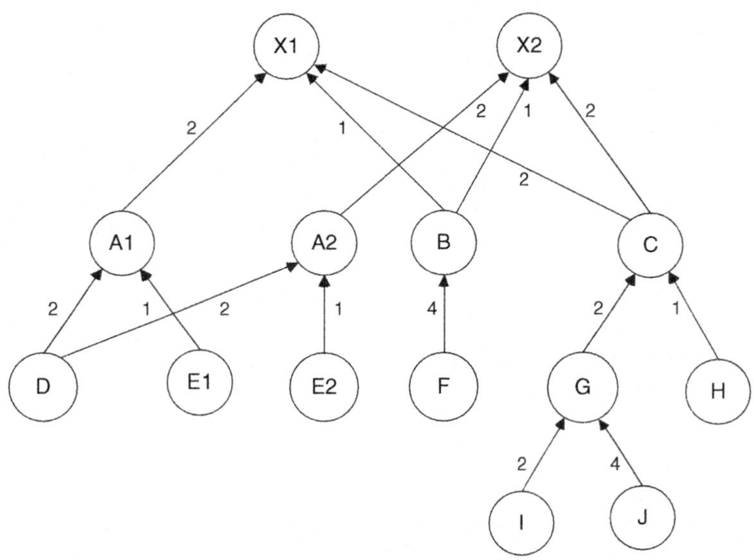

Fig. 2.14 Gozinto graph for variants X1 and X2

While a lot of information is doubled in the product structure trees for X1 and X2 (cf. Fig. 2.13), the Gozinto graph (cf. Fig. 2.14) exhibits less redundancy. Since the database schema for product structures is based on Gozinto graphs and not on trees, there is not much redundancy in the database either.

Figure 2.15 shows that in the "structure" table, redundant branches of the trees appear as rows of the table only once. For example, the subtree for part C occurs twice in the product structures of X1 and X2 but only once in the Gozinto graph and hence only once in the database table.

Nevertheless, some redundancy remains. For example, links from the end product to the assemblies B and C and from the assembly A to part D are duplicated. This might not look like a big problem, but only because our example is very small. In more realistic product structures, the number of redundant links can be quite large.

Therefore, various formats to store static variants have been proposed and implemented in the past. For example, one format uses fictitious common assemblies (combining all invariant parts into one fictitious group); another format indicates where a variant differs from the basic version with plus (additional part) and minus (part to be omitted) indicators.

A popular format for static variants is a *variant family*. In a variant family, the links connecting a variant part with another part are not handled as individual entities in the "structure"

Fig. 2.15 Variants X1 and X2 in a "structure" table

Structure			
Upper-part-id	Lower-part-id	Quantity	...
X1	A1	2	
X1	B	1	
X1	C	2	
X2	A2	2	
X2	B	1	
X2	C	2	
A1	D	2	
A1	E1	2	
A2	D	2	
A2	E2	1	
B	F	4	
C	G	2	
C	H	1	
G	I	2	
G	J	4	

Fig. 2.16 Variant family X in a "structure" table

Structure				
Upper-part-id	Lower-part-id	Quantity for variant		...
		X1	X2	
X	A1	2		
X	B	1	1	
X	C	2	2	
X	A2		2	
A1	D	2		
A1	E1	1		
A2	D		2	
A2	E2		1	
B	F	4	4	
C	G	2	2	
C	H	1	1	
G	I	2	2	
G	J	4	4	

table but together as a group. For our example, this means that the structure table has several columns that contain quantity coefficients.

Figure 2.16 shows the structure table for a variant family X, which contains the variants X1 and X2. The product structures of X1 and X2 are now defined by those links between "upper parts" and "lower parts" that have an entry in the respective row.

Variant families are also known as "multiple," "complex," or "type" bills of materials. They are used both for structure and quantity variants. In any case, the number of possible variants should be small because each variant will add a column to the structure table.

Dynamic variants are often used when products can be customized. Suppose an end product has 50 customizable features, each one coming in 4 different variations. The number of possible feature combinations, and hence the number of variants, is 4^{50}. Storing all variants statically does not make sense, seeing that many of the potential combinations will never occur. Instead, a variant is only created when it is actually requested for a particular order.

Practical solutions often implement an *attribute-value-based approach*. This means that variants are defined with the help of the attributes in which the variants differ. Links in the "structure" table are then uniquely identified by the part numbers

Fig. 2.17 Key attribute "variant code" in a "structure" table

Structure					
Upper-part-id	Lower-part-id	Variant code		Quantity	...
		Attribute	Value		
X	A	C	gr	2	
X	A	C	re	2	
X	A	C	bl	2	
X	B			1	
X	C			2	
A	D			2	
A	E	P	40	1	
A	E	P	60	1	
A	E	P	80	1	
B	F			4	
C	G			2	
C	H			1	
G	I			2	
G	J			4	

of the upper and the lower parts, plus a variant code that defines the attributes of the specific variant under consideration. (In relational terminology, this means that the variant code is also a key attribute.) In this way, variant-specific parts can be marked and tracked down the product structure any number of manufacturing levels.

As an example, let us assume that variant X2 differs from X1 in that the color of assembly group A2 is green (instead of red in A1 or white in another variant) and the power of E2 is 80 kW (instead of 40 kW in E1 or 60 in another variant):

Attribute	Value
Color	Green
	Red
	White
Power	40
	60
	80

The variant code describing specific variants can be constructed from the attribute name (e.g., "C" for color and "P" for power) and the desired value (e.g., "gr" for green and "40" for 40 kW).

The product structure for this variant is generated only when an order for a particular variant, say "C = gr/P = 80," is placed. This happens in such a way that all rows exhibiting the variant code "C = gr" or "P = 80" are considered plus all rows that have no entries in the variant-code columns. Parts without a variant code go into all variants.

Figure 2.17 shows the structure table including variant codes. Because the variant parts are not listed as independent entities in the part master data, variant-specific part numbers such as X1, A1, and E1 do not no longer appear.

The variant problem is very complex. More advanced solutions employ *rule-based approaches*, especially for automatically generating variant bills of materials. Decision tables and knowledge-based solutions for this purpose have been integrated into ERP systems. For example, *Infor ERP COM* uses a knowledge base in which manufacturing and cost-related knowledge (including plausibilities) are stored. When a bill of materials is to be created, the knowledge base is processed, deriving feasible, cost-effective connections between the parts in question.

The next stage in on-the-fly creation of product structures, beyond dynamic variants, is *product configuration*. In electronic commerce, where customers may put the desired product together online, electronic configurators are especially common. Configuration will be discussed in more detail in Sect. 2.2.2.

2.1.3 More Master Data

While part data and product structure data are at the core of material requirements planning, many additional data structures are needed. These include supplier, customer, and warehouse data.

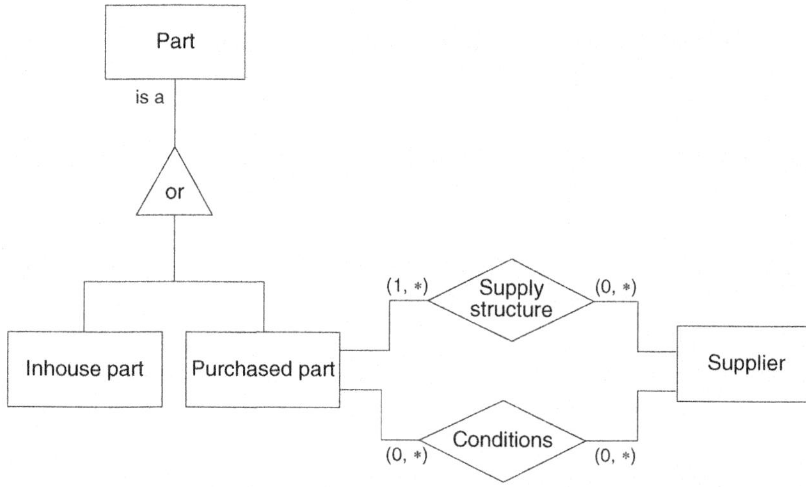

Fig. 2.18 ERM connecting parts and suppliers

Suppliers Supplier data are used in material requirements planning for procurement and purchase orders. Typical attributes of a supplier include:

- Supplier number
- Supplier name
- Address
- Contact person
- Payment data
- Supplier rating (e.g., percent of deliveries being disputed, quality, and average delay time)
- Liability limit

Suppliers are connected with those parts (materials) that are not produced in-house. In Fig. 2.18, these are the parts represented by the "purchased part" specialization of the entity type "part." The relationship type "supply structure" connects a purchased part with one or more suppliers.

In a similar way, these two entity types are again connected with the help of the relationship type "conditions." Attributes of this relationship type are the terms of delivery and payment (e.g., discount and time for payment allowed).

Customers Customer data are required for sales and distribution. Customers have similar attributes as suppliers, for example:

- Customer number
- Customer name
- Address
- Contact person
- Customer rating
- Credit line

Customers and parts (in particular, end products) are related in a similar way as suppliers and parts. Because of these similarities, we will refrain from showing the relationships between these entities again with a separate diagram.

Warehouse Warehousing data structures depend very much on the physical organization of the inventory. Few companies store everything, from raw materials to replacement parts and intermediate products, all the way to the end products, in just one warehouse. Most companies use multiple storage locations and different types of physical storage such as pallet shelves, silos, tanks, and high-bay warehouses. Therefore, different companies in different industries have rather different data models for their warehouse area.

Figure 2.19 assumes that, generally, a given part can be stored in different ways (i.e., different storage forms), for example, on palettes or stacked on a shelf. Storage locations are usually broken up into storage places that allow certain types of storage forms.

2.1.4 Dealing with Missing Data

In describing the MRP master data, we have assumed that either these data already exist or the organization possesses all information

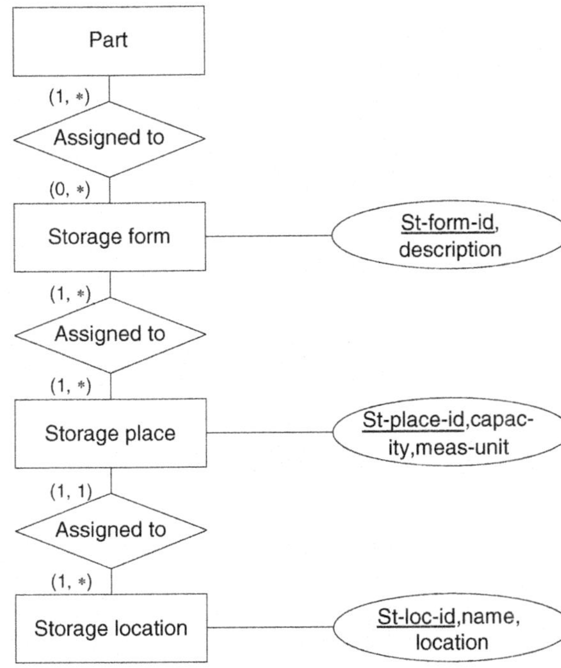

Fig. 2.19 Entity-relationship diagram for warehouse master data

needed to create the data. This assumption is usually satisfied when the organization is similar to the type described in the beginning of the chapter: producing a standard production program in mass or large-series production based on well-defined product structures and well-known demand curves and stocking the products.

Whenever customers are directly involved, the situation can be very different. In *make-to-order production*, the end products are often not predefined, but specified by the customer. For these products, the company will usually not have master data, unless the product has been built in the same way before. In *individual make-to-order production*, and especially in *individual one-time production*, the part and product structure data often have to be created just for the specific customer order.

This does not necessarily mean that every single part going into a customer-specific end product has to be designed from scratch. Make-to-order manufacturers also strive to use standard parts as much as possible, because it is more economical. A typical situation is therefore that the higher levels of a product structure exhibit new (i.e., customer-specific) parts, whereas on the lower levels, standard parts are found. For standard parts, master data exist, but for customer-specific parts, this is not the case.

Normally, an ERP system will require the company to create complete master data before any planning based on these data can be done. However, many make-to-order manufacturers are reluctant to make the effort of establishing new parts and product structures because their organization requires elaborate administrative processes for introducing (and approving) new parts.

On the other hand, an ERP system cannot do any planning without the underlying data structures. Therefore, at least some of the data have to be entered in one way or another. The ERP system can support this work effectively by providing adequate assisting features, including:

- Powerful copying and editing functions allowing existing part or product structure data to be copied and modified to suit the present needs
- Temporary parts and product structures which do not have to meet the same requirements as other database objects
- Product structures which reference incomplete part master data
- Planning features that exploit similarity (i.e., planning in analogy to previous similar orders)

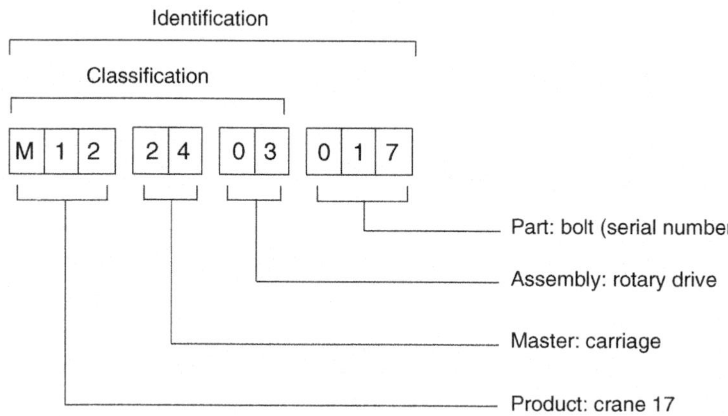

Fig. 2.20 Compound number (example)

2.1.5 A Note on "Numbers"

In the previous sections, so-called numbers were employed to identify the parts (materials) in material requirements planning. These numbers are present in the master data, product structures, bills of materials, where-used lists, and in many more places. Likewise, all other objects of enterprise resource planning, such as machines, routings, tools, orders, invoices, and customers, are identified by numbers.

Although we usually speak of "numbers," these numbers are not meant to be used as numerical values in computations nor are they exclusively composed of numerical digits. In the electric motor example above, the part number was "E10." The reader will find more examples of numbers (i.e., article numbers) by looking at any sales slip printed by a supermarket's cash register.

Many numbers contain long sequences of digits, and also letters, dashes, and other nonnumeric characters. The reason for these long strings is that the numbers serve more purposes than just identifying an object. In general, the purpose of a number can be:

- Identification—the number only identifies an object
- Classification—the number shows which category of objects the object belongs to
- Information—the number tells what the object is (so-called mnemonic number)

According to this distinction, different types of numbering systems have been developed and put into practice:

1. *Identification numbers* serve the sole purpose of uniquely identifying an object. The simplest numbering scheme for this is to use serial integer numbers starting with 1. Although textbook examples sometimes use this scheme, it is not typical for real-world applications.
2. *Classification numbers* categorize objects, that is, they are structured in a way that some places of the number are reserved for the category the object belongs to, other places for the subcategory, etc. For example, a numbering scheme may prescribe that the first two places are for the overall category of the part, the next three places for a form identifier, and the next three places for the basic material the part is made of. A part number would then be composed of three components: xx-xxx-xxx (e.g., 10-C12-133). Obviously such a number is generally not unique because there may be more than one part in the same subgroup.
3. *Compound numbers* extend classification numbers by an identifying number within the subgroup in order to make the number unique. Figure 2.20 shows an example. In addition to the classifying components, a serial number is used to uniquely identify the parts within subgroup 03 (rotary drive) of crane 17's carriage. It should be noted that the identifying part of the number is only unique within the subgroup 03, not within the entire part spectrum.
4. *Parallel numbers* do two things parallel and independently from each other: They classify a part and identify it at the same time. This means that the identifying number is unique

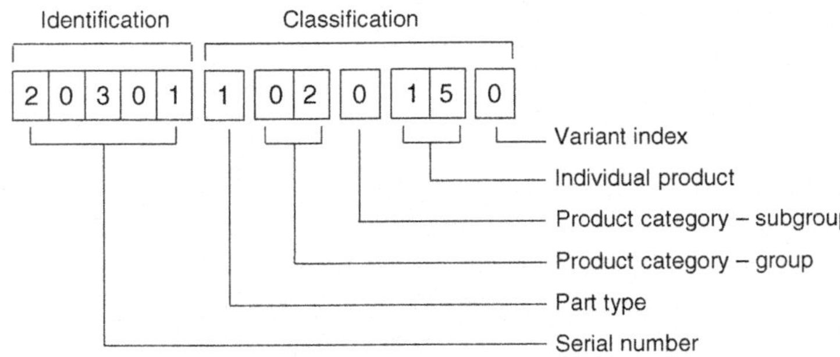

Fig. 2.21 Parallel number (example)

across *all* parts, not only within a group. Figure 2.21 shows an example in which the identifying number is a five-digit serial number and the rest is a classification number. Instead of a classification number, we sometimes find a compound number. This is due to the fact that numbering systems evolve. Often, companies that have been using compound numbers for years and are now going to a parallel numbering system prefer to keep the old numbers and just extend them.

Establishing a numbering system across an entire company is a comprehensive project involving all departments. Part numbers, for example, are needed for production planning, sales, product design, shop-floor control, procurement, cost calculation, invoicing, and many more business areas. These areas have different requirements as to what exactly the part number should express.

Since different interests and opinions on what the numbers should be like collide, it usually takes many years to implement a new system. This is one reason why numbering systems remain in place for a long time. Another reason for this is that the entire organization depends on the system. Experienced consultants recommend keeping a numbering system, once it is installed, for at least 15 or 20 years because of the cost involved with switching. It is very important to build flexibility and adaptability into the design of the system so that it can cope with changing requirements over the years.

2.2 Master Production Planning

Demand for end products can originate from an abstract sales plan or from concrete customer orders. Therefore, we distinguish between planning for anonymous demand (make-to-stock production) and planning for customer orders (make-to-order production).

2.2.1 Planning for Anonymous Demand

When a company produces goods to be sold on the market to customers who are not known at the time the production is planned, we speak of *anonymous demand*. The quantities to be manufactured depend on a sales plan or on expectations as to what the company will be able to sell in the future.

There are basically two approaches to draw up a master production plan: optimization and forecasting. While optimization is the preferred approach in management science, forecasting is the approach mostly taken in practice.

Optimization Model Creating an optimal *master production plan* (also known as *production program*) usually starts from figures taken from the company's sales plan. A *sales plan* indicates which quantities the company intends to sell within the period(s) under consideration. The sales plan can be compiled on an aggregate level (e.g., product groups) or refined down to the level of individual products. Accordingly, a master production plan may refer to product groups or individual products.

Vast numbers of optimization models for master production planning have been proposed in the literature. Many of them are set up as linear optimization models to be solved with *linear programming (LP)*. They are also known as *LP models*.

The following shows a simple LP model taking market, warehouse, and capacity constraints into account. The objective is to compute the quantities of all products to be produced within the given period (e.g., 1 year) so that the total contribution margin is maximized. To keep the model simple, the planning period is not divided into subperiods (e.g., months). This means that only the total quantity of each product for the entire period is computed, not the distribution across the subperiods.

Objective function

$$Z = \sum_{i=1}^{n} (p_i - c_i)x_i \text{ max.}$$

Constraints

$$x_i \leq q_1$$

$$x_n \leq q_n$$

$$\sum_{i=1}^{n} s_i x_i \leq \text{w}$$

$$\sum_{i=1}^{n} r_{i1} x_i \leq a_1$$

$$\sum_{i=1}^{n} r_{im} x_i \leq a_m,$$

with

Z = objective function (contribution margin)
x_i = quantity of product type i ($i = 1, \ldots, n$)
p_i = sales price per unit i
c_i = variable cost per unit i
q_i = maximum quantity of product type i that can be sold
s_i = storage place needed per unit i
w = total warehouse capacity
r_{ij} = required capacity of operating facility j per unit i
a_j = total available capacity of operating facility j ($j = 1, \ldots, m$)

Based on this simplified model, a number of extensions have to be made to represent more realistic planning situations. For example, since MRP has a granularity of quarters, months, or weeks, the total planning period has to be split up into subperiods. This introduces a large number of additional variables and constraints. Furthermore, constraints should be considered not only on the selling market side but also on the buying market (procurement) side. A number of additional modifications are necessary to tune the model. Altogether, this means that the model size grows, and the computability decreases.

Forecasting Methods Instead of optimizing the master production program, most ERP systems offer methods to *forecast* the future demand of end products to be produced. This means that the production program is not set up according to an optimality criterion, but by carrying the planning of the past forward into the future. Common forecasting methods include moving averages and exponential smoothing.

The *moving averages* method computes an average of the past n periods to predict what the demand of the product under consideration in the next period will be. Suppose the current period is $k-1$. Let m_j be the demand that actually occurred in period j and v_k the forecast for period k. Then, v_k is the average of the n most recent actual demands, that is, from period $k-n$ to $k-1$:

$$V_k = \frac{1}{n} \sum_{j=k-n}^{k-1} m_j.$$

This method is called "moving" because one period later, the average of actual demands now includes period k, but not $k-n$, that is, it goes from $k-n+1$ to k. Two periods later, the average refers to periods $k-n+2$ to $k+1$, etc.

Even though the moving averages method is extremely simple, it allows for slower or faster adaption to changing demand. If the parameter n is stipulated with a small value, then demand variations are quickly reflected in the forecast. If n is large, fluctuations are leveled, and outliers do not much affect the forecast.

In the following example, actual demand values from 6 past periods are given. Suppose n is 5 and we want to predict the demand for period 10.

Period j	...	4	5	6	7	8	9	10
Demand m_j	...	100	90	118	110	105	97	–

Computing the forecast for this period yields $v_{10} = 104$. If one period later we know that the actual demand in period 10 was 100, we can compute the forecast for the next period, resulting in $v_{11} = 106$.

Exponential smoothing is a method that can be configured to give recent demand fluctuations more weight than earlier ones. The forecast value v_k is easily calculated: It is equal to the previous forecast v_{k-1} plus the weighted deviation of the actual demand m_{k-1} from this forecast:

$$v_k = v_{k-1} + \alpha(m_{k-1} - v_{k-1}).$$

The weighting factor α is the parameter to influence the method's behavior. α can be stipulated with a value between 0 and 1. If α is close to 1, the forecast will be close to the actual demand in period $k-1$. This means that the forecasting immediately follows demand fluctuations. The opposite is true for a small α. This can be seen by setting α to 0. In this case, demand changes have no effect at all. The next forecast is the same as the previous one.

Between the two extremes, there is a range of possibilities to take recent demand values into account with great or with little weight ($0 < \alpha < 1$). In this way, the demand curve is smoothed to reflect demand variations either more or less quickly.

The table below illustrates the effect of different α values. Starting with period 6 ($v_5 = 100$), v_6 is 98 if $\alpha = 0.2$ but only 92 if $\alpha = 0.8$. Obviously, the drop in actual demand—forecast v_5 is 100 but actual demand m_5 is only 90—is reflected more immediately when α is larger.

Exponential smoothing as described above causes the forecasts to follow demand variations, but not all extreme movements (except if $\alpha = 1$), with a time lag. This is acceptable if there are ups and downs in the actual demand, but if all demand changes go in one direction, it may be preferable to catch up with the trend faster.

This can be achieved by smoothing not only the demand variations but also the forecast variations. Let

$$^2v_k = \text{second-order forecast}$$
$$^1v_k = \text{first-order forecast.}$$

The forecast from second-order exponential smoothing is obtained by first computing the first-order forecast ^1v_k as before, then computing the weighted deviation of the previous period's second-order forecast $^2v_{k-1}$ from ^1v_k and adding this deviation to $^2v_{k-1}$:

$$^2v_k = {}^2v_{k-1} + \alpha({}^1v_k - {}^2v_{k-1}).$$

Period j	...	4	5	6	7	8	9	10
Actual demand m_j	...	100	90	118	110	105	97	–
Forecast v_k								
For $\alpha = 0.2$		–	100	98	102.0	103.6	103.9	102.5
For $\alpha = 0.8$		–	100	92	112.8	110.6	106.1	98.8

In this way, the demand variations are smoothed twice. As a consequence, the forecasts are adapting faster to the actual demand curve, provided that the trend goes in one direction (i.e., continuously increasing or decreasing).

2.2.2 Planning for Customer Orders

Many companies today produce goods according to specific customer orders instead of according to an abstract production program. The previous section showed how a master production plan based on anonymous demand can be created. Now we will discuss what a customer-oriented manufacturing company has to do to determine their primary requirements.

Companies relying in their planning on customer orders are said to pursue *make-to-order production*. The majority of small and medium-sized manufacturing companies work in a make-to-order style. These companies, unlike make-to-stock manufacturers who produce standard goods to be stocked and sold from the warehouse, produce their goods when customers order them. This often implies that the customer specifies what the goods should be like (i.e., the product specification is provided by the customer).

Make-to-order production is common in the investment goods sector (e.g., machine tools, production facilities, cranes, and elevators). Typical make-to-stock manufacturers are found in the consumer goods sector (e.g., television sets, washing machines, and lamps). However, many consumer goods nowadays are made to order as well (e.g., cars and personal computers).

Primary requirements planning in make-to-order production is quite different from make-to-stock production. Instead of optimizing or forecasting a standard production program, all activities are related to specific customer orders. Typical tasks include scheduling the customer order to obtain a delivery date, designing the product the customer wants, calculating the cost of the product, making a quotation, etc.

Make-to-order production is not a uniform approach but includes a wide range of options. These options differ in the degree to which the planning, execution, and controlling actually depend on the customer order or are independent of the order.

For example, a customer may request an end product that needs to be designed in a specific way. This does not necessarily mean, however, that all parts going into that end product must be designed from scratch. Instead, the company will try to use as many standard parts as possible to cut costs. In another company, the situation may be different, requiring the company to manufacture not only the end product but also assemblies and individual parts specifically for the customer.

Thus, the spectrum of make-to-order production ranges from production types close to make-to-stock to one-time individual production, including the following levels:

- *Variant production*—customers can order variants of a basic product as discussed in Sect. 2.1.2.
- *Assemble-to-order*—customer-specific products are assembled from standard parts and subassemblies.
- *Subassemble-to-order*—customer-specific end products as well as customer-specific assemblies are made from standard subassemblies and parts.
- *Individual make-to-order*—in principle, all in-house-production parts of a customer-specific product are manufactured to the customer order.
- *Individual-purchase-and-make-to-order*—all parts needed for a customer-specific product (both in-house production and procured parts) are manufactured and purchased to the customer order.
- *Individual one-time production*—this is a special case of the two previous variants, meaning that the product is only produced once in this form as now specified by the customer (e.g., a ship).

Requirements for Make-to-Order Production Make-to-order production gives the customer a prominent role, in contrast to make-to-stock production where customers are not directly involved.

An important objective for the company is to satisfy the customer. Happy customers will return in the future and place more orders, which pays more for the company in the long term than minimizing production cost or maximizing capacity utilization.

Consequently, the goals of make-to-order production focus on *customer satisfaction*. Essential subgoals for production planning are short lead times, strict adherence to deadlines and delivery dates, high product quality, and flexibility regarding customer wishes. Pursuing these subgoals often increases the cost (e.g., overtime work, machine idle times, and air freight). A make-to-order manufacturer will normally accept this increase because the consequences of losing or disappointing the customer are considered to be more severe.

Another requirement in make-to-order production is that the status of all manufacturing orders connected with the customer order is available at all times. When the customer inquires about their orders, the sales employee must be able to find out on click what the current status is. Whenever problems in the plant occur that affect the customer order (e.g., a bottleneck machine breaks down), the sales employee must be immediately informed.

A precondition for employees to be well informed at any time is transparency of the manufacturing processes. This requires, for example, that all connections between manufacturing and purchase orders related to a customer order are explicitly stored. Likewise, all operating facilities involved must be identified. When all connections are available, it is possible to track the consequences of a problem occurring anywhere in the order network and to find out whether the problem will have an impact on the customer order. In other words, an ERP system suitable for make-to-order manufacturers has to create and maintain all connections between the relevant manufacturing entities.

The ERP system should also be able to work with incomplete master data. This problem has already been addressed in Sect. 2.1.4 above. Working with incomplete master data means that the ERP system can still perform material requirements planning, lead-time scheduling, and capacity planning, even though some of the underlying data structures (e.g., bills of materials and routings) are not complete or even missing. Obviously, the planning results will not be of the same quality and certainty as if they were based on complete data, which is the case in make-to-stock production.

Nevertheless, a make-to-order manufacturer also needs to plan the production, but the conditions under which the planning takes place are different from those a make-to-stock manufacturer is exposed to. Three crucial planning steps are:

- Order calculation
- Order scheduling
- Rough-cut planning

In contrast to make-to-stock production, most make-to-order manufacturers do not have a reliable, cost or profit-based production program from which they can derive the primary requirements. Therefore, they have to go other ways to determine favorable primary requirements that are in line with the company's cost or profit goals.

Two important decisions to make in this process are whether a customer order should be accepted and for what price. In order to be able to negotiate a reasonable selling price, the company needs to know the *cost* of the order.

Accordingly, *order calculation* (precalculation of a customer order) is of utmost importance. Cost calculation is normally based on master data such as parts, bills of materials, routings, and operating facilities (cf. Sect. 3.7.1). If these data are not available, it is difficult or impossible to reliably calculate the cost of a prospective order. Nonconventional approaches have to be applied to obtain even rough cost data (cf. Sect. 3.7.2).

A problem similar to order calculation is *order scheduling*. Scheduling is necessary to be able to agree on a delivery date with the customer. Normally, orders are scheduled using bills of materials and routings, with feasibility of the schedule being established based on capacity data (cf. Sects. 3.3 and 3.4). When these data are not available, other procedures to arrive at a plausible delivery date must be in place.

An important prerequisite for smooth manufacturing conditions in make-to-order production is a good *rough-cut planning*. Since many factors are still unknown, it is not possible to plan the customer orders in detail. Therefore, it is important to at least balance the overall material and capacity situation. If this balance can be established, it is possible later to schedule customer orders without (or with fewer) problems. This is, by the way, one of the fundamental ideas of manufacturing resource planning (MRP II, cf. Sect. 3.2), even though MRP II is targeted more toward make-to-stock than make-to-order production.

Product Specification End products in make-to-order production are typically not standard products but new or at least different products. Because the decisions mentioned above concerning price and time can only be made once the product is "known," one of the initial steps in the order fulfillment process (cf. Sect. 4.3.2) is to create a specification of the product in the ERP system. This may be done by adopting the customer's product specification (if they already have one), by creating a specification from scratch and/or by interacting with the customer, in order to derive the specification together.

A product specification is necessary to check the feasibility of the customer's product idea against the company's technological capabilities before the customer order is accepted. It is also needed to create order-specific master data such as bills of materials and routings, based on which material and capacity planning can be performed.

One relatively easy way to specify a customer-dependent product is to employ *product variants* as discussed in Sect. 2.1.2. This method, however, is only applicable when the product ordered by the customer is within the given spectrum of variants.

Product configuration goes one step farther than variant management. A *product configurator* is a program that allows a knowledgeable user to put together a product interactively from a set of given components. The program checks which combinations of assemblies, individual parts, and possibly raw materials are permitted and may recommend especially beneficial combinations.

When complex products are involved, there may be many rules and regulations that have to be considered. Human experts configuring these products are aware of the rules and regulations that may apply. A good product configurator produces results that come close to those of the human experts or in some cases even exceed them.

Product configuration was one of the first domains in which *knowledge-based systems*, especially *expert systems*, were successfully applied. The first configuration systems were developed in the 1980s for putting together computer systems, such as Digital Equipment's XCON [also known as R1 (McDermott 1981)]. These were followed by a large number of configurators for a variety of products (turbines, elevators, roller blinds, etc.).

Today, configuration systems are very common in *electronic commerce*, allowing customers to select which features of the product they prefer. The configuration program in the background checks whether the selected combination of features is feasible or allows the customer to select only those features that may be combined.

Product configurators can appear as separate systems or be integrated in an ERP system. Typical functionality of an interactive configuration module includes (Hüllenkremer 2003):

- Configuration on the basis of rules
- Immediate notification whether a selection option is permissible
- Automatic explanation of configuration errors
- Suggesting permissible or beneficial alternatives
- Graphic display of the product configuration, allowing the user to directly manipulate the graphic
- Integrated technical computations
- Simultaneous price calculation
- Automatic generation of a quotation (including terms and conditions)
- Internationalization and localization (multilingual settings, different currencies)

- Checking availability and delivery dates with the help of ERP functions
- Automatic preparation and transmission of order data to the ERP system, in case a stand-alone configuration system is used

A product configurator embedded in an ERP system or with interfaces to the ERP system has many advantages. For example, while in the field a sales representative can create and check a product specification together with the customer. Connecting her laptop to the ERP system in the headquarters, she can check immediately whether the configuration is reasonable, how much it costs and when the product will be available. In order to do so, she does not even need specific expertise, because the required knowledge is available in the expert system on her laptop. Based on the configuration result, she can immediately give the customer a quotation and confirm the delivery date.

Product configurators are often connected with *electronic product catalogs*. An electronic product catalog is a digital form of a printed catalog, containing information about products and prices. Today's electronic catalogs offer a wide spectrum of additional functions, for example, advanced searching options. Often the catalog is part of a web shop, which again is connected with an ERP system. In this way, the customer can select products from the product catalog, put them in a shopping cart, and complete the transaction by paying for the products.

If the products are not standard but configurable, the customer is redirected to the product configurator. The product configurator will not only help the customer to put the product together but also calculate the product price depending on the selected options. Afterward, the customer can place the configured product in the shopping cart and proceed to checkout.

2.3 Planning Primary and Secondary Requirements

Primary requirements are derived from the master production plan. Usually, they refer to end products, but other sellable goods (such as spare parts and assemblies) can also be involved. They are the starting point of material requirements planning.

The core of MRP is planning the *secondary requirements*. Secondary requirements refer to the intermediate products, raw materials, and consumables needed to produce the primary requirements.

The main task of secondary requirements planning is to compute the quantities of these materials. This task is closely related with a number of other areas such as procurement and inventory management.

Procurement is relevant because a good deal of the parts needed for the end products have to be purchased from suppliers. Procurement takes time, just as in-house production does. This must be taken into account in scheduling the secondary requirements. Procurement will be discussed in Sects. 4.3.1 and 5.3.2.

Inventory Management Inventory management goes hand in hand with requirements planning because quantities available on stock obviously do not have to be manufactured. Computing the *available stock* depends on what types of stock are kept and how refined the inventory management system is. Typical categories of inventory to be considered include the following:

- *Physical inventory*—the quantity of a part that is actually in the warehouse today
- *Shop-floor stock*—the quantity of a part waiting to be processed in the workshop(s)
- *Reserved stock*—the quantity of a part that is reserved for a customer/manufacturing order and thus not available for planning
- *Open order quantity*—the quantity of a part that has already been ordered from the factory (production orders) or from suppliers (purchase orders)
- *Reorder level*—the quantity of a part that causes a new order to be issued when the stock falls below this quantity (taking into account that the reordering takes time)
- *Safety stock*—the minimum quantity of a part the stock should not fall short of for safety reasons

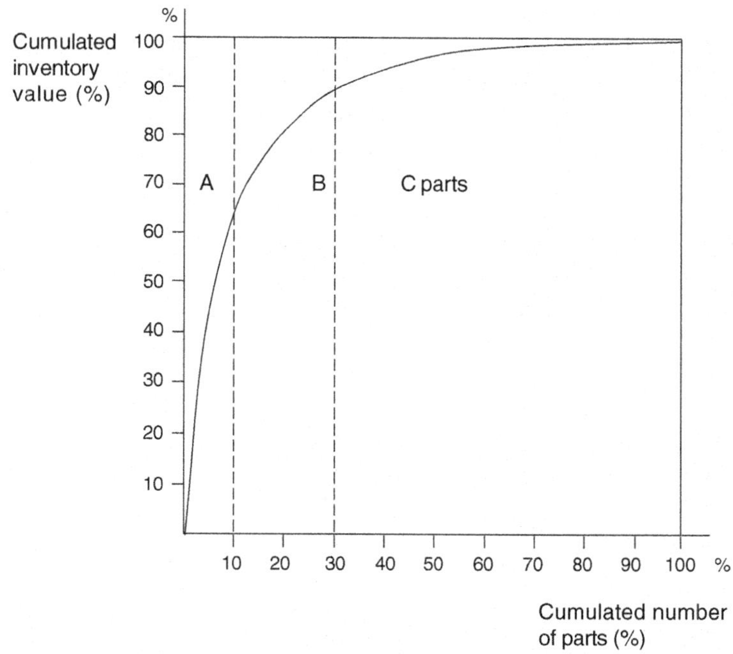

Fig. 2.22 Typical result of an ABC analysis

ABC Analysis The number of parts materials management has to deal with can be very large. The examples given in Sect. 1.5 exhibited figures up to 350,000 parts.

Not all parts are equally important. Some parts represent high values, causing substantial inventory and capital costs. Other parts are cheap, leading to rather insignificant inventory cost. From a business point of view, this means that excess inventory should be avoided as far as expensive parts are concerned but could be tolerated when the parts are cheap.

An approach to discriminate between important and less important parts is called *ABC analysis*. This name indicates that categories A, B, and C are used to classify all parts managed in the company, depending on their value. In order to do so, the inventory value of each part within a given period has to be determined. Then the parts can be arranged according to their value.

The result of arranging the parts is often plotted in the form of a so-called *Lorenz curve* as shown in Fig. 2.22. When doing an ABC analysis, many organizations realize that:

- A small percentage of their total part numbers (e.g., 10 %) account for a substantial share of the total inventory value (e.g., 65 %)—these are the *A parts*.
- Another ca. 20 % of the parts account for approximately 25 % of the value—these are the *B parts*.
- The largest percentage of parts (e.g., 70 %) accounts for only a small share of the total value (e.g., 10 %)—these are the *C parts*.

Since the A parts are expensive, causing high cost, it is essential that the requirements of these parts are carefully planned, using precise methods in order to avoid unnecessary inventory and shortage costs. Shortage cost would occur when not enough parts are available, leading to a disruption of the production process.

On the other hand, the C parts are less critical. Additional inventory to provide for safety buffers is acceptable because the additional inventory cost is low. Therefore, C parts can be planned with less precision using simpler methods.

For *secondary requirements planning*, two basic approaches exist, differing with regard to computation time and accuracy of the results. These approaches are:

- Consumption-driven (stochastic) planning
- Demand-driven (deterministic) planning

Consumption-driven planning is fairly simple but not exact, whereas requirements-driven planning is exact, but requires a lot of computing effort. Taking these characteristics into account, many companies choose to employ the two approaches as follows:

- A parts are planned in a requirements-driven way.
- B parts are also planned requirements driven or partly requirements and partly consumption driven.
- C parts are planned consumption driven.

2.3.1 Consumption-Driven Planning

Consumption-driven planning involves estimating the secondary requirements based on past consumption rates, whereas requirements-driven planning calculates the exact amounts using the bills of materials.

The same methods used to forecast end-product sales can be used to predict future material requirements: moving averages, exponential smoothing, etc. If the forecast value applies to an entire period (e.g., a quarter) and consumption is constant per unit of time, a *consumption rate* can be calculated by dividing the forecast value by the length of the period. This quotient is also known as the *withdrawal rate*.

After the forecasted requirements have been determined, two other issues need to be addressed:

1. When should a purchase order be placed (for purchased parts) or a production order be initiated (for in-house production)?
2. How much should be ordered or produced?

Both questions are interrelated. Shorter time intervals between orders lead to smaller order sizes and vice versa. In practice, the *order date* is often determined by using the reorder point R. When the inventory falls below this level, an order for a certain quantity (usually named Q) is initiated. In inventory theory, this is referred to as an *(R, Q) policy* ("reorder point/order-quantity policy").

Another order policy is the *(s, S) policy*, also known as *periodic review policy*. In this policy, two numbers, s and S, are used. When the inventory is less than or equal to s, the difference between a predefined maximum order quantity S and the inventory on hand is ordered (Nahmias 2008, p. 263).

When using an (R, Q) policy, it is important to set the reorder point high enough so that the safety stock is preserved until the new order arrives. The most important factor in determining the reorder point is the *replenishment time*. It includes (Mertens 2009, p. 76):

- Preparation time (preparation of a purchase order or production order)
- Delivery time (for purchased parts) or lead time (for in-house production)
- Storing time (time from goods received to goods available for consumption)

The relationship between these times is depicted in Fig. 2.23, assuming a linear decrease in inventory. If t_w represents the replenishment time, then an order must be placed when the stock level reaches R. The period of time t_z serves as a buffer. Assuming the same constant withdrawal rate, the production process will not be affected by delivery delays shorter than t_z.

The reorder point can be saved with the parts' inventory or master data in the database, as long as the withdrawal rate is more or less constant. When a withdrawal is booked, the remaining stock is compared with the reorder level. If the remaining stock is below the reorder level, an order is initiated. When there is a great deal of fluctuation in the consumption, the reorder level should not be maintained as a constant but determined period by period to avoid unnecessary stock or shortages.

The risk of running short of inventory can to some extent be countered with *safety stock*. It is important to set the safety stock at an appropriate level. A large safety stock means better protection from risk but leads to high inventory cost. A small safety stock means less inventory cost but a higher risk that missing material will disrupt the manufacturing process. How much safety stock is appropriate must therefore be determined by balancing the cost of inventory and the willingness to take risks.

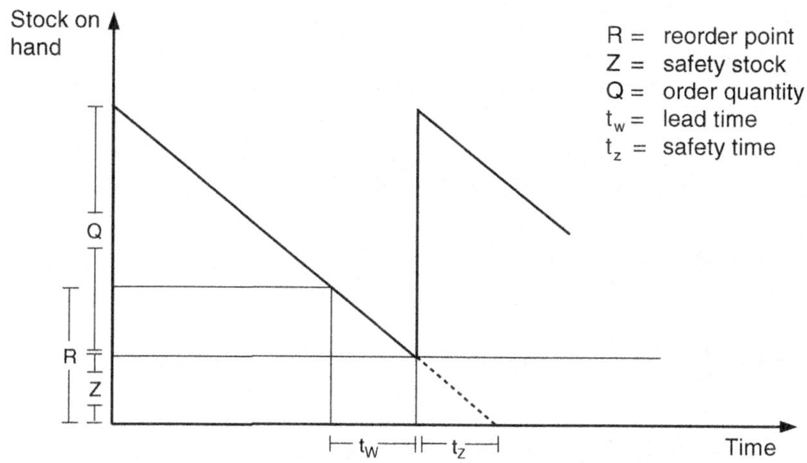

Fig. 2.23 Inventory level with constant withdrawal rate

Calculating Order Quantities In addition to reorder levels and order dates, the quantities to be ordered from suppliers (procurement) or from production planning (in-house manufacturing) have to be calculated. The term *order quantity* stands both for the size of a purchase order and the size of a manufacturing order. In the context of inventory theory, manufacturing orders are usually called production lots, and the quantity is referred to as the *lot size*.

We will mostly be using the terms *order* and *order quantity* to refer to both purchase orders and manufacturing orders. Both cases are similar in that an order is placed—either with a supplier or with the company's production department.

Although purchase orders refer to external procurement and production lots to in-house production, in principal, the same methods can be used. In both cases, conflicting cost relationships are in play, and a decision maker must try to size the purchase order or the production lot in a way that keeps the cost at a minimum. With externally procured parts, this quantity is called the "optimal order quantity" (or "economic order quantity"), whereas for in-house produced parts, the term "optimal lot size" (or "economic lot size") is used in the literature. A *lot* (or production lot) is the amount of parts that are produced together.

In the past, many models and methods have been proposed to calculate the optimal lot size. An evaluation of 30 inventory and lot-sizing models based upon comprehensive simulation experiments can be found in Knolmayer (1985). The 1960s in particular experienced a boom in lot-size research.

In practice, however, only a handful of the research findings have been implemented. Real manufacturing processes are extremely complicated and very difficult to represent in mathematical models and calculations. Only few approaches have made their way into today's ERP systems, namely:

- Fixed period requirements
- Economic order quantity (economic lot size)
- Moving reorder quantity
- Part-period algorithm

Fixed Period Requirements This method is not concerned with calculating any optimal quantities. Instead, the order quantity is set to a fixed value. This value can be saved in the part master data.

Economic Order Quantity The best-known method for calculating an optimal order quantity goes back to the beginning of the twentieth century. It was made popular by several authors—K Andler, FW Harris, and RH Wilson. It is also known as the *root formula*.

This method assumes that the requirements of a planning period (e.g., 1 year) are known and constant over time. During the planning period, the requirements are the same for each time unit (e.g., a day). Parts are withdrawn from the warehouse at a constant rate. The goal of the method is to minimize the sum of the fixed and variable (i.e., quantity dependent) costs within the planning period. *Variable cost* is the cost depending on the size of the order, most of which is inventory cost. *Fixed cost* is independent from the order quantity. For in-house production, this is primarily the setup cost.

Under the preconditions of this model, the optimal order quantity is computed by minimizing a cost function. Let

K_l = the total quantity dependent cost
K_r = the total fixed cost in the planning period
k_l = variable (quantity dependent) cost per unit and period
k_r = fixed cost per order
a = frequency of placing an order within the planning period
T = length of the planning period
y = total demand in the planning period
x = order quantity

Then the total fixed cost is

$$K_r = ak_r$$

or, because $a = y/x$,

$$K_r = y/xk_r.$$

Assuming a constant stock withdrawal rate, the average stock is $x/2$, and thus, the total variable cost amounts to

$$K_l = x/2k_lT.$$

Depending on the order quantity x, the total decision relevant cost K is

$$K(x) = K_r + K_l = y/xk_r + x/2k_lT.$$

The minimum of this function, differentiated by x, is

$$x=\sqrt{\frac{2k_ry}{k_lT}}.$$

x is the *optimal order quantity* (or "optimal lot size," "economic order quantity," and "economic lot size"). In order to meet the demand, x must be ordered a times within the planning period. From $a = y/x$ follows

$$a=\sqrt{\frac{yk_lT}{2k_r}}.$$

Although x is called an "optimal" order quantity, this optimum can be achieved only under restrictive premises, including the following:

- No capacity restrictions are in place regarding the delivery (of externally procured parts), production (of in-house produced parts), and inventory capacities.
- The demand for the entire planning period is known.
- The demand is the same for all periods. The withdrawal rate is constant for all periods.
- The cost price (or the production cost, resp.) per unit is given and independent of the quantity.
- In the case of in-house production, the product is not connected with other parts on higher or lower manufacturing levels, or if so, these connections can be disregarded.

Although in practice these premises are seldom met, the root formula is still acknowledged in inventory theory and remains one of the options available in most ERP systems.

Moving Reorder Quantity Unlike the economic order quantity, the moving reorder-quantity (MRQ) method does not assume that the demand is the same for all (sub) periods across the entire planning horizon. Instead, different demand values per period are considered.

The MRQ method approximates the minimum of the total cost per unit. For a single demand y_i to be met in period j, which is procured or produced in period i ($i \leq j$), the *inventory cost* for storing the quantity y_i amounts to

$$k_ly_j(j - i).$$

Combining the demands of the periods i to $t\,(i \le t)$ into one order results in inventory cost of

$$k_1 \sum_{j=i}^{t} y_j(j-i).$$

The *total cost* of periods i to t, K_{it}, is then

$$k_{it} = k_r + k_1 \sum_{j=i}^{t} y_j(j-i).$$

and the cost per unit is

$$k_{it} = \frac{k_{it}}{\sum_{j=i}^{t} y_j}.$$

The moving reorder-quantity method proceeds step by step, adding up period demands one by one until k_{it} has reached its minimum. In other words, we are looking for that value of t for which

$$k_{it} < k_{it+1}$$

if one more demand (y_{t+1}) were added. Once the value of t has been determined, the *optimal order quantity* is

$$x = \sum_{j=i}^{t} y_j.$$

The moving reorder-quantity method is suitable in practice when the demands of all periods and the cost coefficients k_r and k_1 are known. It does, however, have the disadvantage that minimizing the cost per unit is not necessarily the same as minimizing the total cost of a planning period.

Part-Period Algorithm The part-period algorithm attempts to minimize the cost per order (DeMatteis 1968). It builds on a property of the classical economic order-quantity model, namely, that in the optimum, the inventory cost K_1 and the fixed cost K_r are equal. This can be seen by setting the first derivative of the cost function

$$K(x) = y/x \cdot k_r + x/2 \cdot k_1 T$$

to zero, resulting in

$$y/x \cdot k_r = x/2 \cdot k_1 T.$$

The left side of the equation has the fixed cost K_r, while the right side has the inventory cost K_1.

The part-period algorithm applies this property to a situation where the demand is not continuous, as in the economic lot-size model, but discrete (i.e., individual period demands). In the part-period algorithm, the optimum is approximately reached when an order's inventory cost equals its fixed cost:

$$k_1 \sum_{j=i}^{t} y_j(j-i) = k_r$$

A transformation of this equation to

$$\sum_{j=i}^{t} y_j(j-i) = \frac{k_r}{k_1}$$

shows that both sides have the dimension "quantity multiplied by periods" (or "number of *parts* multiplied by number of *periods*"), hence the name of this method.

Just as in the moving reorder-quantity method, the algorithm proceeds by successively adding period demands y_t and examining whether or not the left side is still less than the right. Once

$$k_1 \sum_{j=i}^{t+1} y_j(j-i) > k_r,$$

the optimum has been passed. Hence, the optimal order quantity is

$$x = \sum_{j=i}^{t} y_j.$$

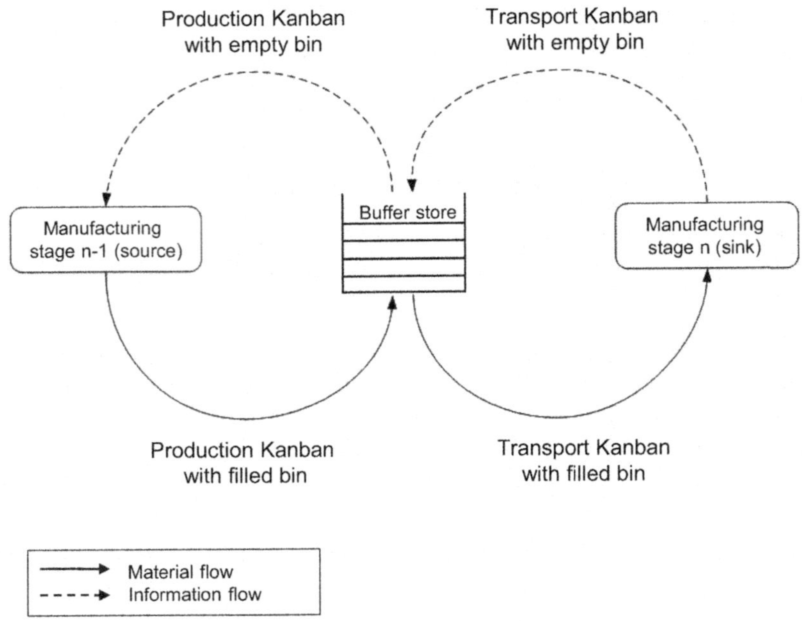

Fig. 2.24 Kanban control cycle (Loos 2011)

To conclude this subsection on optimal order quantities, it is worth noting that the "optimum" is not very sensitive to changes. For example, it does not make much difference whether the fixed and quantity-dependent costs are exactly the same or not. Specifically, increasing the quantity has less effect on the cost than decreasing it. In the economic order-quantity model, the cost increases only by 8 % when the order size increases by 50 % or decreases by one third. For the iterative methods (moving reorder-quantity and part-period methods), this means that it may be acceptable to just add another demand in order to reduce the risk of shortages.

In many companies, optimization of the order sizes is not of central importance, because the costs that can be influenced make up only a relatively small percent of the total production cost.

Excursus: Kanban A special form of consumption-driven requirements planning is based on the *Kanban* principle. Kanban is a Japanese word for a signboard or a card used to indicate something. The Kanban principle stands for a just-in-time form of decentralized control where the consumption of material drives the replenishment of inventory from the source that provides the material.

Applied to production planning and control, the Kanban principle is used to harmonize the flow of parts between two subsequent manufacturing stages and the production of parts. When demand is recognized in stage n, supply from stage $n-1$ is requested. This is accomplished by using *Kanban cards*.

Figure 2.24 illustrates the basic idea with the help of two manufacturing stages communicating through Kanban cards and transport bins. Two types of cards are used in this system: production Kanbans and transport Kanbans.

A *production Kanban* is attached to a bin containing material that is brought from stage $n-1$ to the buffer store located in front of stage n. The transporter leaves the production Kanban behind in the buffer store.

When stage n needs material for its operations, a bin with a *transport Kanban* attached is taken from the buffer store and brought to the manufacturing site. When the buffer is depleted or when a certain number of production Kanbans have accumulated in the buffer store, the Kanbans are returned to stage $n-1$, thereby initiating the production of more parts to eventually fill up the buffer store.

In case stage $n-1$ runs short of parts needed for the production, demand is communicated to stage $n-2$, using the production Kanbans in the buffer store in the front of stage $n-1$. This continues all the way to the raw-material stage. In this fashion, the entire manufacturing chain, from the last stage to the first, is organized according to the "pull principle," demanding supply when it is actually needed.

Conventional MRP and MRP II planning, on the other hand, relies on the "push principle," meaning that supply is provided to stage n by stage n-1 according to previously planned demand and not to actual demand.

Kanban was originally developed by Toyota as a manual approach to lean production (Ohno and Bodek 1988). Meanwhile, electronic versions have been implemented in a number of ERP systems, sometimes called "e-Kanban." Instead of paper cards, they employ electronic media using barcodes or RFID tags (cf. Sect. 11.4.1).

Kanban works best when the flow of production is smooth and uninterrupted, as can be the case in series or mass production. Kanban is actually a means of fine-tuning smooth production. Conditions under which the Kanban approach has proved to be beneficial include the following (Takeda 2006, pp. 185–189):

- Standardized production program, using standard parts as much as possible in order to realize continuous consumption
- Production organization according to the material flow
- Effective transportation system, short transport times
- Small lots (lot size is in fact the amount of parts that fit into one or more bins)
- High availability of operating facilities, short changeover times
- Low defect rate through immediate quality assurance at the workplace

Kanban systems exist in different versions and are used for different purposes. Some applications utilize more or fewer types of Kanbans instead of the two described above. This is the case when external suppliers are included. The most successful applications of Kanban have been reported from supply chains of the Japanese automotive industry.

2.3.2 Requirements-Driven Planning

While consumption-driven planning focuses on assumptions and estimates, requirements-driven planning is based on certainty. Therefore, it is also called *deterministic planning*. As long as the primary requirements are as expected, the secondary requirements can be calculated exactly. For this purpose, product structures (bills of materials) are employed to determine the quantities of subordinate parts needed to produce the primary requirements.

Using bills of materials to determine the secondary requirements is also known as *bill of materials explosion*. Programs exploding bills of materials are called *bill of materials processors (BOM processors)*. A BOM processor is a core component of any MRP system.

Whereas consumption-driven planning treats each part separately, requirements-driven planning must take into account how the parts are related with each other. Because of the hierarchical relationships within the product structures, decisions made on a higher level affect the lower levels as well.

When in Fig. 2.25, for example, the lot size of assembly A is doubled, the secondary requirements for parts that go into this assembly (D and E) are also doubled. On the other hand, if assembly C is still stocked, less of C needs to be produced and also less of all other parts that go directly or indirectly into C (i.e., G, H, I, and J).

This example clearly shows that in requirements-driven planning, calculating gross and net requirements and building lot sizes are closely connected. Principally, each of the following tasks must be completed for every part, before the next part is dealt with:

1. Gross requirements planning
2. Net requirements planning
3. Order-size planning
4. Dependent requirements planning

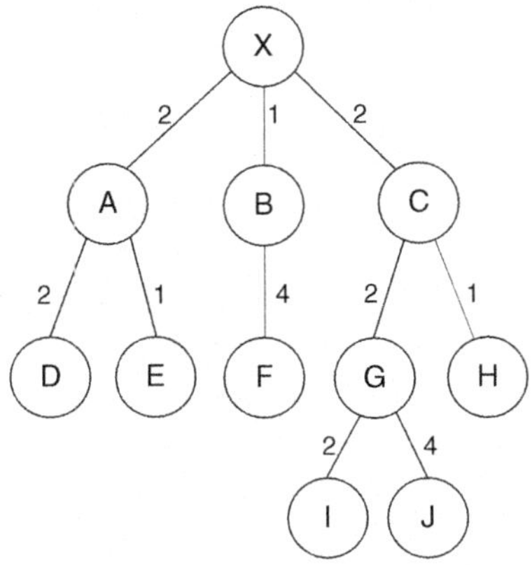

Fig. 2.25 Product structure (example)

5. Forward shifting

When dealing with a leaf of a product structure tree, the last two tasks are omitted.

Gross Requirements Planning For *end products* and sellable intermediate products, planning the gross requirements starts from the primary requirements as determined in primary requirements planning (cf. Sect. 2.3.1). For *dependent parts,* the starting point is the secondary requirements derived from higher-level nodes of the product hierarchy. In addition to these quantities, other components may be added, for example, requirements for replacement parts and estimates based on seasonal consumption patterns.

Net Requirements Planning To determine the net requirements, *available stock* must be subtracted from the gross requirements. Parts planned according to the requirements-driven approach may still be stocked, for example, when inventory orders were included in the plan (i.e., internal orders filling gaps in the capacity utilization), when the gross requirements include consumption-driven components, or when unneeded buffers are left over (e.g., for a previous order, more than the actually needed quantity was produced).

Depending on how differentiated the warehousing structure is, safety stock, shop-floor stock, reservations, and open purchase orders may be taken into consideration. If waste is anticipated, the net requirements must be multiplied by the expected waste factor.

A detailed scheme for planning gross and net requirements is shown in Fig. 2.26 (Mertens 2009, p. 133). It contains sample data for the above-mentioned factors, divided into periods.

Order-Size Planning When the net requirements for a certain number of periods are known, they can either be directly used for planning the requirements on the next level or they can be bundled into *production lots*. In Fig. 2.26, the net requirements from periods 2, 3, and 4 have been combined into one lot (2,208 units) and the net requirements from periods 5 and 6 into another lot (1,887 units).

Order quantities may also be computed for externally procured parts. However, the steps following order-size planning—derived requirements planning and forward shifting—are obviously not applicable to purchased parts. Instead, purchase orders are created and order placement is initiated.

For lot-size planning, basically the same methods as described above are used. From a theoretical standpoint, this is problematic because the presumptions on which the "optimality" of a lot size is based are largely not met. In particular, computing lot sizes without considering the connections with other parts can cause problems later on. The quantity of a lot on a given level of a product structure affects the planning of all parts on the lower levels. This problem will be explored in more detail with the help of Figs. 2.27 and 2.28 below.

Dependent Requirements Planning This process step starts from the production lots computed in step 3. Using the product structures of the parts involved, it derives dependent (or secondary) requirements. Multiplying the lot size with the quantity coefficients results in the quantities of those parts directly needed for the current part.

As an example, let us assume that the planning shown in Fig. 2.26 was for assembly C

Fig. 2.26 Gross and net requirements planning [Mertens 2009, p. 133]

Period		1	2	3	4	5	6
Total dependent requirements for one assembly (from BOM explosion)		700	550	1300	800	900	700
+ Consumption-driven demand		270	400	300	140	340	250
+ Independent requirements (replacements)		130	200	100	60	160	50
= Gross requirements		1100	1150	1700	1000	1400	1000
Warehouse stock - Safety stock - Reserved stock*)	3000 300 900						
= Available stock	1800	1800	700		300	600	
Open production-order quantity - Forecasted rejections	900 90						
- Inflow from recycling			50			100	
= Available stock from production order	810			450	360		
= Net requirements		-	400	1250	340	700	1000
+ Additional requirements for scrap (10%, factor 0.11)		-	44	137	37	77	110
= Extended net requirements		-	444	1387	377	777	1110
Lot sizing		-	2208	-	-	1887	-

*) This reserved stock is released to available stock in periods 4 and 5.

Exact requirements for further planning/explosion

Fig. 2.27 Derived requirements and forward shifting with lot sizes

Period	1	2	3	4	5	6
Net requirements C (after lot-size planning)	-	2208	-	-	1887	-
Dependent requirements G	-	4416	-	-	3774	-
After forward shifting	4416	-	-	3774	-	-
Dependent requirements H	-	2208	-	-	1887	-
After forward shifting	2208	-	-	1887	-	-

Fig. 2.28 Derived requirements and forward shifting without lot sizes

Period	1	2	3	4	5	6
Net requirements C (no lot sizing)	-	444	1387	377	777	1110
Dependent requirements G	-	888	2774	754	1554	2220
After forward shifting	888	2774	754	1554	2220	-
Dependent requirements H	-	444	1387	377	770	1110
After forward shifting	444	1387	377	777	1110	-

of Fig. 2.25. Figure 2.27 continues the planning process, illustrating the dependent requirements for parts G and H.

Forward Shifting Although the focus of MRP is on planning quantities, the temporal structure of the production process is not completely disregarded. Taking into account that executing a production order takes a certain amount of time, the derived requirements needed for the order must be completed earlier by just that amount of time. This time is called a *forward shift* or *lead-time offset*. If, for example, the size of lot C is such that it takes 14 days to manufacture the lot, then all parts that go into C (H and G) must be available 14 days earlier than C, that is, the lead-time offset is 14 days.

The purpose of forward shifting is to give the material requirements plan a rough temporal structure. This, however, is not straightforward, because the actual manufacturing dates depend on decisions that are made later in the planning process. Therefore, rough estimates based on experience have to be used instead, depending on what information is available, how certain the expectations are, and how much computational effort is reasonable. Typical approaches are:

- The lead time is actually calculated, using the setup, transition, and processing times stored in the routing and operating facility data. This time is then used to shift the derived requirements forward (i.e., toward the present).
- The same forward shift is applied across the board for all parts of one manufacturing level. The lead-time offset can be determined, for example, from the average offset that was actually observed in the past.
- The same forward shift (e.g., one or two periods) is applied to all parts and all manufacturing levels.

The first approach is without question the most accurate, provided that the lead-time components can be predicted with sufficient certainty. Unfortunately, calculating a forward shift is often not feasible, because it would basically require a complete lead-time and capacity-scheduling run. Therefore, many manufacturing companies use the same time span as lead-time offset for all parts of the same manufacturing level or even across all levels. The schema of Fig. 2.27 showed an example of a standard lead-time offset of one period.

When all steps of requirements-driven planning for the part under consideration have been completed, the same steps are applied to the next part, as long as the part is not a leaf of a product structure tree. In this way, roughly scheduled derived requirements are created for all parts. In one of the next rounds, for example, the tasks of gross and net requirements planning, lot-size planning, dependent requirements planning, and forward shifting will be executed for assembly G.

Impact of Lot-Size Planning When individual requirements on a higher level are bundled into lots, this changes the requirements and time planning of all lower parts, directly or indirectly.

To demonstrate the effect of lot sizing, we will take up the planning scheme shown in Fig. 2.26. If each period's requirement is produced as a separate lot (i.e., no specific lot sizing), the derived quantities and dates for parts G and H are as in Fig. 2.28, assuming a forward shift of one period. If, however, lots are planned, requirements for lower-level parts going into the current part move up in time. The required quantities are higher in some periods and nonexistent in others. This effect was illustrated in Fig. 2.27.

Another effect of lot-size planning is that assumptions are made regarding the availability of the operating facilities at the implied manufacturing dates. Not only the facilities needed for the current part but also those needed for the subordinate parts have to be available on the right dates so that the production can be completed on time.

To illustrate this effect, let us assume that part H needs only one machine and the capacity requirements are approximately proportional to the quantity. In this case, the allocation of

Fig. 2.29 Consequences of lot-size planning for capacity requirements

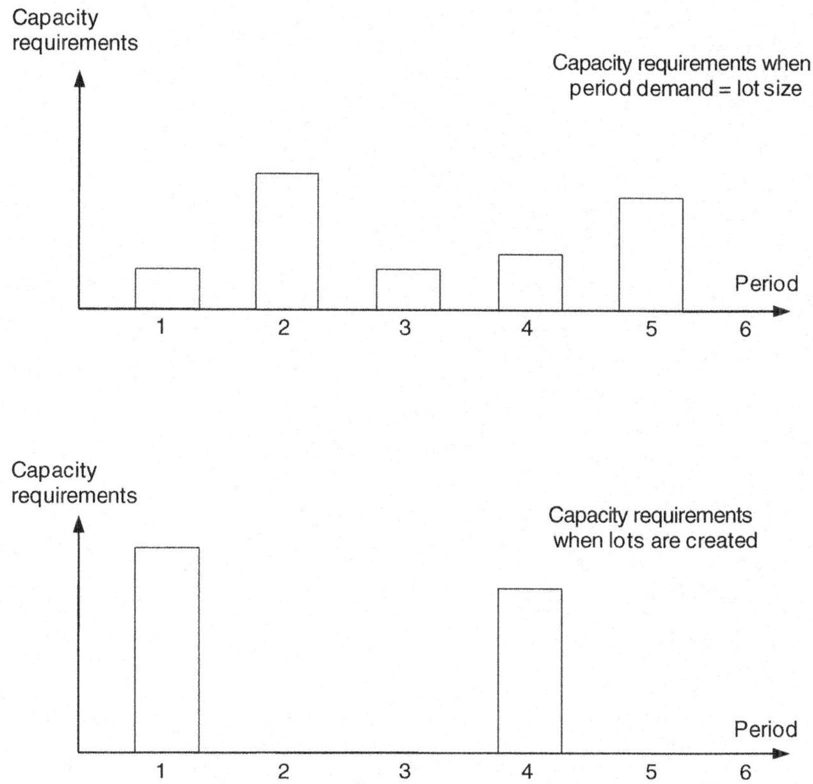

capacity requirements is as shown in Fig. 2.29. On the other hand, when lot sizes are planned, the capacity demand is significantly higher in periods 1 and 4. This means that the higher-level part C can only be produced as planned if the increased capacity necessary for part H is available in periods 1 and 4.

From a theoretical point of view, the connections between lot-size planning and capacity requirements have to be taken into account for all of the parts. Otherwise, any attempt to optimize the production plan will at best end up in a suboptimum.

In practice, however, *feasibility* of the production plan has usually received more attention than optimization. Therefore, material requirements planning focuses only on the quantities, relying on the implicit assumption that the required capacity will be available when the production has to be completed. This assumption, however, is only justified when the production program is basically stable, the demand curves are well known and more or less uniform, and the midterm available capacity is about equal to the required capacity.

Although not without problems, this is also the underlying assumption of the planning approaches supported by MRP, MRP II, and ERP systems. Only in the field of supply chain management (SCM) have interdependencies between different parts, quantities, and capacities been explicitly taken up and are being considered in the planning approaches.

Manufacturing Levels vs. Low-Level Codes

Requirements-driven material planning can be performed in basically two different ways: by manufacturing levels or by low-level codes. The first way is most common when dealing with a single product structure, for example, in make-to-order production. The second way is typical when all products of a standardized end-product program are included, for example, in mass or series production.

Proceeding by manufacturing levels means that one product structure tree at a time is

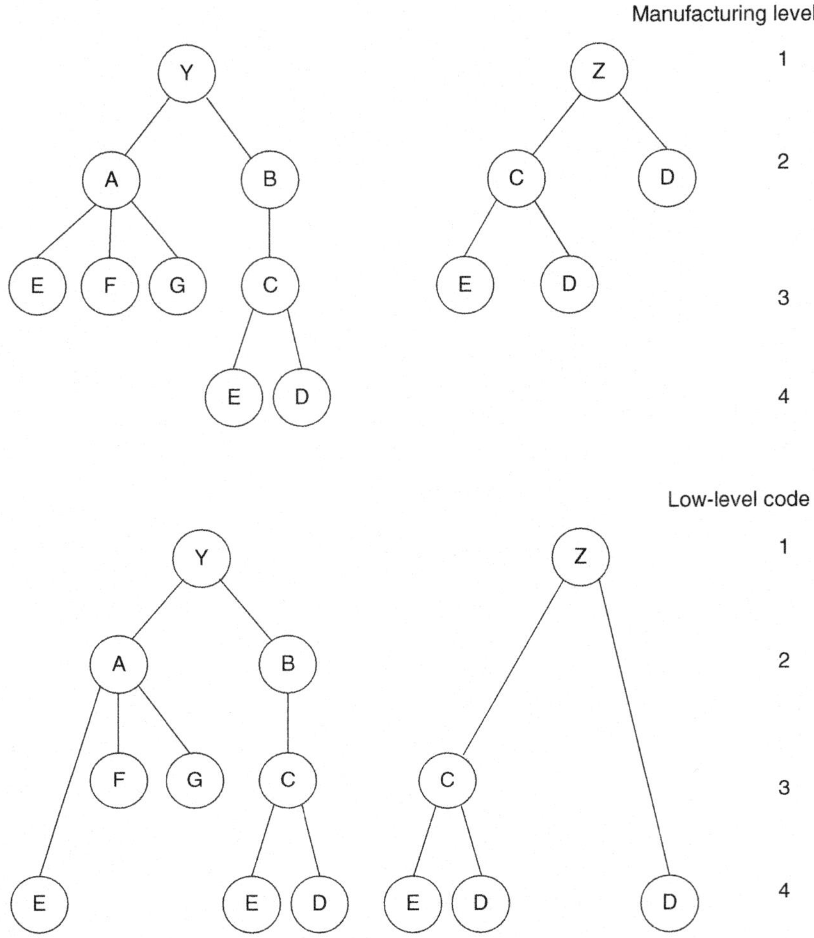

Fig. 2.30 Product structures by manufacturing levels and low-level codes

traversed, branch-by-branch, part-by-part, and from top to bottom. If a part appears more than once in the tree (or in different trees), it is dealt with several times. In Fig. 2.30 (upper section), this is the case for parts C, D, and E.

Calculating net requirements involves subtracting available stock in the course of the process. Since higher-level parts are considered first, the existing stock is assigned to the higher manufacturing levels. This may cause net requirements to appear for the same part on a lower level.

However, the temporal structure of the production process is such that the lower-level parts have to be available *before* the higher-level parts. As a consequence, production of a part that occurs both on a lower and a higher level will be initiated to fill the lower-level requirements, although at the time stock is still available. This stock, however, was reserved to fill the higher-level requirements at a later point in time.

To avoid such misassignments of available stock, so-called *low-level codes* were introduced. In this approach, the product structures are reorganized across all trees in such a way that each part occurs only on one level. Graphically speaking, the trees are stretched vertically so that each node reaches the lowest manufacturing level that the part has in any branch of any of the trees. This level is called the low-level code of the part. In the lower section of Fig. 2.30, parts D and E receive the low-level code 4 and part C the code 4.

Requirements-driven planning by low-level codes starts with the first part on the highest level (code 1), executing:

- Gross requirements planning
- Net requirements planning

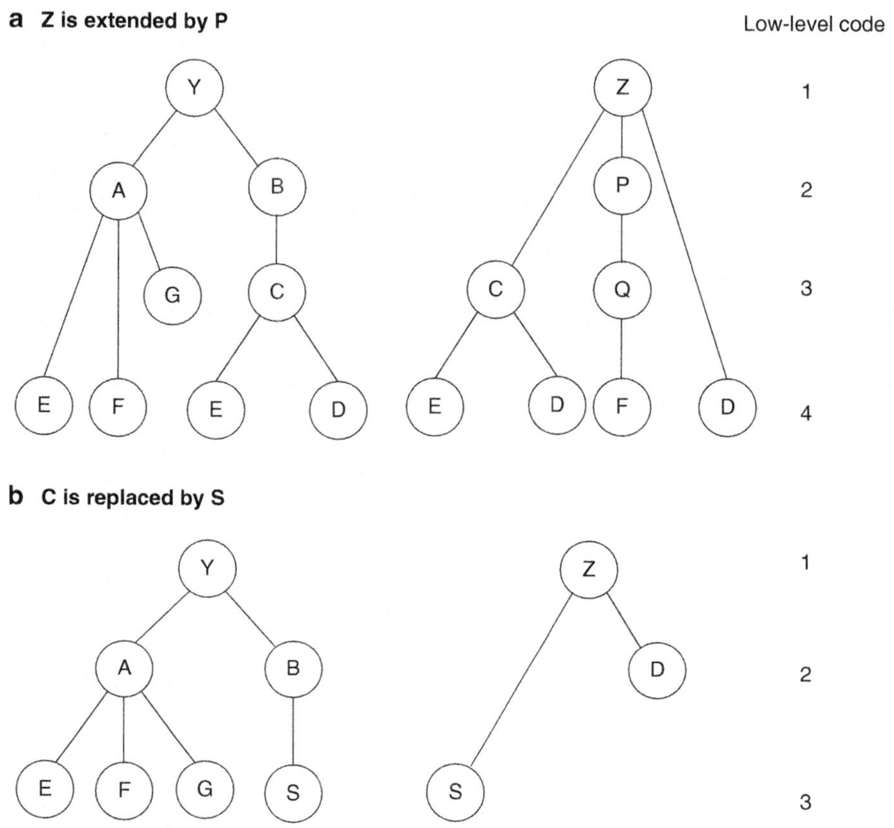

Fig. 2.31 Induced changes of low-level codes

- Lot-size planning
- Deriving requirements for subordinate parts
- Forward shifting

for this part. Then it continues with the next part of level 1, then with the next to the next part of level 1, etc. When all parts of level 1 have been dealt with, the process goes to the next level, treating all parts with low-level code 2 as above, then to the next level, etc.

In this process, requirements for subordinate parts occurring on several levels and/or in several product structures are gradually collected and accumulated, as the process touches the respective nodes in those structures. Requirements planning for a derived part (i.e., gross and net requirements planning, lot sizing, etc.) does not start until the part's low-level code has been reached in the process. When all parts on all levels have been dealt with, the total requirements for all parts are available in the database.

Using low-level codes, the parts shown in Fig. 2.30 would be processed in the following sequence:
Level 1: Y, Z
Level 2: A, B
Level 3: C, F, G
Level 4: D, E

Low-level codes help to avoid mistakes in requirements-driven planning such as inadequate allocation of stock, but they also have *disadvantages*. Worth mentioning is the administration effort. Creating the codes across hundreds of thousands or millions of parts is an extremely time-consuming task, although simple from an algorithmic point of view. Basically, it involves traversing all product structure trees and for each part, storing the lowest manufacturing level ever reached in the part master record.

More problematic than the one-time creation is the *maintenance effort*. Every time a new part is entered into the database, its low-level code must be determined, but what is worse, the codes of all other parts in the database must be reevaluated. The reason is that the codes may need to be changed due to the product structure of the new part. The same applies when an existing part is deleted from the database.

Figure 2.31 illustrates the two scenarios. The top section of the figure shows the case that end product Z is augmented by part P. Part F goes into part Q, which goes into P. Part F was already contained in the product structure of end product Y (with low-level code 3). Introducing P changes the low-level code of F to 4 because in Z's product structure, F is on a lower manufacturing level than in Y's.

The lower section of the figure shows a scenario in which assembly C is no longer produced in-house but replaced with a purchased part S. Since C is not there anymore, D and E are not needed either (for C) but are still needed for Z and A, respectively. They move up according to Y's and Z's product structures, and their low-level codes are now equal to the manufacturing levels.

2.3.3 MRP in Make-to-Order Production

An essential characteristic of make-to-order production is that the product is specific to the customer. This means that important master data such as product structures may not be available and have to be created for the order. Furthermore, customer-specific products are not produced to stock but only when the customer places an order. This is actually an expensive strategy in comparison to mass or series production. The company cannot benefit from cost savings that go along with larger batches if they produce only customer-specific parts. Likewise, it is difficult to meet short delivery dates if for all parts, planning can only start when a customer order is placed.

For these reasons, make-to-order manufacturers strive to use not only customer-specific parts but also standard parts where possible. Since standard parts are typically included in more than one product, they can be planned independently from specific customer orders and produced in larger batches, which saves time and cost.

Planning Levels Different *planning levels* can be introduced to handle customer-specific parts and standard parts. Zimmermann called these levels the *expectation-oriented* planning level and the *customer-order-oriented* planning level (Zimmermann 1989, pp. 74–76).

Figure 2.32 illustrates this distinction with the help of two product structures representing the customer-specific products Y and Z. The company has decided to use the standard parts C, E, and F whenever possible, but A, B, D, and G are parts that must be manufactured just for the customer order.

As the figure shows, planning for the parts Y, Z, A, B, D, and G will be done when a customer order arrives, while planning for the parts C, E, and F can be done whenever suitable, for example, following a consumption-driven approach as described in Sect. 2.3.1. The dashed line between the two planning levels is called the *stock-keeping level*.

Inventory management in make-to-order production has to meet more challenges than in make-to-stock production. The reason is that consumption is not as smooth as in make-to-stock production where the planning can be based on a known, possibly constant withdrawal rate. In make-to-order production, the future customer orders are not known, and hence, derived requirements can at best only be estimated. Consequently, higher inventory levels including safety buffers have to be kept, causing additional inventory cost.

Alternatively, the company may try to keep the inventory (for standard parts) at a reasonably low level and purchase peak demand from suppliers or competitors. In some industries, for example, suppliers exist that have specialized in express delivery of certain materials at substantially increased prices (e.g., special materials which otherwise have long delivery times). If such an option is available, the company may consider a trade-off between increasing the inventory level (i.e., high inventory cost) and

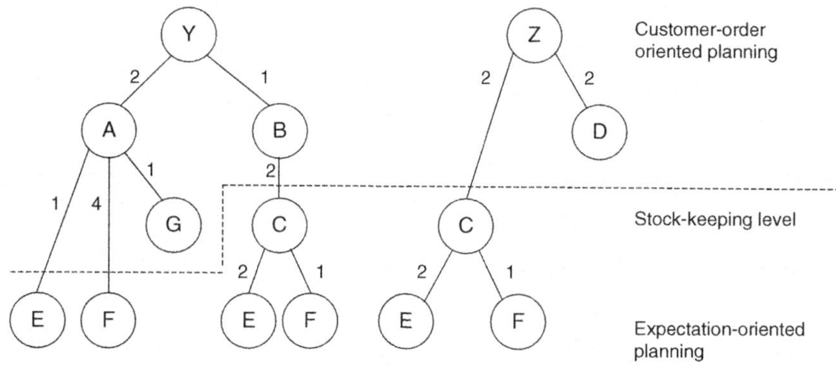

Fig. 2.32 Expectation and customer-order-oriented planning

express delivery when demand peaks arise (i.e., high delivery cost).

As mentioned in Sect. 2.2.2, make-to-order production requires that the status of a customer order, and of all dependent orders, can be retrieved at any time. This is possible when the connections between the orders are explicitly stored and maintained in the database. If standard parts are involved, it is quite likely that secondary requirements resulting from different end-product orders are combined into the same production lot. If the part is on an intermediate manufacturing level, requirements for parts on the next lower level, derived from the current part (and from other parts), may again be aggregated into lots, etc.

Suppose an operating facility needed for any of the lower-level parts in Fig. 2.32 breaks down. In order to check which customer orders might be affected, the production manager needs to know the connections from the machine to the manufacturing orders involved and from there to the end-product customer orders. While the former connections are available in the manufacturing orders (or the routings), the latter ones have to be explicitly created and maintained.

Figure 2.33 contains a general scheme, showing connections on two levels between individual requirements, production orders (lots), and derived requirements. *w*, *x*, *y*, and *z* are part numbers. In order to keep the figure simple, only the "downward" connections are shown completely: from the level n requirements → level n orders → level $n + 1$ requirements → level $n + 1$ orders.

In the opposite direction, only some of the connections have been explicitly included in the figure. For example, an arrow connects one of the three *y* requirements with the first *w* order on level n. Had all connections been drawn, three arrows would be pointing upward from the *y* requirements to the same order. Instead, the letter *p* is used to indicate that the requirement record contains an upward pointer.

Reservations and Availability Checks In make-to-order production, *reservation* of stock plays a more prominent role than in make-to-stock production. The reason is that completing a customer order on time has very high priority. In order to be able to complete an order as planned and confirmed, material (just as other resources) has to be definitely available when it is needed.

Early checking to ensure the availability, followed by a reservation, is typical for many make-to-order manufacturers. In some cases, for example, when an important customer is involved, the reservation may already be booked when an inquiry is received or when the company sends a quotation to the customer.

This is particularly important when purchased parts with long delivery times or in-house parts with long lead times are involved. By the time a customer order has been received, it may be too late to place a purchase or manufacturing order for this part. The delivery or lead time may be longer than the time the customer is willing to wait for delivery of the order. Therefore, a purchase order might already be placed after the

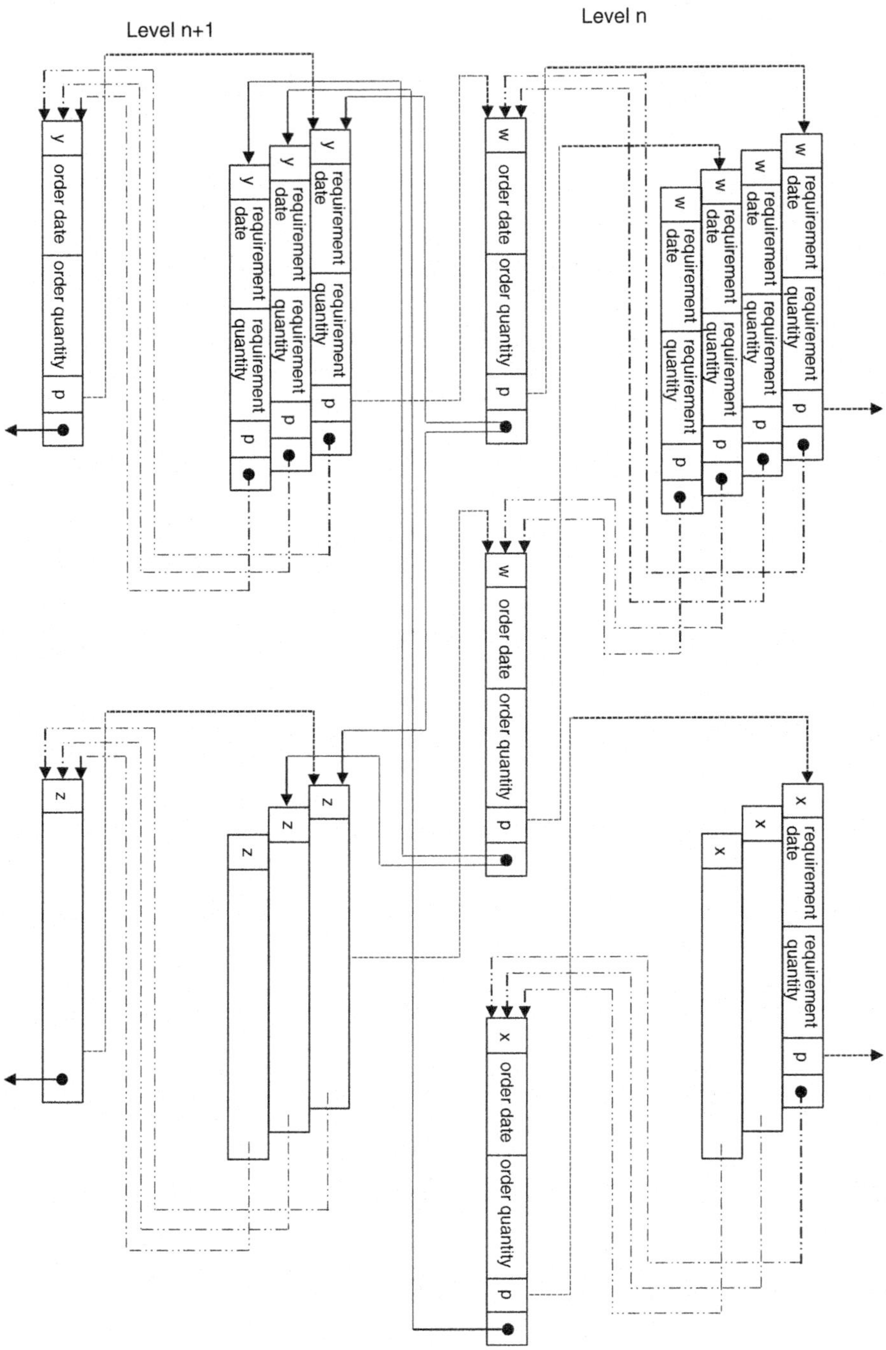

Fig. 2.33 Connections between individual requirements and orders

customer's first inquiry, even if there is a risk that a customer order will not come through.

Advanced approaches for availability checking have been developed in the field of supply chain management (SCM) and included in ERP systems. They are often summarized under the name *ATP ("available to promise")*. ATP and other methods will be discussed in Sect. 10.1.5.

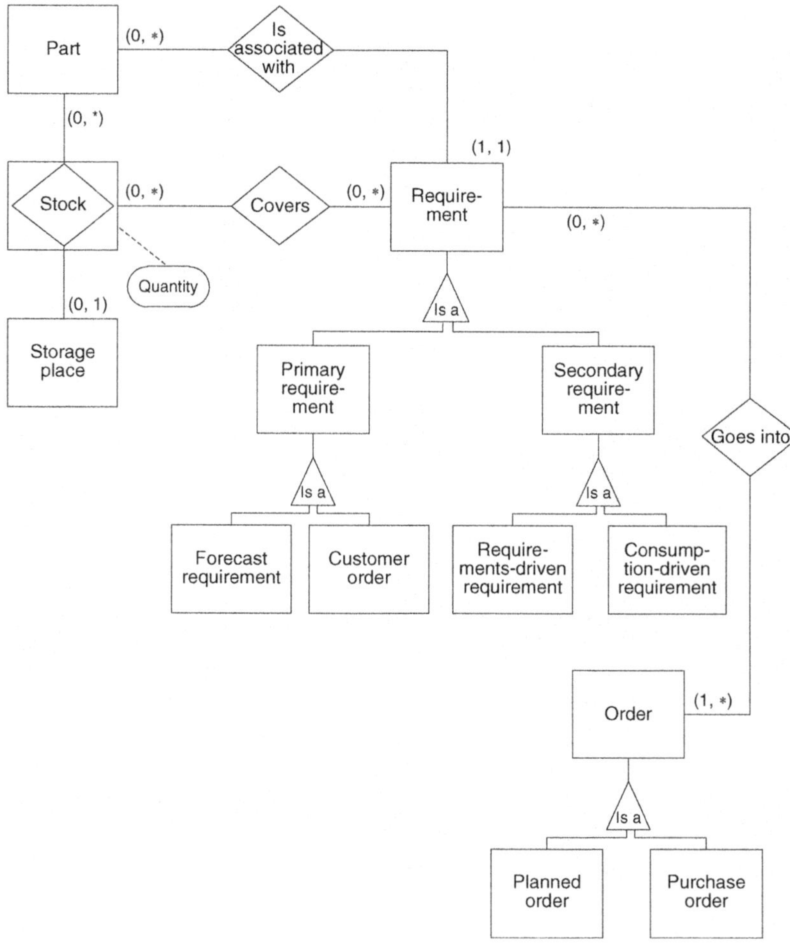

Fig. 2.34 Entity-relationship diagram for key MRP entities

2.4 Outcome of Material Requirements Planning

The main task of material requirements planning is to determine the secondary requirements. Starting from the primary requirements that result from end-product program planning, the required quantities of all subordinate parts are calculated. Inexpensive parts are usually planned based on previous consumption and forecasting, whereas more expensive parts are planned with higher accuracy, using the bills of materials.

One major outcome of MRP is *planned orders* (also called planned manufacturing or production orders) representing either the requirements of individual periods or the requirements of several periods bundled into production lots. These planned orders are later used to create *manufacturing orders* (also called production orders), which are given to the company's manufacturing department.

Another major outcome is *purchase orders* for externally procured parts (also called procurement orders). Like planned orders, they may be based on individual period requirements or on requirements of several periods bundled into an "optimal" order quantity.

To summarize the connections between the key terms of material requirements planning, an entity-relationship diagram is presented in Fig. 2.34. This diagram is highly simplified, showing only the main entity types and their relationships.

Parts are associated with *inventory* data and with *requirements*. Requirements can be primary or secondary requirements. *Primary* requirements come from forecasts or from customer orders. *Secondary* requirements are computed as either consumption driven or requirements driven.

To be satisfied, requirements on all levels finally have to go into orders, which can be *planned orders* (for in-house production) or *purchase orders* (for external procurement).

MRP II: Manufacturing Resource Planning

3

The outcome of material requirements planning is quantities—primary and secondary requirements assigned to different periods. The main disadvantage of the MRP approach is that it is not certain whether the requirements can be fulfilled, because the manufacturing capacities are not taken into consideration. In order to create a feasible plan, material requirements planning has to be augmented with capacity planning and scheduling. For this purpose, further master data are needed than those discussed in Sect. 2.1. In this chapter, we will first describe the most important data structures and then the planning approach of manufacturing resource planning (MRP II).

3.1 Master Data for MRP II

Master data for manufacturing resource planning, in addition to those used in material requirements planning, include routings, operating facilities, factory calendars, shift models, tools, and employees.

3.1.1 Routings

A routing is a list of operations required for the manufacturing of an in-house produced part. It includes processing times, setup times, operating facilities, and other resources that might be necessary to perform the operations.

A routing printed on paper or displayed on a screen usually has a header and a body. The header contains data such as:

- Routing number
- Part the routing refers to
- Parts processed in the operations of the routing
- Organizational data (e.g., date of creation, date of last modification, and person in charge)
- Validity (valid from, valid until)
- Type of routing (initial, normal, maintenance, etc.)
- Reference to a drawing

The body is the main part of the routing. It consists of the operations required to manufacture the part. Important information associated with an operation includes the operating facility or the workplace where the operation is performed, the processing time, and the setup time. A typical operation record contains the following information:

- Operation number
- Description of the operation
- Reference to additional drawings, where applicable
- Necessary operator skills, where applicable
- Operating facility or workplace
- Setup time
- Processing time per unit

K.E. Kurbel, *Enterprise Resource Planning and Supply Chain Management*,
Progress in IS, DOI 10.1007/978-3-642-31573-2_3, © Springer-Verlag Berlin Heidelberg 2013

Fig. 3.1 Example of a routing

Routing					Page 1
Part: Bearing cap with breakout, part no: 860 Material: Bearing cap (aluminum), part no: 880 Created: 12/10/2012, E. Meier					
Operation no	**Operation description**	**Operating facility**	**Setup time**	**Processing time**	**Drawing no**
6200	Setup lathe	D-40	5		
6300	Mount bearing cap	D-40		3	
6400	Lathe bearing cap according to drawing	D-40		16	31
6500	Lathe axle breakout according to drawing	D-40		4	32
6600	Remove bearing cap	D-40			
6700	Mount bearing cap	B-41		2	
6800	Drill fixing hole	B-41		2	33
6900	Remove bearing cap	B-41			

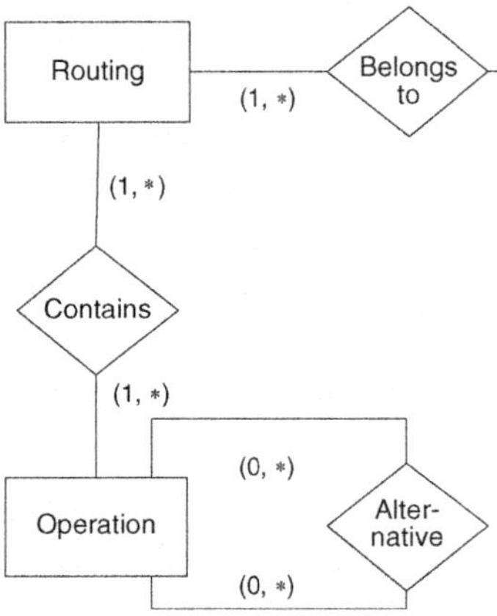

Fig. 3.2 Entity-relationship diagram for routings

- Average waiting time before the operation starts
- Average transition time between operations
- Factors to be used in lead-time reduction
- Average scrap rate
- Organizational and validity data, if operation specific

A simplified example of a routing can be seen in Fig. 3.1. It shows the routing for part number 860 ("bearing cap with breakout"), contained in the product structure of the electric motor E10 as depicted in Fig. 2.1.6. The two operating facilities L-40 and D-41 are a lathe and a drill. Three operations reference a drawing.

In many cases, *alternative routings* exist for a part. Deciding which of the routings to choose can depend on various factors, for example, the desired quality or the size of the manufacturing order.

Additionally, *alternative operations* may exist. A particular result can often be achieved in different ways. A breakout in the bearing cap, for example, can be drilled or punched.

Figure 3.2 shows a data model for routings that takes the above-mentioned aspects into consideration. It includes the fact that one part may have several routings and that alternatives to an operation may exist.

Routings can be printed or displayed on a monitor. They are, however, mostly used in lead-time scheduling and capacity requirements planning because they contain the temporal data needed for these planning steps. Lead-time

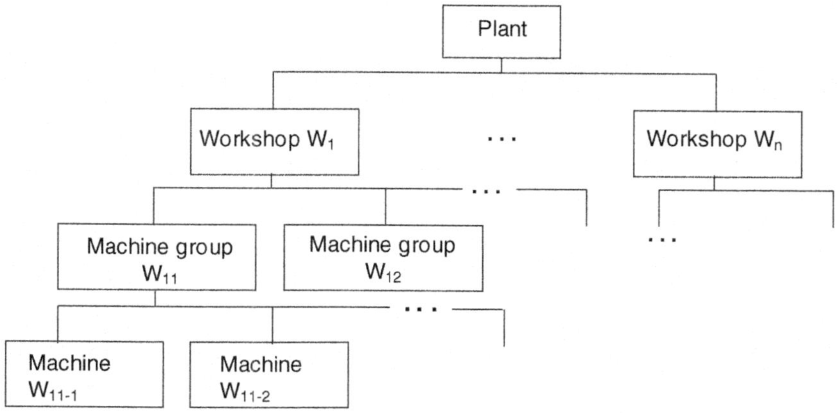

Fig. 3.3 Example of an operating facility hierarchy

scheduling and capacity requirements planning will be discussed later in this chapter.

3.1.2 Operating Facilities

The data for operating facilities and other workplaces are usually maintained in one data structure, collectively referred to as either operating facility or workplace data. We will speak of operating facilities in this chapter.

Operating facilities are often combined into groups and structured in a hierarchy. Figure 3.3 depicts a three-level hierarchy, which can be found in a medium-sized manufacturing company with job-shop production.

For capacity requirements planning, the most important attribute of an operating facility is the *capacity*, measured in terms of the number of units that can be processed per time period or the time the operating facility is available. For rough planning, it is sufficient to maintain the capacity of an operating facility group, whereas for detailed planning, the capacities of all individual operating facilities have to be considered. In addition to the capacity, maintenance data such as regular maintenance intervals are relevant for scheduling and allocating machines.

Operating facility data are also needed in *accounting*. For example, the hourly cost rates of the machines are usually stored with the operating facility master data. They are used when the cost of a product or a customer order are to be calculated.

Attributes used to describe operating facilities usually include the following:

- Operating facility number
- Name and/or description
- Location
- Cost center
- Technical data (e.g., kW and voltage)
- Capacity (e.g., hours or units per shift and number of shifts)
- Worker data (e.g., skills required and number of operators needed)
- Usage/performance rates
- Average setup time
- Machine cost rate (€/h)
- Maintenance data (e.g., maintenance intervals and average downtime)
- Person in charge

Operating facility data are primarily needed for capacity requirements planning. In order to connect operations and operating facilities, the relationships between the two have to be maintained in the database. In Fig. 3.4, the relationship type "man. structure" (manufacturing structure) is used for this purpose. The figure also shows how operating facilities can be combined into groups. Following this approach, an operating facility is either a single facility or a group.

The other two entity types ("shift model" and "factory calendar") are explained below.

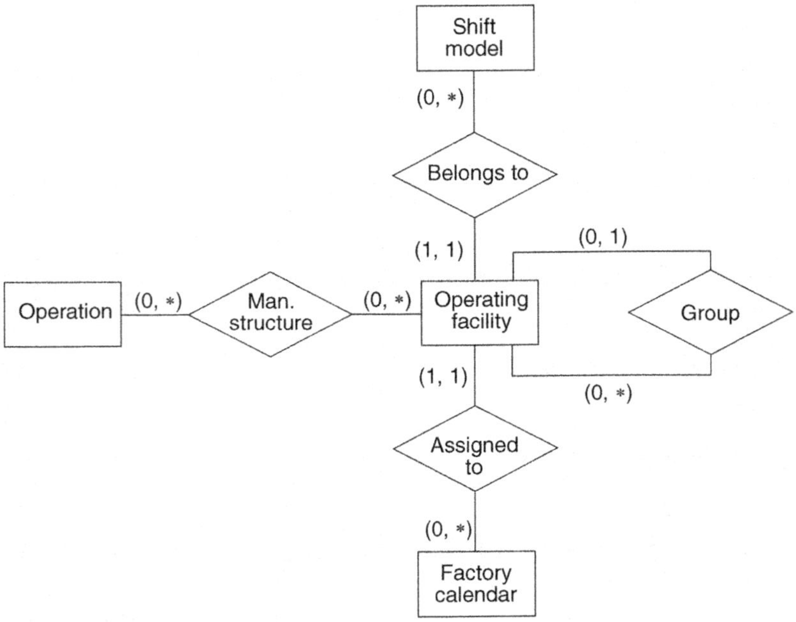

Fig. 3.4 Entity-relationship diagram for manufacturing data

3.1.3 More Master Data

In practice, many more types of master data are used in addition to routings and operating facilities. The most important types for scheduling are factory calendars and shift models. In addition to these, employee data and tools/attachment are discussed in this section.

Factory Calendar Calendar days, hours, and minutes play an important role in planning, scheduling, and controlling. The factory calendar indicates which days are working days and which days are off days (weekends, holidays). Many companies have their own calendar numbering the working days in a year. The year is not necessarily the calendar year, but can also be the company's fiscal year.

Some companies have more than one factory calendar. One reason for this can be that a company uses expensive special equipment that is also operated on the weekends, while the rest of the factory works only 5 days a week. Figure 3.4 takes this situation into account by allowing different factory calendars to be assigned to an operating facility. Another reason can be that the company has locations in different states or countries with different holidays.

Shift Model A shift model describes the daily work times, specifying the beginning and end of a shift, and the breaks during the shift. When a company's operation requires the use of several shifts, different shift models may apply to different sectors of the company or in particular to different operating facilities.

The upper part of Fig. 3.4 shows how this requirement is mapped to the data model. The relationship type "assigned to" allows different shift models to be assigned to different operating facilities. On the other hand, each facility has a unique shift model.

Employees Employee data belong primarily to the human resources function. However, they are also needed in manufacturing resource planning. The main reason is that in shop-floor control, employees with certain skills may also need to be scheduled. Many workplaces require specialists with certain qualifications. The availability of a specialist can impose the same (or even stricter) restrictions as the available capacity of the machine.

Tools/Attachments Restrictions for scheduling and shop-floor control can also arise from the availability of tools and attachments. This is particularly true when special tools are needed in

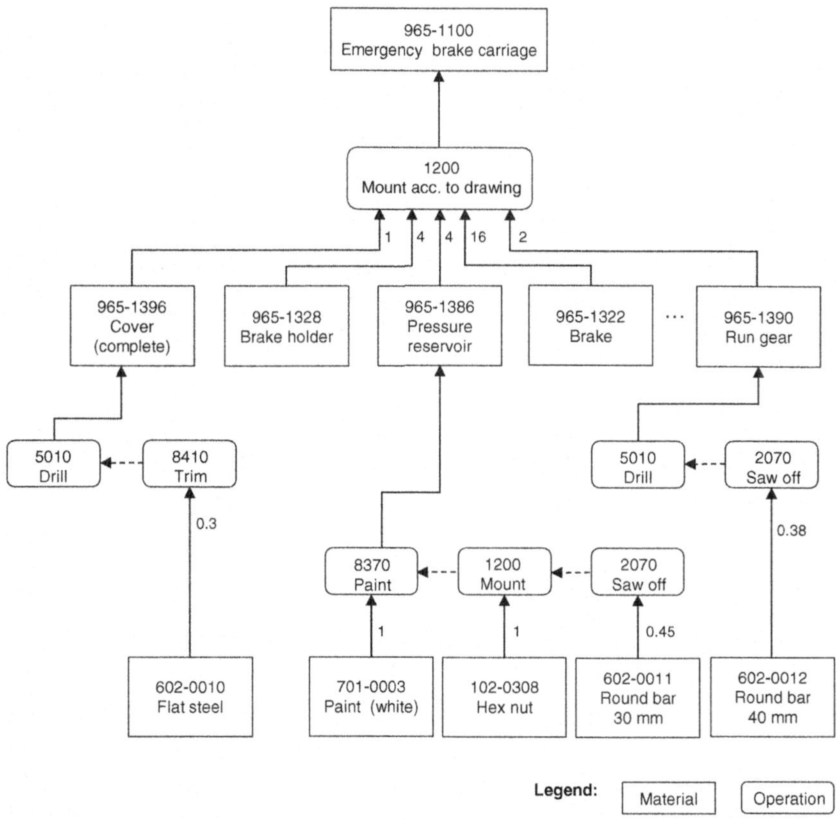

Fig. 3.5 The principle of a resource list (example)

several places. In this case, they have to be scheduled, just as other resources (machines, employees, etc.). Therefore, tools and attachments are often explicitly stored as particular database objects. In other solutions, they are treated like operating facilities, that is, stored as a type of operating facility.

3.1.4 Resource Lists

The most important "resources" considered in manufacturing resource planning are parts (materials) and operating facilities. How they are related is defined in the bills of materials (product structures) and the routings. In conventional MRP II, bills of materials and routings are treated as separate data structures, even though both are needed to create feasible production plans. Quantity-related information is stored in the bills of materials, whereas time- and capacity-related information is stored in the routings. Typically, material requirements planning is done first, using only the bills of materials, and scheduling is done afterwards, using the routings.

In contrast to this, *resource lists* combine the relationships among the parts and between the parts and the operating facilities into one data structure. Resource lists were first proposed by Helmut Kernler in the 1980s (Kernler 2000, pp. 39–40).

The same idea has since been pursued with the so-called *production process models* (PPM) that are used in supply chain management, for example, in the Advanced Planner and Optimizer (APO) of SAP SCM (see Sects. 9.1.1 and 10.1.3).

Figure 3.5 illustrates the principle of a resource list with the help of an example. Normal rectangles represent parts, whereas rectangles with round corners represent operations. The product is an *emergency brake carriage* with part number 965–1100. The emergency brake carriage is built

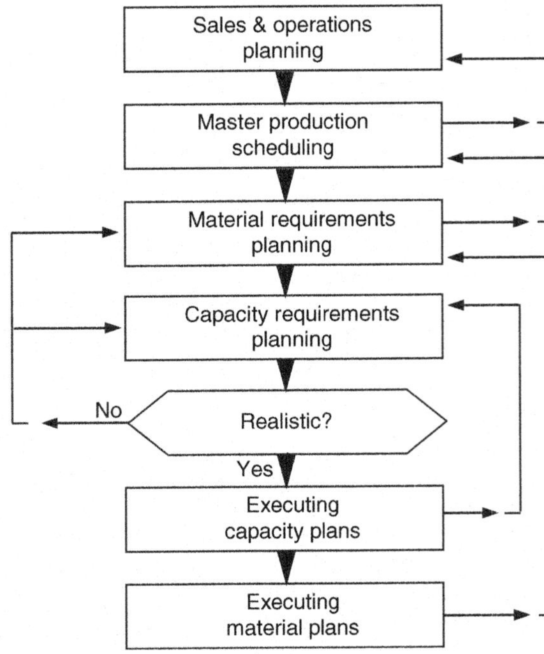

Fig. 3.6 Closed loop MRP [Wight 1984, p. 48]

with the final operation number 1200, "mount according to drawing." In order to perform this operation, one cover (complete) (965–1396), four brake holders (965–1328), four pressure reservoirs (965–1386), 16 brake shoes (965–1322), two running gears (965–1390), etc. are needed. These parts are manufactured using other parts through operations such as drilling, trimming etc.

3.2 From Closed Loop MRP to MRP II

The major benefit of material requirements planning is that primary and secondary requirements are determined with reasonable accuracy. However, it is by no means guaranteed that the requirements can be fulfilled as they were calculated. The reason for this is that the manufacturing capacity and possibly other restrictions are not taken into account in material requirements planning.

An approach to overcome the shortcomings of MRP is *closed loop MRP*. "Closed loop" means two things: Firstly, the capacity requirements implied by the material requirements planning are computed and explicitly included in the planning. Secondly, feedback is generated from the factory (and from other sources) whenever there is a problem in executing the plan.

Oliver Wight, the father of MRP II, describes "closed loop MRP" as summarized in Fig. 3.6 (Wight 1984, pp. 48–50). The main stages are:

- *Sales and operations planning*—establishes the end-product quantities to be produced in each period up to the planning horizon, usually on an aggregate level (e.g., by product groups or families).
- *Master production scheduling*—breaks down the aggregate numbers of the sales and operations plan into quantities of individual products.
- *Material requirements planning*—calculates the secondary requirements as discussed in Sect. 2.3.
- *Capacity requirements planning*—determines how much capacity of the operating facilities and workplaces is needed to fulfill the quantity requirements and schedules the capacity requirements.
- *Realistic?*—this question is the core of closed loop MRP. If the plan is not realistic, adjustments must be made so that the capacity, materials, master production, and/or sales and operation plans become feasible.

Fig. 3.7 Manufacturing resource planning (MRP II)

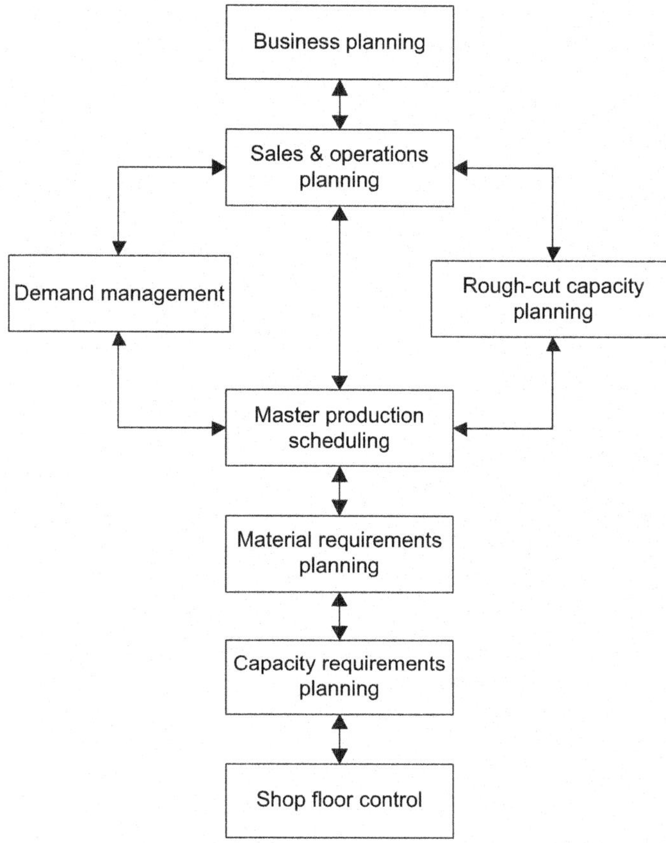

- *Executing capacity* and *material plans*—generating feedback and if necessary, making adjustments to the material and/or capacity plans.

Manufacturing resource planning, MRP II, is more of a paradigmatic step forward from closed loop MRP than a different planning approach. The main concern of MRP II is to involve the top management in the production planning. Before MRP II, the top management made its own business plan, which included the top-level sales and operations plan. The production planning department, however, made its own separate plan down in the factory—while the top management planned in monetary units, the production management planned in quantity units.

The goal of MRP II is *consistent planning* throughout all levels. "MRP II results in management finally having the numbers to run the business. One set of numbers, valid numbers, and everybody using the same set of numbers" (Wight 1984, p. 54). Apart from this paradigmatic aspect, MRP II is technically not much different from closed loop MRP.

In today's presentations of MRP II, the labels of the major steps have changed slightly. Especially the last step (execution) is usually substituted by *shop-floor control* (*SFC*). Figure 3.7 can be regarded as an updated version of the original MRP II workflow as described by Oliver Wight.

Planning and Control in MRP II The MRP II stages shown in Fig. 3.7 are basically the same as the ones supported by today's ERP systems. The first stage (business planning), however, and thus support for the top management, is not at the core of most ERP systems. For this purpose, more specialized systems such as an EIS (executive information system), MIS (management information system), DSS (decision support system), ESS (executive support system), and BI (business intelligence) tools, for example, a dashboard, are available.

On the other hand, an increasing number of ERP systems are enhanced by functionality needed for top management tasks. In particular, business intelligence tools are included or provided along with the ERP system.

In summary, we can say that the core of MRP II as supported by most ERP systems today is *closed loop MRP*. The fundamental idea is a holistic market and resource-oriented planning of sales, production, and inventory.

As shown in Fig. 3.7, a master production schedule is determined based upon long-term *sales and operations planning*. For this purpose, the overall demand is planned (in *demand management*), resulting in a sales forecast and expectations regarding customer orders. At the same time, capacity requirements and capacity supply are balanced on a high level of aggregation (*rough-cut capacity planning*).

Master production scheduling may have two levels: one being the level of product groups (aggregate production planning) and the other the level of individual products. Planning on two levels makes sense when a company offers a large spectrum of end products and variants. In such cases, it is difficult to determine reliable values for each individual product, but it may be possible to derive reasonable estimates for groups of products.

The master production schedule, also known as the *production program*, is the starting point for material requirements planning, as discussed in Sect. 2.2. MRP calculates the quantities of assemblies, individual parts, and raw materials required to produce the production program.

The capacities needed to produce the primary and secondary requirements are planned in detail in *capacity requirements planning (CRP)*. CRP has two main parts: lead-time scheduling and capacity load leveling. The outcome of capacity requirements planning should be a feasible production plan.

This plan is broken down into more detail in *shop-floor control (SFC)*. In this stage, the manufacturing orders that are due in the near future are released and carried out. Tasks required for completing the orders include creating order-specific routings, withdrawing the necessary materials from the warehouse, and scheduling the operations on the operating facilities and workplaces.

MRP II is based on several assumptions. The first assumption is that essential planning parameters such as the available capacities, order lead times, and processing times can be predicted with a high degree of certainty. In addition, it is assumed that manufacturing bottlenecks can be removed by leveling the capacity load through adjustments to the capacity supply and demand. In order for this assumption to be true, the long- and midterm capacity supply and demand must be in accordance, requiring that the rough-cut capacity planning on which the master production schedule is based was realistic.

The most important of the assumptions is that a reasonable master production schedule can be determined. An essential precondition for this is a reliable sales forecast.

3.3 Lead-Time Scheduling

The two main components of capacity requirements planning are lead-time scheduling and capacity load leveling. Lead-time scheduling creates a temporal structure of the manufacturing orders and the dependencies between the orders, whereas capacity load leveling strives to make this structure feasible.

Both components are closely related. Whenever order dates are calculated (in lead-time scheduling), capacity demand is implicitly created on the operating facilities and workplaces on which the order's operations are to be carried out. Vice versa, whenever orders are moved from one period to another (in capacity load leveling), obviously their start and end dates are affected.

Despite these interdependencies, lead-time scheduling and capacity load leveling are two separate steps within conventional capacity requirements planning. First, the order lead times are calculated, disregarding potential capacity constraints. Subsequently, start and end dates of some (or all) orders are adjusted, if required by the capacity situation.

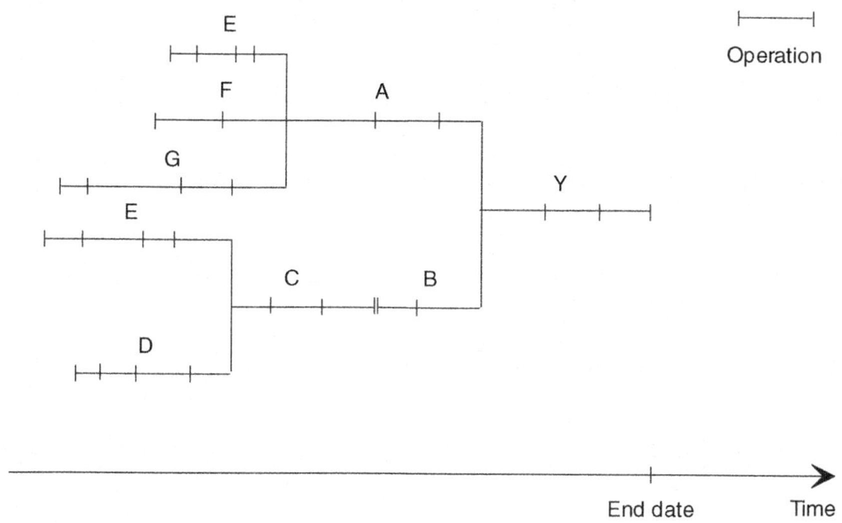

Fig. 3.8 Order network from backward scheduling

3.3.1 Backward and Forward Scheduling

In this section, lead-time scheduling will be described. The main task of lead-time scheduling is to calculate start and end dates of all the operations belonging to a manufacturing order and thus start and end dates of the order itself. Two different approaches exist: backward scheduling and forward scheduling.

Backward Scheduling Backward scheduling starts from the end date of a planned order on the highest manufacturing level. This is typically an end-product order. The date when this order is expected to be completed was established as a result of material requirements planning, as mentioned in Sect. 2.4.

Starting from this date, all the operations required for the end-product order are sequenced, working backward from the last operation to the first. Using the processing times stored with the routings, start and end dates of all operations are calculated. Once the end-product order has been scheduled, the orders for all parts that go into the end product are handled in the same way. Afterwards, the orders on the next manufacturing level are dealt with, operation by operation, etc.

Backward scheduling of an end-product order results in a network of orders and operations, as can be seen in Fig. 3.8. The underlying product structure is the one shown for part Y in Fig. 2.1.1.

It should be noted that the results of backward scheduling are different when material requirements planning has been carried out *using low-level codes* instead of manufacturing levels (see Sect. 2.3.2). In contrast to Fig. 3.8, where only one end product was scheduled, using low-level codes means that all product structures are considered at the same time. The effect of this is that requirements for a particular part may originate from several end products. Therefore, the order quantities tend to be larger than the quantities required when only one end product is considered.

Figure 3.9 illustrates this effect with the help of two end products, Y and Z (see Fig. 2.1). Dealing with more than one end product typically results in lying times for some of the orders. Lying times are caused by the fact that a portion of an order (e.g., a portion of C) is needed earlier in one product structure (e.g., for B) than in the others (e.g., for Y). Therefore, the order has to be completed early enough to meet the requirements of one product (e.g., Y), while the rest of the order has to wait until it is needed for the other products (e.g., Z).

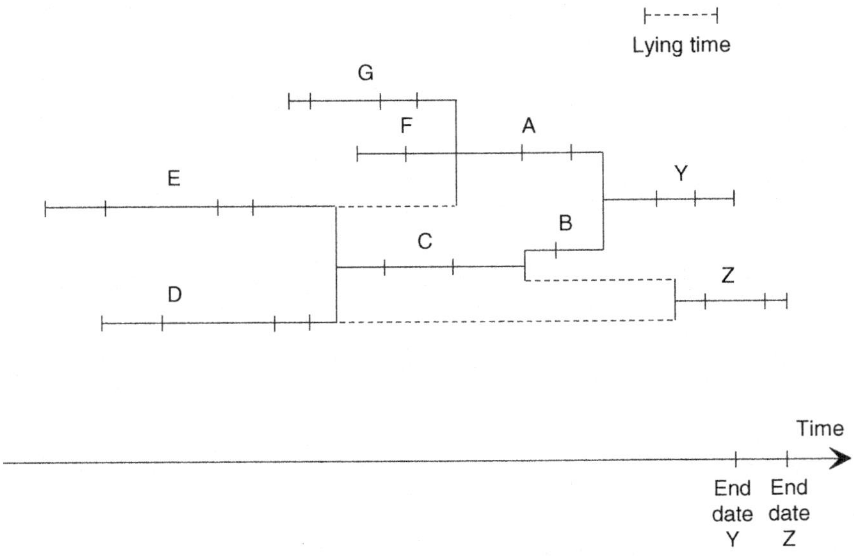

Fig. 3.9 Backward scheduling using low-level codes

The same effect occurs when individual secondary requirements are combined into production lots. In this case, some portions of a lot will be needed earlier while others have to wait.

Backward scheduling can be seen as a form of *just-in-time manufacturing*. All orders are completed at the latest possible time. The main advantage is that inventory cost and capital commitment are minimized. On the other hand, backward scheduling bears the risk that manufacturing processes are disrupted unless sufficient time buffers are built in. If, for example, an operating facility that is a bottleneck breaks down, orders cannot be completed on time. Suppose that such a machine is required for an operation of E in Fig. 3.8 and this machine breaks down. Then it is very likely that E, C, and B cannot be completed as scheduled, and hence, the end date of Y will not be met.

Forward Scheduling Whereas backward scheduling starts with an order on the highest manufacturing level, forward scheduling starts with the *lowest level* and works its way forward toward the future. In terms of a product structure tree, forward scheduling begins with the leaves of the tree and proceeds upward, branch by branch.

In forward scheduling, the first operations of all those orders that correspond to the leaves of the tree receive the same start date, for example, the first day of the planning period. The next operation of such an order can start when the first one is completed, then the next one, etc. Once a lowest-level order has been completely scheduled, the next order up the product structure tree is dealt with, beginning with the start and end dates of the first operation of this order and so on.

As Fig. 3.10 demonstrates, lying times are typical in forward scheduling. They are due to the fact that an order on the next higher manufacturing level cannot start before all subordinate orders are completed. In the example shown in Fig. 3.10, lying times occur for E, F, D, and A.

More frequent and longer lying times arise when *low-level codes* are applied because here some portions of a lower-level order may have to wait until several higher-level orders are ready to be processed. The reason for this is that the higher-level orders may require input not only from this lower-level order but also from others that are completed later.

Figure 3.11 uses two end products, Y and Z, to illustrate this effect. An additional assumption underlying the figure is that individual requirements for some of the parts have been combined into production lots, further increasing the lying times.

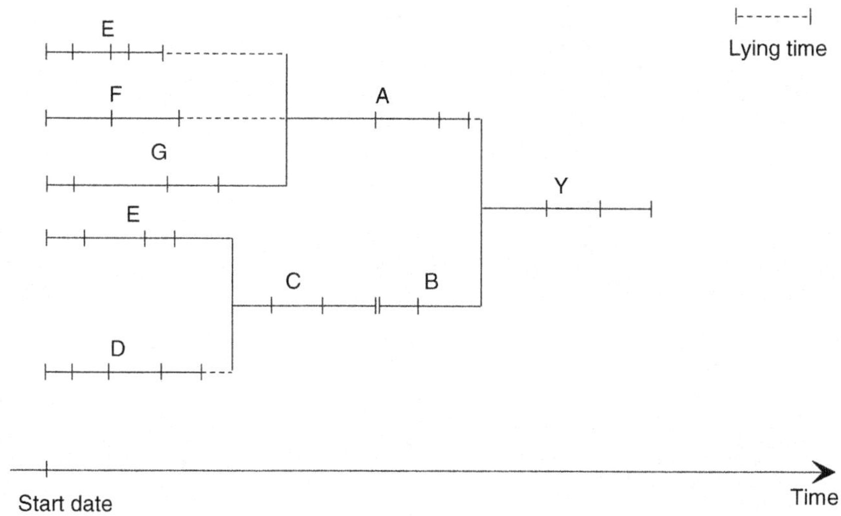

Fig. 3.10 Order network from forward scheduling

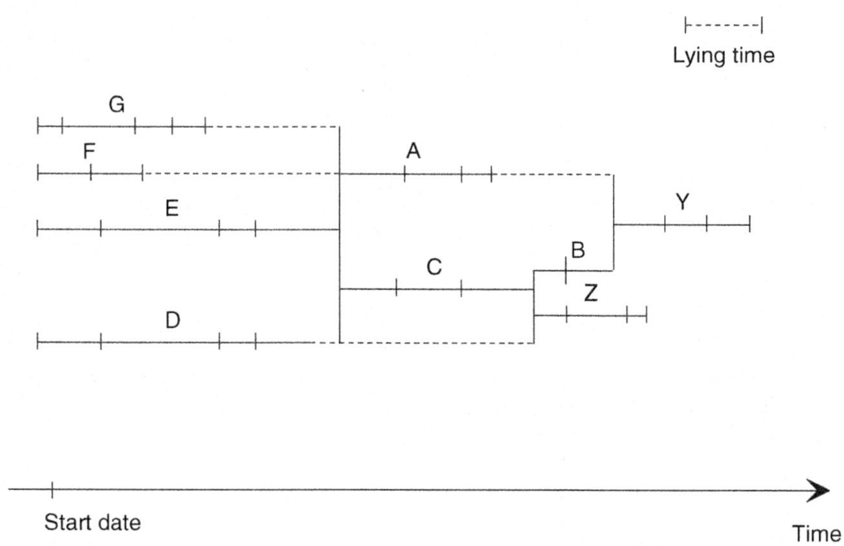

Fig. 3.11 Order network using low-level codes and lot sizes

3.3.2 Determining Buffers Through Double Scheduling

Lying times are not always bad. On the one hand, they increase the capital cost. On the other hand, they help to avoid disruptions to the manufacturing process by serving as time buffers. If problems occur, there is still some time left to fix them.

Following this train of thought, it makes sense to determine the potential time buffers in advance. One way to do so is to schedule all orders both forward and backward. Forward scheduling starts with the beginning of the planning period. Backward scheduling starts with the end of the planning period (or the end dates of the top-level orders, if these are different from the end of the planning period). In this way,

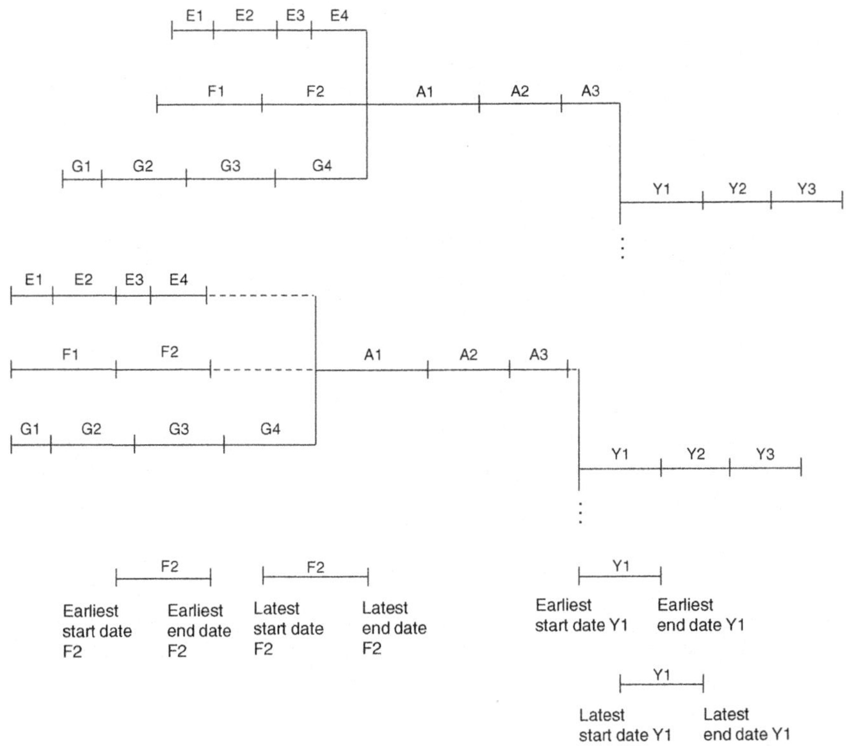

Fig. 3.12 Time buffers from backward and forward scheduling

all orders receive earliest and latest start and end dates.

The difference between an order's latest and its earliest start date is the buffer within which the order may be moved without violating any time constraints. Looking forward, the buffer means that even if the order starts at the very latest date, it will still be possible to complete the end-product order by the given end date. Looking backward, it means that even if the order starts at the very earliest date, none of the orders at the leaves of any product structure tree will fall into the "past" (i.e., need to begin before the beginning of the planning period).

Figure 3.12 illustrates the idea of determining buffers with the help of the order networks for end product Y. In this example, the orders have been scheduled backward (as in Fig. 3.8) and forward (as in Fig. 3.10). The dashed lines represent the buffers within which the orders can be moved.

It should be noted that the problem is much more complicated if more than one end product, or all end products, are scheduled at the same time. These situations offer a variety of scheduling options. A graphical illustration would be rather confusing; therefore, a figure of this case is not included here.

3.3.3 Lead-Time Reduction

Lead-time scheduling often results in infeasible start or end dates because the available time span is insufficient to complete all orders when the given processing times, transition times, and order sequences are used. In the case of backward scheduling, start dates for the first orders might be determined that lie in the past or before the beginning of the planning period. In forward scheduling, end dates calculated for the end products may miss their deadlines.

Fortunately, start or end date violations from initial lead-time scheduling do not necessarily mean that the order network cannot be completed within the given time period. Instead, measures can be taken to reduce the lead times. The standard toolbox of measures includes transition-time reduction, splitting production orders, and overlapping of operations.

Transition-Time Reduction Order lead times used in scheduling are usually historical averages based upon previous experience, with safety buffers added to allow for more flexibility. It is worth noting that the processing times only make up a small portion of the total lead time. The main portion consists of lying times, transport times, and other time components. These are usually summarized under the term *transition time*. Typical components of the transition time include (Mertens 2009, pp. 143–144):

- Average waiting time before an operation
- Process-dependent waiting time before an operation (e.g., for warming up)
- Process-dependent waiting time after an operation (e.g., for cooling down)
- Waiting time for inspection
- Waiting time for transport
- Time for transport to the next operating facility or workplace

Various studies have shown that in practice, the transition time makes up most of the lead time, namely 80–95 %, while the actual processing time is only 5–20 %. Therefore, it is reasonable to start with the transition time whenever lead times have to be shortened.

Transition-time reduction is just a matter of changing planning parameters in the planning system. There are no hard rules for calculating and reducing the transition time. Just as setting it is often based on rules of thumb, the planner may also reduce it in any arbitrary way. However, the planner has to keep in mind that the higher the reduction is, the less buffer remains. Time buffers allow for flexibility that might be needed later.

Obviously, there are limits as to how much can be reduced. For this reason, a maximum reduction factor, for example, 30 % or 50 %, may be defined. This factor will be applied to the transition time in total or only to some components. Many detailed decisions like this have to be made, for example:

- Should different reduction factors be applied to different components of the transition time?
- Should the components be treated one by one, ending the reduction process when a feasible solution has been obtained?
- Should all operations of all orders be reduced or only some?

A common practice is to reduce transition times only until a feasible solution is reached. This allows the company to maintain some of the flexibility hidden in the safety buffers.

There are several ways of storing transition times, depending on how differentiated they are. One method is to store the transition time as a constant value along with the operation's master data in the routings, for example, as a percentage based on the operation's processing time. Another way is to store all components of the transition time as an array. When transportation between the operating facilities takes up most of the time, a common approach is to store the transition times in the form of a matrix (time needed from... to...).

Splitting Production Orders When the order size is very large, the processing time takes up the majority of the lead time. In this case, the order lead time can be reduced by splitting the order up into several parts, provided that several operating facilities are available on which the order can be simultaneously processed.

Splitting an order into n parallel parts, however, does not mean that the lead time is only $1/n$ afterward. Splitting reduces only the processing time, not the other components of the lead time. In particular, the setup time now occurs n times and not just once, reducing the total processing capacity of the operating facilities and multiplying the setup cost.

Figure 3.13 gives an example demonstrating how the lead time is affected by splitting a large

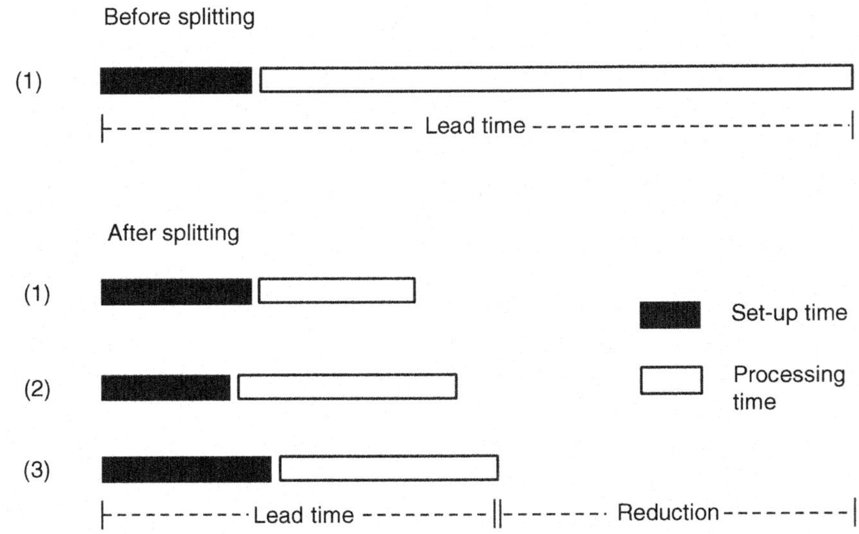

Fig. 3.13 Lead-time reduction through splitting

production order into three parts. One assumption here is that the three operating facilities which share the order are not 100 % identical. This means that the setup times and the processing times per unit are different. Although the three parts of the order are the same size, the bars indicating setup and processing time are different in length. Apparently, it takes less time to set up the second machine than the first one, but processing the same quantity takes significantly longer on the second machine.

The figure shows that splitting saves time, but not as much as might be initially expected. The time saved is not two thirds, but less than half of the lead time. The saving of time is countered with additional setup costs and setup times. Additionally, the total capacity is diminished, and higher administrative effort is incurred. Therefore, the advantages and disadvantages need to be carefully weighed before making the decision to split an order.

Overlapping of Operations Another way of reducing the lead time of a large order is to split transportation of the order to the next operating facility into several parts. In this way, a certain amount of the order can already be sent as soon as it is completed, instead of waiting until the total order is ready. Processing on the next operating facility can then start immediately. Figure 3.14 illustrates this case.

Since the processing times of the various operations belonging to an order are generally different, two cases should be considered. (1) If the processing time per unit on the next operating facility is longer than on the current one, a partial order may have to wait because the facility is still busy with another partial order. (2) If the processing time per unit is shorter on the next operating facility, this facility may be idle for some time because the next partial order has not yet arrived.

Figure 3.14 illustrates a case where the processing time on the second operating facility is longer than on the first, leading to waiting times for the partial orders 2 and 3. This can be seen by observing the horizontal dashed lines, that is, the transition times, which are longer for the partial orders 2 and 3 than for the partial order 1. The partial order 1 can start immediately, once operating facility 2 has been set up. The partial order 2 has to wait until the partial order 1 has been completed. This is due to the fact that processing the same quantity on machine 2 takes longer than on machine 1.

As can be seen in the figure, the amount of time saved may be fairly small. On the other hand, the effort for planning and administration

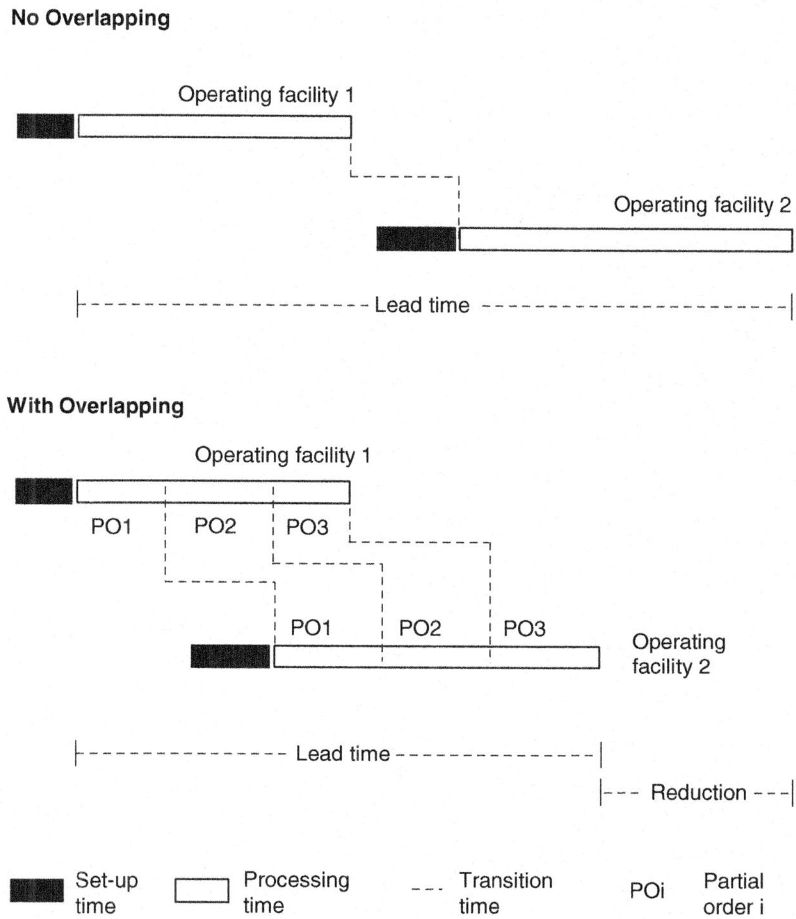

Fig. 3.14 Lead-time reduction through overlapping

is significantly increased. Therefore, it should be carefully considered whether the advantages of reducing the lead time through overlapping outweigh the disadvantages. Some companies apply a predefined minimum overlap time and/or quantity that must be reached in order for the increased planning and administration effort to be worthwhile.

Reducing transition times, splitting, and overlapping are the standard measures for lead-time reduction provided by ERP systems. When it is necessary to shorten order lead times, a typical approach is to start with transition-time reduction. If this is not sufficient, overlapping and/or splitting is considered. When, despite all these measures, deadline violations continue to exist, the end dates of the manufacturing orders have to be moved back to a later date.

3.3.4 Lead-Time Scheduling in Make-to-Order Production

Lead-time scheduling is even more important in make-to-order production than in make-to-stock production. The reason for this is that in order to confirm a *delivery date* to the customer, the sales representative must know how long it takes to complete the order. On the other hand, as mentioned before, it is difficult to make such a statement because of missing data and uncertainty.

In order to estimate a plausible delivery date, the following information must be available:

- The bill of materials for the product the customer wishes to order
- The order lead time, based on the processing and setup times of all parts involved in the product structure

- The delivery times for purchased parts
- The operating facilities needed for all in-house parts in the bill of materials
- The capacity situation (capacity load, free capacity) of these operating facilities

Depending on how "new" the product is, some or all of this information may not be available. The simplest case is a product that is more or less known, for example, a product that can be described with the help of variants, or that is similar to another product that has been built before. In this case, essential master data such as product structures, routings, operating facilities, and the assignment of operations to operating facilities might be available. When this is true, the scheduling algorithm can:

- Explode the bill of materials
- Derive secondary requirements
- Generate manufacturing orders
- Forward schedule the orders
- Calculate the capacity load on the operating facilities involved
- Display the results (especially the order end date and capacity profiles of critical operating facilities) to the user

If the scheduled order end date is later than the date requested by the customer, the planner can take measures to reduce the lead time, as described in Sect. 3.3.3. In case the required capacity is not available, the planner may attempt to reschedule other orders that prevent the current order from being completed within the desired time period. Whether or not such measures are taken depends on how the orders are prioritized by the planner (or the system).

If the product the customer wishes to order is not a "known" product, most of the information needed for scheduling will not be available, meaning that the order lead time and the capacity requirements cannot be determined as above. In this case, it is helpful when the ERP system is at least able to present data from similar customer orders that have been manufactured in the past. The planner can then choose the best-suited order to serve as a basis for the current scheduling task.

To calculate the current order's lead time and capacity requirements, the planner may adjust the details of the old order to the current needs using previous experience and expertise. Alternatively, they may just apply an experience-based correction factor to the data from the previous order in order to be able to quickly offer the customer an estimated end date.

3.4 Capacity Load Leveling

Lead-time scheduling does not take the capacity situation into consideration. The result of lead-time scheduling—start and end dates of all operations—does imply, however, a certain capacity load on all the operating facilities and workplaces involved in the operations. Only through coincidence will this randomly created capacity load be in accordance with the available capacity.

Figure 3.15 uses an example to illustrate the connections between lead-time scheduling and capacity requirements. The operations of three manufacturing orders (parts A, B, and C; see Fig. 3.8) have been scheduled on four operating facilities. An A order consists of three operations (A1, A2, A3), a B order of two, and a C order of three. The assignment of operating facilities to operations is as follows:

Operation	Operating facility
A1	(1)
A2	(2)
A3	(4)
B1	(3)
B2	(4)
C1	(–)
C2	(1)
C3	(2)

The upper part of Fig. 3.15 shows a portion of the order network used earlier, displaying the branches where the orders for A, B, and C are involved. The capacity requirements caused by the lead-time schedule can be seen in the rest of the figure. For example, since operation C3 is assigned to operating facility 2, a certain capacity requirement is created for operating facility 2. This is indicated by the bar segment labeled C3. In other cases, when the duration of an operation

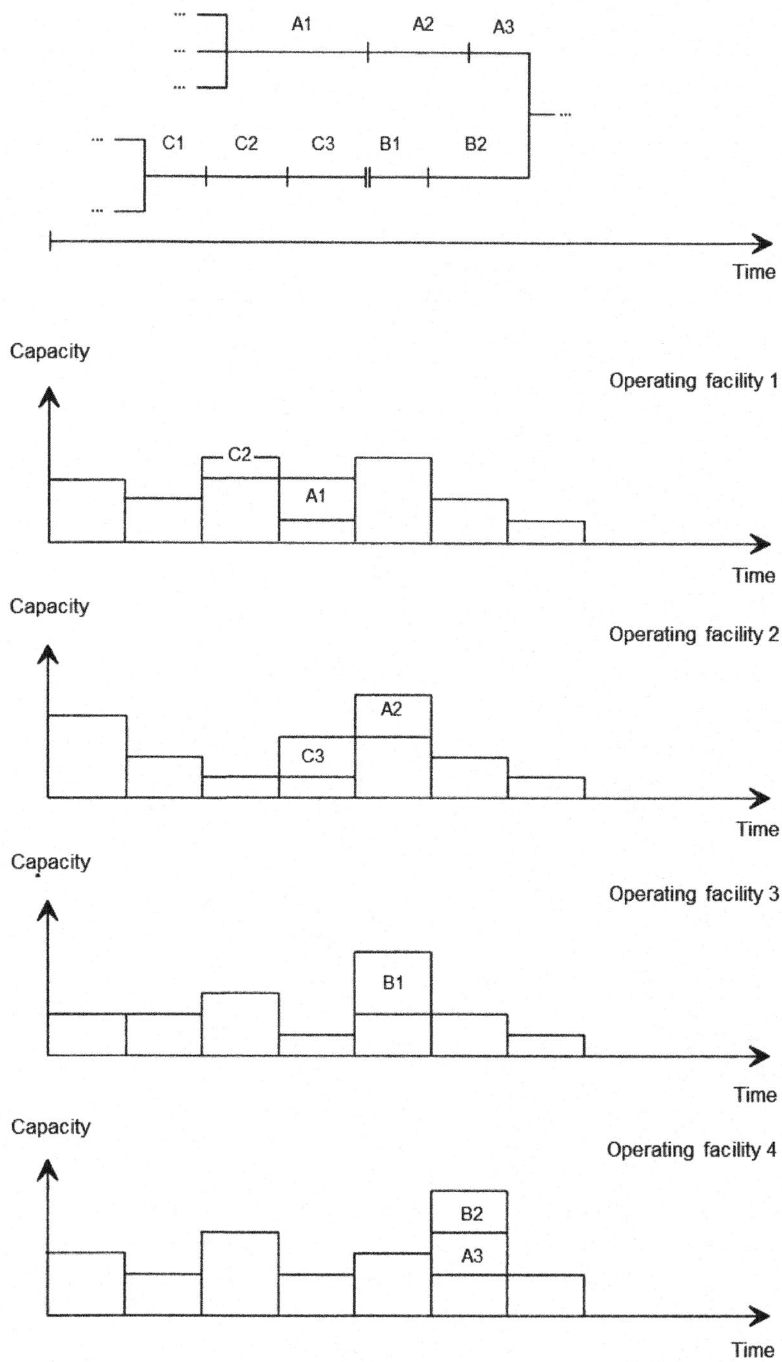

Fig. 3.15 Connections between lead-time scheduling and capacity

oversteps the beginning or end of a period, the respective capacity requirement has been assigned to the period where the major share of the capacity load falls.

3.4.1 Working with Capacity Profiles

Capacity load profiles such as the ones in Fig. 3.15 are implicitly created by the ERP

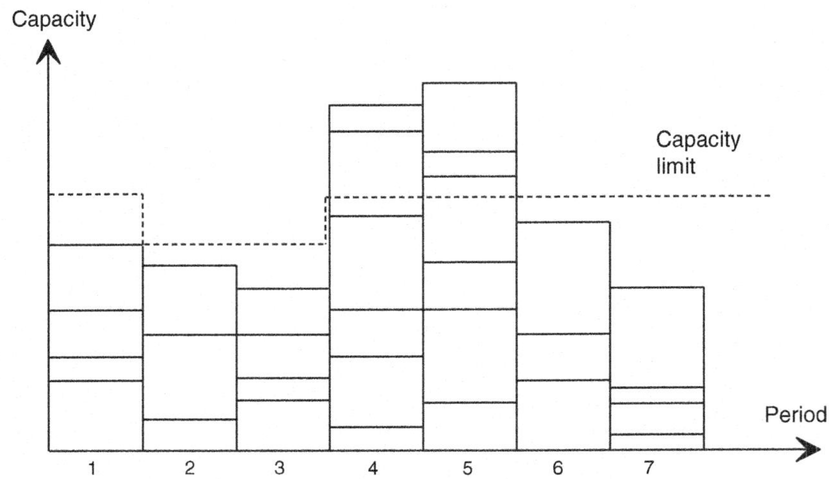

Fig. 3.16 Capacity supply and demand of an operating facility

system for all operating facilities and workplaces, although the user will not explicitly work with all profiles. Capacity load profiles are typically retrieved for operating facilities that are known to be bottlenecks or are otherwise important. For such facilities, special care must be taken to level the capacity load in order to best meet the time and cost goals of production planning as discussed in Sect. 1.4.2.

Since capacity requirements planning (CRP) covers several weeks or months, load leveling is often performed on an aggregate level, for example, for groups of operating facilities or entire workshops. Detailed planning is done later, in shop-floor control (SFC). Another approach is to limit the leveling effort to bottleneck operating facilities.

When lead-time scheduling is done without actually *planning* the capacity utilization at the same time, the chances of achieving a leveled capacity profile are very slim. It is much more likely that the columns are either too high or too low in some or all periods.

A typical capacity profile resulting from conventional lead-time scheduling may look similar to the one in Fig. 3.16. Each segment of the stacked bars represents the capacity requirement of one operation, keeping in mind that the operations usually belong to different manufacturing orders. Two periods of the profile exhibit capacity peaks, whereas in other periods, the capacity is not completely utilized.

The dashed line stands for the available capacity in each period. It is not a straight line because the capacity is not necessarily the same in all periods. For example, some periods may contain holidays or scheduled maintenance work.

When the available capacity ("supply") and the required capacity ("demand") diverge, as is the case in most periods of Fig. 3.16, there are basically two ways to bring them into accordance: adjusting the capacity supply to the demand or adjusting the capacity demand to the supply.

Typical measures for the first case, adjusting the capacity supply, include:

- Implementation/reduction of overtime and extra shifts
- Employment of temporary staff
- Subcontracting ("extended workbench"), purchasing materials
- Varying the rate of production, if technically possible
- Raising or lowering the capacity limit through investments or closing of facilities
- Employment of additional labor, transfer of labor from underemployed plant sections
- Personnel layoff, short-time work, transfer to different plant areas

The other approach, adjusting the capacity demand, employs either quantitative or temporal modifications:

- *Quantitative adjustment* means that the number or the sizes of the orders are changed to accommodate for the amount of available capacity. If, for example, some orders only serve to fill the inventory, without there being specific demand, these orders can easily be canceled, decreased, or increased. Another option is to move orders to an alternative operating facility, if such a facility is available.
- *Temporal adjustment* means that orders are moved from overloaded periods to less busy periods. In Fig. 3.16, for example, orders from periods 4 and 5 would be moved to periods 1, 2, 3, 6, or 7, provided that this can be done without violating time constraints (see below).

Capacity load leveling is the term that is commonly used to describe temporal adjustments. MRP II and ERP systems provide some support for capacity load leveling, but often, it is left to the production planner to manually smooth the capacity profiles of important operating facilities.

The reason for this is that capacity load leveling is a very complex task. Orders cannot just be removed from one column and placed into another one because any operation represented by a column segment is part of an order network. The network imposes restrictions regarding the time when the operation has to begin and end.

Therefore, a good ERP system supports the planner in *manually* smoothing the capacity by maintaining and indicating the limits within which an order may be moved. Systematically calculating the available time buffers in advance, as shown in Sect. 3.3.2, helps to determine these limits. Going back to the example in Fig. 3.16, it is highly unlikely that, for example, an order from period 5 can be moved to period 1 or 3 without violating the start date constraints of the order.

Nevertheless, there are situations in which taking such measures cannot be avoided. Consequently, the initial order network is no longer feasible. Other operations of the same order or of different orders may now need to be shifted, leading to altered capacity demands on all the operating facilities connected with these operations. Previously, feasible capacity solutions may now become infeasible, and another round of capacity load leveling on all operating facilities involved may be needed.

This process does not necessarily come to an end easily, which is why most attempts to automate capacity load leveling have not been successful. Therefore, the task is typically left to a human being. Powerful software tools that support the planner have become available. They will be discussed in the section on manufacturing execution systems (see Sect. 7.1.1).

Data Structures for Capacity Requirements Planning Based on the MRP and MRP II master data, lead-time scheduling and capacity load leveling create and modify *transaction data*. The relationships between the two are illustrated in Fig. 3.17. The left-hand side contains some important master data and the right-hand side the corresponding transaction data.

Routings are used to create the *production orders* (or manufacturing orders) of MRP II. A routing specifies, in general terms, the operations required to manufacture a part. For example, the processing times are related to one unit. A production order contains the same information as a routing, but with reference to a given order quantity and specific start and end dates. The processing time here, for example, is the time per unit (from the routing) multiplied by the order quantity.

The two "used as" relationships link the general concepts "routing" and "operation" with the transactional concepts "production order" and "production operation." Operating facilities have no transactional counterpart, but the "needed for" relationship type will specify when and how much of an operating facility's capacity is required for a production operation.

It is worth noting that the cardinalities on the general concepts' side are (0,*) and on the other side (1, 1). This basically means that the master data ("routing" and "operation") can be used for many production orders, but a specific order will always be derived from a routing in the master data.

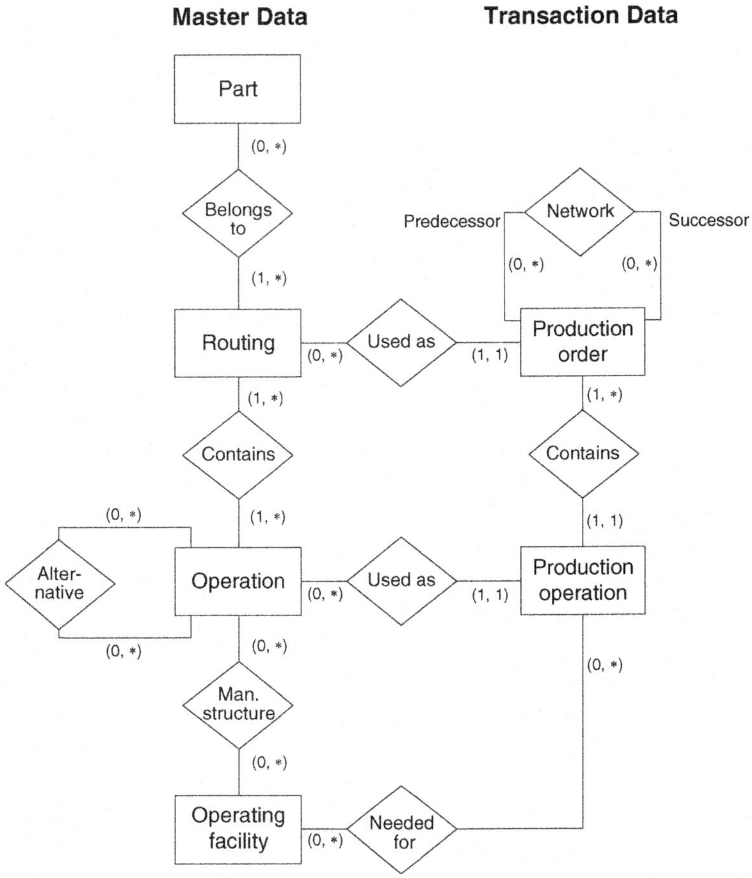

Fig. 3.17 Entity-relationship model for MRP II

Order networks are represented by the "network" relationship type. The two labels "predecessor" and "successor" indicate roles (reading directions), specifying which order precedes or follows which other order. In this way, arbitrary networks can be mapped to the data model.

3.4.2 Capacity Planning in Make-to-Order Production

In make-to-order production, lead-time scheduling and capacity planning must go hand in hand. This is different from the conventional MRP II approach in which lead-time scheduling is done first and capacity planning afterward. When a customer inquiry is processed in order to create a quotation, an essential piece of information to be determined is the delivery date. This delivery date, however, cannot be determined through lead-time scheduling alone. If the capacity situation is not compatible with the end date from lead-time scheduling, this date is useless. Therefore, it is necessary to establish both the order lead time and the feasibility of the order (and of all dependent manufacturing orders) at the same time.

One way of scheduling orders under capacity constraints is *finite scheduling* (scheduling against finite capacity). This approach will be discussed later in the context of manufacturing execution systems (see Sect. 7.1.1).

Further approaches taking production capacities and other capabilities into account were developed in the field of supply chain management. Examples include ATP ("available to promise"), CTP ("capable to promise"), and CTM ("capable to match"). These approaches will be discussed in Sect. 10.1.

A question without a straightforward answer is as follows: When should the capacity requirements of a potential customer order be considered? Capacity reserved for this order is no longer available for other orders (or customer inquiries), restricting the company's options to accept new orders.

If an order's capacity implications are only taken into consideration once the order has been placed, it can happen that the capacities that were free at the time of the customer inquiry have been scheduled for other orders. Consequently, the promised delivery date can no longer be fulfilled.

If capacities are booked directly when the customer inquires or when the quotation is made, these capacities become unavailable for other customer inquiries. Seeing that in some industries, only 30 % or less of quotations actually result in order placements, it is clear that reserving capacities for every potential order is not the best strategy.

Unfortunately, there is no panacea for this dilemma. With sufficient experience, a planner may be able to judge the likelihood that an inquiry will result in a placed order and schedule a percentage of the capacity requirements, according to the likelihood, on the operating facilities involved. For strategically important orders, a company may also decide to schedule the full capacity requirements during the inquiry stage to prevent having to turn the order down later due to booked-up capacities.

Limitations to Simultaneous Planning As discussed above, lead-time scheduling and capacity planning are closely connected. In make-to-order production, scheduling and capacity planning should actually be done at the same time the *primary requirements,* that is, the customer orders, are planned.

The delivery date and the cost of an order (see Sect. 3.7.2) are two essential results in make-to-order primary requirements planning. A reliable delivery date can only be determined when the order lead time and the capacity requirements are planned simultaneously. Since the company most likely processes several orders at the same time, lead-time scheduling and capacity planning should in fact extend to all the current orders.

However, simultaneously planning all orders for a given period is normally not possible, because customers do not place their orders at the same point in time. For this reason, incremental planning of the orders cannot be avoided, even though this means that, from a theoretical standpoint, the final plan will most likely not be optimal.

However, when the planning reaches the level of detailed scheduling, the planning period is fairly short, allowing all manufacturing orders falling into this period to be scheduled together. This is one task of shop-floor control, as described further below (see Sect. 3.6). It is also an issue discussed in the chapter on manufacturing execution system (see Sect. 7.1.1).

3.5 Order Release

All MRP II stages so far have been about *planning*: from very high level, long-term planning down to mid- or short-term planning in CRP. Execution of the plans still lies some distance ahead. Before that, work must be planned in detail on a daily level.

Detailed planning covers a short time period, for example, 1 week. All orders whose start and end dates fall into this period will be included. Scheduling orders in detail obviously makes sense only if the orders are really ready to be executed. Consequently, an important step before detailed planning is to make sure that execution can begin and to provide all documents necessary for the flow of the orders through the plant.

This step is called *order release.* Order release is a commitment that the order will go to the plant and will definitely be carried out. It comprises three major steps:

1. Selecting the orders which fall into the release period
2. Checking the availability of the resources needed
3. Creating documents

When these steps are completed, the orders are released, allowing for detailed planning and preparation of order processing to start.

3.5.1 Availability Check

A precondition for releasing orders is that all resources needed to complete the orders are available. Resources include materials, operating facilities, human experts, machine operators, tools, attachments, and more. Theoretically, these resources should be available because they have been carefully planned through the steps of MRP II. In reality, however, many things can go wrong. Material may be missing because of late delivery, people may fall ill, machines can break down, etc. Practical experience shows that plans usually do not correspond with the reality.

For this reason, it is essential to check if the resources needed for an order are really available. Otherwise, there is a risk that processing will be interrupted, orders will have to wait for operating facilities to become available, and capacity will be wasted. In conventional MRP II, the primary resources to be checked are materials (parts) and operating facilities.

Although checking availability usually takes place after completing capacity requirements planning and before starting detailed planning in shop-floor control, it can also be done at an earlier or later point in time. The best time to check availability depends on the specific production environment.

The later the check is performed, the better the chances are that the resources will still be available when they are actually needed. However, there are situations in which a *late* check may be too late. Consider, for example, an order requiring a special material that takes 2 months to be delivered. If the production manager checks the availability of this material 10 days before the order is supposed to start and finds out that there is a shortage, he or she will realize that the check should have been done 2 months ago. All planning since then, perhaps including a difficult capacity load leveling, has been in vain because now the order will be lying for another 2 months!

Problems like this seem to suggest *early* availability checks. However, the more time passes between the check and the actual demand, the more likely it is that unforeseen things happen that upset the result of the check. In a stable production environment with smooth demand curves, early availability checks may be a reasonable choice. In a dynamic environment with ongoing changes, late availability checks may be more appropriate.

There are many ways to check availability. The simplest way is a *static availability check*. Static means that the availability of the required resources is confirmed only if all the resources are available right now (i.e., when the check is done). Regarding materials, for example, this means that the materials must be physically stored in the warehouse or at least currently booked as available in the computer system.

From a business point of view, static availability is suboptimal because it means that the materials will be lying from the time the check is done until they are needed later, incurring cost. It is more important that the materials are available when they are actually needed than that they are in stock today.

The temporal aspect is taken into account in a *dynamic availability check*. Dynamic means that the things expected to happen up to the time when the order is scheduled are considered. For example, open orders (purchasing orders, production orders) may be filled by then, increasing the inventory, whereas other manufacturing orders may require some of today's inventory and thus decrease it.

Dynamic checking allows the planner to include other factors, such as availability of operating facilities, tools, and human experts. Advanced solutions may even run a complete simulation of the manufacturing processes within the order-release period in order to be able to evaluate availability issues at different points in time.

With the emergence of advanced scheduling approaches in supply chain management (SCM), more advanced types of availability checks have been developed, including ATP ("available to promise"), CTP ("capable to promise"), and CTM ("capable to match"). These types will be discussed in Sect. 10.1.

Excursus: Load-Oriented Order Release A popular technique taking the overall capacity situation into account is the *load-oriented order*

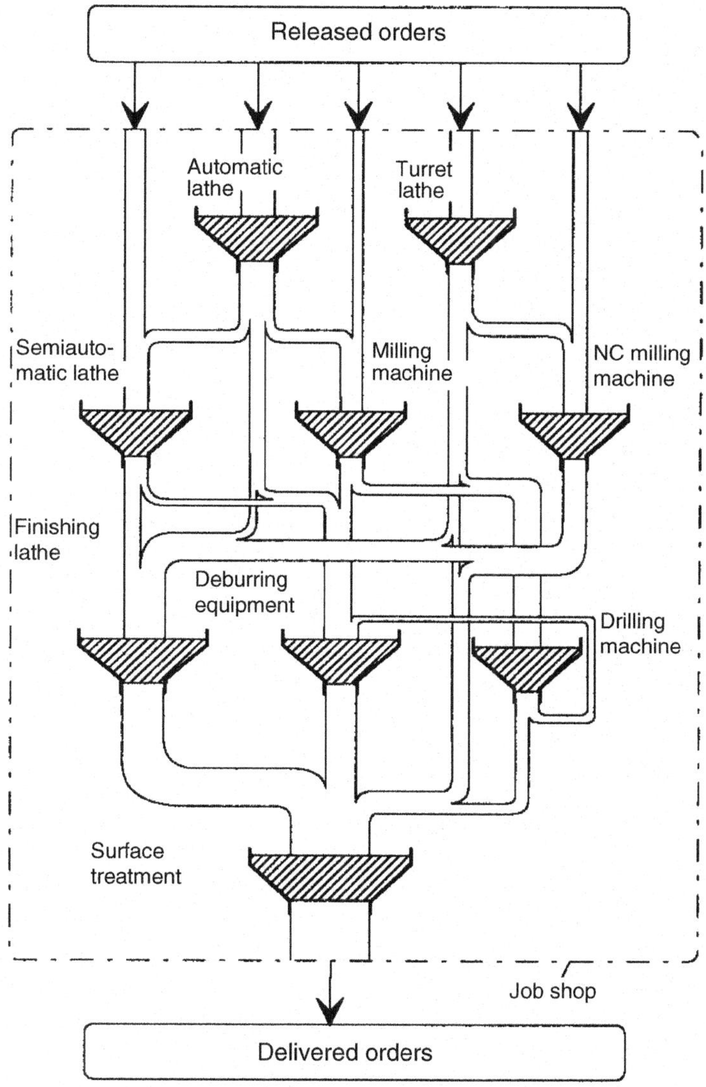

Fig. 3.18 Funnel model of load-oriented order release [Wiendahl 1995, p. 147]

release. This technique has later been extended to a more comprehensive approach, *load-oriented manufacturing control*.

Load-oriented order release was developed at the University of Hannover (Germany) and made popular by Hans-Peter Wiendahl. The development was motivated by the shift of goals in the 1970s and 1980s. Instead of maximizing capacity utilization, the dominating goals were now short lead times, low inventory, and on-time schedule performance (Wiendahl 1995, p. 5). Wiendahl showed through many simulation experiments and practical surveys that there is an interdependence between the four goals. For example, long lead times lead to high inventory and vice versa. High inventory costs money that might be better invested elsewhere.

According to Wiendahl, the main reason why lead times are too long, inventory is too high, and schedules are missed is that too much work is released to the plants, workshops, or operating facilities. Therefore, the basic idea of load-oriented order release is to release only as many orders as can be effectively processed within the next period.

Since many different types of operating facilities with different individual capacities may be involved, the entire system acts and reacts like a system of funnels (cf. Fig. 3.18). The opening of a funnel can be interpreted as temporary stock waiting to be processed, whereas the outlet of a funnel is the operating facility's capacity per time unit.

The overall capacity requirements, the total inventory within the system, the lying times, and thus the order lead times are determined by the amount of work entering the system. Load-oriented order release therefore strives to release orders only up to the point that the system is in balance. This means that no funnel should overflow nor run empty.

The load-oriented order-release method provides detailed techniques for various aspects of steering, monitoring, and controlling the system, for example, how to select the next orders for release and how to fine-tune the funnel capacity and the flow of work from one operating facility to the next. Load-oriented order release has been integrated in a number of ERP systems and implemented in many organizations.

3.5.2 Creating Documents

An important practical issue in the order-release step is to create the documents for the order and related tasks. Typical documents include the following:

- Printed production order (also known as plant order, manufacturing order)
- Job ticket, job schedule ticket (accompanying the order on its way)
- Material slips (for picking materials from the warehouse)
- Wage slips (used as instruction for the machine operator, as feedback on progress monitoring, for payroll accounting, for product cost analysis, etc.)
- Completion confirmation ticket for progress monitoring

Printed completion confirmation tickets are needed when completion information is not automatically created by a machine data acquisition system (cf. Sect. 7.1.2) and sent to the planning and control system. In this case, the feedback must be given manually.

Most documents nowadays are at least semi-automation friendly in that they provide barcodes or other machine-readable codes. Objects carrying RFID (radio frequency identification, cf. Sect. 11.4.1) tags can also return information about the state of an order.

3.5.3 Order Release in Make-to-Order Production

Order release in make-to-order production and order release in make-to-stock production play somewhat different roles. In make-to-stock production, a definite commitment to complete an order is only made when the order is released. In make-to-order production, this commitment is in place a lot earlier, namely, when the customer places the order, when the company sends a quotation to the customer, or even earlier than this, when the company responds with a positive answer to the customer's inquiry.

From this time on, the pressure to complete the order is high. Therefore, a separate step late in the process, named "order release", is often missing. Instead, all activities needed to fulfill the order are already initiated once the inquiry is received, the quotation is prepared, or the order is placed. This includes:

- Issuing the order documents
- Booking material and capacity reservations
- Preparing purchase orders

Availability checks are not omitted, but they are less likely to identify missing resources than in make-to-stock production. The reason for this is that prospective actions to ensure availability have been taken early on.

However, a different source of "uncertainty" is the customer. It is quite common that customers change their minds. For example, they may ask for additional product features, send a new product specification, or request delivery 3 weeks earlier. All these modifications affect the earlier planning. While some changes may have only minor implications, others may require a complete replanning of the customer order (e.g., a change request by the customer requiring a rollback to the product-design step).

Although customer-initiated changes in the order fulfillment process are inconvenient, most make-to-order manufacturers will accept them. Otherwise, they face the risk that the customer is not satisfied, cancels the order, or switches to a competitor next time.

3.6 Shop-Floor Control

Shop-floor control is the final step of planning and control in manufacturing resource planning. Oliver Wright originally called this step "plant scheduling." Other names are also used in the literature. Shop-floor control has two main tasks: one is to decide on which facilities the operations will be processed. The other task is to determine when and in which sequence the processing will take place.

Specifying the operating facilities is relevant when a company performs capacity requirements planning on an aggregate level, for example, for groups of operating facilities (or workshops). Now is the time to decide which individual operating facility out of the group will be used for processing an operation. In addition to this, the main task of shop-floor control is detailed scheduling.

3.6.1 Detailed Scheduling

Detailed scheduling is primarily concerned with in-depth planning of the operations' utilization of operating facilities. A major aspect here is the sequence in which given sets of operations will be processed on the respective operating facilities. Accordingly, a common term for detailed scheduling is *sequencing* (or *order sequencing*). Other terms are *capacity scheduling* and *machine utilization planning*.

Order sequencing is a field that has been investigated by generations of researchers. A plethora of models and methods have been proposed since the 1950s. Optimization methods as well as heuristic approaches were developed in large numbers.

The problem with optimization is that models representing practical scheduling problems are just too complex. Even though today's computers running the optimization methods are much more powerful than earlier computers, they are generally unable to compute a solution within a reasonable amount of time. Optimization methods only work when the problems are fairly small and limited in scope.

For this reason, different approaches are taken in practice. A very popular approach is to use dispatching rules. The rationale for dispatching rules is pursuing or weighting certain goals of production planning more than others. Typical goals as mentioned in Sect. 1.4.2 are:

- Minimizing the total lead times for all production orders (or the average lead time) in the release period
- Maximizing the capacity utilization (or minimizing total idle times) of all operating resources
- Minimizing deadline violations (or maximizing adherence to delivery dates)
- Minimizing the amount of capital tied up in production
- Minimizing setup costs (switching costs) between orders

Since these are conflicting goals, not all of them can be equally realized at the same time. Dispatching rules allow priorities to be set and goals to be weighted.

The scenario for using dispatching rules is as follows: a set of production orders, namely, those that were released in the order-release step, is waiting to be processed on the operating facility under consideration. Now it must be decided which order will be the first to be processed, afterward which order will be the next, etc.

Dispatching rules, also known as *priority rules*, provide criteria for selecting the next order. Common dispatching rules prescribe that the next order will be the one with the:

- Shortest processing time (shortest operating time – SPT/SOT rule)
- Longest processing time (LPT rule)
- Smallest time buffer until the delivery date, i.e., the shortest remaining time ("slack time")
- Largest number of remaining operations
- Longest time waiting for the machine (FIFO rule)
- Shortest time waiting for the machine (LIFO rule)

- Most tied-up capital
- Smallest changeover cost
- Highest external priority ("CEO order")
- Biggest reduction of transition times in the scheduling stage

The number of possible dispatching rules is quite large. For example, 18 rules are listed by Mertens (2009, p. 156). In the 1960s and 1970s, many simulation studies were done to investigate the impact of dispatching rules on the production planning goals. One general finding was that the SPT rule yields good results regarding lead times and capacity utilization but is not effective in meeting deadlines. For this goal, the "slack time" rule is more appropriate, but it does not support short lead times.

An interesting aspect of dispatching rules is that they can be combined. One approach is, for example, adding and/or multiplying several components and weighting the components with appropriate factors. A dispatching rule based on lead-time reduction, slack time, and external priority could be created like this (Mertens 2009, p. 157):

$$G = g_r \cdot R - g_s \cdot (t_1 - t_0 - t_b) + g_p \cdot p,$$

with

G = total priority
R = reduction factor applied to the order in lead-time scheduling
t_1 = end date of the operation from lead-time scheduling
t_0 = today
t_b = remaining processing time of the order
P = external priority
g_r, g_s, g_p = weighting factors

It is worth noting that the priority G is *dynamically changing* as time goes by because the value of G depends on the current date. Another example of a dynamic priority rule is the following:

$$G = g_1 \cdot \frac{n_A}{t_1 - t_0 - t_b} + g_2 \cdot K,$$

with

n_A = number of remaining operations
K = capital tied up in the order
g_1, g_2 = weighting factors

Changeover Sequences In some companies, setting up the operating facility takes a lot of time, using up a significant portion of the capacity. Often the effort to prepare a facility for a particular order depends on which other order (i.e., for which type of part) had been previously processed on the facility. An example for this is dying equipment. Cleaning the equipment takes longer when the dye for the previous order is darker than the dye needed for the current order than vice versa. In the metalworking industry, setting up equipment ranges from simply adjusting an attachment (if the next order is similar to the previous one) to installing new tools, all the way to rebuilding the entire facility (in case the next order imposes completely different technical requirements).

As an optimization problem, dealing with sequence-dependent setup effort means that the sequence of orders that minimizes the total setup cost or setup time has to be determined. While stating this problem is quite simple, computing the optimal solution is generally not possible, because the number of possible solutions is just too large. For n orders, $n!$ possible sequences exist. If $n = 20$, the number is approximately 2.4 quintillion (2.4×10^{18}). This example shows that a complete enumeration of all sequences is not feasible.

Although many optimization and heuristic techniques (see below) have been proposed in the literature, order sequences in practice are often determined with the help of very simple methods or rules of thumb.

An example is scheduling orders according to setup times (from the shortest to the longest). Figure 3.19 illustrates this for five orders involving the parts A, B, C, D, and E. The matrix contains the times required to set up the facility when part i is processed before and part j afterwards.

Suppose that currently (i.e., before the beginning of the planning period) an order for part B is being processed on the machine. In this case, it is advantageous to begin with part B because no setup time is required. Subsequently, the next order to be processed would be the order for part C since C is the part that causes the shortest setup time (35 min) when B was processed

Fig. 3.19 Sequence-dependent setup times

Setup time from \ to	A	B	C	D	E
A	–	120	9	50	75
B	80	–	35	40	70
C	90	60	–	45	110
D	60	40	30	–	50
E	55	80	25	90	–

before. Continuing in this fashion, the result is the following sequence of orders, together with the setup times:
B 0 min
C 35 min
D 45 min
E 50 min
A 55 min
with setup time totaling 185 min. This method quickly produces an acceptable result fast. It may not always find an optimal sequence, but in most cases at least a satisfactory one.

3.6.2 Advanced Scheduling Methods

In the past decades, many approaches to solve scheduling problems have been developed, in particular optimization methods and a variety of heuristic approaches.

Optimization Sequencing and scheduling have been prominent problem domains in *operations research*. Starting in the 1950s, many mathematical optimization methods for specific problems have been proposed. Optimization means that a method attempts to maximize or minimize an *objective function* (e.g., the total lead times) by calculating appropriate values of the *decision variables* (e.g., operation start dates) subject to a number of *constraints* (e.g., operation sequences according to the routings). The method ends with an optimal solution or with the result that no solution exists.

Mathematical optimization uses exact methods, that is, the solution found is guaranteed to be the optimal solution, provided that a solution exists and can be computed within a reasonable time span. Computability, however, has always been a serious challenge. Real-world sequencing and scheduling problems usually lead to very large optimization models, which cannot be solved in a finite or acceptable time.

In response to this problem, many heuristic approaches were developed. These methods do not necessarily end with an optimal solution, but instead try to find one that comes close to the optimum and/or is satisfactory. Many current methods belong to the field of heuristic search, while others have been adopted from neural networks and artificial intelligence.

Heuristic Search In the 1980s and 1990s, various approaches using analogies to biological and physical phenomena were tried out to solve optimization problems. Especially worth mentioning are *genetic algorithms* and *simulated annealing*. Based on the mechanisms of these methods, further efficient search methods such as *tabu search* and *threshold accepting* were developed. All these methods can be summarized under the term "search methods" because their main task is to search for an optimal or at least adequate solution in a large solution space.

Genetic algorithms are based on the principles of evolution theory and the mechanisms of genetics (Goldberg 1989). Similar to natural evolutionary processes, the best individuals survive and reproduce, passing their characteristics on to the next generation ("survival of the fittest").

In an optimization problem such as sequencing, an individual represents a particular solution to the problem. Genetic algorithms employ many solutions at the same time, called a *population*, and continuously create new generations of solutions.

The process of creating the next generation (child generation) applies the genetic operators *mutation, inversion,* and *crossover* to the parent generation. Subsequently, it selects which children survive according to their fitness.

In optimization, this means that new solutions are continuously generated and evaluated and old solutions are discarded. The method ends when all solutions are the same (i.e., when the method converges), when the objective function has reached a satisfactory level, or when the user decides not to spend more computing time.

Many authors have proposed genetic algorithms for sequencing and scheduling problems. The reported results are inconclusive. Some authors have found an improvement compared to other techniques, whereas others noted that alternative techniques performed better than genetic algorithms.

Simulated annealing (Aarts and Korst 1989; Kirkpatrick et al. 1983) is a stochastic heuristic optimization technique based on the physical process of crystallization. In this process, a substance is heated to a very high temperature and then cooled down slowly. When the energy has reached its minimum, perfect crystals are obtained.

In "simulated" annealing, the method starts with an initial solution, modifies the solution, and then continuously creates further solutions. These solutions are accepted for the next iteration with a certain probability. The probability depends on a parameter called "temperature," as in real annealing. The temperature is reduced in each iteration, step-by-step. The smaller the steps, the better the solution.

However, cooling down slowly increases the computing time. On the other hand, cooling down rapidly bears the risk that the method ends up at a local optimum (suboptimum). Just as with other heuristic methods, a trade-off between solution quality and computing time has to be made.

Simulated annealing is a fast and robust heuristic. Applied to detailed scheduling, it performs reasonably well. In a study by the author comparing genetic algorithms, tabu search, simulated annealing, and threshold accepting, simulated annealing was found to outperform the others (Kurbel 1998). However, it should be noted that all results, both those concerning the solution quality and the computing time, depend on how well the user stipulates the respective parameters of the methods.

Neural Networks Neural networks use analogies to structures and processes involved in human thinking. In contrast to the natural neural networks, those dealt with in computer science are frequently called *artificial neural networks* (*ANN*). Artificial neural networks are mathematical models inspired by the biological networks of neurons in the human brain (Singh 1997, p. 65).

Over time, various types of networks have been developed. The best known are multilayer feed-forward networks using backpropagation, Hopfield networks, Boltzmann machines, and self-organizing feature maps, also known as Kohonen networks (e.g., Graupe 2007).

All network types imitate the neurons inside the human brain, the connections between the neurons (synapses), and the neural activity involved in thinking. Each neuron is connected with many other neurons through synapses. Neurons communicate by passing on (firing) electrical charges. When a neuron fires, a signal is sent to other neurons through the synapses. In this way, many neurons are involved in the thought process (or more specifically, in a problem-solving process) at the same time.

Neural networks are systems that function by involving the activity of numerous neurons working in parallel. Accordingly, artificial neural networks are massively parallel information processing systems. The individual processing elements (neurons), on the other hand, are very simple. The "intelligence" of the network results from a large number of neurons working together.

In the 1990s, artificial neural networks were applied to various optimization problems, including sequencing and scheduling of manufacturing orders. Comparisons between artificial neural networks and other techniques, however, have been inconclusive. A comparative study by the author found that Hopfield networks, when applied to scheduling, performed worse than other heuristics (Kurbel and Ruppel 1996, p. 374).

3.7 Excursus: Product Costing

Product costing is one of the tasks of managerial accounting. Today's ERP systems contain comprehensive modules for managerial accounting. Although not really a part of MRP II, earlier MRP II systems have also supported product costing. The reason for this is that product costing can be done very accurately when it is based on the data structures available in MRP II.

A common approach in product costing has always been *overhead costing*. In overhead costing, the total cost is divided into direct cost and overhead cost. *Direct cost* is the cost that can be directly assigned to the product under consideration, whereas *overhead cost* is added as a percentage, because it includes the cost of "everything else" involved (e.g., energy cost, salaries etc.).

3.7.1 Make-to-Stock Products

A popular scheme for calculating the cost of a product is shown in Fig. 3.20. This scheme is based on the assumption that certain cost rates and times are known, as is the case in make-to-stock manufacturing.

The *cost of goods sold (COGS)* is computed from the cost of goods manufactured, plus administration overhead cost and sales cost. The *cost of goods manufactured (COGM)*, consisting of material and manufacturing costs, makes up the largest portion of the cost of goods sold.

Material cost is divided into direct and overhead costs. *Direct material cost* is caused by the use of those materials that can be attributed directly to one unit of the part to be calculated. *Overhead material cost* is also caused by the use of materials, but these materials cannot be directly related to a specific unit of the part in question (e.g., auxiliary materials such as lubricant).

Manufacturing cost is also broken down into direct and overhead costs. The *direct cost* is

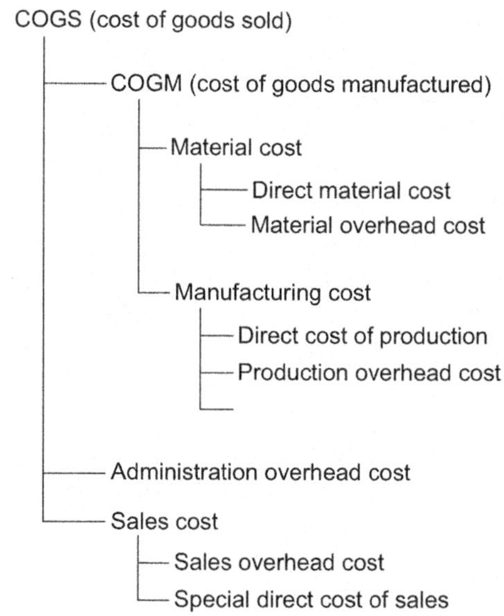

Fig. 3.20 Overhead costing scheme

primarily wages that can be directly associated with one unit of the part (e.g., piecework pay), while the *overhead cost* is caused by the utilization of the operating facilities and the work of employees who are not paid per piece. It is worth mentioning that in today's automated production environments, the machine cost is a lot higher than the labor cost. Nevertheless, the machine cost is traditionally calculated as a (high) percentage of the direct cost of production (i.e., the labor cost). The *special direct cost of production* is the cost associated with an order, but not with a single unit (e.g., specialized tools).

The *cost of goods sold* can be calculated by adding the *administration overhead cost* and sales cost to the cost of goods manufactured. Calculating the cost of goods manufactured and the cost of goods sold as described above is usually the method taught to business students and presented in textbooks.

With the help of an ERP system, the calculation can be carried out much more accurately than by using rough overhead-cost approximations (such as percentage supplements). All data required for a detailed calculation of the material and manufacturing costs are available in the database. For example, the machine cost (per time unit) is stored in the operating facility master data. How much machine time is needed can be found in the routings. Multiplying the time per unit by the machine cost for each machine involved and adding up the products yields an exact figure, so that it is no longer necessary to work with production overhead costs.

Product costing based on an MRP II database means that principally, the manufacturing costs are determined with the help of the *routing* and *operating facility* master data. The direct material cost is computed with the help of the *product structure* and *part* master data. Only the material overhead cost remains to be added as a percentage of the direct material costs. Referring to Figs. 3.2 and 3.4, the entity types "part," "routing," "operation," and "operating facility" would be involved in the calculation.

The essential data needed for the calculation of the *manufacturing cost* are found as follows:

- The *processing times* per unit are stored with the operations in the routings, as mentioned above.
- The *setup times* are either stored with the operations or the operating facilities.
- The *cost of an operating facility* per time unit is usually a field in the operating facility master record. In case a different cost rate applies to setting up the facility, this cost would typically also be stored in the master record.
- For the *amount of human labor* involved in the operations, the processing times per unit and the setup times in the routings can be taken.
- The *cost rates* to be multiplied by the amount of human labor per operation are typically stored in the *human resources* section of the ERP database.
- When the part to be calculated has a multi-level product structure, all the lower-level parts and their routings are identified with the help of the *bills of materials*.

In order to compute the material cost, the product structure tree has to be traversed all the way down to the leaves. The leaves are usually purchased parts (e.g., raw materials) for which purchase prices are known. If the product structure has n levels, the first part to be calculated will be on level $n-1$. The material cost of this part consists of the cost of the purchased parts that go into this part. The cost of a purchased part is obtained by multiplying the price of the part by the quantity coefficient specifying how many units are needed. Totaling the costs of the purchased parts results in the total material cost for the level $n-1$ part.

The direct material cost, material overhead cost, and manufacturing cost are added to calculate the cost of the level $n-1$ part. When the costs of this and other level n parts are known, they can be used in the cost calculation for the next part up on level $n-2$, that is, the part that the level $n-1$ parts go into. Working in this way from the bottom up, the material and manufacturing cost for each part are calculated, step-by-step, before progressing to the next level. Administration overhead and sales costs are added to the cost of the end product (COGM) to yield the cost of goods sold (COGS).

An example is presented in Fig. 3.21 to illustrate the calculation process. This example is based on the end product Y and its product structure (cf. Fig. 2.1.1), which were also used in previous examples.

The calculation starts with the lowest parts manufactured in-house, that is, the parts A and C. It is assumed that D, E, F, and G are purchased parts.

The *material cost* of A, for example, is computed as the sum of the costs of 1 unit of G, 4 units of E, and 1 unit of F (190€) plus 20 % overhead.

The *manufacturing cost* of A is computed from the operations' durations (as specified in A's routing), each one multiplied by the machine cost rate (stored in the operating facility data). Two operating facility groups are involved: OFG 5 and OFG 6. Note that in this example, the machine cost rates for setting up a facility and for processing are different (e.g., 4 vs. 9€/min for OFG 5).

The sum of the manufacturing cost (620.00€) and the material cost (228.00€) yields the *cost per unit of A* (848.00€) that will be used in further calculation steps.

Before the cost of part B can be calculated, the *cost of C* must be known. The cost of C is

Cost Sheet Part A							
	Operation no.	Cost center (OFG	Activity	Dimension	Cost rate (€)	Processing time per unit A/setup time per OFG (min)	Cost per unit
1	1	OFG 5	Setup	€/min	4	10	40.00
2			Produce	€/min	9	20	180.00
3	2	OFG 6	Setup	€/min	10	5	50.00
4			Produce	€/min	35	10	350.00
5	**Manufacturing cost (rows 1+2+3+4)**						**620.00**
	Material/semi-finished product			**Dimension**	**Cost rate/ percentage**	**Required amount per unit A**	**Cost per unit**
6	Direct material cost G			€/unit	20	1	20.00
7	Direct material cost E			€/unit	40	4	160.00
8	Direct material cost F			€/unit	10	1	10.00
9	Material overhead costs			%	20		38.00
10	**Material cost (rows 6+7+8+9)**						**228.00**
11	**COGM (cost of goods manufactured) part A (rows 5+10)**						**848.00**

Cost Sheet Part C							
	Operation no.	Cost center (OFG	Activity	Dimension	Cost rate (€)	Processing time per unit C/setup time per OFG (min)	Cost per unit
1	1	OFG 3	Setup	€/min	6	10	60.00
2			Produce	€/min	18	5	90.00
3	**Manufacturing cost (rows 1+2)**						**150.00**
	Material/semi-finished product			**Dimension**	**Cost rate/ percentage**	**Required amount per unit C**	**Cost per unit**
4	Direct material cost D			€/unit	5	1	5.00
5	Direct material cost E			€/unit	40	2	80.00
6	Material overhead costs			%	20		17.00
7	**Material cost (rows 4+5+6)**						**102.00**
8	**COGM (cost of goods manufactured) part C (rows 3+7)**						**252.00**

Fig. 3.21 Calculating the cost of goods sold

computed from the material cost (102.00€) and the manufacturing cost (150.00€), resulting in 252.00€. Since 2 units of C are needed for 1 unit of B, the direct material cost of B is 504.00€. The manufacturing cost of B amounts to 75.00€, contributing to the total cost of B, which is 679.80€.

Finally, calculating the end-product cost (COGM) means adding up the material cost—two units of A (848.00€ each) and one unit of B (679.80€)—and the manufacturing cost (330.00€). The result is 2,705.80€.

Administration overhead cost and sales cost assigned to the end product Y, computed as

Cost Sheet Part B							
	Operation no.	**Cost center (OFG**	**Activity**	**Dimension**	**Cost rate (€)**	**Processing time per unit B/setup time per OFG (min)**	**Cost per unit**
1	1	OFG 19	Setup	€/min	6	0	0.00
2			Produce	€/min	25	3	75.00
3	**Manufacturing cost (rows 1+2)**						**75.00**
	Material/semi-finished product			**Dimension**	**Cost rate/ percentage**	**Required amount per unit B**	**Cost per unit**
4	Direct material cost C			€/unit	252	2	504.00
5	Material overhead costs			%	20		100.80
6	**Material cost**						**604.80**
7	**COGM (cost of goods manufactured) part C (rows 3+6)**						**679.80**

Cost Sheet Part Y							
	Operation no.	**Cost center (OFG)**	**Activity**	**Dimension**	**Cost rate (€)**	**Processing time per unit Y/setup time per OFG (min)**	**Cost per unit**
1	1	OFG 15	Setup	€/min	10	3	30.00
2			Produce	€/min	30	10	300.00
3	**Manufacturing cost (rows 1+2)**						**330.00**
	Material/semi-finished product			**Dimension**	**Cost rate/ percentage**	**Required amount per unit Y**	**Cost per unit**
4	Semi-finished product A			€/unit	848.00	2	1696.00
5	Semi-finished product B			€/unit	679.80	1	679.80
6	Material overhead costs			%	20		0.00
7	**Material cost (rows 4+5+6)**						**2375.80**
8	**COGM (cost of goods manufactured) part Y (rows 3+7)**						**2705.80**
9	Administration overhead cost (10% of 8)						270.58
10	Sales overhead cost (10% of 8)						270.58
11	Special direct cost of sales						0.00
12	**COGS (cost of goods sold) part Y (rows 8+9+10+11)**						**3246.96**

Fig. 3.21 (continued)

percentages of the COGM value, account for twice 270.58€. The final sum, that is, the cost of goods sold (COGS) for Y, amounts to 3,246,96€.

This example shows that product costing is easy and accurate when a manufacturing database containing times and cost rates is available. If the company is a make-to-stock manufacturer producing the same production program for a long time, the times and cost rates in the database can be expected to be reliable and precise. Well-led companies repeat and tune their product costing in regular intervals. Therefore, initial mistakes and inaccuracies will have been removed in the course of time. When a company knows exactly what producing their products actually costs, they can make better business decisions than if they have only vague cost figures.

3.7.2 Make-to-Order Products

In make-to-order manufacturing, *product costing* is of crucial importance. The cost calculation often refers to an entire customer order instead of one unit of the product (*order costing*). When the company makes a quotation to the customer, it needs to know the cost because the profitability of the order depends directly on the cost of the product.

The problem in make-to-order manufacturing is that the product the customer wishes to buy might have never been built before. In these cases, master data such as bills of materials and routings are not available. If the same product (or a similar product) has been produced before, some master data may be available, but they will not be of the same stability and accuracy as the master data of a make-to-stock manufacturer.

When customer-specific products can be defined using *variants* (cf. Sect. 2.1.2), master data for the variants may be available. However, since it is not likely that a specific variant out of a large spectrum of variants has been used very often (or at all), the master data might be faulty and inaccurate.

If master data are not available, it is difficult to reliably calculate the cost. One way out of the dilemma would be to first create all master data and afterward calculate the product or order cost. However, this is not the approach most companies prefer. The effort needed to establish full-fledged master data is very high. Furthermore, calculation results are needed quickly, namely, when the customer asks for a quotation and, not weeks after, when the master data have finally been created.

For these reasons, many make-to-order manufacturers are forced to apply different approaches to help them quickly obtain a cost figure. Typical approaches use calculations previously carried out for similar products and let the planner modify the parameters underlying the old case to reflect the current case.

Similarity plays an important role in judging whether an old case can be transferred to the current case and in calculating the cost of the current product or order. In order to automate, semiautomate, or just support the user's calculation in one way or another, attempts have been made to formalize and measure the "distance" between old cases and the current case. Distance measures, if available, can be applied to find the closest product (or more generally, the closest manufacturing case), that is, the one that is most similar to the current one.

Human experts doing cost calculations for new products or customer orders usually employ their own experience and knowledge about factors influencing the cost. Such factors include:

- Costing results from other products and orders
- Judgment regarding the new product/order
- Differences between the old and the new product/order
- Problems that occurred with previous orders
- Knowledge about the current production environment, technological changes since the old case, etc.
- General manufacturing knowledge

A problem-solving approach based on knowledge and experience from previous cases is *case-based reasoning (CBR)*. It was developed in the field of artificial intelligence (AI) during the 1980s (Bareiss 1989; Riesbeck and Schank 1989). Ideally, CBR works on a case base containing many cases, uses similarity and distance measures to find old cases suitable for the current problem, and helps the user adapt the best-suited case to the current needs.

While most applications have remained within academia, CBR is nevertheless a promising approach to support product or order costing for make-to-order manufacturers. Since few companies do only things that they have never done before, the new products are usually not completely different from the old ones. Theoretically, a case base could be created, maintained, continuously extended, and used whenever adequate cost figures have to be derived.

4 ERP: Enterprise Resource Planning

Enterprise resource planning (ERP) is a term that was created in continuation of the earlier terms *material requirements planning* (MRP) and *manufacturing resource planning* (MRP II). While manufacturing resource planning focused on the resources needed for manufacturing, the idea behind enterprise resource planning is to consider *all* resources necessary for the success of the enterprise.

Two approaches have driven the development of enterprise resource planning; the first is that companies carry out most of their work within business processes, involving many business functions. In a manufacturing company, some of the business functions are related to manufacturing, while others deal with human resources, marketing, or controlling. The enterprise will only be successful if all of the resources work together effectively. With regard to information systems, this means that IT support for "manufacturing" resource planning had to be extended to support "enterprise" resource planning.

The second factor that led to the development of ERP was the need for effective information systems not only in manufacturing but also in other industries. Much of the functionality that helps manufacturing companies is also beneficial to other companies. Service companies, for example, also require accounting, controlling, marketing, financial planning, etc., but their planning and control needs differ from those of manufacturing companies.

4.1 The Need for Integration

Integration is the key issue in enterprise resource planning. The need for *integrated information systems* grew as more and more business tasks used information systems. In the beginning, most of these systems were stand-alone systems, not connected with each other. This created many problems, because the underlying business tasks are, of course, connected.

Another driving force behind integration was the shift from a function-oriented toward a *process-oriented* outlook on business operations. Business processes cross functional borders, which requires an integrated view of the business functions involved.

Stand-alone systems, sometimes called "silos," cause various problems. The most serious ones are:

- *Redundancy*, meaning that the same information is stored several times in different places
- *Inconsistency*, meaning that information about the same matter stored in different places is not the same
- *Lack of integrity*, meaning that when viewed together, the databases underlying the different information systems are not correct

Additional work, wrong decisions, and planning mistakes are some of the consequences of these shortcomings. A typical challenge many companies have faced is *customer data* being

K.E. Kurbel, *Enterprise Resource Planning and Supply Chain Management*,
Progress in IS, DOI 10.1007/978-3-642-31573-2_4, © Springer-Verlag Berlin Heidelberg 2013

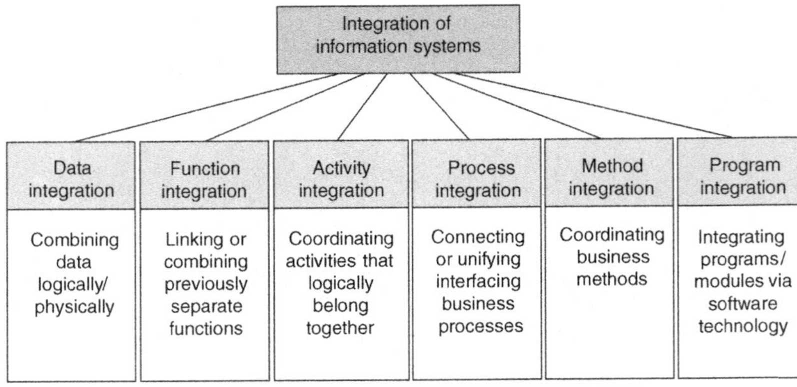

Fig. 4.1 Integration perspectives

stored and maintained within different information systems. Customer data are usually entered or updated in the sales and distribution system when a customer order or an inquiry is received. Other systems also need customer data, for example, the dispatching system (for delivery orders) and the accounting system (for billing).

Having three places where the same data are stored is redundant, causes additional work, and is a source of problems. Most likely, changes in the data will not be updated in all three systems at the same time, if they are even communicated at all. Different business functions may require different attributes to be included in a data record. Even the same attributes do not necessarily have the same meaning or might be structured in a different way. For example, the "address" in the sales and distribution system usually stands for the address of the customer's procurement department, whereas the "address" in the dispatching system is the place where the goods have to be shipped and the "address" in the accounting system is the address where the invoice is sent.

Another example is determining the *delivery date*. Suppose the sales person uses the scheduling method provided by the sales and distribution system to project a reliable delivery date for the customer. If this method is different from the production department's lead-time scheduling method, the customer order might be completed "on time" but according to the production plan and not according to what the sales and distribution department told the customer. Therefore, the date promised to the customer may not be met.

Because of problems like these, the integration of information systems has been one of the major areas of research and development in business informatics for many years.

Integration is a term that includes various aspects. Most people immediately think of integration as a means for eliminating data redundancy, as was the problem in our example above regarding customer data. There are, however, more perspectives from which integration can be considered, as Fig. 4.1 shows:

- *Data integration:* Data models and databases are combined on a conceptual, logical, and/or physical level, so that all departments and/or business processes use the same data entities with the same values.
- *Function integration:* Separate related functions are linked together or combined into one function. An example is connecting computer-aided design (CAD) with product costing, enabling the designer to immediately see the impact of design decisions on the product cost.
- *Activity integration*: Activities that logically belong together are connected or synchronized. This is the case, for example, when one activity triggers the next one, passing all relevant data on to the second activity.
- *Process integration*: Different business processes or subprocesses that interface each other are connected or unified (e.g., order fulfillment and production).
- *Method integration*: Planning methods are coordinated. For example, the method used for calculating order quantities should match

the method used for forecasting in order to avoid unnecessary stock and inventory cost.

- *Program integration*: Different programs or modules can work together. This requires the programs to be based on the same software technology or to use an interfacing technology (middleware) that allows them to collaborate.

From the point of view of the business tasks, the direction of integration is either horizontal or vertical. *Horizontal integration* presents itself when information systems on the same organizational level are integrated, for example, all operational systems or all reporting systems. *Vertical integration* means integration across management levels, usually within one functional area. An example of this would be the integration of systems or modules for procurement, accounts payable, monitoring, controlling, and analytics related to purchasing, on all management levels.

With stand-alone systems increasingly causing problems, many organizations tried to integrate these systems with the help of integration technologies and platforms such as CORBA (Common Object Request Broker Architecture [OMG 2011b]) and other middleware. This was and continues to be a challenging task. Today, the integration problems are dealt with in the field of *enterprise application integration* (EAI).

The alternative to subsequent integration of existing information systems is to develop, buy, or license *holistic systems* that are integrated from the beginning. This is the approach taken in enterprise resource planning. ERP systems are integrated systems, ideally based on an enterprise-wide information systems architecture.

A typical ERP system is very comprehensive. Developing such a system requires significant effort, time, and financial resources. An individual organization is normally not capable or willing to make this kind of investment. Instead, specialized software firms develop standard software for ERP. By selling the standard software to many organizations, the software firm amortizes the high development cost.

For the customer, this means that they have to pay only a share (via the license cost), but on the other hand, they receive only "standard" software that needs to be customized to the company's requirements. This also costs money, but not as much as developing an ERP system from scratch.

An ERP system will usually cover all business functions on all management levels, supporting the essential business processes of the company. Functional areas that ERP systems support include:

- Purchasing and procurement
- Material planning, inventory management, warehousing
- Production planning, manufacturing, quality assurance, maintenance
- Marketing, sales and distribution, shipment, customer service
- Financial and managerial accounting, controlling
- Human resources (payroll, personnel management, staff assignment, etc.)

The names of the ERP modules and the way the systems are structured vary significantly. However, the functionalities of large ERP systems are quite comparable. Small ERP systems are similar as regards the business functions they support, but they are less powerful when it comes to top-management support.

4.2 Mapping the Organization

When a company decides to implement an ERP system, they expect that the system supports their particular needs—not the needs of a "standard" company. However, the standard software vendor could not know the business rules, processes, and strategies of all potential customers when the standard software was developed. Therefore, the standard software needs to be adapted to the requirements of the company before it can be implemented in the organization. This process is called *customization*. It will be discussed in Sect. 6.2.

Before the business processes and the business rules can be adapted, the company "as such," that is, its organizational structure, has to be represented in the system. This is necessary because the responsibility for and the authorization to execute a particular process step or activity are usually bound to an organizational unit.

For example, the right to use the ERP function for lead-time reduction will be assigned to the production management and not to the sales office. The financial accounting department will be responsible for canceling an invoice in the ERP database. The task of creating a purchase order might be assigned to the warehouse manager in one case and to the procurement department in another.

Therefore, one of the first steps in implementing an ERP system is to define the organizational structure of the company within the system. This means that the actual organizational structure has to be described with the help of the organizational elements predefined in the ERP system, using the prescribed terminology.

Mapping organizational structures is a broad and complex task, requiring many discussions and decisions. The essential question is how to arrange the company's actual organizational units so that they can be assigned to the organizational elements available in the ERP system. Once the organizational structure has been defined, it is difficult to change, because it is used throughout all parts of the ERP system. For this reason, the mapping of the organization's structure has to be prepared very carefully.

Although we have been talking about "the" organizational structure, enterprises usually have more than one structure. From the view of accounting, the enterprise looks different than from the perspective of logistics. In accounting, relevant organizational entities are "company," "business area," "controlling area," etc., whereas in logistics, we speak of "plants," "warehouses," "storage locations," "purchasing organizations," etc.

In the following, we will be using the organizational elements provided by SAP ERP as an example to demonstrate the mapping of organizational structures. It should be noted that different organizational structures have to be defined for several application contexts, including materials management and production, purchasing, sales, accounting, and human resources.

4.2.1 Accounting

"Client," "company code," "business area," "controlling area," and "operating concern" are the main organizational elements available to define the organizational structure for accounting. These elements will be explained subsequently.

Client The top element in accounting, and also of all other organizational structures in SAP ERP, is the so-called "client." In a simplified view, a *client* can be regarded as representing a company. In each SAP ERP implementation, there is one client, but there can also be more than one. This is the case when several companies belonging to a group of companies use the same SAP system.

Company Code The *company code* is the most important element in accounting. It stands for an organizational unit for which a complete set of accounts can be drawn up for external reporting. For each company code, documents required for financial reporting (i.e., balance sheet and profit and loss statement) are defined, according to the legal rules and regulations.

The simplest case is one company (client) has one company code. More commonly, a company consists of several legally independent companies, which all need their own company codes. Examples include a company with subsidiaries, a company with branches abroad, and a group holding company.

A *chart of accounts* is assigned to each company code. Having several company codes with the same chart of accounts means that the general ledgers of these companies are structured in the same way.

The company code is used in all transactions that have financial or asset implications. Since this is the case for many transactions in enterprise resource planning, the company code can be found on many ERP screens and reports.

Business Area Many companies monitor and control the success of their various *business areas* separately, not only the success of the entire enterprise. For this purpose, area-specific balance sheets and profit and loss statements are created. An example is a company that is organized by

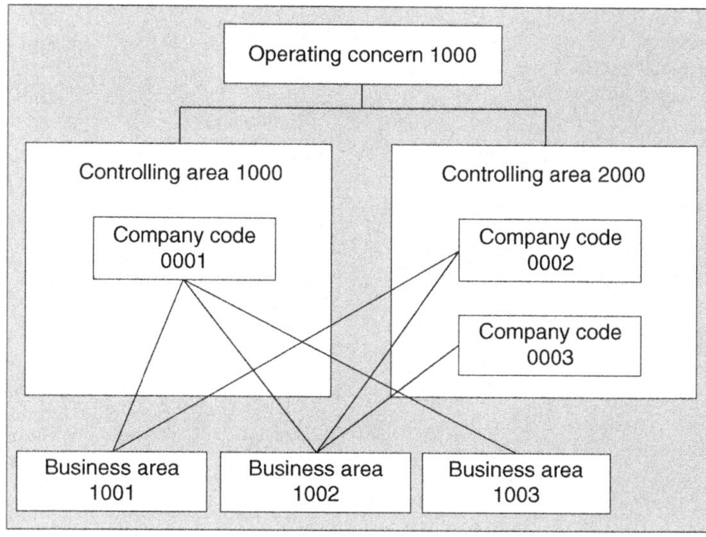

Fig. 4.2 Organizational structure for accounting

divisions, where each division creates their own internal balance sheet. Another example is companies that are subject to legal regulations requiring separate reporting for specific lines of business (e.g., certain products).

In the cases mentioned above, the company will define *business areas* along with the company code(s). The relationship between company codes and business areas is such that one company code can contain several business areas.

Vice versa, one business area can belong to several company codes. An example for this would be a division that is located both at home and abroad. Due to legal requirements, there will be two company codes, but only one business area is involved.

Controlling Area While company code and business area are organizational elements for financial accounting, *controlling area* is an element used for *managerial accounting*.

Costs and revenues are booked and calculated with regard to a controlling area. This means that cost-element accounting, cost-center accounting, product-cost controlling, and profit-center accounting take place within a controlling area.

The simplest case would be a company that has one controlling area and one company code. SAP clients used for training and education usually fall under this category.

However, the legal rules and regulations for external and internal reporting are different. Therefore, it may be necessary to assign more than one company code to a controlling area. An example of this would be a company with several subsidiaries (i.e., several company codes) that nevertheless wants to have a uniform controlling. For this purpose, the company would assign several company codes to one controlling area. One requirement is here that all subsidiaries use the same chart of accounts. Both cases are exemplified in Fig. 4.2.

Operating Concern Operating concern is another organizational element within managerial accounting used for controlling. It represents a part of the organization for which the sales market is structured in a uniform way and a profitability analysis can be carried out.

In the simplest case, there is one operating concern with one controlling area. A more general case is present when multiple controlling areas are assigned to the same operating concern.

Figure 4.2 illustrates the relationships between the terms "company code," "business area," "controlling area," and "operating concern."

4.2.2 Materials Management and Production

In the areas of materials management and production, mostly the same organizational units are employed. In addition to "client" and "company

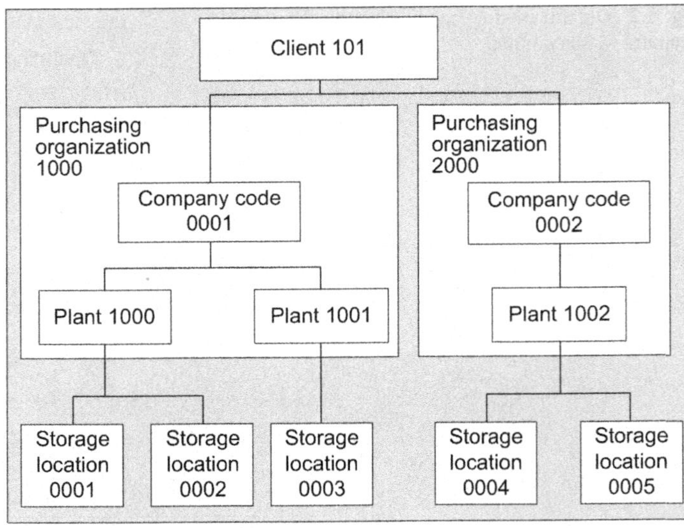

Fig. 4.3 Company-specific purchasing organization (Benz and Höflinger 2008, p. 50)

code," important elements include "plant" and "storage location."

Plant The terminology used to describe the organizational structure for materials management and production is based on a conventional manufacturing company. Products, be they physical products or services, are produced and stored in *plants*. However, the concept of a plant is rather general, comprising all organizational units that create physical or immaterial output, for example, factories, distribution centers, regional offices, and shops.

In the simplest case, a company has one plant, but generally, a company consists of several plants. Each plant is assigned to exactly one company code.

Storage Location Inventory is kept at *storage locations*. These are organizational units including, for example, incoming goods storage and the finished goods warehouse. Storage locations belong to plants, that is, a storage location is always uniquely assigned to one plant.

Storage locations are important for materials management and production because inventory management and stocktaking are done on the storage-location level. This means that inward and outward stock movements are booked with the help of the organizational element storage location.

Purchasing Organization For procurement, additional organizational elements are needed, in particular the elements "purchasing organization" and "purchasing group."

With the help of *purchasing organizations*, a company can be subdivided according to the requirements of purchasing. A purchasing organization is an organizational unit that procures materials and services. In order to do so, the purchasing organization negotiates conditions with the suppliers and oversees the purchasing transactions.

Depending on the company, purchasing can be more or less, or completely, centralized or decentralized:

- A *plant-specific* purchasing organization means that each plant has its own purchasing organization.
- A *company-specific* purchasing organization is responsible for more than one plant.
- An *enterprise-wide* purchasing organization can be chosen when the company has a completely centralized purchasing organization across all company codes.

Figure 4.3 shows how the purchasing organization is related with company codes, plants, and storage locations. In this example, the purchasing organization 1000 is responsible for the plants 1000 and 1001, which are both assigned to company code 0001. The purchasing organization 2000 is responsible for the plant 1002 (within company code 0002).

In Fig. 4.4, the purchasing organization is enterprise-wide, responsible for all plants across all company codes. This is an example of a highly centralized purchasing organization.

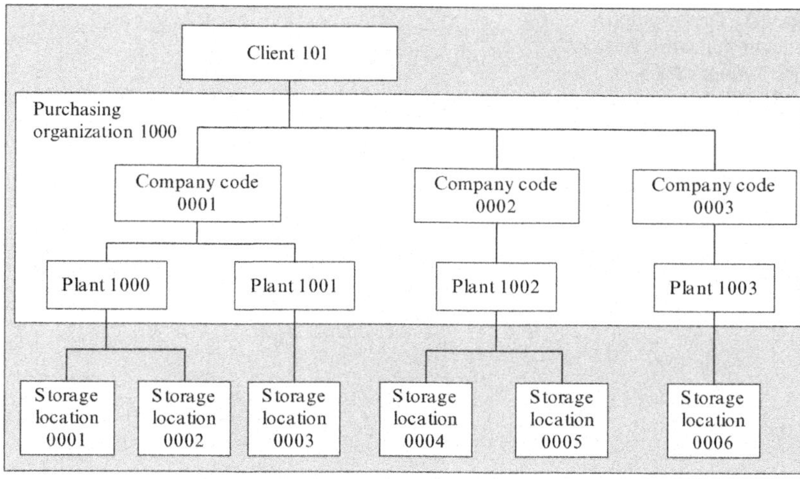

Fig. 4.4 Enterprise-wide purchasing organization

Purchasing Group A *purchasing group* is an organizational unit responsible for certain purchasing activities, in particular for procuring certain materials or services. In larger companies, several persons may be assigned to a purchasing group, but in smaller companies, the purchasing group may be just one person.

By defining a purchasing group, it is also clear who in the company serves as a contact for the suppliers of the materials or services that belong to the scope of the group.

4.2.3 Sales

Regarding the sales function, prominent organizational elements to map the actual organizational structure include, among others, the "sales organization," "distribution channel," "division," and "sales area."

Sales Organization The highest level of the sales structure, below the company code, is the *sales organization*. A sales organization is a legal entity that is responsible for selling goods and is liable for the sales (product liability, compensation claims).

A sales organization is assigned to exactly one company code. On the other hand, a company code can contain several sales organizations, as illustrated in Fig. 4.5. This can be the case when the company has segmented the market into domestic and international markets or into regional markets.

Distribution Channel Most companies use different *distribution channels* to sell their goods to the customers, for example, via retailers, wholesalers, direct sales, or the Internet. A sales organization may have several distribution channels, while the same distribution channel may be utilized by several sales organizations. Figure 4.5 shows both cases.

Companies often connect pricing modes, discounts, responsibilities, and sales statistics with distribution channels.

Division Divisions (sales divisions) are used to group the products and services the company is selling so that they can be treated together. For example, a software company might define divisions such as software licenses, software-on-demand, consulting, and support. A computer vendor may have divisions such as personal computers, printers, and software.

Terms and conditions may be associated with divisions. When negotiating with customers, the company can then refer to division-specific terms and conditions.

Sales Area In a sales area, a *division* is combined with a *distribution channel* used by a *sales organization*. A sales area specifies which products are sold through which distribution channel. A sales area belongs to exactly one company code.

In the Figs. 4.5 and 4.6, some sales areas are presented as collections of shaded rectangles.

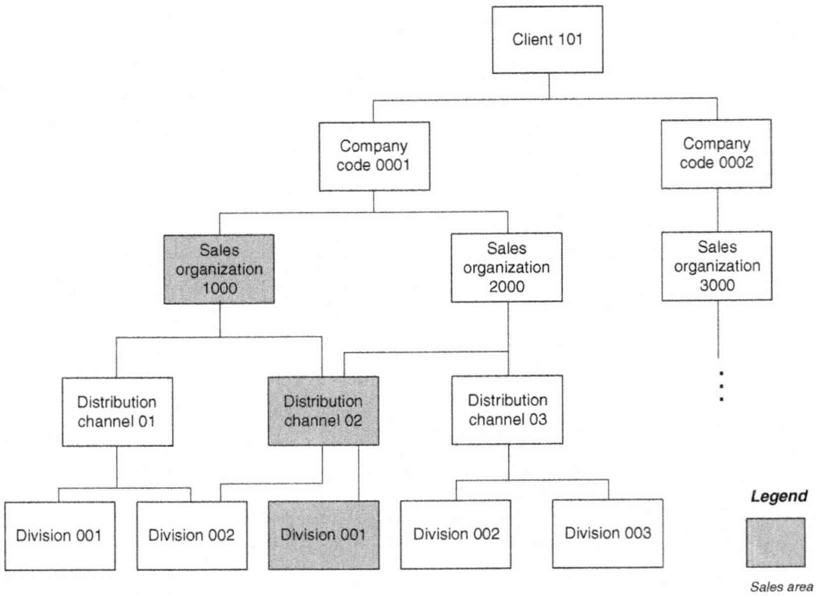

Fig. 4.5 Organizational structure for sales (Benz and Höflinger 2008, pp. 52–53)

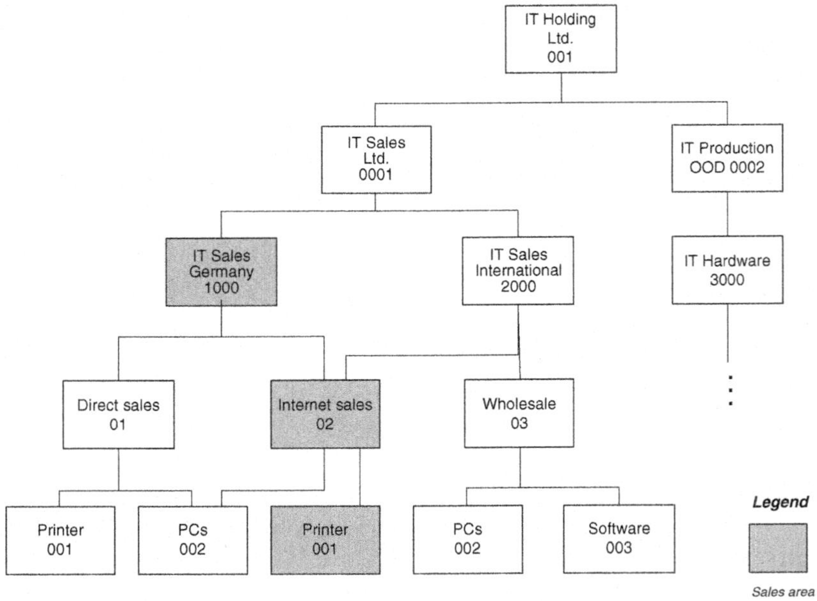

Fig. 4.6 Sales structure (example)

The sample company shown in Fig. 4.6 (IT Holding Ltd. 001) has two company codes (IT Sales Ltd. 0001 and IT Production OOD 0002) and three sales organizations (IT Sales Germany 1000, IT Sales International 2000, and IT Hardware 3000).

Only one sales area in the figure is highlighted, but more exist. Taking into account that on the international market, PCs are sold exclusively through wholesale, the following eight sales areas belong to IT Sales Ltd. 0001:

IT Sales Germany 1000—direct sales 01—printers 001

IT Sales Germany 1000—direct sales 01—PCs 002

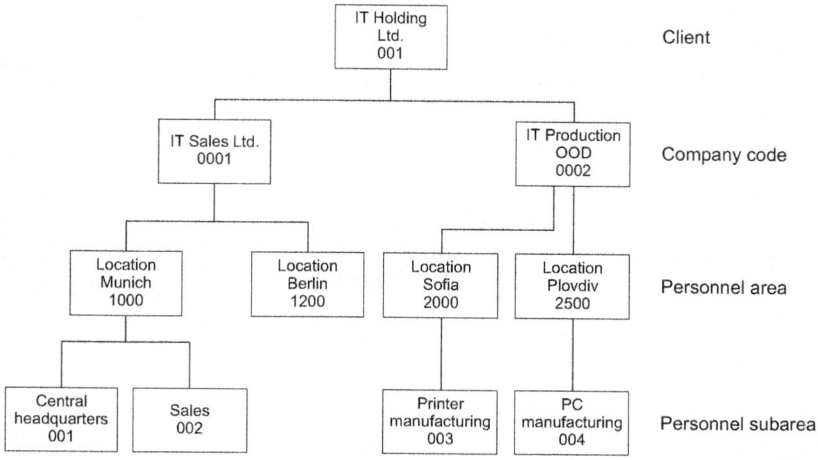

Fig. 4.7 Enterprise structure (example)

IT Sales Germany 1000—Internet sales 02—PCs 002
IT Sales Germany 1000—Internet sales 02—printers 001
IT Sales International 2000—Internet sales 02—PCs 002
IT Sales International 2000—Internet sales 02—printers 001
IT Sales International 2000—wholesale 03—PCs 002
IT Sales International 2000—wholesale 03—software 003

Sales areas play an important role in SAP ERP because sales are booked with reference to a sales area. For example, the documents created during the order fulfillment process (cf. Sect. 4.3.2) are assigned to a sales area. Master data relevant for sales (e.g., portions of the material and accounts-receivable master data) are also organized according to sales areas.

Shipping Point A *shipping point* is an organizational unit for shipping goods to customers. Usually, it is a physical place (e.g., loading ramp, dock, railway freight depot). The same shipping point may be used by several plants.

A shipping point must exist when a delivery is to be shipped to a customer; otherwise, the shipment cannot be completed (at least not in the ERP system).

Sales Office, Sales Group, and Salesperson "Sales office," "sales group," and "salesperson" are organizational elements used to describe how the sales business function is structured with regard to people and locations.

A *sales office* belongs to one or more sales areas. It consists of *sales groups*, which are composed of (individual) *salespersons*.

4.2.4 Human Resources

For the *human resources (HR)* function, nowadays also called *human capital management (HCM)*, different organizational elements are used than the ones mentioned above. With the help of these elements, three organizational structures are defined: the enterprise structure describing legal and financial responsibilities, the personnel structure describing the composition of the staff, and the structural organization.

Enterprise Structure In the enterprise structure, the company (i.e., a company code) is divided into organizational units relevant for personnel administration, time management, and payroll accounting. The main elements available to describe the enterprise structure, below the client and company-code level, are "personnel area" and "personnel subarea."

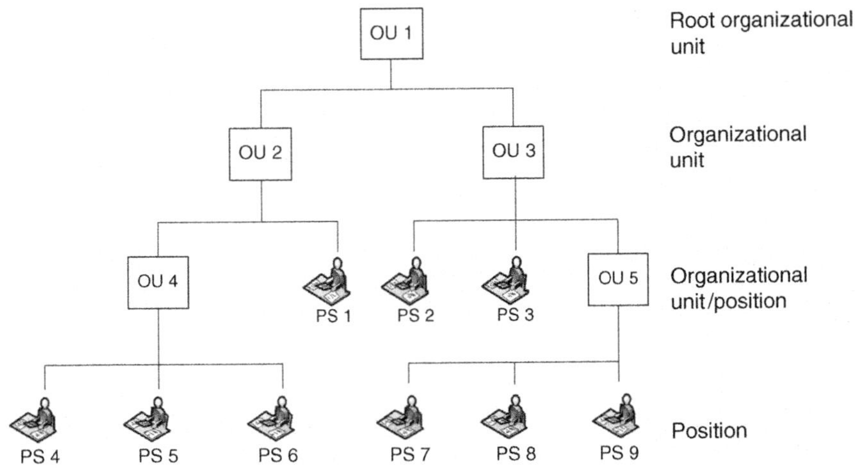

Fig. 4.8 Organizational units and positions

Personnel areas are certain areas of the company defined for human resources purposes, for example, according to the locations of the company. Figure 4.7 exemplifies this case. Locations for which personnel areas are defined are Munich, Berlin, Sofia, and Plovdiv.

Personnel subareas further subdivide a personnel area. HR regulations are made for each of these subareas (e.g., work schedules, salary structures, wage, and salary groups). In Fig. 4.7, personnel subareas for Munich are central headquarters and sales.

Personnel Structure The personnel structure reflects the position and status of individual employees within the enterprise. Organizational elements are "employee group," "employee subgroup," and "payroll area."

Employee groups are used to define the possible status of persons dealt with in human resources. Examples include active employees, pensioners, early retirees, and freelancers.

Employee subgroups subdivide an employee group. For example, active employees could be split up into hourly wage earners, monthly wage earners, pay-scale employees, and non-pay scale employees.

Payroll areas are organizational units comprising all employees for whom the payroll accounting is completed at the same time and for the same period.

Personnel Structure (Organizational Perspective) From SAP ERP's *organizational perspective*, the personnel structure is described as a hierarchy of organizational units, such as departments, subdepartments, and groups. In addition, the positions belonging to these organizational units and the roles they perform are defined.

Within the personnel structure, an *organizational unit* is a user-defined unit that takes on and carries out certain functions within a company (e.g., department, project group). Organizational units can be created using any criteria and related with each other in any way. Through this flexibility, it is possible to map any form of organization (e.g., line organization, matrix organization).

A *position* is an organizational grouping of work that can be performed by one person, for example, "head of the marketing department" or "salesperson." Positions exist, whether or not they are currently filled. Positions are assigned to an organizational unit. In a multilevel organizational hierarchy, positions can exist on all levels, as shown in Fig. 4.8. This means that an organizational unit can contain both positions directly assigned to the unit, as well as other, subordinate organizational units. For example, the department OU 3 has two employees (positions) and one subdepartment (OU 5).

Roles are generally descriptions of tasks, such as department head, accountant, or salesperson. In SAP ERP, the roles are called "jobs." A *job* is a standard description of an activity that can be performed by a person. Jobs are not synonymous with positions. While positions are specific instances in the organizational hierarchy, jobs are generic tasks that are assigned to these positions.

4.3 Business Processes

This section discusses some of the business processes that companies usually carry out with the help of an ERP system. Furthermore, we will explore how and where the MRP and MRP II functions explained in the previous chapters are embedded in a process-oriented context.

Although most ERP systems are structured according to functional areas, the individual functions are used within business processes. This means that the functions have to be applied in a certain sequence and depending on certain preconditions. These preconditions are either given or established by invoking other functions during the execution of the process.

In graphical notations for business process modeling, the connections between preconditions and process steps can be expressed in different ways. In *event-driven process chains (EPCs)*, the concept of events is employed for this purpose. An *event* is a state of the model, which is either established as the result of a function, or has to be in place so that a function can be executed (Mendling 2007, p. 37). *Functions* effectuate transitions from one state to another. EPCs generally start with an event (starting condition) and end with an event (result of the process).

Documents play an important role in enterprise resource planning because the progress of a business process often depends on the existence of certain documents. A document being created or made available is a typical event of an EPC for enterprise resource planning. Examples of documents include customer orders, delivery slips, invoices, quality certificates, etc. In an ERP system, these are usually electronic documents that the user sees as a form on his or her monitor.

Electronic documents are stored in the ERP database. They are identified and retrieved with the help of numbers (see Sect. 2.1.5) or the application context. In this way, documents are available to all users across business functions and processes, provided that they are authorized to access the document.

4.3.1 Procurement

The procurement process primarily applies functionality from *materials management* and *accounting*. The process starts with the event that demand for an external material has been detected. How the demand was detected is outside the process. It may have happened, for example, during inventory control (in consumption-driven planning, cf. Sect. 2.3.1) or when calculating secondary requirements (during requirements-driven planning, cf. Sect. 2.3.2).

The first process step shown in Fig. 4.9 is creating a *purchase requisition*. This process step is initiated by the starting event. A purchase requisition is a document indicating that a demand has to be met. It identifies the material needed, the quantity needed, and the date the material is needed (Magal and Word 2009, p. 52). When manually processed, the purchase requisition would be printed and sent to the purchasing department. In a more automated processing mode, the document is stored in the ERP database and automatically forwarded.

Before the purchasing department can actually place an order, the supplier must be known. For some materials, the supplier will be predetermined and stored in the material master record. For others, the supplier has to be selected. In Fig. 4.9, this step is represented by only one function. In reality, however, supplier selection can be a complex process of its own, including inquiries, requests for quotation, negotiations etc.

After the purchasing department has created a *purchase order* in the ERP system and sent the order to the supplier, the process waits until the goods are delivered. When the shipment has been received, it is controlled with respect to quality, quantity, and price. If there are no issues with the shipment, the goods are stocked, increasing the

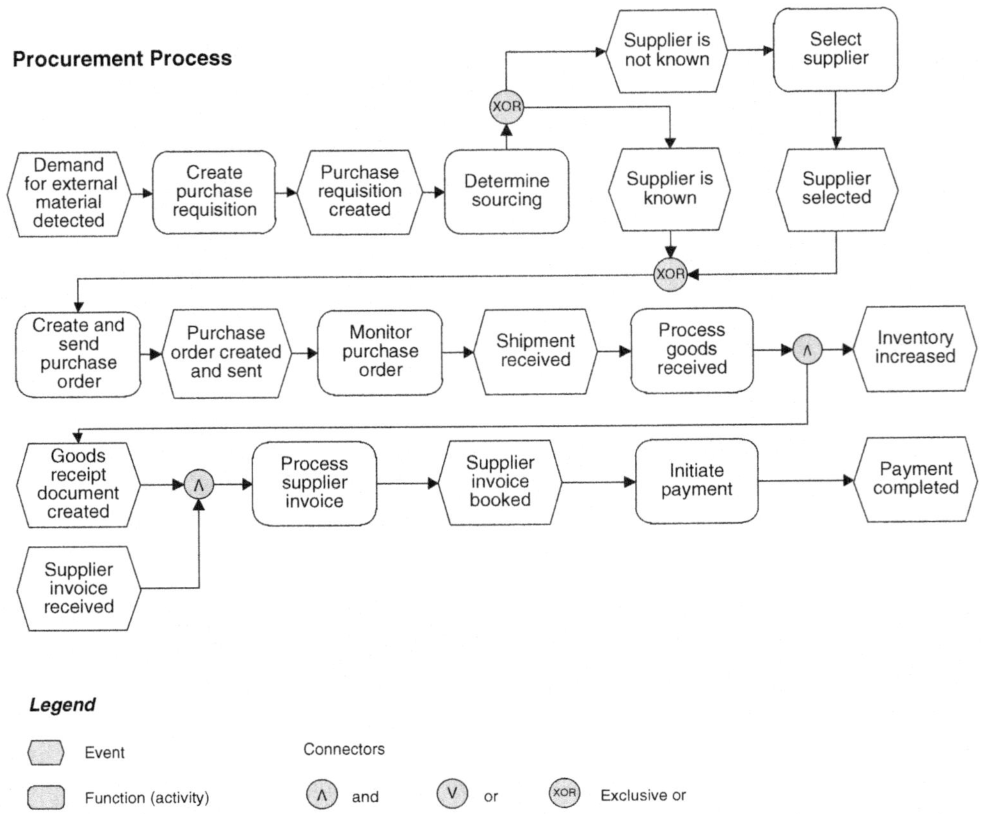

Fig. 4.9 Procurement process

inventory, and a goods receipt document is created. Otherwise, activities such as sending a notice of defects, further treatment, or accepting a partial delivery would be initiated. To keep the figure simple, these activities have not been included.

A precondition for the next step, processing the vendor's invoice, is that the invoice has been received. The process again waits until this precondition has been fulfilled. When the invoice is booked in the system, the payment is initiated, resulting in the final event, the completion of payment.

It should be noted that the process shown in Fig. 4.9 has been substantially simplified. If the process were described in more detail, more events, activities, and perhaps subprocesses would need to be considered. In addition, other EPC elements such as "information objects" (representing the database) and "organizational units" (indicating who is responsible for a function) have not been included. More complete versions of the procurement process that take these additional elements into account will be presented in Chap. 5.

4.3.2 Order Fulfillment

The term "order fulfillment" refers to the process of filling customer orders, starting with the first inquiry, all the way to the shipment of the goods, and receiving the customer's payment. For this process, functions of *sales, materials management,* and *accounting* are needed.

In most cases, the process does not start with a customer order but with an inquiry in which the customer asks for certain goods (or services), prices, delivery dates, terms, and conditions. Therefore, the first activity of the process in Fig. 4.10 is to enter the customer's inquiry into the system ("create customer inquiry"), provided that the event "customer inquiry received" occurred before. If the customer does not yet exist

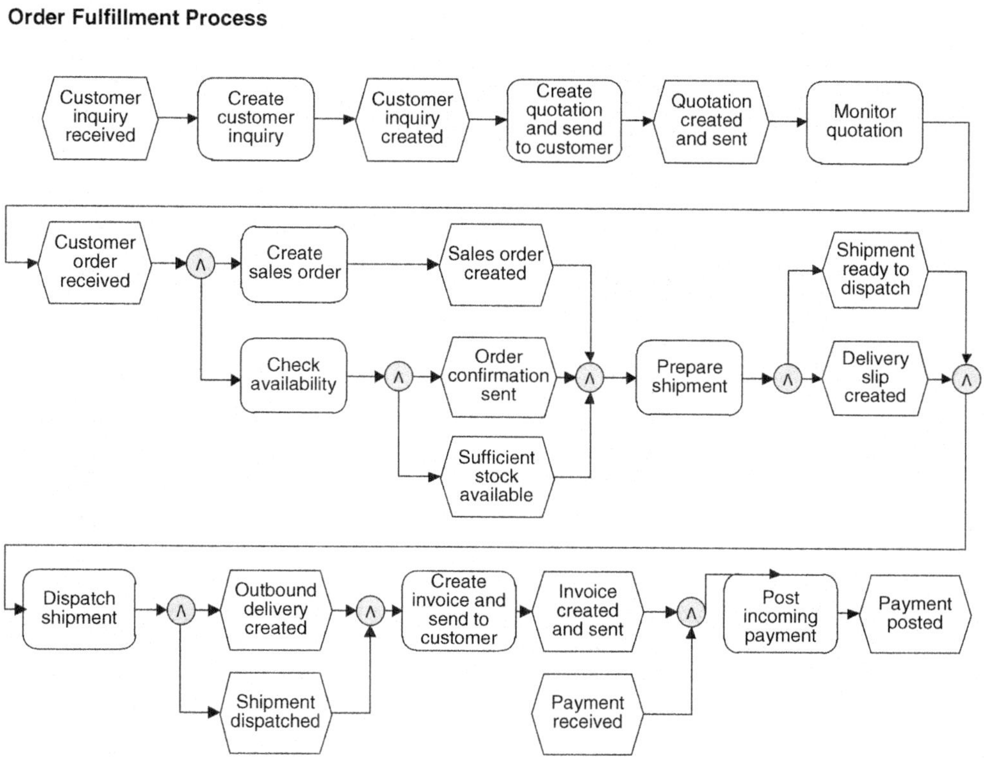

Fig. 4.10 Order fulfillment process

in the system, the customer master data (or at least the most important attributes) should be entered first. This case has been omitted in the figure.

Based on the inquiry, the salesperson creates a quotation, stores it in the system with reference to the inquiry, and sends it to the customer. The quotation contains, for example, quantities and prices of the individual items, sales tax, validity period, terms and conditions of delivery, and more.

If the customer accepts the quotation as sent, they will place an *order*. Otherwise, more negotiations might be necessary, or the customer may decline the offer, which will cause the quotation to be deleted or archived (these two cases are not included in the figure). The salesperson in charge checks the received customer order, comparing it with the quotation issued earlier. The customer order will normally contain the same information as the quotation, plus additional customer-specific information.

However, the customer order is a document issued by the customer's organization, not a document by our company. To be able to process the order, it must be available in the company's ERP system. For this purpose, an internal *sales order* is created. If the customer order was received as an electronic document, the data can be copied to the sales order and adapted. Otherwise, some data items will be automatically transferred from the quotation and others will have to be manually copied from the customer order.

Regarding *availability checking*, certain assumptions have been made in Fig. 4.10:

Firstly, availability is checked after the customer order has been received. As mentioned in Sect. 3.5.1, availability checking can also be done earlier, for example, when an inquiry is received or a quotation is issued. If the salesperson books a stock reservation at the same time, an additional availability check at the time when the customer order arrives is normally not necessary.

Secondly, it is assumed that enough inventory is available to fill the customer order. This means

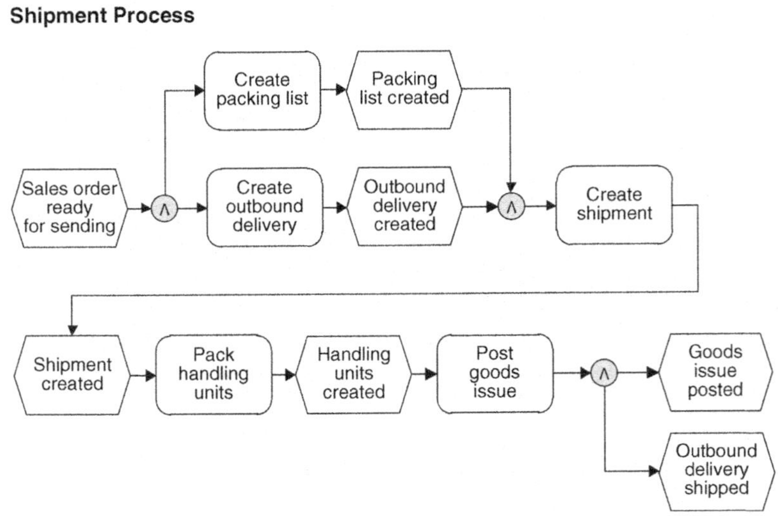

Fig. 4.11 Shipping process

that for all items of the customer order, the salesperson was able to confirm availability invoking the respective MRP function. The case that the amount of stocked goods is not sufficient is not included in the figure. This possibility will be considered later (cf. Sect. 4.3.6).

Thirdly, an order confirmation including the delivery date is sent to the customer when the result of the availability check is positive.

Since availability of all items is assumed in Fig. 4.10, the next step is to prepare the shipment, which includes creating more documents such as *picking* and *packing lists* (internal documents) and a *delivery slip* (document accompanying the shipment on its way to the customer).

Once the shipment has been sent, the customer is *invoiced* with the help of accounting functions, while the invoice is stored in the ERP database. When the customer's *payment* is received, it is also booked in the system. This is the last step of the order fulfillment process.

It should be noted that the process shown in Fig. 4.10 has been substantially simplified in order to present an initial overview of order fulfillment. Some branches have been omitted, as mentioned in the previous paragraphs. A number of process steps are very rough, requiring refinement to become operational. To do so, separate processes would need to be defined and connected with the superordinate process. For example, unless the process step "send shipment" is extremely simple, it would be modeled as its own process. Connecting linked processes will be explained in Sect. 4.3.6.

Make-to-order In make-to-order production, order fulfillment can be more complicated because the first process steps—inquiry and quotation—require more activities than described above or may even need their own subprocesses. This is the case when the product the customer wishes to order is not a standard product but possibly a product that has not been manufactured before and needs to be developed first.

Processing a customer inquiry for a new product includes a feasibility check, determining the delivery date and quotation price, and agreeing on terms and conditions. Some additional difficulties during these steps are:

- *Feasibility check:* Can the product be manufactured as specified by the customers? If the product can be realized as a variant of a standard part, the check is simple; otherwise, product design and planning have to be included in the process.
- *Delivery date:* Lead times, capacity requirements, and procurement times have to be estimated because no reliable master data exist if the product is new.
- *Price quotation:* Here, an estimation is required, too, because the product cost may not be known. As mentioned in Sect. 3.7, product costing also requires reliable master data, which may not be available.

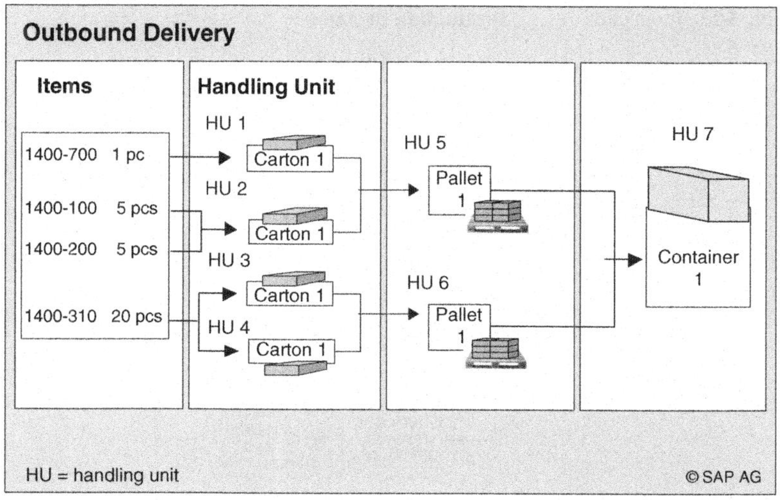

Fig. 4.12 Packing with handling units

- *Terms and conditions:* Since make-to-order production is subject to higher uncertainty than make-to-stock production, some terms and conditions have to be considered more carefully. For example, the risk of not delivering on time has to be assessed before a contractual penalty is accepted.

Despite these difficulties, the offer should be created quickly, because otherwise, the customer may be lost to a competitor. The ERP system should therefore provide features that effectively assist the salesperson in overcoming the difficulties, even if the underlying data are uncertain or incomplete (cf. Sect. 2.2.2).

Shipping A typical shipping process consists of a number of steps as illustrated in Fig. 4.11. In these steps, various types of documents are created. For example, pertinent documents in SAP ERP include a packing list, an outbound delivery document, and a shipment.

A *packing list* contains the items to be packed. It accompanies the shipment when the shipment is sent to the customer. Another common term for a packing list is delivery slip.

All items to be actually shipped together are combined into an *outbound delivery*. An outbound delivery may be created for one or more sales orders. An *outbound delivery document* states what will be delivered to the customer. In case a sales order is too large to be sent in one shipment, it may be split up into several outbound deliveries.

For each outbound delivery, a *transportation order* (called "shipment" in SAP ERP) is created. Before the goods can be transported anywhere, they must be packed. Physical packing follows its own rules, requiring, for example, the creation of larger *handling units* (e.g., cartons, boxes, pallets, containers) than just individual items. Since later, it must be possible to identify which items/units have been packed together, the handling unit is a database object of its own.

Figure 4.12 illustrates how handling units can be used on several levels. Handling units in this example are four cartons, two pallets, and one container.

Booking the *goods issue* is done when the outbound delivery has left the company. This is the last step of the shipping process. The final states established at the end of the process are "goods issue booked" and "outbound delivery shipped."

4.3.3 Production

While the fundamentals of production were described in Chaps. 2 and 3, the next section shows how and where the MRP and MRP II functions are employed when production processes are actually being carried out.

The starting point for the production process shown in Fig. 4.13 is the existence of an order—either a sales order or planned order (cf. Sect. 2.4).

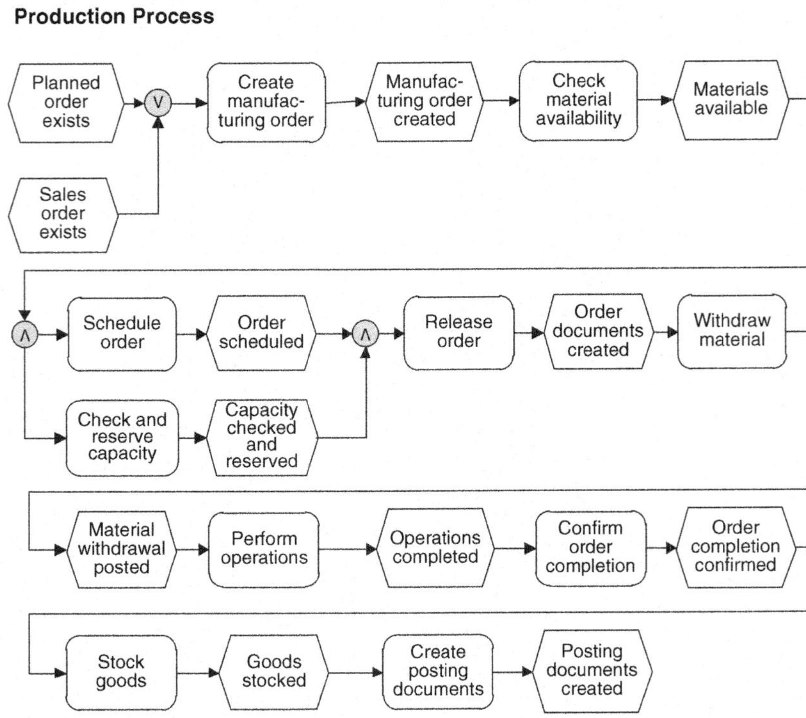

Fig. 4.13 Production process

The first step is to create a *manufacturing order* from the sales order or the planned order. Who is responsible for this task depends on the company's organization. It could be, for example, the production manager or, in an automated environment, the ERP system that routinely transforms end-product orders into manufacturing orders.

In the simplest case, the initial order is transformed one to one into a manufacturing order. However, it may be beneficial to combine several single orders into a larger production lot (or vice versa, to split a very large order into more than one lot). Determining economic order quantities (or lot sizes) is actually a step within material requirements planning, completed long before the production process starts. At this point in time, however, other reasons may call for combining individual orders into a lot. For example, several orders for the same product may have originated from different departments or divisions.

Creating a manufacturing order in the ERP database does not mean that the entire order has to be entered from scratch. In most cases, the manufacturing order will be based on a planned order or a sales order, meaning that most of the data items already exist. An ERP system will copy them automatically into the relevant fields of the manufacturing order.

To avoid disruptions to the production process, all necessary *materials* have to be available. Therefore, the next process step is to check if this is the case. Likewise, the *capacity* of the operating facilities involved has to be available. When, how, and what is exactly checked in the availability checks has to be decided earlier (cf. Sect. 3.5.1). This decision is usually made during the customization of the ERP system (i.e., when the system is implemented in the organization, cf. Sect. 6.3.3).

Scheduling the manufacturing order (lead-time scheduling) is necessary because up to this point, the order has, at best, rough start and end dates (from material requirements planning). The order's operations have not yet been considered and are not equipped with dates.

If the manufacturing order is based on a planned order, the setup and processing times are known from the routings. In this case, the ERP system could even automatically schedule the manufacturing order when it is created. Otherwise, the scheduling procedure has to be invoked explicitly.

In Fig. 4.13, it is assumed that *lead-time scheduling* and *capacity-availability checking* are two separate steps carried out before the order is released. Another option is to integrate the check for capacity availability into lead-time scheduling. This means that an operation is only scheduled in such a way that its capacity requirements are met. The process step "check and reserve capacity" includes both availability checking and booking the necessary capacity reservations.

Another assumption underlying Fig. 4.13 is that only one order is being scheduled. If many orders were to be scheduled at the same time, which is the case in MRP and MRP II based planning, capacity requirements would be accumulated and later treated via capacity load balancing (cf. Sect. 3.4.1) to make the plan feasible.

When the order is scheduled and its capacity requirements have been dealt with, the order is *released*. This means that a commitment is made to carry out the order as planned. Releasing an order normally includes creating the documents that accompany the order on its way through the plant (e.g., picking list, material withdrawal slips, cf. Sect. 3.5.2).

When the necessary materials have been withdrawn from the warehouse and booked, the actual manufacturing takes place ("perform operations"). Once some or all of the operations are completed, this state of affairs is confirmed. (Fig. 4.13 considers only the case that the entire order has been completed). If the ERP system is connected with, or includes, a production data acquisition system, completion confirmations will be created and transmitted automatically. Otherwise, they have to be booked within the ERP system, either manually or in a semiautomated manner (e.g., with the help of barcode and/or RFID readers, see Sect. 11.4.1).

Finally, the finished goods are stocked, and a number of documents are created. Most of these documents are required for financial and managerial accounting. Posting documents initiates further bookings, because quantity- and value-relevant changes to the company's assets have occurred during the production process. In particular, the costs caused by the manufacturing order have to be allocated to the appropriate object (e.g., customer order, end product). These bookings take place in a different process outside the production process (called "order accounting" or "order costing").

4.3.4 Recruitment

In the human resources field, a number of typical business processes exist, including employee recruitment and development. Most ERP systems provide human resources functionality. SAP ERP, for example, is well-known for its comprehensive support of HR processes, including:

- Recruitment (staff requirements, advertising, selection, hiring, etc.)
- Personnel development (qualifications catalog, position profiles, employee qualifications profiles, profile matchup, further training, career, succession planning, etc.)
- Time management (working times, leave, sick leave, business trips, approval of working times, etc.)
- Payroll (wage and salary types, bonuses, tax, and insurance deductions, payment settlement, employee remuneration information, etc.)

This section will describe a recruitment process as an example of a human resources process. This process helps the human resources managers to find, select, and hire suitable applicants. The employee recruitment process requires that a qualifications catalog and a position profile exist that can be used for the job advertisement and the selection of candidates.

As shown in Fig. 4.14, the recruitment process is initiated when a staff requirement occurs. The first step is to create a vacancy in the system, followed by a job advertisement that is published in the appropriate media. Job advertisements are usually not created from scratch but composed of building blocks or based on previous advertisements that can be retrieved from the HR section of the ERP database.

Job advertisements can be published in many ways, both inside and outside the company.

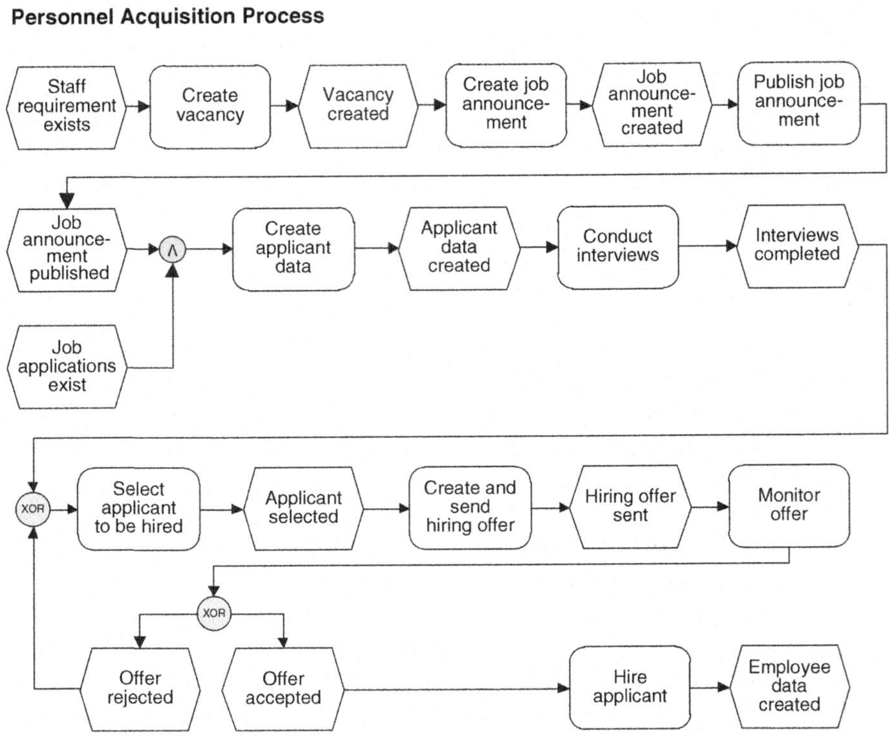

Fig. 4.14 Recruitment process

In addition to conventional media such as newspapers, online media (e.g., job marketplaces and company homepages) are increasingly being used.

Consequently, applications are solicited and received in various formats, including e-mail, paper applications, and online forms. The latter have the advantage that applicant data can be automatically transferred to the HR database. This means that it is not necessary to manually enter the data, as is the case with paper applications.

The process step "create applicant data" frequently comprises not only entering the raw data but also classifying the candidates according to the criteria defined in the enterprise and personnel structures (see Sect. 4.2.4). In this case, the properties of the candidates can be automatically compared with the position and qualification requirements, provided that the vacancy was created with reference to the company's qualifications catalog and that a position profile exists.

The next process step, "conduct interviews," is supported by the ERP system, in that the system generates invitation letters or e-mails and initiates sending the invitations. Likewise, it generates a draft of the written hiring offer when a candidate has been selected.

If the selected candidate declines the offer, the process continues with the selection of another candidate. Otherwise, the "applicant" has to be transformed into an "employee." For this purpose, a large number of data items have to be created. Some of these data items are already available in the system because they were saved when the application was entered. These data can be automatically copied into the employee master record. With the creation of the employee data, the recruitment process is completed.

4.3.5 Other Processes

A company uses many different business processes within and across the functional areas.

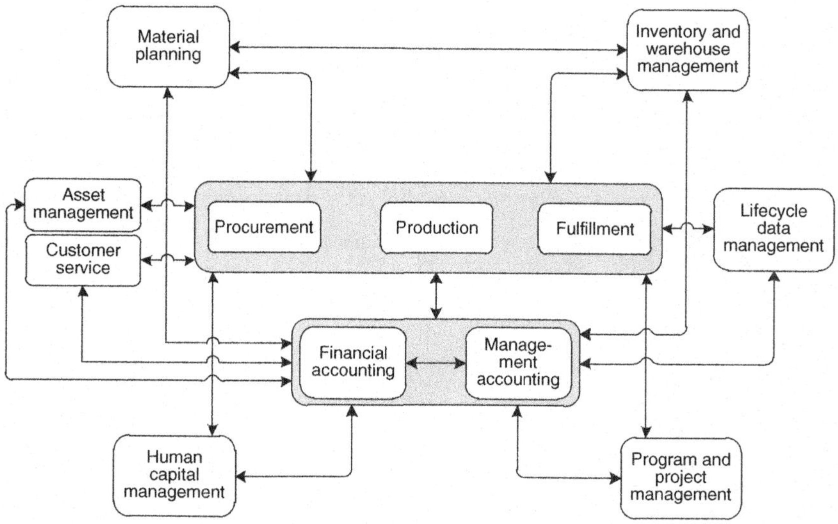

Fig. 4.15 Key business processes (Magal and Word 2012, p. 6)

The essential processes and process areas are summarized in Fig. 4.15.

In the context of this book, accounting processes are particularly important because they have many interfaces with the procurement, fulfillment, and production processes described above.

Within *external accounting* (financial accounting), incoming and outgoing invoices and other documents related with the invoices are processed. The bookings take place in accounts receivable and accounts payable accounting. Financial accounting processes include the following:

- Invoice receipts (booking vendor invoices, treating input tax, offsetting entries, etc.)
- Outgoing invoices (customer invoice handling)
- Canceling invoices, handling credit memos
- Dunning (definition of dunning levels and procedures, dunning selection runs)
- Payment (invoice clearing, applying agreed payment terms, cash discounts, payment methods, etc.)

Internal accounting (managerial accounting) comprises an array of tasks including cost-element accounting, cost-center accounting, product-cost accounting, and activity-based costing, as well as profit-center accounting and profitability analysis. Therefore, a large number of processes exist, including:

- Cost-center planning (i.e., planning of statistical ratios, activity types and quantities, primary and secondary cost-center costs, etc.)
- Product costing (with lump-sum rates or using bills of materials and routings)
- Internal cost allocation (allocation of secondary costs to cost objects)

In addition to the accounting processes, the overview presented in Fig. 4.15 mentions the following process areas, which are typical for most organizations (Magal and Word 2012, pp. 6–7):

- Material planning—using historical data and sales forecasts to plan materials quantities to be procured or produced
- Inventory and warehouse management—storing, tracking, and retrieving materials in the warehouse
- Asset management—acquiring, deploying, maintaining and replacing assets, and preventive and corrective maintenance
- Customer service—delivering after-sales service to the customer, handling service requests (such as repair of a product the customer purchased)

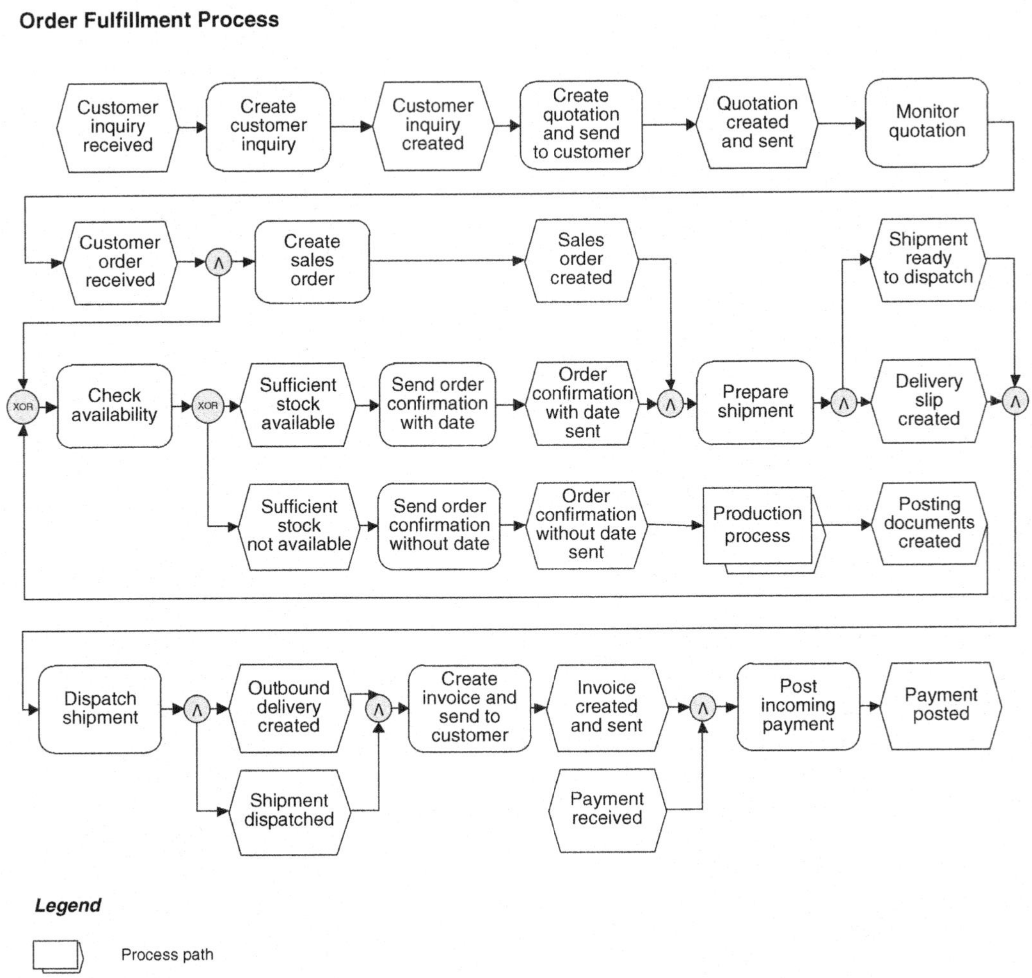

Fig. 4.16 Integrated fulfillment and production processes

- Life-cycle data management—designing, developing, maintaining, and discontinuing a product
- Program and project management—planning, executing, and controlling individual endeavors (projects) and collections thereof (programs)

4.3.6 Process Integration

In the previous sections, a number of business processes were discussed independently of each other. However, in reality, these processes are not isolated but have interfaces with each other, as was already indicated by the arrows in Fig. 4.15.

For example, in the *order fulfillment process* shown in Fig. 4.10, we assumed that sufficient stock of the items needed for the customer order is available in the warehouse. If this assumption is wrong, the missing quantities have to be manufactured before they can be delivered to the customer. This means that the fulfillment process will be interrupted. A *production process* must be initiated and completed before the fulfillment process can continue.

Another example is the connection between the production and procurement processes. Figure 4.13 showed only a simplified case, namely that all materials needed for the manufacturing order are available. If this is not the case, either a procurement process (if the missing material is an external material) or another production process (if the missing material is an in-house material) has to be initiated and completed.

Production Process

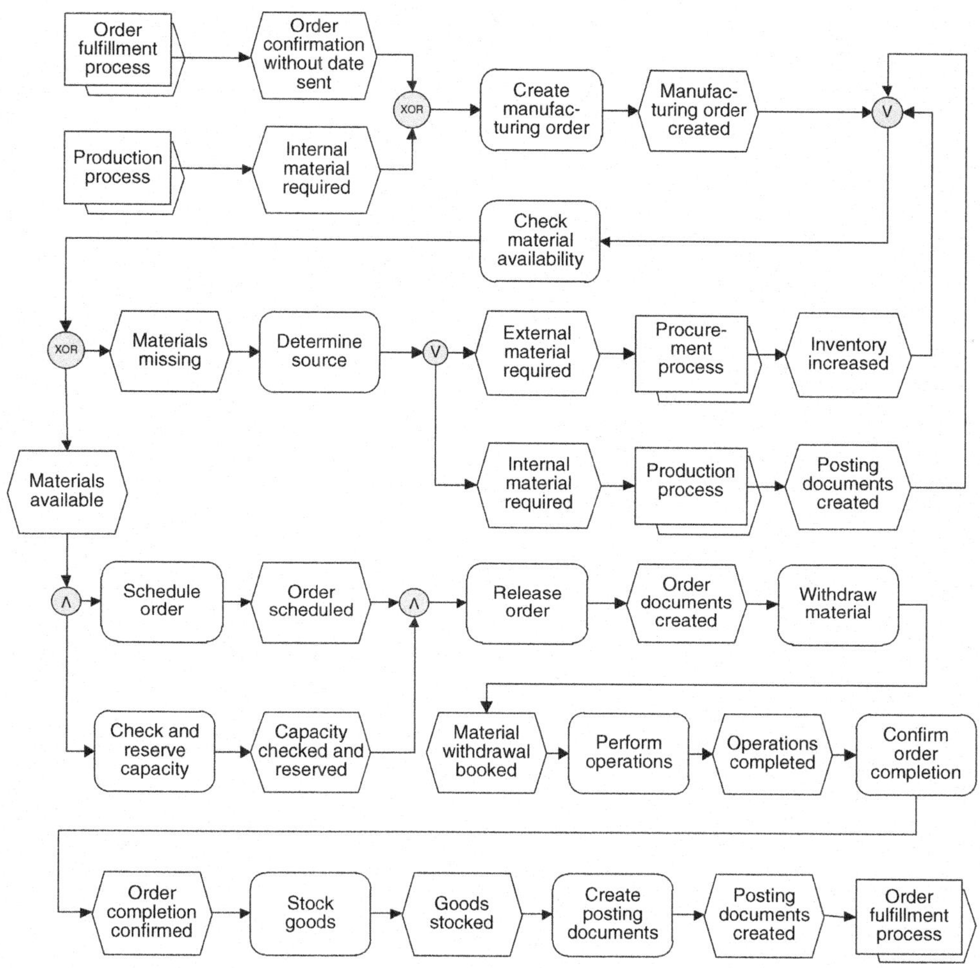

Fig. 4.17 Integrated production and procurement processes

The production process has to wait until the material has been stocked again.

In the following, the connections between *order fulfillment* and *production* will be examined in more detail. In particular, the assumption that sufficient stock is available is removed, resulting in a different process flow following the step "check availability," as shown in Fig. 4.16.

Now there are two cases: The first case is that sufficient stock is available, so that an order confirmation including a shipment date can be sent to the customer and the process can continue as in Fig. 4.10. The second case, however, requires a production process to be completed, because the quantities the customer ordered are not in stock. Therefore, the customer receives only a preliminary order confirmation (without a delivery date), and a production process is started.

The symbol used in event-driven process chains to connect two processes is called a *process interface* (or a *process path*). It is composed of a rectangle overlying a hexagon (event symbol). In Fig. 4.16, the process path leads to an EPC representing the production process. When this process is completed—as is the case when the event "posting document created" has occurred—the waiting fulfillment process can continue.

The next step of the process is again availability checking. Even though a production process was executed, it might have resulted in an amount of goods still too small to fill the customer order.

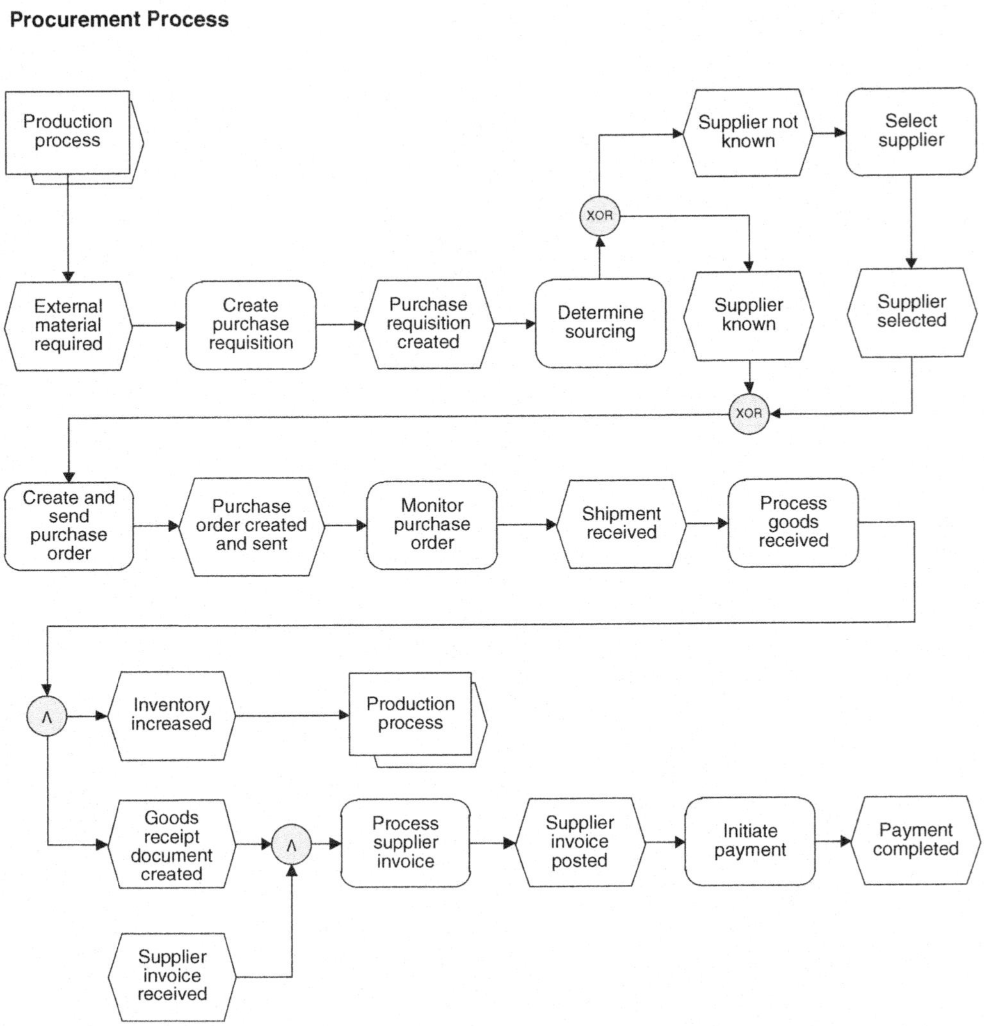

Fig. 4.18 Revised procurement processes

That is why the arrow from the event "posting document created" goes back to the "xor" connector to the left of "check availability." Should the quantity in stock still be insufficient, another production run has to be initiated etc. (This case is not elaborated in order to keep the figure simple. The way the process flow is currently modeled, the customer may receive more than one order confirmation without a definite delivery date.) Otherwise, the customer is notified with another order confirmation including a delivery date, and the shipment is prepared.

In the second example of connecting processes, we will reconsider the production process of Fig. 4.13. The result established in the step "check material availability" is based on the assumption that there is always enough material in stock. If this is not the case, the process should actually make provisions for obtaining the lacking material, because otherwise it cannot continue.

To handle this requirement, two process interfaces are included in the revised process shown in Fig. 4.17. One process interface leads to procurement, the other to production, depending on whether the missing material has to be ordered from a supplier or manufactured in-house.

At the end of the procurement process, the state "inventory increased" must have been established so that the production process in Fig. 4.17 can proceed. Likewise, at the end of

Fig. 4.19 Fulfillment process in BPMN

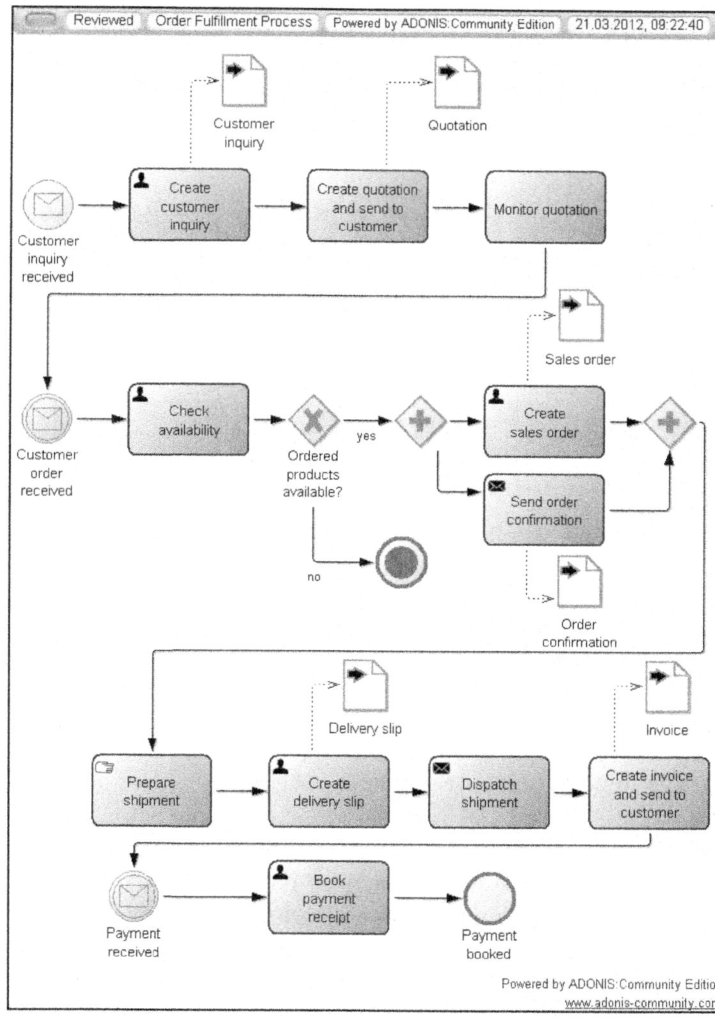

Legend:

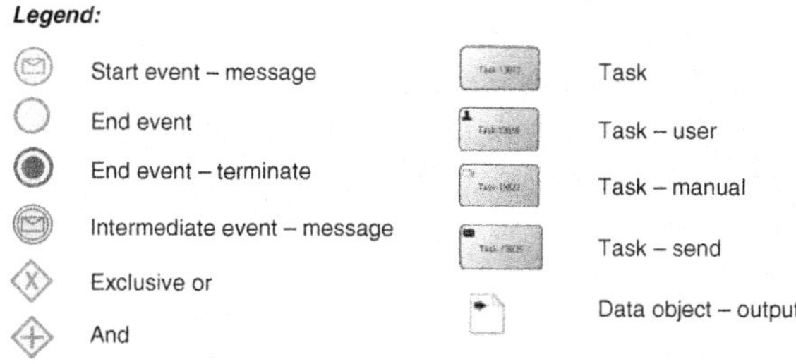

the invoked production process, the event "posting documents created" must have occurred. In both cases, the superordinate production process continues with rechecking material availability.

It should be noted that processes connected by process interfaces need to begin and end, respectively, with the same events. That is, the end state reached by the previous process is the beginning state of the following process. This is indicated by repeating the event symbol at the beginning of the EPC for the invoked process. Likewise, the final state(s) to be reached at the end of the invoked process will be repeated in the outer process, following the process interface symbol.

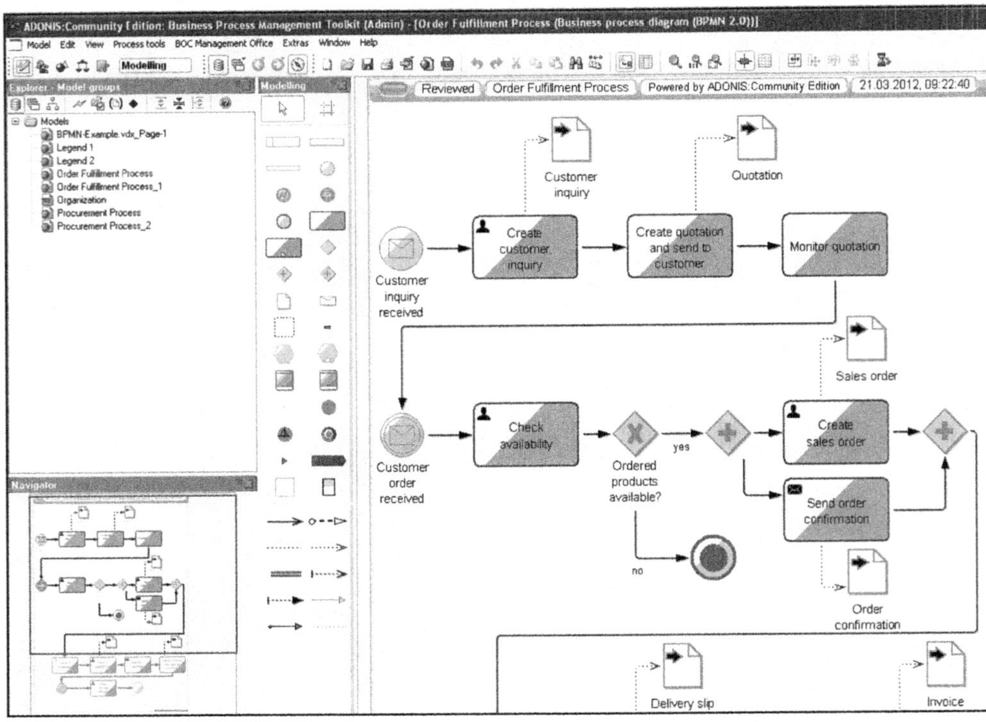

Fig. 4.20 BPM development environment (example)

In Fig. 4.17, for example, the event before the process interface with the procurement process, "external material required," is now also noted at the beginning of the procurement EPC in Fig. 4.18. This EPC starts with the process interface symbol "production process" indicating where the process flow comes from, followed by the event symbol "external material required."

At the end of the procurement process, there are two events. The one relevant for the production process is "inventory increased." This is the same event noted down to the right of the process interface symbol "procurement process" in the production EPC (cf. Fig. 4.17).

4.3.7 Modeling with a Tool

Modeling business processes in a graphical way is rarely done using paper and pencil, because most "real" processes are quite complex, containing many symbols and connecting lines. This means that making changes to a model once it has been created can be cumbersome work. Professionals involved in business process modeling prefer to use automated tools, provided that their company has acquired a modeling toolset.

Event-driven process chains, which have been used throughout the preceding chapters, are supported by various toolsets. One of the best-known ones is contained in the *ARIS platform*, which was originally developed by IDS Scheer AG and is now offered by Software AG, Darmstadt (Germany) (SAG 2012). ARIS is a comprehensive toolset including support for many architectural, design, and implementation issues. Since the concept of event-driven process chains (EPCs) was also developed by A.-W. Scheer, they are the preferred modeling technique in ARIS, supported by graphical tools.

Another graphical notation for business processes, as already mentioned in Sect. 1.3, is *BPMN (business process model and notation)*

(OMG 2011a). It is similar to the EPC technique, providing events, tasks, logical connectors (gateways), and other elements.

To illustrate the BPMN approach and its similarities with EPCs, the order fulfillment process presented in Fig. 4.10 was remodeled in BPMN. The result, created with a tool, is shown in Fig. 4.19. The reason why the diagram appears to be somewhat smaller than the corresponding EPC is that it contains fewer events. In BPMN, intermediate events are only modeled if they provide a notification (message) required for the process to continue.

Another difference to the earlier EPC model of the fulfillment process is that some *data objects* have been included, in particular those that are created by the process activities. Examples include "customer inquiry" and "sales order." (In EPCs, data objects are usually modeled as well, and are called "information objects." This will be discussed in Sect. 5.3.)

Most of the BPMN symbols contain small icons providing further information. For example, the tasks have icons in the top left corner indicating by whom or how the task is solved. Documents that are created in a task have an arrow, etc.

The graphical process model shown in Fig. 4.19 was created with the ADONIS toolset mentioned in Sect. 1.3.3. *ADONIS Community Edition* is available for free download from BOC AG Vienna (Austria) (BOC 2012). Like other toolsets, ADONIS provides a full development environment for the creation and management of business process models (cf. Fig. 4.20).

The screenshot shown in the figure was taken during the modeling of the order fulfillment process. It depicts essential features of the modeler's workplace. The toolbox to the left of the process pane provides the types of elements needed for BPMN modeling. The modeler uses them by dragging and dropping the icons onto the work pane.

4.4 ERP Systems

Enterprise resource planning is a very comprehensive set of functions, processes, activities, and data—beyond what can be handled manually. The tasks to be completed in enterprise resource planning are supported by equally comprehensive information systems (ERP systems). Many systems are available on the market. A company planning to implement an ERP system has to decide first which one to choose.

4.4.1 The ERP Market

The main reason why the number of ERP systems on the market is so large is that business enterprises differ in many ways, including the size, the industry they belong to, the company type (make-to-stock, make-to-order), and the manufacturing organization (e.g., mass, series, or individual production). Because of this diversity, ERP vendors attempting to satisfy their customers' needs have developed many different types of systems.

This was particularly true during the 1980s. Many MRP II systems actually started as systems developed by a small software firm for an individual customer. Since developing an MRP II system requires significant investments, software firms tried to "generalize" the individual solutions and sell them to other customers. Later, many of these MRP II systems were upgraded, continuing their lives as ERP systems.

Interested readers can obtain an overview of the ERP market by looking at surveys and directories published by pertinent magazines and institutions. The numbers of ERP systems listed often range from 100 to 1,000 systems, such as in the following sources:

- Trovarit, a German consulting firm specialized in selecting and implementing ERP systems, maintains a directory containing about 840 ERP systems from more than 600 vendors (Trovarit 2012a).
- The Center for Enterprise Research (CER) at the University of Potsdam, Germany maintains a database of ERP implementation projects (Gronau 2009). In 2012, the database contained close to 1,200 projects in which 250 different ERP systems were used.

Despite the large number of systems on the market, a fairly small number of large vendors

Fig. 4.21 Leading ERP systems and vendors

ERP System	Vendor	Market Segment
SAP ERP	SAP	large
Business ByDesign	SAP	small/mid
Business One	SAP	small
All-in-One	SAP	mid
Fusion Applications	Oracle	large
E-Business Suite	Oracle	large
Peoplesoft	Oracle	large
J.D. Edwards EnterpriseOne	Oracle	large
J.D. Edwards World	Oracle	large
Dynamics AX	Microsoft	mid
Dynamics NAV	Microsoft	small/mid
Infor ERP	Infor	mid
Sage ERP b7	Sage	mid
<several>	Sage	small/very small

dominate the market. This is particularly true for the market for large ERP systems, that is, systems designed for large companies. Following a phase of mergers and acquisitions, this market segment is now led by two major players: *SAP* (http://www.sap.com) and *Oracle* (http://www.oracle.com).

Mergers and acquisitions have also occurred on the market segments for middle and small businesses, where the main market participants are *Microsoft* (small and midrange systems—http://www.microsoft.com) and *Sage* (small and very small systems—http://www.sage.com).

A company offering many ERP systems on all market segments is *Infor*. This is due to the fact that Infor has acquired many competitors over the years. Currently, they own some of the formerly best-known ERP systems, including the original Infor system. (Infor used to be an innovative German IT company before it became part of Infor Global Solutions, now based in New York.)

Figure 4.21 lists some of the leading vendors, including the current names of their ERP systems.

A number of ERP systems are available as *open-source*. This approach will be discussed in Sect. 11.3.1.

4.4.2 Selecting an ERP System

Implementing an ERP system in a company is a complex task that will be discussed in Chap. 6. Deciding which system to choose is one of the decisions that have to be made before the system can be implemented. Because of the large number of systems available on the market, it is difficult and time-consuming for a company to choose the "right" system. In the past, projects for ERP selection used to take many months or even years.

Today, many companies take a different approach. This is partly due to the market consolidation and concentration on a small number of large ERP vendors. Furthermore, the functionalities of the leading ERP systems have become increasingly similar over the years. Therefore, companies seeking to implement an ERP system often limit themselves to checking a few of the leading systems, although there are hundreds of different systems to choose from.

However, the system functionality is only one criterion for the selection. Other factors have become increasingly important for a successful ERP implementation, including:

- Adequate preparation of the organization for the new system

- Simple and effective customization (see Sect. 6.3)
- Appropriate planning and management of the implementation project

Since most companies are not experienced in selecting and implementing an ERP system, they usually enlist the services of a *consulting firm* specialized in this task. A common approach is to set up a project team that starts by developing a requirements specification and deriving a checklist from the specification. Based on the checklist, requests for proposal (RFP) are issued. The project team evaluates the quotations and prepares the final system selection.

A typical project team is composed of (a) employees from the company departments involved who know the functional requirements, (b) IT personnel who will have to run and administer the system later, and (c) external consultants who have experience in selecting and implementing ERP systems from projects with other clients.

Checklists The main purpose of a checklist is to unify the different ways ERP systems are presented by their vendors, allowing the customer to compare the systems. This is not easy to do, because most of the vendors' descriptions are marketing oriented and tend to gloss over the hard facts. Since ERP vendors are trying to sell their products, they emphasize the strengths, not the weaknesses.

A checklist facilitates the comparison of several systems. A checklist comprises many different criteria related to the business processes or functions the company wants to be supported. These criteria must be provided in a very detailed way in order to realistically map the company's requirements. The result, however, is a very long checklist. Some checklists contain thousands of items. For example, the checklists provided by Trovarit can contain up to 2,500 criteria (Trovarit 2012b). They are used for an automated matchup with about 840 ERP systems (Trovarit 2012a).

Shorter checklists are easier to handle, but they are not as useful as lists that are more detailed. Short checklists tend to specify only rough or summarized criteria. This is usually not sufficient. For example, if the company wants to optimize vehicle routing using RFID data, then it is not enough that the checklist contains an aggregated entry "vehicle routing." Instead, the vehicle routing function has to be broken down into several items, one of them specifying that an optimization algorithm should be included and another one requiring an interface to an RFID processing system.

Figure 4.22 presents an example of a checklist (Homer 2007). The excerpt in the figure shows checklist entries referring to advanced planning and scheduling (APS, cf. Sect. 9.2.1). Entries for three candidate systems have been included.

Long and detailed checklists are suited to precisely map the company's requirements. However, they also have a number of serious *disadvantages*:

- Stakeholders tend to specify the current way of problem solving in the checklist and thus prescribe it for the future solution. Subsequently, shortcomings are also carried over to the new solution, meaning that the potential for improvement is missed.
- Not all criteria are equally important. Because of this, there is a risk that good systems may be eliminated from the candidate list, even if the criteria they miss are not so important. The more detailed the list is, the less likely it is that one system will meet all criteria.
- Since no system will satisfy all requirements, many companies, after choosing one, decide to fill the gap with individual extensions. This, however, means additional programming, causing additional cost. What is worse, detailed requirements specified when the checklist is created may be later found not to be so important after all.
- Individual extensions are not part of the standard software. This means that when the vendor provides a new version, the company's extensions are not automatically included. Consequently, the company has to see to it that the extensions are embedded or connected, resulting in even more additional cost.

Ref	Software Product Functionality	Field Type	*Supplier 1 Product 1*	*Supplier 2 Product 2*	*Supplier 3 Product 3*
	⋮				
49	Manufacturing planning & scheduling:				
50	Regenerative schedule	Y/N	Y	Y	Y
51	Incremental schedule	Y/N	Y	Y	Y
52	Resources/constraints that can be modeled:				
53	Labor	Y/N	Y	Y	Y
54	Machines	Y/N	Y	Y	Y
55	Tools	Y/N	Y	Y	Y
56	Subcontractors	Y/N	Y	Y	Y
57	Materials	Y/N	Y	Y	Y
58	Shelf life of product	Y/N	N	Y	Y
59	Warehouse capacity	Y/N	N	Y	Y
60	Transportation	Y/N	N	Y	Y
61	Work centers – machine/labor combination	Y/N	Y	Y	Y
62	Multiple plant sourcing	Y/N	Y	Y	Y
63	All of the above, simultaneously	Y/N	N	Y	Y
64	Modeling capabilities:				
65	Setup time	Y/N	Y	Y	Y
66	Run time	Y/N	Y	Y	Y
67	Wait time	Y/N	Y	Y	Y
68	Move time	Y/N	Y	Y	Y
69	Multiple time fences	Y/N	Y	Y	Y
70	Substitute resources/materials	Y/N	Y	Y	Y
71	Alternate routings i.e. machines	Y/N	Y	Y	Y
72	Rate-based modeling	Y/N	Y	Y	Y
73	Fixed-duration modeling	Y/N	Y	Y	Y
74	Infinite capacity planning	Y/N	Y	Y	Y
75	Finite capacity planning	Y/N	Y	Y	Y
76	Floating bottlenecks	Y/N	Y	Y	Y
77	By-products	Y/N	Y	Y	Y
78	Co-products	Y/N	Y	Y	Y
79	Variable production by part by machine	Y/N	Y	Y	Y
80	Operation overlapping	Y/N	Y	Y	Y
81	Split operations	Y/N	Y	Y	Y
82	Assigns tooling to operation	Y/N	Y	Y	Y
83	Schedule constrained by tooling availability	Y/N	Y	Y	Y
84	Variable delay to force op to start at start of shift	Y/N	N	Y	Y
85	Supports synchronization of operations	Y/N	Y	Y	Y
86	Maintains high utilization of bottlenecks	Y/N	Y	Y	Y
87	Supports sequence-dependent scheduling of setups	Y/N	Y	Y	Y
88	Supports scheduling of development jobs	Y/N	Y	Y	Y
89	Supports scheduling of maintenance jobs	Y/N	Y	Y	Y
90	Rules-based approach for sequencing	Y/N	Y	Y	Y
91	Distribution & inventory planning				
92	Supply network definition:				
93	Supplier	Y/N	Y	Y	N
94	Plant	Y/N	Y	Y	N
95	Distribution center	Y/N	Y	Y	N
96	Customer location	Y/N	N	Y	N
97	Supply network planning tools:	Y/N	N	Y	N
98	Linear programming	Y/N	N	Y	N
99	Heuristics	Y/N	N	Y	N
100	Multi-plant sourcing logic	Y/N	N	Y	N
101	Optimize truckloads	Y/N	N	Y	N
102	Prodn sourcing, inventory build, transport balancing	Y/N	N	Y	N
103	Global supply chain design.	Y/N	Y	Y	N
104	Rules-based order fulfilment	Y/N	Y	Y	Y
105	First come/first served	Y/N	Y	N	Y
106	Fair share deployment	Y/N	Y	Y	Y
107	Prioritized allocation	Y/N	Y	Y	Y
108	Forecast consumption rules	Y/N	N	Y	N
	⋮				

Fig. 4.22 Excerpt of a checklist for APS software (Homer 2007)

- Creating a detailed checklist requires a great deal of effort. It involves stakeholders from different departments as well as external consultants, requiring extensive discussions, compromises, and balancing of competing interests.

Taking the disadvantages of detailed checklists into consideration, *adaptability* appears to be more important than fulfilling all of the original criteria. Here, adaptability means that the system can be easily adjusted to the company's individual requirements. An adaptable system provides appropriate technical and organizational features for *customization*. This will be discussed in Sect. 6.2.

The checklist is given to potential vendors as part of a *request for proposals (RFP)*. The RFP contains more questions than those referring to the system's functionality. A typical request for proposals lists questions regarding:

- System functionality (i.e., checklist)
- Hardware and software requirements (including nonfunctional requirements, such as response time, scalability, etc.)
- Organization of service and support, service-level agreement
- User training and help features (e.g., hotline, help desk)
- Cost (license, upgrade, maintenance, training, etc.)
- Legal issues (contract, indemnification, liability, etc.)

Utility-Value Analysis When the company receives the vendors' proposals, the project team has to evaluate the proposals and decide which would be the best system for the company. This is a very difficult task because it is highly unlikely that one system is better than all the others in all categories.

Regarding the functional requirements, for example, the candidate systems will have their "Y" and "N" entries in different places. In Fig. 4.22, products 1 and 3 do not provide supply network planning tools (row 97). Product 2 does include these tools, but what if it costs twice as much as the other two products? What if products 1 and 3 have features that product 2 does not offer (e.g., first come/first served order fulfillment, row 104)?

Obviously, to come to a decision, the products must be evaluated with regard to the benefits the company expects from certain features, and the drawbacks from missing other features. To do so, the benefits and the drawbacks must be weighed against each other, because most of them cannot be measured directly in monetary or other quantitative units.

A method supporting qualitative judgment in evaluating multiple goals is the so-called *utility-value analysis* (Zangemeister 1976). This approach allows the decision maker to treat qualitative benefits and shortcomings in a more objective manner than by just using personal opinion. An example of benefits that cannot be measured in monetary units is the summary of a checklist, because generally, it is not possible to quantify the value of a "Y" (nor the missed value of an "N") in any of the rows.

In a utility-value analysis, a small number of criteria important for management decisions are established and weighted. The first step is to agree upon which criteria to use and the second to agree upon their relative importance (by weighting the criteria). Both steps require that the members of the project team come to an agreement. This may be a difficult process because the goals, interests, and power of different stakeholders often differ.

Figure 4.23 illustrates the basic structure of a utility-value analysis using seven criteria for three remaining candidate ERP systems. The criteria as listed in the two tables of the figure are functionality, technical requirements, cost, customizing effort, technical service and support, user training and help, and number of reference installations. The second column of the lower table shows the weights the project team has decided to assign to the criteria. (The other columns of the lower table are filled later in the process.)

The next step of the analysis is to evaluate the candidate systems using the criteria. This has been done in the upper part of the figure. For example, it was found that system A provides 70 % of the desired functionality, whereas B comes up to 90 % and C to 60 %. Regarding technical requirements, A was considered to be very good, B just OK, and C good.

When all criteria have been evaluated, the systems can finally be assessed. For this purpose, the results shown in the upper table are mapped to a point scale. Assuming that the scale is from

a Aggregated evaluation results

Criterion	Product assessment		
	System A	System B	System C
System functionality	70%	90%	60%
Non-functional requirements	very good	OK	quite good
Cost (license, hw/sw, maintenance)	1,200,000	1,750,000	1,150,000
Customization effort	10 pm	4 pm	12 pm
Technical service & support	excellent	average	mediocre
User training & help	average	good	good
Reference installations	26	> 500	80

pm = person months

b Assessment

Criterion	Weight (%)	Points from product assessment		
		System A	System B	System C
System functionality	30	7	9	6
Non-functional requirements	10	9	6	8
Cost (license, hw/sw, maintenance)	20	5	2	5
Customization effort	20	4	7	3
Technical service & support	10	10	5	4
User training & help	5	5	7	7
Reference installations	5	2	10	5
Total	100	615	645	520

Fig. 4.23 Utility-value analysis (example)

0 (very bad) to 10 (excellent), each entry of the upper table is given a point between 0 and 10. For example, B gets 7 points for "customizing effort," because 4 person months are considered fairly good, whereas A and B get only 4 and 3 points, resp., because they require a lot more customizing. B is also the best regarding functionality, receiving 9 points.

The last step is to calculate the utility values and add them up, resulting in 615 for A, 645 for B, and 520 for C. The winner in our example is B. If the decision were based exclusively on the utility-value analysis, the company would license ERP system B.

However, companies rarely rely solely on a schematic tool such as a utility-value analysis. Rather, they employ it as one aid in the decision-making process, helping them to make different options comparable. Deciding on an ERP system is a management task that has long-term consequences and requires the consideration of multiple aspects (including strategic implications and long-term perspectives of the choice).

4.5 ERP and the Internet

In the past, an ERP system was usually installed inside the company, for example, on a mainframe or a number of servers. Employees accessed the ERP system through a proprietary frontend, typically a graphical user interface (GUI) that belonged to the system. With the Internet, this situation has changed in several ways.

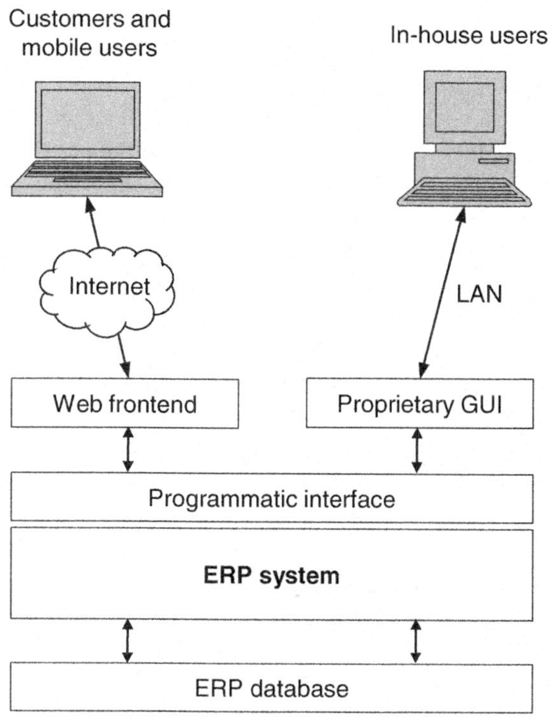

Fig. 4.24 Schematic access to an ERP system

4.5.1 Accessing an ERP System

While accessing an ERP system through a proprietary frontend is still common, other modes have also emerged.

Web Frontends and Enterprise Portals One mode of accessing the system is through a *web frontend*. This means that ERP functionality is made available on web pages on which the user can select options, enter data into forms, etc. One advantage of a web frontend is that the user can access the ERP system from anywhere, not only from within the company (provided that external access to the system is allowed by the system administrator).

Enterprise portals are the next step up. An enterprise portal is a web page providing a uniform point of entry to the company's information offerings. Different kinds of information, services, and functions that are of interest to the employees can be integrated in a portal, including the ERP functionality the employees need to do their work. A portal can be personalized according to the needs of the individual user or workplace.

Companies provide enterprise portals for different target groups: for employees only (via an intranet), for suppliers and partners (via an extranet), or for the general public (via the Internet).

Portals have become increasingly popular. Business software vendors such as IBM, Microsoft, Oracle, and SAP provide powerful toolsets to develop enterprise portals. For example, the technological platform on which SAP ERP is based (SAP NetWeaver) includes an integrated portal component (cf. Sect. 6.4.2).

Electronic Commerce While employees access an ERP system directly, customers usually do not, at least not through a proprietary frontend. However, when they buy goods in a web shop (electronic shopping), they indirectly work with an ERP system, although it is unlikely that they are aware of this. Fig. 4.24 illustrates the technological relationships.

What the customer of a web shop sees in most cases is an electronic product catalog (cf. Sect. 2.2.2), a shopping cart or basket, an order form, and a payment form. Assuming that the company running the shop is not a mini-company, there may be hundreds or thousands of products to show in the catalog. All the product data will, of course, not be stored as static web pages but retrieved from an ERP database when they are needed. This means that the web shop is connected with an ERP system running in the background and doing other work in parallel. The catalog is dynamically created when the user selects options and follows links on the catalog's start pages.

Figure 4.24 shows in a schema how an ERP system can allow different modes of access. The ERP system provides an interface through which programs can use its functionality. Employees inside the company will normally have desktop computers at their workplaces, connected with the ERP system by a local area network (LAN). They communicate with the ERP system through the embedded graphical user interface (GUI). Customers and users outside the company access the system via the Internet and the web frontend.

4.5.2 E-Procurement

With the Internet, electronic forms of purchasing goods have become available not only in the business-to-consumer field (e-commerce) but also in the business-to-business field, that is, between businesses. Here they are summarized under the term *electronic procurement (e-procurement)*. ERP systems increasingly provide e-procurement capabilities and interfaces to e-procurement systems.

In e-procurement, there are primarily four developments worth mentioning: Sell-side systems, buy-side systems, product exchanges, and marketplaces.

A *sell-side system* is a system on the Internet provided by a supplier for the procurement of certain goods. The supplier runs the system, specifies the prices of the goods offered, sets the rules, and prescribes how customers should use the system.

A *buy-side system* is provided by a company inviting offers (bids) from suppliers. In this way, the company gets quotations from different suppliers and can select the best one. Buy-side systems can be found in the automotive industry, for example. In this industry, car manufacturers have usually more power than their suppliers, meaning that suppliers trying to win a deal from the car manufacturer will happily use the system.

A *product exchange* is a website where supply meets demand. Suppliers of goods post their offerings. Potential buyers post requests for the goods they require. The exchange is usually run by an independent third party acting as an intermediary. The intermediary's services include support for matching supply and demand with the help of advanced search functionality. For example, search criteria such as the part numbers of leading manufacturers may be provided.

An *electronic marketplace* is similar to a product exchange but with extended functionality. In addition to providing product catalogs and search features, a marketplace supports negotiations between the market participants, helps them in the preparation and execution of a transaction, and provides a secure payment mode. Business-to-business marketplaces exist both within industries and across industries.

5 Case: SAP ERP

5.1 The Evolution of SAP ERP

The best-known ERP system for years has been that of SAP AG, a German software company based in Walldorf, Baden. The name of the system, however, has changed several times over the years.

For many ERP users, the name "R/3" has long been synonymous with SAP. R/3 is an ERP system implemented worldwide on a wide range of hardware and software platforms. This system has primarily (but not exclusively) been used by mid-sized and large companies.

Although the majority of SAP users still work with R/3 programs in one way or another, this name is no longer used in SAP's marketing and official documentation. The last system version to mention "R/3" was marketed up to 2004 under the name "R/3 Enterprise."

Approximately from the start of the new millennium on, the ERP system became known as "mySAP ERP," presented as a component of the "mySAP business suite." The designation "mySAP" indicated that SAP's application systems were increasingly running on the Internet or an intranet and based upon Internet technology. In 2008, names were again changed from "mySAP xyz" to "SAP xyz."

The *SAP business suite* is a comprehensive package of application systems that include:

- SAP ERP: enterprise resource planning
- SAP CRM: customer relationship management
- SAP SRM: supplier relationship management
- SAP SCM: supply chain management
- SAP PLM: product life cycle management

The largest part of the SAP Business Suite is *SAP ERP*. This system covers four major areas:

- SAP ERP financials: external and internal accounting
- SAP ERP human capital management: personnel management
- SAP ERP operations: procurement, logistics, product development, manufacturing, sales and service
- SAP ERP corporate services: support for administrative processes

The "solution map" (sometimes also called "business map") is a diagram that summarizes the most important areas supported by SAP ERP. It provides an overview of business functions and processes, which according to SAP should help to "...visualize, plan and implement a consistent, integrated and comprehensive business solution" (SAP 2012e).

The descriptions provided for the items on the solution map usually name "processes," although many of the items are actually functions or functional areas rather than processes. Nevertheless, the general perspective taken in the solution map is process oriented, focusing on processes, subprocesses, and process steps.

A completely different question is how the items on the solution map are supported by SAP *software*. When a company wishes to implement the diagram's processes (or subprocesses), it has to employ the SAP ERP software system, which is a *function-oriented* system. This means

K.E. Kurbel, *Enterprise Resource Planning and Supply Chain Management*,
Progress in IS, DOI 10.1007/978-3-642-31573-2_5, © Springer-Verlag Berlin Heidelberg 2013

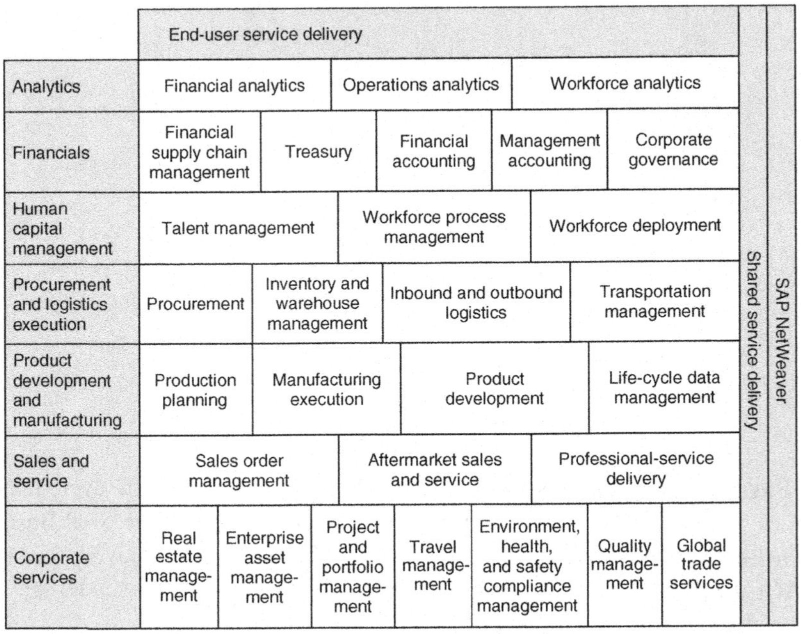

Fig. 5.1 SAP ERP solution map (SAP 2012e)

that, to do their work, the processes utilize the functions of SAP ERP. To put it another way, the company must map the business processes onto functions and invoke them in a correct, process-oriented context.

Accordingly, the user working with SAP ERP sees the system divided into *functional areas* and *individual functions*. The majority of these functions can be traced back to SAP R/3. This legacy can be seen in the system documentation and online help, which predominantly use R/3 terms. The reason for this is the long evolution of SAP ERP from SAP R/3. On the program level, the core of the system consists largely of earlier R/3 code.

SAP R/3 was functionally divided into 12 modules, as shown in Fig. 5.2. A user responsible for the business processes in inventory and warehouse management, for example, would work directly with the functions of the MM (materials management) module. As shown in the figure, the modules are grouped thematically around three main areas: logistics, accounting, and personnel management.

The relationship between SAP R/3 and SAP ERP is illustrated in a simplified form in Fig. 5.3. Since 2004, SAP has been using the technology platform SAP NetWeaver as the basis for their new application systems. Older systems were also migrated to this platform. SAP ERP contains both the "old core" of R/3, now running on the NetWeaver platform and known as *SAP ECC (ERP central component)*, as well as additional components, which were developed directly for NetWeaver.

5.2 Functionality of SAP ERP

This section briefly describes the processes and functional areas contained in the SAP solution map shown in Fig. 5.1. The major sections are:

1. Procurement and logistics execution
2. Product development and manufacturing
3. Sales and service
4. Financials
5. Human capital management
6. Analytics
7. Corporate services

The following description of the processes and functional areas of SAP ERP in Sect. 5.2 is based on information published by SAP AG on their website (SAP 2012a), in particular in the SAP ERP solution map (SAP 2012e).

In earlier versions of the solution map, the first three sections were combined under the term

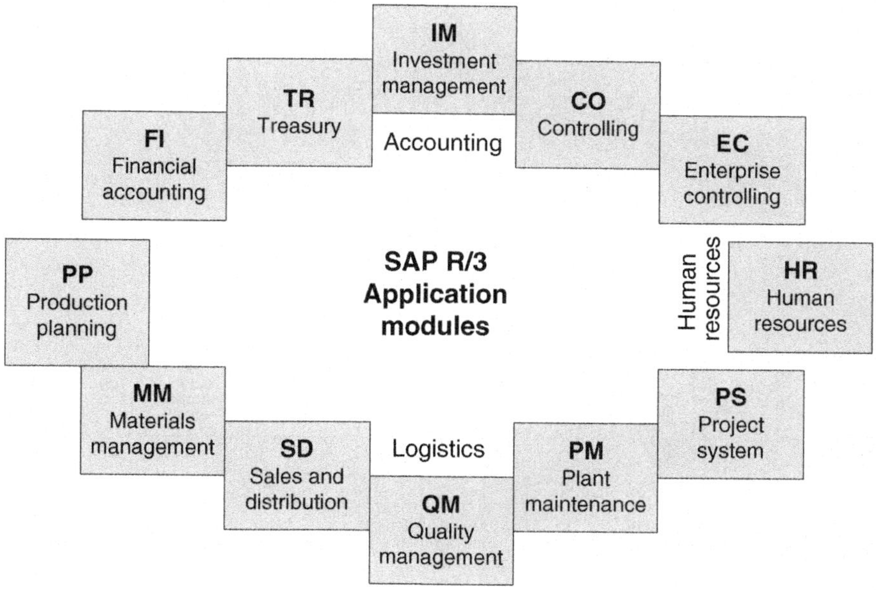

Fig. 5.2 SAP R/3 application modules

"operations," because they constitute the core of the business activities according to the objective of the enterprise. "Operations" incorporate most parts of MRP II. The terminology used by SAP R/3 for this area was "logistics," as can be seen in Fig. 5.2.

5.2.1 Procurement and Logistics Execution

The processes and tasks of *procurement and logistics execution* are primarily supported by functions of the modules MM (materials management) and SD (sales and distribution). This area is divided into:

- Procurement
- Inventory and warehouse management
- Inbound and outbound logistics
- Transportation management

Figure 5.4 exemplifies the relationship between the *processes* in the field of procurement and logistics execution and the SAP ERP *modules* in question.

Procurement The *procurement* part of procurement and logistics execution comprises requisitioning (purchase requisitions), purchase order processing (calculating order requirements, planning, releasing, and monitoring the purchase order), receiving goods, handling returns, and the financial settlement (invoice verification and blocking and releasing invoices).

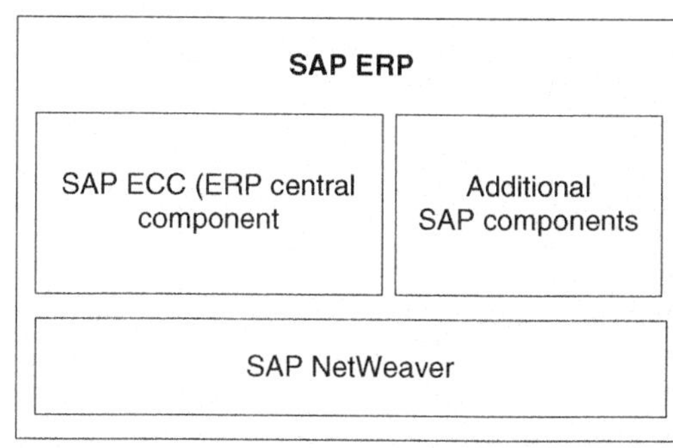

Fig. 5.3 Software components of SAP ERP

Inventory and Warehouse Management The *inventory and warehouse management* part offers support for a variety of tasks, including:

- Inbound processing (i.e., follow-on activities for a purchase order after goods have been received)

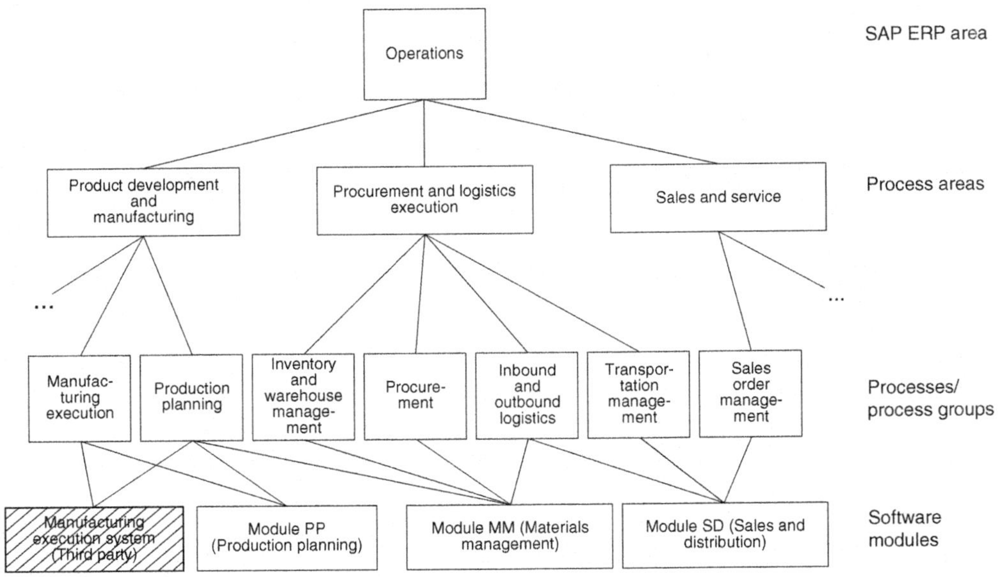

Fig. 5.4 Relationship between solution map and SAP ERP modules

- Outbound processing (delivery processing and distribution, goods issue documents, proof of delivery)
- Cross docking (goods are brought directly from the goods receipt to goods issue without being stored)
- Physical inventory (periodic, continuous, sampling, etc.)
- Warehousing and storage

The scope of inventory and warehouse management is very broad. Different aspects are taken into consideration, including various warehouse structures (e.g., high rack, block storage) and refined types of storage locations and bin structures. Some of the many functions supported are put-away and picking strategies, production supply, handling unit management (i.e., storage functions based on package units), batch and hazardous goods management, including automation features using barcodes and RFID (radio frequency identification; see Sect. 11.4.1) tags.

Inventory management uses a variety of functions provided by the MM module to appropriately manage stock according to quantity and value, supporting goods receipts, goods removal, return deliveries, reservations, and stock transfers.

Inbound and Outbound Logistics *Inbound logistics* cover all steps in procurement after the goods have been received (goods receipt, transportation to warehouses/storage places according to the stock placement strategy, etc.).

Outbound logistics include activities connected with preparing and sending the goods to the recipients (goods removal, goods issue, shipping documents, etc.). When goods are imported or exported, the accompanying documents required by customs are created, and the duty costs are calculated.

While the functions needed for inbound logistics are contained in the MM module, outbound logistics are supported by the SD module. Special functions used for *foreign trade* are connected with the ERP system but provided apart from it (see Sect. 5.2.7).

Transportation Management *Transportation management* also uses SD functions, namely, for transportation planning (route determination, shipper selection, etc.), transportation execution (all activities connected with delivery), and freight costing. Freight costing includes calculating freight charges (considering conditions, payment arrangements, etc.) and freight cost settlement (including settlement for multiple carriers involved in a shipment).

5.2.2 Product Development and Manufacturing

The processes and tasks of *product development and manufacturing* are divided up into the following subareas:

- Production planning
- Manufacturing execution
- Product development
- Life-cycle data management

Production Planning Production planning more or less covers the MRP II functionality, that is to say those parts of MRP II that are not supported by the procurement, inventory and warehouse management parts. Production planning includes determining dependent requirements, forward shifting, creating planned orders, lead-time scheduling, and capacity planning (long-, medium-, and short-term planning).

The functionality related to *material requirements planning*—in particular the consumption- and requirements-driven materials planning, comprising net requirements calculation, lot sizing, forward shifting (lead-time offset), and creating order proposals and planned orders—is provided by the MM module. *Lead-time scheduling* and *capacity planning* (capacity evaluation and leveling) use functions from the PP module (production planning).

Manufacturing Execution Manufacturing execution is another comprehensive part of product development and manufacturing, supporting not only workshop and continuous flow production but also many other forms, such as make-to-order production, make-to-stock production, repetitive and batch manufacturing, and even process production. Special forms of manufacturing organization such as Kanban, lean production, pull production, and integrated product and process development (iPPE) are also available.

PP functions are used for manufacturing execution. Integration of other systems, including both SAP and third-party systems, is made possible by complying with standardized interfaces. Especially important is the integration of dedicated third-party *manufacturing execution systems* (MES, cf. Sect. 7.1).

Product Development Product development is the section providing support for, among other things, defining a product, determining the requirements of the product, developing the product, and identifying potential suppliers. These tasks require effective cooperation from all parties involved (project managers, developers, designers, engineers, etc.).

For this reason, *collaborative work* is explicitly supported through a process called "development cooperation." Special attention is paid to cross-enterprise product development including internal and external project teams.

In order to support the entire process of developing and introducing new products, a special SAP ERP module which is not based on R/3 is available: NPDI (new product development and introduction).

Life-Cycle Data Management Life-cycle data management refers to all aspects of managing and representing product information such as product structures, variants, drawings, recipes, routings etc. It also includes additional specifications like a classification of hazardous substances and goods.

Life-cycle data management involves the administration of a large number of different documents. Therefore, a comprehensive *document management* section is included.

Because product data can frequently change, life-cycle data management contains dedicated functionality for *change and configuration management*. Data changes are often due to engineering changes, possibly affecting production orders, planned orders, and purchase orders. An order change management function helps to identify the affected orders.

5.2.3 Sales and Service

Processes and functions for sales, distribution, and customer service belong to the *sales and service* part of the solution map. This part is broken down into:

- Sales order management
- Aftermarket sales and service
- Professional-service delivery

Sales Order Management Sales order management is the core and largest part of sales and service, supporting processes associated with sales and distribution tasks. The most important functions employed by sales order management are available in the SD module, focusing on quotation and order management: processing inquiries, quotations, pricing (taking into account conditions, surcharges, freights, taxes, etc.), credit card payment, credit checking, substitution products, compliance with minimum order quantities, availability checking, and order scheduling.

Also worth mentioning are the capabilities for *contract management* providing many detailed features and *billing* based on orders and deliveries. *Internet sales* offer a platform with the functionality needed for e-commerce (electronic product catalog, product search, shopping basket, etc.).

Incentive and commission management includes support for creating payment plans, variable remuneration accounting, direct sales commissions, activity-based payment, effectivity analysis and organization management (e.g., specification of regional responsibilities).

Aftermarket Sales and Service Aftermarket sales and service supports all the aspects of service order processing within a service organization—from processing the initial inquiry to confirming the order and billing, all the way to product maintenance and long-term servicing.

Among others things, aftermarket sales and service includes *installation and configuration management* for customers of the company, that is, managing the configurations installed at the client's site.

Furthermore, contractual and warranty-based services, support for maintenance cycles, service requests, and service orders as well as warranty and claims processing, contract management and on-site customer service are provided.

Professional-Service Delivery Professional-service delivery is a subarea for managing *consulting services*. The capabilities provided are designed for selling, planning, delivering, and settling project-based services, including quotation and sales order processing. They support tasks related to consulting projects, such as project planning, project execution, project accounting, as well as resource, time, and travel expense management.

5.2.4 Financials

The *financials* section of the solution map covers all tasks related with planning and controlling finances, costs, and payment transactions as well as analyzing the business operations. The functionality is divided into five sections:

- Financial accounting (external accounting)
- Management accounting (internal accounting)
- Corporate governance
- Financial supply chain management
- Treasury

Financial Accounting For *financial accounting*, the FI module (financials) offers a multitude of functions covering the general ledger, accounts receivable and accounts payable, as well as other types of accounting (asset, inventory, tax, bank-related accounting, and more). Support is available for other functions as well, such as period-end accruals, fast close, year-end closing, and parallel valuation according to different accounting rules.

Management Accounting Management accounting covers all major areas of internal accounting: profit center accounting (profits and losses of organizational units), cost center accounting, internal order accounting (from planning to settlement), project accounting, capital investment management, product cost accounting (calculating and controlling the cost of goods manufactured, COGM, and cost of goods sold, COGS), profitability analysis (revenue and cost analysis), consolidation, and transfer pricing (i.e., determining the prices for goods and services exchanged between different units of a company or different companies of a group).

Accounting functionality for an individual company is contained within the module *CO (controlling)*, whereas functionality needed for groups of companies is addressed by the module *EC (enterprise controlling)*.

Corporate Governance Corporate governance comprises the framework of all the rules and regulations under which a company is operating. The objective of corporate governance processes is to ensure trustworthy and legally compliant behavior of all employees and other parties involved (SAP 2012e) and to achieve transparency and control with regard to a value-oriented management of the company. Complying with the rules and regulations is seen as a means to build up and maintain trust in the company—the trust of shareholders, customers, and employees, as well as other stakeholders and the public.

While features supporting corporate governance are still listed in the "financials" sections of the ERP solution map, most of the functionality is nowadays provided outside SAP ERP. Corporate governance belongs to the "GRC solutions" within SAP's "business analytics" portfolio. GRC stands for "governance, risk, and compliance." It is a part of the SAP BusinessObjects product suite. (BusinessObjects used to be a leading provider of business intelligence and analytics solutions before it was acquired by SAP in 2008.)

Financial Supply Chain Management Financial supply chain management (FSCM) supports the financial management within a company and in company networks. The goal here is to reduce the working capital and to improve the liquidity.

Features provided by FSCM include electronic billing and payment, dispute management (settling payment disputes), collections management and credit management, and contract accounting. The necessary functions are mostly contained in the FI (financials) module and some other SAP ERP components.

Treasury Treasury processes and functions aid the company to oversee cash and payment processes, ensure liquidity, handle financial transactions from deal capturing to accounting, and evaluate interest, foreign exchange, price, and commodity risks. The treasury section is divided into four parts (SAP 2012e):

- Treasury and risk management—supports the principal tasks in a finance department, assisting liquidity, portfolio and risk management.
- Cash and liquidity management—helps in monitoring operational cash flow, forecasting, and planning future cash flow.
- In-house cash—allows diversified companies to optimize their intragroup payment transactions by opening an in-house cash center ("in-house bank"). The in-house cash center processes all payments between company units. Cash resources are kept within the group, saving banking cost and enhancing financial flexibility.
- Bank communication management—provides electronic connections to the bank as well as processing, tracking, and monitoring payments.

The functions needed for the above-mentioned treasury tasks are found in the TR module.

5.2.5 Human Capital Management

The goal of *human capital management (HCM)*, previously known as *human resources (HR)*, is to find the best ways to utilize the potential and productivity of employees. The new name also shows that SAP attaches strategic importance to the change from human resources to human capital management: "Maximizing the investment in the organization's human capital is crucial to business success. This requires transforming the human resource (HR) function from an administration department into a strategic contributor of human capital management (HCM) strategies" (SAP 2012e).

HCM is a vast part of SAP ERP. It offers a comprehensive spectrum, from recruiting to assignment, all the way to qualification and retaining employees in the company. In doing so, country-specific aspects such as the respective legal and business situations are taken into account.

The ERP solution map defines the major areas of human capital management as:

- Talent management
- Workforce process management
- Workforce deployment

Primarily, the functions of the SAP ERP HR (human resources) module are used for these areas.

Talent Management Talent management covers the life cycle of the relationship between employees and the company: attracting and acquiring talent, hiring, allocating tasks and responsibilities, payment strategies, evaluations, training, and qualification (SAP 2012e). The most important processes and tasks include recruitment, career and succession management, company-wide training (including e-learning), employee performance management (tying compensation to performance based on corporate goals and strategies) and compensation management, supporting diverse compensation schemes.

Workforce Process Management Workforce process management supports, among other things, important human resources tasks such as:

- Personnel administration (providing a central repository for employee data)
- Payroll and legal reporting (handling payroll processes subject to legal regulations and collective agreement specifications, taking into account national rules and regulations)
- Organizational management (managing organizational structures and policies)
- Global employment (managing international transfers and assignments)
- Benefits management (defining and administering every type of benefit plan)
- Health benefits management (managing healthcare expenses for benefits)
- Time and attendance (planning, managing, and evaluating the working times and activities of internal and external employees)

Workforce Deployment Workforce deployment provides support for creating project teams based on skills and availability, monitoring project progress, tracking time, analyzing results, eliminating redundant or ineffective projects, making efficient use of resources, and managing the workforce efficiently. The processes and tasks are divided into three parts:

- Project resource planning (targeted toward service companies that work in a project-oriented manner).
- Resource and program management—integrates resource management, project portfolio management, project execution, and skills management and aids in searching and allocating internal and external professionals to projects and service engagements.
- Retail scheduling—supports scheduling of retail staff based on customer volume, shift schedules, and skills.

5.2.6 Analytics

Analytics is the section of the solution map that supports business intelligence and analytics, including financial, operational, and workforce analytics.

Analytics functionality is primarily contained in the so-called information systems of SAP ERP. These are submodules of the former R/3 application modules, providing evaluations based on the data of the respective application area. Examples include the sales information system, production information system, financial information system, controlling information system etc.

Financial Analytics The goal of *financial analytics* is to increase the sales and revenue while decreasing capital investment and operating cost and improving business processes. Financial planning, budgeting, and forecasting are supported. With the help of the financial analytics processes, financial and managerial reports, financial budgets, and forecasts can be created.

Furthermore, profitability management, production and service controlling, overhead cost controlling, payment-behavior analysis, and investment and risk management are supported. Features for analyzing product and service costs and for legal and managerial consolidation are also included.

Operations Analytics Operations analytics is the largest of the three analytics parts because it is responsible for analyzing and improving the business processes and the company's current operations. Available analytics capabilities include procurement analytics, inventory and warehouse management analytics, manufacturing analytics, transportation analytics, sales analytics, customer-service analytics, program and project management analytics, quality management analytics, enterprise asset analytics, and performance management.

In addition, functionality summarized under *sales planning* helps to translate company targets into concrete marketing, sales, and service strategies.

Workforce Analytics The goal of *workforce analytics* is to make sure that the activities of all organizational units and employees of the company are in line with the company's strategic direction. To serve this purpose, a variety of capabilities for workforce planning, cost planning, simulation, benchmarking and analyzing workforce processes (e.g., payroll) are offered.

Additionally, talent management analytics help to monitor talent-related processes. Strategic alignment of all departments and teams with the corporate strategy is facilitated by tools such as *balanced scorecards,* which are built around metrics, targets, and milestones, integrated with management-by-objective goals.

End-User Service Delivery Although listed in the "analytics" section of the solution map, *end-user service delivery* enables the delivery of many kinds of ERP services together with business content to end users throughout the organization. End-user service delivery depends on the roles of the users, their preferences, and the business context.

More than 20 adaptable *roles* are predefined, each providing a work environment that supports the role-specific tasks. Examples of roles include manager, buyer, plant manager, warehouse operation manager, and (general) employee.

A *plant manager,* for example, is provided with a dashboard delivering alerts, key performance indicators (KPIs), manufacturing content, work lists and production confirmations, and with decision support needed in order to respond to exceptions and unforeseen changes in demand or supply.

Another example is the *invoicing clerk* role, providing access to all documents involved in invoice management and search features for related invoices and invoice exceptions. The clerk's workplace environment automates the verification of incoming invoices. If there are no exceptions, the invoices are automatically posted. Otherwise, various workflow and monitoring activities are triggered and tracked, including notifying the vendor about the exceptions.

Some of the capabilities are provided as *self-service.* For example, an employee can invoke a form to apply for a leave or a business trip. The employee's manager will find the application in his or her work list and approve or reject it online.

5.2.7 Corporate Services

Corporate services are services that can be used by the different roles throughout the company. They are made available either centrally or decentrally. Corporate service areas are (SAP 2012e):

1. Travel management
2. Environment, health, and safety compliance management

3. Project and portfolio management
4. Real estate management
5. Enterprise asset management
6. Quality management
7. Global trade services

Travel Management Capabilities supporting *travel management* are provided for all steps of the planning, preparation, and accounting of business trips: travel request and approval, travel planning using global reservation systems (such as Amadeus, Galileo, and Sabre, hotel and railways reservation systems, etc.), travel and expense management (online buying, expense reimbursement, travel accounting), global compliance with travel policies, etc.

Environment, Health, and Safety Compliance Management Environment, health, and safety compliance management supports environmental, occupational and product safety processes, regulatory compliance, and corporate social responsibility (CSR). This area includes solutions for product safety, hazardous materials management, dangerous goods management, industrial hygiene and safety management, occupational health, and waste management.

Project and Portfolio Management Project and portfolio management assists portfolio managers in identifying, selecting, prioritizing, and managing a portfolio of projects, including key performance metrics on budgets, schedules, and staffing.

Project managers are supported by typical project management functionality. Features include:

- Structuring a project (setting up a work breakdown structure, scheduling activities, etc.)
- Resource, time, and budget management
- Project execution (project-based procurement and production, controlling the progress of the project, monitoring costs, etc.)
- Project accounting
- Development collaboration (i.e., cross-enterprise product development with internal and external teams, including the sourcing of complex product components)

Most of the functionality is available from the PS (project system) module of SAP ERP.

Real Estate Management Real estate management supports many different tasks, helping employees plan and administer a real estate portfolio as well as the entire real estate life cycle. Both commercial and legal management aspects (e.g., administering contracts and space, renting and leasing, rent accounting and adjustments, external administration of real estate), as well as technical facilities management are included. Controlling and reporting tools are available to analyze and evaluate a real estate portfolio.

Enterprise Asset Management The job of *enterprise asset management* is to plan, set up, and maintain the technical assets of the company. This includes, for example, technically managing the assets of the company over their life cycle (asset life-cycle management), ranging from the first investment to putting the assets in service, all the way to replacement investment. Other important tasks include planning and executing maintenance (preventive and preemptive maintenance, periodic, activity-based, or other) and processing the release of operating facilities (safety-relevant tasks in restarting technical equipment).

The functions enabling these tasks can be found in the PM (plant maintenance) module of SAP ERP.

Quality Management Quality management supports the company by assuring and managing the quality of products and assets throughout the product life cycle and along the supply chain.

Tasks associated with quality management include quality engineering in accordance with international standards (e.g., ISO 9000), quality assurance and control using several different methods, as well as quality improvement using proven methods, for example, through audit management (ISO 19011) and corrective and preventive action (CAPA).

These functions are available in the QM (quality management) module of SAP ERP.

Global Trade Services Companies involved in worldwide business are subject to diverse regulations, licenses, import tariffs, and an increasing amount of paperwork required by government agencies and other legal entities. Noncompliance with all these restrictions results in costly fines and penalties.

Global trade services (GTS) support export, import, and trade-preference management (shipping products to customers in countries that have trade-preference agreements). GTS features allow for the administration of international logistics chains and for electronic communication with IT systems used by government agencies. In all this, GTS ensure compliance with local laws and foreign trade regulations and create all the necessary documents.

The functionality required for global trade services is not a part of SAP ERP but is included in SAP GRC, a part of the BusinessObjects product suite mentioned above.

5.3 Implementing Business Processes with SAP ERP

In Sect. 4.3, several business processes were outlined but no specific requirements regarding computer-supported execution of the processes or of any particular ERP system were considered.

The following section will demonstrate what these business processes look like when they are implemented with the help of an ERP system, namely, SAP ERP. For our purposes, we will assume that the process flow (i.e., the process steps involved and the order of the process steps) is largely the same as was described in the previous chapter.

The main differences when implementing the processes with the help of an ERP system are (Magal and Word 2009, pp. 16–18) (a) documents are no longer needed or take on different roles, (b) there are fewer and shorter interruptions and delays in the process flow, and (c) visibility of the process, across all process steps, is improved.

(a) Documents If the processes described above are executed manually, that is, without the help of an ERP system, many paper documents are required to connect the process steps with each other. The next process step, which may be carried out by another department, is initiated when the necessary document arrives.

In the procurement process shown in Fig. 4.9, a *warehouse manager* responsible for checking the stock level creates the document "purchase requisition." When the document reaches the purchasing department, it triggers the activity "determine sourcing." The "goods receipt document," which is generated by the *goods receiving* department, and the external document "vendor invoice" together initiate the activity "process vendor invoice" in the *accounting* department, when both of these documents arrive in accounting.

Using an ERP system does not change the basic relationships and dependencies, but there are no (or at least fewer) paper documents. Documents are still created and sent, but now they are electronic documents stored in the database. Occasionally, paper versions may still be printed, but they do not play a central role, as is the case in manual processes.

(b) Interruptions and Delays When the ERP system contains, or is connected with, a workflow management system, no time is wasted between process steps. Since the documents controlling the process are available to the next workplace from the moment they are created and saved, the next step can begin immediately.

Manual processes, on the other hand, must allow time for the documents to be printed and physically sent and received. The next person involved in the process only learns about the transaction after the document has been delivered by the company's internal postal service.

(c) Visibility Since the data is saved in one place, everyone involved in the process has the same information. An example of this can be seen in the order fulfillment process. Compared to manual processing, better visibility significantly reduces the effort involved when processing an order.

When a customer inquires about the status of their order, the salesperson no longer has to call

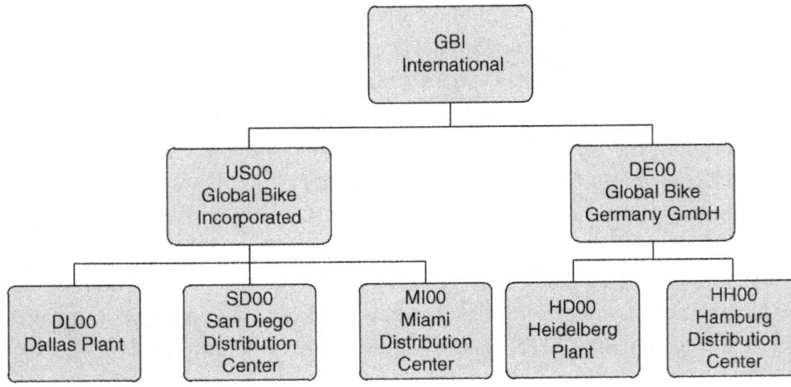

Fig. 5.5 GBI organizational structure (Magal and Word 2012, p. 30)

all the departments involved in the order (e.g., warehouse management, production planning, shop floor, accounting), requesting them to check the order status as noted down in the various documents (e.g., sales order, production order, goods withdrawal slip).

Instead, he or she can examine the status of the customer's order in the ERP system, since status information is maintained in the central database. The customer will promptly receive an answer, instead of having to wait until all the research has been completed, as is the case in manual processing.

5.3.1 The Model Company: Global Bike International

In order to illustrate the implementation of core business processes with the help of SAP ERP, "real" data are required, that is, products, assemblies, bills of materials, routings, a chart of accounts, organizational structures, manufacturing plants, distribution centers, customers, suppliers, etc.

For this purpose, we will use the data of *Global Bike International (GBI)*, a fictitious enterprise created by SAP. "Created" means that SAP (1) implemented the organizational structures as described in Sect. 4.2, (2) defined all of the above-mentioned data entities and their relationships as well as the workflows and database structures, and (3) filled all data items (organizational elements, products, customers, etc.) with appropriate values.

As a result, GBI is available in SAP ERP, just as an SAP customer's enterprise is available once the system has been installed and customized (cf. Sect. 6.3). GBI's companies and all subordinate organizational structures, as explained in Sect. 4.2, are available for training purposes to universities participating in SAP's university alliance program (http://www.sdn.sap.com/irj/uac).

The GBI enterprise produces and sells bicycles and accessories. The backstory created for the company is that it was founded following a merger of two bicycle manufacturers, one in the USA and one in Germany (Magal and Word 2012, p. 15). Consequently, GBI has operations (manufacturing, distribution, etc.) mainly in these two countries.

Due to legal and accounting requirements, GBI consists of two companies: GBI Inc. (USA) and GBI Germany GmbH, with company codes US00 and DE00, respectively. There are two manufacturing sites (Dallas and Heidelberg) and three distribution centers (Miami, San Diego, and Hamburg). The top-levels of the organizational structure are presented in Fig. 5.5. (According to SAP terminology, both the manufacturing sites and the distribution centers are called "plants"; cf. Sect. 4.2.2).

The main products of GBI are different types of touring and off-road bicycles. In addition, a number of so-called trading goods (e.g., helmets) are sold. Touring bikes come as "deluxe touring bikes" and "professional touring bikes," each in three colors. With respect to off-road bikes, men's and women's variants exist. Figure 5.6 provides an overview of GBI's product spectrum.

- Bicycles
  - Touring bicycles
    - DXTR – Deluxe touring bike
      - DXTR1000 – Deluxe touring bike (black)
      - DXTR2000 – Deluxe touring bike (silver)
      - DXTR3000 – Deluxe touring bike (red)
    - PRTR – Professional touring bike
      - PRTR1000 – Professional touring bike (black)
      - PRTR2000 – Professional touring bike (silver)
      - PRTR3000 – Professional touring bike (red)
  - Off-road bicycles
    - ORMN1000 – Men's standard off-road bike
    - ORWN1000 – Women's standard off-road bike
- Accessories
  - Protective gear
    - Pads
      - EPAD1000 – Elbow pad
      - KPAD1000 – Knee pad
    - Helmets
      - OHMT1000 – Off-road helmet
      - RHMT1000 – Road helmet
  - Utilities
    - SHRT1000 – T-shirt
    - RKIT1000 – Repair kit
    - PUMP1000 – Air pump
    - BOTL1000 – Water bottle
    - CAGE1000 – Water bottle cage
    - FAID1000 – First-aid kit

Fig. 5.6 GBI product spectrum (Magal and Word 2012, p. 34)

5.3.2 Procurement

Revisiting the core business processes discussed in Sect. 4.3, we will start with the *procurement process*, demonstrating how this process can be implemented in SAP ERP.

In Sect. 4.3.1, a number of *documents* were mentioned, but these documents were not explicitly modeled. Instead, we implicitly assumed that they are created within a process step or provided from outside the process. For example, in Fig. 4.9, an event "goods receipt document created" must occur for the process to continue. Obviously, it was assumed that this document is created within the process step "process goods received."

When the business process is supported by an ERP system, most documents are stored in the database. They still play an important role because *events* regarding the state of a document (e.g., created, sent, updated) are used to control the flow of a process. This means that the majority of the process steps have to access the database and read, update, or create database objects.

Essential database objects relevant for the procurement process are summarized in Fig. 5.7. Important *master data* are "material" and "supplier." *Transaction data* created or processed during the process include "purchase requisition," "purchase order," "goods received," "supplier invoice," and "payment."

Figure 5.8 shows an event-driven process chain for the procurement process. It is the same process chain as presented in Chap. 4 (cf. Fig. 4.9), but now it has been completed by the relevant data. In EPC terminology, these data are called *information objects*.

The reason why the same information objects are noted down several times is to avoid intersecting lines. For example, a "material" rectangle is connected with the "create purchase requisition" activity, another one with "create and send purchase order" and yet another with "process

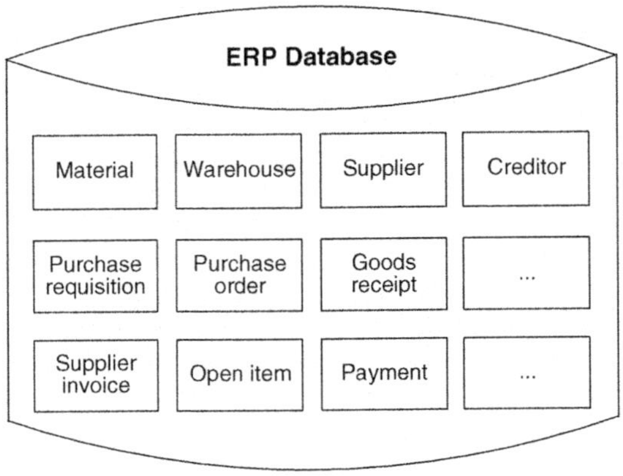

Fig. 5.7 Database objects for procurement

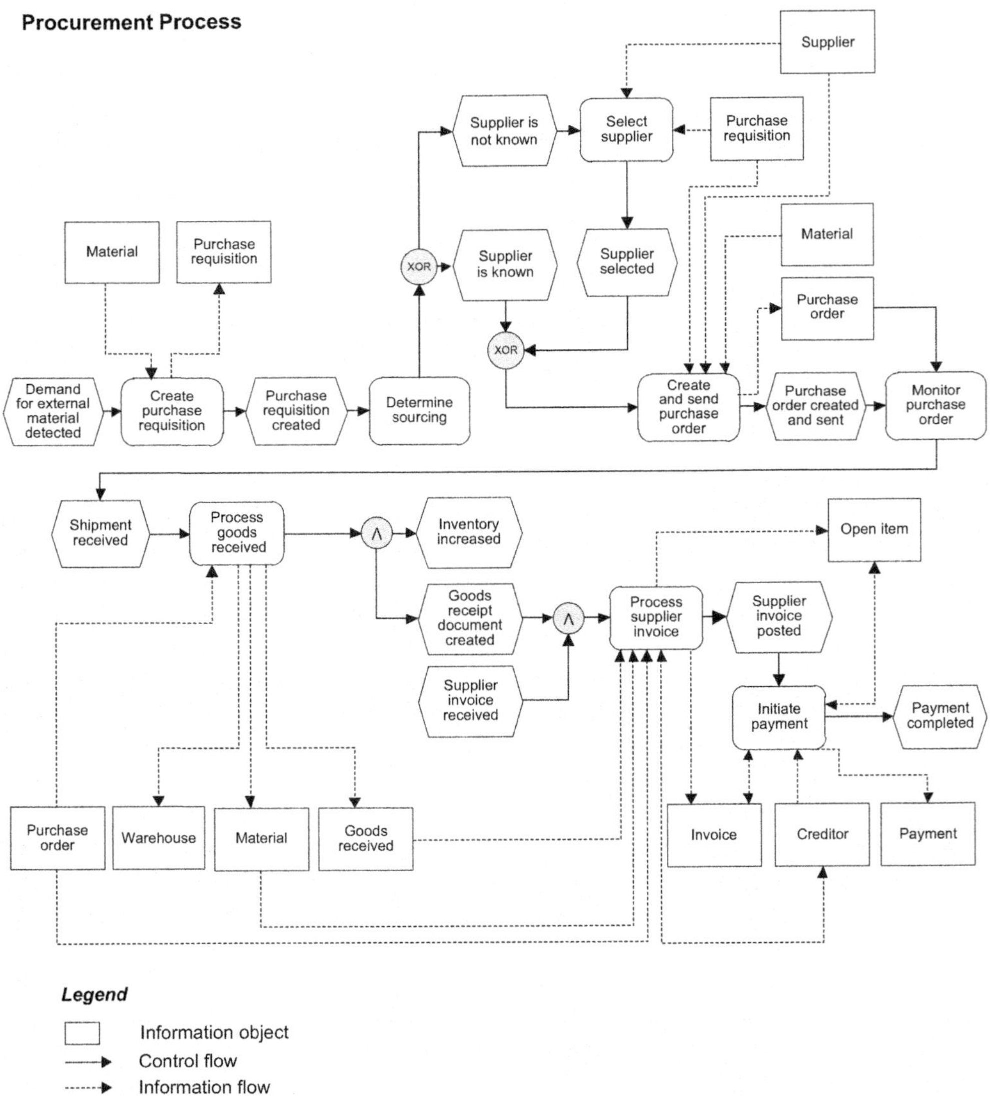

Fig. 5.8 Procurement process including information objects

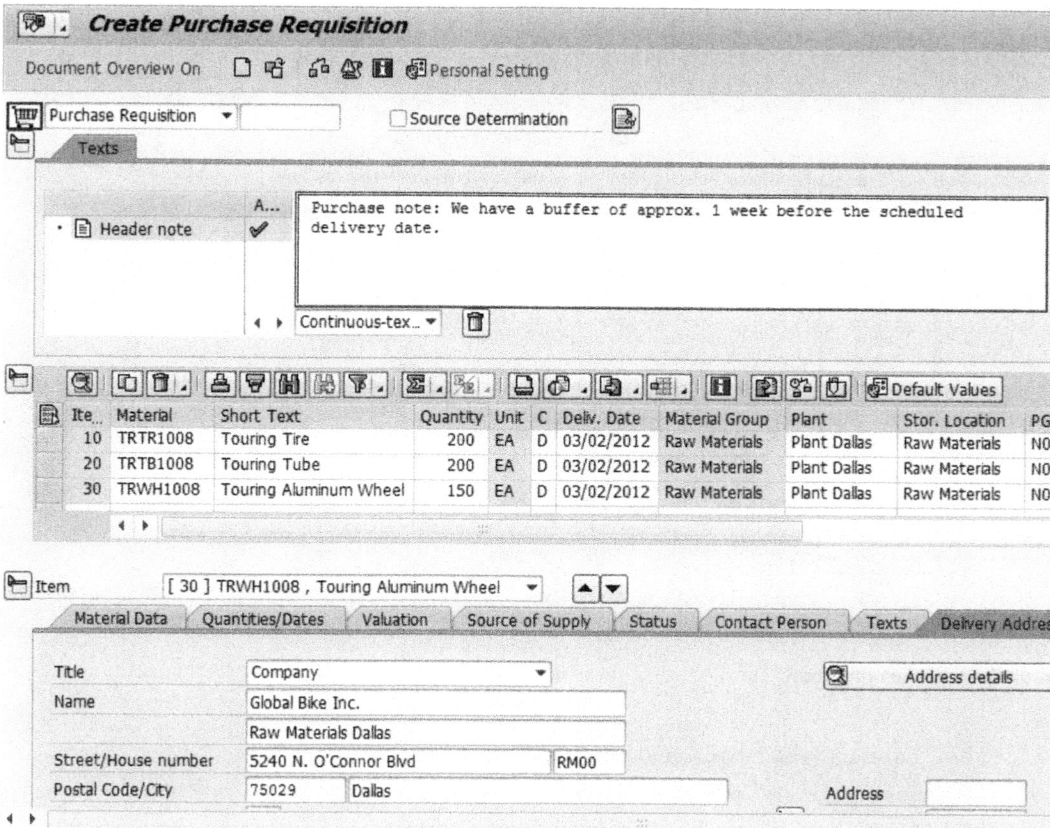

© SAP AG

Fig. 5.9 Purchase requisition form

goods received" and "process supplier invoice." However, all three rectangles represent the same information object.

The process starts when demand for an external material has been detected. In order to create a purchase requisition, the material's master data must be accessed because this is where the details needed to order the material are stored. Through the material master data, the stock on hand is also available. (It should be noted, however, that inventory data in SAP ERP are actually maintained based on storage locations and are just combined for display in the material form.)

An information object called *purchase requisition* is created in the first process step. The purchase requisition is an electronic document that the warehouse manager creates by filling out a form provided by the ERP system. Some fields of this form will be filled automatically with information that is already available in the database, while other fields have to be entered manually. The content of the form is then stored as a purchase requisition object in the database.

Figure 5.9 shows a new purchase requisition created in SAP ERP. The person responsible for the purchase requisition entered three items: 200 touring tires (material number "TRTR1008"), 200 touring tubes ("TRTB1008"), and 150 touring aluminum wheels ("TRWH1008").

The lower part of the form can be used to specify or display details of the items, such as material data, supply sources, and contact details. In the screenshot presented in Fig. 5.9, the warehouse manager specified a delivery address for the third item of the purchase requisition (touring aluminum wheels TRWH1008).

When the purchase requisition is saved, the system creates a number, which can later be used to identify the purchase requisition. In our example, the number is "10000111." It can be

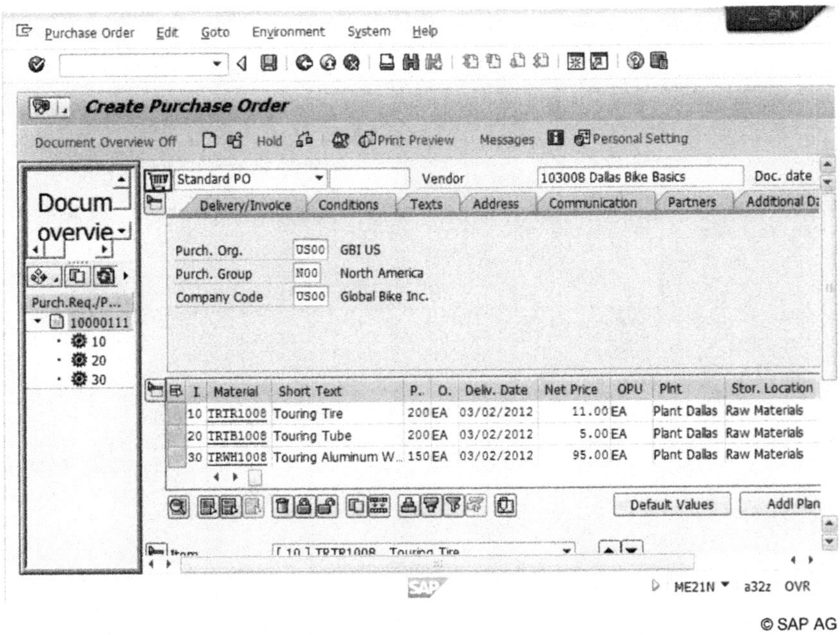

Fig. 5.10 Purchase order form

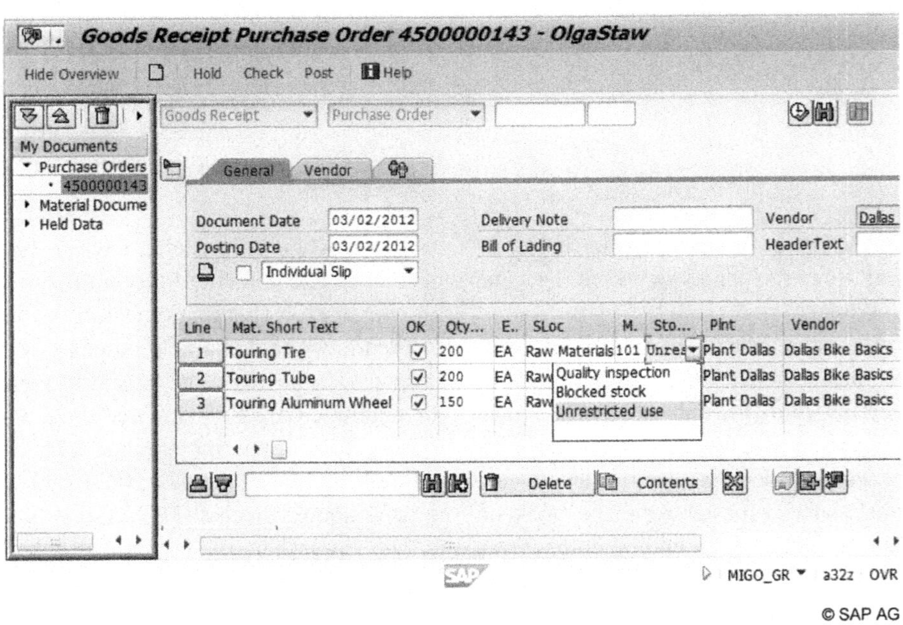

Fig. 5.11 Goods receipt form

found, for example, on the left-hand side of the purchase order shown in Fig. 5.10.

In order to create a *purchase order*, the buyer (or purchasing group) needs to identify the purchase requisition it refers to, while the system resorts to the supplier master data (containing address details, terms, and conditions) and the material master data (providing details of the material).

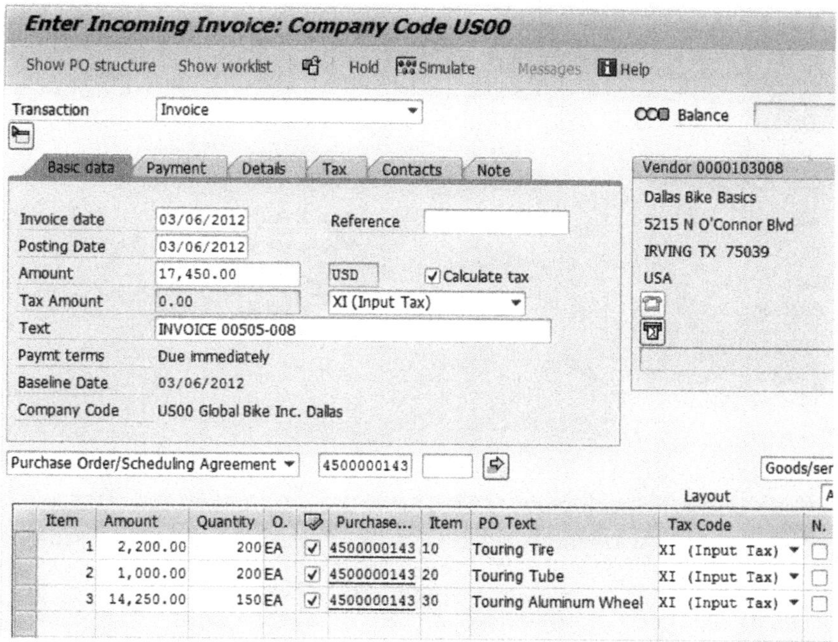

© SAP AG

Fig. 5.12 Adding a supplier invoice

The purchase order contains, in addition to the order items, the prices of the items, the vendor ("103008 Dallas Bike Basics") as well as the purchasing organization ("US00 GBI US") and the purchasing group ("N00 North America"). The company code is "US00," Global Bike Inc.

When the salesperson saves the purchase order, the system creates another number (*purchase order number*). This number can later (e.g., upon goods received) be used to identify the purchase order underlying the incoming goods.

The *goods receipt* is also an electronic document presented to the user as a form on the screen. The title bar of the form (cf. Fig. 5.11) displays the purchase order number ("4500000143") and the buyer's user name ("OlgaStaw"). Some form entries were copied automatically from the purchase order while others have to be entered manually.

The person responsible for goods receiving will confirm (as in our case) or modify the entries in the "OK" column, such as the quantity received (vs. the quantity ordered). Furthermore, information necessary for forwarding the goods received must be provided, such as the plant, warehouse, storage location, and stock type. If this information is available in the purchase order, it is automatically adopted, otherwise it has to be entered (or modified). In the figure, the user is about to identify the stock type, which can be stock in "quality inspection," "blocked stock," or stock for "unrestricted use."

Upon saving the form, this information is used to update the material and inventory data, while the goods received are posted and a *goods receipt number* is generated.

The *supplier invoice* is an external document issued by the supplier. Therefore, an internal document has to be created and stored in the database. If the invoice has been received on paper, the invoice data must be entered manually. If it is an electronic document in a standard exchange format (e.g., EDIFACT, ebXML), most of the entries can be copied automatically.

Figure 5.12 contains the form used for entering an incoming invoice. On the right-hand side, the address of the above-selected vendor no. "103008," Dallas Bike Basics in Irving, Texas, is displayed. On the left-hand side, the invoice date, the total amount, payment terms and the purchase order the invoice refers to (order no. "4500000143") are shown.

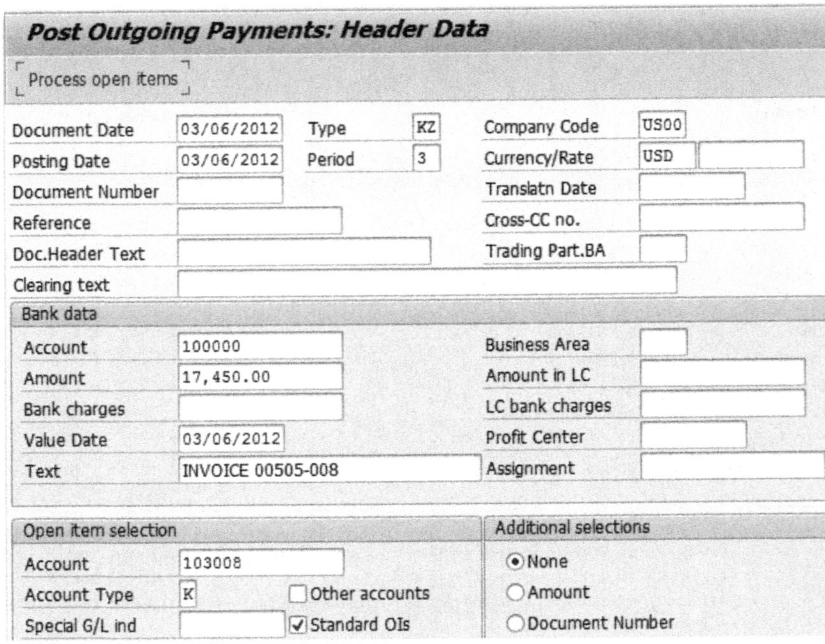

© SAP AG

Fig. 5.13 Outgoing payments form

Since the business process in Fig. 5.8 contains only our company's information objects, the supplier invoice has not been explicitly mentioned in the diagram. It appears only implicitly in the event "supplier invoice received," whereas the information object created within the company ("invoice") is shown explicitly, as an output of the activity "process supplier invoice."

Before creating this object, the accounting department checks the supplier invoice, using the previously saved information objects "purchase order" and "goods received" as well as the material and creditor master data. The information object "invoice" is stored with the help of the form shown in Fig. 5.12.

Upon saving the invoice, an *open item* is automatically created. This open item is booked out later when the payment is processed. The payment is initiated within an outgoing payments form as shown in Fig. 5.13. The form contains, among other things, coded bank data ("100000") and the amount to be paid.

When the open item is booked out, the status of the invoice is changed from open to paid. A *payment* is another information object stored as transaction data in the ERP database.

As the description of the procurement process shows, information objects and events regarding these objects play an important role in the process. Events such as finding or creating a document in the database control the flow of the process. Information objects—documents (transaction data) and master data—are identified by numbers. The numbers of documents are automatically generated by the system and subsequently used to identify related documents.

Following the last process step ("initiate payment"), the event "payment completed" should occur, ending the procurement process.

5.3.3 Order Fulfillment

In the following, the *order fulfillment* process depicted in Fig. 4.10 is reconsidered. While Sect. 4.3.2 provided a general description of the process, this section will show how order fulfillment is carried out with the help of SAP ERP.

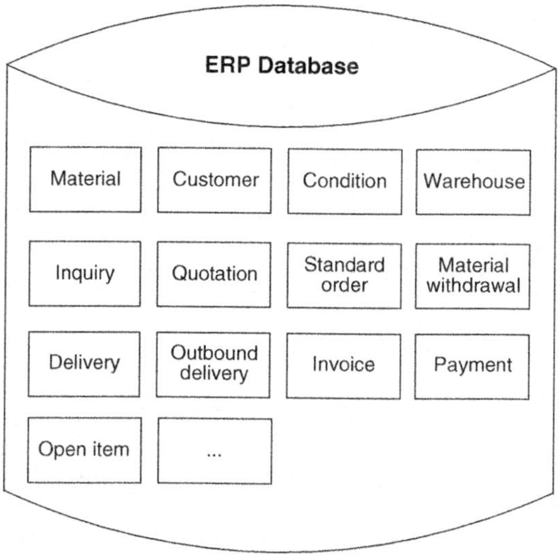

Fig. 5.14 Database objects for order fulfillment

Figure 5.14 summarizes the most important database objects employed in the order fulfillment process. They include *master data,* such as "material," "customer," "warehouse," and "condition", as well as *transaction data* that are created during the process. Transaction data include "inquiry," "quotation," "standard order," "material withdrawal," "delivery," "outbound delivery," "invoice," "open item," and "payment."

In the EPC diagram of Fig. 5.15, the process steps are mostly the same as in Fig. 4.10. However, the information objects related to the activities are now included. For the first step ("create customer inquiry"), "customer" and "material" master data are required as input, while the output is an information object named "inquiry."

Figure 5.16 shows a screenshot of an inquiry in SAP ERP. A customer from Orlando ("The Bike Zone") asked about 20 deluxe touring bikes (red), 10 men's off-road bikes, and 10 professional touring bikes (silver). At the time the salesperson created the inquiry, the ERP system automatically filled master-data items stored in the database into the respective fields and performed necessary computations (e.g., item prices).

An interesting field in Fig. 5.16 is the "expected order value." Provided that historical data about the customer's inquiry/order placement ratio exist, this value is calculated to indicate how much "value" to the company the inquiry actually represents. (An *expected value* is the nominal value multiplied by the probability that the value will be realized.) In our example, the expected value is 34,800 USD, as opposed to the volume of the inquiry, which is 116,000 USD ("net value"). Obviously, historical data suggest that the probability of actually receiving an order from this customer is 30 %.

The next step is preparing a *quotation*. Most data items needed for this step are already available in the database, in particular the customer data, terms and conditions, items, dates, and prices as stored with the inquiry and other details of the materials in question. The ERP system automatically copies available data into the respective fields of the quotation, while requesting the salesperson to enter additional data manually (e.g., special discounts).

Once the customer actually places the order, an internal equivalent (i.e., a *sales order*, called "standard order" in SAP ERP) is created. Before doing this, the salesperson checks whether the customer order matches the quotation. If so, he or she will save the standard order to the database, otherwise the customer will be contacted.

Figure 5.17 shows the form for a *standard order*. The customer has ordered the same items as contained in the inquiry and the quotation. The standard order has a number of entries taken from the quotation and others taken from the material master data (e.g., the weight, which is needed for transportation issues).

Before the delivery can be prepared, *availability* of the materials included in the standard order has to be checked. This may also take place earlier, but it must be done before the delivery is prepared. Different approaches exist. A very simple one is to look at the "stock overview" list. This is a list displaying a product's available stock in all of the company's plants.

The stock overview list of Fig. 5.18 shows the stock of one of the products the customer ordered (deluxe touring bike red) at the various plants and warehouses. The total unrestricted-use stock worldwide is 200 bikes, 10 of which are in Heidelberg, 100 in Hamburg, 40 in Dallas, and 50 in Miami.

Order Fulfillment

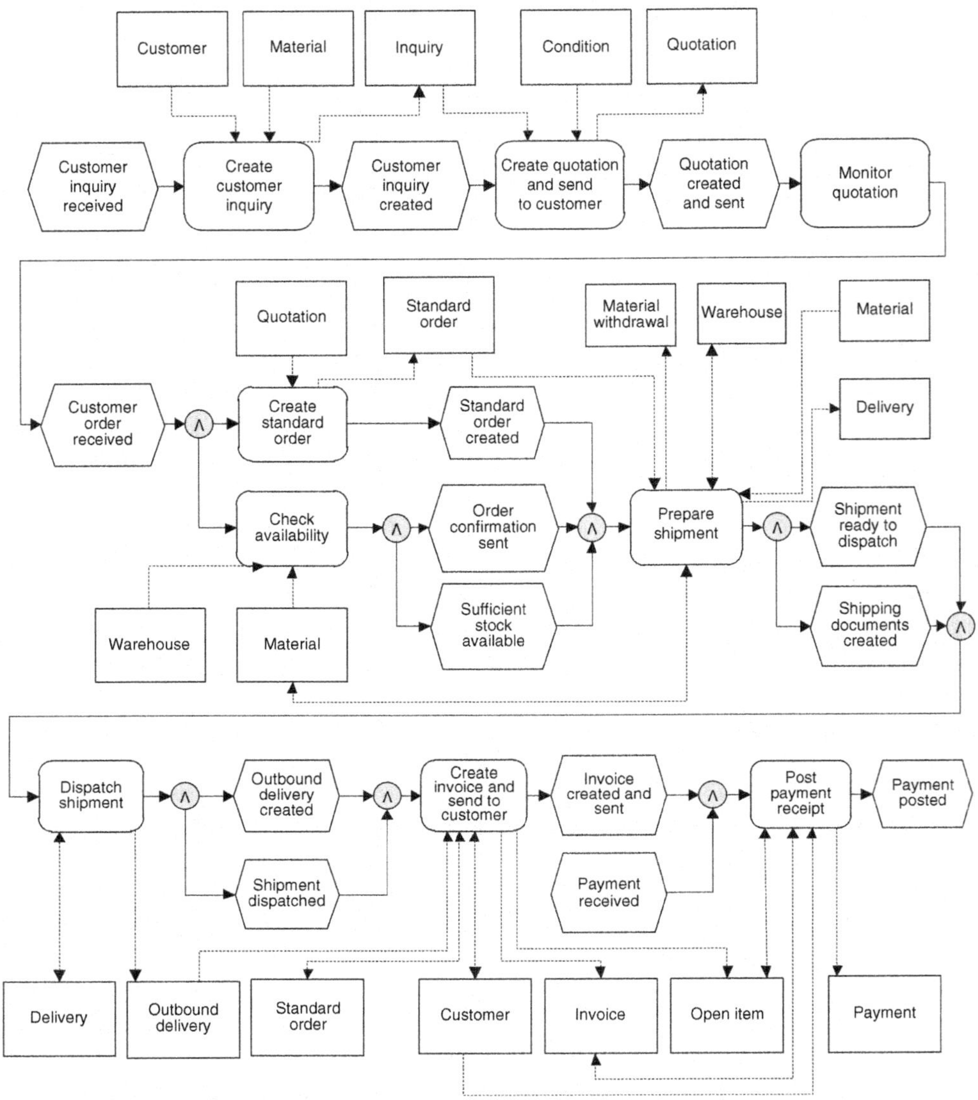

Fig. 5.15 Fulfillment process including information objects

In *preparing the delivery*, the ERP system creates a number of documents needed in further activities and processes (e.g., picking list, transfer order, delivery note). "Delivery" is also an information object stored in the database. A delivery comprises one or more customer orders ready to be shipped to the same customer. For preparing a delivery document, warehouse data is needed because it contains information about which materials are stored in which quantities at which storage locations.

Warehouse workers use the *picking list* to withdraw the listed materials from the respective storage bins. If they detect mistakes in the list, the entries will be corrected. Differences between the list and the actual stock can occur, for example, when the requested materials are not found in the given storage bins (but perhaps

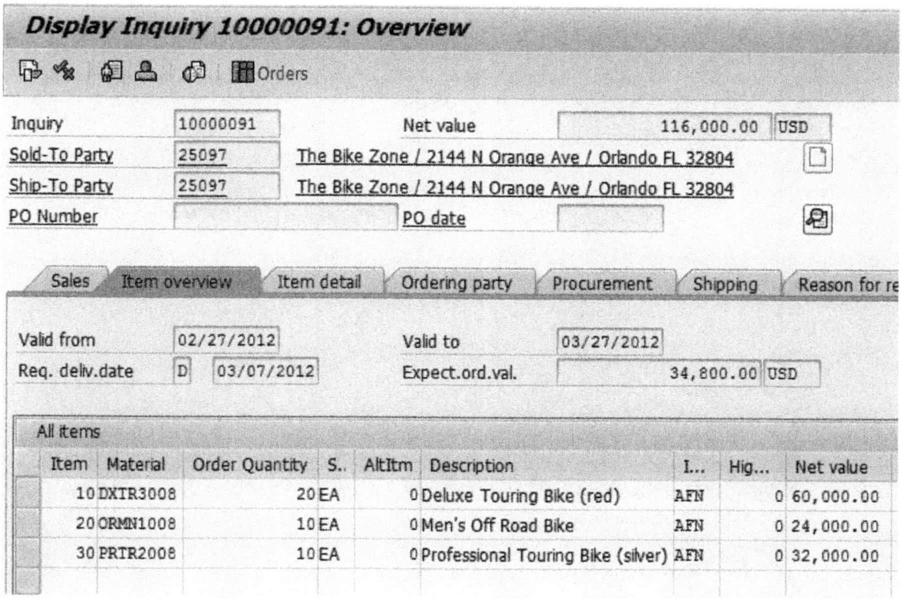

Fig. 5.16 Customer inquiry form

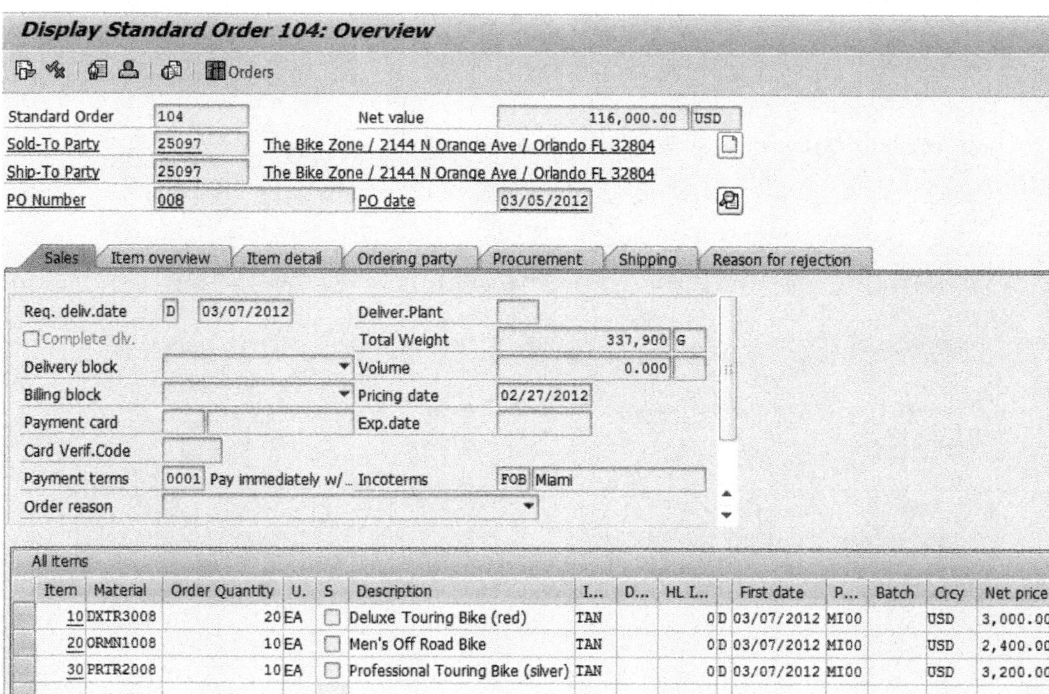

Fig. 5.17 Standard order form

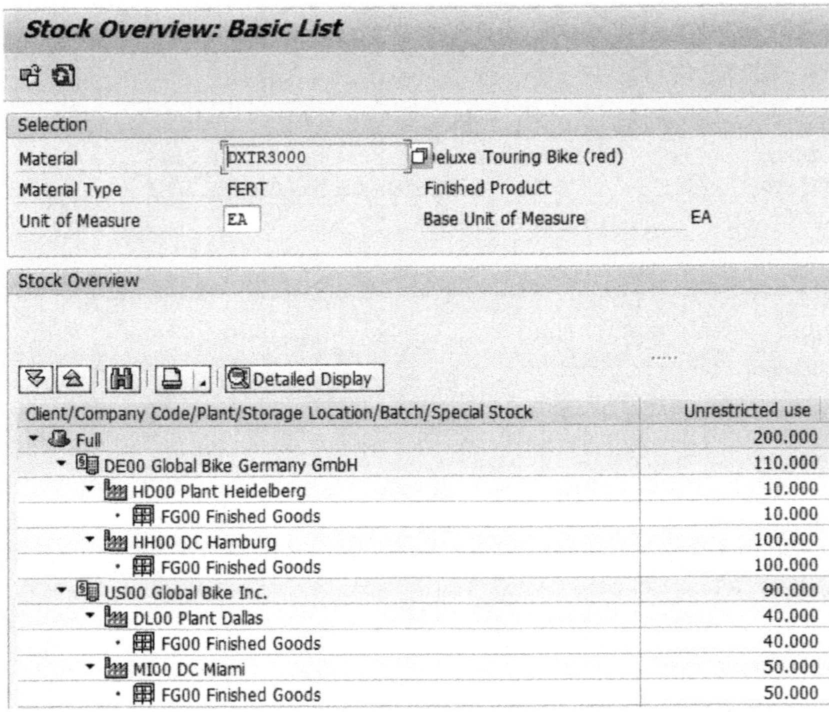

Fig. 5.18 Stock overview list

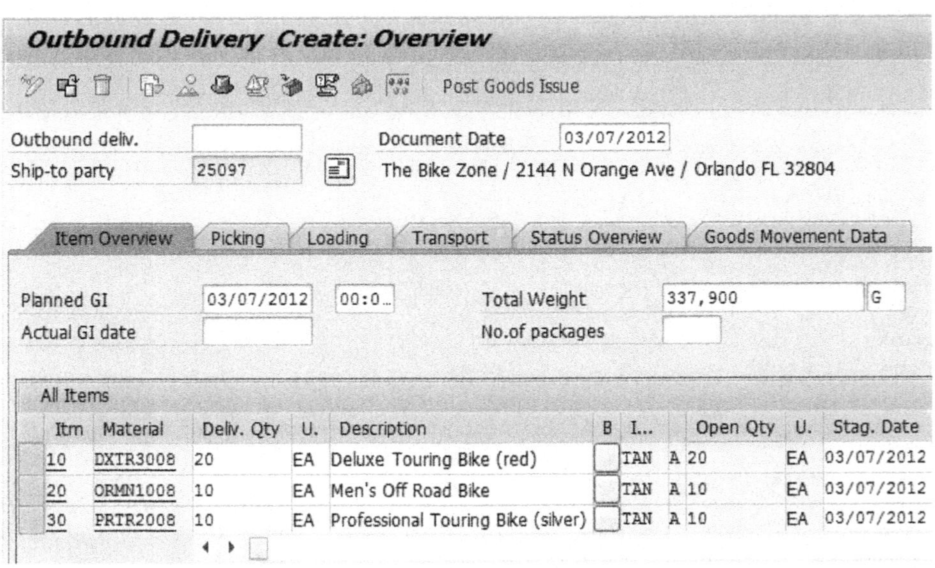

Fig. 5.19 Outbound delivery

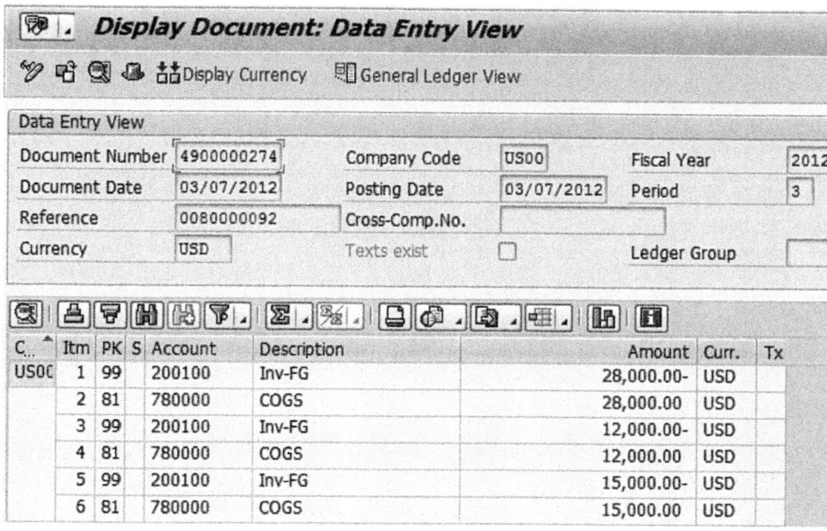

© SAP AG

Fig. 5.20 Posting document for change in inventory value

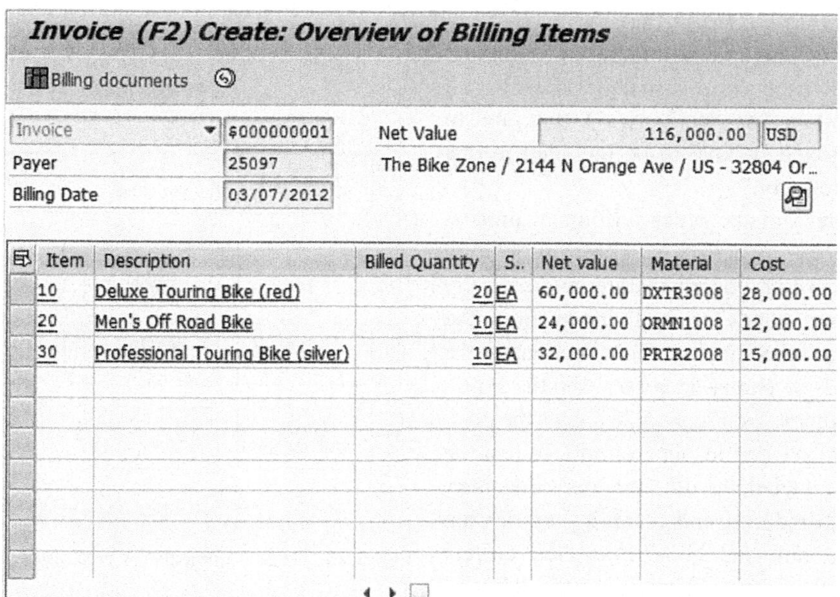

© SAP AG

Fig. 5.21 Invoicing form

somewhere else) or when the stocked quantity is not sufficient.

Withdrawals are transaction data, represented as an information object ("material withdrawal") in the event-driven process chain. As a result of the "prepare delivery" step, withdrawals are created and stock levels in the warehouse and material master data are updated.

In the *dispatch shipment* step, another information object (called "outbound delivery") is created, as shown in Fig. 5.19. This object is required in SAP ERP for actually shipping the

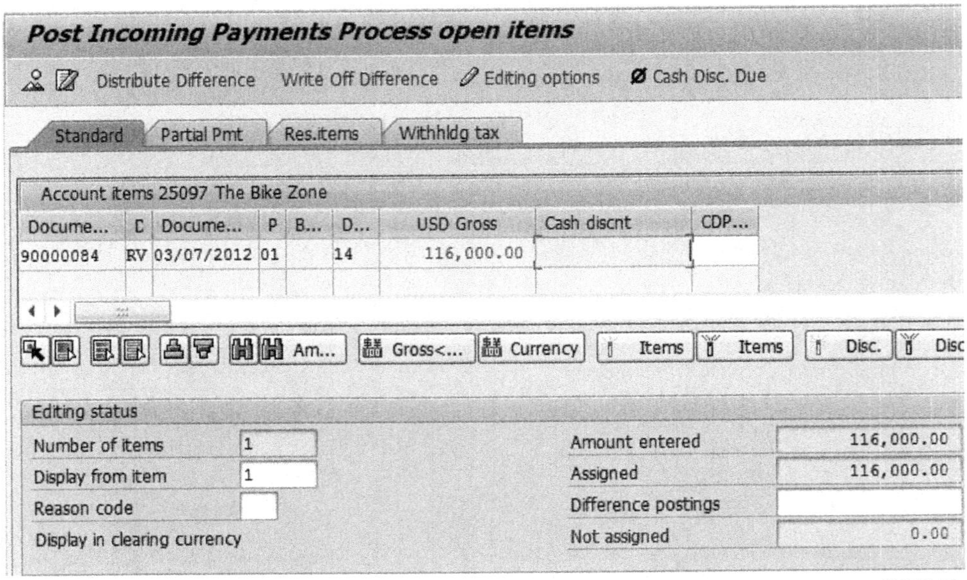

© SAP AG

Fig. 5.22 Payment/open items form

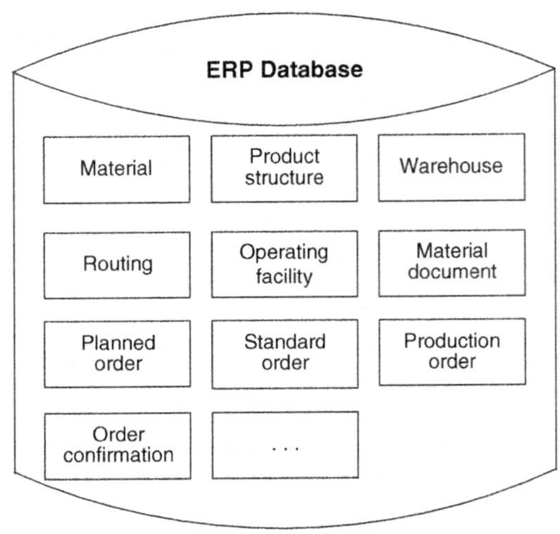

Fig. 5.23 Database objects for production

goods and invoicing the customer. An "outbound delivery" represents the dispatcher's view: all customer orders (or "deliveries") that are to be shipped together have to be included in one "outbound delivery."

Several steps of the order fulfillment process have a financial impact on the company. During these steps, posting documents are automatically created. When goods are withdrawn from the warehouse in preparation of a delivery, the finished goods inventory decreases, and the potential revenue increases. Figure 5.20 shows the posting document created in our example. When the picking is completed, the finished goods inventory ("Inv-FG") is reduced and offsetting entries are created. The amounts booked are the current values of the three items belonging to the delivery, namely, the cost of goods sold ("COGS"). Transfer postings of 28,000, 12,000, and 15,000 USD are made from the account "200100–Inv-FG" to the account "780000–COGS."

For *invoicing*, the accounting department resorts to various documents created earlier in the process (in particular, the standard order and the outbound delivery) and to the customer master data. The customer master data may specify a different payer than the ship-to party (field "payer" in Fig. 5.21). In our example, the recipient of the goods and the payer are the same (customer no. "25097"). An open item is also created.

After the invoice has been sent to the payer, the *payment* will eventually be received. The payment must be checked against the invoice or, more precisely, against the open item created for the invoice. If more than one open item exists for this customer, the proper item(s) the payment

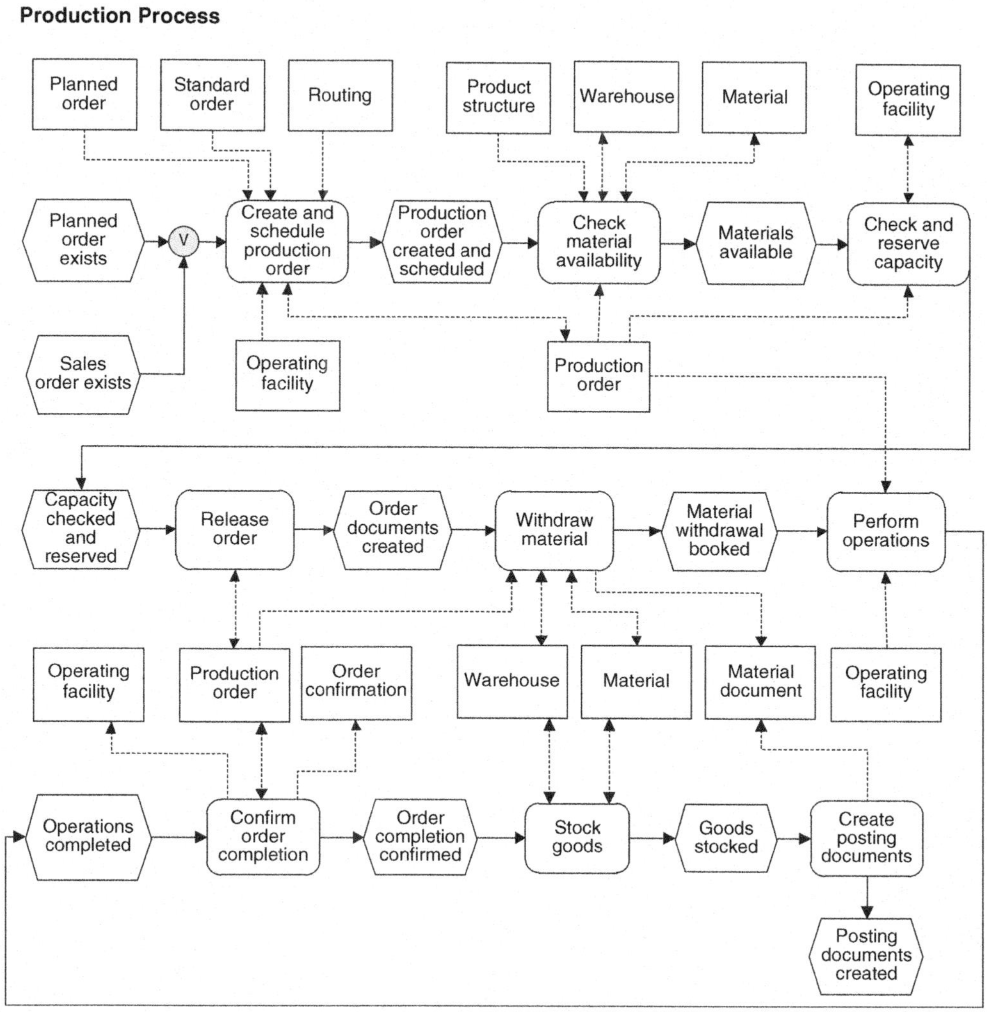

Fig. 5.24 Production process including information objects

refers to must be selected. When the payment has been associated with one or more open items, its status changes from "not assigned" to "assigned." In our example (cf. Fig. 5.22), there is only one open item, which has originated from the invoice of Fig. 5.21.

With the posting of the received payment, the order fulfillment process is completed.

5.3.4 Production

As in the preceding sections, we will continue the production process discussed in Chap. 4 and demonstrate, with the help of screenshots, what the process looks like when it is implemented in SAP ERP. The process steps shown in Fig. 4.13 continue to exist, but the ERP system performs some of them automatically or in the background. That is why a few activities will appear in an aggregated manner or in a different order than before.

Working with an ERP system requires the simple process scheme of Fig. 4.13 to be extended by *information objects*. Most process steps need data from the ERP database. Since the database can be accessed by all ERP modules, the same information is available in all process steps and is up-to-date everywhere.

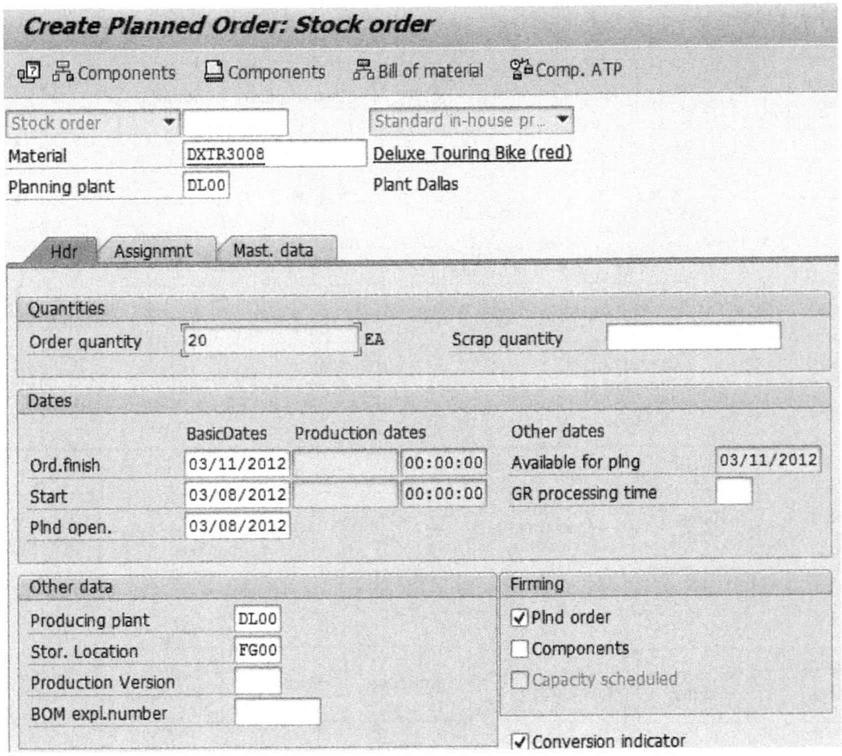

Fig. 5.25 Planned order form

Important information objects stored in the central ERP database are summarized in Fig. 5.23, including:

- *Master data:* material, product structure, warehouse, routing, and operating facility
- *Transaction data:* planned order, standard order, production order, material document, and order confirmation

The production process, complemented by the information objects above, is displayed in Fig. 5.24. It is initiated either by an event "planned order exists" (resulting from requirements planning) or by an event "standard order exists" (from order fulfillment). It is also possible that several such orders exist. If this is the case, the orders can be combined into one production order in the first process step.

Figure 5.25 shows an example of a *planned order* that is created to fill up the inventory. It is a "stock order" specifying 20 deluxe touring bikes (red) to be finished by 11th March 2012. As can be seen from the figure, a planned order already contains a number of items required for a production order (e.g., material, dates, plant). These data are automatically transferred when the production order is created. The "basic dates" displayed within the planned order are the rough dates determined in material requirements planning (cf. Sect. 2.3.2).

The *production order* created from the planned order is shown in Fig. 5.26. A production order consists of a header and many more components. The header shown in the figure contains data referring to the entire production order, for example, the order quantity, material, basic dates (start 8th March, end 11th March) and scheduling type ("backwards").

In addition to the basic dates, the start and end dates resulting from lead-time scheduling (cf. Sect. 3.3.1) are displayed under the heading "scheduled." According to lead-time scheduling, the production is supposed to start on 9th August at 08:00 h and end on 10th August at 10:17 h. These dates were computed when the production

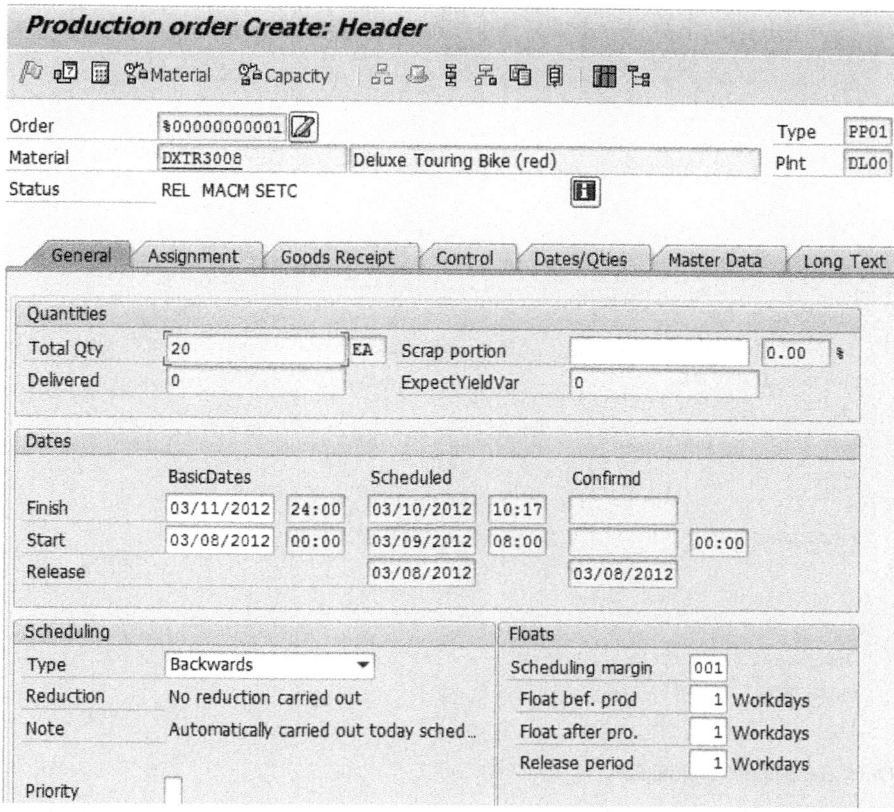

Fig. 5.26 Production order form

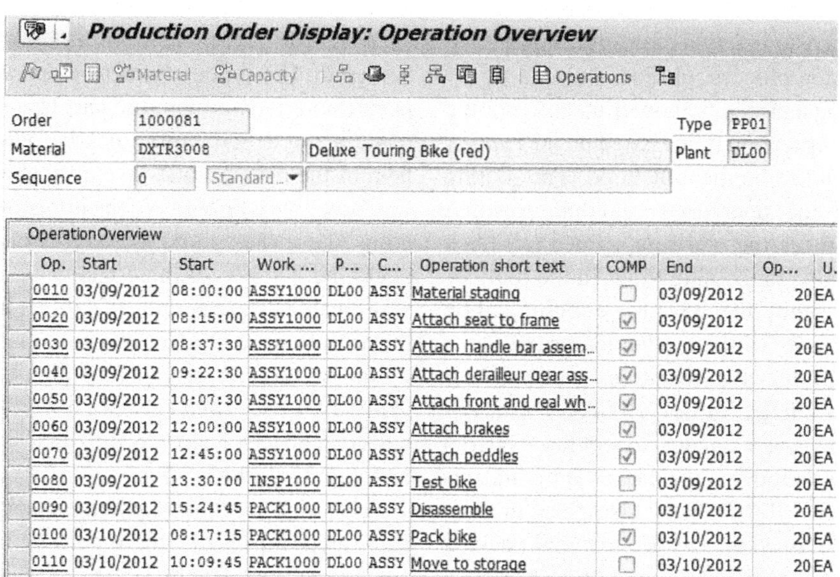

Fig. 5.27 Operations overview

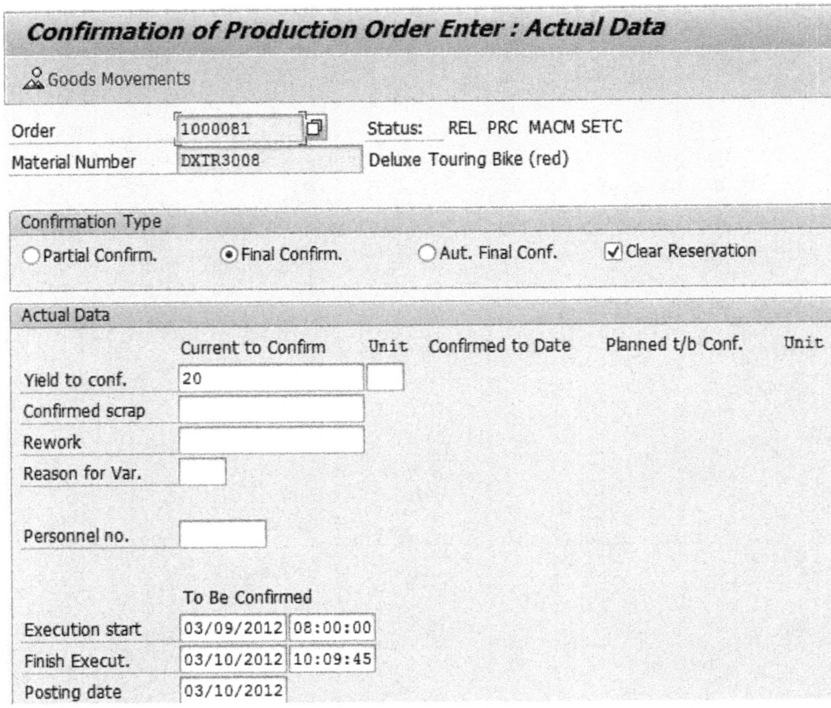

Fig. 5.28 Order completion confirmation

planner started the order creation. The reason why this happened is that our SAP ERP system was configured in such a way that production orders are to be automatically scheduled upon creation. Configuration decisions like this are made in the customization stage during the ERP implementation process (cf. Sect. 6.3).

Scheduling a production order means creating a network of operation times based on the *routing* of the material to be manufactured. The routing contains all the operations required, together with their processing and setup times (cf. Sect. 3.1.1). Since the processing times in the routings are given per unit, they have to be multiplied by the order quantity of the production order.

Figure 5.27 lists the operations scheduled for the above-mentioned order ("1000081"), beginning with material staging (operation "0010") and ending with moving the packed bikes to storage (operation "0110"). They take place in three work centers: assembly, inspection, and packing ("ASSY1000," "INSP1000," and "PACK1000"). The second and third columns indicate when the operations should start and end.

Checking material availability is initiated with the help of the "material" button on the order header form (cf. Fig. 5.26). In order to find out *which* materials have to be available, the *product structure* of the end product "DXTR3000" (deluxe touring bike red) is accessed. The product structure specifies which parts (materials) go into the part (material) to be manufactured. Available stock is found with the help of the material and inventory master data.

Capacity requirements resulting from scheduling the order were already booked in the operating facility master data when the order was created. The operating facilities involved in the operations were identified with the help of the routing. The planner can now check the availability of the required capacity by clicking on the button "capacity" next to the "material" button on the order header.

Assuming that the required capacity is available (as in Fig. 5.24), the order can be released and carried out. The first step is to withdraw the required materials from the warehouse. Material and warehouse data are accessed for this step,

Fig. 5.29 Time ticket including operation completion confirmation

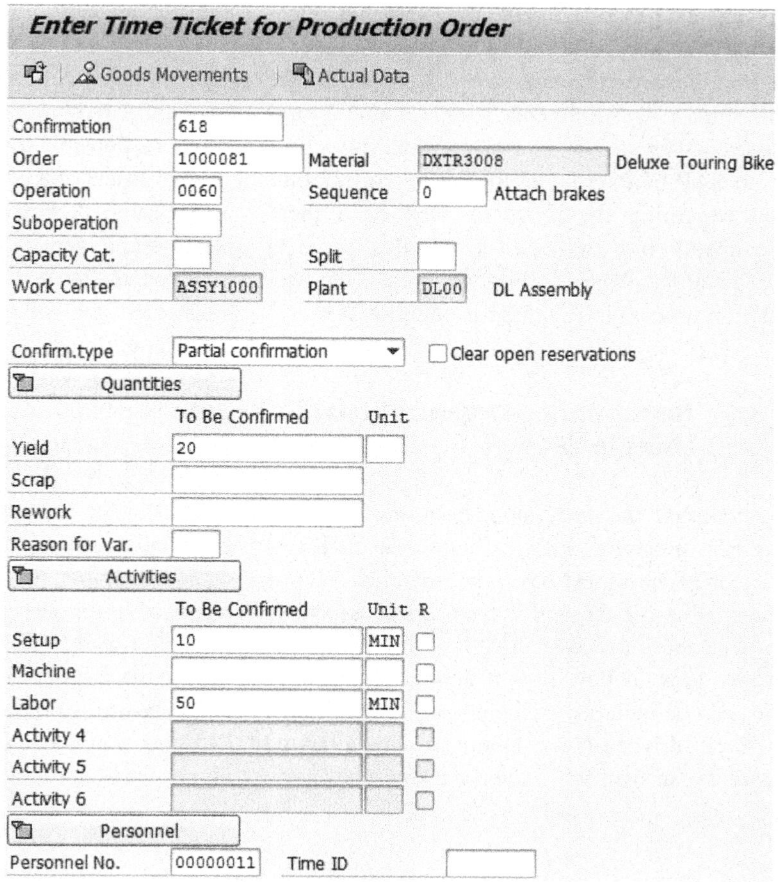

while a material document is automatically created and stored.

When the operations are completed, the completion is confirmed, and a corresponding document is created. In the simplified process, displayed in Fig. 5.24, completion is confirmed only when the entire order is finished. Figure 5.28 shows a screen for "final confirmation" of the order "1000081." The actual execution took place from 9th March, 08:00:00 h, to 10th March, 10:09:45 h, which was within the dates set by lead-time scheduling.

In other cases, it may be meaningful to confirm the completion of each individual operation instead of only confirming the entire order.

Figure 5.29 shows another means of providing completion information, namely a *time ticket* (or wage slip). This is a document workers use to prove the work they did (in order to get paid). At the same time, a company can collect information about order or operation completion by evaluating the time tickets. In our example, worker "00000011" reported that he completed the operation "0060" ("attach brakes"), which took him 1 hour (10 min for setup, 50 min for assembly work).

Along with the completion confirmation, the capacity requirements booked onto the operating facilities are removed, and the status of the production order is changed to "confirmed."

During the process step "stock goods," the finished goods are transferred to the warehouse. This is similar to other warehouse operations described previously. A number of "posting documents" are created and stored. These documents will be used by the accounting department to allocate the cost of the order and to update the accounts involved, for both managerial and financial accounting.

In Fig. 5.24, various accounting documents have been summarized under the term "posting documents." One of them, the "material document," has been explicitly mentioned because it reflects the incoming materials going on stock. The other documents are needed for accounting processes, which are outside the scope of this section.

In SAP ERP, creating the posting documents and triggering the processes that need these documents mostly occur automatically. With the creation of the posting documents, the production process in Fig. 5.24 is completed.

5.3.5 Representing Organizational Units in EPCs

To complete the discussion about implementing business processes with the help of an ERP system, one final aspect has to be included: Who is responsible for the various activities sequenced in a business process? In this section, we will briefly look at how organizational responsibilities can be included in the process descriptions.

Event-driven process chains provide a special symbol—an oval with a vertical line inside—to indicate an *organizational unit* (Scheer 2000, p. 53). This can be a person, a group, a department, or any other unit. Connecting the oval with an activity symbol means that the organizational unit is responsible for the activity (cf. Fig. 5.30).

The procurement process shown in Fig. 5.30 is the same process as in Fig. 5.8, but it has been complemented by the organizational units involved in the process. These units are warehouse management, purchasing, goods receiving, and accounting.

The reason why there are more than four ovals in the diagram is just to avoid intersecting lines. Therefore, the same organizational unit is repeated several times. The same procedure has been applied in the previous EPCs with regard to the information objects.

For example, the purchasing department is responsible for determining the source, selecting a supplier, and creating, sending, and monitoring the purchase order. Similarly, all other activities of the business process have now been assigned to either warehouse management, goods receiving, or accounting.

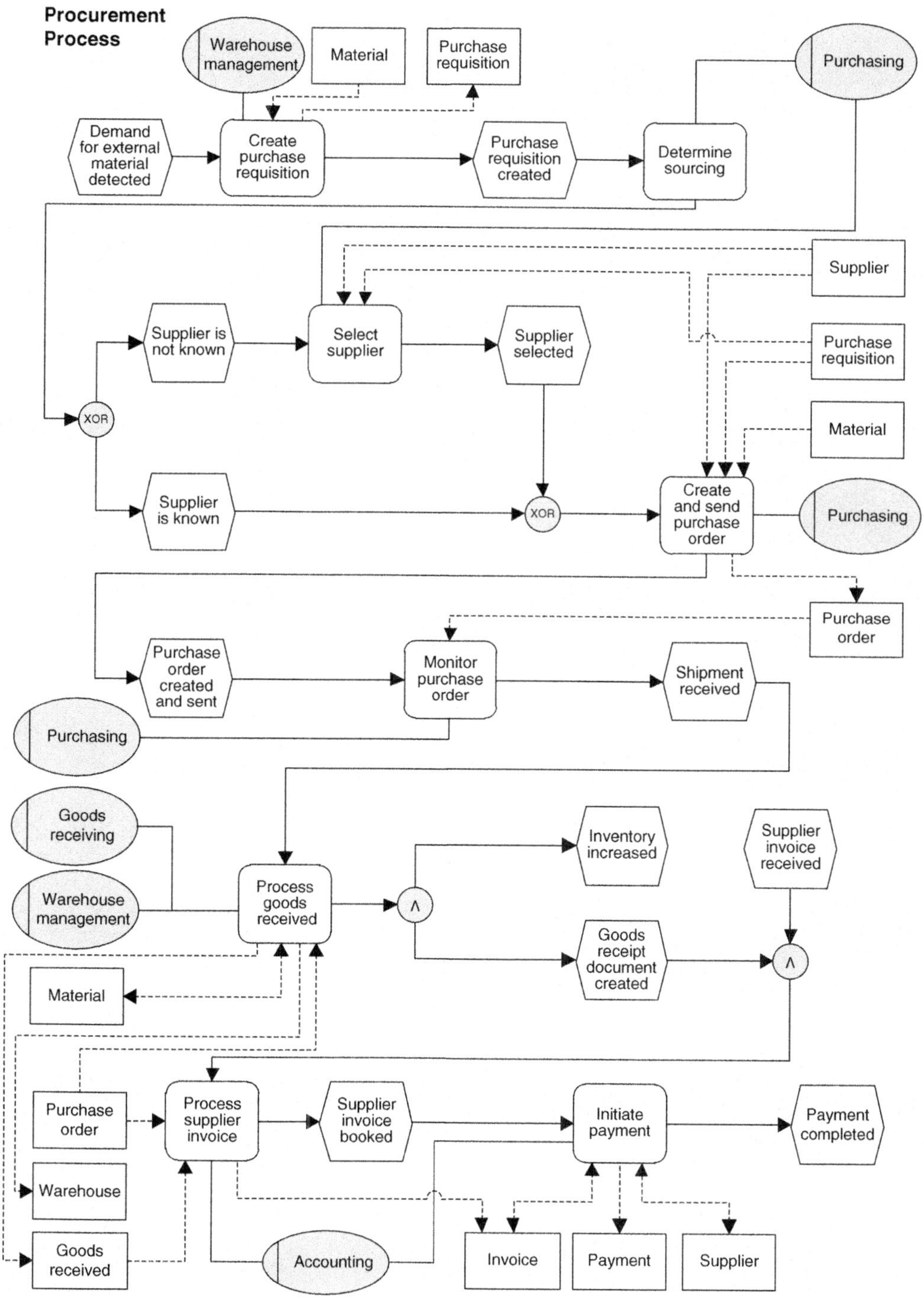

Fig. 5.30 EPC including organizational units

6 ERP System Implementation

Implementing an ERP system in an organization is a complex undertaking due to several factors.

Firstly, the implementation requires comprehensive *preparatory work*. For example, an ERP system is expected to support the company's specific business processes. In order to do so effectively, and in a way that takes the company's requirements into account, these processes must first be explicitly defined before they can be mapped onto the ERP system.

Another task that must be completed before the ERP system can be implemented is to define all the *organizational structures* of the company in terms of the concepts supported by the ERP system. Only afterward can the company's business processes and rules be represented within the ERP system.

Secondly, it is usually necessary to adapt the system. ERP systems are standard software, but this does not mean that the "standard" can be implemented in the company as is. The opposite is true, taking into account that every company has different requirements. The software firm that designed and developed the ERP system could not know and consider every possible requirement that might come up later. That is why the "standard" usually does not fit the company in question and needs to be adapted.

The amount of work needed for ERP system implementation can be seen in the financial reports of typical ERP vendors. In most cases, the revenue from software licenses makes up only a small portion of the total revenue. A larger portion is earned from service and support, with implementation and modification work constituting the major part.

Another indicator is that ERP implementation is an important line of business for the *consulting industry*. Many consulting firms as well as independent consultants earn their money by supporting user companies in implementing ERP systems, especially SAP ERP and other SAP systems.

Relying on the expertise of consultants makes sense because ERP implementation requires comprehensive knowledge on all levels—processes, functions, data, and information technology. A company implementing an ERP system once in 10 or 20 years does not have experts with the necessary knowledge and experience. Therefore, it is reasonable to consult external experts whose daily business is ERP implementation.

The *downside* to this is that the company becomes dependent upon the external consultants, who do not necessarily have the same goals as the company. Wu and Cao quote an information manager who stated that consultants are primarily interested in finishing an implementation project as quickly as possible. The company, however, is interested in obtaining the best possible solution. Because the consultants only present the option they decided upon, the company is often not aware of other possible alternatives (Wu and Cao 2009, p. 50).

K.E. Kurbel, *Enterprise Resource Planning and Supply Chain Management*,
Progress in IS, DOI 10.1007/978-3-642-31573-2_6, © Springer-Verlag Berlin Heidelberg 2013

6.1 Implementation Process and Methodology

6.1.1 Implementation Methodology

In the implementation process, a variety of factors need to be considered. There is a significant risk of forgetting some aspect or not choosing the best possible solution for an issue. That is why both consulting firms and ERP system vendors recommend employing a proven implementation methodology, that is, a methodology that has been successfully applied in other ERP projects.

How can a company planning to introduce a new ERP system find an appropriate methodology? Basically, there are three ways:

1. The *company* has an implementation methodology, which they perhaps developed themselves, improved over the years, and applied when implementing other software systems.
2. The company works with the *vendor* of the ERP system who has an implementation methodology and applies this methodology when contracted by the customer.
3. The company works with an external *consulting firm,* which employs its own methodology based on previous experience in ERP implementation, or the ERP vendor's recommended methodology.

The first case can be observed in large enterprises that frequently introduce and replace software. Although these companies usually have employees experienced in system implementation, applying the same methodology as in other software projects to an ERP project is risky. An ERP system is much larger than most other application systems and has far-reaching implications for the entire organization. A methodology that has worked well for other smaller systems may still fail when applied to an ERP system.

Most implementation projects use the second or third approach. Some large consulting firms have their own methodologies, whereas ERP vendors and many other consulting firms employ the vendor's methodology.

No matter which methodology is used, there is still a risk that some aspect may be forgotten or not considered at the right time. Suppose the company wishes to complete another project—replacing their obsolete numbering system with a new one—together with the ERP implementation. The new numbering system should go live when the new ERP system's warehousing module is launched in the organization. In this case, it would be too late to plan the transition from the old to the new numbering system when the warehousing module is about to be released. Instead, planning the transition should have started many months earlier, including steps such as notifying customers and suppliers, making provisions for the use of both the old and the new numbers during the transition period, training employees, etc.

Due to the complexity and intricacy of the implementation process, most nontrivial implementation methodologies are supported by *software tools*. In these tools, all the factors and the interdependencies between the factors that need to be considered are represented. Based on this information, the user is guided through the implementation process and reminded of open tasks.

In software engineering terminology, an implementation methodology is based on a *process model*. A process model describes a type of process that is divided into separate phases, each phase being characterized by a defined set of tasks to be completed. The process model also specifies the order in which the phases are carried out. Process models are common in application system development but are also used for other undertakings that can be divided into distinct phases.

6.1.2 ASAP: A Vendor-Specific Process Model

The following section describes, as an example, an implementation methodology that is based on a process model used for implementing SAP ERP systems. The underlying approach is called ASAP. While the abbreviation stands for *Accelerated SAP*, the name also intentionally connotes the common abbreviation "as soon as possible." ASAP is not only a process model but also includes a toolbox with computerized tools and many other supporting features.

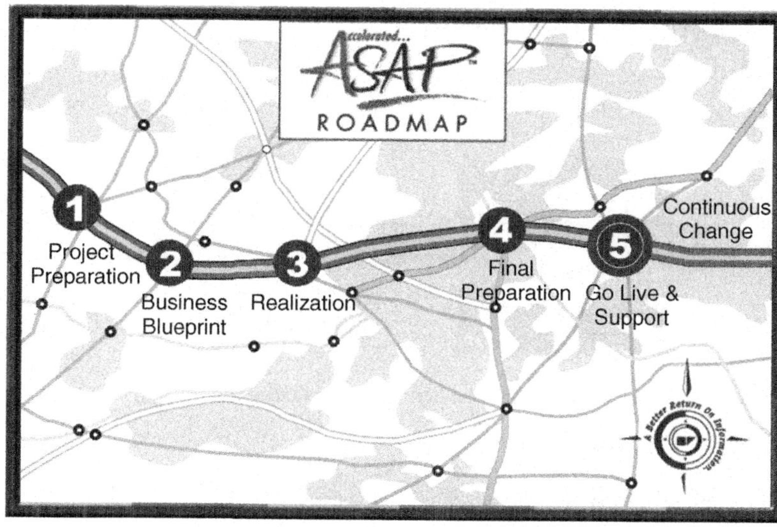

Fig. 6.1 ASAP roadmap (source: SAP AG)

ASAP was developed by SAP in the 1990s based on experiences and insights from customers, consultants, and SAP employees involved in R/3 implementation projects. Many of these projects took disproportionately long, caused high cost, and exceeded their budgets; others completely failed. This was not only a disadvantage for the company but also for SAP because potential new customers were frightened away by the high level of effort and the risk of failure involved.

Therefore, SAP created a methodology that would assist user companies in implementing R/3 more quickly and successfully. ASAP has been available worldwide since 1997. Today, it is employed for the implementation not only of SAP ERP but also of other SAP systems such as SCM, CRM, SRM, and PLM (cf. Sect. 1.2).

A well-known representation of the process model is the so-called *ASAP roadmap*. It visually depicts the five phases of the model on a map, as shown in Fig 6.1. The roadmap describes a reference model, starting with project preparation and including aspects such as business process engineering, technological issues, testing, user training, and productive operation.

Each phase of the roadmap includes concrete specifications for planning the phase (as a subproject) and for the project management within the phase. For this purpose, project management tools are provided in MS Project format. All activities within a phase are supported and supervised by an automated guide.

In the following, the five phases of the ASAP roadmap—project preparation, business blueprint, realization, final preparation, go live, and support—will be briefly outlined. More detailed descriptions can be found in SAP-related literature (e.g., Khan 2002).

Phase 1: Project Preparation The first phase comprises the planning and preparation of the entire implementation project. This includes defining the scope of the project, creating a project plan (time, budget, resources, etc.), setting up the project organization, and assigning members to the project team. Most project teams are composed of internal and external members, including managers, employees from the departments and/or business processes involved, external consultants, IT personnel, quality management personnel, and more.

Furthermore, the *change management* must be planned and communicated to all parties involved. Introducing a new ERP system implies changes in the organization and at the interfaces to the outside (customers, suppliers, banks, etc.). The business partners of the company will certainly appreciate being informed about the transition—and that their interaction with the company will not be disturbed during the transition period (Murray 2009, p. 333).

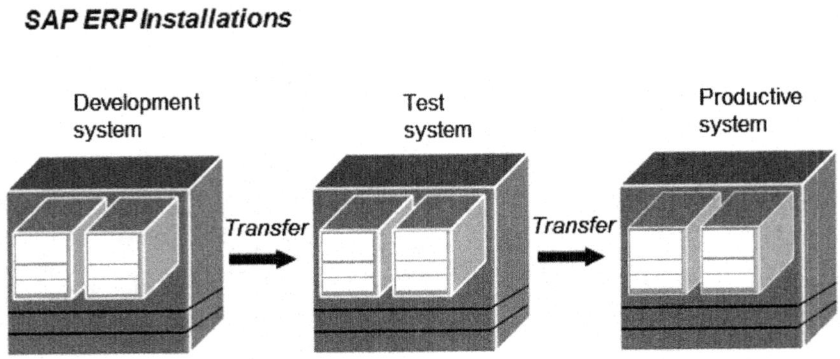

Fig. 6.2 SAP ERP system landscape with three installations

From a management point of view, it is important to define the *metrics* that can be used to evaluate the success or failure of the project. An ERP system is usually implemented in order to improve upon certain business goals, such as lowering inventory levels, reducing the working capital, shortening order lead times, or minimizing outstanding debts. It is important that the project stakeholders and the senior management agree on the desired improvements and on the indicators used to measure the improvements.

Significant aspects of the project are recorded in a *project charter*. This is where the people in charge define the project goals, scope and implementation strategy (e.g., incremental, parallel, "big bang"), the data migration strategy (i.e., transferring the previously used data to the new ERP system), and the decision-making procedure. This phase also defines the technical requirements and converts them into a rough draft of the system landscape.

The term "system landscape" primarily describes the various installations of the ERP system that are used during the implementation phase and later during the operation phase. Usually, there are at least three installations (cf. Fig. 6.2):

- *Productive system* (for the operational use of the ERP system after implementation)
- *Test system* (for quality assurance by the test team)
- *Development system* (for company-specific settings, extensions, and software changes)

During an implementation project, the *development system* is the first to be used. After the system has been configured to meet the functional specifications, it is transferred to the second installation, the *test system*, and thoroughly tested. When the tests have been successfully completed, the tested installation is adopted as the *productive system* and run with the operative data (in SAP terminology, this adoption is actually referred to as "transport").

In addition to these three systems, it can be helpful to utilize more installations for specific tasks so that the company's operations are not affected. Examples include a separate *training system* (for the training of the users) and a *customizing system* (for adapting the system to the company's needs, cf. Sect. 6.2).

The first phase of the ASAP roadmap also encompasses the *project kickoff*, that is, the official start of the project in the company. While work up to now was mostly done by consultants and a few selected employees, the kickoff signals to the company's employees and other stakeholders that the project is starting to really get going.

As is the case with all phases, the "project preparation" phase ends with a *quality check* to make sure that the tasks belonging to this phase have all been carried out, and there have been no undesired side effects.

Phase 2: Business Blueprint In the second phase, the so-called *business blueprint* is created. The blueprint can be seen as an abstract description of the future ERP system. It consists of a set of analysis and design documents to be used as a starting point in the next phase (realization).

Creating a business blueprint requires both analysis and design work. In contrast to other process models, ASAP does not specify an explicit phase for as-is analysis. Instead, the target concept is developed directly. For this purpose, the requirements, which were roughly established in the project charter, are now set down in more detail. Then the requirements are compared with the functionality of SAP ERP. Requirements that cannot be met are identified and discussed separately. The team has to decide whether or not these requirements should be satisfied through other means (e.g., by integrating third-party software or by individual development).

The business blueprint phase is characterized by regular project meetings and workshops. In the workshops, requirements are elaborated in cooperation with experienced consultants and employees who are involved in the business processes.

A large portion of the activities in this phase consists of defining and documenting the company's business processes. SAP provides a *reference model* along with the ERP software, which contains typical business processes and available system functions. The reference model describes the functions with regard to the business processes where the functions are invoked. *Event-driven process chains (EPCs)* are used to graphically map out the business processes. This notation has already been introduced in Chaps. 4 and 5.

In addition to the process specifications, the reference model comprises a number of submodels:

- Process model (flow of the business processes)
- Data model (or object model; data/objects and their relationships)
- Component model (hierarchy of the system functions)
- Organization model (organizational structures, relationships between organizational units)
- Interaction model (communication between the involved parties)

The entity types of the data model (or the object types of the object model) are incorporated in the EPCs as *information objects*. This was already shown in the figures of Sect. 5.3. The *organizational units* (department, group, person, etc.) responsible for carrying out activities are also included in the reference model's EPCs. An example of this was given in Sect. 5.3.4.

In addition to defining the business processes and developing the submodels mentioned above, the business blueprint phase includes other *work packages* such as:

- Training the project team for the tasks involved in the business blueprint phase.
- Developing the system landscape further (e.g., distributing system functionality in the network, installing a development system for the project employees, configuring the implementation guide).
- Defining the company's organizational structures in order to be able to map it in the next phase to SAP ERP's organizational elements.
- Defining the data interfaces with other application systems that will continue to be in use after the ERP system has been implemented.
- Specifying the programs needed for transferring and converting data from the previously used systems (e.g., legacy systems, application systems that will be discontinued).
- Checking the quality at the end of a phase; this is in regard to the business blueprint documents created and whether design decisions, assumptions regarding sizing requirements, the selected system landscape (which, how many installations), and the planned use of certain system functions are appropriate.

Phase 3: Realization In the *realization* phase, the requirements, specifications, and design decisions that have been documented in the business blueprint are implemented. This means that, firstly, a version of the standard software fitting the company will be configured. Secondly, provisions will be made for those functions that are not covered by the standard software.

Realization is a very comprehensive phase, comprising most of the work involved in an implementation project. Especially worth noting, this phase is where *customization* happens, including all the company-specific settings to be made in the ERP software. This will be discussed in more detail below (cf. Sect. 6.2).

Besides customization, the ASAP roadmap specifies a number of other *work packages* for the realization phase, including:

- Training the project team for the tasks associated with the realization phase
- Global settings and representing the company organization in the software system as specified by the business blueprint
- Developing data-conversion and bridge programs, as well as individual system extensions, reports, and forms
- Baseline configuration (i.e., configuring a system representing the business processes, functions, and data that cover approximately 80 % of the requirements), testing, and accepting this configuration
- Detail configuration (configuring a system which covers all of the requirements), testing, and accepting this configuration
- Working out an authorization concept ("who may do what?"), based on role descriptions, functionalities needed by these roles, and authorization profiles
- Designing and implementing the archiving process for data that must be kept (e.g., because of legal requirements)
- Final testing to prepare for the productive operation of the ERP system
- Determining and preparing the necessary user documentation and training documents
- Quality checking, in terms of to what extent the phase 3 goals and the entire project goals have been achieved

Phase 4: Final Preparation The aim of the final preparation phase is to establish a working productive system that is ready to go live. This means that when the phase is completed, the company should be able to use the installed ERP system immediately in their day-to-day operations.

The so-called *cutover*, that is, the changeover from the previous system or status to the new ERP system, has to be carefully prepared.

In order to do so, a *system management* is established, which has to ensure the technical system availability. *Final tests* are performed (especially regarding nonfunctional requirements like recovery, performance, and security), *data* from the previous systems are transferred and converted, and *bridge programs* (interface programs) supplying data to and from other application systems are put in place. Experience shows that problems often occur while migrating data, and correcting these errors can be a time-consuming task.

An important aspect of the final preparation phase is *training the users*. This requires the documents mentioned in phase 3 to be created and afterward the training measures to be executed.

The settings and extensions that were carried out and tested in the development or customization system now have to be transferred to the *productive system*. Before this can be done, however, the productive system has to be set up.

With the *cutover*, the productive operation of the new system begins. A *quality check* at the end of the phase makes sure that all final preparation tasks have been properly completed, and the productive operation can begin.

Phase 5: Go Live and Support The tasks in this final ASAP phase primarily have to ensure that the ERP system runs stably. The main focus is user support (help desk, hotline, etc.). If there is further need for training, then additional training materials must be created and training measures taken.

Errors and shortcomings of the new solution that become apparent only after the system was actually implemented are recorded. They are either dealt with and resolved immediately, or are saved as issues to come back to at a later time.

Furthermore, the metrics that were defined at the beginning to determine the project's successes and/or shortcomings are collected. Where necessary, new approaches and metrics are developed to regularly evaluate the ERP system during its operation.

The final step in the "go live and support" phase is to formally end the implementation project and dissolve the project team.

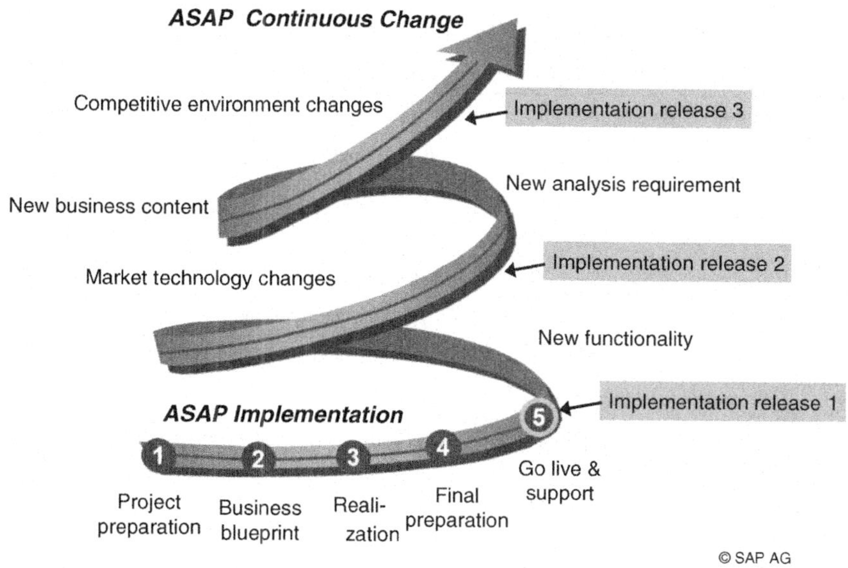

Fig. 6.3 Continuous change to an ERP system (source: SAP AG)

Continuous Change The end of the current project is not the end of the ASAP roadmap. A comprehensive application system such as an ERP system continually changes over the course of its life cycle, as illustrated in Fig. 6.2. After the first system version has been implemented ("release 1"), new findings, experiences, and requirements usually come up. These can stem from a variety of sources, for example, when market-standard technologies change, when the Fig. 6.3 competitive environment of the company shifts, when new business fields are being explored, or when new functionality of the ERP system becomes available.

Therefore, the first ASAP project is only the beginning. More projects will follow. Later projects may be small, for example, when implementing a new system version with limited changes compared to the previous one, or quite large, for example, when installing a new version with different functionality and a new user interface.

In the first case, the business blueprint can more or less be taken as is, whereas in the second, it may be necessary to adjust the models and the realization. This would require external know-how, comprehensive user and administrator training, and possibly data transfer and a complete battery of new tests (function, performance, recovery, and other tests).

6.1.3 Implementation Cost: Total Cost of Ownership

Many different costs are associated with implementing an ERP system. They occur at different times and in different frequencies (one-time, recurrent, etc.).

Total cost of ownership (TCO) is an approach that attempts to capture all cost-inducing facets of an IT project. This approach was originally developed by the Gartner Group, based on an investigation of IT costs. They found that the immediately visible cost (software license or purchase price) is often relatively small in comparison to the "other" costs such as training and supporting the users, maintaining the hardware and software, and coping with system crashes (vom Brocke 2012).

In order to determine the total cost of ownership, a distinction is usually made between direct and indirect costs.

Direct costs are the costs directly associated with implementing an ERP system (e.g., licensing cost, hardware cost). These costs can be further divided into one-time (nonrecurrent) and recurrent costs. *One-time costs* are usually included in the budget of the implementation project, while *recurrent costs*, when foreseeable, are considered in the project proposal and justification (Kurbel 2008, pp. 28–29).

One-time Project Costs	Recurrent Costs
Software licenses	Software licenses
Server hardware	Software maintenance
Infrastructure	Software upgrades
Consulting (external)	End-user support (internal)
Project team (internal)	End-user support (external)
IT support (internal)	Hardware and infrastructure operation
End-user training	Additional end-user training
Administrator training	Additional administrator training
Project team training	Server and infrastructure maintenance
Data adoption and conversion	Server and infrastructure upgrades

Fig. 6.4 Direct costs of ERP implementation (Murray 2009, pp. 342–343)

Indirect Costs
Impact of system downtime
Impact of system errors and poor performance
Retraining of end-users
Additional vendor support
Lower end-user productivity
Inadequate business processes

Fig. 6.5 Indirect cost drivers in ERP implementation (Murray 2009, p. 344)

Figure 6.4 lists the most important one-time and recurring costs associated with ERP implementation (Murray 2009, pp. 342–344). The main reason why some cost types appear in both columns is that these costs can occur both as one-time and as recurrent costs. For example, software licenses depend on the contract model (annual payments, one-time payment to install the software with later payments for upgrades, etc.). User training generally takes place during system implementation, but further training may also be needed later for new employees or when the system is upgraded.

Indirect costs are harder to quantify than the direct costs, which can often be measured immediately in monetary units. In many cases, the indirect costs have to be *estimated*, although it can be quite difficult to obtain reasonable estimates. For example, it is hardly plausible to put a price on a system error because the "price" depends on the consequences the error has for the company's operations or the users' work.

Figure 6.5 shows a few of the common cost drivers associated with ERP implementation. Especially critical are cost drivers that negatively impact customer satisfaction. For example, if orders are delivered late due to initial weak points of the new solution and customers decide to switch to a competitor, the effect can be long-term revenue loss.

Although they are difficult to measure accurately, indirect costs are usually regarded as quite high. Murray quotes a statement made by Gartner Group, who claim that the indirect cost of an IT infrastructure can make up 60 % of the total cost (Murray 2009, pp. 343–344). Taking the difficulty of measuring into consideration, such numbers are certainly disputable; nevertheless, they indicate that the indirect cost is perceived as a significant factor.

Some direct and indirect costs of implementing an ERP system are dependent on each other. Reducing direct costs often results in increased indirect costs. Two examples clearly show the effects of an inappropriate reduction of the direct costs (Murray 2009, pp. 343–344):

1. By purchasing fewer services from external consultants, direct costs are decreased. However, this increases the risk that the system is not installed adequately and requires reworking during the operation phase (including external consulting support), which would increase the indirect costs.
2. The second example is a practical case, where the budget for user training was reduced. Instead of training 40 production and warehouse employees, now only the 4 shift managers were trained. After the system went live, the shift managers were the only ones who knew how to use the system. Because they now had to spend their time entering data and completing business transactions, they had less time to attend to the production, stock keeping, and decision making. This slowed down the processes, resulting in delayed customer shipments and decreased customer satisfaction. In the end, the company had to train all the users at additional costs and, on top of this, also had to deal with the effects of the production delays and missed delivery dates.

6.2 Customizing

Customizing usually refers to tailoring an information system to the specific requirements of the company during the *system implementation* phase. This does not mean, however, that the system will not need to be adapted or extended later on, during the operation phase. The opposite is true.

Subsequent changes to the ERP system may be called for when, for example, new market developments require the company to offer additional services. Other situations may also ask for changes to the ERP system, for example, mergers, setting up virtual enterprises; intercompany cooperations such as collaborative planning, forecasting, and replenishment (CPFR); and vendor-managed inventory (VMI), which will be discussed in Sect. 8.2.3. In all of these cases, the various systems used by the different companies must be brought into agreement.

Modifications and extensions of the ERP system *after* the implementation project is completed are usually not comprised by the term customizing. Instead, they are either considered as part of the system maintenance or as separate change projects. However, modifications and extensions conducted within further ASAP implementation projects may again involve customization.

6.2.1 Forms of Customizing

The term "customizing" describes the process of tailoring a standard software system to individual requirements. In ERP implementation, this means that the company does not use the system "as is" (i.e., the data structures, forms, and processes as given by the ERP vendor). Instead, they configure their own data structures, forms, and processes according to their own detailed requirements.

Although tailoring is usually desirable, departing too much from the "standard" also has its disadvantages. ERP software incorporates best practices and experience gathered by the ERP vendor from many implementation projects. By deviating from the standard, the company cannot benefit from this added know-how. That is why experienced consultants and ERP vendors advise staying as close to the standard processes and data structures as possible. They encourage customers to critically analyze the company's process organization to examine to what extent the company can be adjusted to the standard software.

Customizing can be done on various levels and in different grades. The most important forms are the following:

Parameterization (Customizing in the Narrow Sense) *Customizing in the narrow sense* means that the system is adjusted with the help of settings that the individual company specifies when the system is implemented. This is also called *parameterization* because the user assigns values to predetermined system parameters.

Software companies developing large application systems are aware that different user companies will require different functions and data. Therefore, they include a wide array of functions and data structures in their systems. A particular customer may choose from the available options by setting the system parameters in such a way that they reflect the company's specific requirements.

Parameterization is the preferred approach to tailoring an application system because the software vendor has already implemented the features in question. This means that no additional programming is necessary. The user "only" needs to choose from the available features and enter company-specific values.

However, this approach has certain disadvantages for the ERP vendor as well as for the user. The vendor must consider all of the possible settings in the system design and implement all possible functions. Because of this, systems that can be parameterized are often very large and unwieldy.

For the user, parameterizing a system is an extremely arduous task. The user must be able to judge the effects of the various parameters and their settings. In practice, this is impossible because of the large numbers of parameters and parameter combinations. In SAP R/3, for example, the production planning module (PP) alone offers 150–200 parameters, 40 of which are bound to a particular part. This results in approximately one million parameters for a medium-sized company (Dittrich et al. 2009a, p. 1). All of these parameters have to be set and maintained!

Not only is the sheer number of parameters unmanageable, it also is very difficult to oversee the interdependencies between the parameters. Most users are not aware of how parameter settings impact other parameters.

User Exits (Program Exits) User exits (also known as "program exits" or "customer exits") are predefined places in the program code where external programs can be invoked (Kurbel 2008, pp. 450–452). With the help of such programs, customers can apply their own problem-solving procedures. User exits are often employed when the ERP vendor foresees the need of individual solutions but is unable (or unwilling) to implement them. The reason for this can be that solutions are so customer specific that other customers would not be able to use them, or the implementation is too costly.

Application Programming Interfaces In order to allow other parties besides the organization developing the software to perform changes or extensions, some vendors provide programming interfaces. In software engineering, these interfaces are called *APIs (application programming interfaces)*. By using APIs, programs developed by the user company can employ prefabricated modules provided by the system vendor.

Comprehensive APIs are common in modern software systems. In the Java world, APIs are the predominant interface mechanism. Through APIs and module libraries, reusable software components can be embedded in newly developed information systems.

Changing the Program Code Making changes directly to the ERP system's program code is another way to "bend" the standard solution implemented in the system into an individual solution. In order to do so, the user must have access to the program code (i.e., the source text in the programming language the system is written in), be able to understand the code, and have the right to make changes. Theoretically, this would allow any part of the ERP system to be reprogrammed, but it is not advisable for reasons explained below.

Individual Development Software development outside the ERP system is a way to create individual solutions to problems not covered by the system. It is advisable to embed individual software in the ERP system through features such as user exits, APIs, or an enterprise portal. Otherwise, the end user must work with different application systems and cope with the shortcomings associated with this, such as different user interfaces and perhaps redundant data.

Model-Based Generation When looking at customization from a wider angle, this term also includes the customization of *models* from which program code is *generated.*

In order to reduce the high cost of software development in general and adaptation programming in particular, computer science began early on to work on the generation of software from specifications. For application development, this means that the major share of development work is shifting to a higher level, the level of models.

The foundation of a generated system is an *information model.* Based on this model, the system components are created automatically. Depending on the underlying paradigm, an information model can describe business processes, operations, functions, objects, data, and/or organizational structures.

When adjustments have to be made, they are done on the level of the information model or its submodels. This means, for example, that adjustments regarding data are carried out in entity-relationship diagrams (ER models) or class diagrams (class models), while adjustments regarding activities are carried out in process or workflow models. Provided that the models have been created with a modeling tool and saved in a repository, the program code and the database schema can be automatically generated.

Cutting-edge approaches to model-based generation of information systems date back to the early 1990s, when powerful CASE (computer-aided software engineering) tools were developed. A well-known approach of the time is *information engineering*, which was made popular by James Martin (1989). Information engineering is a comprehensive conceptual framework for an enterprise-wide information systems architecture, including automated models and tools for the construction of operational systems.

Componentware Creating an information system using *software components* is based upon the same idea as model-based generation: reduction of development and maintenance costs and shortening the development time. Software components are put together according to a *component model* in order to create a software system (Crnkovic et al. 2011, p. 24). The corresponding software technology is known as *componentware.*

There are different interpretations of what exactly a "component" is. In the Java world, the term is used to describe *class libraries.* In a Microsoft Office environment, solutions based on one or more *Office programs* (Excel, Access, Word, etc.) have been named componentware. Here, the "components" are the partial solutions created with one of the Office programs. In web-based systems, components can be *web services*, that is, functionality provided on the Internet that can be invoked in another software.

Customizing using componentware means that only individual components need to be modified or exchanged. For example, one web service will be replaced by another.

6.2.2 Disadvantages of Individual Solutions

As mentioned before, parameterization is the preferred form of customizing because it requires less effort than the other types. Compared to parameterization, alternative ways of customizing have serious shortcomings, especially user exits, APIs, code changes, and individual development. They all involve "programming" in one way or another—including all of the time-consuming requirements of programming: specification, design work, testing, solving interface issues, documentation, etc.

These are typical tasks of software engineering. However, the focus is different from "conventional" software engineering, which is usually concerned with the development of new systems. Here, the whole system already exists, so the challenges are basically to understand the system architecture, the interfaces, and the program code that are already in place and then to change or expand upon them as needed.

Special software engineering issues that need to be considered in ERP customization are discussed by Dittrich and coauthors, based upon the customization of the Microsoft ERP systems Dynamics Nav and Dynamics AX (Dittrich et al. 2009b).

Knowledge and experience from previous projects play an important role in the customization of software. Wu und Cao describe an approach to make experience-based customizing knowledge available with the help of a software tool (Wu and Cao 2009). This approach uses *case-based reasoning (CBR)* (Bareiss 1989; Riesbeck and Schank 1989), a branch of *artificial intelligence (AI)*.

In addition to the high effort involved in in-house development, consequences for the future also need to be considered. These consequences show when the ERP vendor brings a new system version to the market and the company decides to install this version. Depending on which customizing form was chosen before, there can be various consequences:

- When the system has only been *parameterized* (customizing in the narrow sense), one can usually expect that the settings defined in the previous version will be automatically carried over to the new version, and no additional adjustments will be required.
- Extensions made with the help of *user exits* are also relatively stable regarding the migration of one system version to the next. Having defined the exit points before, the ERP vendor knows that they exist and need to be considered in the transition. Nevertheless, it is advisable to test the user exists in the new version to see if they are still working properly.
- *APIs* are similar to user exists, in that they are controlled by the system vendor. Customers can expect that the APIs will function properly in the new system version.
- *Code changes* in the ERP system are very risky when it comes to new versions or updates, because the changes exist only in the company-specific variant, and are not a part of the standard software. Obviously, the ERP vendor develops the next version of the system on the basis of the standard version. This means that the user company has to transfer all changes they made to the new version and perform system tests themselves to make sure that the altered ERP modules continue to function.
- *Individual software* developed outside the standard software must also be tested by the user company to see whether the interfaces to the new version of the ERP system are working properly. If the ERP vendor switched to a different software technology, the individual software may also have to be migrated to the new technology and/or partly reprogrammed.

6.3 Vendor-Specific Customizing: SAP ERP

This section will outline the customization of a specific ERP system: SAP ERP. Based on this example, the reader will gain some insights into the actual customization tasks in practice. However, given the complexity of the matter, we will only be able to scratch the surface.

In the ASAP roadmap shown in Fig. 6.1, customization takes place in the realization phase (phase 3). Two forms of customizing are distinguished in SAP ERP: client-independent and client-specific customizing:

- *Client-independent customizing* includes settings that apply to all clients maintained in an SAP ERP system. This can be, for example, setting the currency or the calendars to be used.
- *Client-specific customizing* only affects a single client. Examples of this include company codes and plants that are defined for a specific client only. User data and application data are managed on the client level and cannot be used by multiple clients.

Figure 6.6 shows these differences using three different clients. The *repository* is where programs, forms, menus, and other development objects are saved. Programs created by the user company (see Sect. 6.2.2) are also stored in the repository.

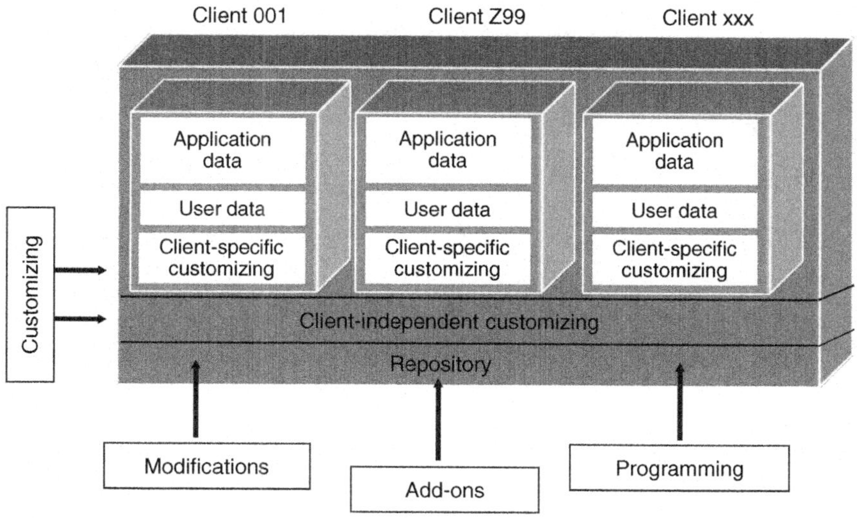

Fig. 6.6 SAP ERP clients and customization options (source: SAP AG)

The settings to be done in customization take place on different levels. They can be roughly divided into three categories:

- *Global settings* such as the definition of countries, currencies, time zones, and measurement units.
- Representing the company's *organization* in SAP ERP terminology, using the generic organizational units provided. This is necessary in order to be able to adjust (and later, to execute) the business processes because processes always refer to certain organizational units.
- Setting the parameters for the various SAP ERP *modules*, covering all functional areas and business processes involved in the company's operations.

To configure the business processes, most companies employ the *reference model* (see Sect. 6.1.2), which contains standardized processes. This model is then altered to fit the company's processes as specified in the business blueprint.

The tool used for customizing is the so-called *implementation guide (IMG)*, which is integrated in SAP ERP. The implementation guide is structured in a similar way as the ERP system itself, that is, according to functional areas. The fact that it is integrated in the system structure means that, among other things, the user customizing the system navigates through menu hierarchies and completes given transactions (called customization transactions). In this sense, the implementation guide actually leads the user through the customization steps.

To a certain degree, the sequence in which the settings should be done is predefined by their order in the implementation guide. Users are expected to work through the steps in the given order because parameters can depend on other parameters that have to be set earlier. By going through the settings in the given sequence, interdependencies are handled in the correct way.

The implementation guide provided by SAP ERP is the so-called *reference IMG*. It includes all of the system's possible adjustments (including the default settings)—for all functional modules and all global settings.

Hardly any company will need the entire functionality of the ERP system. A bank, for example, has no need for shop-floor control. Therefore, most companies create their own specific implementation guides based on the reference IMG, called a *company IMG*. This IMG is a subset of the reference IMG, containing only those customizing transactions that are relevant for the company. A company IMG applies to a complete SAP ERP installation, that is, to all clients of the installation.

Since ERP implementation is a comprehensive and lengthy endeavor, companies often split it up into several projects (or subprojects). For example, the first project is concerned with implementing

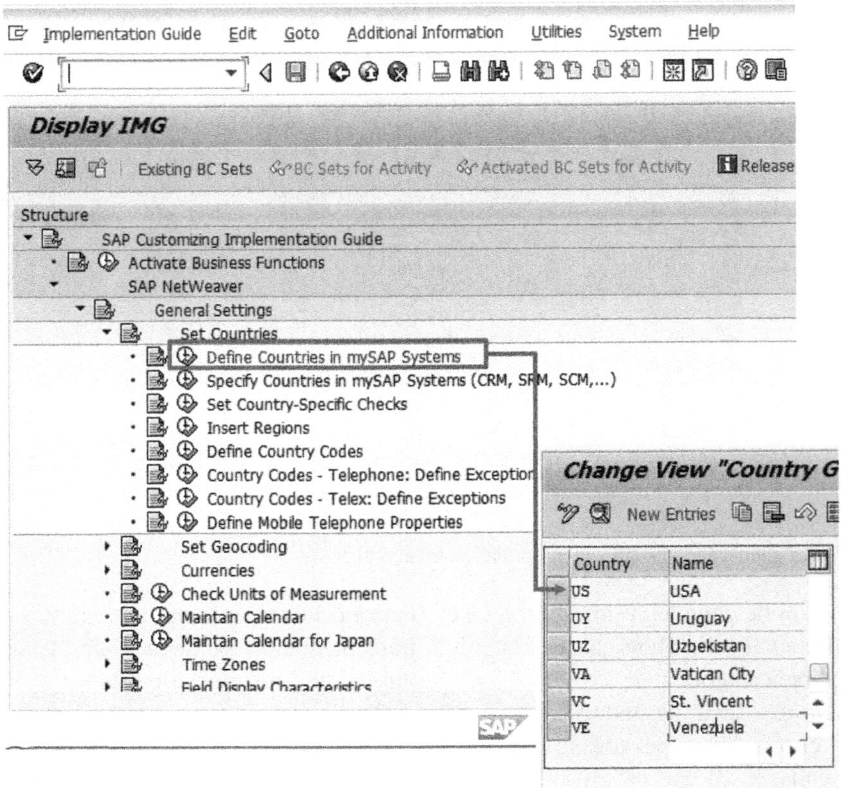

Fig. 6.7 General settings: country definition

material management, the next with implementing sales and distribution. In such a case, a project-oriented implementation guide (*project IMG*) to be used by the projects (or subprojects) can be created from the company IMG.

Furthermore, so-called *views* of a project may be defined. By using views, a project IMG can be narrowed down even further. Subteams within the project team, which are assigned different tasks, will then only see those parts of the project IMG that are relevant for their particular customizing work.

6.3.1 General Settings

In the following, some examples of parameter settings will be explained with the help of the reference IMG. This IMG is provided in the "customizing" section of the "tools" part in the SAP ERP main menu.

Client-independent parameters are set in the SAP NetWeaver section of the implementation guide under "general settings," as can be seen from Fig. 6.7. As an example, the entry "set countries" has been expanded. The user clicked "define countries in mySAP systems" and received a scrollable list of countries to choose from. When a country is selected, the general rules and regulations for that country are activated.

Figure 6.7 shows that a company implementing SAP ERP has to stipulate additional general settings including currencies, calendars, and time zones.

6.3.2 Organizational Structures

In addition to the general settings, one of the earliest customizing tasks that need to be completed is to define the company's organizational structure. This means that the specific

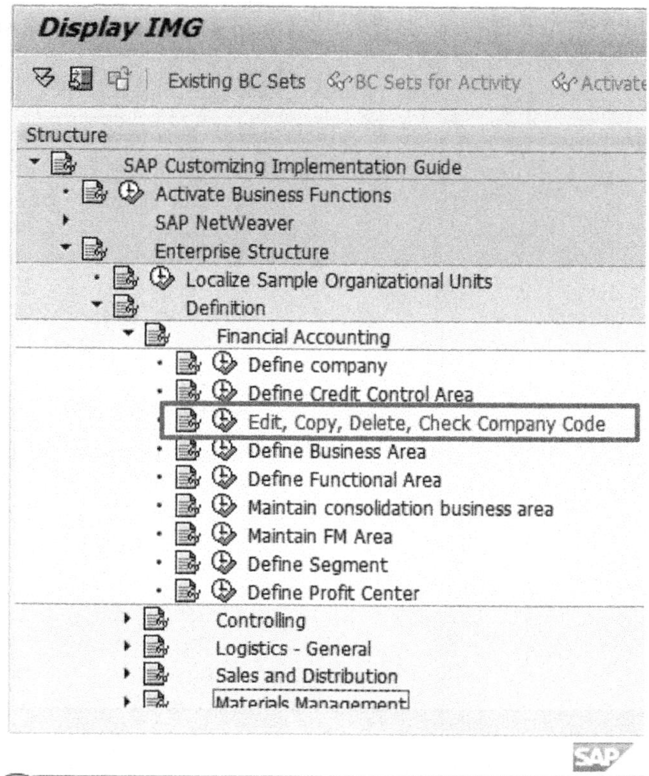

© SAP AG

Fig. 6.8 Enterprise structure: company codes

organization has to be represented using the terminology and organizational elements provided by SAP ERP. This mapping was already discussed in Sect. 4.2.

The following section gives an example illustrating some of the steps, including the definition of a company code and a plant, and assigning the plant to a company code.

The section of the implementation guide where organizational structures are defined is "enterprise structure." Figure 6.8 shows the navigation path to the transaction where a new company code can be created ("edit, copy, delete, check company code").

The company we are looking at is "Global Bike." It already has two company codes, DE00 ("Global Bike Germany GmbH") and US00 ("Global Bike Inc.") as displayed in part (a) of Fig. 6.9.

Suppose Global Bike wants to expand into Eastern Europe and has established a new company for this purpose. This company is located on the German side of the Polish border, in Frankfurt (Oder). The middle part of Fig. 6.9 shows how the company code PL00 is defined for this company, called "Global Bike East KG." Address details, etc. are given in a separate screen that has been omitted from the figure.

The result can be seen in part (c). Global Bike now has three company codes, DE00, US00, and PL00.

In the next step, a plant belonging to Global Bike East will be defined. This takes place in the "logistics—general" section of the enterprise structure definition part, under the item "define, copy, delete, check plant" (cf. Fig. 6.10).

Global Bike already has five plants, as shown in part (a) of Fig. 6.11. The new plant that was defined is "SL00 Zaklad Slubice-Frankfurt." Some entries in the definition of the plant can be seen in the middle of the figure. The result is that now six plants exist (cf. part c).

The next step is to associate the new plant with a company code. As already mentioned in Sect. 4.2.2, a plant must belong to exactly one company code. In our example, the plant "SL00

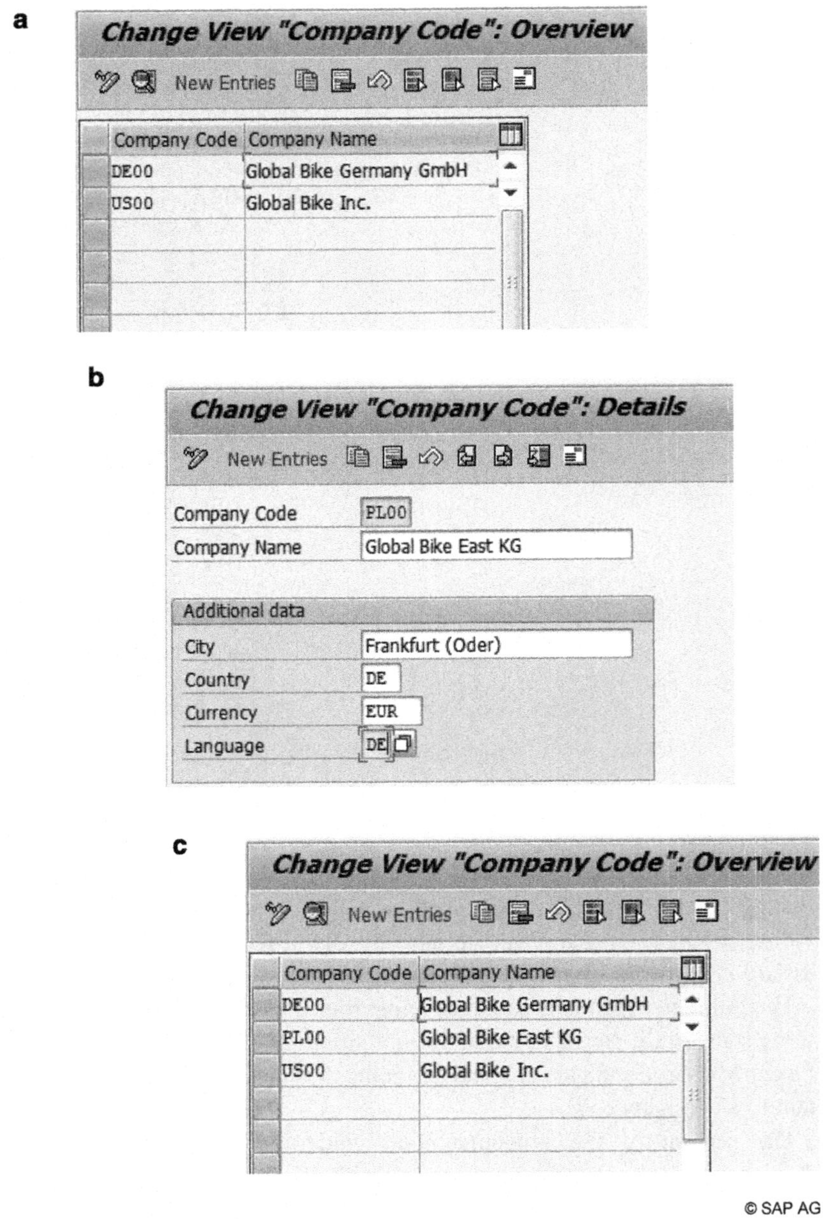

Fig. 6.9 Creating a company code

Zaklad Slubice-Frankfurt" is going to work for the new company "PL00 Global Bike East KG."

Assigning plants to company codes is a menu item that can be reached by following the path "enterprise structure," "assignment," "logistics," and "general," as shown in Fig. 6.12.

When a new entry in the assignment table associating the plant SL00 with the company code PL00 has been created, the organizational structure is as listed in Fig. 6.13. Global Bike has three plants belonging to company code US00 (Dallas, Miami, San Diego), two belonging to DE00 (Heidelberg, Hamburg), and one belonging to the new company code PL00 (Slubice-Frankfurt).

6.3.3 Process and Functional Settings

In theory, companies act according to the economic principle and pursue various goals, as discussed in Sect. 1.4.2. How to reach the goals is a different question because, in practice, the

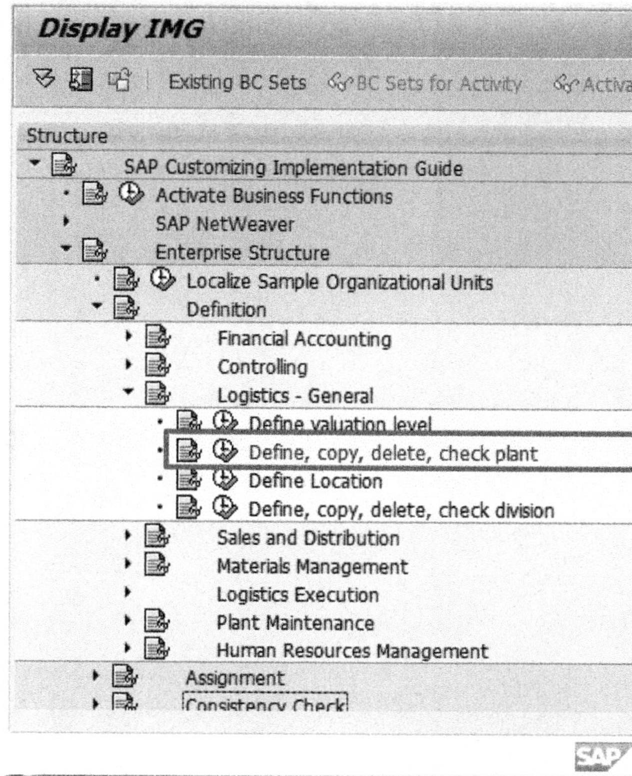

Fig. 6.10 Enterprise structure: plants

© SAP AG

variables are distributed across many business functions and processes. Today, most companies perform their functions and processes with the help of information systems. This means that the information systems must be configured in such a way that they behave according to the company's goals.

In practice, this is done by *customizing*, in particular, setting parameters. For enterprise resource planning, a system such as SAP ERP provides a mass of process- and function-related parameters. With the help of these parameters, companies adjust planning algorithms and ensure compliance of the users' actions with the company's goals and policies.

For example, inventory cost and tied-up working capital are influenced by parameters in the material management and production planning modules. Setting these parameters in an appropriate way will help the company minimize their inventory cost and working capital.

While the basic approach sounds simple, setting parameters in practice can be extremely difficult. This is due to the fact that an ERP system has thousands of parameter types (implying millions of individual parameters, as shown in the subsection on parameterization in Sect. 6.2.1 above), and the interdependencies between the parameters are mostly opaque. Because of these interdependencies, parameter settings may even be counterproductive and have negative effects on the company's goals.

Dittrich and coauthors have identified a number of reasons for inappropriate parameter settings (Dittrich et al. 2009a, pp. 16–20):

- Time pressure to complete the implementation project
- High cost of external consultants and employees released from other work
- Leaving the system's default settings unchanged
- Lack of controlling regarding configuration quality
- Lack of experience and business knowledge of the implementation team
- Inappropriate consulting

Fig. 6.11 Creating a plant

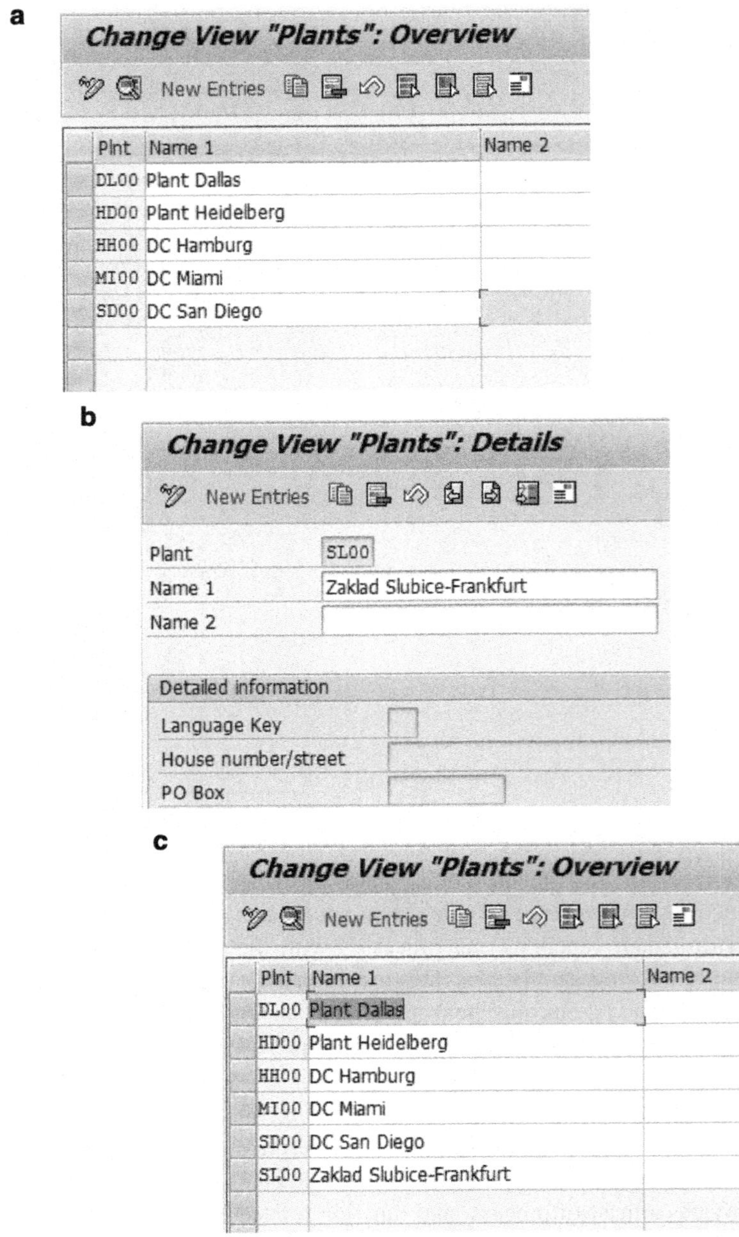

- Unreflected adoption of parameter settings from a previous system or from other companies

An additional problem arises when employees are allowed to override parameters set in the system. If the initial parameter setting was actually suitable, an employee may end up making things worse by changing these settings.

As an example of process-related parameters, we will demonstrate the steps required to define a *material availability check*. This type of check is involved in the order fulfillment and production processes as explained in Sect. 5.3 (e.g., Fig. 5.3.9).

In SAP ERP, several steps are required involving so-called checking groups, checking rules, a scope of check, and a checking control. These terms and how they are related will be described and illustrated subsequently.

A*checking group* specifies a particular treatment for all the materials belonging to the group.

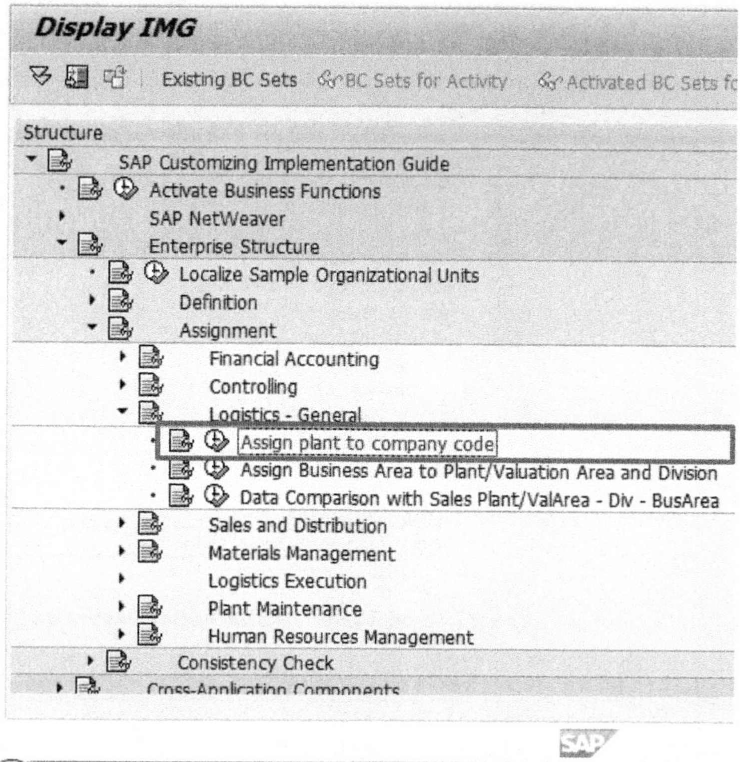

© SAP AG

Fig. 6.12 Assigning a plant to a company code

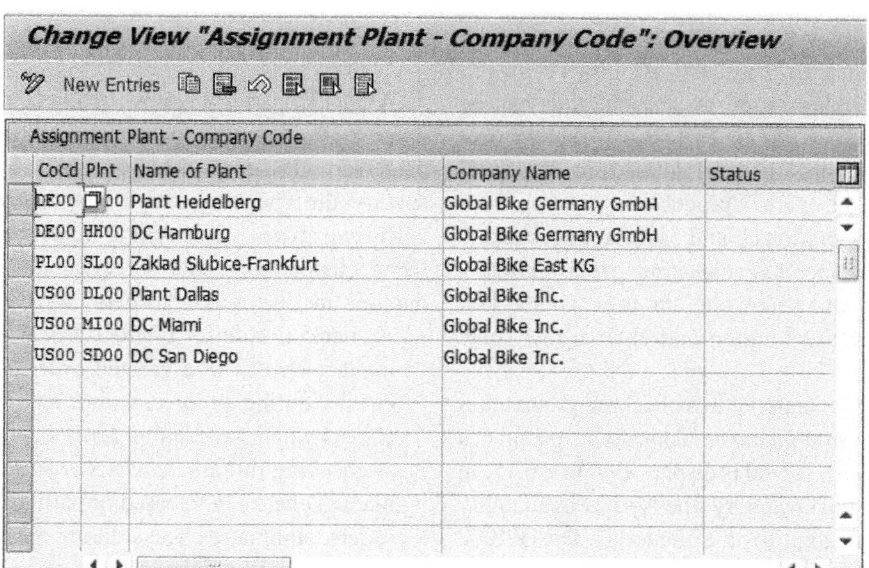

© SAP AG

Fig. 6.13 Plants assigned to company codes

Fig. 6.14 Checking groups

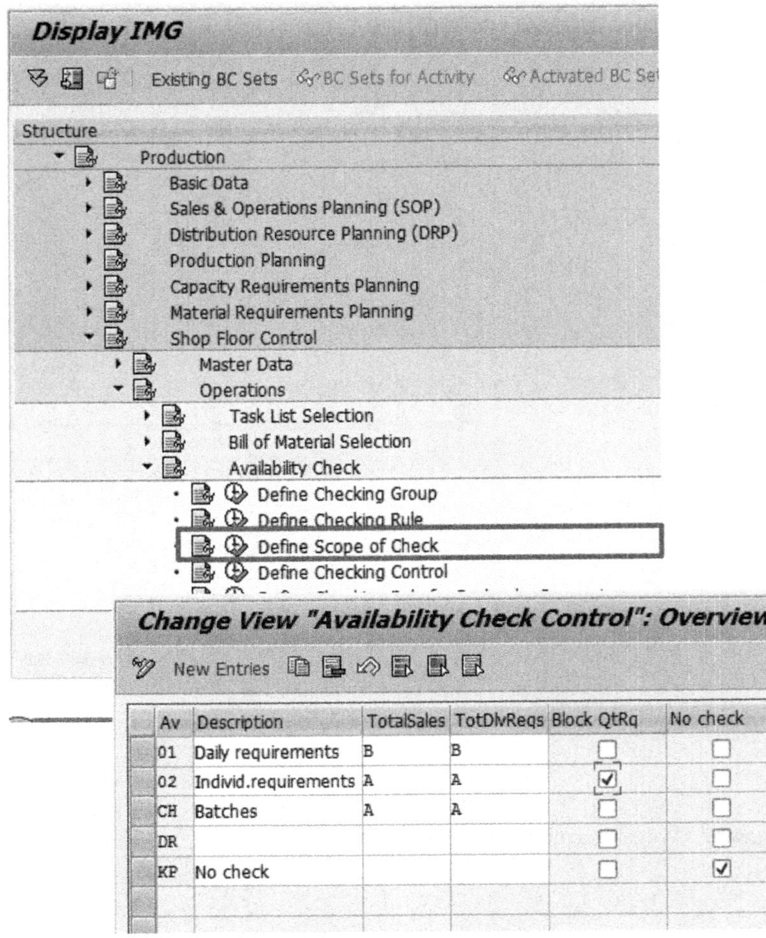

© SAP AG

Once a checking group exists, materials can be assigned to the group. Figure 6.14 shows that checking groups can be defined in the IMG following the path "production," "shop-floor control," "operations," and "availability check." In our example, five checking groups already exist. To create a new one, the user would click the "new entries" button and enter a few basic settings.

Assigning a material to a checking group takes place in the *material master* data. As an example, a material master record is displayed in Fig. 6.15. In the general data category, the type of availability check applicable to the material DXTR1007 (a black deluxe touring bike) is specified as "02." As the additional description indicates, "02" stands for the checking group "individual requirements" that was also displayed in Fig. 6.14.

A *checking rule* defines the checking procedure to be applied to an availability check. Together with a checking group, it is used to specify the checking scope (see below). Basically two types of checking rules can be set when customizing, one for created orders and another one for released orders (SAP 2012b):

- A checking rule for *created orders* applies to manual checks in a created order, automatic checks during order creation, and automatic checks when a created order is saved.
- A checking rule for *released orders* applies to manual checks in released or partially released orders, automatic checks during the release of an order, and automatic checks when a released or partially released order is saved.

The *checking scope* is determined by a checking group and a checking rule. It specifies

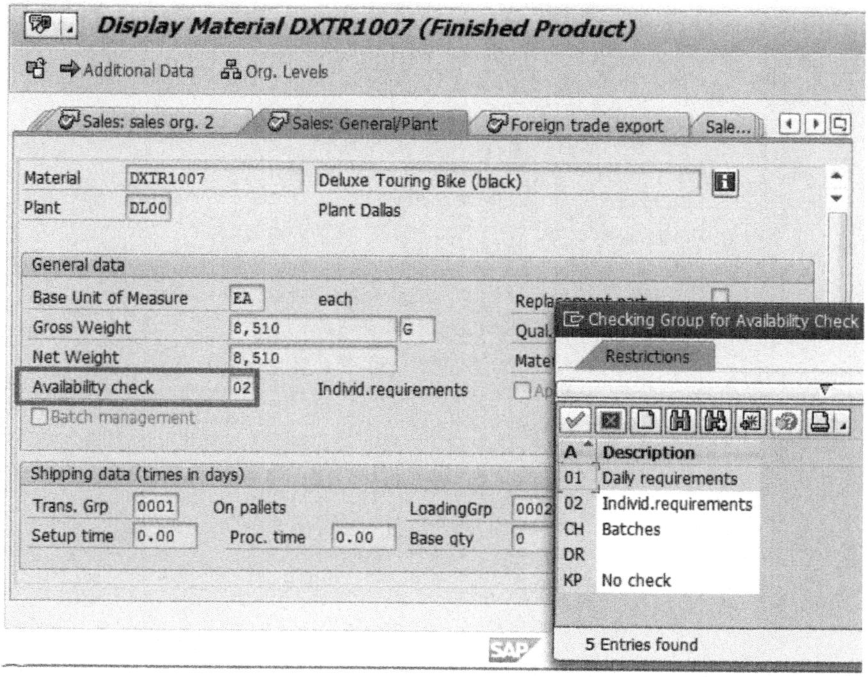

© SAP AG

Fig. 6.15 Material master record

how the check is to be done (SAP 2012b), that is:

- Which types of stock (e.g., safety stock, stock in inspection) are considered in the check
- Whether and which types of goods receipt and goods issue are taken into account (dynamic availability check)
- Whether the check includes the replenishment lead time or not
- Whether the check is only carried out at plant level, regardless of whether a storage location is specified in the reservation

Figure 6.16 gives examples of checking scopes. The first six items refer to the checking group 01 ("daily requirements") and the others to the checking group 02 ("individual requirements"). For example, the second row states that the checking rule "PP" can be applied to the checking group 01 ("daily requirements").

Finally, a *checking control* specifies for each order type and checking rule of the material availability check:

- Whether the availability should be checked automatically or not when an order is created, released, or partially released
- Which type of check is to be used (ATP check, cf. Sect. 10.1.5, or check against planning)
- Whether a check should be carried out when an order is saved

Figure 6.17 shows that for a standard production order (order type "PP01") processed in the Heidelberg plant, availability checking will be done during order creation. (Alternatively, availability could be checked later, during order release). As far as material is concerned, availability will be checked upon saving the order, according to the "PP checking rule." Availability of production resources and tools (PRT) and capacity is not included in the check.

The effect of setting the parameters in the way described above will be evident later on, in the operations phase. Any standard production order created in the Heidelberg plant will be subject to

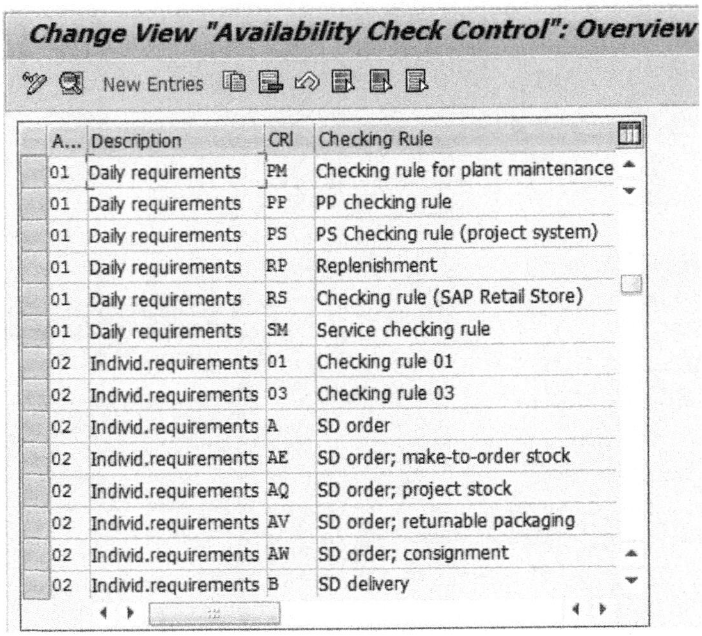

Change View "Availability Check Control": Overview

New Entries

A...	Description	CRl	Checking Rule
01	Daily requirements	PM	Checking rule for plant maintenance
01	Daily requirements	PP	PP checking rule
01	Daily requirements	PS	PS Checking rule (project system)
01	Daily requirements	RP	Replenishment
01	Daily requirements	RS	Checking rule (SAP Retail Store)
01	Daily requirements	SM	Service checking rule
02	Individ.requirements	01	Checking rule 01
02	Individ.requirements	03	Checking rule 03
02	Individ.requirements	A	SD order
02	Individ.requirements	AE	SD order; make-to-order stock
02	Individ.requirements	AQ	SD order; project stock
02	Individ.requirements	AV	SD order; returnable packaging
02	Individ.requirements	AW	SD order; consignment
02	Individ.requirements	B	SD delivery

Fig. 6.16 Checking scope

the "PP checking rule." Before the order is saved, the "PP checking rule" is executed. If the result according to this rule is that material is not available, the creation of the order will be rejected. The user will receive a message stating that the order completion date could not be confirmed because of missing material.

The above description of customizing material availability checks shows that parameterization is a lengthy process. Checking rules and scopes have to be defined, and all materials to be checked in one way or another have to be assigned to a checking group.

6.3.4 User Exits

Not all customizing needs can be satisfied through parameter settings. In many cases, in particular when extensions of the ERP system's standard functionality are involved, company-specific programs have to be written and embedded. For this purpose, SAP ERP provides a large number of predefined user exits.

The list of user exits that is available in SAP ECC (ERP central component) contains 3,178 entries. Figure 6.18 shows the beginning of the list. The user exits have coded names. The first two characters often indicate the ECC module where the user exit is located (e.g., "AC" = accounting, "PP" = production planning).

Customizing with the help of user exits usually involves three steps:

1. The developer has to find the right user exit for the extension to be included. The user exit has a name, an export interface (i.e., data provided by SAP ERP that can be used in the custom program), and an import interface (i.e., data expected by SAP ECC to be available when the custom program is finished).
2. The custom program has to be designed, coded, and tested. Testing especially involves examining whether the data created in the program to be transferred to SAP ECC are correct.
3. The custom code has to be embedded at the prescribed position in the code of the respective SAP ECC module.

Fig. 6.17 Checking control

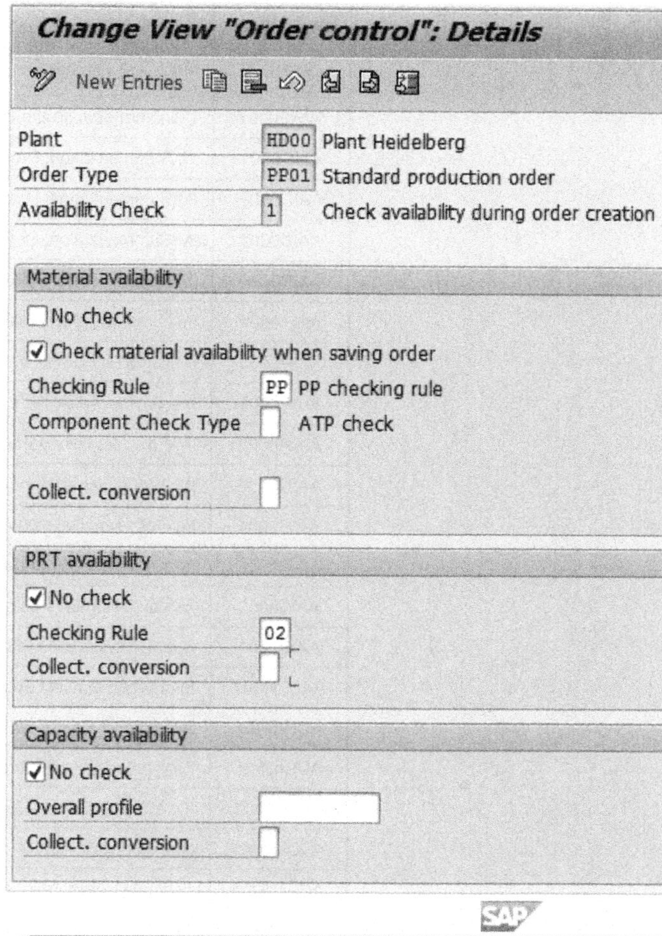

© SAP AG

Custom code usually has to be written in ABAP, SAP's own programming language, since most of the SAP ERP modules are also written in ABAP. This means that the developer has to observe SAP's ABAP-specific programming conventions and restrictions.

Figure 6.19 shows a user exit in the code of the FI (financials) module. The name of the user exit is SAPMF02D. This exit allows the company to extend customer master data. At the beginning of the code, a number of data tables that can be used in the custom code are made known to the programmer. The custom code will be included under the name "ZFX04U01," that is, the programmer will actually code all necessary actions in an ABAP program with this name.

Programming user exits is an arduous task. This is evidenced, for example, by the number of help requests posted by exit programmers in Internet developer forums, blogs, and wikis. However, since user exits are well defined and documented, it is much easier to use them than to make changes in the complex source code of SAP ERP.

6.4 SAP ERP Technology

The SAP ERP solution map shown in Fig. 5.1 listed not only the processes and tasks supported by SAP ERP but also indicated in the right-hand column the technology that SAP ERP is based on. This technology will be discussed below. Before doing so, however, it is necessary to point

Fig. 6.18 List of user exits in SAP ECC 6.0 (source: SAP AG)

Exit Name	Short Text
/SAPHT/E	Menu exit with MES menu items
0VRF0001	Customer-spec. route determination
AAIC0001	IM Summarization: Processing values after selection
AAIC0002	IM Summarization: Processing of assigned entities after sel.
AAIC0003	IM Summarization: Definition of User-Defined Characteristics
AAIP0001	IM Drilldown: Assignment of Actual Values to Budget Categories
AAIP0002	IM Drilldown: Definition of User-Defined Key Figures
AAIP0003	IM Drilldown: Definition of User-Defined Characteristics
AAIR0001	IM-IS: User value fields in app.req. reporting
AAIR0002	IM-FA: User fields for app. requests
AAIR0003	IM: Workplace assignment when creating PM order from app.req.
AAIR0004	IM Drilldown: Definition of User-Defined Characteristics
AAIR0006	IM-FA-IA: Data Transfer from App. Req. to WBS Element
AAIS0003	Actual settlements of investment measures to assets
AAIS0004	Supplements to overall plan value or budget value
AAPM0001	Integration of asset accounting and plant maintenance
ACBAPI01	Accounting: Customer Enhancement to BAPI Interfaces
ACCID001	IDoc processing for Accounting
ACCID002	IDoc Processing for Outgoing Accounting
ACCOBL01	Customer exits for PAI and PBO in coding block
ACCR0001	Accruals/Deferrals: User Exists for Master Data
AD010001	Change object list and its hierarchy
AD010002	Delimit selection and/or filter data that is determined
AD010003	Create user-defined DI characteristics
AD010005	Create user-defined sources
AD010007	Change DI Processing Information
AD010010	Modify print header

out some aspects of the technology that was used previously.

6.4.1 History and Background

The contemporary SAP ERP system has its roots in the earlier systems R/3 and R/2. SAP R/3 used to be a typical client–server system with a three-layer architecture. In this type of architecture, the tasks of the layers are as follows:

- The *presentation layer* is responsible for the communication between the user and the system. It provides a graphical user interface, accepts and interprets user input and invokes application programs accordingly.
- The *application layer* contains the business-oriented ERP functionality, decoupling the application logic from the user interface and the database.
- The *database layer* is in charge of the data the application layer works with. It stores and

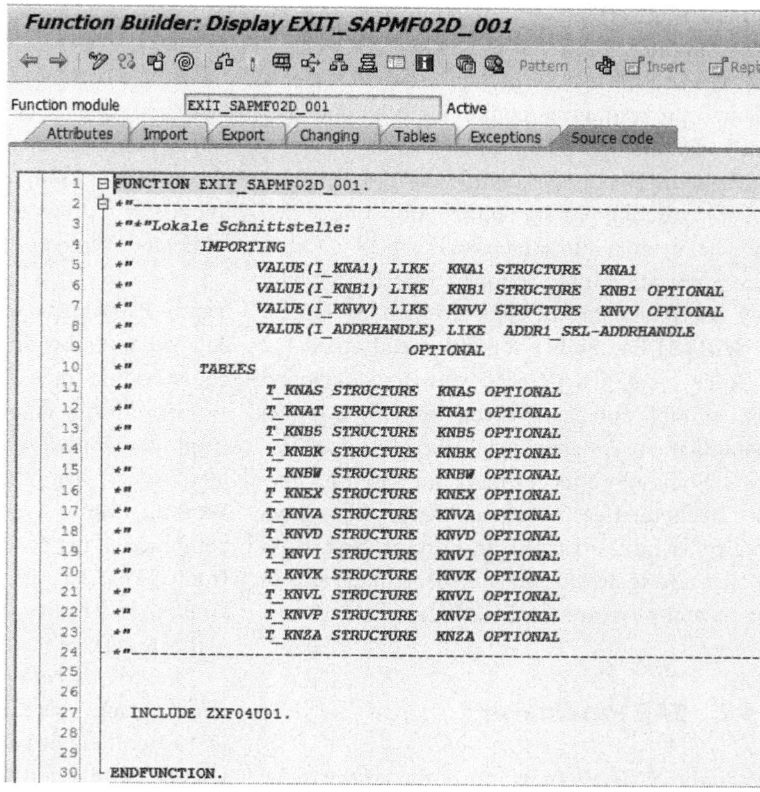

Fig. 6.19 User exit for extending customer data (source: SAP AG)

manages these data, usually with the help of a database server.

Ideally, the functionality of the presentation layer is assigned to the user terminals (e.g., personal computers), the application modules are provided by one or more department servers, and the data are stored on a central database server. All computers involved are connected by a local area network (LAN).

This "ideal" architecture has since been modified and extended. One reason for this is that the IT landscape has become increasingly heterogeneous. The second reason is that access to the ERP system via the Internet and intranets was required. In the late 1990s, SAP used four- and five-layer architectures, including an Internet layer.

The software technology R/3 is based on was largely developed by SAP itself. The foundation is a development environment called *ABAP workbench.* It contains a programming language of its own (ABAP) and a repository for all objects (forms, application programs, data models, process models, etc.) that are created during application development. ABAP used to be a German abbreviation before it was renamed to "Advanced Business Application Programming."

Since R/3 is a transaction-oriented system, programs are executed in dialog steps, connected with so-called *dynpros* ("dynamic programs"). A typical transaction is realized by several linked dynpros.

In contrast to the "old" software technology R/3 was developed with, *object-oriented technology* has promised significant advantages such as software reuse and loose module coupling, resulting in easier maintenance, simpler extensions, and lower cost. Therefore, some parts of R/3 were later redesigned according to object-oriented principles, while new systems (e.g., supply chain management, customer relationship management) were developed in an object-oriented way outside R/3.

In 1997, SAP presented a new strategic architecture for component-oriented business applications called *business framework.* At the core of this framework are so-called *business objects*, for example, "customer," "order," "invoice," etc. These are objects in the sense of object-oriented programming, containing both data and functions.

Business objects are composed into *business components*, comprising entire application areas. They have defined interfaces called BAPIs (business application programming interfaces), and they communicate via a mechanism developed by SAP (ALE—application link enabling).

Since today's SAP ERP was not developed from scratch but has evolved from R/3, it still contains many modules using the older technologies. Some more recent parts are based on current technologies such as Java EE (Java Enterprise Edition) and web technologies. Both old and new technologies have been integrated in the current platform SAP NetWeaver.

6.4.2 SAP NetWeaver

Not only SAP ERP but also the entire SAP business suite as well as new developments are based on SAP NetWeaver. This is a comprehensive platform, integrating information and applications from diverse sources. It brings together users and business processes across the enterprise and the technologies used. When NetWeaver was introduced, SAP described the motivation for developing this platform as follows (SAP 2003):

- The total cost of a company's IT landscape is primarily influenced by how well the most important vendor-provided application systems work together.
- Large SAP customers realize that most of their integration effort is expended on integrating SAP solutions with other, customer-specific business systems.
- Despite a multitude of applications systems, end users expect all systems and components to be seamlessly integrated and to provide limitless access to the system and to all data from any location.

NetWeaver is intended to satisfy the requirements derived from this by a comprehensive set of components and tools. In the following, a brief summary is given based on SAP's description of NetWeaver (SAP 2012c). As summarized in Fig. 6.20, NetWeaver supports activities in five areas, namely, team productivity, information management, composition environment (including business process management), SOA middleware, and foundation management.

Team Productivity This area primarily includes support for different user interfaces and collaboration tools.

Portal: An enterprise portal provides the employees with a personalized unified *web interface* for accessing the systems integrated in NetWeaver. Many types of information can be combined in the portal, for example, information from SAP ERP, non-SAP systems, data warehouses, and user's desktop, as well as internal and external web content.

The *collaboration* component allows people to access and share information and applications in a collaborative environment. This part includes integrated tools (e.g., wikis, discussion forums, instant messaging, and web conferencing) as well as virtual collaboration. Virtual collaboration means people working together, regardless of where they are located.

Knowledge management provides services for finding, organizing, and accessing unstructured information stored in repositories and content management systems (CMSs). Such information may be available, for example, as text, audio, or multimedia files. Classification tools help to automate the organization of information.

Mobile is the component that supports the development and modification of mobile applications that are connected with back-end systems (such as ERP). An important feature is scalability, that is, deploying mobile applications to and running data realignments on any number of mobile devices. Users can work both when they are connected and disconnected. In the latter case, they can store data offline on their devices and synchronize the information with the back-end systems later.

Enterprise search provides users with searching functionality, enabling them to

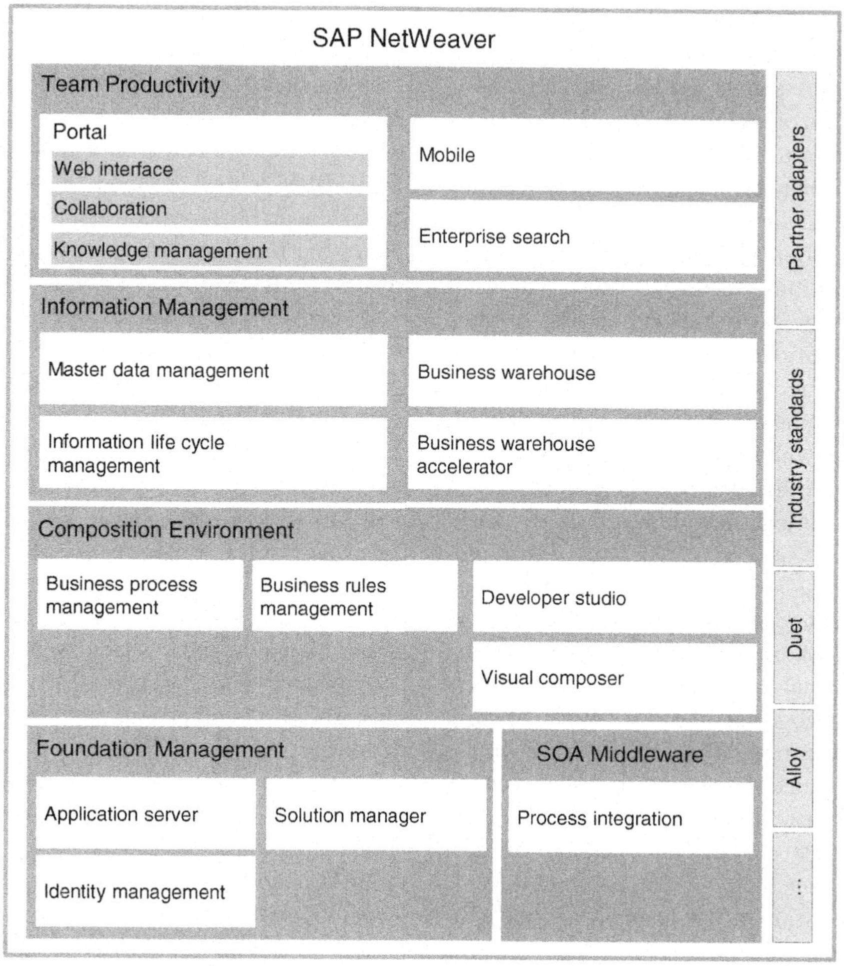

Fig. 6.20 SAP NetWeaver platform

extend the search across different systems. In the past, information was sometimes difficult to retrieve because it was stored in disparate systems ("islands of information"). The enterprise search tool helps business users by providing seamless access to SAP and non-SAP information.

Information Management The purpose of the *information management* area is to provide fast access to business information to the right people at the right time in order to improve their decision making. The main components and tools are master data management, information life-cycle management, and the business warehouse.

Master data management (MDM) helps to unify master data in heterogeneous environments, providing the same data for supplier-, product-, customer-, or user-defined data objects. This area includes support for:

- Consolidation of master data from disparate systems into a centralized repository (including data cleansing and normalization)
- Synchronization and distribution of the data, ensuring that all systems receive consistent master data
- Central creation and management of master data, supporting enterprise-wide data governance
- Management of unstructured content, including PDF files and images

- Integration of customer data in a repository to efficiently coordinate customer processes across business units and locations
- Management of vendor data from SAP and non-SAP sources to eliminate administrative mis-communication and reduce supply chain delays

Information life-cycle management (ILM) provides solutions for archiving and time-dependent validity of data. This component enables companies to manage access, storage, and retention of data from legacy SAP systems, while complying with legal and regulatory mandates. Information retention rules can be defined, according to which different business records will be kept for different periods of time according to policy or legal requirements.

The *business warehouse (BW)* component provides data warehousing capabilities on which business intelligence can be based, including data acquisition, business-oriented modeling, and multidimensional data analysis. The business warehouse recognizes the life cycle of data (current, near-current, older, archival), allows the merging of structured and unstructured data (in particular textual data), and includes metadata, which facilitate finding the location of data (Inmon 2009, pp. 3–5).

Connected with the BW component is the *business warehouse accelerator (BWA)*. This tool deals with the need for fast access to multidimensional warehouse data stored in a relational database management system (RDBMS). BWA addresses this problem by storing the data in a column-based, vertical-decompositioned way, unlike the tuple-based relational way (Inmon 2009, p. 7). All data operations are executed in memory, as BWA provides very high compression rates.

Composition Environment The *composition environment (CE)* is a software development environment for the design and implementation of composite applications. A *composite application* is based on existing information systems, reusing software components and combining them to support cross-functional processes.

The composition environment contains components for business process and business rules management as well as a number of technology-oriented components.

Business process management (BPM) helps process architects model, execute, and monitor business processes based on a common process model. BPM allows the modeler to create *executable* business process models. Each model defines the rules and exceptions governing the process steps that are performed by people or systems in response to specific business events. The modeling technique included in the "process composer" uses BPMN, the "business process modeling notation" (see Sect. 1.3.3). The "process server," a Java-based runtime execution engine, executes process models written in BPMN (Silver 2009, p. 10).

Business rules management (BRM) helps to manage the growing set of business rules in an organization. It provides support for the various phases of a rule life cycle: design, execution, modification, and improvement of business rules. The BPM component provides the following tools:

- Rules composer—creating and modifying business rules via decision tables and other rule representation formats
- Rules analyzer—testing, refining, analyzing, and improving rules
- Rules manager—editing and managing business rules
- Rules repository—an environment for rules versioning, permissions management, access control, alerts, and additional services
- Rules engine—executing business rules

Developer studio is an integrated environment for developing Java EE-based, multitiered business applications. This tool is based on Eclipse (http://www.eclipse.org), an open-source development environment using Java and web services. SAP has enhanced the standard Eclipse with design, construction, and maintenance tools that cover the full software life cycle.

Visual composer is a model-driven tool, allowing developers to compose model-based business applications without manual coding. When a model is deployed, this tool translates the model into executable code. Developers do not need to write any code themselves.

The visual composer is not only integrated with the composition environment but also with the business warehouse and the portal components.

SOA Middleware In contrast to the historical portion of SAP ERP (cf. Sect. 6.4.1), more recent parts are based on a *service-oriented architecture (SOA)*. An information system with a service-oriented architecture essentially consists of *services*. Nowadays, these services are provided as web services or, on a higher level of abstraction, as *enterprise services* (Kurbel 2008, p. 118). Enterprise services are highly integrated web services, combined with business logic and harmonized semantics, which can be accessed and used repeatedly to support different business processes. SAP delivers SOA via the technology platform NetWeaver.

Process integration (PI) is a SOA middleware component performing application-to-application and business-to-business integration and facilitating composite application development. PI supports process-centric collaboration among SAP and non-SAP systems, both within and beyond the boundaries of the enterprise.

More SOA middleware components are shown on the right-hand side of Fig. 6.20. So-called *partner adapters* are provided to integrate with application systems from other vendors using different technologies. The motivation behind adapters is to reduce the integration cost and to extend connectivity across the business networks. A number of adapters are provided for other common application software (e.g., Lotus Notes, Siebel CRM, and some ERP systems), while other adapters are technology oriented (e.g., for SWIFT and various EDI standards).

Industry standards are supported to facilitate business-to-business integration with partner solutions and custom-built applications. These standards span the professional Java world (Java EE, EJBs—Enterprise JavaBeans, etc.), web service standards (SOAP, WSDL, UDDI), other open XML-based standards, and more (Kurbel 2008, pp. 107–112).

Worth mentioning are features to support *interoperability* with Microsoft and IBM software. Since the majority of businesses use, and will continue to use, not only SAP software but also other common software, it is essential to be able to easily integrate SAP's software with this software. For office programs, the market leader is Microsoft, while for professional middleware and high-end IDEs (integrated development environments), it is IBM. Therefore, features are provided which enable interoperability with the *.NET platform* on which Microsoft's programs run and with the software portfolio contained in IBM's *WebSphere* product suite.

Duet and *Alloy* are two tools that have been available before SOA middleware was introduced.

Duet is an interface program that exposes selected functions and data from SAP systems through *Microsoft Office*. This means that SAP content is delivered through Excel, Word, and Outlook. For example, reports and analytical data created by SAP ERP can be displayed and processed as Excel spreadsheets, and relevant time entries made in Outlook calendars are automatically recorded in SAP ERP.

Alloy makes similar functionality available to business users working with *IBM Lotus Notes*. It provides access to selected functions and data from SAP systems through Lotus Notes.

Foundation Management With the components and tools provided in the *foundation management* area, diverse application systems can be run on a unified platform. This includes both programs from the SAP business suite (such as SAP ERP) and programs from partners certified by SAP.

The *application server* component can be used to deploy scalable web applications and web services. It provides an open infrastructure that supports high availability, reliability, scalability, and security throughout the application's life cycle.

The task of *identity management* is to manage user identity and access to information systems across the enterprise. This component helps companies manage the users' access to applications securely, while meeting audit and compliance requirements.

The *solution manager* is a tool facilitating technical support for distributed systems. Its functionality covers many aspects of deploying, operating, and continuously improving solutions, for example, implementation and upgrades of application systems belonging to the SAP business suite (see also Sect. 6.3), testing (test preparation and execution), and proactive monitoring of solutions.

Note The NetWeaver platform is continuously evolving, just as other SAP software is. New components are being integrated and others renamed. The way NetWeaver is being presented by SAP today has changed from the first release in 2004. The summary given in this section is based on the picture of NetWeaver at the time this book was being written. Although most of the components and tools are likely to be the same a few years later, the arrangement in which they are presented by SAP may have changed.

Manufacturing Systems

7

In this chapter, information systems that are closely connected with manufacturing will be described, including manufacturing execution systems and engineering information systems used for the technological preparation of manufacturing and products. Related with these are systems for the management of master data over their life cycle. All these systems are not part of a conventional ERP system, but they have many interfaces with enterprise resource planning.

7.1 Manufacturing Execution Systems

Manufacturing execution systems (MES) close the gap between the planning done with the help of an ERP system and the execution of the plans in the real world. Execution is often supported by technical systems that automate manufacturing steps (e.g., NC—numerical control, industrial robots). Figure 7.1 shows the role of manufacturing execution systems, connecting engineering systems with the business systems.

The rationale for manufacturing execution systems is mitigating one of the shortcomings of MRP II systems. These systems just create *plans*—rough plans, detailed plans, but still only plans. There is no guarantee that the plans will be implemented as is. Many things can happen to prevent a plan from being realized: changes in the planning parameters, events outside the company, and especially unforeseen events on the shop floor, such as machine breakdown, material shortage, worker sickness, etc. Changes and events occurring after the plan has been completed are, of course, not covered by the plan.

Most of the former MRP II systems did not support short-term execution planning and control. To compensate for this, dedicated solutions were developed which also included connections to the mid- and long-term planning systems. The first solutions, developed in the late 1980s, were "electronic leitstand" systems, which will be discussed in Sect. 7.1.1.

Compared to the short planning horizon in manufacturing execution, planning in an ERP system covers a long time period. Since it is only rough planning, it needs to be refined in order to be operational for the shop floor. In addition, feedback from the execution level is required so that the rough plans can be updated. Creating very short-term plans and collecting feedback are the tasks of manufacturing execution systems.

Figure 7.2 shows the functional areas and time horizons covered by enterprise resource planning, manufacturing execution, and CAx systems (the latter will be described in Sect. 7.2). Whereas master production planning spans several months or years, execution planning and control is concerned only with the next few days or hours.

K.E. Kurbel, *Enterprise Resource Planning and Supply Chain Management*,
Progress in IS, DOI 10.1007/978-3-642-31573-2_7, © Springer-Verlag Berlin Heidelberg 2013

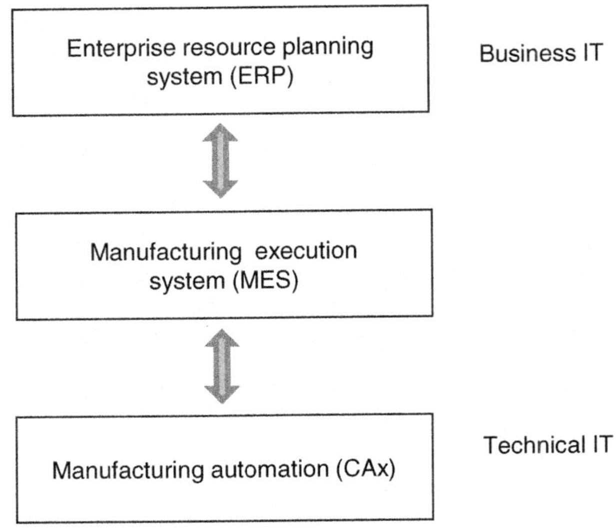

Fig. 7.1 MES connecting ERP and manufacturing

Fig. 7.2 Distribution of work between MES and ERP

Task	Time Horizon	System
Rough planning		Enterprise resource planning system (MRP II)
Master production planning	years/months	
Sales planning	years/months	
Material planning	months	
Detailed planning		
Lead-time scheduling	months/weeks	
Capacity planning	months/weeks	
Shop floor control	weeks/days	
Execution planning and control		Manufacturing execution system (MES)
Short-term planning	days/hours	
Control	hours/minutes	
Monitoring	minutes/seconds	
Manufacturing processes		CAx systems

The figure also shows that the functionalities of enterprise resource planning and manufacturing execution systems overlap. For example, shop-floor control is usually supported by both ERP systems and MESs. Additionally, a number of ERP functions have been included in manufacturing execution systems. This requires a decision to be made as to how exactly the work will be distributed between the two systems, that is, a company has to decide which functions of the ERP system and which functions of the manufacturing execution system they will use.

Some companies make this decision according to which type of system they are currently using and which they are planning to implement. Since most companies already have an ERP system, the new system is usually the MES. This means that the previously used functions and data remain with the ERP system, while the MES is in charge of the additional functionality and the data related with this functionality.

Several definitions of the term "manufacturing execution system" exist. The most common ones are those used by *MESA International* (MESA =

Manufacturing Enterprise Solutions Association), a nonprofit organization of production companies and software vendors (http://www.mesa.org), and *APICS* (formerly American Production and Inventory Control Society; today, Association for Operations Management; http:http://www.apics.org). Accordingly, an MES can be defined as follows:

A *manufacturing execution system (MES)* is an information system that extends ERP, CAx, and other technical systems by detailed planning, monitoring, and control of the manufacturing resources and production orders. Its main functionalities include:

- Short-term scheduling of manufacturing processes, operating facilities, maintenance, and personnel placement
- Administration, monitoring, and control of manufacturing resources and production orders
- Acquisition, preparation and processing of plant, machine, and personnel data, adjusting short-term plans, and providing feedback to other information systems
- Monitoring of orders, materials and batches, as well as tracking and tracing
- Quality management, document management, and performance analysis

In a guideline provided by the Association of German Engineers, the tasks of manufacturing execution systems are divided into eight major areas (VDI 2007):

- Detailed scheduling and process control
- Equipment management
- Material management
- Personnel management
- Data acquisition
- Performance analysis
- Quality management
- Information management

The terminology indicates that, in this guideline, the tasks of a manufacturing execution system are very broadly defined. Likewise, the guideline lists a wide range of "enterprise processes" that benefit from an MES (VDI 2007): operations scheduling, production, transports, material logistics, quality assurance, personnel logistics, traceability, maintenance, continuous improvement, and controlling. Despite a questionable use of the term "process," the list shows essential areas of enterprise resource planning which can benefit from an MES.

Manufacturing execution systems are quite different regarding their functionality. This is due to the diverse origins of the systems. Many were developed based on dedicated shop-floor control or leitstand systems (cf. Sect. 7.1.1), while others were based on time and attendance, plant data acquisition, or quality control systems. This means that missing functionality was added to an existing core to upgrade the respective system to an MES. While manufacturing execution systems are separate systems, they are usually connected with other application software (including ERP).

As shown in the center of Fig. 7.3, the main components of an MES are a manufacturing leitstand, plant/machine data acquisition (PDA/MDA), personnel management, and quality management. Many MESs provide additional components, for example, document management, analytics, and reporting.

From the above-mentioned list of tasks, it is clear that a manufacturing execution system has interfaces with many other information systems. In Fig. 7.3, the most important of these systems have been placed around the MES: enterprise resource planning, supply chain management, customer relationship management, as well as technical systems such as transport logistics, computer-aided design and manufacturing, product data management, and machine control.

There are two major differences between "conventional" production planning in an ERP system and execution-oriented planning in an MES.

Firstly, although the capacity situation is considered in one way or another in the various MRP II stages, capacity is not scheduled in detail. Capacity load leveling (cf. Sect. 3.4.1) remedies some of the problems on an aggregate level, but there is still no guarantee that weeks later the machines will be free exactly when an individual production order needs them. In contrast, a manufacturing execution system schedules both the capacities and the orders in such a way that the plan is really feasible. This is also known as *finite capacity scheduling*.

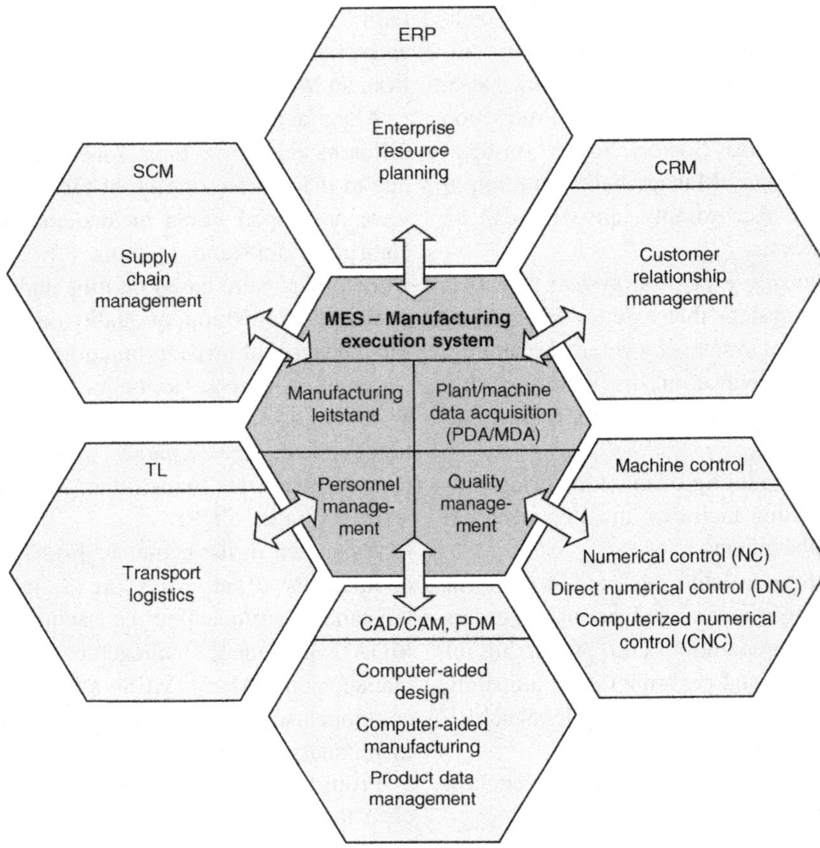

Fig. 7.3 Core and environment of an MES

Secondly, an enterprise resource planning system does not know what happens on the shop floor, that is, it does not have the actual production data. Therefore, it cannot keep the plans created earlier up-to-date, according to the actual situation in the factory. A manufacturing execution system, on the other hand, captures the production data and is therefore able to schedule orders and capacities according to the actual manufacturing situation.

Planning and updating plans with the help of an *MES* means that (1) the resources that are really available are taken into account, (2) actual production data are captured, (3) short-term plans are adapted according to the real situation, and (4) feedback to the ERP system and other relevant application systems is provided.

It is worth mentioning that the concepts combined under the term "manufacturing execution system" are not all new. Short-term planning and scheduling on the plant level has been addressed since the late 1980s with dedicated solutions called "electronic leitstand" systems. Dedicated production data and personnel time acquisition systems have been in use even longer. Quality management has been included in the CIM (computer-integrated manufacturing) approach since the 1990s.

What is new in manufacturing execution systems is that previously separate solutions for the tasks mentioned above have been *integrated* into one system. Integration enables better solutions for short-term planning and control than those created with stand-alone components.

The *benefits* from using an integrated manufacturing execution system include (Fauser 2012) better planning quality; improved transparency within production planning and control; better adherence to planned delivery dates, lead times, capacity utilization, and costs; and early warning and identification of problems and bottlenecks.

7.1.1 Finite Capacity Scheduling: Manufacturing Leitstand

From a planning and scheduling perspective, the most important MES component is a *manufacturing leitstand*. Leitstand systems have been available as stand-alone systems long before manufacturing execution systems were introduced to the market. The first leitstand systems were developed in the mid-1980s.

"Leitstand" is originally a German word meaning *control post* or *control center*. In a conventional manufacturing organization, a manufacturing leitstand is an organizational unit that is responsible for monitoring and controlling the shop floor, in particular overseeing the execution of production orders, short-term capacity scheduling, monitoring the progress of the orders, and giving feedback to other departments.

Tasks of a conventional manufacturing control center include scheduling operations, assigning operations to operating facilities, sequencing production orders on each operating facility, determining start and end dates of operations and orders, monitoring order progress, receiving progress information (e.g., start, end, delay of an operation, machine defects) from the shop floor, forwarding this information to other organizational units, initiating action, and replying to inquiries regarding the order status.

The main instrument to complete these tasks is a *planning board*. In a conventional leitstand, one or more of these boards hang on the wall, filled with cards (routing cards) or folders (containing order documents).

Most companies have used several planning boards, keeping orders for different manufacturing areas (e.g., different workshops) on different boards. Another criterion to split up orders is to distinguish them by their status, for example, planned orders (with basic dates from lead-time scheduling only), scheduled orders (with start and end dates from short-term planning), orders in execution, disrupted orders, etc.

The *planning-board metaphor* inspired the first application systems for manufacturing control centers. They were named "electronic leitstand" or "graphical leitstand" (Adelsberger and Kanet 1991; Kurbel 1993) because they mapped the manual work style based on a planning board to an electronic system, and they had a graphical user interface. This was considered a significant step forward at the time, since the user interfaces of common business information systems (e.g., MRP II systems) were text-oriented and not very user-friendly.

The first *leitstand systems* were developed in Germany, both by university institutes and manufacturing-oriented software firms. A very popular system and market leader for a long time was AHP's "CIM leitstand," better known as "AHP leitstand" (Factory Solutions 2012).

The tasks supported by a leitstand system are similar to those covered by a conventional manufacturing control center. They can be roughly assigned to the following areas:

- Capacity scheduling (machine-utilization planning) and sequencing of production orders with the help of a planning board
- Short-term capacity requirements planning using capacity profiles
- Releasing orders and creating documents
- Event-driven updating of capacity schedules and order sequences
- Monitoring production progress and handling exceptions

Since ERP and leitstand functionalities overlap, a division of work between the two types of systems has to be organized. This problem will be discussed later. For the moment we will assume that the responsibilities are as follows:

- Rough planning including lead-time scheduling is done by the ERP system. In particular, the ERP system creates manufacturing orders and operations and gives them basic start and end dates.
- Scheduled orders within a certain period of time are downloaded to the leitstand. In the leitstand, the orders' operations are assigned to operating facilities, sequenced, and monitored. Any short-term problems are resolved in the leitstand.
- The leitstand gives feedback (regarding completion of orders and/or operations) to the ERP system so that this system can update its order- and capacity-related data.

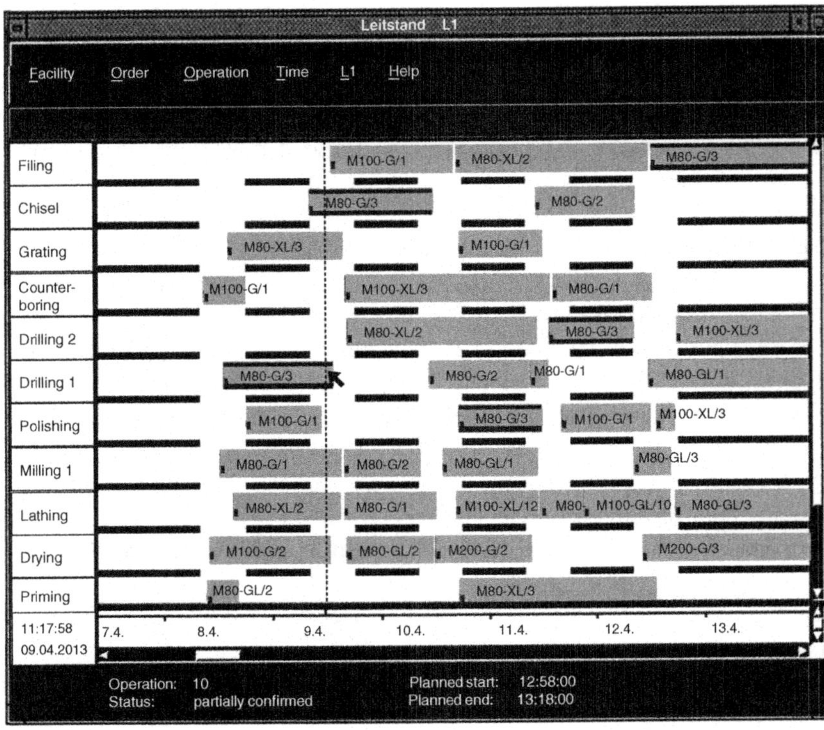

Fig. 7.4 Electronic planning board

Capacity Scheduling and Order Sequencing

The main tool for capacity scheduling and order sequencing is an *electronic planning board*. This tool provides a visual representation of orders assigned to operating facilities, similar to a Gantt chart.

To simplify things, we will use the term "operating facilities" to mean machines as well as other workplaces and equipment to be scheduled. Likewise, it should be noted that "orders" in the context of capacity scheduling actually means "operations belonging to different manufacturing orders." What is assigned to an operating facility is an *order*, but what is displayed as a bar in the planning table is the duration of one *operation* of this order, namely, the specific operation that has to be performed on the operating facility in question. Other operations of the same order may be performed on different operating facilities.

Before orders can be scheduled with the help of the planning board, they have to be available in the leitstand. This means that manufacturing orders have to be downloaded from the ERP system and stored in the leitstand. There, they will be available as a *pool of operations* waiting to be scheduled.

Since the planning horizon of the ERP system's capacity requirements planning is usually much longer than the leitstand's planning horizon, only a certain number of manufacturing orders are downloaded, namely, those with start and end dates falling within the next planning period.

Figure 7.4 shows an electronic planning board with orders scheduled on a number of operating facilities. The thick horizontal bars represent operations. The length of a bar indicates the duration of the operation. The thin bars stand for breaks (e.g., nights, weekends). Obviously, the workshop that uses this planning board operates with only one shift.

If an operation is not finished before a break, the bar is extended by the length of the break. This means that operations that in actuality only take a short amount of time appear to take much longer on the graph because of the breaks.

The total elapsed time of an operation thus consists of the setup time, the actual processing time, and the breaks that occur during the operation.

The reason why the thick bars may appear in different shades of gray is that, in the original leitstand, the operations are color-coded. Colors indicate the status of an operation, such as inconsistent, fine scheduled, delayed, released, started, interrupted, partially confirmed, roughly scheduled, and being a maintenance operation.

In the example shown in Fig. 7.4, 15 individual operating facilities are involved, 11 of which are currently visible. Obviously, the available space on a leitstand screen is not sufficient to display all of the company's individual operating facilities. Although monitors and resolutions have significantly improved over the years, dozens or hundreds of operating facilities will not fit.

Apart from this, most enterprises organize their plants into separate manufacturing areas such as different workshops (for different manufacturing stages) or different assembly lines (for different products). In these cases, each department will have its own leitstand. In other cases, the organizational structure is even more decentralized; not only does each workshop have its own leitstand but also each foreman's office.

Taking the size of a computer monitor into account, only a limited number of operating facilities can be reasonably displayed at one time. How, then, should operating facilities be selected for inclusion? Some options are as follows:

- *Individual selection*: The user manually selects from the list of available facilities which facilities he or she wants to see together.
- *Hierarchical selection*: When the user selects an aggregate, for example, a workshop or an operating facility group, all the individual operating facilities belonging to this aggregate will be automatically included in the planning board.
- *Order-related selection*: The user identifies a manufacturing order. Subsequently, all operating facilities where operations of this order have to be performed will be automatically selected and displayed. This is possible when the relationships between the operations of the order (i.e., the order networks from lead-time scheduling) are available.

The third option is particularly useful for order tracking, resolving issues, and schedule modifications, because it makes the connections between the operating facilities and the order's operations transparent.

An issue that we have not yet addressed is how the planning board is initially filled with operations. Basically, there are two approaches, one manual and one automatic.

Manual means that the production planner picks the relevant operations from the pool of operations downloaded from the ERP system and places them at appropriate positions on the planning board. "Appropriate" means that technological and schedule constraints are observed, for example, the preceding operation must be completed beforehand, the facility must be available, and it must be possible to complete all remaining operations of the order on time. An "intelligent" planning board will assist the user in this task by preventing impermissible actions and/or issuing warnings.

Figure 7.5 shows an example of a pool of operations to be scheduled on the planning board. The operation currently selected is highlighted. The potential operating facilities where it can be placed ("drying," "priming," "varnishing 1," and "varnishing 2") are automatically indicated by the leitstand.

Filling the planning board manually with a large number of operations is tiresome. Therefore, the manual approach is only applied in special cases and when an existing schedule has to be modified or extended by additional orders. Otherwise, *automated methods* for creating an initial schedule are preferred. The various methods differ in their capabilities and performance.

A simple scheduling algorithm sequences all or a part of the operations pool according to a given strategy (e.g., scheduling each operation for the latest possible date and time). When placing an operation on the planning board, the algorithm maintains the consistency of the order networks by observing predecessor-successor relationships.

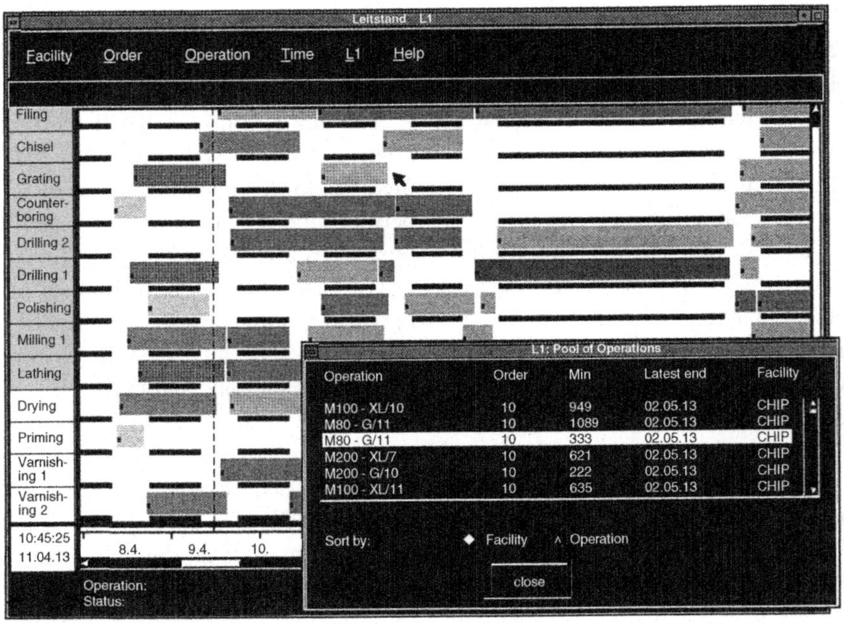

Fig. 7.5 Pool of operations to be scheduled

More powerful algorithms take into account that some sequences have advantages over others. They try to avoid, for example, high changeover costs or times when the machine setup effort is sequence-dependent.

Operations research methods have also been included in leitstand systems. Capacity scheduling and order sequencing are "classical" problems of operations research. In the 1960s and 1970s, a plethora of optimization and heuristic approaches were developed. However, due to the limited power of the computers of the time, most of these approaches could not be applied to practical problems.

Today, the situation has changed. Workstations have become so powerful that even optimization models can be solved within a reasonable amount of time. Furthermore, if only a limited number of operating facilities are considered, the size of an order-sequencing model is not too large (in terms of variables and constraints). Therefore, an algorithm can compute the optimal solution in an acceptable time frame.

Other solution approaches that have been included in leitstand systems are heuristic search methods (such as genetic algorithms, simulated annealing, and artificial neural networks). These approaches were already described in Sect. 3.6.2.

Schedule Changes Down in the factory, a "finished" schedule is unlikely to remain unaltered. On the contrary, schedules usually have to be changed due to a number of reasons. For example, urgent new manufacturing orders may arrive, operations may be canceled due to missing material, or unplanned maintenance may be scheduled because a machine is not working properly.

This means that the initial capacity schedule and order sequence have to be modified. Typical actions performed by the production planner include the following:

- Moving a scheduled operation to an earlier or later time—This requires that a time slot exists in the schedule for when the operation should now take place. If no sufficient time slot is available to accommodate the change, the production planner can either move operations that are in the way, or the planning board will do this automatically, maintaining the consistency of the order networks.
- Moving a scheduled operation to a different operating facility—This can be useful when an additional operation has to be scheduled on the operating facility in question, but there is not enough capacity. In this case, an already scheduled operation of lower priority might be moved to a different facility, if alternatives are available.

- Scheduling a new operation—This happens fairly often when a company creates a complete schedule only in certain time intervals. In between, they may want to schedule important orders immediately and not wait until the next planning run. If the scheduling is done manually, the production planner will proceed as described above (see Fig. 7.5). In case he or she does not find a suitable time slot, other operations may need to be moved, as has already been discussed.
- Removing an operation from the schedule—This may be necessary when there is not enough capacity for scheduling higher priority operations or when an operation cannot be carried out because material is missing or the machine operator is sick. An operation removed from the planning board will be returned to the pool of operations.
- Searching an operation—Since it can be difficult to find a particular operation out of the hundreds on the planning board, a search function helps to locate the operation and center the planning table around it.

Schedule changes may result not only from rescheduling but also from feedback the leitstand receives from the MES system's plant data acquisition component. This feedback includes changes to an operation's status (e.g., from "started" to "interrupted") and completion confirmation for an order or an operation.

A useful feature provided by many leitstand systems is *schedule simulation*. The production planner may be interested in trying out scheduling alternatives and seeing what effect certain actions would have on other manufacturing orders and operating facilities. This type of simulation is a "what if" simulation.

Simulation can also be used to automatically generate complete capacity schedules. In this approach, a large number of schedules may be created. In order to be able to select an appropriate schedule, an objective function is required (e.g., minimizing total order lead times or maximizing capacity utilization). If such a function has been defined, the schedule that produces the best result will be chosen.

Capacity Planning in a Leitstand Capacity planning is actually a part of MRP II and supported by ERP. The reason why it is also available in leitstand systems is that MRP II capacity schedules are mid- and long-term. Even if the capacity load was leveled and a feasible capacity schedule was determined within MRP II, the situation may have changed weeks later when it comes to shop-floor control.

On the other hand, working with the electronic planning board does not make much sense when the overall capacity during the time period in question is not sufficient. Trying to find an optimal order sequence is pointless if, due to lacking capacity, no feasible sequence exists. Therefore, it is very important to first strive for a realistic capacity load before turning toward the planning board.

For these reasons, *capacity planning* has been included in some leitstand systems as an additional module. While most systems provide features for displaying the capacity load of the operating facilities in question, only few systems allow the planner to actually change it by rescheduling orders.

The capacity situation is visually represented with the help of column charts, as has already been shown in Sect. 3.4. A chart like this represents the capacity load of an individual operating facility, a group of operating facilities, or some other aggregate.

When capacity planning is included in a leitstand, the planner will manually select operating facilities for review. Usually this will be facilities that are known to be bottlenecks, or that are very expensive and should be used to their full capacity. Provided that the leitstand allows changes to be made, the planner will interactively modify the capacity load.

Figure 7.6 shows a screenshot of a capacity profile created for a particular operating facility. The vertical axis represents the capacity per day (in hours). The horizontal axis represents the time (in days). The line that starts at 40 h on the y-axis on the first day and continues for 5 days before going down to zero for a period of 2 days and going up again and so on stands for the available capacity. Obviously, this operating

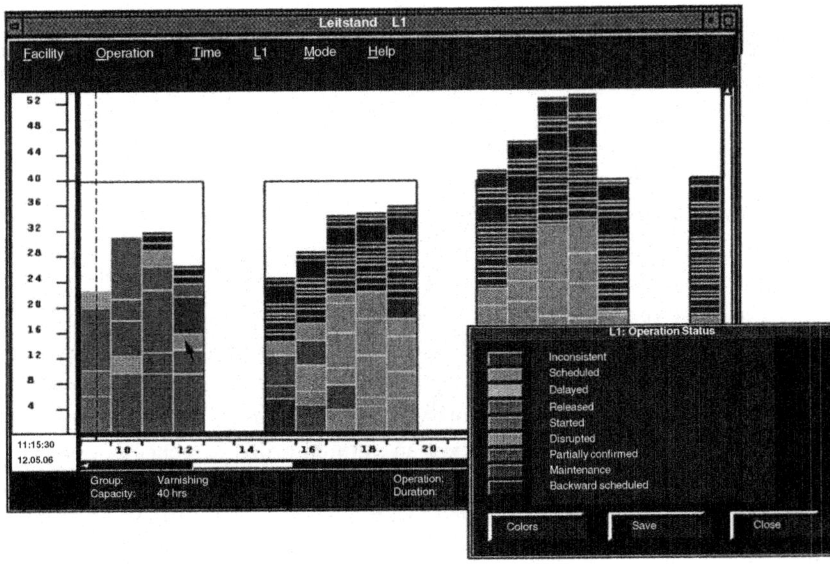

Fig. 7.6 Capacity profile

facility is being operated in one shift, and only from Monday to Friday. On Saturday and Sunday, the capacity is zero.

The columns of the load profile are composed of different manufacturing orders. To be more precise, each of the small rectangles stands for the capacity required for one operation to be executed on this operating facility, with operations belonging to different manufacturing orders. As in the planning board, colors are used to indicate the status of an operation. In print, the colors have been mapped to shades of gray.

In order to cope with the limited size of a computer monitor, many leitstand systems support different timescales. Another option is to use multiple monitors.

Visualizing the capacity load is one thing, changing the load, however, is another. In an interactive system, the planner could, for example, move an order from one column to another. In the capacity profile shown in Fig. 7.6, the planner would perhaps drag an operation from April 24 and drop it in one of the columns between April 15 and 19.

Whereas the graphical manipulation is state-of-the-art today, changing the underlying schedules continues to be a problematic undertaking. In the background, the leitstand system has to check if the consistency of the order networks is maintained despite the change. If the consistency is violated, the system will prevent the user from making the change unless the issue is resolved.

An operation can only easily be moved if there are sufficient buffers between the earliest start date and the latest end date of the moved operation. Otherwise, predecessors or successors in the order network may also need to be shifted. Shifting these operations can mean, however, that they are moved to time periods in which there is not enough capacity on the operating facilities they are to be processed on. Then, these problems would also need to be dealt with, initiating a chain reaction.

If, however, moving an operation is inevitable, some leitstand systems provide features for rescheduling an order network around the moved operation. In the AHP leitstand, this feature is called "center planning" (Factory Solutions 2012, p. 10). It is also known as "bottleneck scheduling" (Kurbel and Meynert 1989, p. 77). In this approach, lead-time scheduling starts with the operation in question and then schedules predecessors backward and successors forward.

While rescheduling orders is a common feature of electronic planning boards, it is rarely available for capacity profiles. This means that

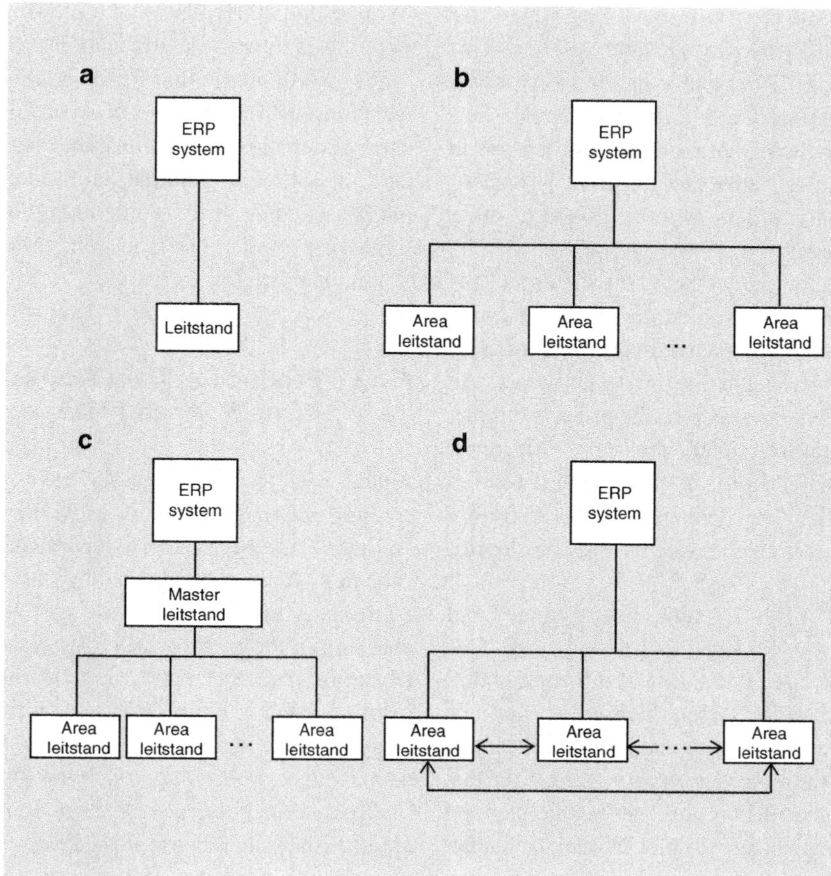

Fig. 7.7 Cooperation between ERP and Leitstand systems

the user may display a profile, but if they want to make any changes, they would have to turn to the ERP system, use the ERP capacity load leveling function, and again download the orders to the leitstand.

Relationship Between Leitstand and ERP System Under the assumption made above, that the ERP system is responsible for the rough, midrange planning, and the leitstand is responsible for short-term execution planning, a natural interface between the two systems is *order release*. Most companies use the order release functionality provided by the ERP system. However, since order release is also available in many leitstand systems, some companies prefer this option.

As has already been mentioned, many companies utilize *multiple leitstand systems* depending on the manufacturing organization. In this case, the exchange of information not only between the ERP system and the leitstand but also between the various leitstand systems, has to be coordinated.

Figure 7.7 illustrates some basic forms of cooperation between an ERP system and possibly multiple leitstand systems.

Part (a) of the figure depicts the simplest case, that is, only one leitstand exists. This system is responsible for all shop-floor-related planning and control tasks. The ERP system creates manufacturing orders and releases these orders. A complete pool of released orders is given to the leitstand for further processing. The leitstand then sends feedback to the ERP system, especially in order to confirm the completion of orders, operations, or both.

More typical is the case that different manufacturing areas, for example, different workshops or different manufacturing stages, are equipped with their own leitstand systems. This means that the ERP system hands over only a part of the released orders to a particular leitstand, namely those that have to be processed in the manufacturing area this leitstand is responsible for. Other orders will be given to other leitstand systems.

While handing orders over to different leitstand systems is no problem, a challenge arises from the fact that orders and manufacturing areas are interconnected via the order networks. An order completed in one workshop, for example, has to be transferred to the next. An order delayed in one workshop can affect the schedules of other workshops. The question is therefore how the decentralized systems can be coordinated.

In *part (b)* of Fig. 7.7, it has been assumed that the ERP system does the coordination work. This means that each relevant piece of information has to be sent to the ERP system. Examples would be the start and end of each operation, delays, interruptions, partial completion, etc. Based on this information, the ERP system can update planned order dates and release or block orders intended to go to other workshops.

Part (c) shows the case where the manufacturing execution system takes over the coordination work from the ERP system. This constellation is usually more flexible because coordination remains in the factory, avoiding the overhead of involving the ERP system, uploading order information, downloading orders, etc.

In *part (d)* of the figure, coordination is integrated in the decentralized systems. Instead of employing an additional master node, the various leitstands coordinate themselves. This means that the functionality needed for the coordination task is included in the leitstand software.

While the one-leitstand solution depicted in part (a) is rarely found, most manufacturing companies use configurations as shown in parts (b) and (c). Self-coordinating leitstand systems as in part (d) have been a subject of research and development in academia, employing artificial-intelligence approaches [e.g., multiagent systems (Wooldridge 2009)]. However, they are not commonly used in real-life applications.

It is worth noting that Fig. 7.7 shows just four basic forms of relationships between ERP and leitstand systems. Combinations and extensions are also possible. For example, large manufacturing enterprises may have a hierarchy of systems, employing master leitstands on more than one hierarchical level.

7.1.2 Production Data Acquisition: PDA, MDA, and TDA

Actual data from the factory are essential for creating and updating plans, as well as for taking corrective measures when the plans are being executed. While this sounds obvious, in practice there has always been a wide gap between the planning in the ERP (or MRP II) system and the execution on the shop floor. Consequently, planned dates in the ERP system were often far away from the actual dates in reality. Production data acquisition is an approach to close the gap.

Production data, also known as *plant data*, are the data that come into being during the manufacturing process. These are data about quantities (e.g., actual numbers of good and scrap parts), times (e.g., actual start, end, duration of an operation), status of operating facilities (e.g., running, maintenance, broken down), movement of goods, quality, employee attendance, and more.

Production data acquisition (PDA, also called *plant data acquisition)* comprises all measures required to make production data available in a machine-processable form to other application systems and/or decision makers.

A *PDA system* consists of the hardware and software needed for fulfilling the tasks of production data acquisition. The hardware often encompasses special hardware components, beyond normal office technology (see below).

Nowadays, most nontrivial machines are controlled by computers or microprocessors. This means that a great deal of production data is generated automatically and can be captured directly from the machine controllers, for example, the operating time, speed, quantities produced, cycle time, and temperature. Other data can be collected from sensors (e.g., at a conveyor belt) or dedicated reading terminals (e.g., RFID readers, cf. Sect. 11.4.1).

Data captured directly from technical devices are usually called *machine data*. In a manufacturing environment, this kind of data constitutes most of the production data. Therefore, the term *machine data acquisition* is often used instead of production data acquisition. Even more common is the combination PDA/MDA.

Just as leitstand systems, PDA/MDA has existed long before manufacturing execution systems came into being. PDA/MDA has been available both as a stand-alone solution and as a component of other systems. For example, it was integrated in CAx systems, in leitstand systems, and in timekeeping systems.

Timekeeping Systems *Timekeeping systems*, also known as *time and attendance* or *time data acquisition (TDA) systems*, have originally focused on attendance and absence times (comes, goes), taking leaves of absence and sickness into account. In addition, these systems have allowed the company to track employee assignment to production orders, projects, operating facilities, etc. This information is useful, for example, in cost object accounting, where exact labor times are needed for calculating the direct cost, and in future staff allocation planning.

Timekeeping systems use a variety of technologies. While conventional time clocks have been employed for a long time, most TDA systems now use electronic devices. These devices read the person's data from swipe cards using magnetic strips or RFID chips, or from different kinds of contactless media. In special areas, biometric data (e.g., finger print, retina) are captured. Conventional solutions may also allow form-based data entry on a regular computer monitor.

Just as leitstand systems have been expanded by ERP functionality, many TDA systems have been expanded by HR (human resources) capabilities, including staff allocation and payroll. However, a company working with an ERP system is more likely to use this system's HR functionality than that of the TDA system.

Therefore, most stand-alone TDA systems provided interfaces with common ERP systems. When TDA is a component of a manufacturing execution system, as is the case today, this system provides the interface between the timekeeping component and the ERP system.

Types of Production Data What kind of production data a company decides to capture depends on the type of company and what the data are needed for. A company building machine tools make-to-order may be more interested in accurate operation times than in quantities (because the lot size is 1). On the other hand, a company engaged in mass or series production might want to closely monitor the process output (in terms of quantity per time unit) or the process speed.

Many different types of data are summarized under the term "production data" (see, for example, (Kletti 2010, pp. 126–129)). They can be grouped into the following categories:

- *Order data:* In contrast to order data in ERP, order data maintained in the PDA part of an MES are much more detailed. This is due to the fact that they reflect the progress in the various stages of manufacturing. In addition to operation start and end dates, order data include time components such as lying, transport, processing, controlling and disruption times, manufacturing states, output (numbers of conforming and nonconforming parts), allocated staff (names of employees, qualification, time), material data (type, quantity), contracted services, etc.
- *Operating facility data:* This category comprises machine running and down times, utilization ratios, cycle-time adherence, disruptions and causes, numbers of pieces per time unit, etc.
- *PRT data*: Data about production resources and tools (PRT) inform about the usage of these appliances: when they are issued; how, where, and when they are used in the process; what defects occur; when and why they occur; etc.

- *Inventory* and *material data:* These data capture the consumption of raw materials and supplies as well as other materials planned in a consumption-driven way.
- *Process data:* In highly automated manufacturing processes, the quality of the output often depends on the quality of the technical process. Therefore, it is important to capture the values of various process parameters (e.g., temperature, pressure). Legal regulations may also require the company to prove evidence of certain process parameters.
- *Quality data:* These data include measured values, such as the results of a quality analysis, as well as defect indices and ratios, reasons why defects occur, etc.
- *Personnel data:* The second main reason why personnel data are captured—in addition to payroll needs (e.g., for piece-work wage)—is that this data is required for order and product costing. Personnel assigned to operating facilities and/or manufacturing orders can be accounted accordingly.

Usage of Production Data Within a manufacturing execution system, the principal consumers of production data are the *leitstand* and the *quality management* subsystems. Obviously, feedback from the shop floor is immediately useful for the short-term execution planning and control a leitstand is responsible for. When PDA/MDA and leitstand are well integrated within the MES, production data can even be automatically adopted by the leitstand and reflected in its planning board and capacity profiles.

In *quality management*, production data are employed for the planning of quality-assurance measures and the controlling of technical systems. Production data may also be needed for the tracking of individual orders for which an uninterrupted proof of quality is required.

Beyond the MES limits, production data are primarily needed by enterprise resource planning and technical systems (CAx systems).

Enterprise resource planning uses production data for most planning areas:

- In primary and secondary *requirements planning* and other material management tasks, actual data such as the consumption of material, inventory levels, and inbound and outbound goods movements are needed.
- In *lead-time scheduling,* order networks will be rescheduled according to the progress reported through completion (or disruption) information.
- For *capacity load leveling,* the available capacity as well as the actual capacity requirements resulting from planned manufacturing orders have to be determined. In order to do so, machine data, actual machine loads, and orders scheduled for the coming periods are required.
- *Rough planning* within ERP can be improved based on feedback from the factory. With this feedback, generic parameters such as machine-utilization ratios, external subcontracting rates, and the variance of order lead times can be adapted, leading to better results of manufacturing resource planning.
- *Payroll accounting* receives employee and time data (presence, absence, performance, etc.) for the calculation of gross wages. These data are particularly important for piece-rate wages.
- For *end product* and *order costing*, exact data are necessary regarding material consumption, machine utilization, running and down times, personnel allocation (duration, qualification), and more. In general, cost accounting and controlling make intensive use of production data.
- For *maintenance and repair planning,* machine data such as intensity levels, disruptions, and how long the machine has been running are important. Based on these data, preventive maintenance and repair work can be scheduled.

Technical systems (cf. Sect. 7.2) also use production data, in particular machine data. This is the case in CAM (computer-aided manufacturing) and CAP (computer-aided planning) as well as in other areas.

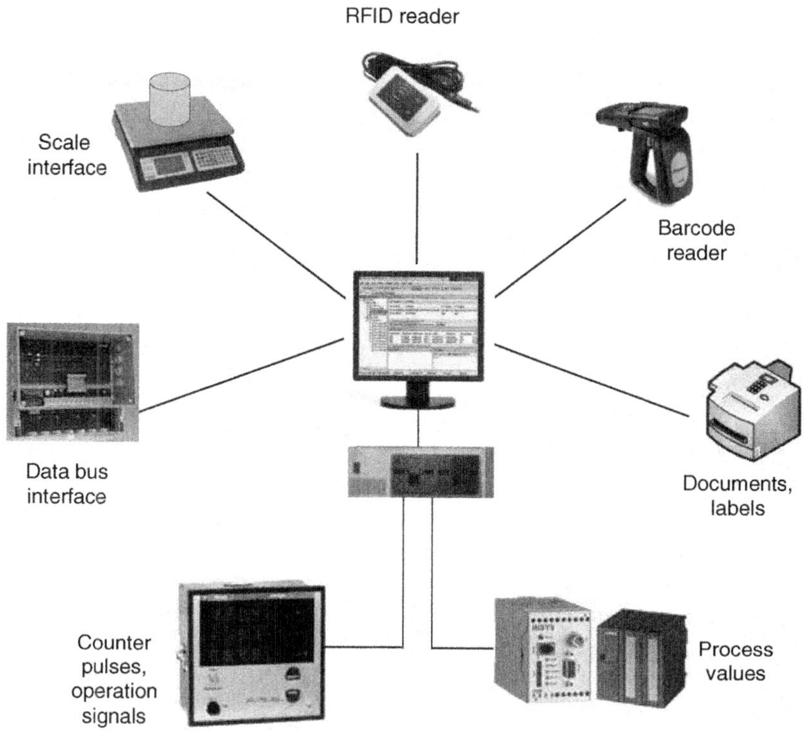

Fig. 7.8 PDA/MDA hardware

For example, when a DNC (direct numerical control) machine issues a confirmation regarding the completion of an operation, an automated transport system connected with the DNC machine can process this information. It may initiate several actions, such as automatically providing a container, filling the container, and transporting it to the warehouse.

Organization and Technology of PDA/MDA Capturing of production data is normally decentralized, while processing the data can be centralized or decentralized. When machine data are involved, these data are created and collected automatically at the location where the machines are installed. For time and attendance data, both central (e.g., at the gate) and decentral solutions (e.g., in the workshop) are available.

Due to the many different types of production data, the components of a PDA/MDA system can be quite diverse (e.g., Kletti 2010, p. 131). Figure 7.8 summarizes a number of hardware devices used for production data collection.

There are basically three different ways for storing and transmitting production data: through paper, plastic, or electronic media.

While machine data are usually transmitted and stored in electronic form, conventional production data are often reported with the help of paper documents. As has been mentioned before, various documents accompanying a manufacturing order are issued when the order is released (cf. Sect. 3.5.2). Examples of paper documents include wage slips and order and/or operation completion slips.

Wage slips (also called time tickets) actually serve the purpose of calculating the worker's pay. However, when workers are on a piece-rate plan, they will return the wage slip when they are done with the work. In this way, the completion of an operation (or order) is implicitly reported with the wage slip. Wage slips have long been used as completion confirmation documents. This is somewhat problematic because the worker may not return the slip immediately when the operation is completed, but later when it suits them better. The worker's interest is in optimal pay, whereas the company's interest is in timely and accurate feedback.

A better alternative to wage slips are special order or operation *completion slips*. These documents are filled out and returned when the order (or operation) is finished.

Today, electronic documents have replaced paper in many areas. For example, completion information is often entered in a form on the screen and not on a piece of paper. Some of the information will already be provided when the form is loaded, while other information have to be entered by the user.

Entering information manually requires a lot of effort. Therefore, even paper documents have been increasingly made "machine-friendly," meaning that information on paper can be read and processed automatically. Typical technologies used for this purpose include barcodes, optical marks, magnetic strip cards, chip cards, and RFID tags:

- *Barcodes* can be found on all kinds of documents (order, goods issue, delivery slip, labels, etc.). They are printed with special printers and read by special readers (barcode readers, cameras, scanners, etc.).
- Documents with *optical markings*, in OCR font and even in plain writing, are also used to enable automated reading and processing.
- *Plastic cards* can be equipped with barcodes, but also with magnetic strips storing information and with chips containing small microprocessors. With chip cards it is possible, for example, to store an order's way through the factory and successively add data as the order passes different stations on its way.
- *RFID tags* are labels capable of reflecting or sending electromagnetic waves (cf. Sect. 11.4.1). RFID readers are used to transmit the received information to the places where it can be processed. RFID technology is nowadays employed in many business areas.

Machine data are captured electronically, in many cases directly from sensors or machine controllers. The Hydra MES, for example, collects quantities, counting pulses, and disturbance signals directly from sensors connected with the machines (MPDV 2009). As an alternative, this MES uses data communication interfaces with machine and system controllers to directly upload data saved by the controller, for example, quantities, machine states, and malfunction periods. The communication is based on common protocols and standards such as Euromap E63, OPC (object linking and embedding for process control), and Profibus.

Devices for Production Data Acquisition While machine data are often captured directly via interfaces, other production data have to be collected with the help of special devices. Many of these devices are equipped with appliances capable of accepting data in a machine-understandable format, for example, handheld optical scanners, voice input, touch screens, and special monitors.

Taking into account that production data are usually not created in a "clean" office environment, devices must be robust and function under conditions of dirt, noise, fluctuating temperatures, vibrations, magnetic fields, and so on. When keyboards are used as input devices, they are often plastic-foil keyboards, preventing dirt from falling between the keys. The keys may be oversized so that a worker wearing protective gloves can press them.

A good deal of production data acquisition happens wherever the objects to monitor are and not where stationary reading devices are installed. In this case, *mobile devices* are used, connected to a stationary PDA terminal or server (e.g., via Bluetooth, infrared). Both special PDA equipment as well as devices for general usage (e.g., PDAs, smartphones, notebooks) are employed for mobile PDA.

Further means available for production data acquisition include the following:

- *RFID tags:* Information stored or transported by RFID tags is obtained from RFID readers. While many readers are stationary, mobile equipment is also in use.
- *Biometric data:* Biometric data are often employed for access control to security-sensitive areas. They are read, for example, by retina or fingerprint scanners, transmitted to a server, and compared with the stored patterns.
- *Alarm generators:* Alarm generators are special devices creating an event in the

MES, a message and/or an acoustic or optical signal when a critical situation occurs. Additionally, the employee in charge can be notified by SMS, email, or pager.

Processing Production Data While production data are captured using all kinds of devices, the data are normally transmitted to a dedicated server *(PDA server)*. Taking into consideration that a large number of data items are created (especially in MDA), the server tasks may be distributed to a multilevel server configuration.

Tasks involved in *processing production data* include preparation and preprocessing of the collected data, condensing, aggregating, and evaluating the data. Feedback to the other MES components, to the ERP system, and to other information systems is created and transmitted.

Typical reports and statistics that can be generated from the data include (MPDV 2009):

- Machine-utilization ratios
- Performance reports regarding quantities and times
- Evaluation of downtime and disruptions for each machine and for the entire plant
- Machine time profiles
- Performance indicators such as the overall equipment effectiveness (OEE), total productivity and manufacturing cycle effectiveness

7.1.3 Quality Management

The third main component of a manufacturing execution system is *quality management (QM)*. Just as the other components, quality management is not a new thing. It has always been considered an important task long before manufacturing execution systems were invented.

In the 1980s and 1990s, quality management was discussed under the name *CAQ (computer-aided quality assurance)* as one of the CA techniques within the comprehensive CIM (computer-integrated manufacturing) approach.

Quality management is concerned with the planning, execution, and controlling of all measures that have an effect on the product and/or process quality. It covers several stages, starting with product planning and design and continuing through all stages of manufacturing. Quality flaws caused by inadequate product design are difficult to remove later, usually causing high cost.

A systematic quality management, on the other hand, costs money. Accompanying all steps of manufacturing preparation and execution, quality management is responsible for a significant share of the total production cost.

Master data for quality management include inspection plans and test programs. An inspection plan is similar to a routing, specifying the steps required to verify the quality criteria that have been defined for the end products, assemblies, or individual parts.

Quality management modules of an MES cover not only the creation and administration of inspection plans and test programs but also quality data acquisition (such as confirmation of actual output, scrap and machine downtimes) and evaluation.

For example, Hydra MES, a well-known manufacturing execution system, provides quality management functionality such as the following (MPDV 2010; Kletti 2010, pp. 180–185):

- Inspection and test planning: definition of inspection plans, sampling, creating and processing inspection orders, etc.
- Statistical process control (SPC): automated acquisition of measurements and analysis of process data during the process
- Nonconformance management: tracing back nonconformant products based on technical aspects, manufacturing conditions, and input materials, and taking countermeasures
- Incoming goods: capturing and checking properties of incoming goods, evaluating, and rating supplier performance
- Equipment management: managing the inspection, measurement and testing of equipment, ensuring that the equipment meets the required standards, and that it is appropriate for the planned tests and inspections
- Capturing or acquiring process data (e.g., temperatures, pressures) directly, checking the data against tolerances and recommending countermeasures

Quality Management–ERP Interfaces Basic quality data are often specified as early as in product design, when the product properties are decided on, for example, temperature resistance, material thickness, and tolerances. These properties serve as parameters for the planning of quality-assurance measures in the MES. On the other hand, feedback from quality management (actual quality data and correction needs) is used to update quality parameters in the ERP system.

Material requirements planning (MRP) needs quality information for gross and net requirements planning (cf. Sect. 2.3.2), because it makes assumptions about quality parameters. For example, the waste factor used in Fig. 2.25 is obviously based on expectations that have been derived from quality data evaluated earlier.

Procurement works with supplier ratings when selecting a supplier for a purchase. These ratings are based on quality data from incoming goods inspection.

In *MRP II scheduling* and *capacity planning*, quality data are required for several purposes. Inspection operations take time, just as manufacturing operations do. This means that they have to be scheduled and included in capacity planning with their respective durations.

Quality requirements may influence the choice of operating facilities, because one facility may be capable of fulfilling certain criteria while others are not. For example, when a company has a number of universal lathes and one special lathe, and the product in question requires tolerances that can only be guaranteed with the special lathe, this lathe will be the only choice.

Furthermore, the ERP system's capacity planning module may be involved when the measuring and testing equipment is needed in many places. In this case, availability of the equipment has to be scheduled. Therefore, the company will include the equipment in the capacity requirements planning and administer it in the same way as an operating facility.

7.2 Engineering Information Systems

Most manufacturing processes and operating facilities in today's factories are run or supported by computers. Software for manufacturing usually comes from the engineering sciences. Therefore, it is often summarized under the terms "engineering information systems" or "technical information systems."

The information processed or created by engineering systems is in part the same as the information used in the business systems. Examples include bills of materials, routings, and part master data. Because of the many interfaces with the business systems, this section will discuss engineering information systems, including their relationships to enterprise resource planning, manufacturing execution, and other business systems.

7.2.1 CAx Systems

Technical information systems are often called CAx systems because their names include the words "computer-aided" (CA). In the 1980s, various CA techniques were combined under the term "computer-integrated manufacturing" (CIM).

Computer-Integrated Manufacturing *Computer-integrated manufacturing (CIM)* is a comprehensive approach, integrating business and technical information systems of a manufacturing enterprise. The business part is primarily represented by production planning and control (or MRP II), while the technical part is composed of CAx systems:

- Computer-aided engineering (CAE)
- Computer-aided design (CAD)
- Computer-aided planning (CAP)

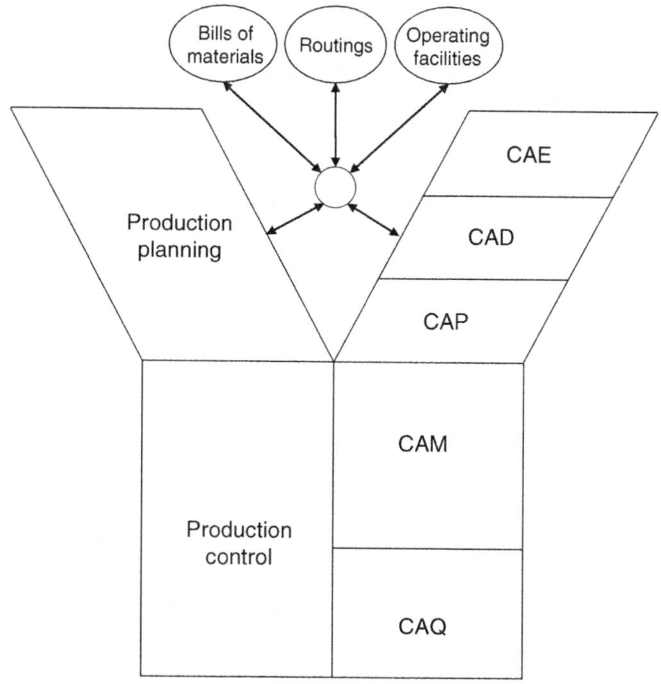

Fig. 7.9 Y-model for computer-integrated manufacturing (Scheer 1994, p. 2)

- Computer-aided manufacturing (CAM)
- Computer-aided quality assurance (CAQ)

For manufacturing planning and control, the business and the engineering perspectives are equally important. Figure 7.9 illustrates this rationale with the help of the so-called *Y-model*. This model was developed in the late 1980s by August-Wilhelm Scheer at the Institute of Information Systems at the University of Saarbrücken in Germany (Scheer 1994).

The most important aspect of CIM is the letter "I" (for "integrated"). It means that the data, the functions, and the processes are integrated across all subsystems involved. General benefits resulting from integration have already been discussed in Sect. 4.1.

Specific benefits of the *CAx techniques* include the ability to quickly remove errors (e.g., errors in the product design) or even to prevent them from occurring in the first place. Figure 7.10 illustrates the relationships between the probability of detecting an error and the effort needed to remove the error, depending on whether CAx systems are employed or not. The later an error is detected, the more effort is needed to remove it. CAx systems help to recognize errors early, thus reducing the cost and effort involved in eliminating the errors.

Integrating *all* the systems shown in Fig. 7.9 turned out to be a too ambitious endeavor for most companies. For this reason, the term "computer-integrated manufacturing" is not as common any more as it used to be. Instead, the individual CIM components are nowadays just referred to as "CAx systems."

Figure 7.11 provides an overview of the most common CAx systems and where they are used in the product life cycle. CAE, CAD, and CAM will be described subsequently.

CAID (computer-aided industrial design) is a special approach for technical product design and styling (Vajna et al. 2009, p. 12).

CAE (computer-aided engineering) is a term that is used with different meanings but generally refers to computer systems that support product engineering, in particular numerical methods for design computations. It is closely related to computer-aided design, which is why the abbreviation CAD/CAE is quite common.

Computer-Aided Design (CAD) *Computer-aided design* systems support design engineers in their work. CAD includes approaches both for

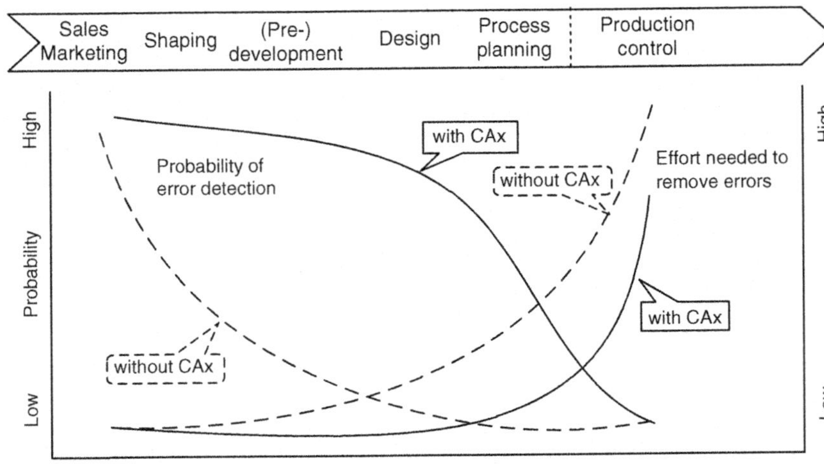

Fig. 7.10 Detecting and removing errors (Vajna et al. 2009, p. 14)

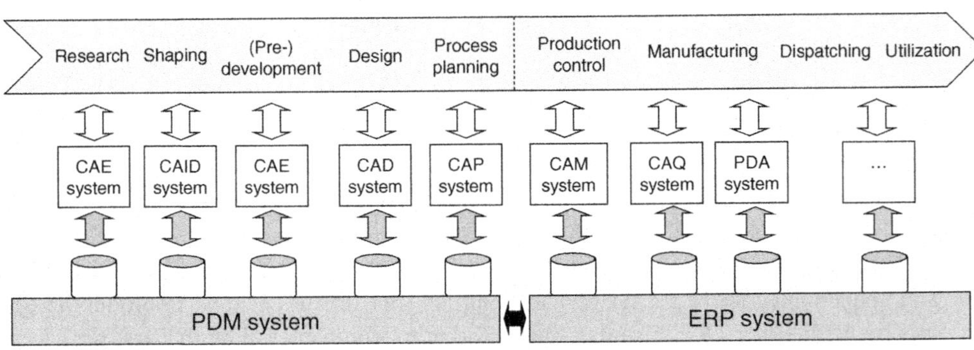

Fig. 7.11 CAx systems in the product life cycle (Vajna et al. 2009, p. 11)

mechanical and for electrical and electronic design. The latter is also known as PCB (printed circuit boards) design.

In all phases of designing a product (or a part), drawings play an important role. For this reason, the core of a CAD system is a graphical editor, that is, a tool for creating, manipulating, and displaying multidimensional technical drawings.

CAD systems have gone through several stages of evolution. The first generation was characterized by *2D systems*. These systems were mainly used to create drawings, reducing three-dimensional physical objects to a two-dimensional representation on a computer screen. Although the objects can be viewed from different perspectives, each perspective is only a two-dimensional top view.

The next generation encompassed so-called *2½D systems*, allowing two-dimensional objects to be projected onto a three-dimensional representation. This means that the design engineer had to decompose three-dimensional objects into two-dimensional components and define connecting points so that the components could be joined to be displayed in three dimensions. The main disadvantage of this approach is that it requires a high level of abstract thinking by the design engineer. He or she has to mentally disassemble the object and define the connecting points.

3D systems show the objects in a three-dimensional space with *x*, *y*, and *z* axes. Common models to display the objects include wire-frame, area, volume, solid, and parametric models. A major difference between these models is the amount of data that must be gathered, stored, and considered in the calculations.

Advanced CAD systems have a higher level of automation. If, for example, a design parameter

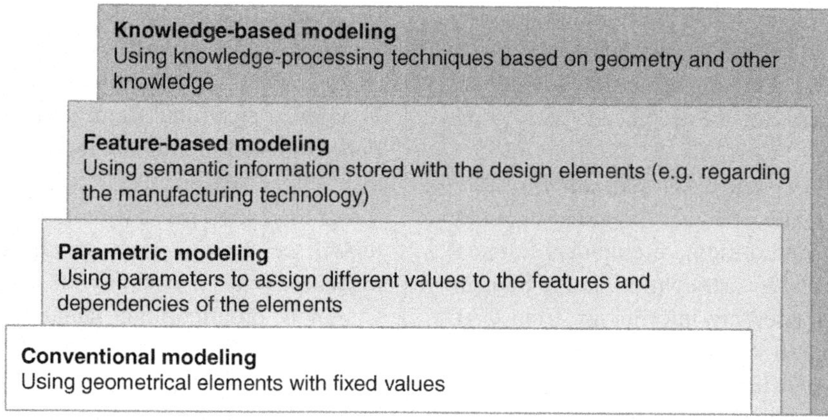

Fig. 7.12 Stages of 3D modeling (Vajna et al. 2009, p. 173)

changes, the system adjusts the design process fully or partly automatically. In addition, today's object-oriented software technology allows design elements to be reused. For example, certain standard elements such as drill holes or coils are needed again and again. They can be automatically generated by referring to stored information and adapting it to the characteristics of the object in question.

A powerful *archiving* component that allows drawings and other data from earlier design processes to be easily retrieved is important for the performance of a CAD system. Functions for *component classification* help engineers to design new parts by searching a component database. For this purpose, components must be classified according to appropriate criteria before they are stored.

Using a CAD system requires careful modeling of the products. The fundamentals of 3D modeling are described in a guideline by the Association of German Engineers (VDI 2209/2006). Based on this guideline, Fig. 7.12 illustrates the stages of 3D modeling (Vajna et al. 2009, p. 172):

Parametric modeling means that the features and dependencies of the elements can be assigned different values. Parameters apply to, for example, the geometry (form of the product), the topology (structure of the product), the technology, as well as the physical properties.

Feature-based modeling takes not only the geometric aspects but also semantics into account (meaning additional information that is stored with the design elements). "Features" are abstractions of geometric elements that are semantically tagged and available from a library. The semantics refer to, for example, the production technology or properties of the manufacturing process.

Knowledge-based modeling uses knowledge-processing techniques to reach conclusions based on stored geometry knowledge and other knowledge.

Interfaces with Enterprise Resource Planning: A design process can be initiated by the decision to create a new product or by accepting a customer order. At this stage, the type and the properties of the product as well as—implicitly or explicitly—the parts required for the product are specified. With regard to the latter ones, it must be decided which parts need to be designed from scratch and which existing parts can be reused and/or modified, and in what way.

In *make-to-order manufacturing*, customer-specific product features are determined and recorded in the ERP system when the customer places an order. If the specification of the product requires new parts to be designed, the necessary data provided by the customer have to be transmitted from the ERP system's *sales and distribution (S&D)* module to the CAD system.

For completely new parts, bills of materials that could be used to calculate the product cost and to plan the material requirements are not available. Therefore, planning in ERP must start with imprecise data or based on broad assumptions. Later, when the product design is completed and bills of materials have been established (in CAD), the preliminary estimates created earlier can be replaced with more precise data.

Interfaces between CAD and *material management (MM)* are obvious. Exploded drawings in computer-aided design are graphical forms of bills of materials. It is straightforward to transmit geometry and assembly information from CAD to ERP, include it in the ERP master data (parts and product structures), and make it available for material management. In many cases, CAD generates preliminary bills of materials, which are later completed in the ERP system.

From a business point of view, an important connection exists between *product-cost calculation* and computer-aided design. When the design engineer is provided with cost information regarding needed parts (e.g., cost of goods manufactured, purchase prices), he or she can take this information into consideration when making design decisions. Since up to 70 % of the production costs are determined during design, this is a way to significantly save cost. The same applies when the design engineer knows the inventory costs or procurement options of critical parts.

Computer-Aided Planning *Computer-aided planning (CAP)* is a term used in engineering to describe the planning of the technical operations needed for manufacturing a certain part with the help of computer-supported tools. CAP starts with the product structures and/or specifications provided by the customer. Master data needed for CAP, in addition to parts and product structures, include operating facilities, design features, material characteristics, quality specifications and allowances, drawings, and more.

CAP is sometimes considered a part of CAM (computer-aided manufacturing, see below). On the other hand, CAP modules have also been included in CAD systems.

The primary *output* of computer-aided planning consists of work instructions in the form of routings, NC programs, and programs for industrial robots:

- For conventional manufacturing technology, *routings* as described in Sect. 3.1.1 are created. They are printed out and passed on, in paper or electronic form, to production.
- For automated production facilities, the work instructions are realized as *NC programs* (programs for numerically controlled machine tools, see below) and transferred to the machines via a network or data carrier. Common programming languages for NC programs are APT and EXAPT.
- Programs for *industrial robots (IRs)* are similar to NC programs, but industrial robots differ from machine tools. They can be programmed not only using textual instructions but also through "learning" (for example, observing a movement and saving the coordinates and the speed) (Vajna et al. 2009, p. 378).

CAP systems support different forms of planning (Mertens 2009, p. 38):

- *Repetitive planning* means planning based on standard routings. This happens usually when a manufacturing order (i.e., an order-specific routing) is created. It involves copying the standard routing and adding order-related information (quantities, deadline, etc.).
- *Adjustment planning* means that routings available in the database are manually changed or expanded upon.
- *Variant planning* refers to part families (cf. Sect. 2.1.2) using basic data of the part family to generate a new routing. Preexisting operation groups are copied from the part-family routing, modified if necessary, and combined into the new routing.
- *New planning* means that the routings are created from scratch. This is usually the case in extreme make-to-order manufacturing where the parts and/or order-specific details are specified by the customer.

CAP systems comprise components for data management, graphic editors for routings and work pieces, a simulation component for controlling and improving routings that were created manually, a programming environment for NC and industrial-robot programs, as well as a program administration component.

Interfaces with Enterprise Resource Planning: The overlapping of ERP components and CAP is especially visible in the routings. Although the routings created in CAP are not identical with the routings maintained in ERP, they do have many things in common. When the business and technical information processing are not integrated, data are redundantly kept in two systems. A similar problem is that functionality for completing manufacturing orders can be found in both ERP and CAP systems.

The reasons for these redundancies lie mainly in the different origins of the two types of system. While ERP systems have their roots in the business field, CAP systems originated in the engineering sciences.

Uncontrolled redundancy between the two systems leads to inconsistent databases, causing errors when manufacturing orders or NC programs are generated. For example, scheduling in ERP may be negatively affected, resulting in long order queues or missed deadlines. CAP may suffer in that NC programs are compromised, leading to scrap and high rejection rates when the programs are executed.

Integration of CAP and ERP helps to avoid these problems. The best option is when the ERP and CAP systems are built on the same database. Otherwise, they may be loosely coupled using well-defined interfaces. Loose coupling means that data are systematically exchanged as follows:

Primary requirements planning (in ERP) and computer-aided planning are connected through customer orders and internal orders. These orders—in particular the quantities, dates, and possibly product specifications—are transferred from the ERP to the CAP system for further processing. Processing here means entering into repetitive, adjustment or new planning (see above) in order to create the required routings and NC programs.

Vice versa, the ERP system may require *routings* from the CAP system for primary requirements planning. This is the case when a preliminary cost calculation has to be carried out during the inquiry or quotation steps of order fulfillment.

Material management and *master data management* are connected with computer-aided planning by the fact that ERP master data can contain information relevant for CAP. Examples include material characteristics and standard routings stored in the part or product-structure master data.

When both the ERP system and the CAP system provide *order-scheduling* functionality, the company must check whether the scheduling methods are compatible. Different methods may lead to contradictory results, for example, due to different priority rules. A better way is to assign the responsibility for scheduling to only one of the systems:

(a) If the ERP system has been declared responsible, it is still necessary to maintain a consistent communication between the two systems. For example, the CAP system may create a routing for an order, transfer this routing to the ERP system's lead-time scheduling module, and trigger the execution of the scheduling procedure.
(b) When order scheduling is under the responsibility of CAP, the ERP system is nevertheless affected because it manages the capacity loads. *Capacity planning*, in particular capacity load leveling, is a typical ERP task, which is influenced by the scheduling decisions made in CAP. If the company uses a *manufacturing execution system (MES)* for short-term planning and control, this system is also affected, because the order and operation dates the MES works with now come from the CAP scheduling.

Computer-Aided Manufacturing While CAD and CAP deal with tasks to be completed *before* the production begins, *CAM (computer-aided manufacturing)* systems are employed directly in the manufacturing process. It is here that the business and engineering information processing meet. For some planning and control functions, it is even difficult to say whether they are part of the technical or business branch.

This is one reason why the term "computer-aided manufacturing" is not uniquely defined. Some authors refer to CAM as comprising all

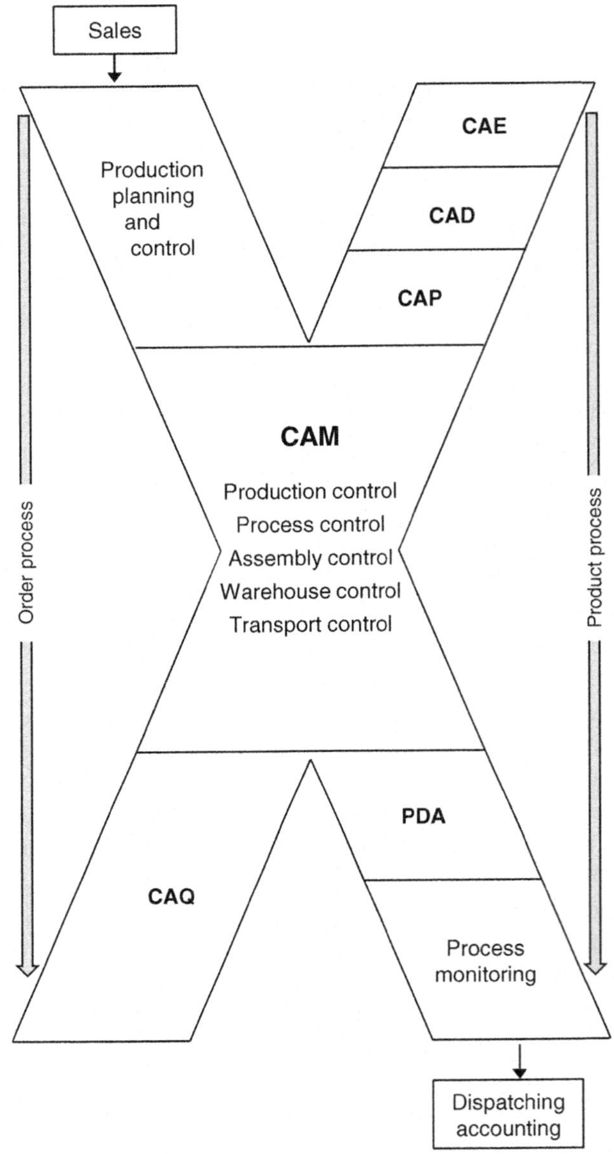

Fig. 7.13 CAM in business and engineering (Mertens 2009, p. 267)

execution-related tasks—including business-oriented tasks—while others summarize under CAM only the technical execution of manufacturing.

CAM's execution-oriented focus in both business and technical information processing is highlighted in Fig. 7.13. The X leg that has production planning and scheduling on top represents the business perspective, while the other leg, starting with CAE, arranges the engineering subsystems in a logical order. CAM is embedded in both legs, although it primarily contains technical control functions: manufacturing, process, assembly, warehouse, and transport control.

Major technical systems belonging to CAM include numerically controlled machine tools (NC machines), robots, driverless transport systems, mechanical handling systems as well as flexible manufacturing systems, and automatic stock and logistic systems.

- *NC machines* (NC = numeric control) come in different variants (Suh et al. 2010, p. 3–31), depending on how much support is provided by computers: simple NC machines, CNC machines, and DNC machines. All are basically controlled with *NC programs*. These programs describe all the steps that the machine must carry out in succession. While early NC machines read the control programs from punched tape, later more modern data carriers came in use.

- *CNC machines* (CNC = computerized numeric control) contain one or more microprocessors (Suh et al. 2010, p. 7) and operating software. This means that programs can not only be read, but also modified on the machine. However, CNC machines are not capable of communicating and automatically coordinating their actions with other machines since they are basically stand-alone units.
- *DNC machines* (DNC = distributed numeric control, also known as direct numeric control) are CNC machines connected via a network, usually communicating with a central computer. This computer monitors, controls, and coordinates the machines. NC programs are usually transmitted to the individual machines over the network.
- *Industrial robots* (IRs) (Kandray 2010, pp. 257–287) are handling units controlled by a program that can move in all directions. Most robots are found in the automobile industry. Robots are capable of orienting themselves and positioning work pieces, tools, and tensioning means. They usually have graspers, tools, and sensors. With the help of sensors, they can, for example, determine surface textures. Industrial robots complete complex and varied operations. They are used in areas such as automatic assembly and variant manufacturing, where single-purpose assembly machines are not flexible enough. Welding is another area where industrial robots are employed. The performance and application areas of robots are constantly growing. This is due to the general fact that machines have increasingly been enriched with "intelligence." *Robotics* is a major research area in artificial intelligence (AI).
- A *flexible manufacturing system (FMS)* is made up of a number of work stations (usually CNC machines), which are connected to each other through an automated transport and storage system (Alavudeen and Venkateshwaran 2010, pp. 43–49). An FMS is capable of processing work pieces from a specific spectrum of parts in any sequence, without significant delays from setup.
- *Automated guided vehicles (AGVs)* and *automated inventory systems* are used for transporting and provisioning work pieces, tools, and materials for the operating facilities and work places (Alavudeen and Venkateshwaran 2010, p. 227). AGVs, also known as driverless transportation systems, are conducted through induction loops and are controlled by process computers. Automatic inventory systems use computers for placing and removing work pieces, tools, and materials from stock. The control programs often include optimization methods, for example, to minimize the number of stock placing and removing steps.

Interfaces with Enterprise Resource Planning: Information about an automated inventory system's storage and removal actions is important for *material management* in ERP (inventory control, net requirements planning, purchase requisitions, etc.). Furthermore, actual material movements are needed for tracking orders and checking invoices.

Warehouse structures are maintained within the ERP system, including information such as how the warehouse is divided up into smaller units and how materials are assigned to storage places. This information is essential for planning, executing, and controlling stock placement and removal by an *automated inventory system*.

Rough planning in MRP II, especially *capacity planning*, requires information from CAM about the mid- and long-term availability of operating facilities (including transport facilities). ERP master data such as standard routings and operating facilities must be updated whenever the actual times in production differ significantly from the times stored in the master data. This is primarily true for the processing and setup times in the routings. Regarding the operating facilities, the capacity, utilization ratio, and performance level might be affected.

The *transportation times* of automated guided vehicles can be of importance for the scheduling functions of ERP, unless they are so small that they can be neglected. If fragile or time-sensitive goods are to be transported, the availability of suitable transport resources is an essential information item maintained in the ERP system.

For *highly detailed planning,* transportation requirements can be considered in the routings through separate transport operations and explicit assignment of transportation resources. For this case, the ERP system has to maintain basic times and resources needed for transport operations, as it does for manufacturing and setup operations.

In *less detailed planning,* transportation is included in the transition times between production operations. This was already mentioned in Sect. 3.1.1.

Estimates of the transportation times can be continuously tuned by processing feedback received from production/machine data acquisition (PDA/MDA, cf. Sect. 7.1.2).

Input to CAM includes production orders, operation sequences, assignment of operating facilities, as well as start and end dates of operations. If an integrated database exists, these data are available to the CAM system, otherwise they have to be exported from the ERP system and imported into the CAM system.

Another essential input to CAM consists of the NC programs created in CAP. For the sake of data consistency, only one of the systems, either the ERP, the CAP, or the CAM system, should be responsible for storing and maintaining the NC programs (preferably the ERP system). However, since not all ERP systems are capable of managing NC programs, an option is to employ a *product data management (PDM) system* as a single point of storage (see Sect. 7.2.2).

Data from CAM regarding the execution of manufacturing operations are especially interesting for the short-term tasks of a *manufacturing execution system.* For example, the planning board of an electronic leitstand can be kept up-to-date by directly coupling the automated manufacturing facilities and the leitstand, or by making machine data continuously available to the leitstand. In this way, the leitstand can immediately react to disruptions of the manufacturing process by rescheduling operations and/or transferring them to alternative facilities.

In some cases, the functionality of an electronic leitstand, in particular its scheduling and capacity-planning features, is embedded in an automated manufacturing system. The reason for this is that automated manufacturing systems are usually quite expensive. Therefore, it is important to utilize them at their optimal capacity.

Computer-Aided Quality Assurance CAQ (computer-aided quality assurance) is a set of activities spanning multiple phases. While CAQ has always been considered a part of CIM (computer-integrated manufacturing), today its functionality is usually provided by a manufacturing execution system (MES). For this reason, *quality management* was already discussed above in the context of MES (cf. Sect. 7.1.3).

Relationships Between CAx Components Figure 7.14 illustrates the relationships discussed above between CAx systems and between the CAx systems and the ERP system. Wide arrows indicate the flow or exchange of data, while narrow arrows express function- and data-oriented coupling.

The overall process from strategic planning to manufacturing execution touches the various areas as follows: Strategic production planning as a part of business planning provides product requirements, based on which CAE creates an overall product design. Subsequently, the ERP system's sales and distribution module passes preliminary part and variant master data, and possibly customer orders, on to the CAD system, where the product is designed. When the design is completed, geometry data and engineering bills of materials are handed over to the CAP system. This system generates routings and NC programs, referring back to the operating facility master data and standard routings stored in the ERP system.

While the routings are made available to the ERP system, NC programs are transferred to the CAM system for execution. Notifications about

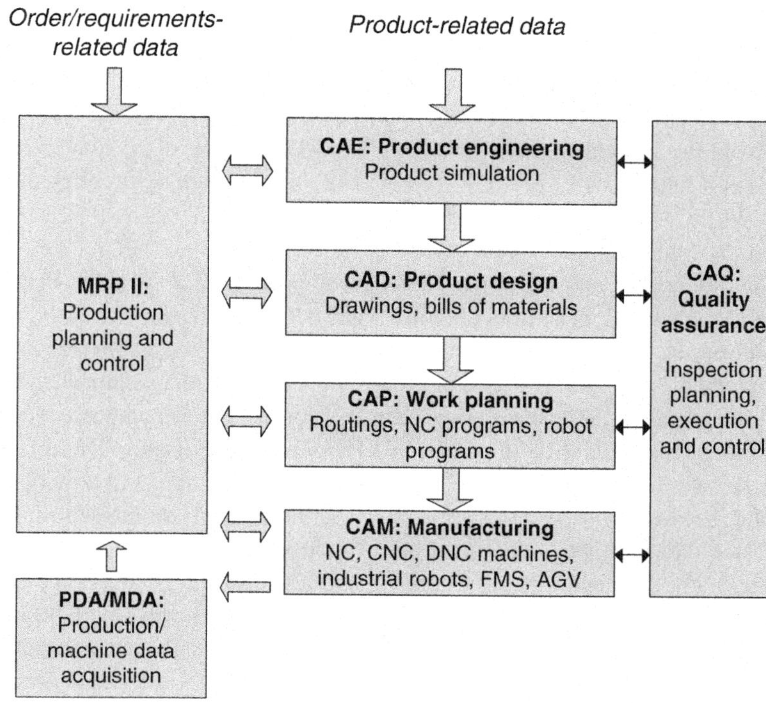

Fig. 7.14 Connections Between CAx, ERP and MES modules

finished parts, errors, and interruptions are communicated to the ERP system via the production/machine data acquisition (PDA/MDA) system.

Quality assurance (CAQ) accompanies and supervises the entire process. It takes in the quality requirements from primary requirements planning as well as the quality to-be data that were created in CAD based on the quality requirements. CAQ assures that quality inspection plans are created in CAP and oversees their execution in CAM. Finally, CAQ processes the inspection data and initiates corrective measures if needed.

The process outlined above maps out a best-case scenario. Typically, only parts of this process are realized in practice. The reasons for this may be that only some CAx components were implemented in the organization, that the CAx and ERP systems are not connected, or that the various CAx components are based on different technologies, because they were purchased from different vendors.

In order to be able to work smoothly together, all CAx systems, and also the ERP system, must support common standards for product-defining data, for example, STEP ("standard for the exchange of product model data").

CAx Implementation and Integration Implementing CAx systems is a comprehensive project, similar to implementing an ERP system. It has an impact on all business areas that are related with manufacturing. Implementation projects usually follow a process model, just as ERP implementation projects do (cf. Sect. 6.1).

A typical process model for CAx implementation includes phases like the following (Vajna et al. 2009, p. 444):

→Project motivation
→Setting up the project team
→Selecting a partner (e.g., an external consultant)
→As-is analysis
→To-be concept and requirements profile
→System evaluation and selection
→Estimation of cost-effectiveness
→Implementation
→Migration from the old system to the new system
→Installation of CAx support

Before migrating from the old to the new system, the company must decide whether the cutover shall take place in one step ("big bang"), or whether both systems shall operate in parallel for some time. Furthermore, employees have to be trained, the old databases have to be reviewed and converted, and the necessary hardware has to be installed.

Just as in an ERP implementation project, not all modules will be installed at the same time, but instead the individual CAx systems are handled one at a time.

When a company proceeds step by step, certain implementation sequences may be better than others. The starting point, before turning to the CAx systems, is an integrated ERP and MES solution. A meaningful first step would be to implement CAD and CAM, and to integrate these systems if they come as separate solutions. The next step would be to connect ERP—MES, on the one hand, and CAD—CAM, on the other hand, because these systems are related via their master data (e.g., bills of materials, routings). Afterward, production data acquisition (PDA) can be coupled with CAM.

Once the ERP, MES, and CAx systems have been integrated, the company will benefit in many ways. Bills of materials and routings are usually created by engineers using CAD and CAP. Afterward, however, they are primarily needed by business people working in enterprise resource planning. This means that the bills of materials and routings must be available in the ERP system where they are used for material requirements planning, accounting, lead-time scheduling, and many more tasks as discussed in the previous chapters.

Vice versa, with integration, data from the business systems are available to the engineers. For example, design engineers can access material cost data when they draft a new product. They can take this information into account and select a less expensive material if a choice is available.

The next step after intracompany system integration is to deal with business processes that include customers and suppliers. Integration means here, in the first place, data exchange with the partners in standard formats. For example, order data can be transmitted using EDIFACT or ebXML, while geometric data may be sent using a STEP format.

It is worth noting that it usually takes a long time to implement a CAx system. Implementing a complete CAx suite is an extremely time- and energy-consuming endeavor. Therefore, companies often stay with one CAx component for years before they move on to the next.

7.2.2 PDM: Product Data Management

Product data management (PDM) is an approach for the technical and organizational integration of data management with the company's business processes. PDM refers to storing, archiving, maintaining, and providing all product-describing data that are created during the product development process, as well as the relationships between the data. It covers the entire life cycle of a product, extending to all business processes where the data are relevant. In addition, data integration between CAx and ERP systems is nowadays often realized with the help of a PDM system.

A number of different *terms* have been used for and around product data management, including:

- *Engineering data management (EDM)*: This term focuses more on the processes (e.g., product release, change management) during the product life cycle than on the documents (e.g., drawings).
- *Engineering management (EM)*: This term indicates that the main concern is not product data but the management of the entire product development process.
- *Product data and process management (PDPM)*: This approach claims that not only product-describing data and activities but also the production processes and production facilities have to be included.
- *Collaborative product definition management (CPDM)* and *collaborative product commerce (CPC)*: These and similar approaches emphasize the computer-supported collaboration of work groups. They are based on insights from the field of CSCW (computer-supported cooperative work).

A term related with product data management is *product life cycle management (PLM)*. Unfortunately, this term is also used with different meanings.

- Some authors and vendors speak of PLM when they mean the *strategic management* of a product throughout its entire life cycle. In this sense, PLM comprises requirements generation, product planning, product development, process planning, procurement, production, operation, and recycling (Theuer et al. 2010).
- Sometimes, this term is used to describe an extension of product data management by an *integrated configuration, requirements, and project management*. Configuration management is responsible for a complete documentation of a product structure at any time of the product life cycle. The task of requirements management is to capture and maintain all product requirements and changes of the requirements during the life of the product. Project management in this context is mainly concerned with coordinating the groups involved in the product development.
- PLM is also applied as an umbrella term that encompasses multiple application areas. In the *SAP business suite*, for example, PLM covers several modules, one of which is product data management.

Product data management was originally created as a response to the growing requirements concerning the management of engineering data. This increase is due to several reasons. Firstly, the complexity of the products has substantially increased and is still increasing. Secondly, companies have to meet more and more documentation requirements, regarding both the products and the manufacturing processes. Examples include product liability and quality standards such as ISO 9000. With these requirements, the amount of information that needs to be stored and retrieved has grown significantly.

Another reason for the development of PDM systems is the problems resulting from lack of data integration. Before PDM, product and process data were stored in many different systems, including ERP, CAD, CAP, DTP (desktop publishing), and document management systems. All these systems had their own databases. A good deal of the information that is nowadays stored in a PDM system is created by *computer-aided design*. The most important integration step regarding PDM is, therefore, coupling the PDM system with the CAD system. Subsequently, other CAx components should also be connected with PDM.

The interaction between PDM, CAx, and ERP systems is shown in Fig. 7.15. This figure is based on a guideline by the Association of German Engineers (VDI). It can be interpreted as follows.

All relevant data from product planning, design, work planning, manufacturing, and sales should be stored in an integrated product and process data model and managed with the help of a PDM system. The product structure is generated step by step in the PDM system using information from the various CAx systems. The PDM system is subsequently responsible for any modifications, versioning, and archiving.

Later, in manufacturing resource planning, when a specific version of a product structure is needed, the ERP system accesses the data managed by the PDM system. Data and documents are transferred from the PDM system to the ERP system via a well-defined interface, including the product structure and routing of the released product version as well as data referring to the manufacturing order in question.

Functionality of PDM Systems PDM tasks include master data management (e.g., parts, bills of materials), document management (e.g., drawings, 3D models), keeping track of process-related properties of data and documents (e.g., release status, version, valid from), and supporting release and change processes.

An integrated PDM database allows the company not only to store but also to retrieve data and documents efficiently. It helps to avoid problems many companies have been exposed to, such as struggling with multiple releases and different numbers for the same part.

Based on a guideline by the Association of German Engineers, Vajna et al. list a number of *core functionalities* PDM systems should provide

Fig. 7.15 Interaction of PDM, CAx and ERP (Vajna et al. 2009, p. 424)

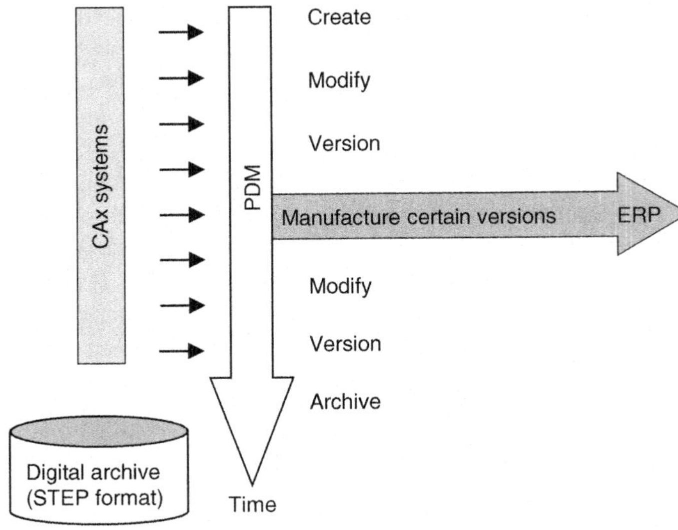

(Vajna et al. 2009, pp. 425–426). The list includes the following:

- Product data and documents: supporting the management of data and documents (including input/output of CAD models, drawings, multimedia, etc.), and maintaining the connections with the systems where these objects were created
- Product structures and configurations: creating and modifying product structures, generating bills of materials and where-used lists, change management (configurations, versions), and management of product variants
- Part classification and part families: classifying parts using property lists, searching and retrieving part and product information, providing a numbering system (e.g., based on standards such as eCl@ss, ISO 13584 and ISO 61355)
- Workflow management: mapping and monitoring processes, activities and information flows, forwarding documents to the next person, providing process information, etc.
- User management: representation of organizational structures, administration of users and user groups (e.g., roles, access rights)
- Project data management: administration of activities, dependencies, timetables, and other project management information (e.g., project-specific roles, access rights, and milestones)

Additionally, a PDM system should provide administration, customization, and configuration tools, helping the company to set up a PDM environment and tailor the system (cf. "customizing" in Sect. 6.2).

Integration issues arise when the PDM system is to be embedded in a typical work environment. Interfaces should be available for common office programs (e.g., MS Office), CAx systems, and ERP systems. If the company requires interfaces with systems not supported by the PDM vendor, they have to arrange for an effective coupling themselves.

With regard to ERP, the coupling may be realized in a specific customizing project. ERP and PDM have many logical interfaces, because an ERP system, being the backbone of business information processing, uses a large number of data structures. As has been discussed in Sects. 2.1 and 3.1, these data are usually stored in an ERP database.

When a PDM system comes into the game, responsibilities for the data have to be redefined. The basic principle behind product data management is that all relevant data are created, stored, and distributed under the control of the PDM system (cf. Fig. 7.15). This means primarily that the ERP system will have to access product data through the PDM system.

Process and *workflow support* are other important features of PDM. Examples of processes, in this context, include releasing a new product and changing a product structure. Many organizational units are involved in these processes. The workflow component of the PDM system will see that the necessary process steps are initiated in the right sequence. For example, when one person or department has finished their activity, the system will automatically notify the next person or department that is responsible for the next step and forward them the needed documents. When the status of an object changes, the system will trigger pertinent actions and/or inform the persons involved.

In addition to the functionalities mentioned above, PDM systems provide extensions such as the following:

- Support for *requirements management*, especially during the early stages of the product development process; linking requirements documents (e.g., functional specification) with later process stages (this is sometimes called "requirements traceability management," RTM).
- A *product configurator* based on product variants, possibly integrated with an electronic product catalog and coupled with a CAD system. A configurator assists the sales personnel, allows the design engineer to create customer-specific CAD models, and facilitates configuration management according to ISO 10007.
- *MRO management* (MRO = maintenance, repair, and operations), connecting maintenance, repair, and service data from operations with product development information.
- *Engineering portals*, providing all PDM relevant sources of information in a web portal that serves as a "single point of information" (including both company-internal and external information).
- Interfaces for coupling PDM with electronic market places, product catalogs, standard-part libraries, etc.

Benefits and Shortcomings Companies can significantly benefit from implementing a PDM system. Frequently mentioned *benefits* include:

- Unified data structures due to data integration, reducing redundancy-related problems
- Avoiding multiple data entry, resulting in fewer errors
- Efficient storage and retrieval of very large amounts of data and documents
- Company-wide access to the same information pool, reducing the effort of gathering information
- Transparency, increasing the reusability of parts
- Shorter product development processes, increased productivity, lower design and modification costs
- Better product quality and product documentation, improving the traceability of products (e.g., for product liability issues)

Despite these benefits, many companies do not yet utilize product data management systems. This is due to a number of problems and *shortcomings*:

- Uncertainty among potential users about the benefits, because the functionalities of PDM systems and other systems (in particular, CAx systems) partially overlap.
- PDM involves high cost for software licenses, implementation, and operation.
- Cost-benefit analysis is difficult, because the benefits of having "better data" are difficult to measure in quantitative figures.
- Implementation projects are very complex and costly, because PDM affects the entire organization and information system landscape.
- Implementation of a PDM system may require organizational measures before it can start. For example, if different numbering systems and/or terminology are used in different departments, they need to be unified first. Likewise, if the product-related processes are not clear, they must be defined first, which requires business process reengineering.
- Acceptance problems can occur because users may fear being monitored or losing some of their previous tasks.

PDM Market A significant number of PDM systems are available in the market today. In addition to vendors specializing in product data management, the large vendors of CAx and ERP systems are also market participants, having extended their software portfolios with PDM systems. Examples of ERP vendors offering PDM systems include:

- *SAP*—delivering product data management as a part of SAP PLM (http://www.sap.com)
- *Oracle*—offering several solutions, including "JD Edwards EnterpriseOne Manufacturing (PDM)" and "Agile Engineering Data Management" (http://www.oracle.com)
- *Infor*—providing Infor PDM as a part of PLM (product lifecycle management, http://www.infor.com)

SCM: Supply Chain Management

8

Enterprise resource planning (ERP), as well as the earlier approaches manufacturing resource planning (MRP II) and material requirements planning (MRP), focuses on an individual company, in particular on the planning and control *within* the company. In contrast to this, supply chain management (SCM) looks at *chains* (or networks) of companies connected with each other through supplier-customer relationships.

8.1 Motivation for Supply Chain Management

The reason why supply chain management came about is because industrial relationships have become increasingly complex over the last decades. Manufacturing still happens "within" an enterprise, but not exclusively. Nowadays, hardly any manufacturing company produces all parts and assemblies of their goods entirely in-house. On the contrary, an increasing share of the end product is manufactured by, and purchased from, other companies. In most industries, the production depth has significantly decreased.

Suppose a company manufactures a product that used to have a seven-level bill of materials when the entire product was manufactured in-house. Since the company now purchases the majority of parts and assemblies from suppliers and only performs pre-assembly and final assembly in-house, the production depth is down to two levels. Compared to seven levels, in-house production planning and control is much simpler, but now the company is dependent upon suppliers for obtaining the needed parts and assemblies in the right places, at the right time, and at the lowest cost.

Let us assume the company accepts a customer order and confirms the delivery date. In order to meet the date, not only must the company's own activities (requirements planning, scheduling, shop floor control, etc.) be effectively planned and executed but also those of the suppliers. Furthermore, the supplier's activities must be coordinated with the company's planning. The company will only be able to complete the customer order on time if all purchased parts and assemblies arrive as scheduled and in conformant quality.

From the perspective of one of the suppliers, the situation is perhaps the same. Our company is the supplier's customer placing an order. The supplier does not manufacture all parts of their product themselves. Rather, they have to order input materials from their suppliers and coordinate their own production planning and control with the suppliers' delivery schedules. This process continues all the way back to the producers of the raw materials, hence the name "supply chain."

With the globalization of economic relationships, today's supply chains are not limited to the home country, but cross-national boundaries and

K.E. Kurbel, *Enterprise Resource Planning and Supply Chain Management*, Progress in IS, DOI 10.1007/978-3-642-31573-2_8, © Springer-Verlag Berlin Heidelberg 2013

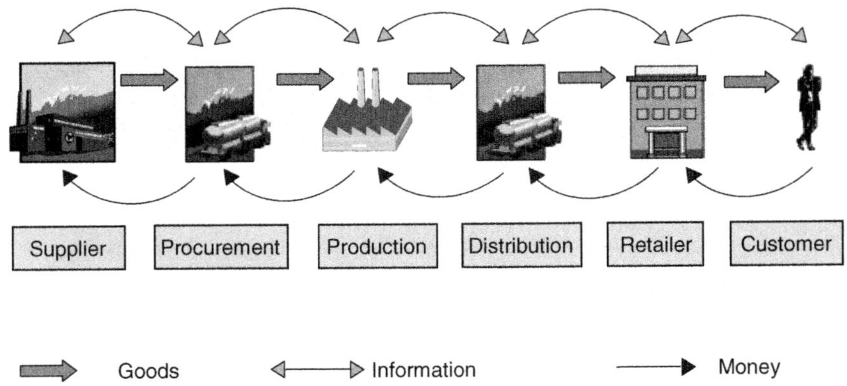

Fig. 8.1 A simple logistic chain (Kuhn and Hellingrath 2002, p. 10)

continents. For example, most computer chips come from Taiwan or the USA, personal computers are assembled in China, and transmission parts are manufactured in India.

A critical success factor for all participants in a supply chain is *customer satisfaction*. At one end of the supply chain is the end customer who creates the demand for the end product. This demand indirectly produces the demand for the intermediate and preliminary products and ultimately for the raw materials.

The better the supply chain works, the stronger the partners' competitive position on the market. When the chain runs efficiently, the utility for the customer increases in terms of price, quality, and delivery time. This in turn leads to happier customers, who generate more demand for the end product and thus increase the revenue of all supply chain partners.

Supply chain management is an approach that deals with the *flows of goods* and *information* across entire logistic chains. Figure 8.1 gives an example of what the stations of such a chain can look like: suppliers of the company, various departments (e.g., purchasing, manufacturing, dispatching), distribution centers, merchants (wholesale, intermediaries, retail), and customers. Additional stations that are not shown in the figure include shippers and their depots.

The figure also shows that the objects that flow through the chain include not only goods and information but also money. The flow of money goes in the opposite direction from the flow of goods. Although the exchange of money is an important part of the business relationships between the partners, it is usually not explicitly considered in supply chain management. That is, SCM focuses more on the flows of goods and information.

In the field of *logistics*, the flows of goods and information have been examined for a long time. A traditional differentiation of logistics was according to business functions, for example, into procurement logistics, production logistics, distribution logistics, and disposal logistics. Later, the integration aspect was also taken into consideration, and the term "logistic chain" came into use.

Supply chain management has evolved from logistics, but it has a stronger focus on the *management* of the chains, crossing business processes, business functions, and even the boundaries of the company. This means that supply chain management deals with the proper functioning of the entire supply chain with all partners included, not only with effective processes of one company.

The partners of a supply chain are tightly connected, as Fig. 8.2 shows. One company's supplier is at the same time another supplier's customer, etc. For this reason, supply chain management has to look at all the steps and stations involved in the chain, starting with the very first supplier all the way to the end customer.

The following *definition* of supply chain management summarizes the above-mentioned aspects. It has been adopted from Kuhn and

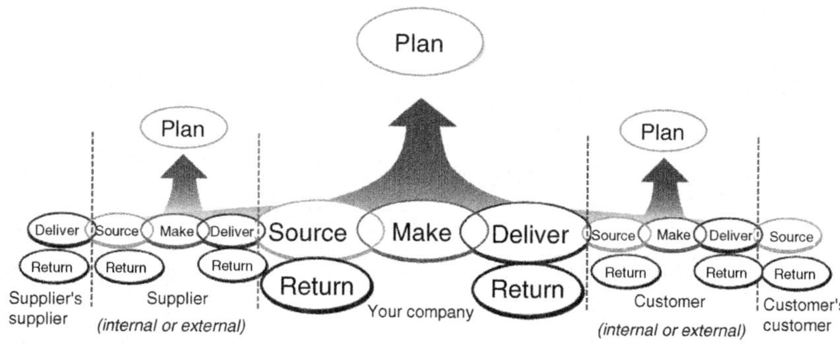

Fig. 8.2 Supplier-customer relationships in a supply chain (SCC 2010, p. 6)

Hellingrath's definition (Kuhn and Hellingrath 2002, p. 10).

Supply chain management is defined as the integrated, process-oriented design, planning and control of goods, information, and cash flows along the entire value chain from the customer to the raw-material supplier with the aims of:

- Improving customer orientation
- Synchronizing supply with demand
- Making the production more flexible and responsive to the demand
- Downsizing of the inventory along the value chain

Highlighting the *process-oriented* approach to supply chain management is important. Process orientation has many advantages that have already been discussed in Sect. 1.3. In supply chain management, it is even more relevant because the business processes involve various departments, not just in one company, but in different companies. The attribute "integrated" in the definition expresses that all partners in the processes have to coordinate their activities. It is worth noting that supply chain management includes not only the planning but also feedback and monitoring, controlling, and adapting the supply chain.

Whereas enterprise resource planning concentrates only on the internal processes of a company, supply chain management also seeks to exploit the optimization potential that exists between the companies. In particular, it focuses on the effective collaboration of all elements participating in a supply chain, both inside and outside the company.

As an example, let us consider the overall goal of reducing the inventory levels. This goal can be better reached when all partners in a supply chain are provided with adequate information. In this way, the partners can avoid producing too much too early, that is, earlier than actually needed for the next step in the chain. Consequently, inventory levels and tied-up capital will decrease, as well as the storage, labor, and transport capacities required. Trying to optimize the entire supply chain instead of concentrating on local optima usually leads to better overall results.

Zara, a Spanish chain of fashion stores, gives an example of this. Zara has an integrated supply chain that starts with capturing actual demand in the stores worldwide and extends all the way to the designers and the sewing factory in La Coruña, Spain. While focusing on an efficient supply chain, Zara's managers accept the fact that manufacturing and transport capacities are insufficiently exploited. The bottom line is that they enjoy higher profit margins than the rest of the industry (Ferdows et al. 2004).

It's worth pointing out that the term supply "chain" management is actually an oversimplification. Any company that is part of a supply chain is likely to have many customers and many suppliers. This means that the company is not only involved in one supply chain but in many or, in other words, in a supply network, as shown in Fig. 8.3. Therefore, a better term than supply chain management would be "supply network management." However, even though this term

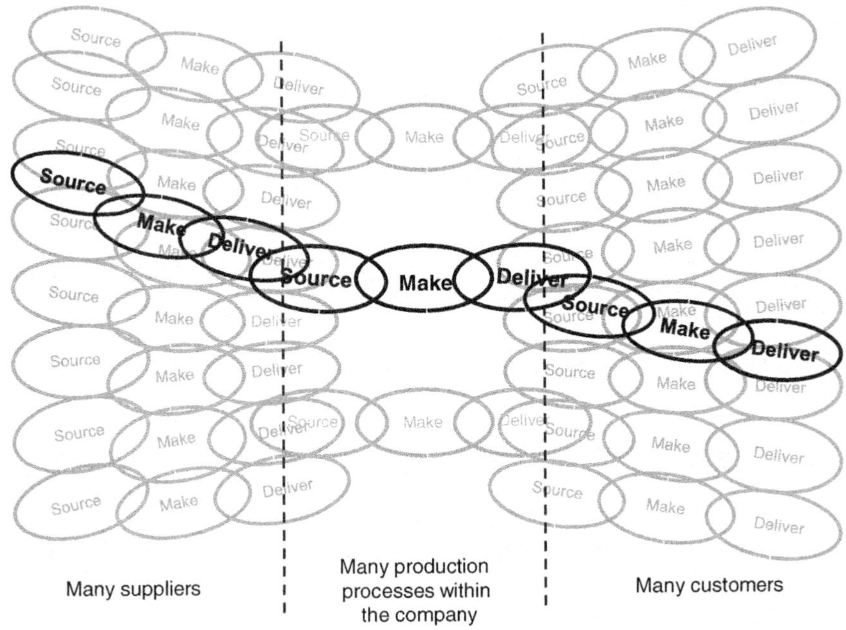

Fig. 8.3 Supply network (source: Supply Chain Council)

better reflects the reality, "supply chain management" is still the term that is used by most authors.

8.2 Coordination and Cooperation

When each company involved in a supply chain only strives to optimize their own processes, there is a considerable risk that the supply chain as a whole will not perform in the best way and that problems in the system will occur. Assuming each company plans their requirements independently and places orders with their suppliers upstream, even small variations in demand downstream can build up into large fluctuations, gaining momentum farther up the chain.

This is mainly due to the *lack of information*. Suppose one company notices that they are receiving more orders from their customers than before. They will increase their production and order more material from their suppliers. Since they don't know why the demand has increased, they will order even more than they immediately need just to be on the safe side for the future. Subsequently, the supplier is put into the same situation as the first company and so on.

Another problem is the *delays* across the supply chain. There are several reasons for this issue. The first is that it takes a certain amount of time before a company realizes that there is a variation in demand. Usually, this variation is recognized only after a significant change of the inventory level has been recorded. The second reason is that material management needs time to decide how to adapt to the new demand. Thirdly, delays occur between detecting a variance, ordering more stock, communicating the order to the supplier, and the supplier's processing of the order.

8.2.1 Industrial Dynamics

Jay W. Forrester, one of the pioneers of industrial management, already attacked these problems in the 1950s. Forrester argued for a theoretical foundation of production management, demanding that management should discover the underlying principles interrelating the flows of information, materials, manpower, money, and capital equipment (Forrester 1958, pp. 37–38). This would enable them to anticipate clearly "how small changes in retail sales can lead to large swings in

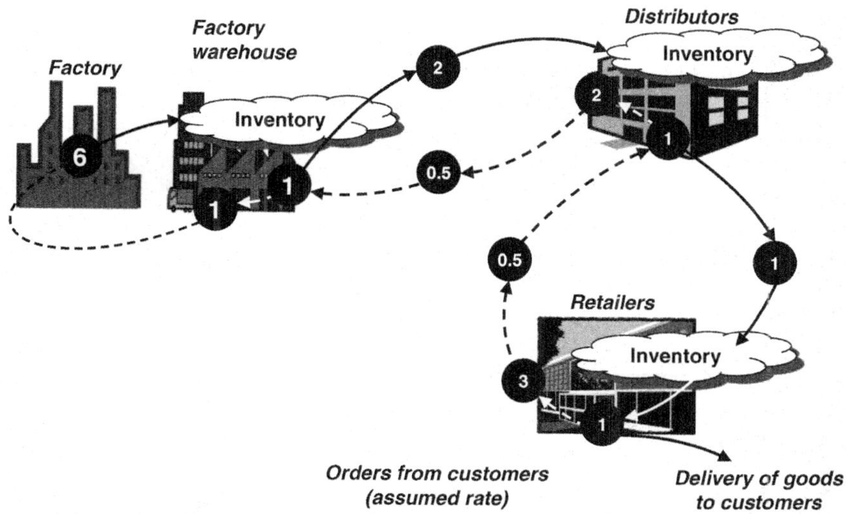

Fig. 8.4 Production-distribution system (Forrester 1958, p. 41)

factory production" and "how a factory manager may find himself unable to fill orders although at all times able to produce more goods than are being sold to customers" (Forrester 1958, p. 38).

To support his argument, Forrester performed detailed investigations and simulation studies according to the new field of research he was establishing—*industrial dynamics*.

Figure 8.4 shows a simple production-distribution system used by Forrester to derive certain conclusions. This system contains retailers, distributors, a warehouse, and a factory. Solid lines represent the flow of goods and dashed lines the flow of information between the elements.

In this system, *delays* occur in the decisions and actions of the parties involved. These delays are indicated by the numbers on the arrows (weeks):

- Delivery from the warehouse to the customer usually takes place 1 week after the order is placed.
- Retailers usually require 3 weeks for bookings, checking inventory, and the procurement department actually creating a stock replenishment order.
- Sending the order through postal service to the distributor takes ½ week on average.
- The distributor needs around 1 week to process the order and an additional week to deliver the order to the retailer.
- Similar delays exist (3 weeks in total) between the factory warehouse and the distributor.
- Factory lead time requires a period of 6 weeks from the point in time when the decision is made to increase the production speed, until the production output has actually reached the target level.

In this system, three *inventory levels* exist: the factory's warehouse, the distributor's warehouse, and the retailer's warehouse. A number of *assumptions* as to the ordering and inventory policies are made, such as (Forrester 1958, p. 41): orders to the next higher level of the system include the actual sales made by the ordering level, the number of orders in progress are proportional to the level of business activity and the length of the time required to fill an order, and an increased sales volume and an increased delivery lead time results in increased total orders in the system.

System Simulation In a number of *simulation studies,* Forrester investigated various effects occurring in the production-distribution system outlined above. Taking the computing capabilities

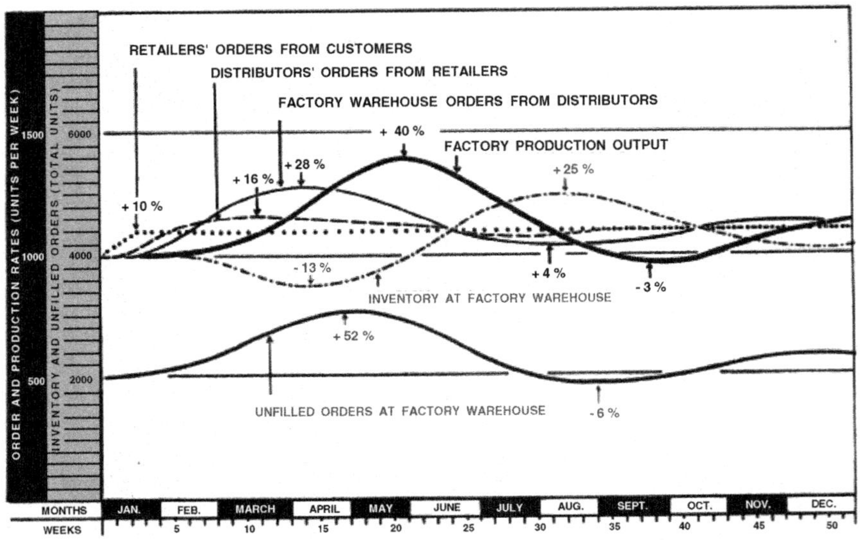

Fig. 8.5 Simulation of production-distribution system (Forrester 1958, p. 43)

of the time into account, the results are impressive. In the original publication in Harvard Business Review, some 5–10 charts per study are presented, each full of curves and values covering several years with weekly period split. Some of the charts extend across several folded pages.

As an example, a chart showing the effect of a sudden increase in end-customer demand is shown in Fig. 8.5. The initial increase with the retailer's, stimulating the system in January, is 10 %. This increase leads to a number of reactions including:

1. Following the 10 % increase in the curve of the orders the retailers receive from customers, it takes about 1 month until the orders placed with the distributors have also gone up to this level.
2. However, the rise of this curve ("distributors' orders from retailers") does not stop at 10 % but reaches 16 % in March. This is partly due to the fact that the retailers increase their inventory levels to be on the safe side and partly due to model assumptions (i.e., more orders are in the system).
3. The curve of the orders the factory warehouse receives from the distributors exhibits an even larger swing. It reaches its maximum of 28 % in April. The main reasons are that the distributors have placed 16 % more orders, the factory warehouse manager adds a safety supplement, and more orders are in the system (according to the assumptions).
4. Inventory at the factory warehouse drops by 13 % (in April) because more has to be shipped to the distributors than before.
5. After a lead time of 6 weeks, the output from factory production rises to a peak in June. This is 40 % above December, while the retail sales are still at 10 %.

Since production has now been increased four times more than the actual rise of end-customer demand, *reverse movements* eventually begin:

1. The retailers see that they can satisfy the demand from their inventory. Therefore, they decrease their orders with the distributors.
2. The distributors realize that they ordered too much and now have too much inventory. They reduce the orders they are placing with the factory, actually dropping to only 4 % above the level before it all started (i.e., previous December). Compared to the 10 % increase in customer demand, the distributor now actually orders 6 % less.
3. The factory output drops to 3 % below the initial value (previous December), which is actually 13 % below the 10 % increase in customer demand.
4. In total, it takes more than 1 year before the production-distribution system has again

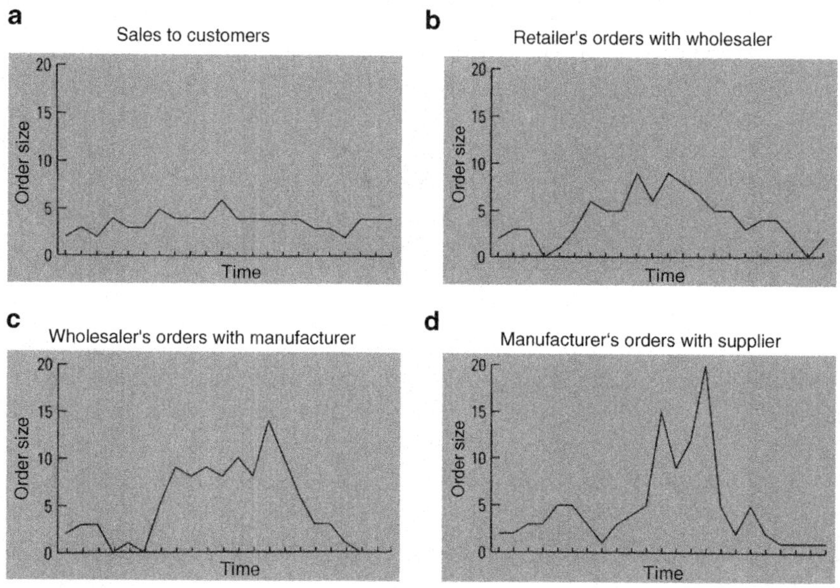

Fig. 8.6 Demand fluctuations in a supply chain (Lee et al. 1997a, p. 94)

reached a stable state. This means that all ordering and manufacturing rates are at their proper levels, corresponding to the initial 10 % retail sales increase.

It is worth noting that the increase in end-customer demand was fairly small compared to the fluctuations it triggered in the business activities of the parties involved.

Forrester performed numerous other investigations regarding causes and effects of demand variations in both directions as well as capacity restrictions. Most of them are more complex than the simple study presented above. The interested reader is advised to consult Forrester's original publications (Forrester 1958, 1961).

8.2.2 The Bullwhip Effect

Almost four decades later, many of Forrester's findings were rediscovered and have since been discussed under the name "bullwhip effect." This term goes back to a famous article in Sloan Management Review, published by Lee, Padmanabhan, and Whang under the title "The Bullwhip Effect in Supply Chains" (Lee et al. 1997a).

In a similar line of reasoning, Lee and coauthors discuss how demand fluctuations can build up along the nodes of a supply chain. The main effects are summarized in Fig. 8.6.

Part a of the figure shows the end-customer demand as observed by the retailer. While the fluctuations are fairly small, the retailer still wishes to avoid the risk of stockouts and therefore increases the safety stock, placing larger orders with the wholesaler.

In *part b,* the retailer's orders reaching the wholesaler are displayed. While noticing that there is higher demand than before, the wholesaler does not know why the demand has increased nor whether the increase is a one-time occurrence or permanent. Therefore, they also raise their inventory level by the increase in demand, plus a safety margin.

From *part c* of the figure, it can be seen that the wholesaler's orders with the manufacturer go up significantly. The manufacturer, not knowing the reasons, raises their production by a little more than the demand increase, just to be on the safe side.

Consequently, more material is needed, requiring more to be ordered. To minimize the risk of stockouts and subsequent disruption of the production process, the manufacturer places larger orders than actually needed. The situation of the suppliers receiving the orders is shown in *part d* of the figure. Compared to the fairly small fluctuations of end-customer demand, the amplitude in the suppliers' demand curve is quite dramatic.

Lee and coauthors identify four *major causes* of the bullwhip effect (Lee et al. 1997a, pp. 95–98):

1. *Demand forecast updating:* As each entity along the chain places an order, it replenishes stock and includes some safety stock. With long lead times, there may be weeks of safety stocks, which make the fluctuation in demand more significant.
2. *Order batching:* Companies may place orders in batches, often to avoid the cost of processing orders more frequently or the high transportation costs for less-than-truckload orders. Suppliers, in turn, face erratic streams of orders, and the bullwhip effect occurs. When order cycles overlap, the effect is even more pronounced.
3. *Price fluctuation:* Special promotions and price discounts result in customers buying in large quantities and stocking up. When prices return to normal, customers stop buying. As a result, their buying pattern does not reflect their consumption pattern.
4. *Rationing and shortage gaming:* If product demand exceeds supply, a manufacturer may ration its products. Customers, in turn, may exaggerate their orders to counteract the rationing. Eventually, orders will disappear and cancelations pour in, making it impossible for the manufacturer to determine the real demand for their product.

Similar to Forrester's arguments, Lee et al. ultimately attribute the bullwhip effect to the lack and distortion of information (Lee et al. 1997b, p. 53). Fixed order quantities and fixed order dates contribute to this distortion.

Fixed order quantities mean that the quantity to include in an order has been determined beforehand, for example, using the economic order quantity approach (cf. Sect. 2.3.1). This quantity is stored in the material master record, implying that orders with the supplier will always be placed in this quantity.

When the company observes a small increase in demand, they will still order the full amount as specified by the fixed order quantity. Since actually less is needed, the rest will be stocked, implying that the next order will be placed much later. What the supplier observes—and will react to—is a fluctuating demand pattern, even though the end-customer demand is actually not fluctuating (Kuhn and Hellingrath 2002, p. 19).

Fixed order dates contribute to the order-batching effect mentioned above. If a customer places an order with the supplier only once a month, the supplier has a strong increase just this one day. When many customers do the same, on the same day, the increase reaches a peak.

This effect can be observed when customers use MRP systems for secondary requirements planning. In the past, the planning was usually done in a batch run, taking many hours (or days). Therefore, companies let the program run over a weekend, for example, at the end of the week or the month, and processed the results next Monday morning, including issuing purchase orders. Being technology driven, the ordering dates do not reflect the actual customer demand pattern.

The bullwhip effect has a number of *negative consequences* for companies, including:

- Extra shifts, overtime, or short-time work due to fluctuating demand
- Safety stock that is higher than actually needed
- Increased inventory cost and capital lockup
- Orders not completed on time, long delivery times, and delays
- Unsatisfied and/or lost customers

The farther up the company is in the supply chain, that is, the farther away from the end customer, the more severe these consequences are.

Lee and coauthors propose a number of measures to counteract the bullwhip effect (Lee et al. 1997a, pp. 98–101):

1. *Avoid multiple demand forecast updates:* Companies can make demand data from downstream available upstream, or they can bypass the downstream site by selling directly to the consumer. Also, they can improve operational efficiency to reduce highly variable demand and long resupply lead times.

2. *Break order batches:* Companies can use electronic data exchange to reduce the cost of placing orders and place orders more frequently. And they can ship assortments of products in a truckload to counter high transportation costs or use third-party logistics companies to handle shipping.
3. *Stabilize prices:* Manufacturers can reduce the frequency and level of wholesale price discounting to prevent customers from stockpiling. They can also use activity-based costing systems so they can recognize when companies are buying in bulk.
4. *Eliminate gaming* in shortage situations: In shortages, suppliers can allocate products based on past sales records rather than on orders, so customers don't exaggerate their orders. They can also eliminate their generous return policies, so retailers are less likely to cancel orders.

While all of these measures are relevant, the first is the most important for avoiding the consequences of missing information. When all parties have the same information regarding the future demand, they can better adjust their production and inventory policies to the actual demand.

8.2.3 Cooperation and Trust in Supply Chains

Companies cooperate in supply chains in order to avoid negative consequences such as the bullwhip effect. They expect to achieve certain benefits from their collaboration, including the following (Kuhn and Hellingrath 2002, pp. 41–43):

- Risk mitigation—lower market and investment risks through cooperation
- Economies of speed—shorter time to market through common utilization of resources, research, and development
- Economies of scale—benefits from bigger size and all supply chain partners acting as a group ("virtual enterprise")
- Economies of scope—lower cost because multiple marketing, service, and sales activities are avoided
- Know-how transfer—learning effects from the exchange of technology, management, and market know-how
- Reduction of horizontal competition—former competitors now cooperate and act together in a larger group (horizontal cooperation)
- Reduction of vertical competition—suppliers and customers communicating closely mitigate the impact of demand fluctuations

Cooperation in supply chains is based on *trust*. Partners must be ready to disclose and exchange information, enter into long-term agreements, and harmonize their work. This means not only that they adjust their processes throughout the entire supply chain but also that they plan the capacity requirements together, level the capacity load across the supply chain, agree on common standards, and establish interfaces for their information systems so that these systems can collaborate.

A prerequisite for an effective collaboration is that companies make internal information available to the other supply chain partners. Today, this means that they exchange electronic information (e.g., customer orders, inventory levels, capacity load) with the partners or that they grant them access to their in-house information systems. When an upstream partner (i.e., a supplier) gains insight into the company's production plan and inventory levels, they can prospectively adapt their own production and procurement planning early on.

Many companies have used EDI (electronic data interchange) to send business information to suppliers and customers, as shown in the upper part of Fig. 8.7. In most cases, this information was limited to orders, quotations, invoices, and similar documents. In supply chain cooperations, information exchanged between the partners, or granted access to, is much more detailed and often rather sensitive. It includes sales plans and forecasts, inventory levels, resource utilization, status of orders, shipments, and more.

Obviously, companies are concerned about this information. Disclosing it to other companies, be they partners in supply chain management or not, is a sensitive matter. What if the partner uses internal information to the company's disadvantage? For example, if the customer sees that the

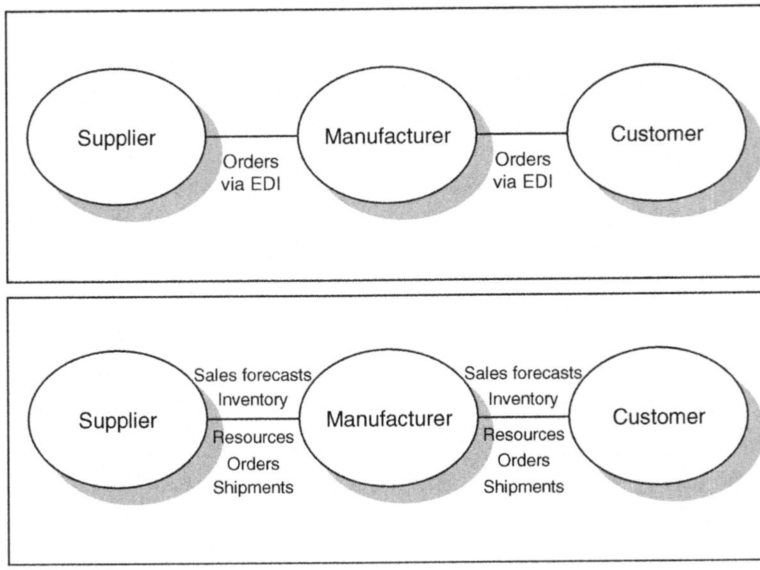

Fig. 8.7 Exchange of information in SCM (Knolmayer et al. 2000, p. 14)

supplier's inventory level is too high, they might use this information to negotiate a price reduction that the supplier otherwise would not have given.

Despite the risk of making internal information available, an increasing number of companies perceive the advantages they derive from exchanging information with their supply chain partners. They realize that the benefits they receive from effective supply chains outweigh the potential disadvantages from disclosing information.

Two prominent approaches that unleash the benefits of information exchange between two partners are VMI (vendor-managed inventory) and CPFR (collaborative planning, forecasting, and replenishment). These approaches will be discussed next.

Vendor-Managed Inventory *Vendor-managed inventory (VMI)* is an approach for close cooperation between a supplier and a vendor, based on trust. The supplier takes on the responsibility for the customer's inventory, making a commitment to act in the interest of the customer. An early project that made VMI popular in Europe was the cooperation between *dm-drogerie markt*, a chain of drug stores, and their suppliers Colgate, Melitta, L'Oreal, and Henkel.

In the VMI approach, the supplier monitors and maintains the customer's inventory at an appropriate level (Baily et al. 2008, pp. 180–182). This requires the customer to allow the supplier to access their inventory data and provide the supplier with up-to-date point-of-sales data. The customer also entrusts the supplier with creating the purchase orders. This means that the supplier is in control of the customer's stock quantities, the replenishment time, and delivery of the goods to the customer.

In traditional inventory management, in contrast, the customer places an order with the supplier when demand for the goods is noticed. The order time and quantity are under the control of the customer because the customer monitors the inventory levels.

It is worth noting the fact that the supplier's total control of inventory management does not change the ownership of the goods. The customer still has to purchase the goods from the supplier to become the owner, or if the goods have only been commissioned, they remain the property of the supplier.

VMI has *advantages* for both partners: Important demand and sales information is available to both the retailer and the supplier, transmission errors are reduced, stockouts are avoided, the service level is improved, etc.

Nevertheless, VMI has failed to become widely implemented (Behrenbeck et al. 2003, p. 43). This is due to several reasons: *Firstly*, no one can decide on appropriate inventory levels as well as the customers themselves. *Secondly*, disruptions in the information flow may occur, and it can happen that important information, such as losing a major customer, is not transmitted to the supplier. *Thirdly*, when the customer's and supplier's information systems are not well integrated, data may need to be explicitly exported from one system and imported into the next, requiring manual editing and conversion to fit the format of the new system. *Fourthly*, the effort needed to implement this approach is relatively high, requiring high revenues to make the venture worthwhile. This means that VMI is better suited for large partners than for small.

CPFR: Collaborative Planning, Forecasting, and Replenishment Collaborative planning, forecasting, and replenishment (CPFR) is an approach for the collaboration of manufacturers and merchants that starts with sales planning. Instead of planning separately, both sides exchange their forecasts in the planning phase and discuss diverging estimates in order to come to a single forecast. Later, when the sales processes are running, both sides actively work together, allowing them to quickly recognize and correct planning mistakes (VICS 2004).

CPFR was initiated in 1995 in a pilot project by Walmart, the world's largest chain of department stores, and one of their suppliers. In this project, the partners realized that further benefits from industry-trade collaboration would require a standardization of business processes. For this reason, Walmart initiated the *CPFR Committee* of VICS ("Voluntary Interindustry Commerce Standards Association"). VICS is an interindustry association, focusing on the improvement of the efficiency and effectiveness of the entire supply chain and the development of cross industry standards (http://www.vics.org). Members of the CPFR committee are well-known manufacturers and retailers of consumer goods.

The mission of the CPFR committee is "... to develop business guidelines and roadmaps for various collaborative scenarios, which include upstream suppliers, suppliers of finished goods and retailers, which integrate demand and supply planning and execution" (http://www.vics.org/committees/cpfr/). By integrating processes on the sides of supply and demand, CPFR aims to improve the efficiency, increase revenue, lower tied-up capital, and reduce inventory levels throughout the entire supply chain.

In order to achieve these goals, a reference model is provided, as shown in Fig. 8.8. This model defines eight major activities where the parties involved should cooperate. It includes important steps such as creating a common sales forecast and how to handle exceptional situations, namely:

1. Sales forecasting
2. Order planning/forecasting
3. Order generation
4. Order fulfillment
5. Exception management
6. Performance assessment
7. Collaboration arrangement
8. Joint business plan

During the execution phase, the forecasted requirements are automatically translated into delivery orders, provided that no exceptions apply. If, however, a situation is exceptional, the responsible employees on both the retailer's and manufacturer's sides have to be informed and work together to find a solution.

Essential advantages of CPFR include the following (Kuhn and Hellingrath 2002, pp. 113–114):

- A common forecast of customer demand guides the activities of both partners.
- Collaboration is coordinated, from establishing a common forecast to finding common solutions for operative problems.
- Companies are enabled to operate proactively, with respect to customer requests, as opposed to reacting to problems when they occur.
- Manufacturers receive guaranteed orders from retailers, while retailers can rely on guaranteed deliveries by the manufacturers because both parties operate on the basis of a common forecast.

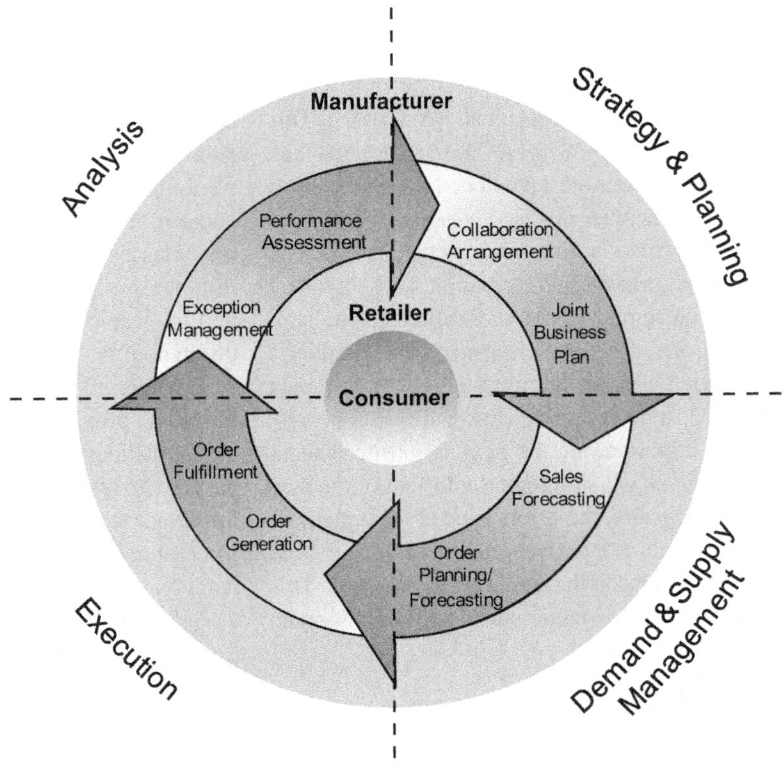

Fig. 8.8 CPFR reference model (VICS 2004, p. 9)

For the manufacturer, CPFR implies a reorientation—from anonymous and inventory-based production toward customer-focused and order-based production.

Today, software vendors offer solutions and support for VMI and CPFR, although CPFR does not depend on specific software. However, since CPFR partners normally exchange information in electronic form, they should employ common standards (e.g., XML-based standards such as EAN.UCC or EDIFACT (VICS 2004, p. 21)).

8.3 Modeling Intercompany Business Processes: SCOR Model

When talking about unifying their business processes, the partners need a common understanding of the supply chain matters they are discussing. All parties involved must understand how the partners are connected, what the consequences of their own actions and the actions of others are for the entire network, and that they need to develop their processes in a cooperative manner. In order for this to happen, members of the supply chain must work together to detect and analyze weak points, identify possible improvements, and document their findings and results.

A common "language" plays an important role in the discussion, documentation and communication of suggestions, plans, and decisions. Since Hammer and Champy introduced "business process reengineering" in 1992 (Hammer and Champy 1993), many modeling approaches and languages have been developed expressly to describe business processes. Common techniques available today include BPMN (business process modeling notation), EPCs (event-driven process chains), SA (structured analysis), SADT (structured analysis and design technique), Petri nets, and workflow definition languages.

When the partners use different modeling approaches, there is a risk that the different notations, levels of detail, and scope of interpretation lead to misunderstandings. Therefore, it is very important to decide upon a common notation.

Reference models serve to create this common basis. While various reference models have been suggested for supply chain management, the most well known today is the SCOR model.

8.3.1 Overview

At the initiative of the consulting company Pittiglio Rabin Todd and McGrath (PRTM), the *Supply Chain Council (SCC)* was founded in 1996, with the aim of advancing supply chain management through the institution of standards. The Supply Chain Council is a nonprofit organization, which currently claims around 1,000 members worldwide, including well-known companies such as Siemens, Daimler, Nokia, IBM, Intel, Coca Cola, BASF, Hewlett Packard, Unilever, UPS, and Toshiba (http://www.supply-chain.org).

The Supply Chain Council provides a reference model including modeling techniques, the so-called *SCOR model (supply chain operations reference model)*. This model can be used on different planning levels, to describe intercompany business processes. The SCOR model is a process reference model, which means that it serves as a uniform reference for subjects and terms related with SCM processes.

The following description of SCOR has been compiled and adapted from the SCC's publicly accessible information (SCC 2008, 2010, 2011). More detailed descriptions are available to SCC members.

The Supply Chain Council defines a *process reference model* as a model that integrates familiar concepts of business process reengineering, benchmarking, and measuring process efficiency in a cross functional framework. It consists of:

- Standardized descriptions of processes and subprocesses
- A framework for the relationships between subprocesses
- Standardized metrics for measuring process performance
- Best practices for improving performance
- Training and skills requirements aligned with processes, best practices, and metrics

Implementing the SCOR Model Implementing the SCOR model in a network of organizations requires a structured approach, that is, a process model. An example of a structured approach is the so-called *SCOR project roadmap*, an earlier proposal by the SCC. This roadmap specifies the following phases (SCC 2008):

Phase 0—Organize: Identifying the organizational support and who will be the project sponsor.

Phase 1—Discover: Defining the supply chain, the priorities regarding business strategies, and the necessary resources, as well as passing the project guidelines and the project charter.

Phase 2—Analyze: Analyzing the competition with the help of scorecards, benchmarks, and competition requirements, aiming to derive key indicators and metrics for assessing the supply chain.

Phase 3—Material: Analyzing the current material flows and defining future flows, including geographic locations. Means to do so include the "geographic map" and the "thread diagram" (see Sect. 8.3.4). 26 predefined process categories (e.g., "S1 source stocked product") and 500 process elements are available as building blocks. Processes or process categories are further broken down into tasks and activities (e.g., "schedule material delivery," "accept material," and "check material"). The inputs and outputs of the process elements are determined.

Phase 4—Work: Describing in detail the as-is and to-be processes and information flows.

Phase 5—Implement: Describing the workflows and activities for implementing supply chain management with regard to the organization, technology, and persons involved.

8.3.2 SCOR Processes

The processes of the SCOR model are differentiated according to the types of products the company deals with. Generic product types are:

- Stocked product
- Make-to-order product
- Engineer-to-order product

The top three levels of the SCOR model contain standardized processes, process categories, and process elements. How the companies involved in a supply chain are connected via their processes can be seen in Fig. 8.2 (presented in Sect. 8.1). Procurement ("source") in one company is connected with dispatching ("deliver") in another. The chain continues over several stages, from the company's supplier to the supplier's supplier, etc.

The SCOR model defines five top-level processes called "management processes," namely planning, sourcing, making, delivering, and returning (SCC 2010):

- *"Plan"*—these processes describe the planning activities associated with operating a supply chain. Planned capabilities and resource gaps are determined by establishing customer requirements, finding available resources, and balancing requirements and resources. If gaps are found, possible corrective actions are identified.
- *"Source"*—these processes describe the ordering, scheduling, and receiving of goods and services, including issuing purchase orders, scheduling deliveries, receiving, shipment validation and storage, and accepting supplier invoices. As for engineer-to-order products, identification and selection of supply sources are also included. Additionally, source processes also cover management tasks such as assessing supplier performance and controlling the working capital and capital assets.
- *"Make"*—these processes describe the activities associated with the conversion of materials or creation of the content for services. They focus on manufacturing and all other types of material conversion, including assembly, chemical processing, maintenance, repair, overhaul, recycling, refurbishment, and remanufacturing. These processes are recognized by the fact that one or more items (e.g., materials, services) go in, and one or more items (e.g., end products) come out.
- *"Deliver"*—these processes describe the activities associated with the creation, maintenance, and fulfillment of customer orders. They span receipt, validation, and creation of customer orders; scheduling order delivery; pick, pack, and shipment; and invoicing the customer.
- *"Return"*—these processes describe the activities associated with the reverse flow of goods back from the customer to the company or from the company to the supplier. They encompass identifying the need for a return, making the decision regarding product disposition, scheduling the return, and shipping and receiving the returned goods.

8.3.3 Process Decomposition

The top-level processes of the SCOR model are decomposed on four levels, as shown in Fig. 8.9. In SCOR terminology, the objects dealt with are management processes, process categories, process types, process elements, tasks, and activities.

The *management processes* described in Sect. 8.3.2—plan, source, make, deliver, and return—are the starting point.

For each management process, several *process categories* are defined. These categories depend on the product types mentioned earlier (stocked, make-to-order, and engineer-to-order products). Some examples of categories are shown in Fig. 8.10, for example, "S1 source stocked product" and "D3 deliver engineer-to-order product."

Each level 2 process can be further described by a so-called *process type* as being a planning, execution, or enabling process (SCC 2010, p. 13). A *planning process* aligns expected resources to meet expected demand requirements. An *execution process* is triggered by planned or actual demand that changes the state of material goods. An *enable process* prepares, maintains, or manages information or relationships on which the planning and execution processes rely.

The categories on the second SCOR level are refined on the third level. Figure 8.11 illustrates this refinement using the process category "S1

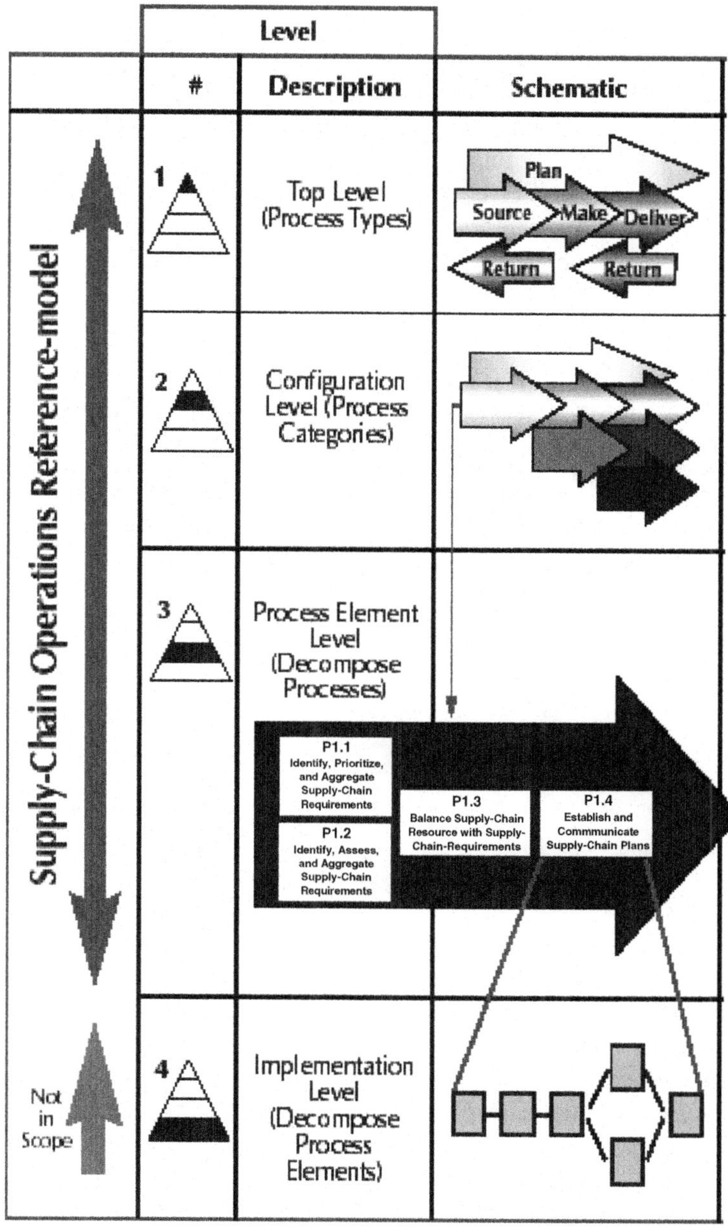

Fig. 8.9 SCOR process decomposition (SCC 2008, p. 7)

source stocked product" as an example. The following *process elements* are defined on level 3:

S1.1 schedule product deliveries
S1.2 receive product
S1.3 verify product
S1.4 transfer product
S1.5 authorize supplier payment

All process elements have inputs and outputs. However, for the sake of clarity, only the inputs and outputs of the process element "S1.2 receive product" are shown in the figure.

Further levels, beyond level 3, are not within the scope of the SCOR model, that is, they are not standardized in the reference model. Every company or industry using the SCOR model may implement these levels as they see fit. This means that other common process decomposition techniques such as SA (structured analysis) and

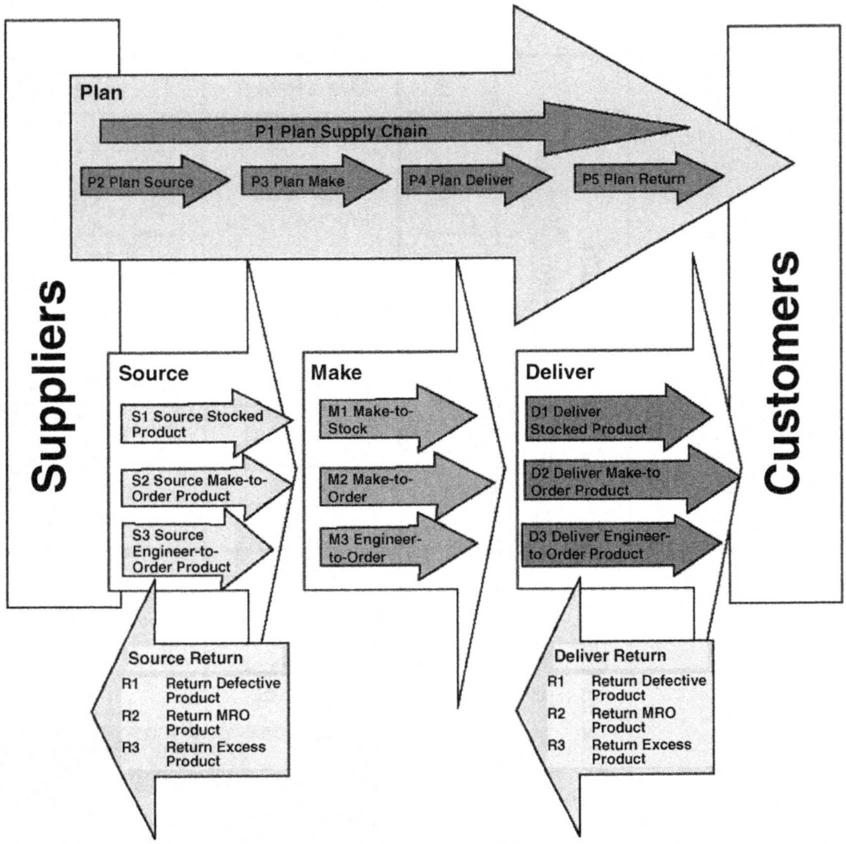

Fig. 8.10 Level 2 SCOR process categories (SCC 2008, p. 10)

SADT (structured analysis and design technique) may be used. On level 4, the SCOR process elements are decomposed into tasks, which are broken down into activities and activity steps on further levels.

In Fig. 8.12, an example is presented showing how a SCOR level-3 process element can be refined. In this example, the process element "S1.1 schedule product deliveries" is detailed into one subprocess ("create order") and two tasks ("select supplier" and "approve and send order"). The subprocess is specified on level 5, containing the two activities "create purchase requisition" and "sign purchase requisition."

The screenshot in Fig. 8.12 was created with the *ADONIS* toolset, which was already mentioned in Sect. 4.3.7 (BOC 2012). The notation used in the example is proprietary, as this toolset supports both BPMN and its own techniques for process modeling.

8.3.4 Modeling a Supply Chain

In this section, we will show how the SCOR diagrams can be used in order to model a specific supply chain. The example illustrated in the Figs. 8.13, 8.14, and 8.15 is taken from an earlier edition of the Supply Chain Council's overview of the SCOR model (SCC 2008, pp. 17–20). This example shows a supply chain involving several suppliers (Flash, Inc., Battery Ltd., and component suppliers), one manufacturing company (MP3, Inc.), and one customer (Retail, Inc.).

Business Scope Diagram A *business scope diagram* is used to identify the key partners of the supply chain, including the involved organizational units within the company, and to connect them with the help of material and information flows. The schema shown in Fig. 8.13 provides three different columns for the different types of nodes.

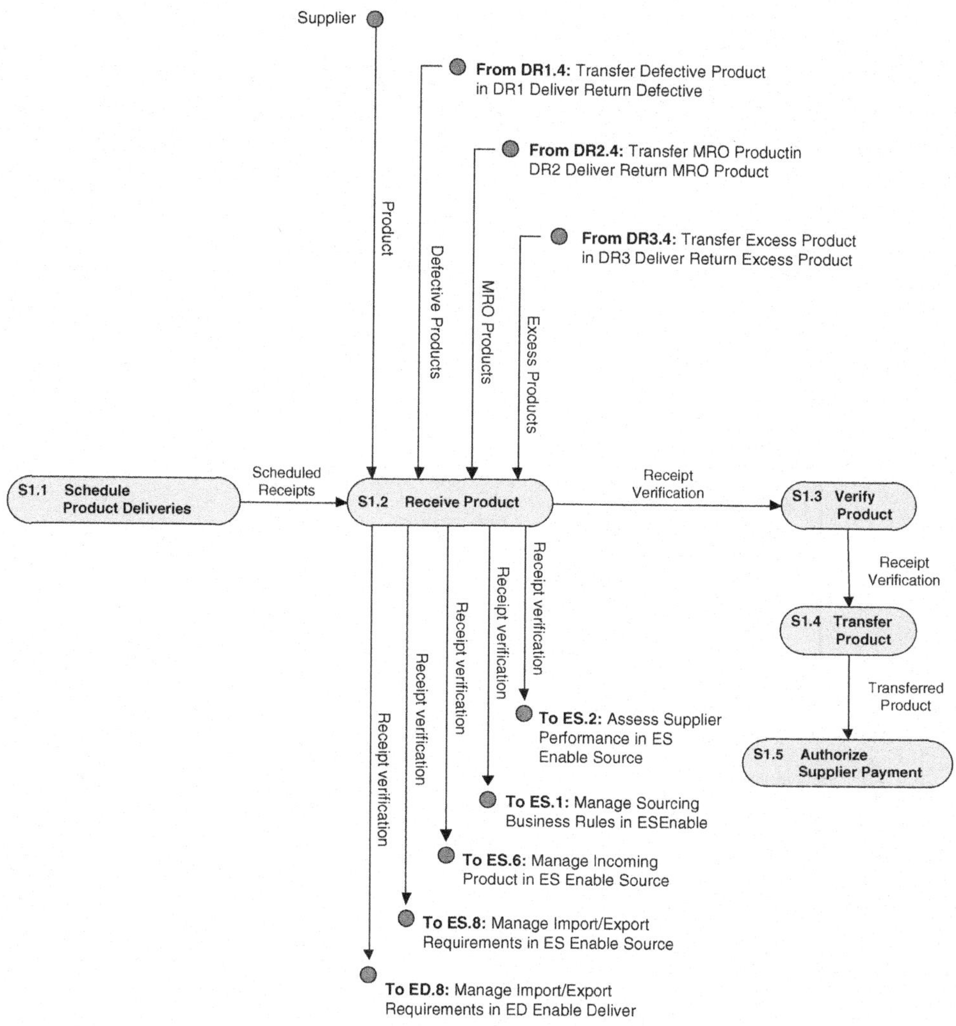

Fig. 8.11 Level 3 process elements (SCC 2008, p. 11)

Solid lines in the business scope diagram indicate both material and information flows, whereas dashed lines indicate only information flows.

Geographic Map With the help of a *geographic map*, the modeler describes the flow of material between the nodes as shown in Fig. 8.14. The major steps to create a geographic map are:

1. Identifying the geographic locations of production sites ("make"), distribution nodes ("deliver"), and procurement ("source")
2. Identifying all important material flows (point-to-point connections between nodes), starting at the end of the supply chain (customer) and then going backward, node by node, to the suppliers of the node
3. Identifying the relevant level two process categories (S, M, D, P) for each node

Thread Diagram A *supply chain thread* connects source-make-deliver chains for a product family. This term includes the planning processes and how they are connected with the execution processes.

The thread diagram shows the connections between the level two processes, as can be seen from Fig. 8.15.

Workflow Model A *workflow model* describes the connections between the level three process

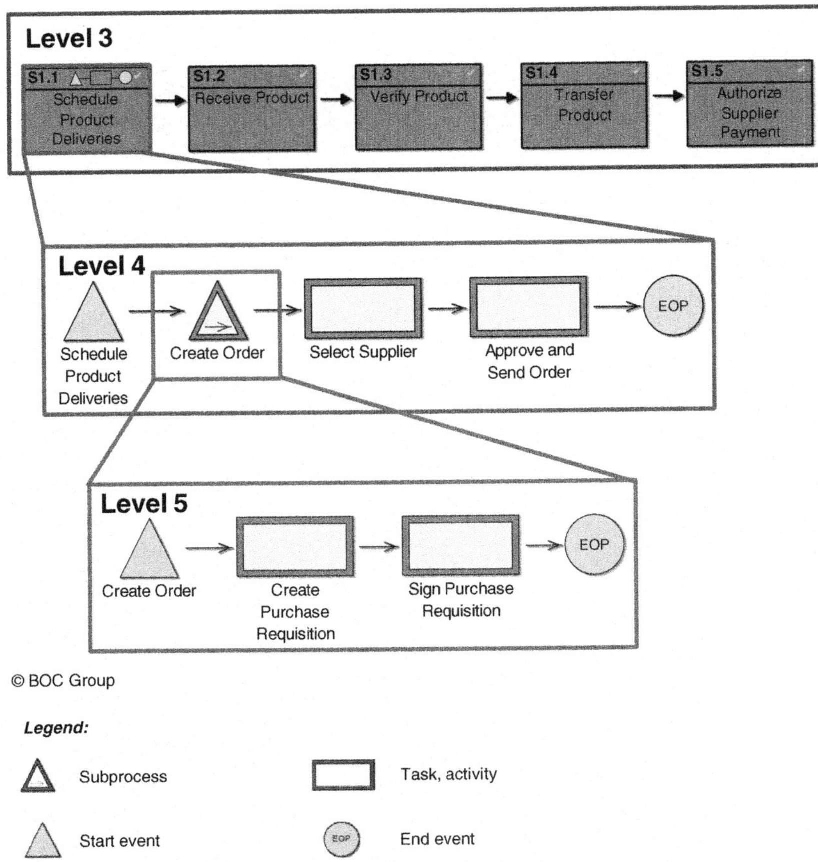

Fig. 8.12 Refining a SCOR level 3 process element

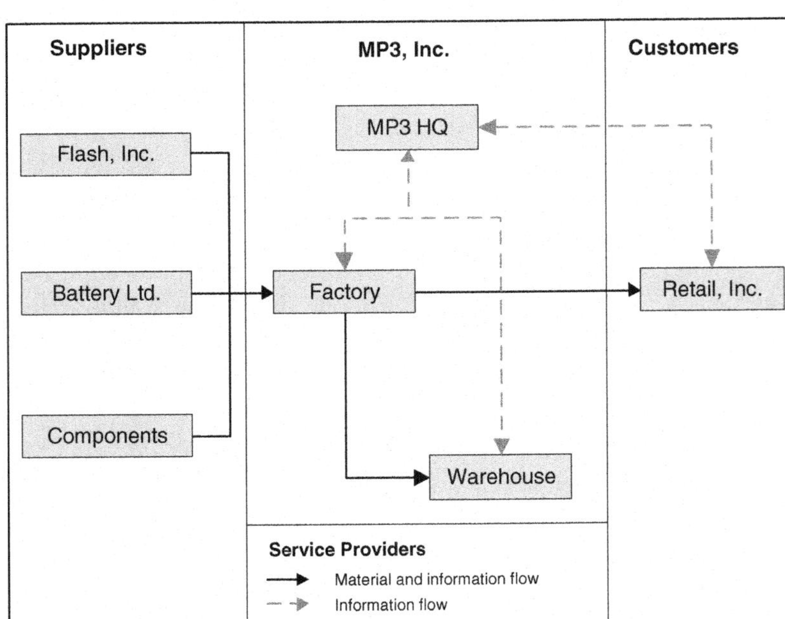

Fig. 8.13 Business scope diagram (SCC 2008, p. 17)

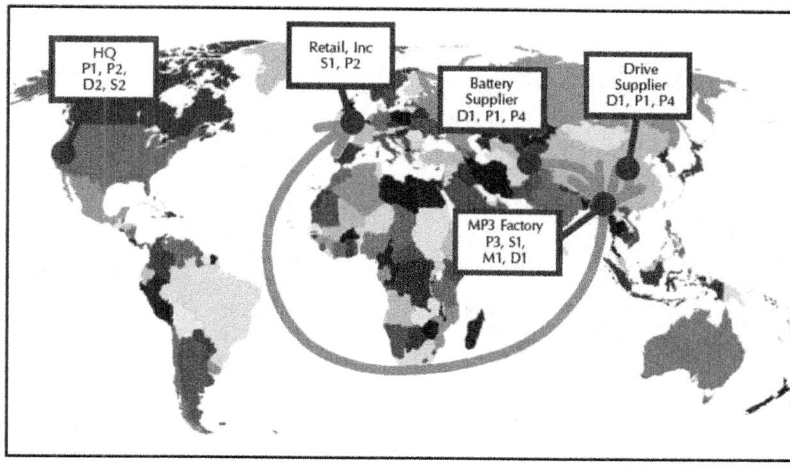

Fig. 8.14 Geographic map (SCC 2008, p. 18)

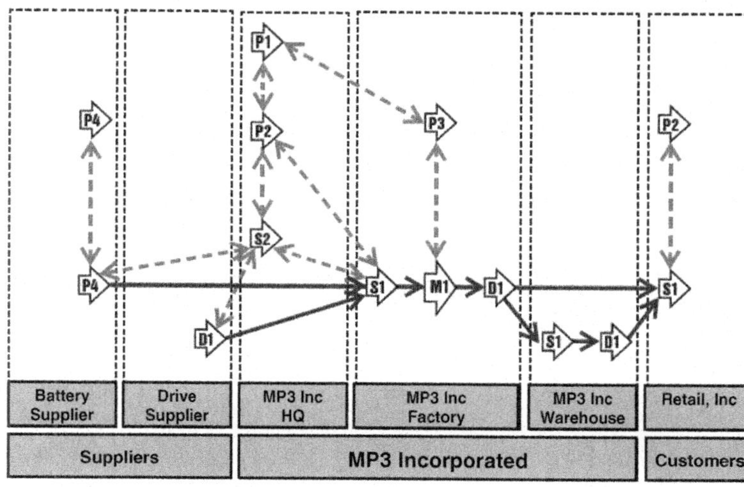

Fig. 8.15 Thread diagram (SCC 2008, p. 19)

elements using work, information, and material flows. Organizational responsibilities are expressed with the help of so-called *swimming lanes* (different sections of the diagram).

In the example of Fig. 8.16, three swimming lanes for the organizational units (Retail, Inc.; MP3 headquarters; and MP3 factory) are shown. Information objects related with the workflows (e.g., customer order) are noted on the arrows of the diagram.

In a dynamic environment, a supply chain that has been configured will not remain unchanged over time. For example, a supplier may be eliminated or an important production site may cease to be used. In these cases, the supply chain has to be *reconfigured*. Obviously, this process is facilitated when explicit models on all levels are available.

8.3.5 Supply Chain Performance and Risks

While the focus of the SCOR model is on processes, measures to keep up on the *performance* of the supply chain and the *risks* involved are also included in the model. Just as processes are identified and refined on several levels, metrics to monitor the performance and risks connected with the processes can also be specified level by level.

Performance is characterized by five attributes: reliability, responsiveness, agility, costs, and asset management. For measuring the performance of a process, *metrics* are defined. In the SCOR model, metrics are used as diagnostics for the performance attributes. Many metrics are

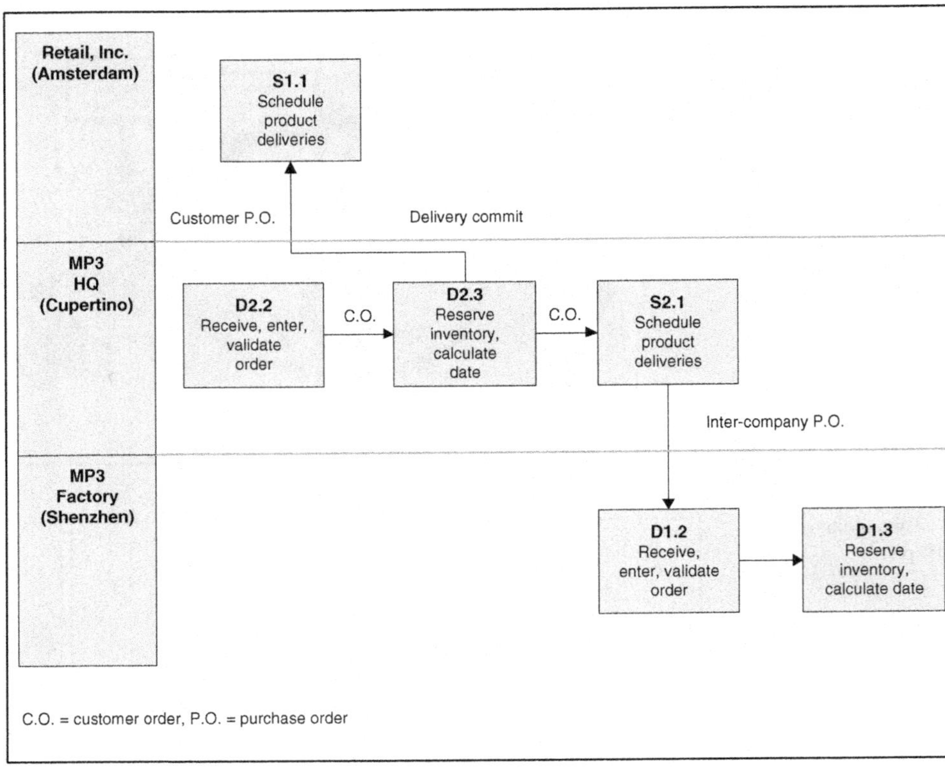

Fig. 8.16 Workflow model (SCC 2008, p. 20)

hierarchical, that is, higher-level metrics are decomposed into lower-level metrics.

The SCOR model recognizes three levels of predefined metrics (SCC 2010, p. 8):

- Level 1 metrics are indicators of the overall performance of the supply chain. They are called strategic metrics and are also known as key performance indicators (KPIs).
- Level 2 metrics are diagnostics for the level 1 metrics, serving to identify the causes of a performance gap for a level 1 metric.
- Level 3 metrics are used to diagnose level 2 metrics.

Many of the metrics are decomposed from level 1 down to level 3. Because of the hierarchical structure, a higher-level metric is created from lower-level calculations.

In the two Figs. 8.17 and 8.18, an example of modeling metrics is presented. The screenshots were created with the modeling toolset *ADOlog* (BOC 2009).

Figure 8.17 shows a level 1 metric, "perfect order fulfillment," used for diagnosing the performance attribute "reliability" and how the level 1 metric is decomposed into level 2 metrics "% of orders delivered in full," "delivery performance to customer commit date," "documentation accuracy," and "perfect condition."

All metrics modeled on level 1 are shown in Fig. 8.18. In this excerpt of a screenshot, the metrics associated with the level 2 process "S1 source stocked product" are listed because these metrics need to be considered and refined in the process. (For example, the level 1 "perfect order fulfillment" metric will be refined into the level 2 metrics "delivery quantity accuracy" and "delivery item accuracy.")

Similar to performance attributes and metrics, *risks* that could negatively impact the supply chains should explicitly be captured and modeled. In SCOR, risk management is seen as one of the *best practices,* comprising the systematic identification, assessment, and mitigation of potential disruptions in logistics networks (SCC 2010, p. 18). The roots of the problems can lie both within the supply chain (e.g., insufficient quality, unreliable suppliers, machine breakdown, and uncertain demand),

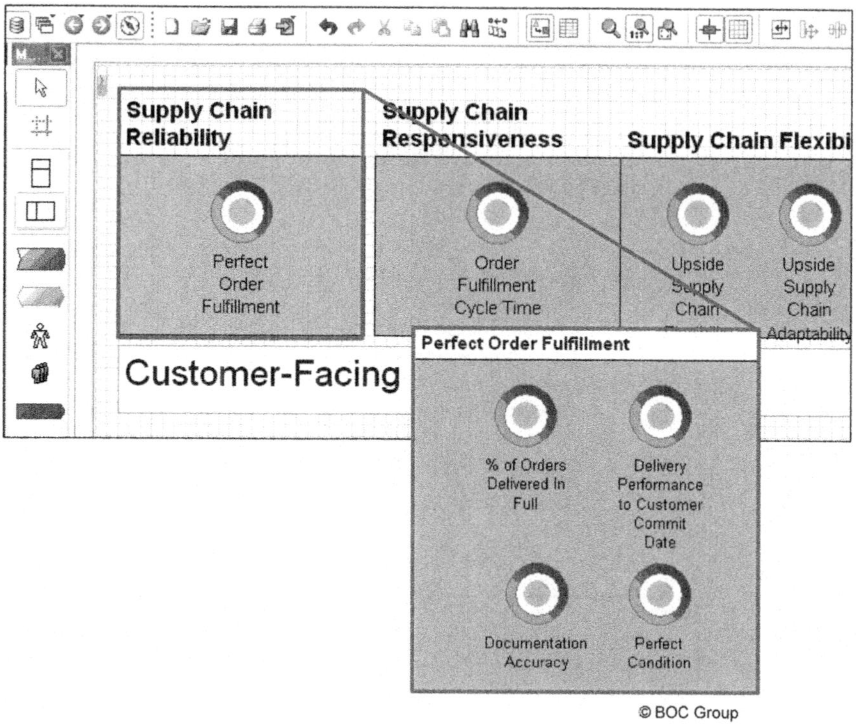

Fig. 8.17 Performance attributes and level 1 and 2 metrics

and outside (e.g., flooding, earthquake, and labor strike).

When the company uses a modeling tool, risks can be modeled in a similar way as metrics, beginning with a high-level definition of the risks and subsequently refining the risks. In Fig. 8.19, which was again created with the *ADOlog* toolset (BOC 2009), the major risks have been identified as "environmental," "supplier-related," "transport," "company internal," and "customer-related" risks. For the "transport risks" category, more specific risks detailing this category (e.g., damage and accident risks) have been identified. This risk map was created based on risk perspectives described by McCormack et al. (2008, p. 7).

Controls to mitigate (i.e., to eliminate or reduce) the risks may be defined in a risk mitigation plan (Supply-Chain Council 2010, p. 18). With the help of a SCOR-based modeling tool, the controls will also be represented in the model. For the example mentioned above (i.e., transport risks), the list of possible controls includes careful definition of transport way and time, access control at stock location, adequate packaging, transport and forwarding insurances, and many more.

8.4 Tasks of an SCM System

The discussion of the SCOR model showed that a variety of tasks on different levels of detail and abstraction are involved. The time horizons of the various tasks range from several years (e.g., for strategic planning of the supply chain) down to minutes, when it comes to execution of individual steps.

Architectural models allow the supply chain architect to assign the tasks an SCM system should support to different levels, for example, a strategic level, one or more planning levels, and an execution level.

8.4.1 Strategic Level

The major task on the strategic level is forming the intended supplier–buyer network, in accordance

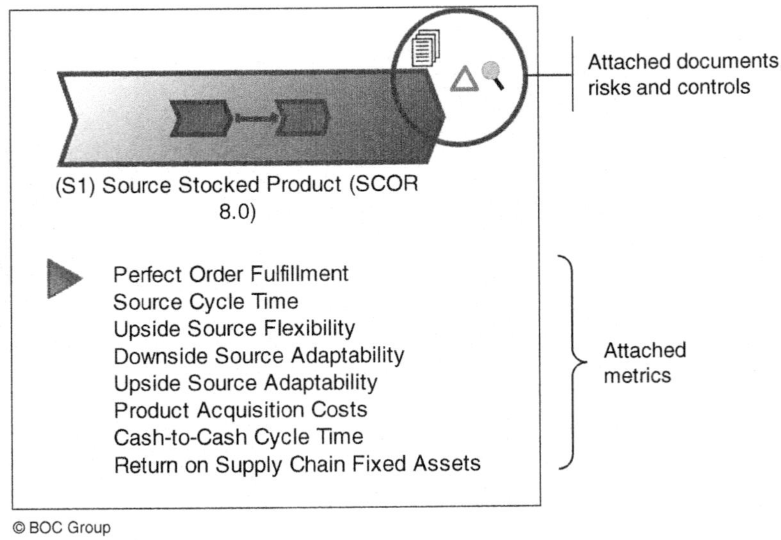

Fig. 8.18 Metrics in "S1 source stocked product" process

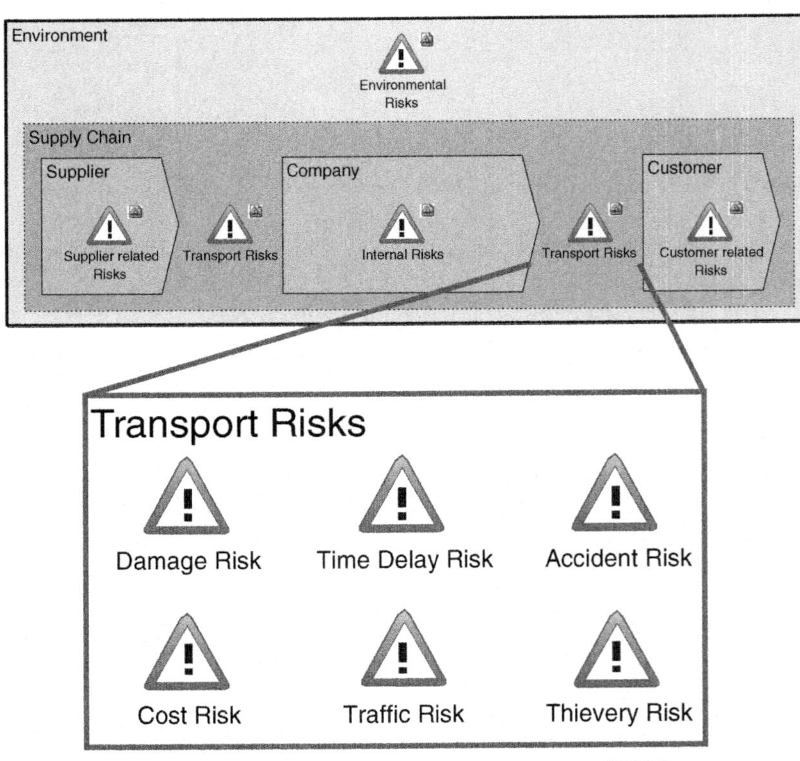

Fig. 8.19 Supply chain risk map (created with an SCM tool)

with the strategies of all partner companies involved.

The strategic level requires decisions on the sources of supply, anticipating supply needs and evaluating the capacity of suppliers that can deliver goods to match those needs.

It also includes the assessment of alternative revenue and cost options as well as decisions about strategic investments, for example, investing in new production facilities, distribution centers, or marketing channels.

An important management tool on the strategic level is *simulation*, in particular, what-if simulation. With the help of simulation tools, the company's management can try out different constellations, for example. which product will be manufactured in which plant or which sales region should be served by which distribution center? By simulating various options and assessing their implications, the constellation that fits the company (or the entire supply chain) best can be elaborated.

8.4.2 Planning Level

A large number of tasks are ascribed to the planning level. Although different classifications exist, the types of tasks on the planning level usually refer to long-term and midterm planning.

It is worth noting that a number of planning tasks addressed in supply chain management are the same or similar to those addressed in enterprise resource planning. For example, SAP SCM includes, on the top planning level:

- Demand planning and forecasting
- Safety stock planning
- Supply network planning
- Distribution planning

On levels further down, tasks are found such as:

- Production planning
- Detailed scheduling
- Transportation planning
- Route optimization

Figure 8.20 illustrates the overlapping functionalities of ERP and SCM systems with the help of a simplifying schematic distinction between long-term and short-term tasks (Corsten and Gössinger 2008, p. 162). Long-term tasks are summarized under "supply chain planning," whereas short-term tasks are assigned to "supply chain control."

From the figure, it becomes evident that SCM systems provide more support for "planning," whereas ERP systems better support the "control" tasks. Ignoring the oversimplified terminology, Fig. 8.20 also gives an impression of how companies deal with the overlap of SCM and ERP systems.

Whenever a certain functionality is available in both types of systems, the company must decide which one to use. As the figure suggests, this decision can be made in favor of the system that provides the better support. This means that long-term tasks, in particular, tasks involving external partners, are handled with the help of the SCM system, whereas short-term tasks use the ERP system's functionality.

One reason why ERP and SCM systems overlap is that many of the solutions implemented in ERP are not really satisfactory. This is partly due to the long history of enterprise resource planning. At the time when MRP and MRP II solutions were developed, computer performance was weak and planning methods were less advanced than today.

Consequently, some of the weaker solutions have been reconsidered in supply chain management and re-implemented using more powerful approaches. Both technological and methodological advances have enabled much better solutions within SCM software.

An example is *mathematical optimization*, which was mostly beyond the limits of MRP II. In SCM, however, various problems are now being solved using optimization.

Another example is *availability checking*. With the help of SCM functions, much better checking and much more reliable assertions regarding the availability are possible. This is being reflected in advanced capabilities with new names, including:

- *ATP ("available-to-promise"):* Is the product on stock or will it be available when it is needed?
- *CTP ("capable-to-promise"):* Are we capable of manufacturing the product on time, taking capacity and material requirements into account?
- *CoTP ("configure-to-promise"):* Is the product configuration the customer requires feasible on time and according to CTP?

These types of availability and capability checking will be further discussed in Sect. 10.1.

More advanced functionality than that available in enterprise resource planning is often summarized under the term APS ("advanced planning and scheduling"). APS will be described below (cf. Sect. 9.2.1).

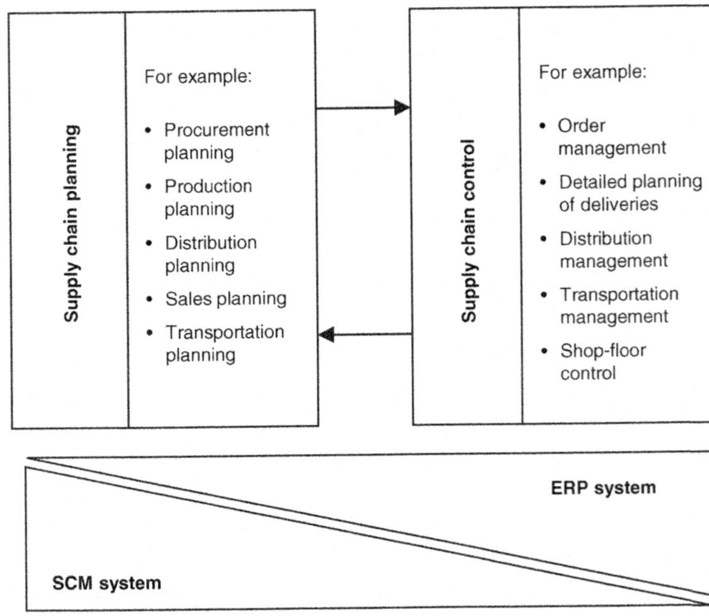

Fig. 8.20 Overlapping ERP and SCM functionality (Corsten and Gössinger 2008, p. 162)

8.4.3 Execution Level

The execution level contains all the functions needed for the operation of the supply chains. Sometimes, the term *SCE (supply chain execution)* is used. On the execution level, a number of familiar terms reappear, such as order fulfillment; material, inventory, and transportation management; warehousing; and production planning.

The main difference in the usage of these terms is that enterprise resource planning looks at a single company, whereas supply chain management takes an intercompany perspective. With regard to methodology, more optimization and suboptimization approaches to the same problems are found in SCM than in ERP.

Despite the different perspectives and approaches, on the execution level, it is more common to use ERP functionality rather than specific SCM functionality. Vendor-specific solutions tend to integrate existing ERP functionality with SCM functionality in one way or another. For example, SAP SCM relies largely on SAP ERP, meaning that functionality already available in SAP ERP is invoked from SAP SCM. Other SCM vendors also use their own ERP system, if available, or provide interfaces with common ERP systems.

Another option is that the vendor provides interfaces to a manufacturing execution system (MES). In this case, the MES is responsible for the short-term, production-related planning and control tasks within a company.

Supply Chain Event Management An important task on the execution level is monitoring the supply chains with regard to their proper functioning and performance. Whenever events happen that cause the supply chains not to work as planned, additional actions have to be taken.

Supply chain event management (SCEM) encompasses all tasks regarding the monitoring, measuring, notification, decision making, and control within and between the partner companies of a supply network.

One prerequisite for supply chain event management is that all relevant intra- and intercompany business processes are explicitly represented in the SCEM system. Another prerequisite is that all data about the things happening along the supply chain are continuously captured and interpreted. Useful tools for this purpose are *tracking and tracing systems* (T&T systems).

Tracking means following logistics objects (such as packages, palettes, containers, etc.) on their way from one point to another, including the capability of finding out the object's current location and state at any time. *Tracing* means following an object across the business processes and activities it is involved in. This may be required, for example, when products have to be called backed due to defective parts or when special treatment has to be proven (e.g., an uninterrupted cooling chain).

Tracking and tracing systems are common in the logistics industry. While earlier only the logistics companies themselves used tracking and tracing, nowadays, this functionality is commonly available to customers. For example, courier companies such as FedEx, DHL, and UPS allow customers to track their shipments online, via the web front end of the company's T&T system.

Tracking and tracing is an enabler for supply chain event management, meaning that the T&T system provides the data needed for SCEM. However, these as-is data are neither filtered nor evaluated and are unrelated to the to-be data. Suppose a process owner receives the message, "container x left the loading dock A at 10:30 a.m." It is left to him or her to evaluate the message—was it on time, too early, too late, planned, unplanned, etc.—and to take actions if necessary. T&T systems are usually passive, that is, they do not point out problems nor do they initiate any actions.

Supply chain event management (SCEM) encompasses much more than merely tracking and tracing. It not only captures status information and makes it available but also filters and checks this information and creates events or alarms if applicable (SAP 2010). An ideal SCEM system behaves proactively, advising the decision maker of relevant events, suggesting possible actions, and perhaps even initiating a solution procedure.

As an example, consider the case that a manufacturer in Hong Kong runs into a production delay, causing the shipment to the US customer to miss the freighter to San Diego (SAP 2001). Since the delayed shipment is on the critical path, the SCEM system suggests two alternatives: air freight or waiting for the next cargo ship. It also evaluates the alternatives, calculating the costs and elaborating other possible consequences such as shortages and interruptions to the customer's production.

A prerequisite for timely and proactive actions is that the relevant business processes have been represented in the system and that points of control have been defined in the processes. These points are often called "milestones." An example of a milestone is "goods received." Here, the system would check whether the order was received on time, complete, free of defects, etc. Other examples of milestones include order release, order completion, dispatching, tendering of a load, goods issue of an order, truck departure, goods receipt at the customer's location, and receiving the payment.

Events monitored and handled by an SCEM system can be divided into:

- Expected events (e.g., delivery on time, complete, in suitable quality, and free of defects)
- Expected events, albeit in a different form than expected (e.g., different quantity or quality level)
- Overdue events (e.g., delivery has been expected but has not taken place)
- Unexpected events (e.g., machine breakdown)

Depending on the type of event, different measures have to be taken. Figure 8.21 shows the relationships between actual and expected events. Events no. 1, 2, and 4 have been expected. The actually occurring events no. 1 and 2 take place within the specified time period, but event no. 4 does not occur at all. Event no. 3 is an unexpected event that was never planned.

An SCEM system monitors actual events ("as-is") and compares them to the expected events (planned events, "to-be"). It also handles unexpected events like event no. 3.

Figure 8.21 is a schema indicating the steps involved in SAP's solution for supply chain event management (SAP 2010, pp. 6–7): Actual events are *tracked* and *monitored* against relevant expected milestones. Any problems that occur are identified and dealt with, for example, when a specific event is overdue, an unexpected event is reported or a measurement value is outside the tolerances.

When a problem occurs, a predefined set of persons are *notified* and supplied with the information needed to resolve the situation either locally or across the supply chain. Depending

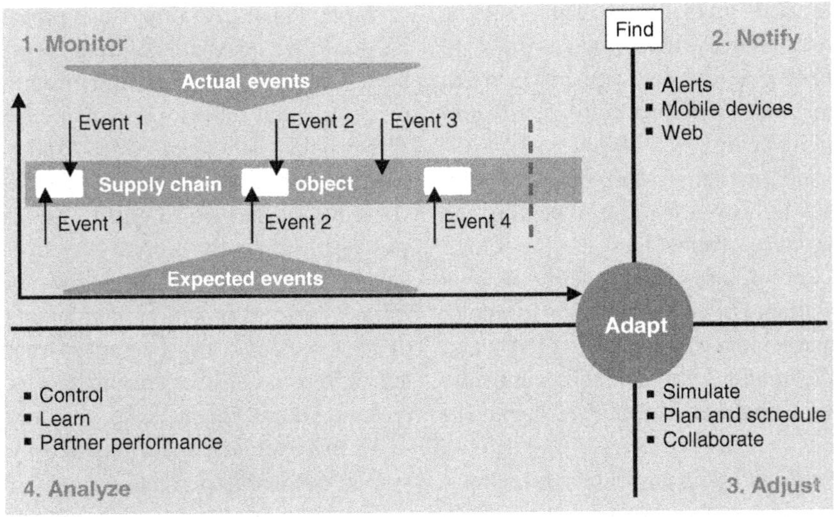

Fig. 8.21 Actual and expected events (SAP 2010, p. 6)

on the type of problem, both manual and automatic resolutions are supported.

The "adjust" part of the figure denotes that the event management system generates and proposes alternative solutions to problems. Finally, in the "analyze" part, time-specific data and data specific to the context of the events are captured and stored. These data can be given to the business intelligence module of SAP NetWeaver for further analysis.

Both a milestone model and rules for interpreting messages and initiating actions are stored within an SCEM system. Figure 8.22 shows the main components of an SCEM solution using *SAP event management* as an example. As a prerequisite, each relevant business object or process has to be represented by an event handler. Likewise, milestones and expected measurements containing information about what is planned to happen to the object or process have to be provided (SAP 2010, p. 8). Subsequently, actual events and measurements are posted manually or captured from within SAP SCM or an external system.

The *event processor* accepts messages on events that have occurred and checks, evaluates, and stores the events. The *event controller* administers the events and passes them on to processing. The *event monitor* supervises and examines expected, required, and overdue events. The *rule processor* applies the given system of rules to the events and creates actions. For example, it issues alerts or invokes further monitoring functions.

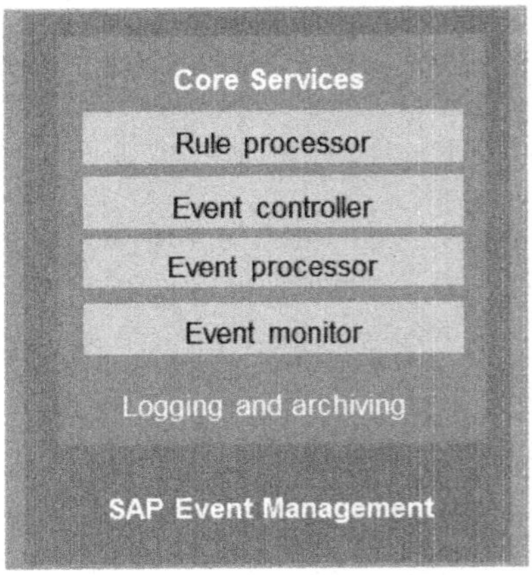

Fig. 8.22 SAP event management (SAP 2010, p. 8)

A side aspect to be pointed out is that SAP event management is not only available for supply chain management but also for other applications within the SAP business suite where processes or objects have to be monitored and tracked (SAP 2010, p. 8).

Supply Chain Performance Management *Supply chain performance management (SCPM)* is related to SCEM in that both oversee the supply chains. However, SCEM refers to the execution level, whereas SCPM provides analysis and early warning tools on higher levels. Supply chain performance management depends on data captured and evaluated in supply chain event management.

Based on the SCEM data, SCPM can perform analyses (e.g., causes, length, and frequency of disruptions) and identify developments or trends. This was already mentioned in the left bottom corner of Fig. 8.21.

Modeling for SCPM usually includes the definition of indicators and thresholds along the SCM business processes, for example, indicators and thresholds regarding the time, accuracy, and quality of deliveries as well as the capability to deliver. If these indicators and thresholds are available, SCPM can determine shortages or overages and send off an early warning so that appropriate measures can be taken at the right time.

The modeling of performance attributes and metrics to diagnose the performance is part of the SCOR model, as discussed above (cf. Sect. 8.3.5). Companies can use the reference metrics to monitor and evaluate their own supply chain performance.

9 SCM Data Structures and Advanced Planning

In this chapter, extensions regarding the ERP data structures and the methods used to solve planning problems will be discussed. While the basic data and the solution approaches of ERP continue to be employed in supply chain management, additional data structures and new approaches are also needed.

The first part of this chapter focuses on additional data structures required for supply chain management. Afterwards, methodological improvements as compared to the current state of enterprise resource planning in practice are discussed.

9.1 Data Structures for Supply Chain Management

In this section, essential data structures for supply chain management are described. Basically, we assume that the data structures known from enterprise resource planning are also available in supply chain management. However, additional data structures are required because typical SCM matters cannot be represented by conventional ERP data alone.

In order to demonstrate the practical relevance of the data structures and to better illustrate the topic, we will use the data structures available in SAP SCM as examples. Although this will make the discussion somewhat SAP specific, similar data structures are employed in other SCM systems as well.

9.1.1 Master Data

In fact, many of the SCM master data are the same as ERP master data, only extended by additional attributes. Other entity types, however, are completely new.

ERP master data are usually adopted from the ERP system in order to make them available in the SCM system. In SAP SCM, this is completed with the help of the *core interface (CIF)*. This interface connects SAP's ERP and SCM systems. It will be described in Sect. 10.2.

Essential SCM master data include the following (Dickersbach 2009, pp. 17–23; Wood 2007, pp. 63–124; Hoppe 2007, pp. 209–228):

- Location
- Product
- Resource
- Production process model (PPM)
- Production data structure (PDS)
- Transportation lane
- External procurement relationship
- Quota arrangement
- Hierarchy
- Model and version

Location Locations play a more prominent role in supply chain management than in enterprise resource planning because, by their nature, supply chains extend over many places. While in enterprise resource planning, these places are

K.E. Kurbel, *Enterprise Resource Planning and Supply Chain Management*,
Progress in IS, DOI 10.1007/978-3-642-31573-2_9, © Springer-Verlag Berlin Heidelberg 2013

mostly inside the company, in supply chain management, different partners outside the company are also involved.

A *location* is a physical or logical place where products are manufactured, stored, or transported or where resources are managed. Some predefined location types in SAP SCM are:

- Plant
- Distribution center
- Stock transfer point
- Customer
- Vendor
- Subcontractor
- Transport service provider
- Transportation zone
- Storage location/MRP area
- Terminal
- Geographic area
- Store

Some of the location types correspond directly to ERP master data, for example, plant, customer, and vendor. These master data can be automatically adopted from SAP ERP, while others have to be manually transferred and modified.

Important attributes of a location include the *time zone* and the applicable *calendars*, for example, the production, storage, and shipping calendars.

Product Products in SAP SCM correspond to *materials* in SAP ERP. However, they are not limited to physical products but also include services. Product master data are extremely large, comprising more than 100 attributes that are required in the different subareas of supply chain management.

An important new aspect regarding products is that, to some extent, products depend on locations. More precisely, product *attributes* are divided into global and location-dependent attributes.

Properties of a product, such as the weight or volume, are *global* attributes. Most global attributes are automatically adopted from the ERP material master data. *Location-dependent* attributes include the procurement type, settings for goods receipt and goods issue, and settings for the calculation of lot sizes and order quantities. These attributes have to be created in SAP SCM.

Resource Resources are entities on or with which operations are performed. Resources have a finite capacity that has to be scheduled, and they belong to a category such as production, transport, handling, or storage. Examples of resources include machines, machine groups, workers, teams, means of transport, and storage containers. Resources and their capacities are required, for example, for scheduling planned orders.

Production resources in SAP SCM correspond to *work centers* in SAP ERP. Work center data are adopted via the core interface (CIF), and their capacities are mapped onto the capacities of the production resources.

Production Process Model, Production Data Structure Production process models and production data structures are similar. Some differences between them exist as far as the flexibility of usage is concerned.

The idea underlying both data structures is the same as the rationale behind *resource lists* described in Sect. 3.1.4, namely, to combine information that is otherwise distributed among a bill of materials and a routing into one data structure. The reason for doing so is that in order to create a feasible production plan, information about *all* required resources should be available at the same time. Critical resources are, in particular, the required materials and operating facilities.

If only materials are considered in the first planning step (as in conventional MRP) and operating facilities in a later step (as in conventional MRP II), it is difficult to create a feasible plan—and even harder to create a good plan.

A *production process model (PPM)* consists of a header and a PPM plan. Header information includes the planning location, temporal validity, a lot-size interval, and the cost.

The *PPM plan* is an order-independent plan, describing the work steps and components required to manufacture the output products of the plan (Hoppe 2007, p. 218).

Fig. 9.1 Structure of a PPM plan (Wood 2007, p. 109)

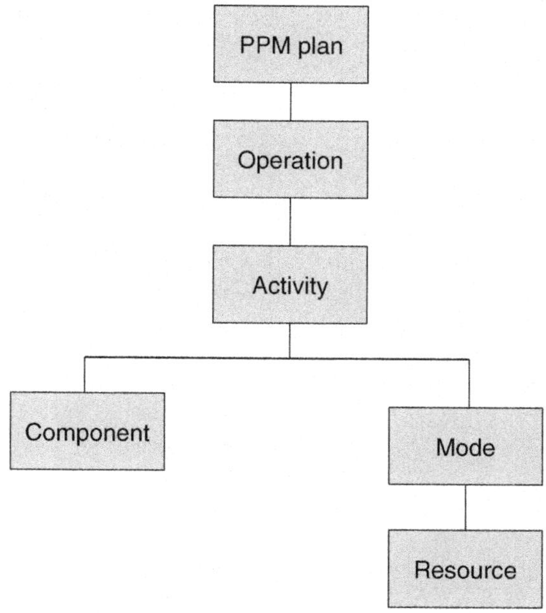

As shown in Fig. 9.1, a PPM plan contains one or more *operations*, with each operation consisting of one or more activities (Wood 2007, pp. 108–109). *Activity* types are "setup," "produce," and "teardown."

The relationship between operations and activities is illustrated in Fig. 9.2. The costs incurred by the PPM plan are single-level cost (i.e., cost of the operations defined in the plan) and multilevel cost (i.e., including the cost of providing the required components) (Hoppe 2007, p. 219).

Activities are connected with resources through modes. A *mode* specifies in which way, i.e., on which resource, an activity is to be carried out.

Resources are primary resources or secondary resources. *Primary resources* are resources on which the activities are scheduled in the first place (e.g., the machine needed for the activity). *Secondary resources* are resources that may also be considered in the plan because they may become bottlenecks (e.g., the machine operator).

Components are the parts (materials) that are input to the activities. The output of an activity can also be a component, for example, a finished good.

Activity relationships specify dependencies between activities, such as sequence constraints (Dickersbach 2009, p. 269). A sequence constraint is, for example, that a particular activity has to be completed (or started) before the next activity can start (or end). Typical sequence constraints thus include end-start, start-start, end-end, and start-start relationships. Other constraints refer to the time buffers of the activities and the mode linkage (e.g., whether the next activity must be performed on the same resource as the previous one or not).

A screenshot of a production process model taken from SAP SCM is presented in Fig. 9.3. It shows a portion of the PPM for an intermediary product ("casing with handlebar"). The upper part contains the operations "drill screw thread" and "screwing" with the required activities and components. Activities for "drill screw thread," for example, are "setup: clamp drill bit," "drilling," and "shutdown." The components needed are "handlebar," "mounted casing," and "screw M5."

The lower part of the figure graphically visualizes the connections between the operations, activities, resources, and components. The "activities" pane on the right-hand side displays all the activities that belong to a particular operation, allowing the user to modify, delete, or add activities.

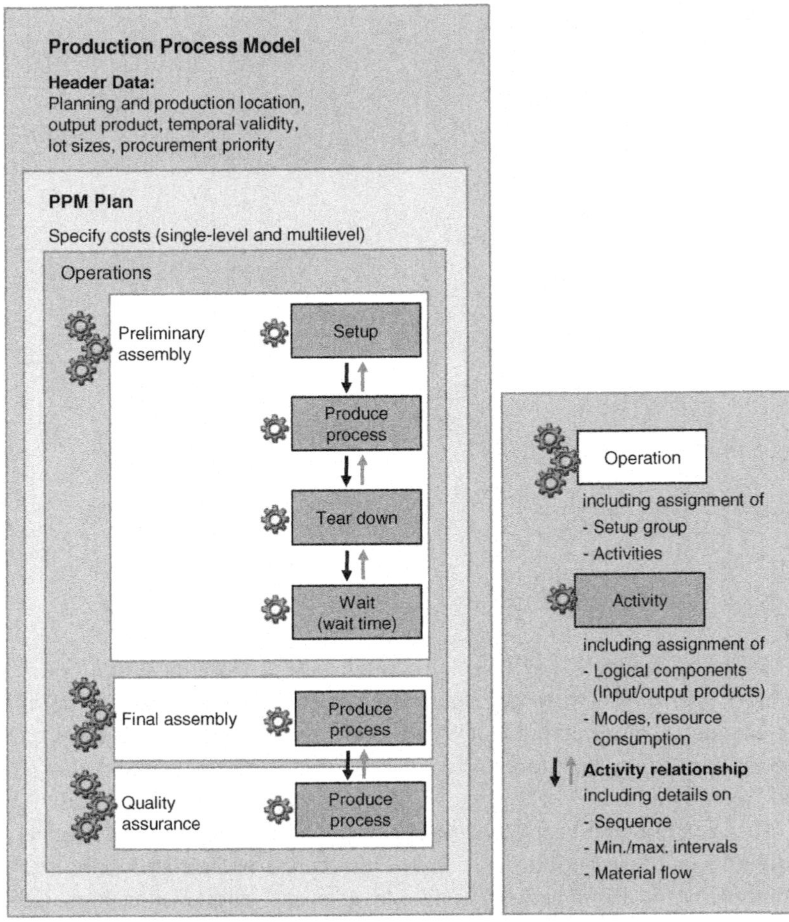

Fig. 9.2 PPM operations and activities (Hoppe 2007, p. 219)

Costs can be associated with a PPM plan as a whole (cf. Fig. 9.2) and with the individual activities and resources. In SAP SCM, these costs are employed by the planning and optimization modules to create schedules.

The *production data structure (PDS)* introduced later in SAP SCM is similar to a production process model (PPM). It also combines routing and bill-of-material information into one data structure. A PDS is more flexible than a PPM in that it supports engineering change management (Dickersbach 2009, p. 270) and allows for more flexible options for combining and reusing existing routings and BOMs (Hoppe 2007, p. 222).

Transportation Lane A transportation lane specifies that a product can be transported from a sender A to a recipient B. It connects locations and defines the means of transport (e.g., airplane, truck, rail, ship). The means of transport have durations and costs associated with them. These are used, for example, by the planning algorithms to select the best means of transport or to switch to a different one when a shipment is delayed.

In Fig. 9.4, a transportation lane from location 3100 to location 3500 has been created, applicable to two product types (pumps P-102 and P-103). Because a transportation lane is product oriented, the products to which it refers must be specified when the lane is created. The selected means of transport for both products is "truck," as specified in the middle section of the form. Product-specific entries can be made in the lower section, for example, product-specific transportation costs and lot sizes.

Transportation lanes are required whenever business relationships with suppliers and customers or stock transfers between locations are to

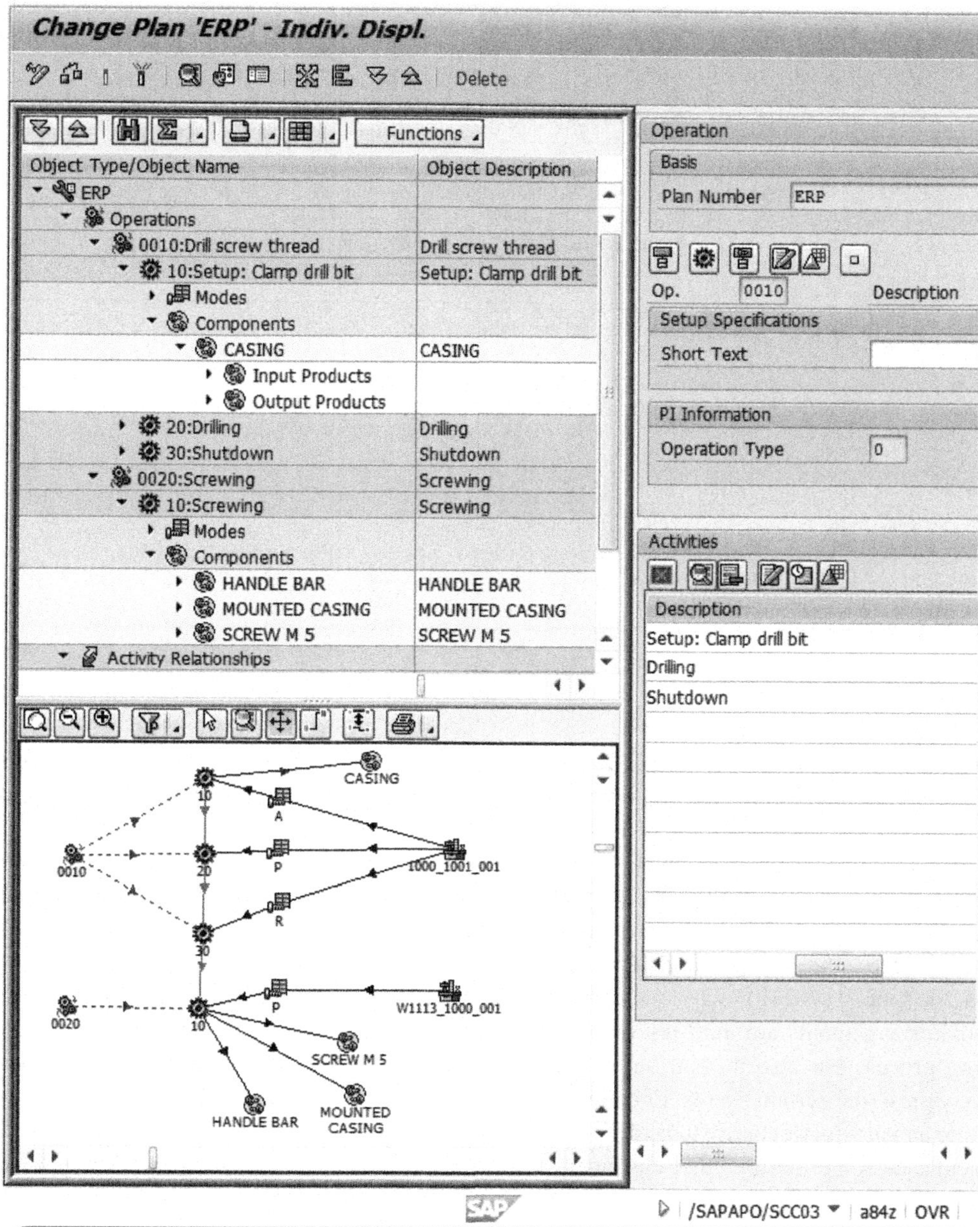

Fig. 9.3 Production process model in SAP SCM

be planned. Products can only be procured, for example, if a transportation lane exists between the supplier's and the company's locations.

External Procurement Relationship and Quota Arrangement External procurement relationships are usually based on information that is already available in SAP ERP, namely, in the form of a so-called purchasing info record or an outline agreement with a supplier (i.e., a contract or a scheduling agreement). In SAP SCM, this information is automatically adopted and mapped to an external procurement relationship and to a transportation lane.

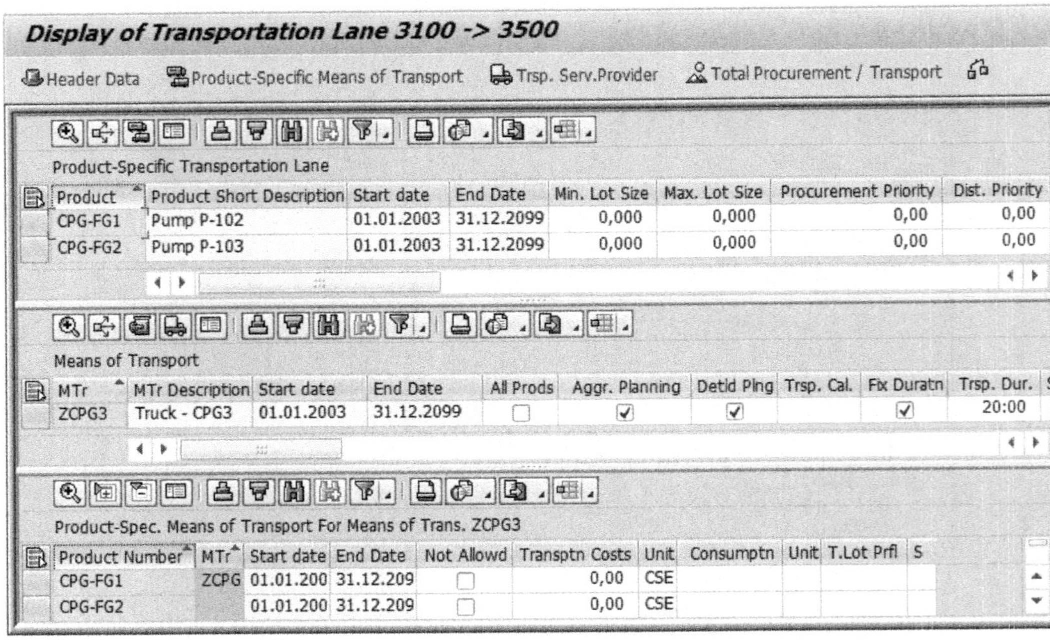

Fig. 9.4 Transportation lane in SAP SCM

Quota arrangements are used when a product is regularly procured from more than one supplier. A quota arrangement may define which share of a total procurement quantity should be purchased from which supplier or which supplier has to be considered first with a guaranteed quantity before other suppliers receive orders (Wood 2007, pp. 117–118).

Quota arrangements are used not only in the sourcing process but also in distribution. Here, they may prescribe certain shares for certain customers or a mandatory quantity to be delivered to a particular customer before other customers are served.

Hierarchy Hierarchies are required for aggregate planning. For this purpose, products must be combined into product groups and locations into location groups. Based on a product hierarchy and a location hierarchy, a so-called *location product hierarchy* can be defined. *Location products* are products that exist at a particular location, that is, their master data are maintained depending on the location.

Figure 9.5 illustrates these relationships. The products B and C are combined into product group A. There is one location group (group 1), which has only one location (2). Another location (3) is not included in the hierarchy.

In this example, the *location product hierarchy* is created using the product group A and the location 2. The location product C/2 is part of the hierarchy, while the product B/3 is not.

Because different products and/or locations generally have different characteristics, standardization must take place before the groups can be created. For example, the planning horizons, procurement types, lot-size parameters, and transportation lanes must be standardized for all products of a group.

Model and Version Planning in SAP SCM is based on models and versions. Generally, a model contains the master data and a version the transaction data (although there are some exceptions). Several different models may exist at the same time – one active model and several inactive models.

An *active model* is the basis for the current planning. It includes the data needed to execute a plan, which is mostly done with the help of SAP ERP. For this purpose, the planning results for the active model are sent over the core interface

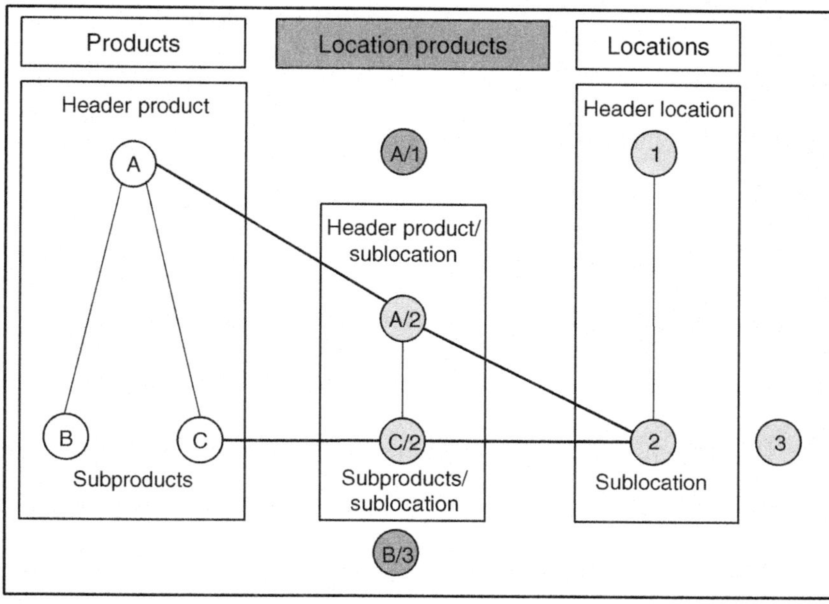

Fig. 9.5 Location product hierarchy (Hoppe 2007, p. 228)

(CIF, cf. Sect. 10.2) to SAP ERP, where they initiate specific transactions. In the other direction, data that are relevant for SCM are sent from SAP ERP to the active model.

Inactive models are primarily used for what-if simulations. Frequently, an inactive model is created as a copy of the active model and then modified as needed. Any number of inactive models may exist at the same time.

Versions are different instances of the same model with varying characteristics. Versions are used, for example, to create different planning variants based on the same supply chain. As with the models, active and inactive versions may exist. The *active version* of the active model, which may also have inactive versions, is the version that is communicated to SAP ERP.

A planner running what-if simulations on an inactive version, having decided on a particular plan, may then transfer the planning results either fully or partially from the inactive version to the active version (Gaddam 2009, p. 36; Wood 2007, p. 120). This version will subsequently be used for carrying out the plan in the ERP and SCM systems.

Simulations can be run both in inactive models and in inactive versions of the active model. The latter ones are often used when a company wants to try out different situations within the same model (i.e., same supply chain). Different models (i.e., different master data configurations) are created when the underlying supply chains are also different.

9.1.2 Transaction Data

Transaction data are created and maintained during the execution of the business processes. In the context of supply chain management, the major categories of transaction data are stock data, goods receipts, demands, and forecasts.

The majority of transaction data are associated with various kinds of orders: planned orders, production orders, stock transfer orders, transportation orders, etc. Transaction data in SAP SCM, for example, include the following:

- Stock
- Forecast
- Stock transfer reservation
- Sales order
- Planned order
- Production order
- Purchase requisition
- Independent requirement
- Dependent requirement
- Schedule line

- Subcontractor requirement
- Purchase order
- Transportation order

Most of these transaction data are straightforward, similar to the entities used in MRP, MRP II, and ERP. In supply chain management, different attributes may be required, but basically, the data structures are the same as already explained in the Chaps. 2–5.

Stock comes in several types: unrestricted-use stock, blocked stock, safety stock, stock in quality inspection, etc.

Two data structures that have not been mentioned before are schedule lines and subcontractor requirements.

A *schedule line* is associated with a scheduling agreement between the company and a supplier. If such an agreement exists, schedule lines represent partial deliveries within the agreement. A schedule line is similar to a purchase order. In an SCM system, it is usually created automatically based on the quantities and dates stored with the overall agreement.

A *subcontractor requirement* is created when parts are to be manufactured by a third party. Subcontracting means outsourcing one or more production steps to another company.

This is different from *procurement*, which normally means that parts are purchased from a supplier who produces the parts. Since the production process is in the supplier's responsibility, the company does not need to worry about the components needed for the purchased part (i.e., the bill of materials).

In *subcontracting*, the outsourced production steps are inside an order network (cf. Sect. 3.3.1) or product structure (cf. Sect. 2.1.1), respectively. This means that production steps before and after the outsourced step are carried out inside the company, requiring the company to provide the subcontractor with components and to include deliveries from the subcontractor in the material requirements and production planning.

Subcontracting comes in many different variations. Three basic forms are depicted in Fig. 9.6, assuming a simple product structure with C going into B, B into A, and A into X. The subcontracted part is A.

Normal subcontracting as shown in part a means that the company has to provide the subcontractor with components B, enabling the subcontractor to produce A and supply A to the company.

More difficult is the situation depicted in part b, requiring the subcontractor to procure the components needed for A from a *third-party* supplier. This can continue over several levels, as shown in part c. If the company wishes to capture and maintain all relationships in their SCM system, the modeling process is rather complex. The reader interested in more detail is referred to (Dickersbach 2009, pp. 401–411).

In supply chain management, it is essential to know and explicitly maintain the connections between the various types of orders, stocks, and requirements. From a process-oriented perspective, a supply chain is ultimately formed by linking different types of orders. In supply chain management, this aspect is known as *pegging*.

9.1.3 Pegging

Pegging is a common approach to realize and maintain the concatenation of orders (or transaction data in general). In this approach, requirements and allocations of material are used to connect different types of orders. Figure 9.7 illustrates pegging with the help of a simple example. Arrows represent the material flow (called *pegging relationships*). Diamonds represent quantities (required and actually allocated quantities).

This example shows how purchase orders, production orders, and stock transfer orders interact to satisfy the demand from customer orders. The component quantities received from two purchase orders (80 units each) are used for three manufacturing orders (50 units each), leaving a surplus of 10 units. 30 units of the first production order go into the first stock transfer order, and 20 units go into the second transfer order.

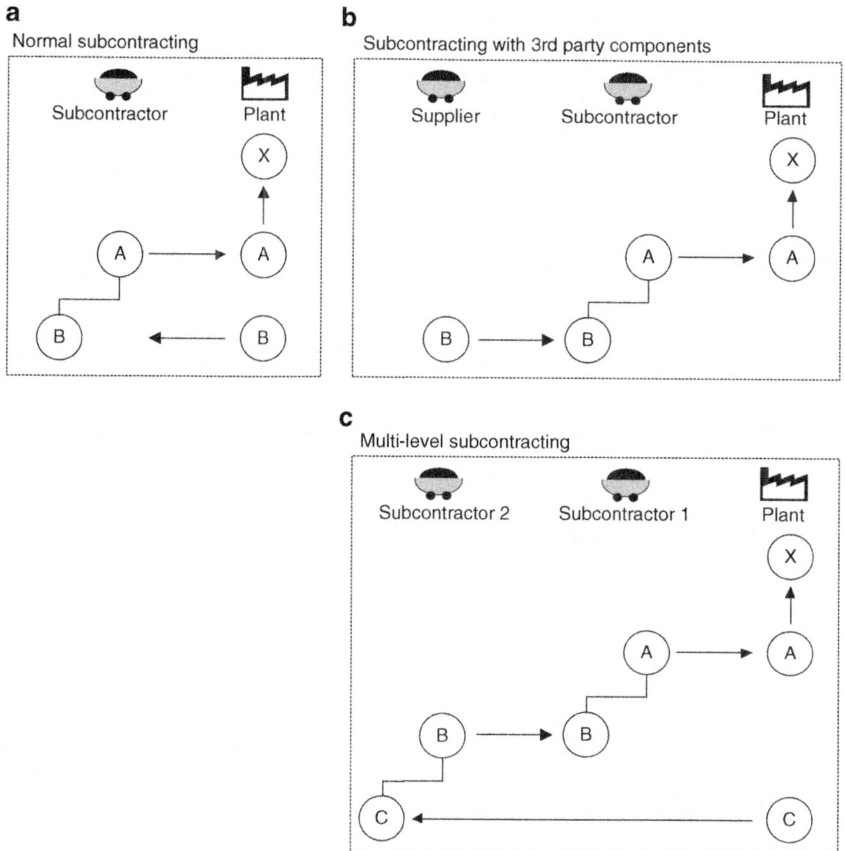

Fig. 9.6 Subcontracting variants (Dickersbach 2009, p. 401)

The second transfer order is additionally filled with 50 and 30 units, respectively, from the other two production orders. 20 units of the third production order are left over, that is, they are not used to fill the two stock transfer orders.

Four sales orders are filled with the quantities received from the stock transfer orders. Since the total requirement of 140 units (10 + 20 + 10 + 40 + 60) for the four sales orders cannot be satisfied with the two stock transfer orders (130 units together), a shortage of 10 units remains.

There are different possible strategies for visiting supplying nodes to meet the requirements of receiving nodes. One such strategy is FIFO (first-in-first-out), another is LIFO (last-in-first-out).

These two strategies differ as to when and where excess supply is recorded. Figure 9.8 illustrates the effect with the help of a small example—two sales orders S_1 and S_2 to be satisfied by three planned orders P_1, P_2, and P_3. The first planned order to become available is P_1 and the last is P_3.

In the *FIFO strategy*, quantities are allocated in such a way that 5 of the 10 units from P_1 are used for S_1 and the other 5 for S_2, while the entire amount of P_2 (10 units) and half of P_3 (i.e., 5 units) are used for S_2. Obviously, the excess supply of 5 units remains with planned order P_3.

In the *LIFO strategy*, the entire amount of P_3 (10 units) is used, then all of P_2 (10 units), and afterwards 5 units of P_1, leaving 5 units with P_1.

In SAP SCM, pegging can be dynamic or fixed. *Dynamic pegging* means that requirements for a location product are automatically linked with suitable stocks or receipts for the location product (SAP 2012b). The pegging relationships

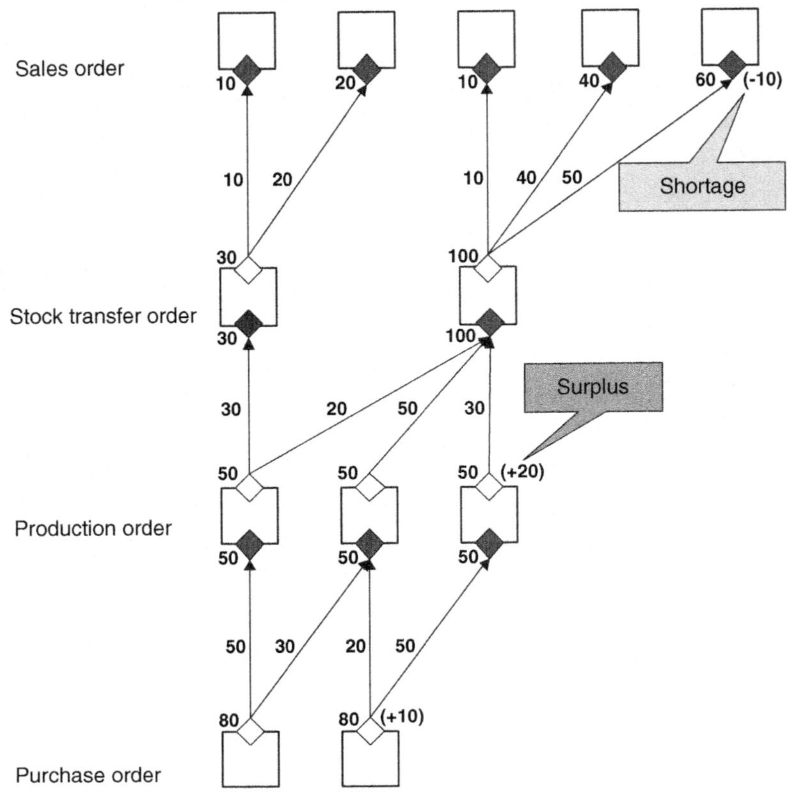

Fig. 9.7 Pegging structure (SAP 2012b)

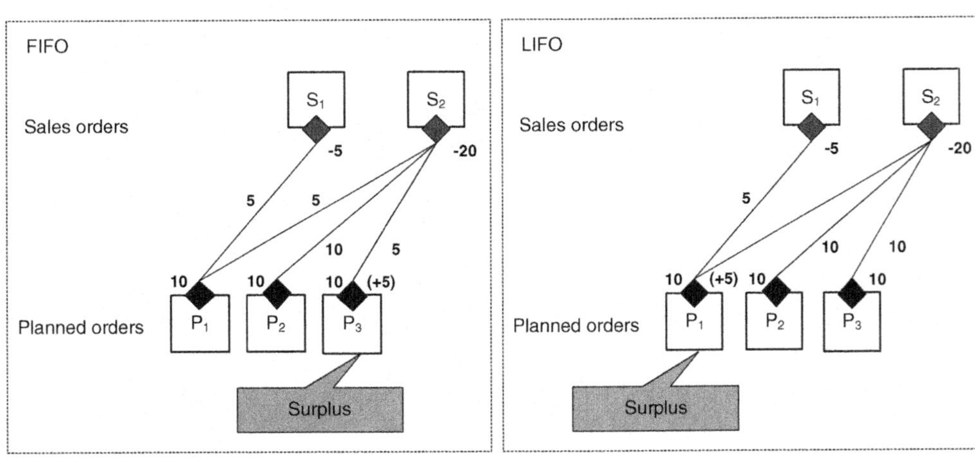

Fig. 9.8 Pegging with FIFO and LIFO strategies (Dickersbach 2009, p. 26)

are adapted by the system whenever requirement or allocation data change, that is, any association of a requirement element with a material-allocation element may be discarded as soon as the planning is modified.

In *fixed pegging*, the assignment of a material-allocation element (receipt) to a requirement element remains untouched when the planning changes. This means, for example, that components that have been assigned to an order via fixed pegging will not be available to other competing orders.

9.2 Advanced SCM Planning Approaches

Today's SCM systems provide advanced approaches to planning compared to those available in ERP and MRP II systems. This is due to both methodological and technological advancements. More efficient models and solution methods have been developed over the last decades, and much more powerful computers have become available, capable of solving even optimization problems in a reasonable amount of time. Recent approaches have often been summarized under the abbreviation APS.

9.2.1 APS: Advanced Planning and Scheduling

APS is a summary term that many authors use as an abbreviation of "advanced planning and scheduling," while others use it to mean "advanced planning system" (e.g., Kallrath and Maindl 2006, p. 6). APS offers (1) a number of extensions and improvements of ERP functionality and (2) additional functionality needed for intercompany business processes.

The first category includes, for example, more powerful methods for order sequencing, scheduling, and resource allocation than those available in a typical ERP system. The second category provides support for common tasks where several partners are involved, for example, planning a supply network.

Providing "advanced" methods and tools, the typical functionality of an APS system includes:

- Distinctive modeling capabilities, with a strong focus on bottlenecks and constraints
- Powerful algorithms, for example, linear and mixed-integer programming as well as heuristic approaches such as genetic algorithms, simulated annealing, and neural networks
- Dealing with complex data structures (multi-level bills of materials and routings)
- Pegging, that is, maintaining the connections between procurement, production, transport, and customer orders (see Sect. 9.1.3)
- Simulation capabilities, in particular, what-if simulation, for testing and evaluating different production and supply scenarios
- ERP interfaces

APS functions support both planning within the company as well as across the network. Figure 9.9 illustrates the various planning areas with the help of a so-called supply chain planning matrix. This matrix was initially introduced by Rohde, Meyr, and Wagner in 2000 and has since then been republished several times (e.g., Meyr et al. 2010, p. 109).

The supply chain planning matrix covers both strategic and operative planning within and across functional areas (Fleischmann et al. 2010; Meyr et al. 2010, p. 110):

- The main task of *strategic network planning* is configuring the entire supply chain or supply network. Decisions on this level are strategic and long-term, for example, which distribution centers should be established in which locations and which customers should be served by which distribution centers.
- *Demand planning* has the main role of generating forecasted demand figures for end products. For this purpose, various statistical methods, aggregation/disaggregation, and what-if simulation can be used.
- The task of *master production planning* is to create a feasible midterm production plan, synchronizing the flow of material along the supply chain. In this planning area, procurement, production, and distribution quantities are centrally harmonized, taking available and required capacities into consideration (Kallrath and Maindl 2006, p. 7). When an appropriate level of aggregation is chosen, optimization methods can be used for this purpose.
- *Material requirements planning* is primarily a task within the individual enterprise. It comprises conventional consumption and requirements-driven material planning but also includes approaches such as VMI (vendor-managed inventory) and CPFR

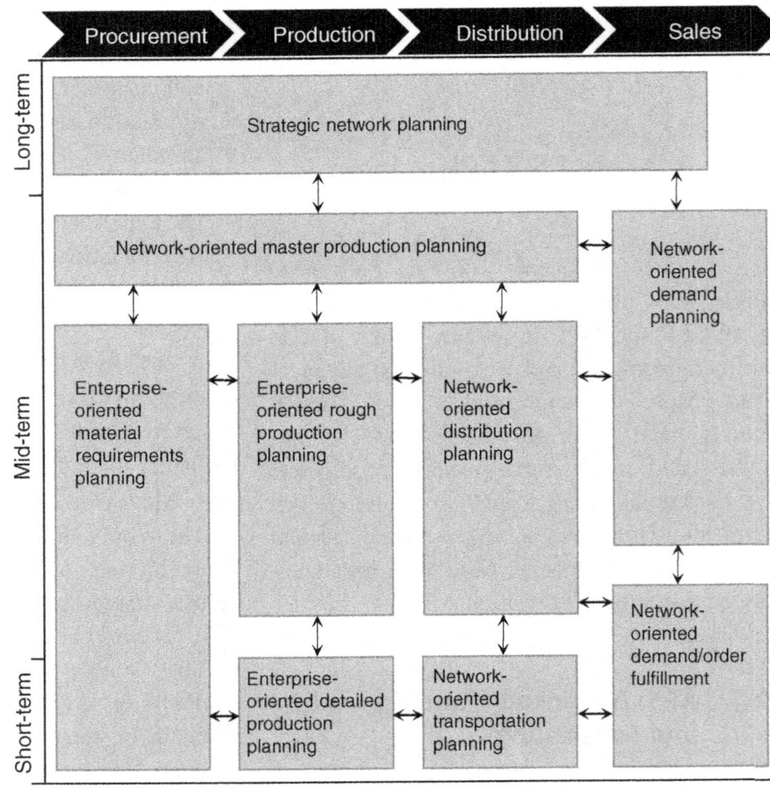

Fig. 9.9 Supply chain planning matrix (Meyr et al. 2010, p. 109)

(collaborative planning, forecasting, and replenishment) (cf. Sect. 8.2.3).

- *Production planning* and *scheduling* create rough and detailed production plans for the individual enterprise, based on the network-wide master planning.
- In *distribution planning,* end-product quantities are allocated to deliveries, in accordance with the production and demand plans.
- *Transportation planning* deals with route planning, load planning, selecting the means of transport, and assigning end-product quantities to individual customer shipments.
- *Demand/order fulfillment* comprises availability checking and order scheduling. In some versions of the supply chain planning matrix, this area is directly referred to as *ATP ("available-to-promise")* (Meyr et al. 2010, p. 109).

Network-wide planning areas are strategic network planning, master planning, demand planning, distribution planning, transportation planning, and demand/order fulfillment. *Company-specific* planning areas are material requirements planning, production planning, and scheduling.

Figure 9.10 illustrates how the planning areas are related in terms of the interfaces where the supply chain partners have to collaborate. Similar to the SCOR schema depicted in Fig. 8.2, one interface is where the supplier's demand planning and fulfillment meet the planning of the company in question (e.g., purchasing). The other interface is on the customer's side, where the company's demand planning and fulfillment meet the planning of the customer. Strategic network planning interfaces both the supplier's and the customer's strategic network planning.

Optimization A remarkable feature common to most of the above-mentioned fields is that solution approaches increasingly employ optimization methods, for example, linear, nonlinear, integer, and mixed-integer programming. In addition, sub-optimizing heuristics such as genetic algorithms,

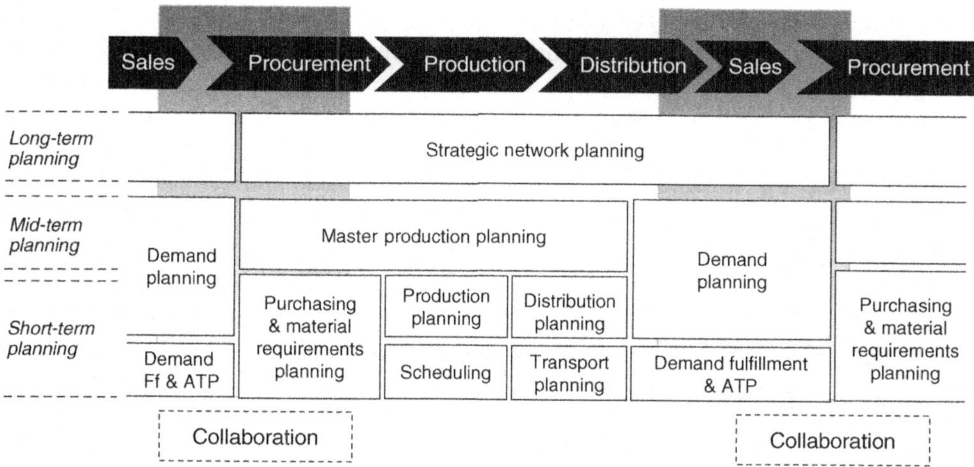

Fig. 9.10 Supply-chain collaboration in APS (Meyr et al. 2010, p. 111)

simulated annealing, and constraint propagation have become quite common.

These approaches are not only popular in academia, but they have also been implemented in real-world supply chain management systems. For this reason, we subsequently discuss some optimization models reflecting typical SCM problems. Chapter 10 deals with a practical SCM system and points out where optimization models are used.

The models presented in the following subsections support three examples of long-, mid-, and short-term planning decisions, namely, planning the locations of distribution centers (long-term), planning a complete supply network (mid- to long-term), and ordering reasonable quantities from suppliers (short-term).

9.2.2 Planning Locations

The model presented in this section reflects a typical decision problem when setting up a supply chain or network: The partners have to decide where they want to install distribution centers (DCs) and which customers (or regions) should be served from which distribution centers. They have already identified several possible locations for distribution centers and determined the location-dependent costs.

The answers to the two questions above depend on several things, in particular, on the *costs* of:

- Running a distribution center (depending on the location, e.g., rent, insurance)
- Storing and handling goods (depending on the location and the good)
- Transportation (depending on the distance between a distribution center and the customer)

The following symbols will be used in the model:

f_n = fixed cost of running a distribution center at location n ($)

v_n = variable cost of storing and handling one unit at location n ($/unit)

t_{nj} = variable cost of transporting one unit from location n to customer j ($/unit)

d_j = demand by customer j (units/day)

y_n = 1, if a distribution center is installed at location n, otherwise 0

x_{nj} = 1, if customer j is served from location n, otherwise 0

We are assuming that we have N candidate locations ($n = 1, \ldots, N$) and J customers ($j = 1, \ldots, J$). On a sufficiently high level of aggregation, we may consider an entire sales region as a "customer." This interpretation is acceptable when the transportation cost is mainly determined by the cost of reaching the region, while the cost of going from one individual customer to the next within that region is negligible.

Basic Model Using the notation introduced above, we can formulate the decision problem as a mixed-integer optimization model as follows (see, e.g., (Thonemann 2010, pp. 112–114)):

The decision variables are y_n and x_{nj}. This means, for example, that if the solution algorithm computes the value 1 for y_3, a distribution center will be established at location no. 3. If the value is 0, no distribution center will be installed there. Likewise, if $x_{35} = 1$, customer (region) no. 5 will be served from location no. 3. If $x_{35} = 0$, customer no. 5 will not be served from this location (but from some other one).

The goal of the model is to select locations for distribution centers (y_n) and options for serving customers from locations (x_{nj}) in such a way that the total cost C is minimal:

$$C = \sum_{n=1}^{N} \sum_{j=1}^{J} (v_n + t_{nj}) d_j x_{nj} + \sum_{n=1}^{N} f_n y_n \rightarrow \min,$$

subject to

$$\begin{aligned} \sum_{n=1}^{N} x_{nj} &= 1 & j &= 1, \ldots, J, \\ x_{nj} &\leq y_n & n &= 1, \ldots, N; j = 1, \ldots, J, \\ x_{nj} &\in \{0, 1\} & n &= 1, \ldots, N; j = 1, \ldots, J, \\ y_n &\in \{0, 1\} & n &= 1, \ldots, N. \end{aligned}$$

The *objective function* specifies C as the sum of all variable costs (storage, handling, and transportation) and all fixed costs (running distribution centers). Variable costs occur whenever $x_{nj} \neq 0$, that is, when customer j is served from location n. A fixed cost of f_n is incurred if a distribution center is operated at location n ($y_n = 1$); otherwise, it is 0 for this location.

The *constraints* of the model ensure that all customer demand is satisfied, that a customer can only be served from a location if a distribution center exists at that location, and that a customer is not served from more than one location.

More specifically, the first set of constraints requires that exactly one distribution center ships goods to a customer j. If the sum of all x_{nj} is equal to 1, then exactly one x_{nj} will be 1 and all others will be 0. This has to hold for all customers $j = 1, \ldots, J$.

The second set of constraints ($x_{nj} \leq y_n$ for $j = 1, \ldots, J$; $n = 1, \ldots, N$) ensures that a customer only receives deliveries from location n if a distribution center is operated at location n ($y_n = 1$). Only in this case, x_{nj} values can be greater than 0.

The third set of constraints (integer constraints) requires a customer to be served from no more than one distribution center. Allowing only 0 and 1 values means that partial serving is excluded.

Likewise, the fourth set of constraints makes sure that a distribution center at any location is either run or not run, that is, "partial openings" are not allowed.

Finding the optimal solution to the problem stated above is not too difficult when the problem size is small but extremely time-consuming when the size is large. As long as the number of locations and the number of customers are small, all possible options of serving customers from this or from that location can be evaluated by computing the objective function. When the numbers are very small (e.g., two locations and three customers), this can even be done with pencil and paper.

However, when the problem size is larger, a complete enumeration of all solutions would take a lot of time—due to the large number of possible combinations of locations and customers—and for realistic problem sizes, it is not even possible to compute all solutions within a reasonable time frame.

A common technique to solve optimization problems containing integer decision variables is the *branch-and-bound technique* (Land and Doig 1960). *Branching* means that the decision problem is divided into smaller subproblems.

These subproblems are also split up, etc., that is, the entire solution space is divided into subsets. *Bounding* means that for each subproblem, upper and lower bounds of the values the objective function can possibly reach are computed. With the help of the bounds, branches of the solution tree that obviously cannot contain the optimal solution are discarded early. In this way, the number of solutions to check decreases rapidly.

Extensions The basic model described above is very simple because it makes a number of *assumptions* that may not be satisfied in practice:

1. The company deals with only one product, or the level of aggregation is so high that different products do not matter.
2. The company is ready to actually open N distribution centers, one at each potential location, if the optimal solution says so.
3. Even if a distribution center serves only one customer, it will be installed.
4. The distribution centers are able to deliver any amount of products. Their capacities are unlimited.
5. No matter if there are logical relationships between the locations and no matter how far or close locations are away from each other, distribution centers will always be established if the computed solution says so.

To make the model more realistic, these assumptions should be lifted. This will be shown subsequently, starting with the single-product restriction (cf. Thonemann 2010, pp. 119–121).

Multiple products can be considered by defining deliveries not only with regard to the location (n) and the customer (j) but also the type of product (p) to be delivered: x_{pnj}. Thus, the objective function of the basic model has to be extended as follows:

$$C = \sum_{p=1}^{P} \sum_{n=1}^{N} \sum_{j=1}^{J} (v_{\text{pn}} + t_{\text{pnj}}) d_{\text{pj}} x_{\text{nj}} + \sum_{n=1}^{N} f_{\text{n}} y_{\text{n}} \rightarrow \min$$

with

v_{pn} = variable cost of storing and handling one unit of product p at location n ($/unit)

t_{pnj} = variable cost of transporting one unit of product p from location n to customer j ($/unit)

d_{pj} = demand for product p by customer j (units/day)

y_{n} = 1, if a distribution center is installed at location n, otherwise 0

x_{pnj} = 1, if customer j is served with product p from location n, otherwise 0

subject to

$$\sum_{n=1}^{N} x_{\text{pnj}} = 1 \quad p = 1,\ldots,P; j = 1,\ldots,J,$$

$$x_{\text{pnj}} \le y_{\text{n}} \quad p = 1,\ldots,P; n = 1,\ldots,N; j = 1,\ldots,J,$$

$$x_{\text{pnj}} \in \{0,1\} \quad p = 1,\ldots,P; n = 1,\ldots,N; j = 1,\ldots,J,$$

$$y_{\text{n}} \in \{0,1\} \quad n = 1,\ldots,N.$$

The second term of the objective function is the same as in the basic model because the fixed cost of a location (f_{n}) does not depend on the products.

The constraints are similar as above. The first set of constraints requires that a customer (j) demanding a certain product (p) is actually served from exactly one location (and not from more, i.e., only one x_{pnj} must be equal to 1). The second and third sets of constraints are analogous to the constraints of the basic model but take the differentiation by product types into account.

More constraints result from lifting assumptions no. 2–5:

- The number of *open distribution centers* can be limited to a maximum number M by requiring

$$\sum_{n=1}^{N} y_n \le M$$

- Lifting the third assumption allows the company to avoid the risk of having an open distribution center but no customers to be served from that center. This case might occur, for example, when the only customer assigned to that center decides not to buy from the company anymore. The risk of running into such a situation can be reduced by requiring a minimum number R_n of customers for each distribution center n:

$$\sum_{p=1}^{P}\sum_{j=1}^{J} x_{pnj} \leq R_n \quad n = 1, \ldots, N$$

- The *unlimited-capacity assumption* can be treated by formulating capacity constraints such as the maximum quantity Q_n a distribution center at location n can handle:

$$\sum_{p=1}^{P}\sum_{j=1}^{J} d_{pj}x_{pnj} \leq Q_n \quad n = 1, \ldots, N$$

- Regarding the *dependencies between locations,* we can introduce constraints specifying bilateral relationships, such as a distribution center may be installed either at location n or at location m but not at both:

$$y_n + y_m \leq 1,$$

  and, if a (no) distribution center is installed at location n, then there must also be one (none) at location m:

$$y_n = y_m$$

Of course, there are many more model assumptions that have to be elaborated and removed to meet practical requirements. When a company or a network of companies plans the locations of distribution centers, plants, transport hubs, etc., an optimization model will be much more complex than the simple model presented in this section.

9.2.3 Planning Inventory and Orders

A problem that all partners of a supply chain are exposed to is to decide *how much* to order from their suppliers. That this is a difficult decision has already been shown in the sections on industrial dynamics and the bullwhip effect (cf. Sects. 8.2.1 and 8.2.2).

The reason why the bullwhip effect takes place is that a company—due to lack of information about the "true" demand—orders more than is actually needed, just to be on the safe side. This behavior leads to an increase in inventory, which in turn causes high inventory cost.

What if the company took the risk of *running short of material* but, on the other hand, saved inventory cost? In operations research, optimization models allowing for shortages were also developed. While the majority of these models assume known demand rates (deterministic demand), the model discussed subsequently takes *stochastic demand* into account. This is a realistic situation in a supply chain, where the downstream partners generally are not sure about the orders they will receive from upstream.

Newsvendor Model A simple model allowing for stochastic demand is the so-called *newsvendor model.* The model is named after news vendors because their business model best illustrates this approach to dealing with demand: A newspaper vendor has to decide each morning how many copies to order from the distributor to meet the day's demand. From past experience, the vendor has, of course, some idea of what would be a reasonable quantity, but he or she does not know what exactly will be the demand for this period (day).

Ordering too little means that the newspaper vendor loses money that he or she could have earned, had more papers been ordered. On the other hand, ordering too much is a loss because the unsold papers are worthless one day later. However, they can be returned to the supplier for a lower price than the purchase price.

Cheng and coauthors provide a brief summary of the newsvendor model in a supply chain management context (Cheng et al. 2011, pp. 211–213). In the following, we will use Thonemann's notation for the explanation of the model (Thonemann 2010, pp. 209–218).

All decision-relevant costs in the newsvendor model are variable costs. Suppose the newspaper vendor buys the paper for \$0.80 per copy, sells it for \$2.50, and receives \$0.45 per copy returned to the supplier. Then, ordering too much results in a cost of \$0.35 per copy. This cost is called *unit overage cost* (c_o).

Ordering not enough means that the vendor could have sold additional copies and earned \$2.50–\$0.80 = \$1.70 per copy. This cost is called *unit underage cost* (c_u).

Suppose the newsvendor knows the probabilities of selling 1, 2, …, 199, 200, 201, etc., copies per day, that is, $p_1, p_2, \ldots, p_{199}, p_{200}, p_{201}$, etc. Then, it is simple to compute the expected values of the total overage and total underage. With

S = order quantity
d = demand value (number of copies)
D = possible demand values (random variable)
p_d = probability of demand equaling d copies
$E[]^+$ = expected value (only positive values in the bracket are considered)

the *overage* is

$$E[S-D]^+ = \sum_{d=0}^{S}(S-d)p_d,$$

and the *underage* is

$$E[D-S]^+ = \sum_{d=S}^{\infty}(d-S)p_d.$$

Multiplication of the overage by the unit overage cost c_o and the underage by the unit underage cost c_u yields the *decision-relevant cost* $C(S)$ to be minimized (*objective function*):

$$C(S) = c_o E[S-D]^+ + c_u E[D-S]^+ \text{ min}$$
$$= c_o \sum_{d=0}^{S}(S-d)p_d + c_u \sum_{d=S}^{\infty}(d-S)p_d$$

Obviously, the model is straightforward, but the crucial question remains: What will the period's demand be like? In other words, what is the probability distribution of the demand? Depending on this distribution, the optimal order quantity can be computed.

In the literature on the newsvendor model (e.g., Cheng et al. 2011, p. 213), it has been shown that the optimal order quantity S^* is equal to the value of the distribution function's inverse function F^{-1} at the point $c_u/(c_u + c_o)$:

$$S^* = F^{-1}\left(\frac{c_u}{c_u + c_o}\right)$$

The point $c_u/(c_u + c_o)$ is also called the *critical ratio* (*CR*) (Thonemann 2010, p. 211).

The value of S^* depends on the particular probability distribution that suits the actual problem. In the original newsvendor problem, the number of units per day is fairly large, so a continuous distribution function can be used.

If the level of certainty about the distribution is low, a *normal distribution* is often a good approximation. Figure 9.11 shows the density function $f(d)$, the distribution function $F(d)$, and the inverse function F^{-1} of a normal distribution with mean $\mu = 200$ and standard deviation $\sigma = 25$ copies. For the above-mentioned values of $c_u = 1.70$ and $c_o = 0.35$, the optimal order quantity is

$$S^* = F^{-1}(1.70/1.70 + 0.35) \approx 224 \text{ copies}$$

When more information on the probability distribution is available, a more specific distribution function than the normal distribution can be used. For example, an exponential distribution or a hyperbolic distribution may better fit the demand pattern.

Continuous distributions are appropriate when the number of units is large. For small numbers, the demand will be measured in discrete units, and a *discrete distribution* function will be better suited, for example, a Poisson distribution.

A Supply Chain Management Scenario Mapping the newsvendor model to a *supply chain management scenario* leads to the following interpretation: A manufacturer has to decide

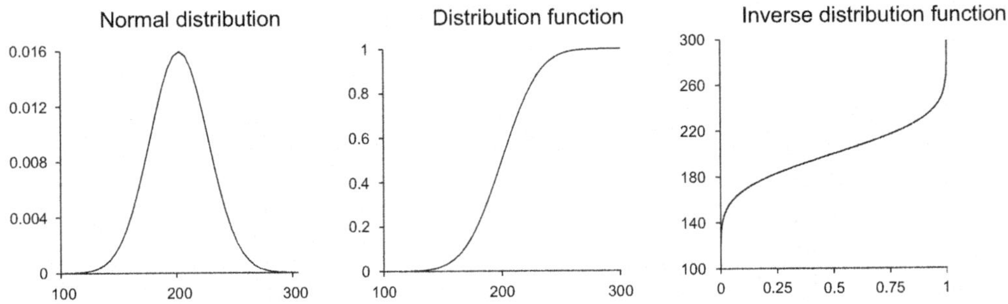

Fig. 9.11 Normal distribution ($\mu = 200$, $\sigma = 25$)

how much of a material to order from a supplier at or before the beginning of a period. The manufacturer uses the material to produce a sellable good. The optimal order quantity depends on the customers' demand for the good, which is not exactly known.

If the manufacturer orders too much, the overage cannot be used for anything else and will be salvaged. The *salvage value* reduces the manufacturer's "loss" which would otherwise be equal to the purchase price. If the manufacturer orders too little, customer demand cannot be satisfied, inducing lost profit in the same way as for the newspaper vendor.

In the original newsvendor model, the manufacturer makes the purchasing decision independent of the supplier's decisions. In particular, the supplier sets the price of the material, and the manufacturer tries to optimize the order quantity (as well as the production level) based on this price. The supplier performs their own optimization planning, which is not connected with the manufacturer's planning in any way.

It has been shown in the literature that both the supplier and the manufacturer can achieve better results when they integrate their planning (Cheng et al. 2011, pp. 213–215). Instead of each party attempting to maximize their own profit independently, *integrated planning* means maximizing the profit of the total (two-stage) supply chain. This profit (P_I) is greater than or equal to the sum of the supplier's profit (P_S) and the manufacturer's profit (P_M) when the two parties plan independently:

$$P_I(S_I^*) \geq P_S(S^*) + P_M(S^*),$$

with S_I = order quantity in integrated planning.

This is mainly due to the fact that the supplier has different options for remaining quantities than the supplier, for example, selling them to other buyers. In model terms, this means that the salvage values of the supplier and the manufacturer are different. Therefore, it can make sense if the supplier retains certain quantities instead of selling them to the manufacturer. In integrated planning, the optimal order quantity (S_I^*) is not decided only by the buyer but also by the seller.

Planning for Service Levels The objective function of the newsvendor model is a rational guideline for ordering when the demand is not known with certainty. However, it takes only the immediate overage and underage costs into account. In a real supply chain scenario, the situation is much more complex. Shortages may have indirect consequences that cannot be captured by a simple cost figure such as c_u.

If the company in question is at the end of the supply chain (selling to end customers), there is a significant risk that customers will be dissatisfied if they are not served. A consequence may be that they buy somewhere else and do not return in the future.

If the company is a node in the middle of the supply chain (manufacturing intermediate products), a material shortage can mean that the production must be discontinued until the material is again available.

Indirect costs resulting from losing customers to the competition and from disruptions of the production are difficult to measure or estimate. Grounding an optimization model on vague estimates would not make much sense.

Instead of following the newsvendor model's cost function, many companies use a different guideline. They attempt to purchase goods in such a way that they can maintain a certain service level. The term "service level" generally describes to what extent requests can be fulfilled. It is often expressed as a percentage or a probability.

In the ordering problem, a reasonable definition of "service level" is "the probability that all of the period's demand can be satisfied." A service level of $\alpha = 95\ \%$, for example, means that the company has to compute their order quantity S in such a way that the total demand will be met with a probability of 95 %. Since producing more units than are actually needed to meet the 95 % level will cause unnecessary cost, the optimal order quantity is obviously the smallest possible value of S that meets the 95 % criterion.

Increasing S gradually, the threshold where it satisfies the criterion can be determined with the help of the probability distribution function $F(S)$, namely, at the point where $F(S) \geq \alpha$ for the first time (Thonemann 2010, p. 219). Setting $F(S) = \alpha$, the optimal order quantity S^* is $F^{-1}(\alpha)$. This is the same solution as in the newsvendor model described above, except for CR being replaced by α.

Summarizing the ordering model with a service level as objective function is as follows:

$$S \rightarrow \min$$

subject to

$$F(S) \geq \alpha$$

The optimal order quantity is

$$S^* = F^{-1}(\alpha)$$

Assuming that the demand is *normally distributed* as above ($\mu = 200, \sigma = 25$), the optimal order quantity for a service level of 95 % is

$$S^* = F^{-1}(0.95) \approx 241 \text{ units}$$

As a reminder, we have used the term "service level" as indicating the probability that the demand of the period can be satisfied. Other views of what a "service level" exist as well. One common definition is "the expected share of the period's total demand that can be met." A service-level model using the expected share of satisfied demand as a guideline is described by Thonemann (2010, pp. 219–220).

9.2.4 Planning Supply Networks

Planning order quantities or locations is only part of the task at hand. Far more challenging, with respect to the modeling and solution approach, is *simultaneously* planning procurement, production, distribution, and transportation so that customer demand is met. The subtasks of this problem involve the suppliers', the manufacturer's, and the customers' sides of the network. In other words, the problem is planning a supply-manufacturing-distribution network, or in short, a supply network. Subsequently, we will use the short form: *supply network planning (SNP)*. As will be seen in Sect. 10.1.3, this is also the term used in SAP SCM.

To illustrate the problem, we will take up an example presented by Kallrath and Maindl (2006, pp. 43–50). Figure 9.12 shows a simple supply network consisting of two suppliers (S1, S2), one production site (factory F1), and three customers (C1, C2, C3). In general, there can be more suppliers, more factories, and more customers. Instead of individual customers, we may think of distribution centers or homogeneous regions where demand is created.

Input materials (components) X1 and *X*2 are required for the products manufactured in the factory and delivered to customers (P1, P2, P3). The quantities needed are derived from customer demand using the quantity coefficients of the bills of materials. As the figure indicates, the same material may be purchased from different

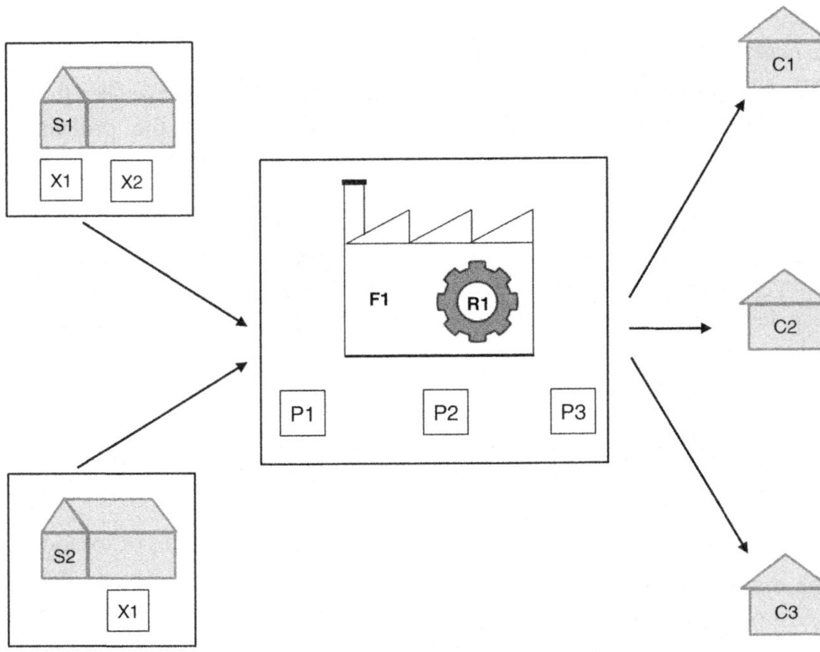

Fig. 9.12 Supply network example (Kallrath and Maindl 2006, p. 43)

suppliers, and obviously, not every supplier provides all materials.

Production resources are considered on an aggregate level, such as an entire production line. In our example, the (only) factory contains just one production resource (R1). The regular capacity of this resource is limited, but it can be extended (e.g., doubled by implementing a second shift) at an additional cost.

To summarize, the model framework consists of the following sets of objects:

Suppliers:	$\mathcal{S} = \{S_s \mid s = 1, \ldots, n^S\}$
Factories:	$\mathcal{F} = \{F_f \mid f = 1, \ldots, n^F\}$
Customers:	$\mathcal{C} = \{C_c \mid c = 1, \ldots, n^C\}$
End products:	$\mathcal{Y} = \{P_p \mid p = 1, \ldots, n^Y\}$
Components:	$\mathcal{X} = \{X_p \mid p = 1, \ldots, n^X\}$
Products:	$\mathcal{P} = \mathcal{X} \cup \mathcal{Y}$, elements numbered by $p = 1, \ldots, n^P$ with $n^P = n^X + n^Y$
Resources:	$\mathcal{R} = \{R_r \mid r = 1, \ldots, n^R\}$
Locations:	$\mathcal{L} = \mathcal{S} \cup \mathcal{F} \cup \mathcal{C}$, elements numbered by $l = 1, \ldots, n^L$ with $n^L = n^S + n^F + n^C\}$
Time buckets:	$\mathcal{T} = \{t \mid t = 1, \ldots, n^T\}$
Demands:	$\mathcal{D} = \{d \mid d = 1, \ldots, n^D\}$

Note that the term "product" is used for both components (input materials) and end products.

"Time buckets" are periods into which individual demand dates and other dates are combined. In the model, they are numbered 1 to n^T.

"Demands" are also numbers starting with 1, identifying customer demand through 4-tuples "product, customer location, time bucket, and quantity."

Objective Function The *objective function* of the supply network planning model is to minimize the cost. In this model, the total cost C that can be influenced by planning decisions comprises:

- Procurement cost C^B
- Production cost C^P
- Capacity expansion cost C^X
- Inventory cost C^I
- Cost of late delivery C^D
- Cost of nondelivery C^N

In order to formulate the objective function, the following notation is used:

C^B_{lp}=cost of procuring one unit of product p at location l

C_p^P=cost of producing one unit of product p

C_r^X=cost of extending the capacity of resource r by one time period (time bucket)

C_p^I=cost of storing one unit of product p for one period

C_{dt}^D=cost of late delivery of demand d in period t (penalty)

C_d^N=cost of not delivering demand d to the customer (penalty)

r_{lpt}=quantity of product p purchased at location l in period t

L_p=lot size of product p

$\propto_{lpt}$=positive integer number indicating a multiple of the lot size L_p, if product p is produced at location l in period t, otherwise 0

c_{rt}^X=extended capacity of resource r used in period t

s_{lpt}=stock of product p at location n at the end of period t

f_{dt}=quantity delivered to satisfy demand D_d in period t

D_d=quantity of demand d

Objective Function

$$C = C^B + C^P + C^X + C^I + C^D + C^N \rightarrow \min$$

$$= \sum_{l=1}^{n^l} \sum_{p=1}^{n^p} \sum_{t=1}^{n^t} C_{lp}^B r_{lpt} + \sum_{l=1}^{n^l} \sum_{p=1}^{n^p} \sum_{t=1}^{n^t} C_p^P L_p \propto_{lpt}$$

$$+ \sum_{r=1}^{n^r} \sum_{t=1}^{n^t} C_r^X c_{rt}^X + \sum_{l=1}^{n^l} \sum_{p=1}^{n^p} \sum_{t=1}^{n^t} C_p^I + s_{lpt}$$

$$+ \sum_{d=1}^{n^d} \sum_{t=1}^{n^t} C_{dt}^D f_{dt} + \sum_{d=1}^{n^d} C_d^N \left(D_d - \sum_{t=1}^{n^t} f_{dt} \right).$$

Most of the terms are straightforward. The last two (costs of late delivery and nondelivery) show that partial deliveries are allowed. In the case of nondelivery, the penalty applies only to the difference between the demand (D_d) and the actual deliveries (Σf_{dt}).

Since in all terms the summation goes across the entire range of elements, some obvious *restrictions* regarding the *domains* of the variables apply:

- *Procurement* costs $\neq 0$ only exist for components and only at supplier locations, that is, all other values have to be zero:

$$r_{lpt} = 0 \quad \forall p \in \mathcal{Y}, 1 \in \mathcal{L}, t \in \mathcal{T}$$

$$r_{lpt} = 0 \quad \forall l \in \mathcal{C}, p \in \mathcal{P}, t \in \mathcal{T}.$$

- *Production* costs only occur at factories where end products are produced, that is, all other values have to be zero:

$$\propto_{lpt} = 0 \quad \forall p \in \mathcal{X}, 1 \in \mathcal{S} \cup \mathcal{C}, t \in \mathcal{T}.$$

- *Inventory* is considered only at supplier and factory locations, not at customer locations; hence,

$$s_{lpt} = 0 \quad \forall l \in \mathcal{C}, p \in \mathcal{P}, t \in \mathcal{T}.$$

Restrictions like these actually apply to, and have to be implemented for, all decision variables. These variables may only be created with values > 0 if the respective combination of location and product exists.

Constraints The major part of the model, in addition to the objective function, is constituted by the system of constraints reflecting the connections between and within the areas of procurement, production, inventory, transportation, and delivery.

To state the constraints referring to *demand and delivery*, we use the notation introduced in Kallrath and Maindl (2006, pp. 47–48):

I_{pd}^P=1, if demand d is for product p, otherwise 0

I_{ld}^L=1, if demand d is at location l, otherwise 0

T_d^D=last time period in which deliveries to satisfy demand d are possible (afterwards, demand will be lost)

d_{lpt}=delivered quantity of product p at location l in period t

$T_{l_1 l_2 pt}^X$ =maximum quantity of product p that can be transported from location l_1 to location l_2 in period t

$t_{l_1 l_2 pt}$=quantity of product p (transport volume) that is transported from location l_1 to location l_2 in period t

The constraints are then as follows:

$$d_{lpt} - \sum_{d=1}^{n^D} + I_{ld}^L I_{pd}^P f_{dt} = 0 \quad \forall l \in \mathcal{L}, p \in \mathcal{P}, t \in \mathcal{T}, \quad (9.1)$$

$$\sum_{t=1}^{n^T} f_{dt} \le D_d \quad \forall d \in \mathcal{D}, \quad (9.2)$$

$$f_{dt} = 0 \quad \forall d \in \mathcal{D}, t \in \mathcal{T} | t > T_d^D, \quad (9.3)$$

$$t_{l_1 l_2 pt} \le T_{l_1 l_2 pt}^X \quad \forall l_1, l_2 \in \mathcal{L}, p \in \mathcal{P}, t \in \mathcal{T}. \quad (9.4)$$

These constraints specify that (9.1) a delivery d_{lpt} is used to satisfy one or more f_{dt} values (i.e., quantities delivered to satisfy one or more demands d in period t), (9.2) all quantities delivered to satisfy demand d (i.e., Σf_{dt}) must not exceed the quantity of the demand (D_d), (9.3) deliveries after the acceptance deadline T_d^D are not possible, and (9.4) the transport volume between a source location l_1 and a destination location l_2 does not exceed the maximum transport capacity available for l_1, l_2, p, and t.

For the constraints regarding *material flow* and *production,* the relationships between components and end products as well as the quantitative impact on the capacity are needed. With:

$B_{p_1 p_2}$=quantity of component p_2 to make one unit of p_1 (BOM input coefficient)

b_{lpt}=quantity of product p consumed in production at location l in period t

R_r^C=regular capacity of resource t per period

R_r^X=extended capacity of resource t per period

R_{pr}=capacity of resource r needed for one unit of product p

c_{rt}=capacity of resource r used in period t,

the *material balance* equation must hold, requiring for any product at any node and time that the sum of incoming quantities (left side) is equal to the total output (right side):

$$\sum_{l_1=1}^{n^L} t_{l_1 l_2 pt} + L_p \propto_{lpt} + s_{lpt-1} + r_{lpt} = \sum_{l_2=1}^{n^L} t_{l_1 l_2 pt} + d_{lpt} + s_{lpt} + b_{lpt} \quad (9.5)$$

$$\forall l \in \mathcal{L}, p \in \mathcal{P}, t \in \mathcal{T},$$

where s_{lp0} is provided representing the initial stock level of product p at location l.

Incoming quantities can be the volume of the product brought in from other locations ($t_{l_1 l_2 pt}$), the lots produced ($L_p \propto_{lpt}$), stock from the previous period (s_{lpt-1}), and purchased amounts (r_{lpt}).

The *output* of the node comprises the number of units transported to other locations ($t_{l_1 l_2 pt}$), demand fulfillment (d_{lpt}), stock at the end of the period (s_{lpt}), and consumption in the production (b_{lpt}).

Constraints for *production* capture MRP and MRP II matters, that is, input relationships (how many component units are needed?) as modeled in the product structures (cf. Sect. 2.1.1) and capacity requirements (cf. Sect. 3.4):

$$\sum_{p_1=1}^{n^y} L_p \propto_{lpt} B_{p_1 p_2} = b_{lp_2 t} \quad \forall p_2 \in \mathcal{X}, l \in \mathcal{L}, t \in \mathcal{T}, \quad (9.6)$$

$$\sum_{p=1}^{n^y} R_{pr} L_p \propto_{lpt} = c_{rt} \quad \forall r \in \mathcal{R} l \in \mathcal{L}, t \in \mathcal{T}, \quad (9.7)$$

$$c_{rt} \le R_r^C + c_{rt}^X \quad \forall r \in \mathcal{R} t \in \mathcal{T}, \quad (9.8)$$

$$c_{rt} \le R_r^X \quad \forall r \in \mathcal{R} t \in \mathcal{T}. \quad (9.9)$$

Constraint (9.6) ensures that the quantities of all components needed for end product p match the production lots for that product. Capacity consumption is modeled in (9.7) and (9.8), ensuring that the used capacity does not exceed the available capacity. Constraint (9.8) says that if the needed capacity c_{rt} is greater than the regular capacity limit R_r^C, an additional amount of c_{rt}^X can be used beyond R_r^C, provided that the total amount c_{rt} is not greater than the extended capacity limit R_r^X (9.9). (Remember that in the objective function above, utilization of extended capacity was considered with an additional cost of C_r^X. The cost of utilizing the regular capacity was not included in the objective function because it is not relevant for the decisions to be made.)

It is worth noting that *restrictions* regarding the planning *parameters (data)* apply, similar to the restrictions on the domains of the variables mentioned above:

- *Input coefficients* only exist for end products, not for components. Hence, all $B_{p_1p_2}$ have to be set to zero if p_1 is a component:

$$B_{p_1p_2} \geq 0 \quad \forall p_1 \in \Upsilon, \forall p_2 \in X$$

$$B_{p_1p_2} = 0 \quad \forall p_1 \in X.$$

- *Resource consumption* R_{pr} can only occur when end products are manufactured. Hence, all other R_r^P values are zero:

$$R_{pr} \geq 0 \quad \forall p \in \Upsilon.$$

$$R_{pr} = 0 \quad \forall p \in X.$$

- *Transportation* is only possible between suppliers and factories (components) and between factories and customers (end products). All other $t_{l_1l_2pt}$ values must be zero:

$$t_{l_1l_2pt} \geq 0 \quad \forall (l_1 \in S, l_2 \in F,\ p \in X) \vee (l_1 \in F, l_2 \in C, p \in \Upsilon)'$$

$$t_{l_1l_2pt} = 0 \text{ otherwise.}$$

This completes the brief overview of a simple supply network planning model. The model is a mixed-integer linear programming (MILP) model because production takes place in multiples of the lot size L_p only. This restriction was modeled above with the help of the $\propto_{lpt}$variables, which can take on only integer values. To solve the MILP model, an algorithm for discrete optimization has to be employed.

It is worth mentioning that the model presented in this section, although it might look voluminous, is still oversimplifying the real-world problem. For example, product structures have been limited to one-level bills of materials, and neither transportation nor production alternatives have been considered.

Making the model more general increases its size substantially. Capturing all aspects of a real-world problem in an optimization model requires significant efforts. Solving an optimization model of real-world problem dimensions has long been impossible. However, with today's advances in both methodology and technology, comprehensive practical problems are being modeled as optimization models and solved with powerful algorithms (and computers). Section 10.1.3 will outline a practical approach to supply network planning using optimization.

10 Case: SAP SCM

In this chapter, an example of an SCM system will be presented—SAP SCM. This umbrella term combines several solutions for different parts of supply chain management. The core module is *SAP APO (advanced planner and optimizer)*. Since APO is a very comprehensive solution, and was the first available SCM component by SAP, many people still equate it with SAP SCM.

Later on, additional modules were subsumed under the name SAP SCM, leading to the following set of modules:

- SAP APO (advanced planner and optimizer)
- SAP SNC (supply network collaboration)
- SAP F&R (forecasting and replenishment)
- SAP EM (event management)
- SAP EWM (extended warehouse management)

The *SAP SCM solution map* provides an overview of the total functionality available as part of SAP SCM. As with other solution maps, the SCM solution map is not divided into software modules. Instead, it largely assigns the available functionality to business processes and subprocesses (Fig. 10.1).

SAP SCM is closely connected with SAP ERP. Many of the APO's planning and scheduling functions access SAP ECC (ERP central component), which basically represents the core of the earlier SAP R/3 system. This is a reasonable approach because a large portion of the master and transaction data needed in supply chain management have already been created and maintained in enterprise resource planning. Similarly, many planning and controlling functions available in SAP ERP are also useful for supply chain management.

Because the functionalities required for supply chain management and enterprise resource planning generally overlap, it was necessary to decide which function should be implemented in which system. Seeing that R/3 existed long before APO, it was an obvious decision for SAP to utilize the already available R/3 functionality also for APO.

Most companies working with SAP SCM also use SAP ERP. Therefore, the roles are basically divided between the systems as follows: SAP APO serves as a planning, controlling, and analysis system, while SAP ERP's main role is that of a transaction system. The interface between SAP SCM and SAP ERP is the *CIF (core interface)*, which will be discussed in Sect. 10.2. In addition, SAP BI (business intelligence) is used for evaluating information and for analysis tasks (Knolmayer et al. 2009, p. 60).

K.E. Kurbel, *Enterprise Resource Planning and Supply Chain Management*,
Progress in IS, DOI 10.1007/978-3-642-31573-2_10,

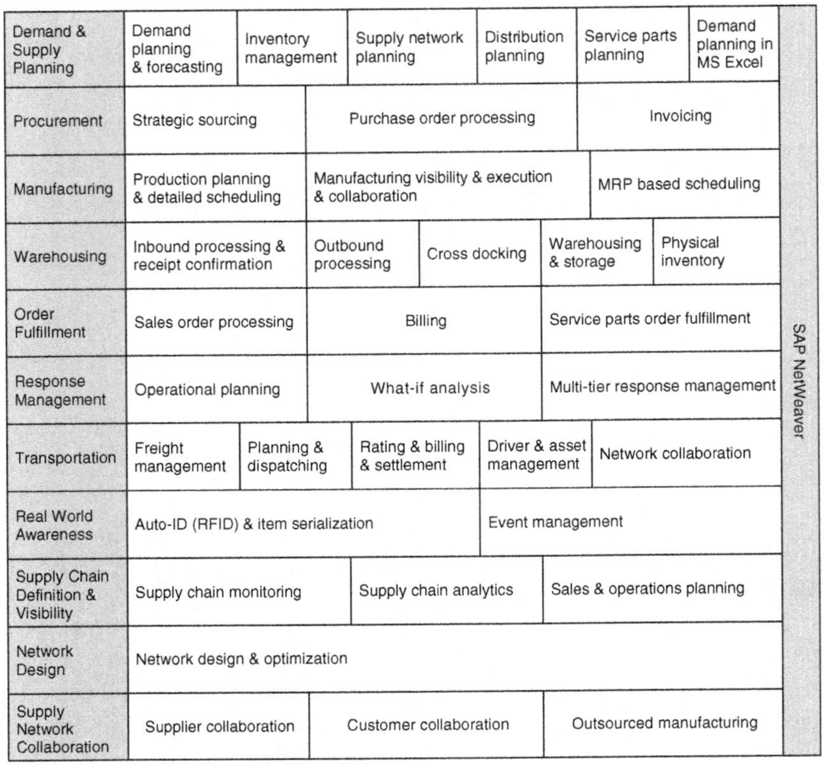

© SAP AG

Fig. 10.1 SAP SCM solution map (SAP 2012d)

10.1 SAP Advanced Planner and Optimizer

The core of SAP SCM is the *advanced planner and optimizer (APO)*, which provides advanced planning functionality, including optimization methods and powerful heuristics. In contrast to the sequential planning approach used in MRP II, APO modules attempt to simultaneously consider all relevant planning areas, parameters, and restrictions.

SAP APO is sometimes labeled an *APS system* (advanced planning and scheduling system, cf. Sect. 9.2.1), but it is not identical with the common perception of APS. Although APO covers many parts of APS (including the tasks arranged in the supply chain planning matrix in Fig. 9.9), it has additional functionalities that are not usually included in an APS.

The main modules of SAP APO are listed in the column headings of Fig. 10.2. The figure contains the top-level tasks assigned to the APO modules, namely, demand planning, sales, transportation planning, VMI (vendor-managed inventory), integrated distribution and production planning, distribution planning, replenishment, production planning, detailed scheduling, production execution, purchasing, and subcontracting.

The tasks mentioned in Fig. 10.2 obviously have different temporal extensions. For example, demand planning typically spans 1–5 years, whereas automatic inventory replenishment only covers a few days or weeks (Dickersbach 2009, p. 10).

The temporal extension of the planning tasks is illustrated in Fig. 10.3, positioning the APO modules as follows:

- Demand planning (DP): long term
- Supply network planning (SNP): midterm

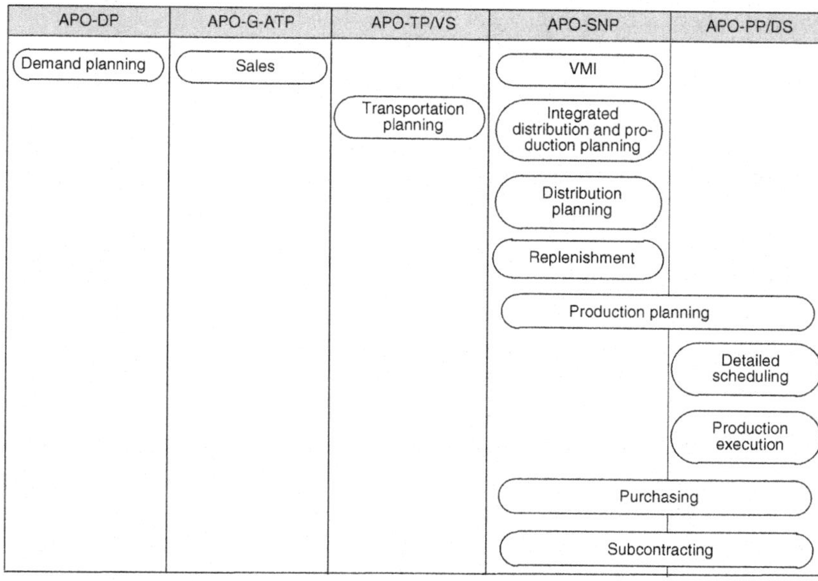

Fig. 10.2 SCM tasks assigned to APO modules (Dickersbach 2009, p. 12)

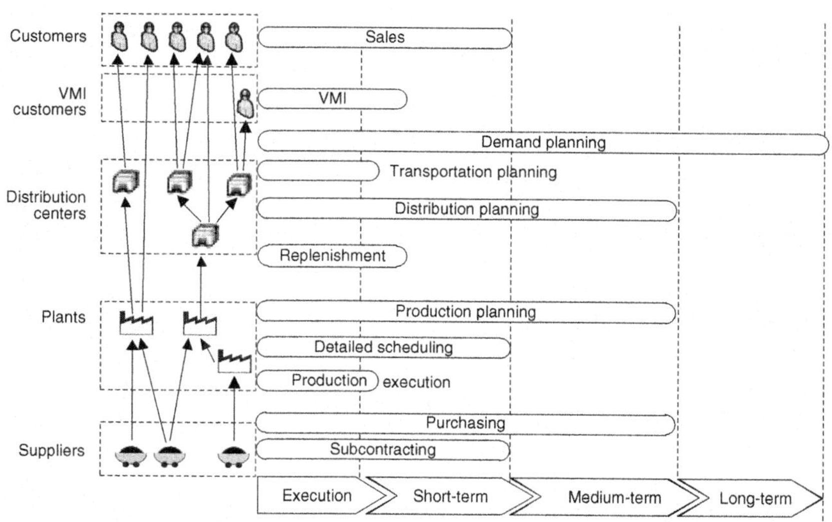

Fig. 10.3 Time horizons of SCM tasks (Dickersbach 2009, p. 11)

- Production planning (PP): midterm
- Detailed scheduling (DS): short term
- Global ATP (available-to-promise): mid- to short term
- Transportation planning/vehicle scheduling (TP/VS): short term

10.1.1 Supply Chain Engineer, Cockpit, and Alerts

Although SAP APO supports many planning tasks with powerful methods, algorithmic support for strategic network planning (top level of the supply chain planning matrix, cf. Fig. 9.13) is limited. The main instrument for strategic tasks is the supply chain engineer (SCE).

Supply Chain Engineer The *supply chain engineer (SCE)* is used to create and maintain models and versions. As explained above (cf. Sect. 9.1.1), a model represents a specific supply chain, consisting of nodes and links. Nodes are locations were business entities are located (e.g., plants, distribution centers, customers, suppliers). They are connected through the transportation lanes described in Sect. 9.1.1.

The data characterizing the nodes of a supply chain are usually available in SAP ERP and/or other source systems. With the help of SCE features, they can be assigned to an SCM model or removed from the model.

Supply Chain Cockpit With the help of the *supply chain cockpit (SCC)*, a high-level overview of an entire supply chain can be obtained. The cockpit provides a panel of graphical instruments for managing and controlling the supply chain.

The supply chain cockpit supports not only high-level tasks but also short-term planning, control, and execution tasks. Typical users of the cockpit include (SAP 2012b):

- *Strategic planners*, setting up and modifying supply chains according to the business strategy, monitoring the key performance indicators (KPIs)
- *Demand planners*, viewing the demand situation for the entire supply chain, launching demand planning runs
- *Supply network planners*, viewing and controlling the entire supply network, using optimization and heuristic algorithms for planning
- *Production planners and schedulers*, viewing and manipulating detailed planning data, using optimization and heuristic algorithms for their planning problems

All categories of users, with the possible exception of the strategic planners, will also use the supply chain cockpit to perform multidimensional data analysis, drill down to examine details, and receive and react to alerts.

The supply chain cockpit can be configured to exhibit various kinds of information, in particular a *graphical overview* of the supply chain as shown in Fig. 10.4. In addition, details of the *data* in question can be displayed in another pane of the cockpit, for example, master data such as locations, products, resources, transportation lanes etc. More panes often include *alerts* relevant to the user.

Alert Monitor An *alert monitor* is available either as a separate tool or embedded in the supply chain cockpit to facilitate exception handling. The alert monitor compares to-be and as-is data, computes performance metrics (based on SCOR, cf. Sect. 8.3.5), and issues alerts when situations occur that require the person responsible to be notified and/or to take action. In this way, the alert monitor supports management by exception (Wood 2007, pp. 175–178).

A number of alert types are predefined, but companies can also define their own alerts. Predefined alert types include (Dickersbach 2009, pp. 429–433):

- Forecast alerts (relating to forecast errors)
- Supply and demand planning alerts (relating to demand planning and supply network planning problems)
- Transport load builder alerts (relating to deployment, shortage, load violations, etc.)
- Production planning/detailed scheduling alerts (relating to shortage, surplus, lateness, pegging constraints, etc.)
- ATP alerts (mostly relating to shortages in availability checking)

10.1.2 Demand Planning

Demand planning (DP) comprises forecast methods and planning functions to calculate the future demand. As a result of demand planning, independent requirements are created, triggering further production, distribution, and procurement planning.

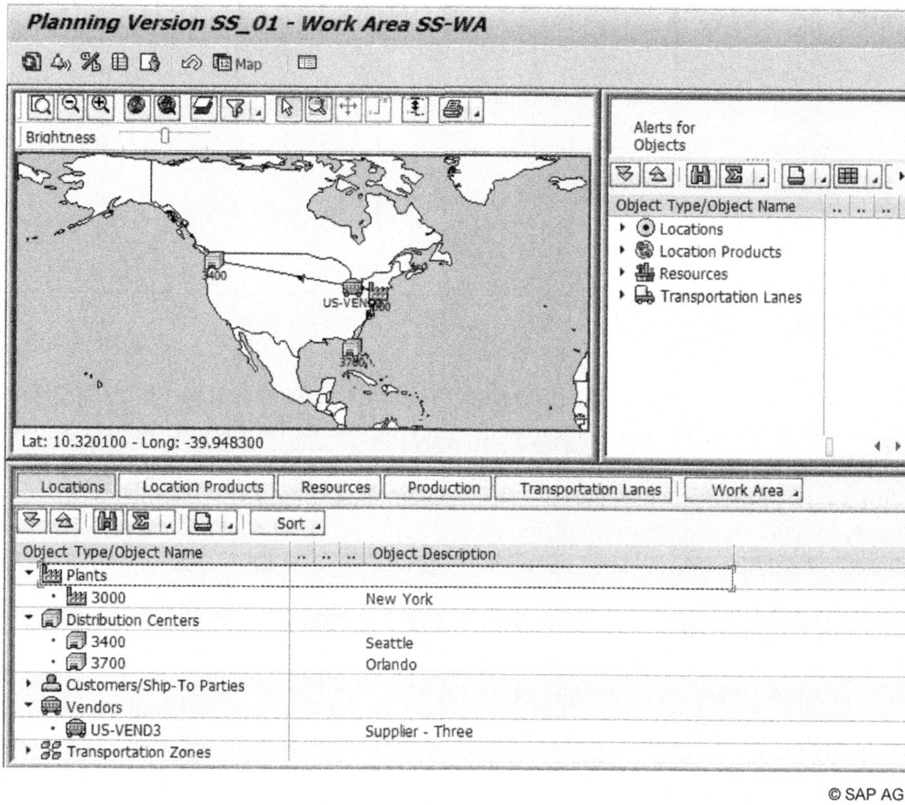

Fig. 10.4 Supply chain cockpit (SCC)

Frequently, the starting point of demand planning is a sales forecast. This forecast is consolidated, checked for plausibility and compliance with statistical forecasts and personal experience of the planner, and modified if needed (Dickersbach 2009, p. 33). The released forecast serves as input to other planning areas such as distribution and production planning.

Forecast Methods Several models and methods are available for demand planning, including univariate methods, causal models, and composite approaches.

Univariate forecast methods are useful when historical data (time series) are available that exhibit a typical demand pattern, for example, constant, trend, seasonal, or intermittent demand. This category of forecast methods comprises (Hoppe 2007, pp. 111–131):

- Moving averages (for stable demand)
- First-order exponential smoothing (for stable demand)
- Linear regression (for demand trends)
- Holt method (first-order exponential smoothing for trend patterns)
- Winters method (second-order exponential smoothing for seasonal patterns)
- Seasonal linear regression (for seasonal demand)
- Croston method (for intermittent demand)

Causal models (using *multiple linear regression*) are applied when several independent factors determine the demand. The method of least squares is employed to estimate the model parameters.

Composite forecasts combine different forecast methods, for example, exponential smoothing and multiple linear regression, to exploit the advantages of both methods.

Readers who wish to learn more about these methods are advised to consult a textbook on statistical forecasting.

Life-Cycle Planning In marketing, the *life cycle* of a product is often divided into *phases*

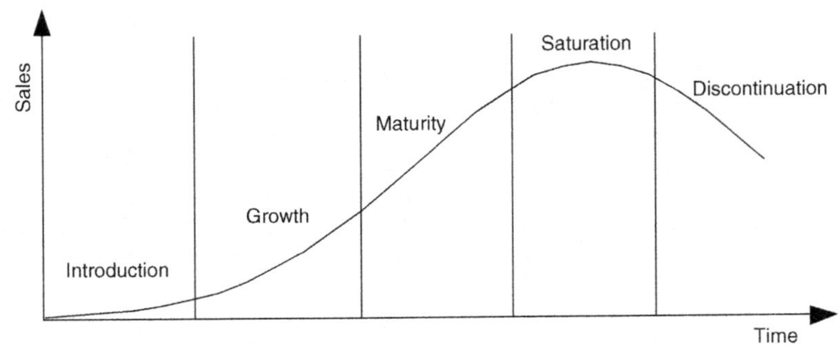

Fig. 10.5 Product life-cycle curve

such as introduction (i.e., introducing the product on the market), growth, maturity, saturation, and discontinuation. Figure 10.5 shows these phases together with a typical product sales curve.

For supply chain management, different product phases mean different demand patterns. Hence, it is not appropriate to use the same uniform forecast for all phases. In the growth phase, for example, sales are likely to increase progressively and much faster than in the introduction phase. The forecast method for "introduction" will most likely not produce good results for "growth." Likewise, since the demand patterns for "saturation" and for "discontinuation" are completely different, the methods to predict the demand should also reflect this difference.

Another factor to consider is that the introduction of a new product may have a "cannibalization" effect on another product. This means that the new product may to some extent push aside an old product already in the saturation or discontinuation phase.

Product life-cycle modeling is supported by *profiles*—so-called like, phase-in, and phase-out profiles.

A *like profile* consists of similar products and weighting factors to adapt the other products' profiles to the current product. The idea behind a like profile is that for a new product, historical data are not available; therefore, data of existing products that are similar are used.

A simple example of using a like profile is the introduction of a new ice cream flavor (almond, article no. T-FV 300) (Hoppe 2007, p. 165). Since the company has so far only sold vanilla (T-FV 100) and chocolate (T-FV 200) ice cream, they have data for these two flavors, but not for almond. Therefore, a like profile for almond ice cream is created:

Like Profile for T-FV 300	
T-FV 100	80 %
T-FV 200	20 %

This profile says that 80 % of the demand forecast for almond-flavored ice cream should be based on the forecast of vanilla-flavored ice cream, and 20 % on the forecast of chocolate-flavored ice cream.

Phase-in and *phase-out profiles* are used to adapt the forecasted demand according to the increasing and decreasing parts of the sales curve in the product life cycle. A *phase-in* profile simulates the increasing sales curve, reflecting the curve in the introduction and growth phases. A *phase-out* profile simulates the decrease of the sales that is expected in the discontinuation phase.

Phase-in and phase-out profiles are primarily represented by time-dependent factors (percentages). These factors are multiplied by the respective forecast values from the statistical forecast to obtain the adapted forecast.

Aggregation and Disaggregation Between Planning Levels Both demand planning and demand forecasting can be carried out on different levels, for example, in a:

- Product-oriented view: by individual products, product groups, product families, or brands
- Regional view: by sales offices, zip codes, states, countries, or continents

- Temporal view: by days, weeks, months, quarters, or years

Since data are stored with the finest granularity, any level of aggregation and disaggregation can be addressed. This means that planning and forecasting can be carried out with more or with less detail, just as required.

Aggregation means that the values of the most detailed level are summed up and displayed or used in calculations according to the desired (higher) level. For example, when the level of aggregation is "countries," all forecast data to be displayed (e.g., demand by product families, sales channels, brands, etc.) would be added up for each country.

Disaggregation means that demand values on a higher level (e.g., country) are detailed into lower-level demand values. If an aggregation structure has been defined, disaggregation happens at runtime according to this structure. For example, a higher-level demand value that has been computed is automatically broken down into product families, sales channels, brands, etc., for the countries involved.

Additional Demand Planning Functionality In addition to the areas discussed above, SAP APO supports demand planning in various ways (Dickersbach 2009, p. 67–79; Hoppe 2007, pp. 180–190; Knolmayer et al. 2009, pp. 79–84):

- *Promotion planning:* Promotions are measures to increase sales through special events and actions. Examples include trade fairs, gift certificates, raffles, and special discounts. The advantage of planning promotions separately from regular demand planning is that the effect of a promotion can be isolated and the regular sales (i.e., without the promotion) can be better compared to the sales forecast.
- *Secondary requirements planning:* Using bills of materials, dependent requirements can also be forecast. Although demand planning primarily refers to end products, in some cases it is advisable to extend the forecast to subordinate parts. One example of this is when there is a limited supply of a key component that is required for several end products. Then it is helpful for the planner to see what effect the end-product demand has on the demand of the limited component. Another example is extreme variant production (see Sect. 2.1.2), where the demand actually occurs on the level of components and not on the level of the assembled end product.
- *Collaborative demand planning (CLP):* Companies wishing to coordinate their logistic activities with their business partners can use the collaborative planning features of demand planning. CLP support ranges from a common sales forecast all the way to joint transportation planning. The business partners, e.g., manufacturers and retailers, collaborate in a similar way as in CPFR (collaborative planning, forecasting, and replenishment) described in Sect. 8.2.3. As illustrated in Fig. 10.6, the partners create their own forecasts, exchange forecasts, and cooperate when defining and handling exceptions.

The results of demand planning are used for midterm procurement, distribution, production, and transportation planning and short-term scheduling. For this purpose, the results are transferred to the APO modules SNP (supply network planning) and PP/DS (production planning/detailed scheduling).

Companies using only demand planning but not the other APO modules can adopt the planning results in SAP ERP for further processing. In SAP ERP, the demand forecasts serve as primary requirements for material requirements planning (MRP).

10.1.3 Supply Network Planning

The APO component *supply network planning (SNP)* supports integrated planning on a tactical level across procurement, manufacturing, distribution, and transportation.

The planning is initiated either by a demand plan created by APO DP (demand planning) or by primary requirements specified in some other way, for example, with the help of SAP ERP SD (sales and distribution) or an external application system.

SNP calculates a feasible medium-term plan to cover the forecast demand. This plan

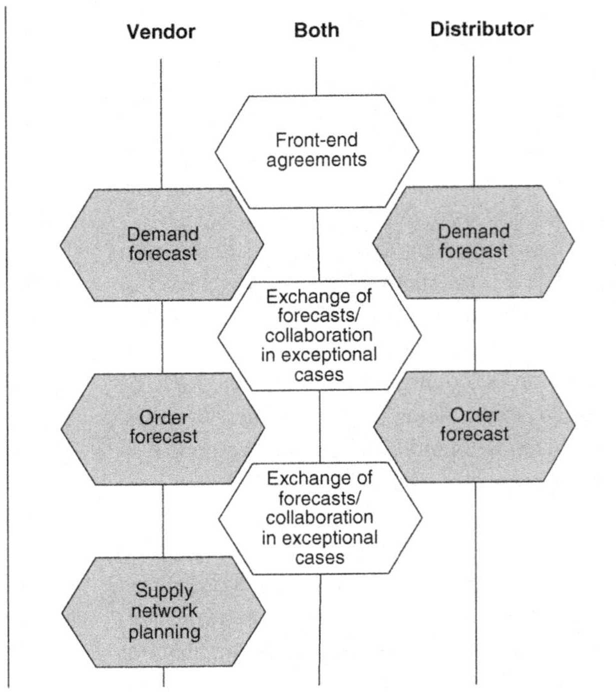

Fig. 10.6 Collaborative demand planning (Hoppe 2007, p. 182)

comprises all quantities to be procured, produced, and transported between locations (Hoppe 2007, p. 199).

The *deployment* part determines the quantities to be sent to distribution centers and customers, as well as the shipment dates. A distribution plan is created, which takes restrictions (such as transportation capacities) and business rules (such as replenishment strategies) into account. The *transport load builder (TLB)* is responsible for creating transport loads that optimize the utilization of the total transportation capacity.

SNP Planning Process The process of supply network planning and the collaboration between APO components can be seen in Fig. 10.7. The most important steps are as follows (Hoppe 2007, p. 201):

1. *Administrate the planning area:* The basis for all SNP activities is a so-called *planning area,* which needs to be set up before completing any other steps. A planning area is primarily defined by parameters that specify the scope of the planning tasks, such as key indicators for planning the volume (e.g., the planned demand), planning levels, relevant objects (e.g., product, location), parameters indicating how to aggregate and disaggregate, and basic information like currency, units of measurement, time grids, etc.
2. *Configure the APO master data* that are needed for SNP: These data include locations, products, resources, production process models, production data structures, transportation lanes, and data required for hierarchical planning (e.g., regarding product groups).
3. *Create a model* and assign a *version* (or several versions for simulations) with the help of the SCE (supply chain engineer, cf. Sect. 10.1.1).
4. *Configure the supply chain model:* For this, the locations, products, resources, and production process models are attributed to a model, and transportation lanes are created.

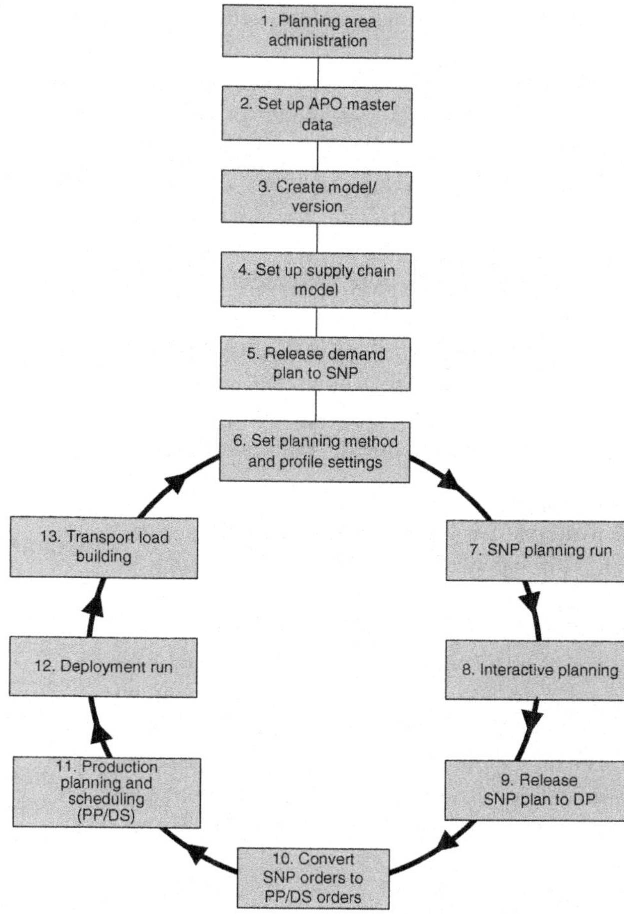

Fig. 10.7 SNP process flow (Hoppe 2007, p. 201)

5. *Release the demand plan to SNP:* The demand plan that was created during demand planning is released to supply network planning.
6. *Define the planning method*—optimization-based, heuristics-based, CTM (capable-to-match, see below)—as well as the *profile settings* for the selected planning method.
7. *SNP planning run:* A medium-term production and distribution plan is created with the selected planning method. Planned orders are also created.
8. *Interactive planning:* The planner viewing the result of the SNP run, in aggregate or detailed form, can interactively modify the plan that was created. For example, infeasibilities may need to be removed. When the planner decides to change planning parameters, he or she can initiate a new SNP planning run.
9. *Release the SNP plan to DP:* The final SNP plan, which was created with capacity restrictions in mind, can be released back to DP to compare the constraint-free demand plan with the constraint-based SNP plan. If there are major discrepancies between the two plans, it may be necessary to make adjustments to the demand plan.
10. *Convert SNP orders to PP/DS orders:* The manufacturing orders created in supply network planning are sent to production planning and detailed scheduling and converted into PP/DS orders.
11. *Production planning* and *detailed scheduling (PP/DS)* take place outside of SNP. A feasible production plan is created on the

basis of the planned orders generated in SNP.

12. *Deployment run:* Once production planning is completed and the system knows what will actually be produced, these quantities are allocated to the various locations and finally to the customer. In doing so, stock transfer orders are created, specifying the transfer of the finished goods from the production plant to the distribution centers.
13. *Transport load building (TLB):* In a transport load builder run, the deployment stock transfers and manually generated transfers are combined into so-called TLB transports.

Planning Methods Several different methods are available for supply network planning, especially for calculating medium-term production and distribution plans. Capacity and delivery limitations as well as other restrictions can, but do not have to be taken into account. The user can influence the desired quality of the solution, thereby affecting the program runtime.

The three primary planning types are based on optimization, heuristics, or CTM (Knolmayer et al. 2009, pp. 87–92; Hoppe 2007, pp. 235–305):

- *Optimization* results in the highest-quality solution. However, it is also the slowest and most complex approach because it calculates a total optimum subject to all constraints specified in the optimization model.
- The so-called *SNP heuristic* delivers the fastest but lowest quality solution, because capacity restrictions, material availability, etc., are not included in the calculation. When these factors cause problems, the planner is only alerted.
- *Capable-to-match (CTM)* falls between the other approaches when it comes to quality and speed. This approach is rule based and is controlled by priorities.

Optimization Various optimization methods are available for supply network planning, depending on the type of problem to be solved. Continuous linear optimization problems are solved with the simplex algorithm, whereas problems containing discrete variables or piecewise linear cost functions are solved using branch-and-bound methods and mixed-integer programming.

The *objective function* to be minimized is a cost function that includes various components. The weights of the cost components have default settings, but the user can make changes to the proportions. The costs function includes:

- Production, procurement, inventory, and transportation costs
- Costs for increasing the production, inventory, transportation, and handling capacities
- Costs of falling short of safety stock, resulting in shortages and delayed deliveries

The result produced with the help of an optimization method is an integrated plan, which specifies:

- How much of which products should be manufactured, procured, stocked, transported, and delivered on which dates?
- Which resources and which production process models or production data structures should be used?
- Where should manufacturing, procurement, inventory, and delivery take place and which locations should products be sent from and delivered to?

Because computation times can be very long when using optimization, SAP APO offers the option of decomposing the total problem into smaller subproblems, which are solved sequentially. Several decomposition types exist:

- *Time decomposition*: The initial problem is divided into subproblems that succeed each other in time.
- *Product decomposition*: The problem is divided according to product groups that are optimized together.
- *Resource decomposition*: The problem is divided according to resources, which are scheduled one at a time.

The drawback of decomposition is that only local optima for the subproblems are computed. These local optima do not necessarily represent the overall optimum, that is, decomposition usually decreases the quality of the solution.

The upside, on the other hand, is that the program runtime is shorter.

Production, transport, handling, and inventory resources can limit the options in supply network planning. During optimization, some or all of these restrictions are taken into consideration, depending on which settings and upper/lower bounds the user specifies. The required production capacity is calculated based on the production process models, which identify the manufacturing resources through the so-called mode (see Sect. 9.1.1).

In addition to taking capacity restrictions into account, SNP optimization allows the planner to compute cost-minimal manufacturing, procurement, and transport lot sizes and to keep inventory levels within given upper and lower limits (inventory planning).

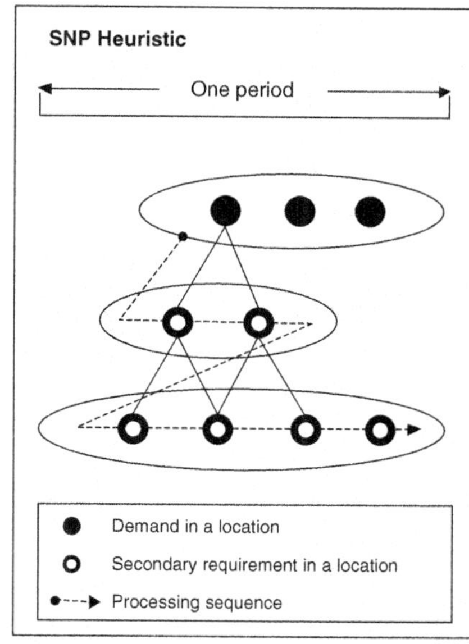

Fig. 10.8 SNP heuristic processing levels (Hoppe 2007, p. 236)

SNP Heuristic The so-called *SNP heuristic* is a heuristic method that calculates the net requirements based on the demand for a product or family of products, taking inventory, products in transit, and previously scheduled manufacturing orders into account.

For each location, the SNP heuristic adds up all requirements for a product. Then it determines the sources and options to fulfill this total requirement, taking quotas, lead times, calendars, and rules for lot-size and order-quantity calculation into consideration.

When planning for multiple levels, the heuristic works level by level according to locations and product structures, as shown in Fig. 10.8. It starts at the highest location level (usually the location of the customer, i.e., last node of the supply chain) and schedules all products on that level (usually end products). Then it moves on to the next level (e.g., distribution centers) and schedules all products on that level, etc. Manufacturing, procurement, and transportation orders are created for each level in the network.

Since the SNP heuristic does not take capacities into account, it creates a plan that is not necessarily feasible. Therefore, the planner must check the resulting capacity load. If the required capacity is not compatible with the actually available capacity, the planner can interactively look at each location's bottleneck resources and create a feasible plan by leveling the capacity.

An example illustrating the SNP heuristic is presented in the following figures (SAP UA 2011). In this example, supply sources to meet the demand for a finished good need to be established. In order to distribute the risk and ensure a high level of service, several plants and distribution centers are involved to satisfy the customer demand.

The basic relationships between the locations have been specified in the master data as follows (see also left part of Fig. 10.9):

- The customer, residing at location US-CUS1, is served from two distribution centers: DC 3500 and DC 3700.
- The product in question (product number CPG-FG1) is manufactured in two production plants (locations 3000 and 3100).
- To reduce the risk and improve the service levels, demand from the customer is distributed to the two distribution centers 3500 and 3700 via VMI (cf. Sect. 8.2.3) in such a way that DC 3500 covers 80 % and DC 3700 covers 20 % of the total demand.

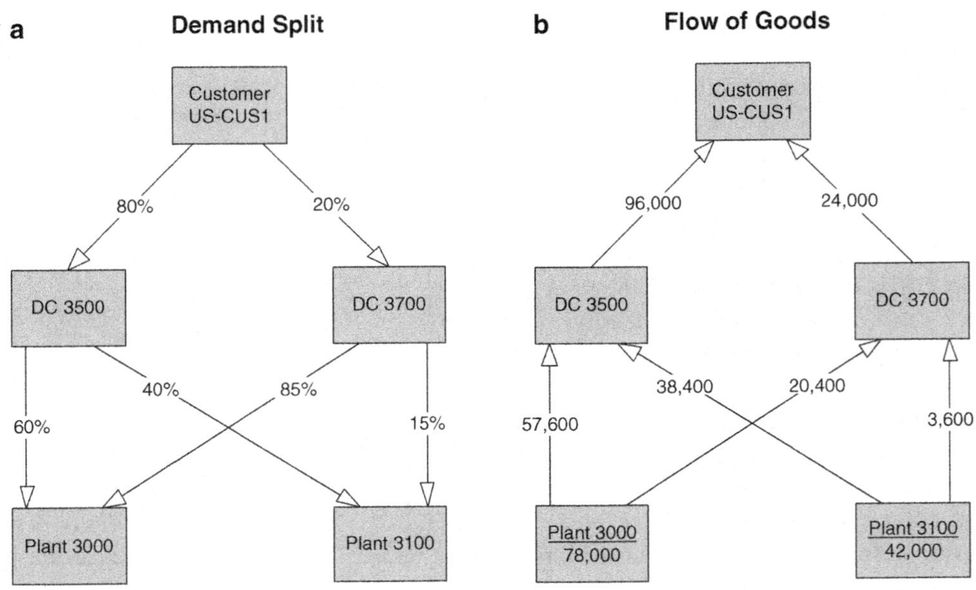

Fig. 10.9 Relationships between locations for SNP

- To fill up the stock needed to satisfy its share of the customer demand, DC 3500 requests 60 % of the stock to come from plant 3000 and 40 % from plant 3100.
- Likewise, DC 3700 requests 85 % from plant 3000 and 15 % from plant 3100.

In the end, 65 % (= 80 %× 60 % + 20 % × 85 %) of the customer demand comes from plant 3000, and 35 % (= 80 % × 40 % + 20 % × 15 %) comes from plant 3100.

The tool used for planning and visualizing results is the so-called *planning book*. It provides a multipane tabular overview with features for interactive planning, showing details of the planning situation. This so-called interactive planning desktop is available both in demand planning (DP) and supply network planning (SNP).

Figure 10.10 illustrates the top level of a planning book using the relationships between the locations that were described above. The planning problem was initiated by a customer demand of 120,000 units of product CPG-FG1 forecasted for week 11. As shown in the top left pane, the customer is US-CUS1.

The navigation area on the left allows the planner to specify which planning book should be displayed. Our example uses the "SNP PLAN" planning book. The relevant objects for this planning book are displayed in the "info objects area" (as "selected objects"). The "selection profile" section below assists the planner by listing frequently used selections (e.g., heuristics).

In the right top corner of the planning book's main pane (called the "workspace"), three buttons for selecting heuristics are partly visible: "Network" invokes the SNP heuristic for a specified product (or for several products) at all locations where this product exists. "Location" does the same but for product(s) and locations that the user explicitly selects. "Multilevel" (cut off in this screenshot, but visible in Fig. 10.12) additionally takes the components needed for the finished product into consideration, according to the bill of materials.

Figure 10.10 shows the planning situation after the "multilevel" heuristic has been executed. The planned receipt from distribution, resulting from the total demand of 120,000, has been split up in the lower pane of the workspace into 96,000 and 24,000. This is according to the relationships discussed above, that is, 80 % should come from DC 3500 and 20 % from DC 3700.

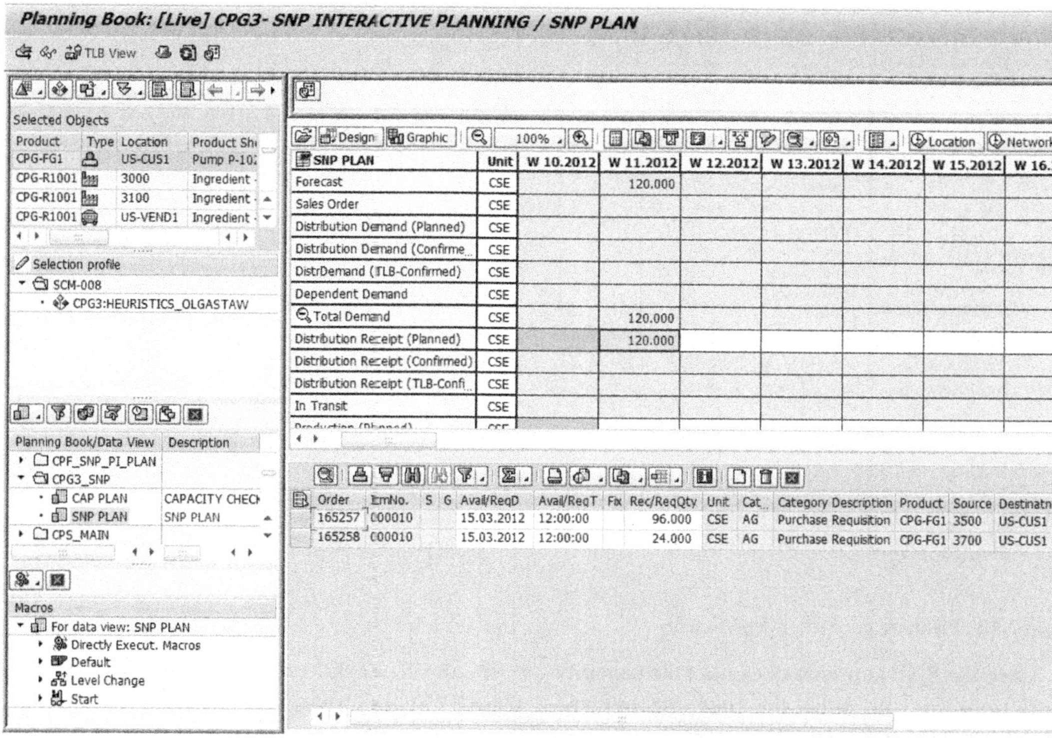

© SAP AG

Fig. 10.10 Planning book showing top level of SNP

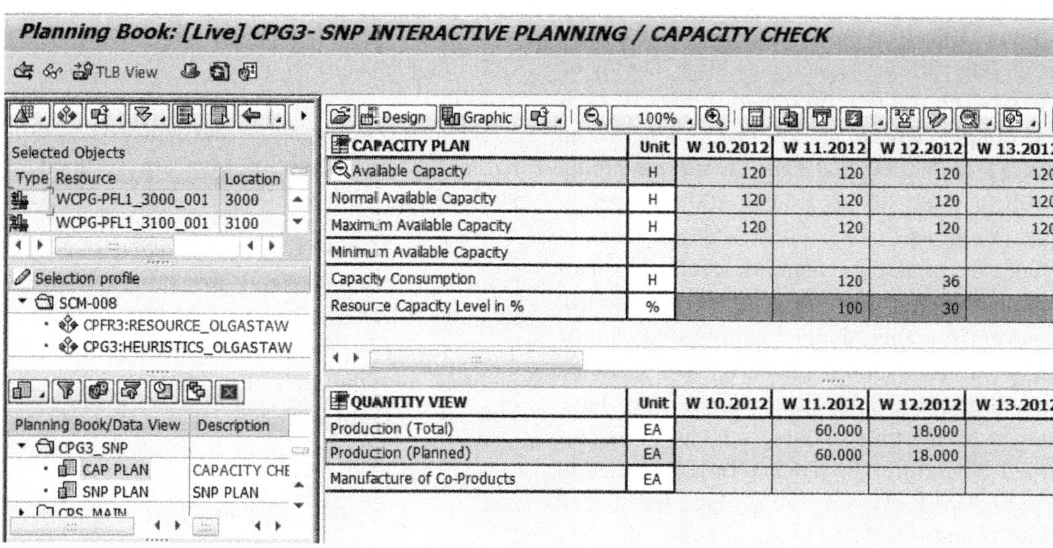

© SAP AG

Fig. 10.11 Planning book after capacity leveling

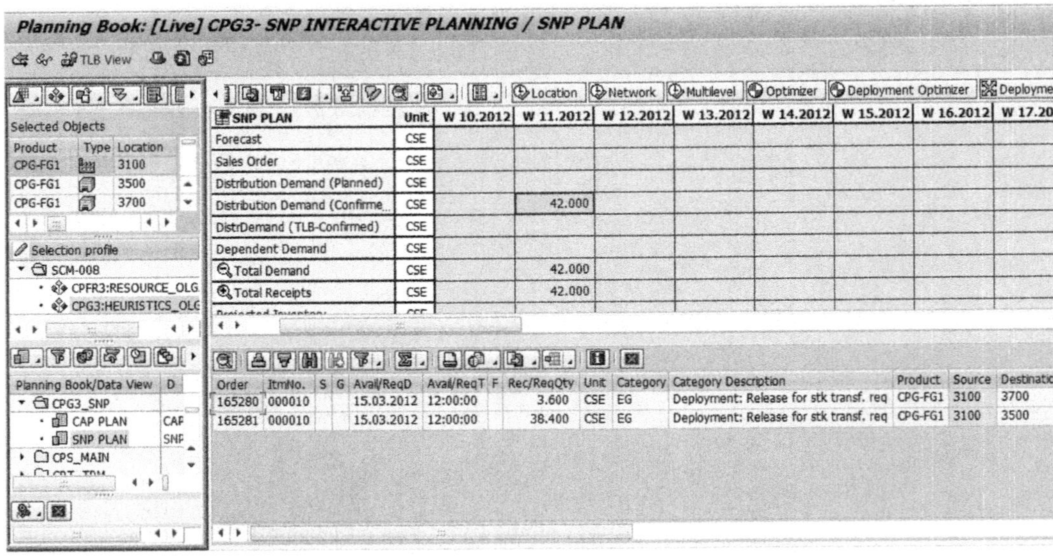

© SAP AG

Fig. 10.12 Planning book after deployment

Since the SNP heuristic does not take capacity restrictions into account, the outcome may be infeasible. In our case, the capacity of plant 3000 required to produce 78,000 units of CPG-FG1 (= 65 % of 120,000) in week 11 is 156 standard hours. However, only 120 h per week are available, as Fig. 10.11 shows.

Since 156 h would exceed the available capacity by 30 %, capacity leveling has to be invoked. The solution presented in Fig. 10.11 is quite simple: Reducing the total production in week 11 to 60,000 and shifting the remaining 18,000 to week 12 has lead to 100 % capacity utilization in week 11 (and 30 % in week 12).

Once the production plan is feasible, the quantities planned for distribution could be *deployed*. However, in reality, deployment depends on the results of production planning and detailed scheduling (PP/DS) because things may have changed by the time detailed scheduling is performed. Therefore, the planned orders created in supply network planning are actually transferred to PP/DS and scheduled in detail before they are ready for deployment (cf. Fig. 10.7).

To complete our example, we assume that PP/DS does not change the SNP planning, leaving 60,000 and 42,000 units in week 11 and 18,000 in week 12 ready for deployment.

Figure 10.12 shows the situation for production plant 3100 (see "selected objects")—42,000 units to be deployed in week 11 ("distribution demand (confirmed)"). This quantity is deployed according to the relationships described above, meaning that 3,600 units are to be sent to distribution center 3700 (3,600 = 15 % of DC 3700's demand of 24,000) and 38,400 units to distribution center 3500 (38,400 = 40 % of DC 3500's demand of 96,000).

The quantities produced and deployed according to the given relationships are outlined in part b of Fig. 10.9.

Capable-to-Match *Capable-to-match (CTM)* is another heuristic method for supply network planning. CTM is used to schedule *individual requirements*—in contrast to the optimization methods and the SNP heuristic, which work with a period split and aggregated period requirements (e.g., derived from a demand forecast; cf. Sect. 10.1.2).

CTM uses a constraint-based, multilevel, finite, top-down planning approach for cross-location checks of supplies, production, and transport capacities (Gaddam 2009, p. 21). The main idea behind CTM is an iterative approach based on (1) predefined supply categories,

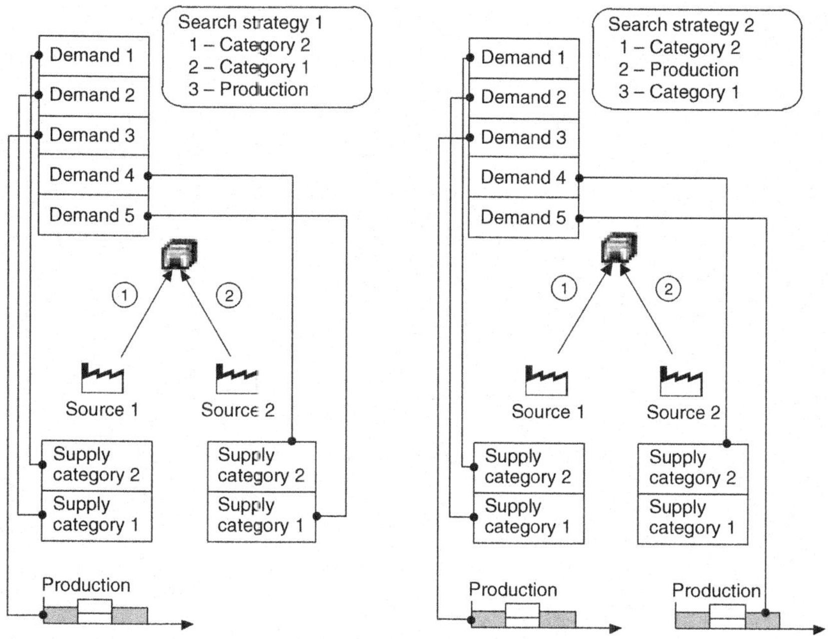

Fig. 10.13 Effect of CTM search strategies (Dickersbach 2009, p. 197)

(2) prioritized demands, and (3) a search strategy used for leveling supply and demand.

It should be noted that in CTM, the terms "supply" and "demand" are not used in exactly the same way as in other parts of SAP APO. "Demand" is an end-product requirement that has to be fulfilled, whereas "supply" stands for any source that products can be obtained from, for example, available stock or open production orders.

The planner can choose the *criteria* to be applied to determine the *demand priorities* from a list of over 250 predefined criteria, and/or create custom criteria and add them to the list. Examples of criteria include:

- Date of material requirement
- Priority of the product
- Priority of the location
- Delivery group (items are delivered together)
- Date when an order was placed

The CTM method categorizes the supply available for a planning run. *Categories* influence the order in which the supply is used to meet the demand. Examples of categories are:

- Unrestricted stock
- Planned orders
- Reserved stock
- Categories based on supply limits

The fourth point, categories based on supply limits, refers to the fact that stock can be divided into quantity intervals, which may also be considered as categories (Gaddam 2009, pp. 95–96). Using supply limits, it is possible to split a single supply into multiple supplies and assign them to different categories.

A *search strategy* specifies the order in which supplies are used to cover the demand and create new orders. It is up to the planner to define a search strategy and thus the order of demand fulfillment.

Figure 10.13 illustrates the impact of the search strategy, using a simple example (Dickersbach 2009, p. 197). There are five demands, with demand 1 having the highest priority and demand 5 having the lowest; two locations, with location 1 having a higher priority than location 2; and two supply categories.

Search strategy 1, as shown in the left part of the figure, specifies that for demand fulfillment, first supply category 2, then supply category 1, and finally newly manufactured products should be used. When *search strategy 2* is applied, the

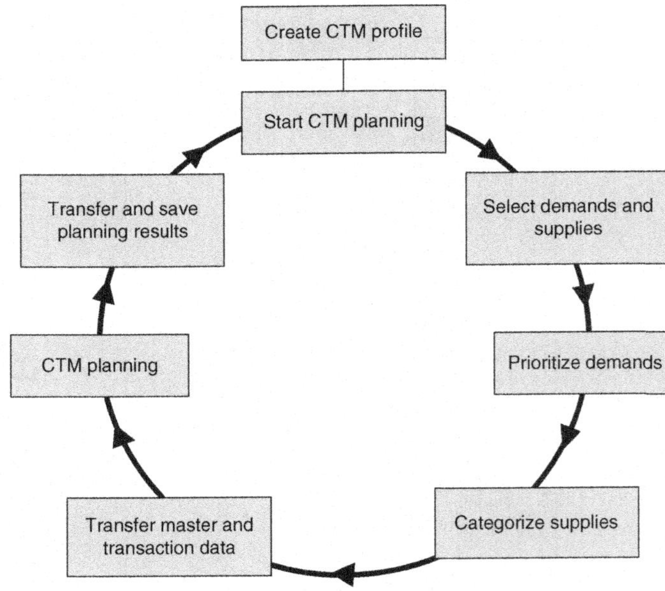

Fig. 10.14 CTM planning process (Hoppe 2007, p. 290)

sequence is first category 2, then production, and after that, category 1. Since location 1 has a higher priority than location 2, all capabilities of location 1 are exploited to satisfy the demand before starting on location 2. This is independent of the search strategy.

In this example, *search strategy 1* results in the following assignment of demands and sources of supply:

Demand 1: supply category 2 in location 1
Demand 2: supply category 1 in location 1
Demand 3: production
Demand 4: supply category 2 in location 2
Demand 5: supply category 1 in location 2

Search strategy 2 leads to the following results:

Demand 1: supply category 2 in location 1
Demand 2: production
Demand 3: supply category 1 in location 1
Demand: supply category 2 in location 2
Demand 5: production

The process of CTM planning is illustrated in Fig. 10.14. Before the planning can start, a so-called *CTM profile* has to be created (Gaddam 2009, pp. 22–24). This profile specifies the planning horizon and the strategies to be used in the planning. Then, the demands and supplies that fall within the planning period are selected. The demands are prioritized based on the criteria defined in the profile. Likewise, the supplies are assigned to the supply categories, which were defined earlier. Next, the master and transaction data required for the planning are selected and uploaded to the CTM engine running the planning algorithm.

The most important step is of course the *CTM planning run*. The CTM engine determines the dates, supply sources, and quantities to satisfy each individual demand. It also creates the orders needed for demand fulfillment. The planning algorithm uses heuristic methods such as constraint propagation and goal-oriented programming.

The planning algorithm processes the demands in the order of their priorities, according to the given search strategy. It determines optimal (or at least favorable) supply sources and schedules the demands and the resulting secondary requirements either backward or forward, depending on the chosen setting. In doing so, the algorithm attempts to meet all demand dates. If this is not possible, the demands are scheduled for a later time, with either higher or lower priority in comparison to other demands in the demand list, depending on the chosen strategy.

The planning results are transferred from the CTM engine to the *SAP liveCache*. This is an SAP-specific internal computer memory, containing all SCM-relevant planning data. All other SCM modules can access the created orders and the pegging relationships maintained in the liveCache. When a company uses SAP ERP, relevant planning results are also transferred to this system.

Planning the safety stock in the supply chain is supported by SAP APO in general, and also with special features for CTM. It is a complex task, due to the large number of possible locations and the many options as to how much safety stock should be kept at each location. The goal of safety stock planning is to ensure certain service levels across the supply chain while maintaining the inventory of all intermediate and end products at all locations at a minimum level.

Deployment The results of supply network planning are processed by the PP/DS (production planning and detailed scheduling) module. This will be discussed in a separate section below. Once a feasible production plan is available, *deployment* can be planned. Deployment is also known as *replenishment planning*.

The main task of deployment is to determine which demands can be fulfilled by the supply that will actually be available according to the PP/DS results. The need for deployment arises from the fact that in reality, many things could have changed since the supply network planning run both on the demand side (e.g., additional customer orders) as well as on the supply side (e.g., failure to deliver). Once the production planning and detailed scheduling have been completed, the exact quantities that will be produced and available are known with greater certainty.

The deployment run now distributes these quantities among the various sources of demand, that is, it decides which demand will be covered by which supply. Both heuristic and optimization methods are available for this step.

The primary concern of the deployment run is to examine the stock transfer orders created in supply network planning, to modify these orders if needed and to convert them into so-called *deployment stock transfers*. Based on these transfers, the transport load builder (TLB) can create short-term transport loads (see below).

The *deployment heuristic* creates a distribution plan referring to *one* product and *one* location. Before doing so, it has to determine the available product quantities at the different locations. The total amount of these quantities is called the ATD quantity (ATD = available-to-deploy). The ATD quantity is the quantity that can be distributed to the demand sources.

In rare cases, when the available quantities are the same as those calculated in supply network planning, deployment basically confirms the SNP plan. More commonly, however, the ATD quantity is smaller or larger than the total demand. If the available quantity is not sufficient, it must be shared among the demand sources.

For this purpose, certain rules can be applied, for example, sharing the ATD quantity proportionally, based on quota or according to due dates. Rule types available for sharing are push, pull, and fair share rules (Hoppe 2007, pp. 337–343).

Figure 10.15 illustrates the distribution problem using an example of an ATD quantity of 1,000 units. The demands to be satisfied are 100 units due on the 5th of January, 500 units due on the 6th of January and 800 units due on the 7th of January. The demands come from two distribution centers, DC 1 and DC 2.

Obviously, the ATD quantity is not sufficient to completely meet all demands, because after the demands of the first two days have been satisfied, only 400 units are available on the third day. According to a *fair share rule,* these 400 units are shared between the two demand sources based on the ratio 200:600, that is, DC 1 gets 100 and DC 2 gets 300 units. The result of deployment can be seen in the lower part of the figure.

In *deployment optimization,* a deployment plan covering *all* the products and locations the user wishes to include is created. The optimization procedure minimizes the relevant costs, that is, transport costs, inventory costs, and penalty costs for delayed delivery or nondelivery. Constraints of the optimization model include transport capacities, storage capacities, and transport lot sizes, as well as the distribution rules mentioned above.

Transport Load Builder The main task of the *transport load builder (TLB)* is to create transport loads (transport orders) based on the deployment stock transfers generated in the deployment run.

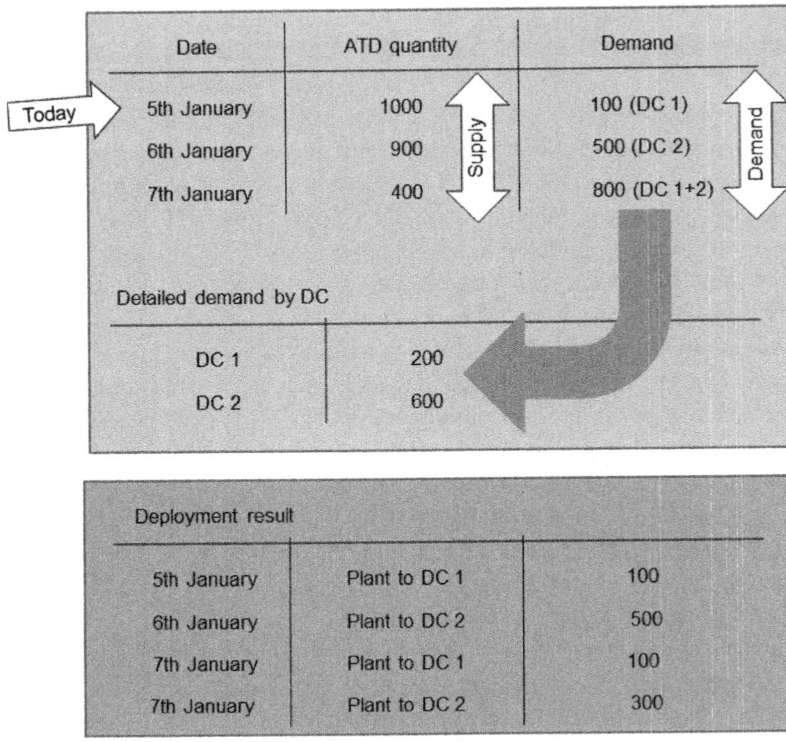

Fig. 10.15 Deployment example using a fair share rule (Hoppe 2007, p. 338)

Whereas deployment primarily operates from a product-oriented perspective, the focus of TLB is to combine goods to be shipped into advantageous transport loads, regardless of the products involved. The goal is to fully exploit the available transport capacity. On the other hand, half-empty truckloads can be avoided by requiring that a transport can only be started when a minimum load is reached.

The transport load builder is usually considered a part of supply network planning, but it can also be used as an independent module. For example, SAP SNC (supply network collaboration) also employs the transport load builder.

10.1.4 Production Planning and Detailed Scheduling (PP/DS)

The results of supply network planning, as far as products and components manufactured in the company are concerned, are transferred to the *production planning* module (PP). Since this module is closely connected with the *detailed scheduling* module (DS), both names are often used in conjunction (hence, PP/DS).

In contrast to supply network planning, which covers the material flow across a supply chain, production planning and detailed scheduling focus on manufacturing within the company's plants, including short-term procurement. This means in particular that the midterm master production schedule (MPS) created in SNP has to be refined for a shorter time period. Whereas in supply network planning, locations are considered as a whole production planning and detailed scheduling have to look at the individual resources (e.g., machines, workplaces) within each location. Furthermore, orders must be scheduled for production.

The goal of PP/DS is to establish a feasible production plan and a plan for external procurement. PP/DS attempts to (1) utilize limited resources in the best possible way, (2) calculate optimal order sequences (with respect to sequence-dependent setup costs), and (3) account for unexpected events that affect scheduling within the company (and possibly other companies in the supply chain).

The tasks of production planning and detailed scheduling in SAP APO are similar to those of production planning and shop-floor control in SAP ERP. However, PP/DS focuses more on *integrating* the MRP II subtasks while taking the *supply chain* context into account.

The granularity of PP/DS is rather fine, and the planning horizon is short. While supply network planning works with periods of days, weeks, or months, PP/DS uses a continuous timescale (hour, minute, second), resulting in much higher accuracy. Order dates are maintained with exact times down to the second.

Production Planning (PP) SAP APO provides a variety of production-planning approaches, which are all based on so-called *heuristics*. Single heuristics can be invoked interactively, or they can be configured in different ways into a *planning run*. This is the crucial difference to production planning in SAP ERP and most other ERP systems. The planning procedures of these systems are usually hardwired, and any changes can only be made when the system is installed (i.e., through customizing, see Sect. 6.2).

A *heuristic* in SAP APO is a planning function or rule that can be parameterized and that can be used to execute one, several, or all planning steps for a planning object (Balla and Layer 2007, p. 153). Planning objects include products, resources, orders, and operations. When the planner selects a heuristic (or a combination of heuristics), the production planning module knows how to perform the planning and which methods (algorithms) to use.

Heuristics are available on different levels, including both the general planning approach and details of individual planning steps. Many heuristics are related to products (e.g., methods for calculating lot sizes), while others are related to the connections between products (e.g., bill-of-materials explosion). Yet others serve specific tasks, such as rescheduling orders. Figure 10.16 shows the beginning of the list of standard heuristics available in SAP APO. The user can also define additional heuristics.

The following is an example of a typical planning run using five heuristics (Balla and Layer 2007, pp. 162–164; Wood 2007, p. 212). This planning run basically specifies MRP II-like planning.

- *Heuristic 1:* SAP_PP_20 ("stage numbering algorithm"): Low-level codes for the materials involved are created to guarantee consistent planning.
- *Heuristic 2:* SAP_MRP_001 ("product planning (comp. according to low-level code)"): The material requirements for the selected products are planned. This includes creating planned orders and purchase requisitions.
- *Heuristic 3:* SAP001 ("schedule sequence"): Lead-time scheduling and capacity requirements planning are completed. The planned orders are scheduled backward (see Sect. 3.3.1) and assigned to operating facilities or work places. The capacity needed for the orders is determined.
- *Heuristics 4 and 5:* SAP_PP_009 ("rescheduling: bottom-up") and SAP_PP_010 ("rescheduling: top-down"): Capacity is leveled by moving orders, if possible. Otherwise, alerts are generated and sent to the responsible person.

The last two heuristics deal with induced capacity problems on the assembly level, requiring rescheduling of production orders on this level. As a consequence, order dates on lower levels may also need to be rescheduled. The two heuristics SAP_PP_009 and SAP_PP_010 compute a consistent solution to the rescheduling problem by proceeding either bottom-up or top-down through the product structure.

In addition to MRP II-oriented planning, the PP module provides two more approaches: CTM planning and interactive planning. CTM planning was already discussed in Sect. 10.1.3. It is not only available in supply network planning but also in production planning and detailed scheduling.

Interactive planning allows the user to manually plan an individual product. Graphical and tabular tools to support the user include:

- Product view (view of a single location product)
- Product overview (simultaneous view of several products)

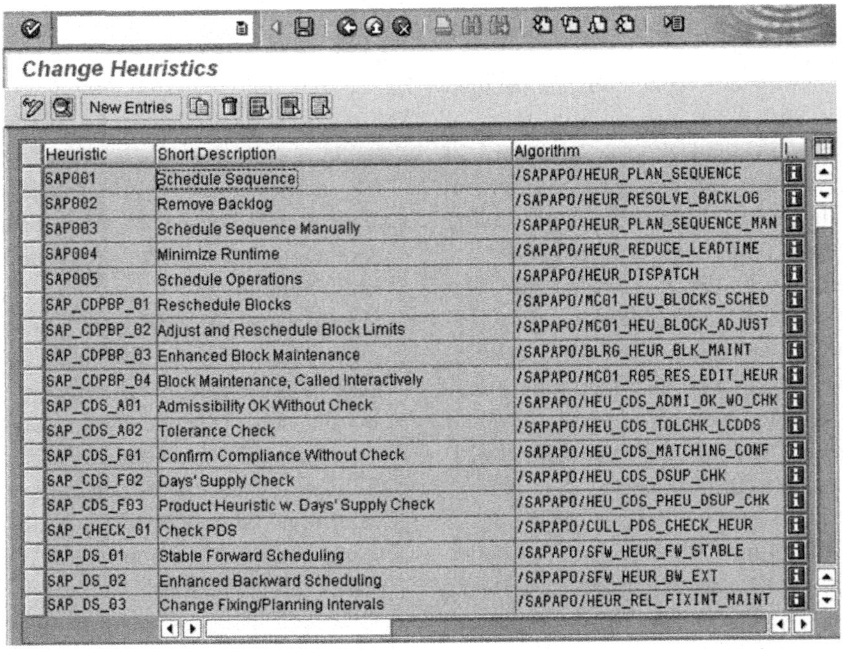

© SAP AG

Fig. 10.16 List of SAP APO heuristics

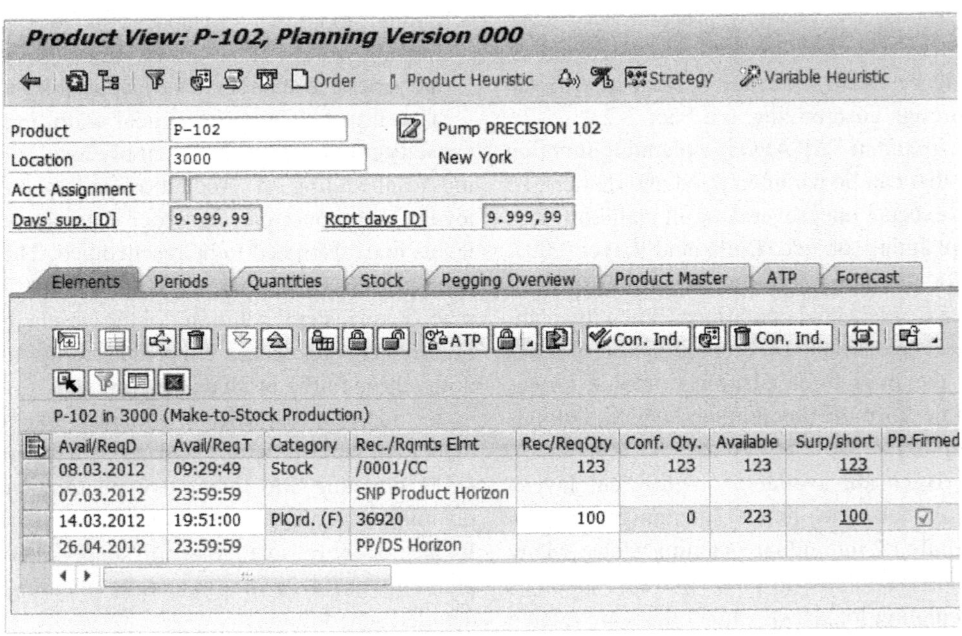

© SAP AG

Fig. 10.17 Product view in PP/DS

- Product planning table (view of different planning objects)

The *product view* actually combines several different views that the user can select, including an "element," "period," and "stock" view.

The *element view* is an order-related view of the planning results, listing orders (both demand and supply) in chronological order. An example of the element view is shown in Fig. 10.17. The product in question is P-102 ("pump precision 102") at location 3000. Supply elements are 123 units available on stock and 100 from a production order.

The *period view* shows requirement and receipt elements aggregated by periods, whereas the *stock view* displays the stock types according to (sub)locations.

The *product overview*, as the name suggests, provides an overview of a number of products selected by the user. Each product is displayed in a row containing a large number of fields with the most important information related to the product.

The *product planning table* is a flexible tool used to display and manipulate products, locations, and resources over time.

Detailed Scheduling (DS) Detailed scheduling covers a short planning horizon. Its main task is to schedule the relevant production orders on the resources (operating facilities, workplaces) involved. This task was already discussed in detail in the context of MRP II (cf. Sect. 3.6.1) and MES (cf. Sect. 7.1.1).

The most important graphical tool is the *detailed scheduling planning board*. It basically provides the functionality of a leitstand system, as described in Sect. 7.1.1. Production planners can configure the planning board according to their needs.

The planning board provides a number of display options and additional functionality, including:

- *Simulation* of order sequences and machine schedules. The result of a simulation run can be fixed and transferred to the transactional system (i.e., SAP ERP) that will execute the schedule.
- *Scheduling* and *rescheduling* production orders and operations, taking capacity restrictions and existing machine load into account (finite scheduling). This can be done manually or automatically.
- Creating *optimal order sequences* according to objective functions selected by the user.

PP/DS uses both optimization techniques and heuristic methods, including constraint propagation and genetic algorithms. The user can decide which objective function to pursue, for example, minimizing the maximum delay or minimizing the average setup cost. A typical application of genetic algorithms is searching for order sequences with minimal setup cost.

Constraint propagation is an approach coming from logical programming and artificial intelligence. It investigates existing restrictions in order to derive from them possible further restrictions and to identify inconsistencies within possible solutions. Constraint propagation is suited for complex planning problems that are subject to many dependencies and restrictions.

In detailed scheduling, constraint propagation assists the planner in finding a *permissible* solution. While the planning board is a convenient graphical tool, it displays only the surface of the problem. The planner still needs to mentally keep track of all the dependencies and restrictions limiting the decision space when scheduling or rescheduling orders. Constraint propagation helps the planner by observing all these factors and coming up with a solution.

PP/DS planning methods require information about the connections between products, locations, and resources. This information is obtained from *pegging*, as described in Sect. 9.1.3. Detailed scheduling connects procurement, production, transportation, and customer orders in such a way that the relationships between product receipts (e.g., planned orders, stocks) and product requirements (e.g., sales orders) become evident.

Fig. 10.18 Dimension of ATP checking (Mertens 2009, p. 272)

Possible ATP Checks

1) Is checking limited to one location (warehouse, plant), or should transfers from other locations also be considered?
2) Should only physically present and free stock be checked (static view), or should planned inflow and outflow also be included (dynamic view)?
3) Are reservations "cemented" or can they be reassigned?
4) Is the check limited to the end product or does it include (main) assemblies etc., perhaps even externally procured raw materials?
5) Is producing the goods an option when the available quantity is not sufficient?
6) Should production capacities also be queried for availability?

10.1.5 Global Available-to-Promise (Global ATP)

Global ATP comprises a number of approaches to check short- or midterm product availability and related functions. ATP (available-to-promise) is a general term used by SAP to determine delivery dates based on the availability of the requested products. The essential question is: Can the product be delivered to the customer on the promised date?

A considerable variety of possible checks can be employed to answer this question. Mertens lists a number of checking dimensions that could be taken into consideration, as shown in Fig. 10.18 (Mertens 2009, p. 272).

ATP checks are available in both SAP ERP and SAP APO. They are often initiated in SAP ERP during a fulfillment process, when a customer inquiry or order is received. SAP APO provides more extensive ATP functionality than SAP ERP, such as multilevel ATP checks (including bill-of-materials explosion) and global location or product substitution.

"Global" ATP refers to availability checking involving several companies in a supply network. While simple checks (called "local ATP") only include information that is stored within one company's ERP system, global ATP extends across several nodes of the network and several levels of the product structure. This means that the availability of end products and components is checked based on multiple SAP systems or even on application systems provided by other software vendors. In simulation mode, alternative products, components, or delivery locations can also be considered.

Basically, there are three different types of ATP checks:

- Product availability check
- Product allocation check (i.e., allocating limited supply to customers)
- Forecast check (i.e., allocating supply to cover forecasted demand)

The most important of these checks is the *product availability* check. When a customer order or inquiry is received, a delivery date can only be confirmed if there is enough time to complete all necessary activities prior to that date. In other words, the goods must be available for dispatching early enough so that all activities related with dispatching (e.g., ordering the transport with a shipper, picking, packing, loading) can be completed.

If, however, the check shows that not enough of the product is available, the production and procurement departments must be informed so that the product can be manufactured and components can be ordered on time. In addition, the expected receipts must be marked as reserved in material planning.

A *multilevel ATP check* is employed when the availability of lower-level components is important. This is primarily the case when *assembly* plays a dominant role in a production process. Because production or procurement of lower-

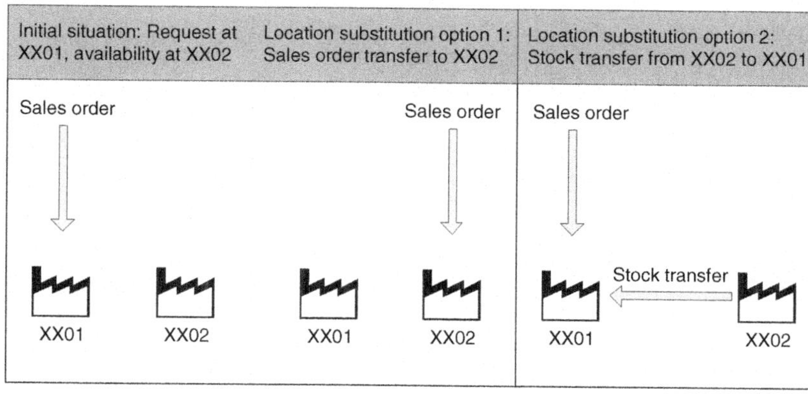

Fig. 10.19 Options for location substitution (Dickersbach 2009, p. 125)

level components often takes longer than the customer is willing to wait, components are produced or procured to stock, independently of customer orders.

Once a customer order is placed (or expected), availability of the components required to manufacture the end product is checked so that the final assembly can start shortly thereafter. This requires an ATP check on multiple levels, usually entailing a bill-of-materials explosion.

Multilevel checks are especially important in *make-to-order* production. In particular, when customers are provided with configuration capabilities, end products will only be specified in detail on demand. Due to the vast number of possible combinations, the availability of all needed parts can only be checked after the customer has completed the configuration.

Rule-Based ATP *Rule-based ATP* means that availability checks are conducted according to rules defined by the user. For example, options regarding location and product substitution may be specified using rules.

Figure 10.19 illustrates this approach: Location XX01 cannot cover the demand, because there is not enough stock available, but location XX02 would be able to fulfill the demand. There are two main options:

- Transfer the order to location XX02 and fulfill the demand at this location (secondary location)
- Initiate a stock transfer from location XX02 to location XX01 to allow XX01 (primary location) to fulfill the order

In this scenario, a rule can be used to specify the conditions under which either the location is substituted or a stock transfer order is created.

Instead of the location, the product might also be substituted if its availability cannot be ensured. A checking rule taking both *location and product substitution* into consideration could look like this [cf. similar rules in SAP (2012b)]:

1. Is the product available at this location?
2. If not, is an alternative product available at this location?
3. If not, is this product available at a different location?
4. If not, is an alternative product available at an alternative location?
5. If not, production is triggered.

In this example, the result of one step determines, in conjunction with certain predefined parameters, whether a solution has already been found or whether further checks need to be carried out.

Possible alternatives for products and locations are defined using so-called substitution lists. These are in turn created using a designated "access strategy" while taking into consideration any given product and/or location constraints (Dickersbach 2009, p. 125).

In principle, *production process models* may also be substituted with alternatives. PPM

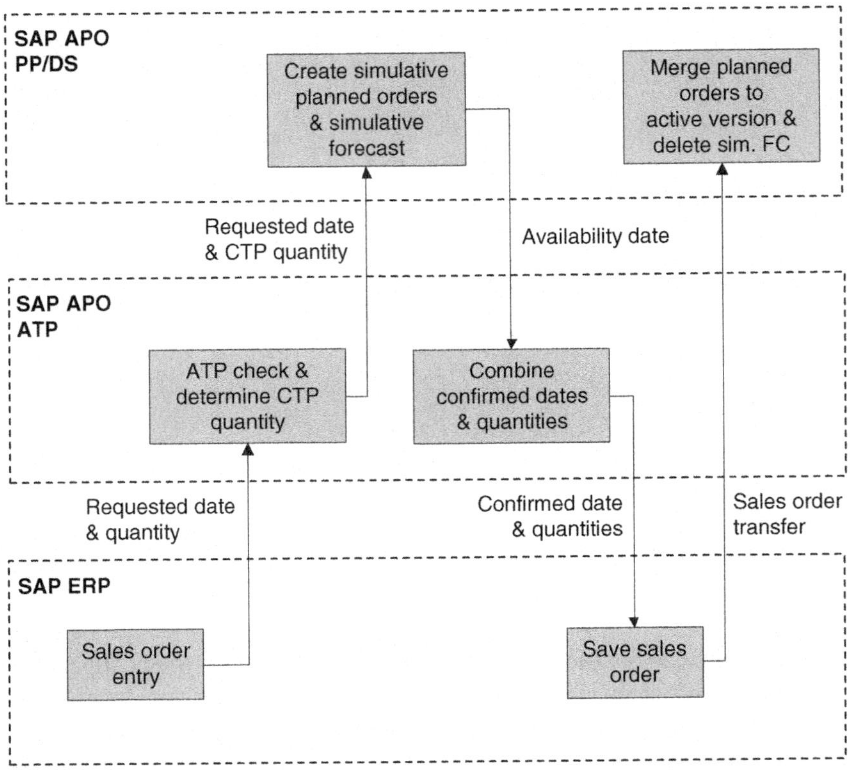

Fig. 10.20 Capable-to-promise (Dickersbach 2009, p. 328)

substitution means that the product is manufactured using a different combination of materials or according to a different routing.

Capable-to-Promise ATP is primarily used for make-to-stock production, matching planned stock levels, receipts, and demands. In *make-to-order* production, these types of planned values are often not available. Therefore, instead of checking product availability, it makes more sense to check whether the capacity needed to manufacture the requested product by the requested delivery date is available.

Consequently, a so-called *CTP (capable-to-promise) check* examines whether sufficient capacity is available, both on the end-product level and the levels of important components (e. g., assemblies). Although this type of check can also be used for make-to-stock production, it is most significant in make-to-order production.

Capable-to-promise is a part of global ATP and also uses the standard ATP checks. When the required amount of the end product or component is unavailable, CTP prompts production or procurement. Figure 10.20 demonstrates the collaboration between SAP ERP and the APO modules G-ATP and PP/DS.

Once a standard order (customer order) has been created in SAP ERP, as described in Sect. 5.3.2, it is passed on to the APO module G-ATP, including the delivery date requested by the customer. G-ATP then determines the required CTP quantity, possibly deducting available ATP quantities, and relays it, together with the desired delivery date, to the PP/DS module.

PP/DS simulates the corresponding planned orders—along with a demand forecast to prevent other demands from using this planned order (Dickersbach 2009, p. 327)—and initiates an ATP check. PP/DS schedules the planned orders according to the available capacity. Global ATP stimulates production and procurement processes if the CTP quantity is not sufficient.

The results of the ATP check and the PP/DS simulation are then combined. The confirmed quantities and dates are sent to and saved in

SAP ERP, while in APO, they are used as a basis for further SCM planning.

10.1.6 Transportation Planning and Vehicle Scheduling

The *transportation planning/vehicle scheduling (TP/VS)* module helps the transportation planner to combine orders that need transporting (e.g., deliveries to customers, stock transfers, returns etc.) into shipments. As a result, planned shipments are created (SAP 2012b).

The planner must choose the most suitable means of transport and use it as efficiently as possible while determining the quickest or most cost-effective delivery route (route planning).

At the same time, there are various restrictions to keep in mind: availability and capacities of transport means, order delivery dates, time windows for loading/unloading set by the sender or recipient, fragility of the products, and special shipment instructions (e.g., refrigeration, dangerous goods). The submodule *"vehicle scheduling"* assists the planner in observing all these restrictions and constraints, while he or she configures routes and schedules vehicles.

TP/VS is mainly used for operative shipment planning, with a short-term planning horizon of a day or less. For midterm transportation planning within SNP (supply network planning), TLB (transport load builder) functionality is used instead (Knolmayer et al. 2009, p. 113).

A common way of SAP ERP and SAP APO collaborating is creating deliveries in ERP and then having APO carry out a planning run. The shipments created by TP/VS are then sent back to SAP ERP, where they are processed further. If no matching deliveries in the ERP system exist, TP/VS automatically triggers their creation (Dickersbach 2009, p. 146).

The main tool used in transport planning and vehicle scheduling is the interactive *TP/VS planning board*. The planner uses the planning board to manually schedule transport loads and to invoke an optimization component (TP/VS optimizer).

Transportation planning and vehicle scheduling are an optimization problem. For this reason, the TP/VS module includes an optimization component, the so-called *TP/VS optimizer*. Strictly speaking, the optimizer does not employ true optimization methods but local search heuristics such as genetic and evolutionary algorithms (Dickersbach 2009, p. 156).

The optimizer uses these methods to generate the best possible *shipment, vehicle, and route plan*, taking into account the costs associated with transportation, late or early deliveries, and nondeliveries. It provides for hard restrictions (e.g., transport capacities, product incompatibility, loading and unloading time windows) as well as soft constraints (e.g., delivery dates that incur penalties if not met) (Knolmayer et al. 2009, p. 114).

Additional functions for transportation planning and vehicle scheduling include carrier selection and predefined routes (Dickersbach 2009, p. 160).

Carrier selection [official name: "transportation service provider selection" (SAP 2012b)] means assigning transportation service providers to planned shipments, either manually or automatically. The selection can be based on different criteria, such as priority level, cost, or percent of total transport volume. If a carrier turns down the order, the planner either receives a message in the "alert monitor" of the supply chain cockpit (cf. sect. 10.1.1), or the next carrier is automatically selected, depending on how the system was configured.

Predefined routes allow transportation resources to be included in an ATP check as early as when a customer inquiry or order is received. Otherwise these resources are only checked after transportation planning has been completed. A salesperson processing the inquiry (or order) can thus inform the customer immediately about transportation possibilities and times.

10.2 Core Interface (CIF)

Many companies that use SAP APO for supply chain management also use SAP ERP for their daily business processes. This means that both

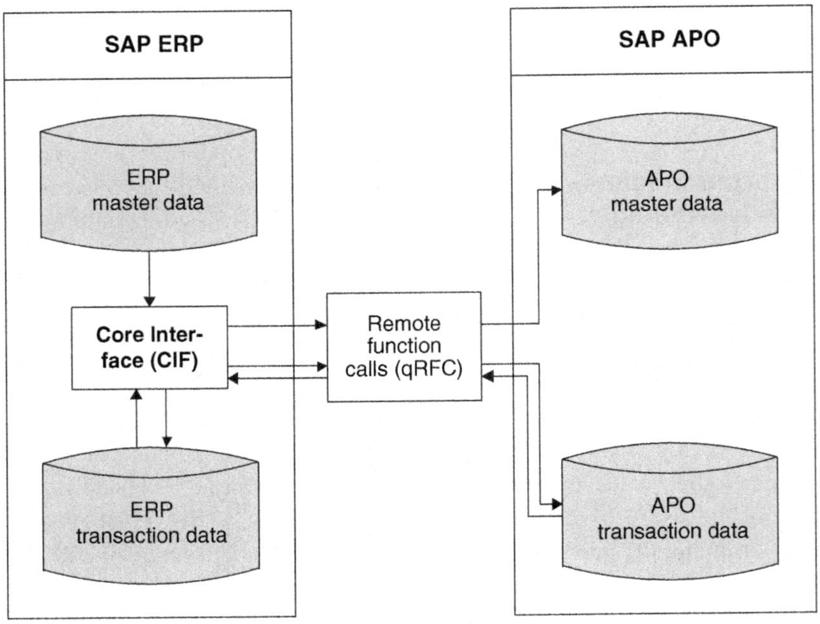

Fig. 10.21 Core Interface SAP ERP–SAP APO

systems must work well together with minimal redundancies, despite the fact that they perform similar and/or complementary tasks. Integrating the two systems requires not only proper organizational but also technical measures.

Within an SAP landscape, the technical interface between ERP and SCM is the so-called *core interface (CIF)*. It is responsible for data exchange between SAP ECC and SAP APO, including (Hoppe 2007, p. 398):

- Initial transfer of relevant master and transaction data from SAP ERP to APO
- Transfer of changes to the master and transaction data
- Adopting the planning results from SAP APO in SAP ERP

It is worth noting that master data are not maintained in multiple places but only in the system that was originally responsible for the data. This means that most master data and transaction data (e.g., customers, suppliers, orders, invoices) are maintained in SAP ERP, while data specific to SCM (e.g., production process models, locations, transportation lanes) are maintained in SAP APO. Master data are only transferred in one direction, meaning that in SAP APO, copies of the ERP master data are created.

In SAP ERP, the core interface has to be implemented as a plug-in, as shown in Fig 10.21. In SAP APO, the corresponding functionality is always available. The interplay of the two systems is basically organized in such a way that an event is generated whenever the two systems need to communicate (e.g., when a customer order is created). The event triggers an action with the help of a *remote function call* (qRFC—queued remote function call).

Because function calls are continuously generated—with every relevant event, such as a data change in SAP ERP—the SCM system is always working with up-to-date data. Changes to the data are registered in SAP APO as soon as they are made, and new planning runs are initiated immediately if necessary. This means that SCM planning essentially occurs in real time.

Integration models define which information should be transferred from SAP ERP to SAP APO when an event occurs. An integration model specifies the objects to be transferred, for example, materials, customers, plants, deliveries, or manufacturing orders. When an integration model is created, the relevant objects are selected. When the model is activated, they are effectively sent to SAP APO.

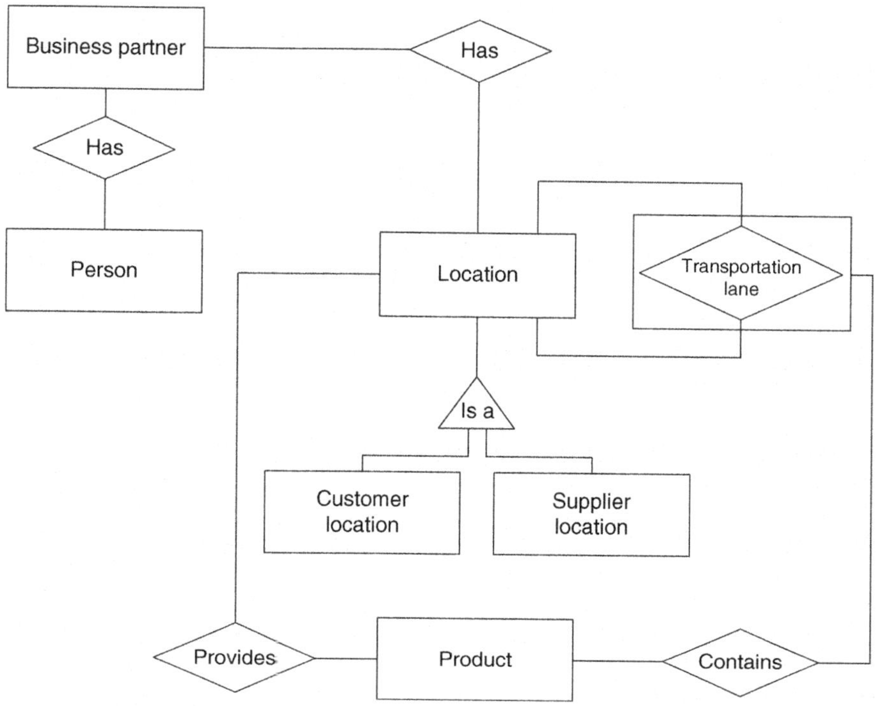

Fig. 10.22 Connections between master data in SNC

In the other direction—from SAP APO to SAP ERP—only *transaction data* are sent. Transaction data reflect the SCM planning results computed in APO: demand forecasts, stocks, transportation orders, shipments, etc. Transaction data consistency is controlled by the core interface.

10.3 Other SAP SCM Modules

While SAP APO is the most important subsystem, SAP SCM also contains other components: SAP SNC (supply network collaboration), SAP F&R (forecasting and replenishment), SAP EM (event management), and SAP EWM (extended warehouse management).

10.3.1 Supply Network Collaboration

SAP SNC (supply network collaboration) supports various processes in the collaboration of suppliers and customers. This module provides the functionality that used to be called *SAP ICH (inventory collaboration hub)* in earlier versions of SAP SCM.

The partners modeled in SNC are suppliers and customers. SNC considers both organizations and people, as shown in Fig. 10.22. Organizations (i.e., companies) are assigned to locations (supplier or customer locations), while people are assigned to organizations. In this way, it is possible to find out the relationships between employees and their locations (i.e., the location of the company they work for) (Hamady and Leitz 2009, pp. 53–54).

Supply network collaboration aims to implement the concept of *adaptive supply chain networks* (Hamady and Leitz 2009, p. 21). This term refers to networks that are flexible and can be dynamically adjusted to changing circumstances. Adaptability is essential today, given that supply chains are becoming increasingly complex and vulnerable. Factors such as transportation risks, capacity problems, new material sources, and cost pressure can all be reasons to change an existing network.

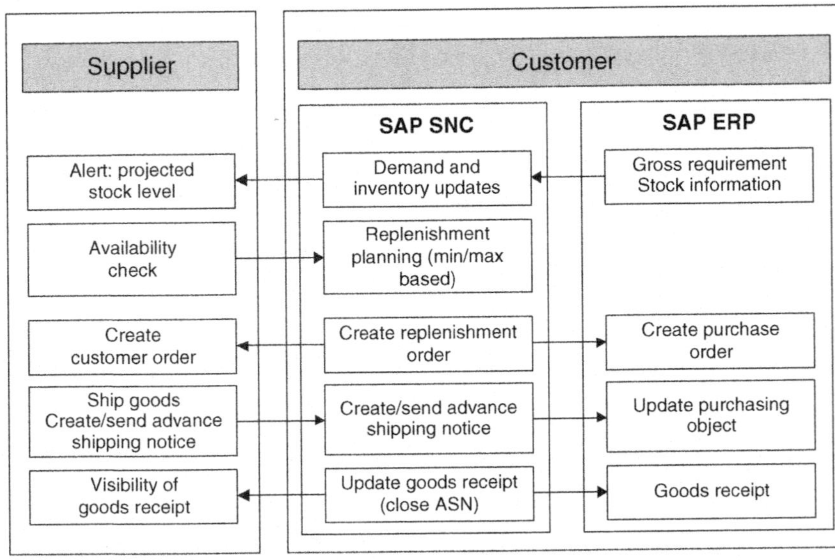

Fig. 10.23 Replenishment collaboration in SMI (Hamady and Leitz 2009, p. 58)

The SAP SCM solution map names three main areas of SNC that provide functionality for working with suppliers ("supplier collaboration"), customers ("customer collaboration"), and subcontractors ("outsourced manufacturing"). The following explanations are adapted from the process descriptions in the SAP SCM solution map (SAP 2012d).

Supplier Collaboration The *supplier collaboration* part of SNC offers web-based functions that allow close collaboration with suppliers. These functions use capabilities from the SAP NetWeaver platform (see Sect. 6.4.2). Exchanging information, which in many companies still relies on paper documents (e.g., fax) or EDI (electronic data interchange), is carried out on the basis of Internet protocols.

According to the solution map, supplier collaboration supports the following business processes (SAP 2012d; Hamady and Leitz 2009, pp. 26–28):

- *Release* and *purchase order processing:* SNC functions support releases within scheduling agreements, as well as explicit purchase orders placed by customers who execute their own replenishment planning. In both cases, the supplier performs some checks and creates an advance shipping notice (ASN). This notification informs the customer that the delivery is planned to arrive shortly, allowing them to prepare for goods receipt on time.
- *Supplier managed inventory (SMI):* This SAP-specific variant of VMI (vendor-managed inventory (cf. Sect. 8.2.3) is offered as a part of SAP SNC. (VMI is also available in SAP SCM but within SAP APO; more specifically, within SNP—supply network planning, cf. sect. 10.1.3). The main difference between SMI and VMI is that the customer runs the system instead of the supplier (Knolmayer et al. 2009, p. 120). The customer determines the material requirements and inventory levels in their ERP system and communicates this data to the supplier. The supplier is then responsible for replenishing the customer's inventory within upper and lower levels or according to a target range of coverage. Figure 10.23 illustrates the collaboration between the partner systems.
- *Dynamic replenishment:* This process allows for a comparison of customer and supplier planning data, making deviations between the customer's plan and the supplier's plan transparent. The customer's planned data (e.g., planned orders and purchase requisitions) are

taken from the customer's ERP system and transferred to SAP SNC. The supplier does the same regarding planned or scheduled deliveries.

Based on these data, SNC updates its supply and demand data. It evaluates the differences and warns the user of critical situations—depending on how the system was configured during customization (see Sect. 6.2). Through dynamic replenishment, both supplier and customer become aware of mid- to long-term deviations of supply and demand, enabling them to take appropriate action early on to avoid delayed shipments or surplus production.

- *Kanban* (cf. Sect. 2.3.1): Kanban replenishment signals—generated as part of the customer's MRP run or created manually—can be transferred to SNC. The supplier receives this information through SNC and creates ASN messages that are used to update the customer's SAP ERP system. SNC handles goods receipt posting and invoicing. The customer and the supplier can monitor the Kanban cycle by, for example, the status of a Kanban, Kanban ID, product number, etc., and react accordingly.
- *Delivery control monitoring (DCM):* In contrast to SMI (supplier-managed inventory), where the supplier reacts to demand notifications from the customer, delivery control monitoring allows the supplier to react directly to the customer's current stock levels on a short-term basis. The supplier can use DCM functions to keep track of the customer's stock levels, even several times a day if need be. The system also creates alerts when levels fall beneath a certain threshold so that the supplier can initiate a shipment. Replenishment is based on upper and lower inventory limits. DCM functions calculate the suggested replenishment quantities using the maximum level as an upper limit.
- *Invoicing:* This process allows suppliers to create invoices for the orders and shipments that have been processed through SNC. A supplier can, for example, respond to a purchase order, create an ASN, create the resulting invoice and send it to the customer's ERP system. In this system, a supplier invoice is automatically created and ready for further processing by accounts payable functions. Once the payment has been processed by the customer's ERP system, the supplier is notified.
- *Self-billing invoicing:* This invoicing capability is also known as "evaluated receipt settlement" (ERS). In ERS, the customer's ERP system recognizes consumption of the supplier's materials and directly generates an invoice for the supplier. Once the invoice has been created in the customer's ERP system, the supplier receives a notification indicating the products, amounts, and dates for payment. The main business value is derived from the fact that the invoicing process is automated. The supplier no longer needs to create an invoice and mail it, while the customer does not need to manually enter the invoice in the ERP system.

Customer Collaboration The *customer collaboration* part of SAP SNC allows companies to share information and collaborate with their customers on the finished goods level. Four business processes are defined. The focus is on a "responsive replenishment" scenario, which is achieved through the combination of the two processes "responsive demand planning" and "responsive replenishment" (SAP 2012d):

- *Responsive demand planning*: This process allows forecasting and collaboration on baseline and promotion demand between the business partners. It supports the exchange of data about product activities and forecasts. Functionality is available for statistical forecasting, as well as projecting short-term sales.
- *Responsive replenishment planning:* This process allows replenishment planning to fulfill the daily supply target at the customer's ship-to location. It helps to build truckloads, attempting to optimize the transport with methods such as load balancing. Baseline and promotion demand can be planned separately, taking into account safety stock levels and lot sizing. Through integration with SAP ERP, an availability check can be executed before triggering the logistic execution. By

exchanging a replenishment order and an advanced shipping notification, visibility over the replenishment situation (on-order, in-transit) and over changes within the distribution chain is provided.

- *Min-max replenishment:* This process provides data exchange and forecasting functionality as in responsive demand planning. Replenishment planning is based on minimum and maximum stock levels, maintained at the ship-to location of the customer. All process steps are aligned to be automated. Exceptions that require the planner's manual input are shared using alerts.
- *Demand forecast collaboration:* This process allows comparison and consensus building between a consumption-based forecast and a forecast created by the customer. Techniques used include visualizing absolute and percentage differences as well as applying rules to calculate a consensus forecast. The consensus forecast can then be used to drive the downstream demand and replenishment processes. Automation and exceptions are handled as above.

Outsourced Manufacturing In many industries, outsourced manufacturing relationships (also known as "contract manufacturing" or "subcontracting") have become increasingly important. Managing these relationships is the goal of the SNC part *outsourced manufacturing*.

Capabilities aim to support information sharing, collaboration, and monitoring of activities that are needed to effectively manage the relationships with contract manufacturers. According to the SAP SCM solution map, this part includes the following processes (SAP 2012d):

- *Contract manufacturing purchasing:* In this process, purchase orders with attached bills of materials are used. The contract manufacturer can access the subcontracting purchase order in the customer's ERP system and collaborate on both the finished goods and component levels.

  Any changes update the customer's ERP system, allowing internal planning functions to use the latest supply commitments from the contract manufacturer. The main business value is derived from the fact that suppliers and customers communicate their respective requirements and responses in real time, while their ERP systems remain up-to-date.
- *Supply network inventory (SNI):* SNI enables visibility of the inventory and the supply and demand planning situation across independent business partners such as the customer, component suppliers, contract manufacturers, and third party logistics providers. Visibility is filtered, allowing partners to only see information for which they have been authorized.

  The customer can view the inventory of a certain product across many locations belonging to different partners in the supply chain network, including stock in transit at the component supplier's and the contract manufacturer's locations. Projected stock is calculated and displayed along with the planned replenishments and planned outtakes (e.g., for production orders) with min and max stock limits and associated alerts. This allows for proactive monitoring of changes in supply and demand, early discovery of exceptions, and fast response times.
- *Work order:* Through the work order process, SNC provides a granular way of collaborating and tracking contract manufacturer activities. A work order is a high-level collaborative order representing the production activities at the contract manufacturer's site. It is based on a purchase order that was generated by the customer's back-end system, enriched with manufacturing instructions and production phases.

  The work order serves as a means to communicate the finished goods requirement to the subcontractor. At the same time, it enables high-level tracking of the production progress by means of milestones, as well as projecting the date and quantity of finished goods according to the current production status. A work order allows the subcontractor to capture the consumption of components and materials provisioned by the customer.

  The main advantages for the customer are visibility of the production activities at the contract manufacturer's location and early

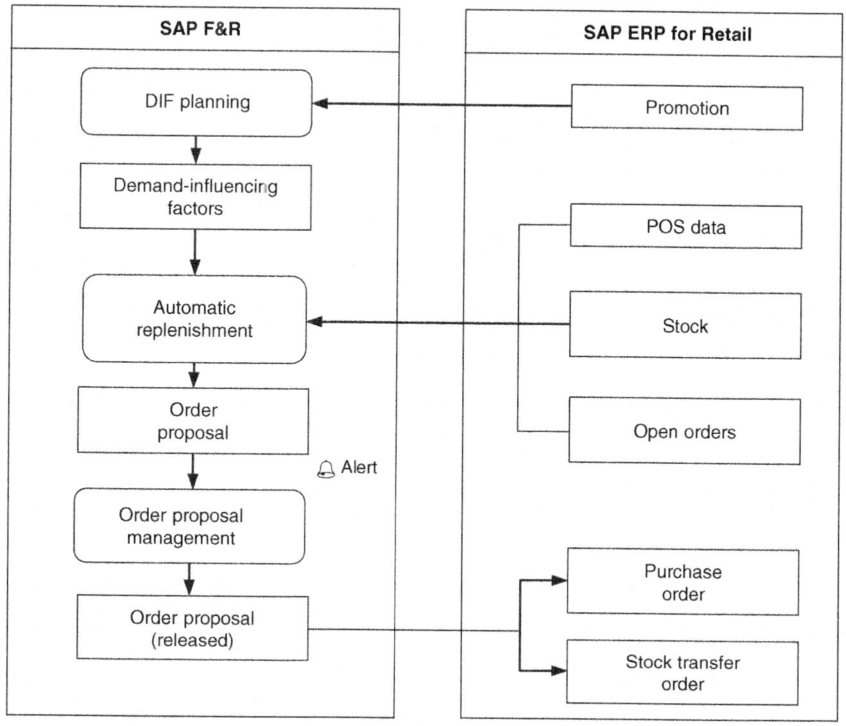

Fig. 10.24 Interplay of F&R and ERP for retail (Knolmayer et al. 2009, p. 151)

information about changes that affect the shipping date and final quantity of the finished goods. The customers also get more up-to-date information relating to their own components being used by the contract manufacturer.

10.3.2 Forecasting and Replenishment

SAP forecasting and replenishment (F&R) is responsible for planning short-term stock replenishment in retail stores and distribution centers. Many retailers handle a very high number of articles (often in the millions) so that tasks like master data administration and demand forecasting involve mass data processing. Capturing POS data (POS = point of sale, e.g., cash register terminal) adds an enormous amount of data to be dealt with.

Sales planning in the retail business differs from "normal" sales planning due to a number of factors: Advertising campaigns, holidays (e.g., Christmas), vacations, sporting events (e.g., World Cup, Olympics), unusual weather conditions (e.g., heat waves), etc. have a major impact on sales. In SAP terminology, these factors are called "demand-influencing factors" (DIFs).

Due to the special requirements in retailing, SAP F&R was designed to efficiently deal with large volumes of data. It is used together with SAP's industry solution *SAP ERP for retail*. Figure 10.24 shows how the two systems work together, using a promotion as an example.

The promotion is created in *SAP ERP for retail* and sent to *F&R*, where it is planned using demand-influencing factors. During automatic replenishment, demand forecasts are created on the product and location level. These forecasts are used to determine the net requirements, taking available quantities into account, and to calculate the order, delivery, and availability dates.

The outcomes of F&R are order proposals, which are then transferred to SAP ERP to be processed as stock transfer or procurement orders. Order proposal management deals with exceptions such as not meeting the minimal order

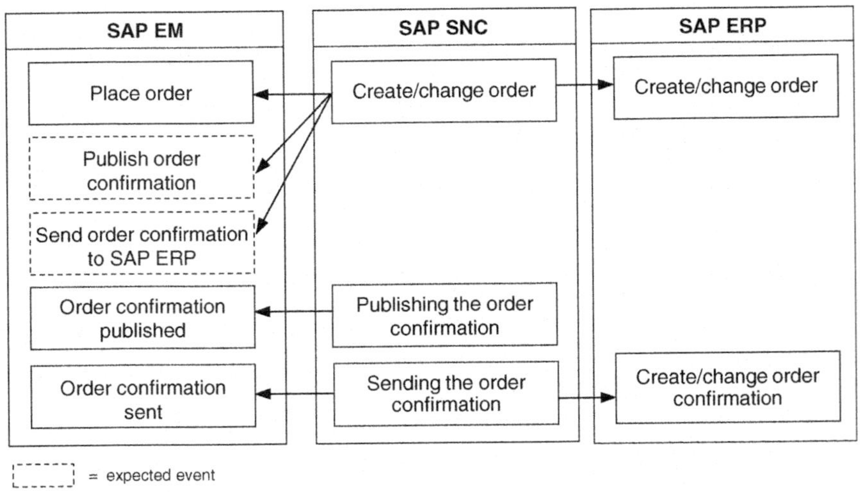

Fig. 10.25 Events in SAP EM, SNC and ERP (Hamady and Leitz 2009, p. 251)

quantity or exceeding the maximal possible quantity before sending the proposal to the ERP system.

10.3.3 Event Management

Event management (EM) in SAP SCM is used to monitor the supply chains, especially the locations outside the company. Monitoring is carried out based on planned and unplanned events.

When a *planned event* occurs (e.g., a carrier loads the goods at the supplier's), checks are made to see whether or not the event takes place within the given time frame.

Deviations from what was originally planned, as well as *unplanned events* (such as a missing transportation resource) need to be handled differently, either by defining rules specifying how to deal with this situation or by addressing the events manually.

SAP's approach to event handling has already been outlined in Sect. 8.4.3. Events can originate from a variety of sources. Predefined interfaces for communicating events exist for SAP ERP and for other sources. An example of integrating *SAP event management* with *SAP SNC (supply network collaboration*, cf. Sect. 10.3.1) is shown in Fig. 10.25. This example deals with the planned event "confirmation of an order by a supplier," which must take place within a certain time frame) (Hamady and Leitz 2009, p. 251).

A planned event is automatically generated when SAP SNC receives a new purchase order that was created in SAP ERP. Afterwards, event management checks whether or not the order confirmation has been completed ("published") within the defined time frame. A second event, "send order confirmation to SAP ERP," is also contained in this example.

10.3.4 Extended Warehouse Management

SAP extended warehouse management (EWM) is a comprehensive module offering a broad range of functions for goods transfer and inventory management. EWM functionality goes far beyond the warehousing capabilities available in SAP ERP. While SAP ERP manages stock separately depending on storage locations, EWM allows for comprehensive management of the entire warehousing complex, even down to the level of the individual storage bins.

An entire physical warehouse complex can be assigned a single *warehouse number*. This number can cover different warehouse facilities, which are differentiated by *storage type* (e.g.,

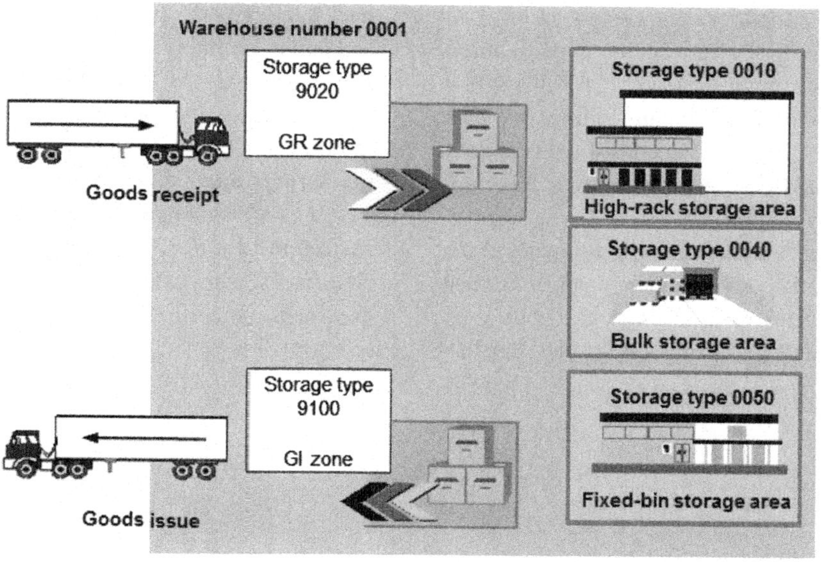

Fig. 10.26 Storage types in SAP EWM (SAP 2012b)

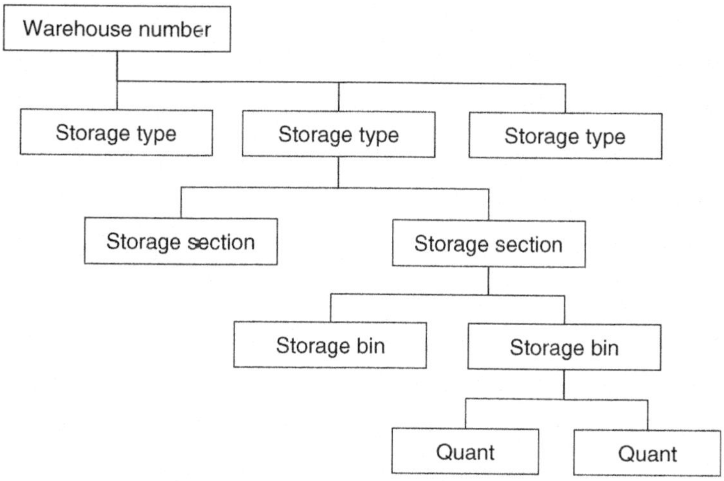

Fig. 10.27 Warehouse structure in SAP EWM (SAP 2012b)

high-rack storage, bulk storage, fixed-bin storage). In the example shown in Fig. 10.26, five different storage types (0010, 0040, 0050, 9100, 9020) are defined within warehouse number 0001 (SAP 2012b).

The *warehouse structure* is hierarchical, as can be seen in Fig. 10.27. Each storage type is divided into *storage sections*. A storage section has *storage bins*, that is, storage places with common characteristics, for example "bins for fast-moving items." In the example above, this type of bin is likely to be used near the goods receipt zone (storage type 9020).

Goods are stored in bins. Stock is booked with reference to bins, that is, inventory accounting is done on the bin level. Storage bins can be located through coordinates. In this way, it is possible to find out exactly how much of a product is in stock and where it can be found. The stock of goods stored in a storage bin is called a *quant*.

EWM functionality supports a number of *processes* for goods movement and inventory management. Among these are (SAP 2012b):

- *Goods receipt*: including unloading, put-away strategies, counting, deconsolidation, cross docking, add-ons (e.g., mounting, labeling), and quality control
- *Goods issue*: including picking management (bundling delivery positions), replenishment control (reserving sufficient stock for picking), managing and optimizing storage bins, handling unit management, packing, loading, slotting, and taking inventory
- *Supporting processes*: including planning and control (using the "warehouse management monitor"), radio frequency transmission (gathering data through RFID, cf. Sect. 11.4.1), barcode reading, warehouse resources management, and warehouse automation (interfaces with external systems/warehouse control computers).

11 Current and Future Trends

Throughout this book, methodological and technological approaches to enterprise resource planning and supply chain management have been presented. Most of these approaches are supported by current ERP and SCM systems and are implemented today in many companies.

In this final chapter, we will point out some recent developments that are likely to reshape, complement, or extend the current ERP and SCM landscape. Among these are technological advancements allowing for the creation of new, flexible system architectures, Internet-based approaches for on-demand computing, and the networking of physical entities. In particular, we will discuss various aspects of software-as-a-service, on-demand solutions, open-source ERP, federated ERP, and the so-called Internet of Things.

11.1 Service-Oriented Architecture

Since the end of the 1990s, *service orientation* has become a dominant paradigm in software development and management, initiating a shift in the business software world as well. Modern software systems increasingly build on this paradigm.

We start this section with explaining some fundamental terms (such as service and service-oriented architecture), before proceeding to the related concepts in enterprise resource planning software. The following outline is based on (Kurbel 2008, pp. 105–122).

Using a *service-oriented architecture* (SOA) (Sweeney 2010), a software system is made up of services. Application software is considered a *service* (or a collection of services) and not a piece of software installed on the company's computers. For both the developer and the user of the software, it is normally more important to get the specified work done (i.e., obtaining a service) than to actually own software modules that are capable of performing the work.

In contrast to a conventional system, SOA-based software is not necessarily installed on computers inside the company. There is no need for the code behind the service to reside on a local server. Instead, the service may be invoked via the Internet from anywhere in the world. The same service may be used in different information systems, even by different organizations, independent of their geographic location.

The rationale for a software service is similar to that of services in a business context. Clients demand services from businesses, for example, getting a quotation, booking a flight, or opening a bank account. Likewise, a software service provides a functionality that is useful to (software) clients.

To be more precise, the service is provided by a *server* that receives *requests* from clients, as

K.E. Kurbel, *Enterprise Resource Planning and Supply Chain Management*, Progress in IS, DOI 10.1007/978-3-642-31573-2_11, © Springer-Verlag Berlin Heidelberg 2013

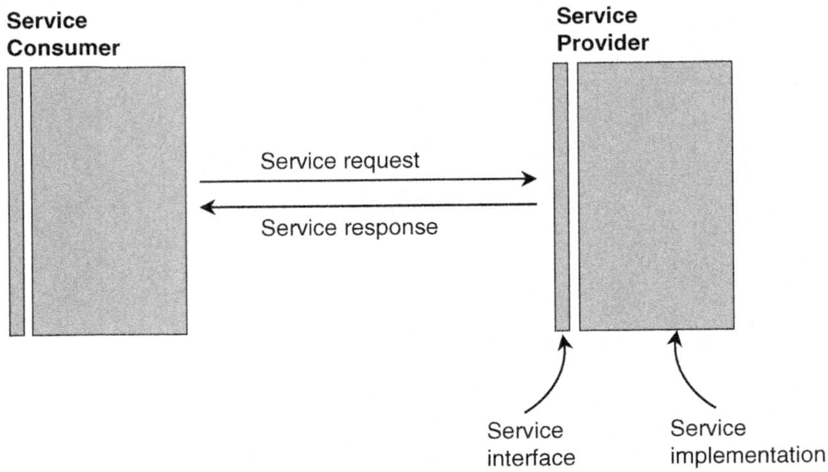

Fig. 11.1 Service request and response

illustrated by Fig. 11.1. The "consumer" (e.g., a sales and distribution module) requests the "provider" to perform a service (e.g., create a quotation) by invoking a function specified in the provider's interface. The narrow rectangle to the left of the "service provider" box indicates this interface. It is worth mentioning that the "consumer" does not need (nor want) to know how exactly the "provider" will solve this task (i.e., the service implementation). A software system with a service-oriented architecture is essentially a collection of services that are capable of communicating with each other.

The simple scheme of Fig. 11.1 also illustrates why a service-oriented architecture is so *flexible*: The service consumer and provider can be located anywhere, as long as there is a mechanism available to connect them. Nowadays, this mechanism is provided by so-called web services.

Web Services Based on the W3 (World Wide Web) consortium's definition (W3C 2004), a *web service* can be described as a software component designed to support interoperable machine-to-machine interaction over a network. It has an interface described in a machine-processable format (WSDL). Other software components interact with the web service in a manner prescribed by the web service's interface description, using SOAP messages.

The *web services framework* specifies how services communicate in order to use other services' functionality via the Internet. Communication is based on *message exchange*. A web service receives a message containing a request. It processes the request and sends a response message back to the requester.

The web services communication infrastructure uses XML-based standards, in particular SOAP and WSDL:

- *SOAP* (formerly an acronym for "simple object access protocol," now considered a name) defines a common syntax for data exchange. Any program on the web can send a SOAP message with the service name and input parameters via the Internet, and will obtain another SOAP message with the results in return.
- *WSDL* (web services description language) addresses the question: How does the service consumer know what exactly to send in the request? This information is specified in WSDL and contained in the web service's public interface. Every web service has a WSDL description specifying how to communicate with the service. Any programmer invoking the web service needs to know this specification in order to employ the service correctly.

Since a SOA-based system may invoke a large number of web services, possibly provided by

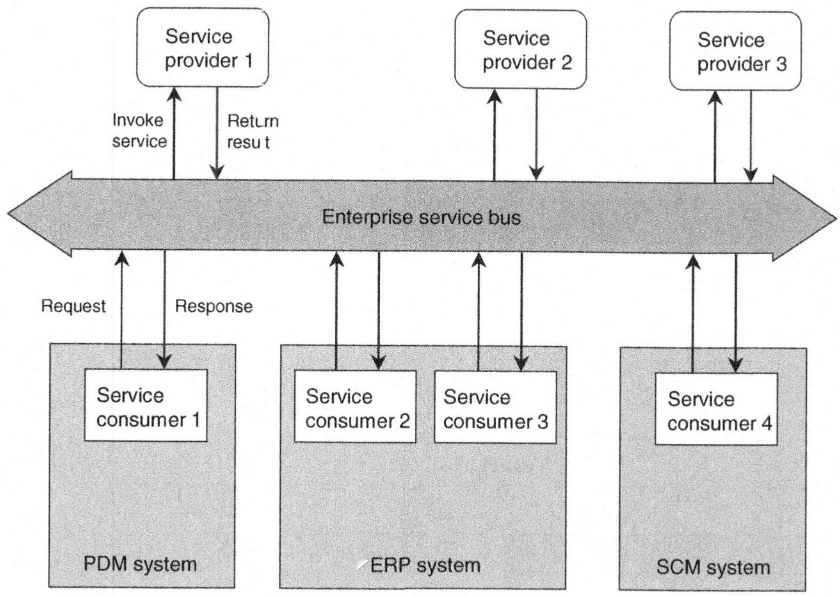

Fig. 11.2 Service-oriented architecture with an enterprise service bus

different servers, it is common to use a middleware functioning as a mediator between the service consumers and service providers. This middleware is usually an *enterprise service bus* based on a messaging system, as shown in Fig. 11.2.

Basically, the service consumers—different information systems, modules, or other services—communicate only with the enterprise service bus by sending requests to and receiving responses from the bus. The service bus is responsible for connecting to the appropriate service providers and exchanging information with them.

Enterprise Services *Enterprise services* are business-level web services. This term has been particularly stressed by SAP when they introduced SOA for their new products.

Most web services expose low-level functionality and/or functionality delivered by a single information system (or a specific module of such a system). While web services are for programmers, enterprise services are defined on a higher level, where they can also be understood by business analysts.

Since business activities are part of business processes and processes often cross business functions, an enterprise service is likely to employ functionality from different information systems, modules, or web services. Accordingly, SAP's approach to enterprise services is to combine them to form so-called *composite applications*. A composite application composes functionality and information from existing systems to support new business processes or scenarios (cf. Sect. 6.4.2).

The following scenario demonstrates the difference between a web service, on the single-system level, and a business-level enterprise service (SAP 2006, p. 7):

Consider a business-process step such as canceling an order that originated in the finance department in response to a customer's credit standing. Carrying out the task requires more than just deleting the order record in the sales management system. From a business perspective, several activities involving multiple business functions and information systems are needed, including sending a confirmation to the customer, removing the order from the production plan, releasing materials allocated to the order, notifying the invoicing department, and changing the order status to "inactive" or deleting it from various systems.

For each of these activities, a single web service might be offered by one of the modules

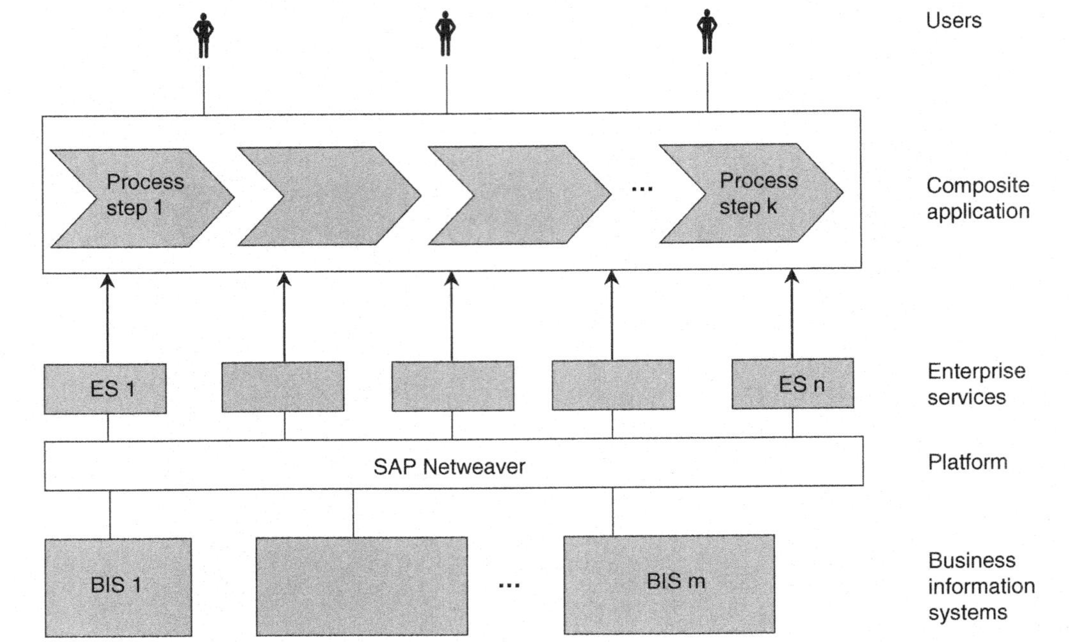

Fig. 11.3 Service-oriented architecture and composite applications

of the company's ERP system. If just these web services were provided, an employee responsible for the cancelation of the order would have to go to each module one after the other, start a screen, and carry out the necessary action.

An enterprise service, on the other hand, might combine the tasks performed by the various web services and the employee's steps into one service. The employee would just have to initiate the process, for example, start a screen that invokes the enterprise service "cancel order."

Enterprise services can be reused in different contexts, both for developing new information systems and reusing existing ones. Thus, they can be looked at as building blocks for creating larger solutions based on existing and on new components. Enterprise services can be assembled to compose new systems and enable new business processes.

This idea, illustrated in Fig. 11.3, was propagated by SAP when they launched the NetWeaver platform (cf. Sect. 6.4.2). It shows the flexibility a service-oriented architecture is intended to provide. Services based on different information systems can be assembled to support new business processes that need functionality from different existing systems.

The SOA paradigm has gained a lot of popularity in software development. Many information systems have already been created with a service-oriented architecture. SAP, for example, began basing future developments on SOA with the introduction of the NetWeaver platform in 2004.

11.2 On-Demand Solutions

A typical IT landscape in the past, and up to now, has been characterized by the fact that the company installs the needed hardware, networks, and software on their premises. While the hardware is usually owned by the company, application software such as an ERP system is licensed from a vendor but nevertheless installed and running on the company's hardware—on a mainframe or midrange computer, or on a number of networked servers.

This scenario is about to change. New technological developments and software options allow companies to buy or license the software (or certain parts of it) "as a service," but only when they actually need it, that is, "on demand."

11.2.1 Software-as-a-Service and Cloud Computing

Software-as-a-service (SaaS) takes the idea of service-oriented computing even one step further than SOA. Using a service-oriented architecture in most cases still means—although this is not at all a precondition—that the software system is hosted within the company. Some of the services belonging to the system may be obtained from the outside, but the majority are still provided from servers within the company.

In contrast to this, software-as-a-service usually means software that is *not* hosted by the company—although this is also not a precondition for the concept. For example, an ERP system available "as a service" is hosted and operated by an ERP provider, on the provider's premises. The client only receives "services" (such as inventory management, order fulfillment, and invoicing) from the provider. Instead of paying license fees, the client pays according to a usage scheme.

Historically, similar solutions have been implemented where the installation is not inside the company but outside, provided and run by a service firm working for the company. This constellation is known as *application service providing (ASP)*. Although an established approach, most ERP vendors and service companies generate only a small portion of their revenue with ASP.

Nowadays, software-as-a-service is available for a wide range of application areas. Office programs (such as Google Docs, Gmail, Calendar; http://www.google.com/apps) are among the most popular, but heavyweight applications such as customer relationship management, enterprise resource planning, and supply chain management are also available as services.

Typical *features* of software-as-a-service include the following:

- The software is *web based*, meaning that it is hosted on a server on the web. Users normally just need a web browser to access it, instead of a proprietary GUI (graphical user-interface) tool. This delivery model has been made possible by the increasing availability of broadband Internet.
- The software system has a *multi-tenant architecture*, meaning that the system is designed to serve many users simultaneously and to partition the users' data accordingly.
- At the same time, multi-tenancy requires the software and/or infrastructure that the software runs on to be *scalable*. Scalability means that the system is capable of smoothly handling increasing (or decreasing) numbers of users.
- Software offered as a service is typically developed and run by the *vendor* of the software (in contrast to traditional ASP, where the provider usually hosts and runs third-party software).
- Common *pricing schemes* are subscription based, requiring the customer to pay, for example, a monthly or annual fee. This fee may or may not depend on the usage rate.
- Although *customization* features (e.g., parameterization, cf. Sect. 6.2) are available, they are not as comprehensive as for conventional standard software.

Using software-as-a-service has not only many advantages but also serious challenges. The most important *advantages* are:

- The company does not need to worry about system operation, maintenance, user support, or acquisition of the needed expertise and know-how, because these tasks are taken care of by the SaaS provider. Consequently, the company can focus on their core tasks and competencies.
- Upgrades and new releases are easier to handle, both for the user company and the provider, because there is only one configuration (i.e., the provider's).
- Customers benefit from frequent new releases, which are "automatically" obtained.

The most serious challenge for software-as-a-service adoption is *data security*. While private users seem to be less concerned about their personal data being stored and maintained "somewhere" (i.e., not on their own computer), many potential business users regard this as risky. Companies are concerned because they need to keep their data confidential. Many companies do not believe that the data will be as

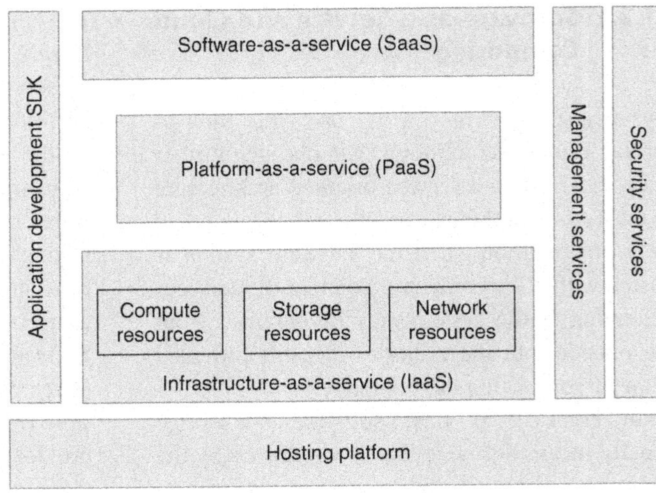

Fig. 11.4 Cloud-computing layered architecture

secure when they are hosted outside the company as they are when they are locked up in-house.

Cloud Computing Nowadays, software-as-a-service is considered a part of cloud computing because most of today's software services run "in the cloud." However, it is worth mentioning that the basic concept is independent of this implementation.

The notion of a "cloud" in which the computing takes place may appear somewhat nebulous, but the term can be defined quite succinctly:

"A *cloud* is a type of parallel and distributed system consisting of a collection of interconnected and virtualized computers that are dynamically provisioned and presented as one or more unified computing resource(s) based on service-level agreements established through negotiation between the service provider and consumers." (Buyyaa et al. 2009, p. 601)

In other words, the "cloud" appears to the customer as a computer of appropriate size and performance, and it is up to the two parties (customer and provider) to agree on the level of service (e.g., service availability, response times, mean time to repair) the customer should get.

The *cloud-computing paradigm* provides three distinctive new aspects that set it apart from previous developments in distributed computing, such as the client–server model (Armbrust et al. 2009, p. 1):

1. The illusion of a seemingly unlimited resource pool, eliminating the need to plan far ahead for a possible increase or decrease in computing demand.
2. No need for an up-front commitment to a particular level of service, allowing companies to adjust the hardware resources according to their actual needs.
3. The granulation of services—the user pays only for the actual amount of resources used and may release the resources when no longer needed.

While the term "cloud computing" is often used to describe a type of elastic infrastructure ("infrastructure-as-a-service"), other services are also summarized under this term, namely, "platform-as-a-service" and "software-as-a-service." Figure 11.4 illustrates the layers of cloud computing, based on a similar scheme as used by Joseph (2009).

- *Software-as-a-service (SaaS)*, as described above, is the highest layer of cloud computing. "Software" usually means "application software" that runs in a cloud environment. End users access this software over the Internet via a web browser.
- *Platform-as-a-service (PaaS)* generally refers to Internet-based software development and delivery platforms. Programmers can create multi-tenant, web-based applications on and for these platforms. The applications are

hosted on the provider's infrastructure and are offered as a service to customers. PaaS supports tasks such as code editing, deploying, running, and managing applications (Lawton 2008).

- *Infrastructure-as-a-service (IaaS)* is the foundation of the cloud-computing stack, offering a scalable, on-demand, elastic computer infrastructure—including virtual machines, storage or processor time—normally based on a pay-as-you-go pricing scheme.
- A *hosting platform* provides the underlying physical, virtual, and software assets, including physical machines, operating systems, network systems, storage systems, power management, and virtualization software (Joseph 2009).

Users of IaaS can utilize computing power and storage that is ready to be commissioned and, when no longer needed, decommissioned on short notice. Access to the computing resources is normally provided with the help of web tools. On top of this elastic infrastructure, companies/users can set up their own platforms and applications, use the cloud infrastructure as an outsourced storage device or perform resource-intensive computing tasks.

Cloud computing gives companies many *advantages*, including flexibility, no need for an up-front commitment as to the amount of computing resources needed in the future, and usually lower cost than buying the hardware and licensing the necessary software.

On the other hand, a number of *problems* go along with cloud computing, which have up till now hindered its widespread adoption for business information processing. These problems include uncertainty about the actual level of service, data security, reliability, and privacy protection the cloud service vendor is able to provide to the customer.

Obviously, a crucial prerequisite for cloud-computing adoption is *trust*. The potential customer must trust the provider (and the underlying technology) that the required service will be delivered as required by the customer—reliably, securely, quickly, and whenever needed. Since it is hardly possible for a potential customer to systematically check and audit all relevant aspects of a particular cloud service offer, other ways of establishing trust must be in place, for example, the reputation of the provider or performance figures the provider is able to prove.

Well-defined *service-level agreements (SLAs)* may also serve as a means to create initial trust between potential customers and providers. The role of SLAs as an instrument to enhance trust in cloud computing is discussed in Stankov et al. (2012) (see also Goo et al. 2009).

11.2.2 ERP on Demand

"ERP on demand" stands for a mode of providing or utilizing (from the vendor's or the customer's standpoint, respectively) ERP functionality in the form of a service. An example of an on-demand system including ERP is SAP Business ByDesign. This system will be discussed in Sect. 11.2.3.

An on-demand ERP system is hosted by an ERP vendor or a service firm. ERP functionality is available on web pages, which the customer can open on any workplace with Internet access and a web browser. Figure 11.5 illustrates this situation. The on-demand ERP provider hosts the ERP system and makes its functionality available to authorized users on the Internet. For this purpose, a web front end is provided on a web server.

Corporate users, inside their company, are normally connected by a local area network (LAN). Any request for ERP functionality is therefore routed through a gateway to the public Internet to reach the provider's web server.

For the user, working with an on-demand ERP system is not much different from working with a system installed in-house—except perhaps for a more modern graphical user interface. The ERP system allows users to carry out their specific business processes using the company's data, even though the company's business rules, settings, and data are not stored in-house.

When the provider uses a virtualized technological infrastructure, for example, based on *cloud computing* (cf. Sect. 11.1.1) as assumed

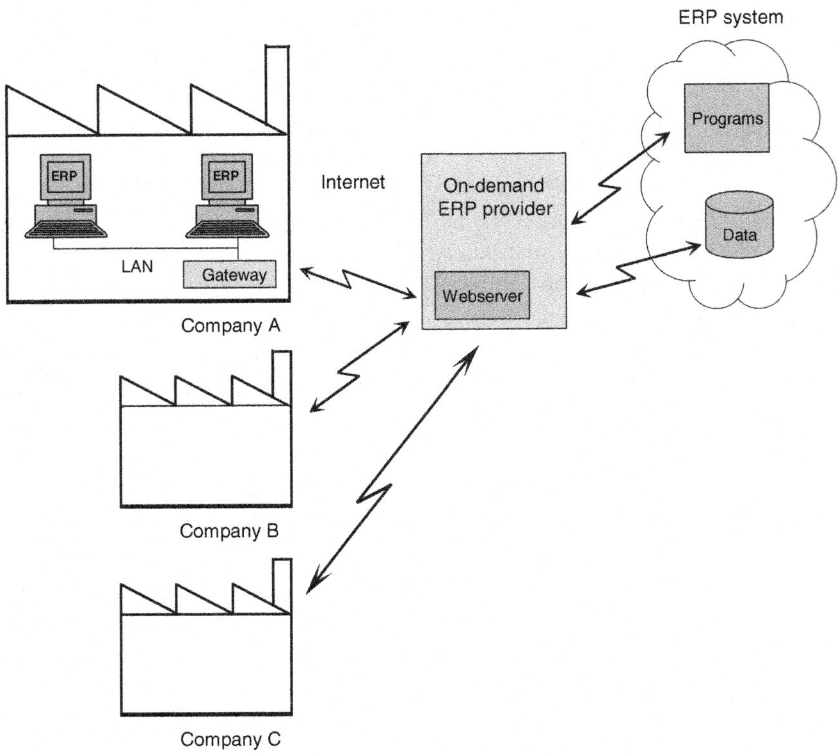

Fig. 11.5 ERP on-demand architecture

in Fig. 11.5, the user company will not even know exactly where their data is stored and where their processes are being executed. This situation requires a substantial amount of trust on the user company's side, in particular trust in the provider's solidity (Khan and Malluhi 2010).

Since virtualized infrastructures and external hosting are not in line with conventional business information processing, potential customers are hesitant to implement it. Despite its substantial cost advantages, on-demand ERP based on cloud computing is still in its infancy.

11.2.3 Case: SAP Business ByDesign

SAP Business ByDesign is an on-demand solution, in contrast to the SAP systems discussed so far—SAP ERP and SAP SCM. These are *on-premise* systems, meaning that they are usually installed on the company's premises. Servers, platforms, and the application software are operated inside the company. The company's IT personnel are in charge of running and administering the system and helping end users with technical problems.

A completely different approach was taken when *SAP Business ByDesign* was developed. (An often-used, yet not officially endorsed, abbreviation of Business ByDesign is *ByD*. In the interests of brevity, we will occasionally use this short form as well.)

Being an *on-demand* system means that the system's functionality is provided by SAP "on demand"—whenever and whatever the customers demand. With ByD, SAP is targeting the small and medium-size business market, including subsidiaries of large enterprises. The SAP business suite (including ERP and SCM) is primarily intended to be used by large companies.

Functionality ByD is not only an enterprise resource planning system, but it also covers many other business applications. An overview of the functionality is given in Fig. 11.6. As this overview shows, the main components are the following (Hufgard and Krüger 2012, pp. 68–85):

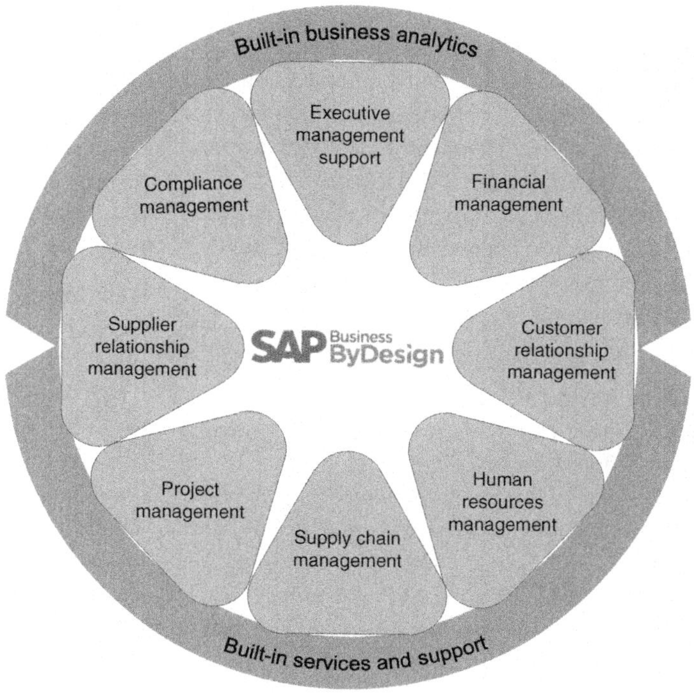

Fig. 11.6 SAP Business ByDesign functionality (Kagermann 2009)

- *Financial management*—supporting financial processes and accounting, using an integrated accounting system for managerial and financial accounting. A key feature is the use of different accounting schemes in one system (e.g., IAS, US-GAAP, HGB).
- *Customer relationship management*—providing tools that allow the company to strengthen the ties with their customers (e.g., providing a salesperson with a factsheet on the customer when he or she accepts a call from this customer).
- *Human resources management*—supporting time management, personnel administration and payroll, as well as interfaces for outsourcing payroll accounting.
- *Supply chain management*—comprising both supply chain planning and supply chain execution, including support for outsourcing of shipments to service companies.
- *Project management*—providing project planning, scheduling, and controlling tools, integrated with human-resources and supplier-relationship management, allowing the project manager to search for qualified project members inside and outside the company.
- *Supplier relationship management*—automating supplier-related processes such as selecting the best supply source, purchasing, incoming goods, invoice verification and payment, as well as supporting decision making when exceptions occur.
- *Compliance management*—allowing the company to implement their specific internal controlling processes and to obey up-to-date legal rules and regulations (being centrally hosted, any legal changes are implemented by SAP and thus immediately available in every company's ByD system). Since year-end closing is audited, a balance created by ByD can be directly submitted to the financial authorities.
- *Executive management support*—satisfying the information and analysis needs of the company's management and owners through predefined reports and analytics functionality.

Business analytics (business intelligence) features are not only available for executive management but also for lower management and other employees. These features are embedded in all modules of the system, supporting real-time analysis of transaction data. In ByD, this analysis is provided within the system and not through a separate business-intelligence system, as is the case in conventional solutions. Managers can use dashboards, key performance indicators, and other business-intelligence tools directly within Business ByDesign.

The core functionality of ByD is often extended and enhanced by add-ons created by the customer or supplied by SAP partner firms. This aspect will be discussed below.

Design Principles The essential *design principles* of Business ByDesign include user orientation, process automation, and the push principle in workflows (Faisst 2011a, p. 25).

In contrast to previous SAP systems, ByD is not function- or process oriented but *user oriented*. This is not to say that business processes are not supported. On the contrary, many business processes are implemented. The difference is that in ByD, the processes are *automated*, requesting user interference only when exceptions occur. Otherwise, default settings, or settings that were stipulated when the system was implemented, are employed to execute the process automatically.

User orientation means that the users set up their workplace the way they need it. This includes not only the system functionality required for their daily work but also common tools such as MS Excel, which can be connected with ByD in their work environment. Furthermore, users are able to create their own customized forms and reports.

The third key principle, in addition to user orientation and automation, is active user notification according to the *push principle*. This means that employees are proactively provided with tasks when a process workflow requires them to become involved. In contrast to this, conventional systems create tasks that the user has to fetch (pull principle). An employee working in purchasing, for example, has to remember to check the purchase requisitions to be processed herself. If she forgets, the task will not be completed until later.

The approach underlying the push principle is based on so-called *work centers*. A work center is a collection of functions needed by a role (which is filled by an employee) to complete the tasks the role is responsible for. An employee can be assigned to different work centers. This approach implies that an organizational model of the company composed of work centers has been defined, and authorizations and access rights have been connected with the work centers.

User Interface Since there is a strong focus on the user's workplace, various tools and solutions are available to customize the user interface.

On a desktop computer, the user interface is browser-based and composed of GUI (graphical user-interface) components that are reused throughout the system. With the help of so-called *patterns*, the available GUI components (e.g., work lists, quick start menus) can be combined into an arrangement called a *floor plan*, specifying where the components are placed on the user's screen (Hufgard and Krüger 2012, p. 58). Since the same patterns are applied throughout the system, it is easy for a user to learn and understand the general behavior of the system.

The user interface integrates access to the ByD functionality as well as to the extensions and enhancements, including (Faisst 2011a, p. 27):

- Forms and reports created by key users or by SAP partner firms, including MS Excel sheets
- Mashups, for example, Google Maps (to show a customer's location), route planner, web search, RSS news, etc.
- Third-party solutions, for example, credit card processing, shipping, or payroll service
- Add-ons for ByD, created with the same software technology as the Business ByDesign core (ByD Studio)

Mobility With increasing mobility in the business world and society in general, many business users are concerned about work-related issues not only when they are in their office but also when they are on the move or away from their normal place of work.

Providing access to business data and functionality from mobile devices—beyond office matters such as e-mail, calendars, and contacts—has been an issue in research and development since the beginning of the century. Taking into account that essential business information is maintained in ERP systems, mobile access to ERP has received particular attention. While the first comprehensive approaches to mobile ERP were developed in business informatics research [e.g., (Kurbel et al. 2003)], some ERP vendors have provided solutions for specific problems such as travel support and procurement.

Business ByDesign focuses on the needs of mobile business users (including managers on the move), supporting intuitive usage via touch screen. As smartphones and tablet PCs have become increasingly popular in the business world, ByD functionality has been made available on devices such as the iPhone, iPad, and Blackberry, as well as smartphones using Microsoft or Google software. Due to the model-based approach in the development of Business ByDesign, the user interface can be adapted more easily to diverse front end devices than would be possible using conventional software technology. ByD functionality can be accessed from mobile devices supporting Apple, Microsoft, RIM, and Google operating systems.

Figure 11.7 illustrates the alternative front ends, including a customized desktop user interface, an Excel report, and various smartphones displaying Business ByDesign content.

Cloud Strategy Business ByDesign is one of the constituents of SAP's strategy for exploiting the potential of cloud computing. This so-called "cloud strategy" comprises other on-demand solutions, a service-oriented provision of content and collaboration features, cloud operations, an e-commerce platform (called "commercial platform") as well as a development platform, and ecosystem for the extension of ByD. The development and commercial platforms are briefly outlined below.

The physical infrastructure of SAP's cloud consists of several large data centers run by SAP. This means that security and availability issues are handled by SAP and not by an anonymous cloud provider—mitigating the problem of trust in the cloud solution that user companies may otherwise feel exposed to (cf. Sect. 11.2.1).

IDE Through Platform-as-a-Service (PaaS): SAP adopted the PaaS concept mentioned above (cf. Sect. 11.2.1) to make a software development environment available to their partners. This environment, named *ByD Studio,* is based on MS Visual Studio, a powerful IDE (integrated development environment) for all types of software development in the Microsoft ecosystem.

As a development platform, ByD Studio is hosted by SAP. Partners can download a software development toolkit (SDK) and create add-ons to the core ByD system. In order to do so, developers use a scripting language ("SAP Business ByDesign Scripting Language") and resort to code libraries, the ByD core, patterns for GUI components and a user-interface design tool (Hufgard and Krüger 2012, p. 57–60).

When working in ByD Studio, developers can create add-ons with the same (or similar) look-and-feel as the core ByD system by employing the available patterns according to SAP's design guidelines. This approach to developing add-ons is expected to require substantially less time and cost compared to conventional application development. The time-to-market of an average add-on is about one month (Faisst 2011a, pp. 27–28).

Commercial Platform: An innovative feature of SAP's on-demand solutions is the so-called *SAP commercial platform* (Faisst 2011c). As Fig. 11.8 indicates, partners offer add-ons (usually functionality that is otherwise not available in Business ByDesign) on this platform and potential customers can buy the add-ons. This is similar to an "app store" in the smartphone ecosystem (e.g., Apple iTunes—http://www.apple.com/itunes), where customers can download apps (i.e., small application programs) provided by a large developer community. However, ERP add-ons are more "demanding" than consumer apps, as compatibility with other ERP components has to be checked and ensured.

Despite the differences between ERP add-ons and smartphone apps, the business model supported by the platform is similar. Customers download the add-ons, which are installed immediately and are ready for use ("plug and play").

Fig. 11.7 Frontends for SAP Business ByDesign (Faisst 2011b)

Invoicing the customer and paying the vendor are handled by SAP.

Many ERP-related problems are too complex to be covered by ready-made apps, requiring expertise, discussion, and customization. Therefore, add-ons traded on the platform tend to provide solutions to simpler problems. In order to help the customer make an informed purchase, details of the add-on are provided on the platform, including selected scenarios visualizing how it works.

Figure 11.8 illustrates the role of the commercial platform. Solution partners (on the left) use the development platform to develop add-ons, which are certified and published. Customers using Business ByDesign (on the right) search the app store and subscribe to a solution, provided they find what they are looking for. When the deal is closed, the add-on is deployed, and billing and payment are initiated.

On-demand solutions such as Business ByDesign provide a number of *advantages* over on-premise solutions, including:

- *Time-to-operation:* Implementation projects take less time. The software can go live in the company's operations shortly after installation.
- *Subscription model:* Initial investment is much lower due to a pay-per-use payment scheme.
- *Expandability:* The basic functionality can easily be extended and enhanced, both through capabilities for end users and add-ons provided for plug-and-play download.

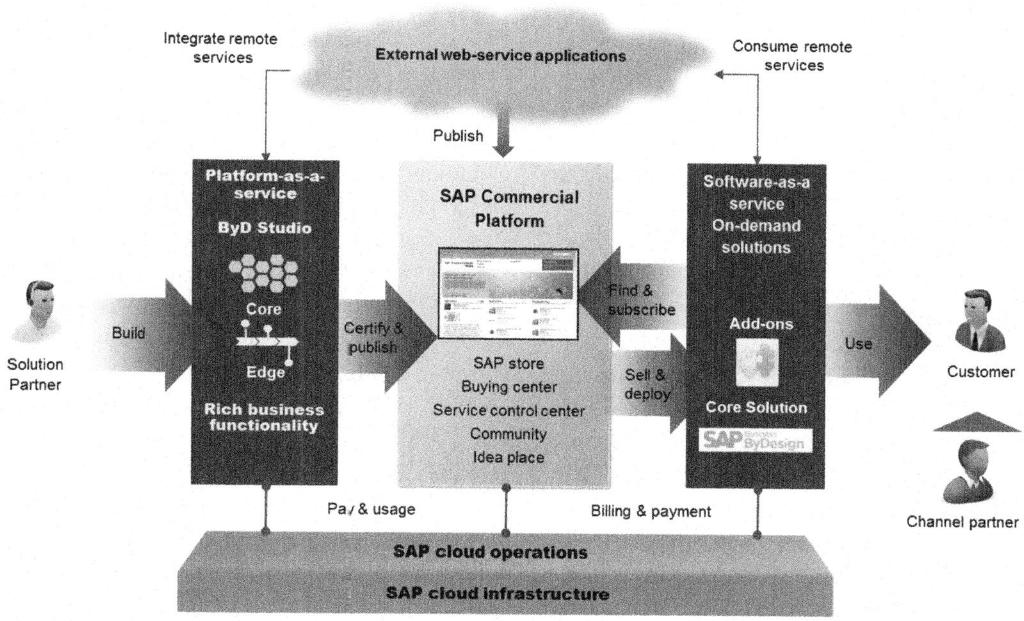

Fig. 11.8 SAP commercial platform (Faisst 2011a, p. 28)

- *Up-to-date:* Because only the provider hosts the software (software-as-a-service model), it is centrally updated. Customers do not need to worry about new versions and releases.
- *Scalability:* When the on-demand system is operated on a cloud infrastructure, additional requirements regarding computing power, storage capabilities, number of users served, etc., can be easily satisfied. (The same is true in the opposite direction, when the company is shrinking instead of growing.)

11.3 Alternative Approaches

In this section, two approaches to providing enterprise resource planning functionality are discussed: open-source ERP, an approach to avoid paying license fees to a vendor, and federated ERP, an approach to connect different ERP systems.

11.3.1 Open-Source ERP

ERP systems are also available as open-source software (OSS). "Open source" means that the program code (source code) can be used by anyone free of charge.

OSS is often developed around a nucleus—a software system—that was initially created by an organization or individual and then made available to whoever is interested in the code. Many developers around the world revise and add to the code. Some open-source systems started out from hobbyist programming by individuals who wanted to do good for the world. Other OSS was initially created by a professional organization and later made available to the rest of the world.

The primary reason why organizations make code available free of charge is normally not altruism. While they do not earn money from license fees, they do earn from services and customized software based on the OSS.

This is particularly true for open-source ERP systems. The need for "service" around the bare software (e.g., in implementation projects and customization) was already discussed in Chap. 6. Implementing any ERP system in an organization requires plenty of consulting services and customization work. Later on, when the system is in operation, external support is also needed. Many user companies are not able to administer an ERP system themselves. As a consequence, software and service firms create their revenue from service, support, and customization, even though the software as such does not require the user company to pay a license fee.

The development of open-source software has changed over the years, evolving from anarchic to structured (which has been labeled FOSS versus OSS 2.0):

- *FOSS* ("free and open-source software") refers to software created by many volunteers (or what has been called a "crowd of anarchist programmers") who collaborate over the Internet. The basic ideas underlying this approach go back to Eric S. Raymond, who formulated 19 rather idealistic principles for FOSS. The first one, for example, states "Every good work of software starts by scratching a developer's personal itch" (Raymond 2000). Since many people are involved in the development, FOSS advocates point out that errors will be found and fixed quickly, thus increasing the software quality.
- *OSS 2.0* is used for software created by professional organizations in a more rigorous way. When software firms and commercial organizations enter the open-source market, they pursue strategic goals such as gaining a competitive advantage or adversely affecting competitors (Fitzgerald 2006, p. 591). Their goal is not to scratch a personal itch but to make money. Companies sometimes make formerly proprietary software open-source or sponsor the development of new open-source software.

Open-source ERP systems tend to fall into the second category. The reason for this is that enterprise resource planning requires not only software but also a good deal of service and support. For software and consulting firms, it can be attractive to give away the software for free and create revenue from service and support. Another business model is to help clients (user companies) with open-source ERP software that was developed by someone else.

A number of open-source ERP systems are listed in Fig. 11.9. The list is sorted alphabetically, because comprehensive overviews of market shares and installation numbers are not available. Some of the older and widely distributed systems have "spin-offs," that is, new open-source systems based on a previous system. Examples include Adempiere (based on Compiere), Opentaps (based on Apache OFBiz), and Tryton (based on OpenERP).

It is worth noting that most open-source ERP systems are not really comparable with proprietary ERP systems and by far not as powerful as the systems listed in Fig. 4.21. Some of the systems in Fig. 11.9 just cover selected areas of ERP and lack the rest (Schatz et al. 2011, pp. 19–53). For example, WebERP basically provides support for purchasing, sales, and accounting. SQL-Ledger, as the name suggests, specializes in accounting, whereas AvERP is focused on manufacturing.

11.3.2 Vision: Federated ERP

The vision of "federated ERP" (FERP) was proposed by Brehm and Marx Gómez (2007). This approach is based on the assumptions that (1) different ERP systems have strengths and weaknesses in different areas, and (2) while some of a company's requirements may be best served by a component of system A, others would be better served by components of B and C.

The authors based their assumptions on an empirical study in which they found that small- and medium-size German enterprises on average run four business systems in parallel. Not surprisingly, 47 % observe serious redundancy problems (Brehm and Marx Gómez 2008, p. 29). The reason for this is usually that the various systems are not well integrated.

The FERP vision basically demands that a company can use features of different ERP systems as if they were provided by one ERP system. This requires ERP components from different vendors to be integrated in such a way as to appear as one system to the user.

Figure 11.10 illustrates the collaboration of various ERP components using a simplified production process that is triggered by a customer order. Material requirement planning is

Fig. 11.9 Open-source ERP systems

ERP System	Website
ADempiere	www.adempiere.org
Apache OFBiz	ofbiz.apache.org
AvERP	www.averp.de
Compiere	www.compiere.com
ERP5	www.erp5.com
IntarS	www.intars.com
OpenBravo	www.openbravo.com
OpenERP	www.openerp.com
OpenPro	www.openpro.com
Opentaps	www.opentaps.org
SQL-Ledger ERP	www.sql-ledger.com
Tryton	www.tryton.org
WebERP	www.weberp.org
xTuple ERP	www.xtuple.com

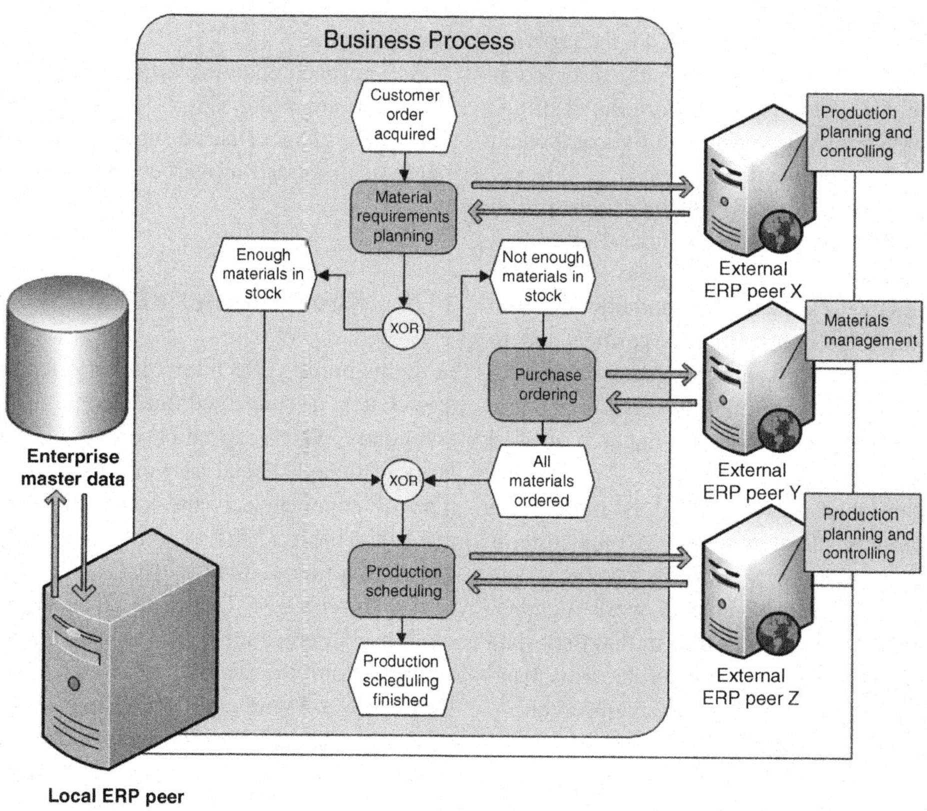

Fig. 11.10 ERP peers involved in a business process (Brehm and Marx Gómez 2008, p. 39)

performed with the help of a component of ERP system X, but for the purchasing tasks, a different ERP system (Y) is employed. Production scheduling seems to be best served by ERP system Z. In this approach, the various ERP nodes are called "peers," because it is assumed that the underlying network connecting the nodes is a peer-to-peer (P2P) network.

Obviously, this approach can only work if there is a coordinating mechanism supervising the collaboration and handling the data exchange with the external systems. This task is assigned to an in-house component called the "local ERP peer" in the figure.

A federated ERP system thus consists of a local base system and a set of application components provided by various ERP vendors. The base system executes the company's processes, invoking services from the different vendors in the respective workflows.

The application components are expected to be available as *services* (cf. Sect. 11.1), implying standardized interfaces. Ideally, the user company would be able to choose from the offerings of several vendors in order to get the component that best suits their needs.

Implementing the FERP vision requires a lot of standardization and agreements on interfaces among the partners involved. Figure 11.11 illustrates these needs showing a hypothetical system architecture. The consortium of partners has to agree on the standards and interfaces so that the components can work together and make the system appear as one system under a unified graphical user interface.

As mentioned above, FERP is more of a vision than a practical approach. All the systems involved must support uniform interfaces and exchange formats to be able to work together. Moreover, they must be similar in that their data and process models are compatible. This basically requires the systems to be developed anew. In order to do so, up-front agreements between a number of partners are needed. This means that a consortium willing to collaborate and develop exchangeable ERP components has to be set up. It remains to be seen whether such an effort can be successful.

Taking into consideration that (1) the development of an ERP system requires a substantial investment and (2) many ERP systems are already available on the market, an alternative to developing from scratch would be to connect existing systems in order to achieve a "federation." This can be done by equipping the systems with additional interfaces to be used by other systems.

A software engineering approach supporting this idea is the so-called *façade pattern*. According to this pattern, the program code is encapsulated with the help of a "façade," providing a well-defined interface through which the functionality of the system can be accessed.

Creating a façade on top of an existing system is still a lot of work. This is due to the fact that all of the system's functions that should be available to other systems must be captured and their interfaces must be formally described. However, building a façade on top of a software system is still less effort than creating the entire system from scratch.

An approach enabling different ERP systems to collaborate using a web-services façade—in the context of agent-based supply chain management—is discussed in Kurbel (2006).

11.4 The "Internet of Things"

In the beginning, the Internet connected computers. Later it connected the people using the computers, which can be observed by the popularity of today's social networks. Another recent type of connection is the connection between material objects. This is sometimes referred to as the "Internet of Things" (IoT).

The *Internet of Things* is considered to be of high significance for the businesses, the economy, and the society in general. In a report for the US government, the IoT was named one of six disruptive technologies that may have an impact on US interests out to 2,025, creating the potential to enhance or degrade US national power (NIC 2008). (The other five technologies are biogerontechnology, energy storage materials, biofuels and bio-based chemicals, clean coal technologies, and service robotics.)

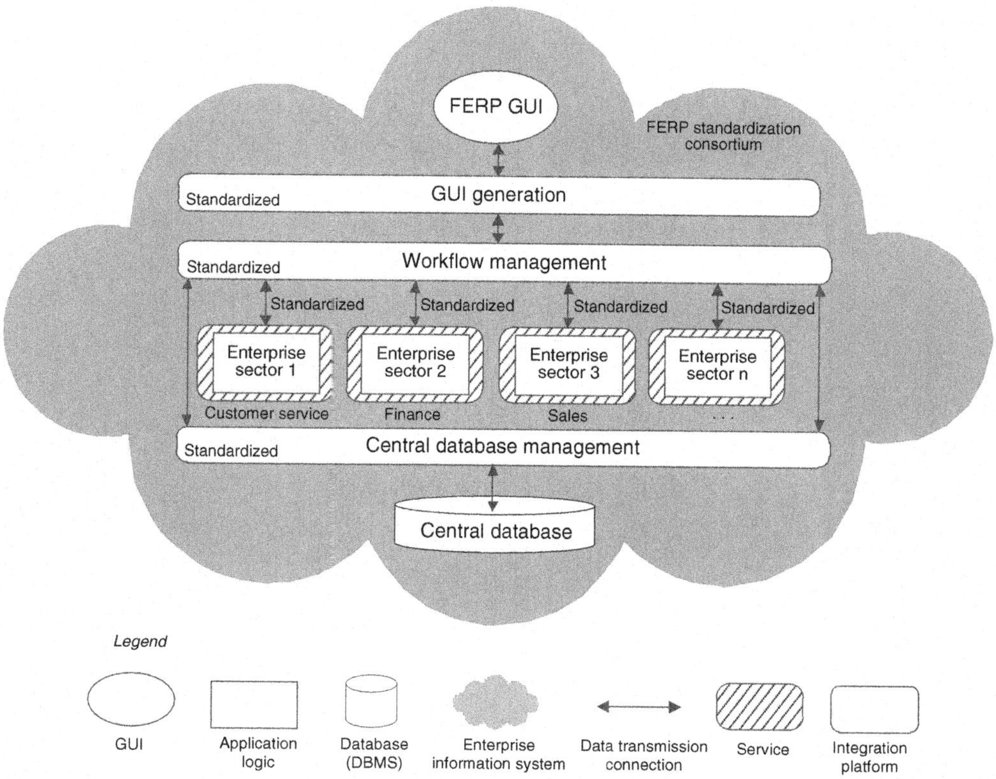

Fig. 11.11 Architecture of a federated ERP system (Brehm and Marx Gómez 2007, p. 6)

A European Commission roadmap looks even farther ahead, outlining a vision of the future Internet. In this vision, the IoT is just one part, in addition to the *Internet of media* (IoM, supporting multiplayer mobile games, digital cinema, and virtual worlds), the *Internet of services* (IoS, improving cooperation between service providers and consumers), and the conventional Internet of computers (Guillemin et al. 2009, p. 7).

The Internet of Things became possible when products (or actually any kind of material object) turned "smart." This means that objects are equipped with electronic devices (i.e., very small low-end computers) allowing them, among other things, to communicate via the Internet. Instead of humans entering, forwarding, or producing information about the objects, the objects do this themselves.

The technology on which the Internet of Things is based enables advancements in everyday life as well as in business and, in particular, in the fields this book is centered around—enterprise resource planning and supply chain management.

11.4.1 Background and Technology

The vision laid down in the European Commission roadmap is the IoT connecting things (and people), any time, any place, and with anything and anyone, using any path/network and any service. This vision is summarized in Fig. 11.12.

What is meant by "things," i.e., what features of "things" are relevant for the IoT, is spelled out in detail in the table presented in Fig. 11.13. While many of these features are available today, others are still subject to research and development.

A *definition* based on the characteristics of things listed in Fig. 11.13 is as follows: The

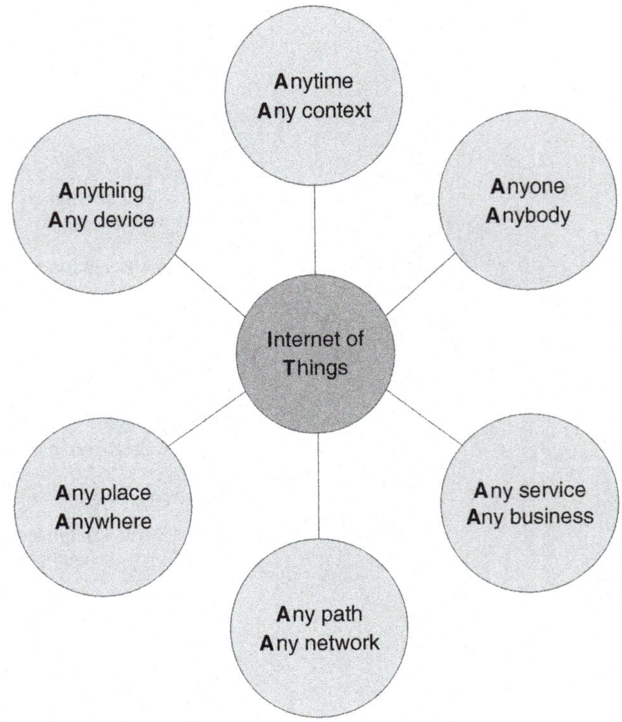

Fig. 11.12 Aspects of IoT connections (Guillemin et al. 2009, p. 8)

Internet of Things is "… a dynamic global network infrastructure with self configuring capabilities based on standard and interoperable communication protocols where physical and virtual 'things' have identities, physical attributes and virtual personalities and use intelligent interfaces, and are seamlessly integrated into the information network" (Guillemin et al. 2009, p. 6).

To elucidate the *main differences* between the Internet of Things and the conventional Internet, we refer to six aspects presented by Fleisch (2010, pp. 3–5):

1. Invisible versus flashy hardware: In the Internet, the end nodes ("nerve endings") are full-blown computers, ranging from workstations to smartphones, with regular access to the public power supply network. In the IOT, the "nerve endings" are very small, often invisible electronic devices with low energy consumption. Their functionality is limited compared to Internet computers, and they usually cannot interact directly with human beings.
2. Trillions versus billions of network nodes: It is estimated that, today, several billion devices are connected to the Internet. In contrast to this number, the total number of "things" that could reasonably be connected on the IoT reaches trillions. A network with trillions of nodes poses different requirements than a network with "only" billions.
3. Last-mile bottleneck versus highway: On the Internet, not only the long-distance connections but also the "last mile," that is, the connection to the individual end point where the user is, have become very fast (in the range of megabits/s). In contrast to this, the speed on the last mile to an RFID (radio frequency identification) tag is slow (in the range of kilobits/s).
4. Lack of standards versus global identification and addressing: On the Internet, there are globally accepted identification and addressing schemes (e.g., IP and MAC addresses). However, they cannot be employed for IoT devices in most cases because they require too much energy. Since standards are lacking, many vendor-specific solutions exist for the last mile. This prevents objects from being globally identified and addressed.
5. Machine-centric versus user-centric: On the Internet, the largest share of the functionality

Domain	Characteristics
Domain 1 - Fundamental characteristics	"Things" can be "real world entities" or "virtual entities" "Things" have identity; there are means for automatically identifying them "Things" are environmentally safe "Things" (and their virtual representations) respect the privacy, security and safety of other "things" or people with which they interact "Things" use protocols to communicate with each other and the infrastructure "Things" are involved in the information exchange between real/physical, digital and virtual worlds
Domain 2 – Common characteristics of all things, even the most basic (applies to all higher classes too)	"Things" can use services that act as interfaces to "things" "Things" would be competing with other "things" on resources, services and subject to selective pressures "Things" may have sensors attached, thus they can interact with their environment
Domain 3 - Characteristics of social things (applies to all higher classes too)	"Things" can communicate with other "things", computing devices and with people "Things" can collaborate to create groups or networks "Things" can initiate communication
Domain 4 - Characteristics of considerate autonomous things (applies to all higher classes too)	"Things" can do many tasks autonomously "Things" can negotiate, understand and adapt to their environment "Things" can extract patterns from the environment or to learn from other "things" "Things" can take decisions through their reasoning capabilities "Things" can selectively evolve and propagate information
Domain 5 - Characteristics of things that are capable of self-replication or control	"Things" can create, manage and destroy other "things"

Fig. 11.13 IoT relevant characteristics of "things" (Guillemin et al. 2009, p. 9)

is targeted toward human users, for example, the World Wide Web (WWW), e-mail, chat, and electronic shopping. On the IoT, devices usually interact directly, without human intervention. If human users are involved, they normally communicate through a computer.

6. Focus on sensing versus on communication: While the Internet brought about a breakthrough in human communication and interaction, the IoT is about "sensing" the physical world. Sensing enables measuring, which in turn facilitates managing the matters sensed and measured.

The Internet of Things imposes a number of *technological requirements* that are different from, or additional to, those of the Internet of computers (i.e., the conventional Internet). The following requirements are worth noting (Fleisch 2010, p. 6):

On the Internet of computers, common mechanisms to *identify and address* the nodes include DNS (domain name system), IP (Internet protocol), and MAC (media access control) addresses. On many IoT-end devices, these mechanisms cannot be used because they require more computing power than the devices have. Therefore, alternative ways of identifying and addressing the sensors have to be employed.

Another challenge is *bridging the "last mile"* and connecting it to the Internet. The communication technology on the side of the end nodes must be wireless, robust, and energy efficient. Sometimes it is also necessary that the technology enables security features and allows

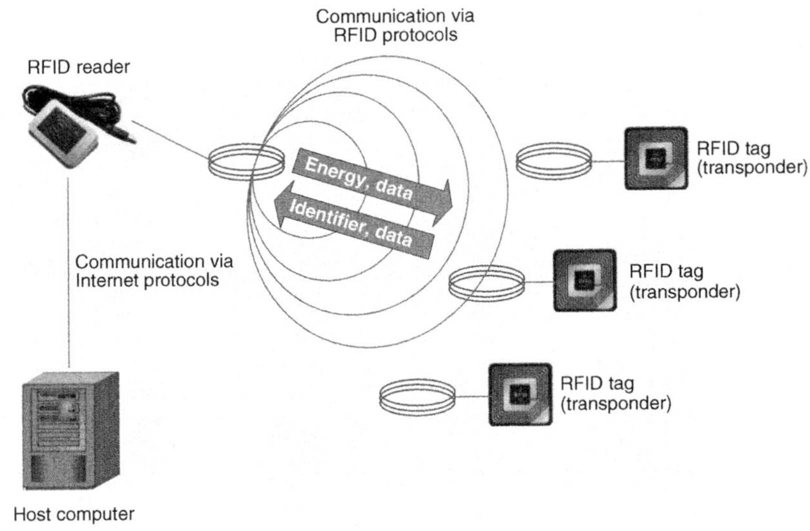

Fig. 11.14 Components of an RFID system

measuring the distance (ranging) and localizing the object.

A *gateway to the Internet* is required because long-distance transport of information coming from an end node is normally based on the conventional Internet. This means that the collected information, which is transported from the end node with the help of IoT or vendor-specific technologies, has to be converted. The first step required is establishing a connection with the object's "homepage" (i.e., the place where "master data" of the object are stored). To be able to do so, the IP address has to be looked up so that information on the homepage is available for further processing.

Radio Frequency Identification The major IoT technology applied on the end-device side is *radio frequency identification (RFID)*. The concepts of the Internet of Things actually do not depend on RFID, but this technology is nowadays the most common.

An *RFID system* has basically three types of components: transponders, readers, and host computer. This is illustrated in Fig. 11.14.

A *transponder* is the device that actually carries the data. It consists of a microchip and a microwave antenna. A typical microchip is small (less than half a millimeter) and does not have a controller or a power supply (battery) of its own. It is not very powerful, just capable of storing a few bytes of data. The antenna connects the chip via microwaves to a reading and transmitting device. Most transponders are passive, that is, they are only activated when they are supplied with electric power from outside.

Transponders are usually mounted on a substrate and covered by plastic or other material, depending on where and how they are to be used. In this form, they are often referred to as *RFID tags* (or smart tags, smart labels) because they are tagged to physical objects such as a single product, a box, or a pallet.

An *RFID reader*, also known as an *interrogator*, is a device that sends and receives radio waves via one or more antennas. The radio waves carry not only data but also small amounts of electrical current that are used to power the RFID tags. In this way, transponders are activated and can start to work.

The RFID reader basically interrogates a transponder about its identity ("Who are you?"). The transponder then replies with an answer such as "I am product XYZ from company ABC" (Winkler 2006). Another benefit of radio waves is that they do not require a line of sight between the tag and the reader. This means, for example, that tags inside a container can also be identified.

Fig. 11.15 RFID portal

An important capability of RFID technology is *bulk reading*. Using an RFID portal, for example, many items can be read and separately identified at the same time. Suppose a pallet full of cartons, each one filled with a dozen of items, passes through a loading dock which is equipped with RFID reading capabilities. Bulk reading means that all items of the "bulk" are reliably recognized when it is pulled through the portal, even though the items are packed inside other handling units (see Fig. 11.15).

This is, by the way, an important improvement over barcode technology. When barcodes are used, each item needs to pass the barcode reader individually and visibly.

A *host computer* is needed to process the data received from the reader. The host computer will either interpret the data with the help of special RFID software or scan and route it to some other computer where the processing will take place (Holloway 2006).

RFID tags as described above are *passive*, because they only respond to requests when they are questioned by a reader and under current. Since they have no power supply of their own, they can only communicate over a short distance (several meters). Passive tags are inexpensive, which makes them attractive for tracking low-cost items.

Active RFID tags are tags that have a battery. They are more powerful than passive tags but also much more expensive. Active tags broadcast signals to the reader themselves, covering distances up to several hundred meters or even kilometers. Due to the cost, active tags are mainly used to track high-value goods such as vehicles and large containers of goods, for example, shipboard containers.

In a business context, it is important that products (and other objects) can be identified uniquely, not only within the company but also across supply networks. Therefore, *standardization* plays an important role in the identification of objects.

With this aim in mind, *EPCglobal* developed a standardized "electronic product code" (EPC). EPCglobal is a not-for-profit organization that continued the product-code standardization efforts of MIT's *Auto-ID Center*. EPCglobal is also a part of *GS1*, an association developing standards that are intended to improve the efficiency and visibility of supply chains globally and across sectors (http://www.gs1.org).

The electronic product code (EPC) is similar to a barcode, containing information about the type of unit (e.g., item, carton), manufacturer (or vendor) and article number, plus a serial number used to uniquely identify an item within the classification established by the previous entries.

A possible way of processing EPCs is outlined in Fig. 11.16. In a real application, billions of individual EPCs on RFID tags may exist. Taking the sheer volume into account, the data created by these tags are not passed directly to the business systems involved but buffered with the help of a middleware (Lewis 2004, p. 24). This middleware (called *savant* in Auto-ID terminology) manages the readers, processes the raw data, and directs it to the respective information system, for example, to an ERP, SCM, or inventory management system. Processing includes the detection and removal of reading errors. Such errors often occur in real applications, in particular with bulk reading.

Savants also initiate queries to a so-called *object naming service (ONS)* in order to be able to retrieve product information from the ERP system or other systems involved. The ONS has similar tasks as the DNS (domain name system)

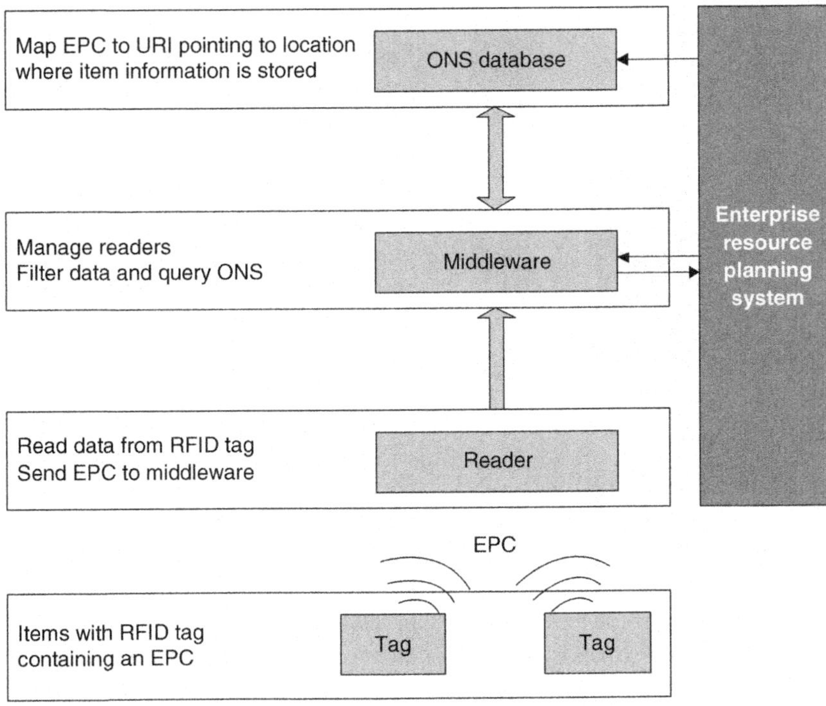

Fig. 11.16 EPC processing including middleware

on the Internet. It matches an EPC to a place on the network [i.e., a URI—uniform resource identifier (W3C 2006)] where information about the product is stored. A savant can then retrieve the product information and pass it on to the business system that needs it for further processing, for example, a tracking and tracing (T&T) system or an SCM system.

11.4.2 RFID Applications in Business

Applications of RFID technology are as manifold as there are business areas. In this section, we present some typical scenarios, in particular applications that are related to enterprise resource planning and supply chain management.

As the Internet of Things refers to physical objects, typical applications involve tasks in which material things are stored or moved, such as inventory management and logistics.

Inventory Management If all articles (in a supermarket) or parts (in a factory warehouse) are tagged with RFID labels, they can be automatically supervised, counted, and moved. Additional activities such as accounting and replenishment can be triggered automatically.

The supermarket manager, for example, is provided with information about the products, their state, storage conditions, expiration date, remaining stock, and changes in the products' locations (Presser 2011, p. 26). In addition, the number of units taken off the shelf is recorded, allowing a program to produce statistics on which products are favored by the customers.

If the shopping carts are also equipped with RFID transponders, the customers' buying behavior can be monitored and evaluated. For example, the customers' decision to buy a product (or not) can be correlated with the fact that they pick up the product or with the time they spend in front of the product shelf. All monitoring and evaluation can be done automatically, without any manual work.

Supply Chain Tracking The following example illustrating how the EPC network is intended

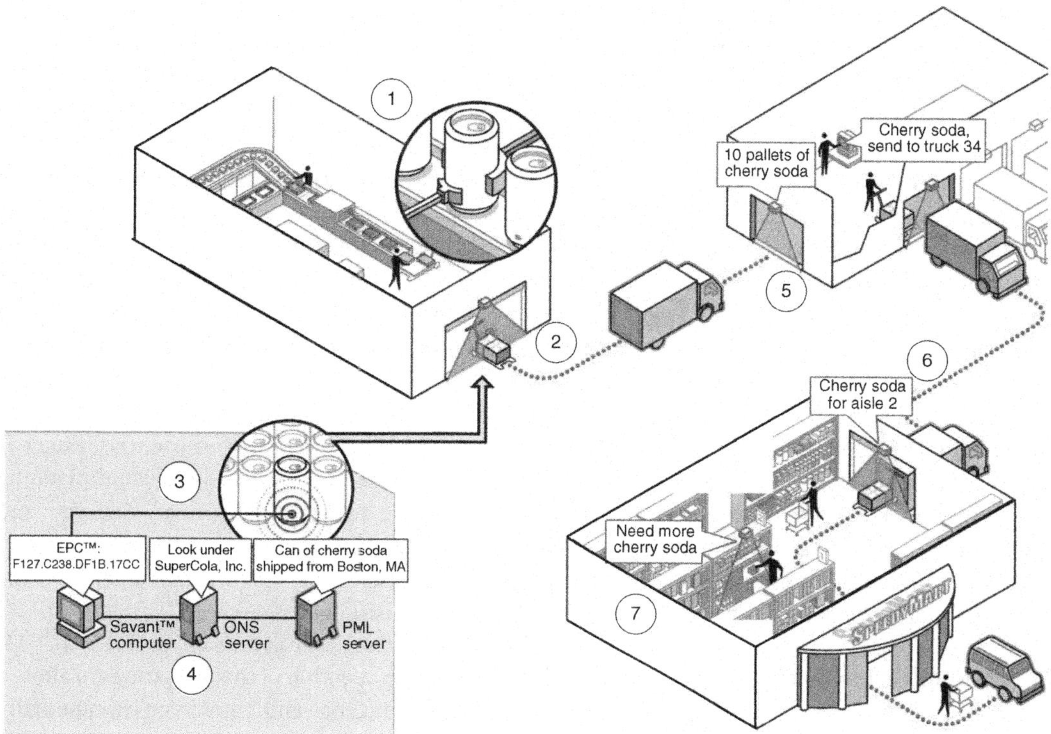

Fig. 11.17 EPC processing in the supply chain (Auto-ID 2002)

to work was originally presented by the Auto-ID Center at MIT. It has since been reproduced and adapted by many authors. In the following, we compile various aspects of the example from Auto-ID (2002, 2003), and Lewis (2004, p. 25). The case uses soda production, shipping, and delivery to a supermarket, as illustrated in Fig. 11.17.

The supply chain starts at the soda producer's, continues at a distribution center (warehouse), and ends at the supermarket shelves:

1. At the producer's assembly-packaging line, each item has an RFID tag with a unique EPC stored in its memory. Cases and pallets also carry their own unique tags
2. As pallets leave the manufacturer's site, an RFID reader positioned at the loading-dock door beams a radio signal that activates the tags
3. The tags broadcast their individual EPCs to the reader, which rapidly switches them on and off in sequence until all are read
4. The reader sends the EPCs to a computer running middleware software (savant). This middleware sends the EPC over the Internet to an ONS database, which produces an address. The ONS matches the EPC to another server where comprehensive information about the product is stored
5. At the distribution center, the unloading area is equipped with an RFID reader. There is no need to open packages and examine their contents. The middleware provides a cargo list, and the pallet is quickly routed to the appropriate truck
6. As soon as the shipment arrives at the supermarket, retail systems are updated to include every item. In this way, stores can locate their entire inventory automatically, accurately, and at low cost
7. Reader-enabled "smart shelves" can automatically order more products from the system and therefore keep stock at cost-effective and efficient levels.

The *efficiency* of this supply chain is much higher than in a supply chain without RFID (Auto-ID 2003):

- The *manufacturer* has up-to-date information and knows an item's destination as it comes off the line. If an incident involving a defect or tampering arises, only the affected products need to be recalled.
- In the *distribution center,* the warehouse manager is able to quickly route shipments to the right place because he or she can look up what is in the warehouse and on every truck.
- On the *retail floor*, when a customer takes a product from a "smart shelf," replenishment is automatically ordered. In this way, stock people and distributors can keep the shelves full all the time.
- The supermarket's *back office* knows exactly what is on the shelf and in the stockroom as well as what is rolling off the truck. The need for costly buffer stock is reduced.

More Examples From the vast number of RFID applications on the Internet of Things, we briefly outline 3 of 25 future scenarios presented in the "IoT Comic Book" (Presser 2011). This is an illustrative brochure containing innovative scenarios for the Internet of Things, compiled within a research program of the European Commission.

- *Intelligent shopping* (Presser 2011, p. 24): In this scenario, products are augmented with multimedia information that is transferred from a server to the customer's device. For example, a supermarket customer pointing their mobile phone at a product gets additional information about the product such as origin, expiry date, and alerts ("this product contains traces of nuts"). Passing nearby products, the customer may get personalized advertisements from the store's ERP system, considering their profile as well as their recent buying behavior. Whenever the customer places a product in the shopping cart, the bill is updated. Checkout and payment then happen automatically, to avoid lengthy lines at checkout.
- *Smart orchard* (Presser 2011, p. 40): In this scenario, IoT infrastructures are employed to improve agricultural production. Managing a farm requires various activities that can be supported by IoT applications. This is sometimes referred to as "precision agriculture." For efficient farming, the manager must always have a detailed picture of weather, crop, and soil conditions. If the farm is equipped with sensors that monitor the conditions of the crops (duration and level of sunlight, temperature, humidity, level of rainfall, wind speed, etc.), the state of the plants (size, humidity in the ground, ripeness of the fruits—size, color, sugar level, etc.), the workers' position in the area, and the equipment in use, the farmer is able to make better decisions when planning upcoming activities. Moreover, data gathered by these sensor networks can also be sold to organizations such as weather agencies, the crop industry, or researchers.
- *Smart urban waste management* (Presser 2011, p. 4): The intention of this scenario is to allow a more efficient and more environmentally friendly way of collecting waste. This can be achieved by identifying and emptying bins and containers when they are close to their fill level but not overflowing. "Intelligent" bins notify people approaching with their garbage what the current load level is, advising them which bin to use. Garbage collection can be optimized, for example, in terms of choosing optimal routes based on fill levels. Empty bins are bypassed and full bins are emptied.

The list of Internet of Things applications compiled in the IoT brochure exhibits many more scenarios, including smart urban planning, smart urban environment, smart renewable energy, help for Alzheimer's disease, continuous care, emergency response, intelligent commuters, smart meters, secure mobile payment, smart events, and home automation.

The last mentioned scenario, *home automation,* includes devices and equipment that are monitored by a "home central control" (HCC) (Presser 2011, p. 32). This tool controls access, energy, heating, and more according to the residents' profile, environmental conditions, and prices. The HCC triggers the heating system by combining data from outdoor and indoor temperature, weather forecast from the Internet, and user preferences. It recognizes which appliances (washing machine, dishwasher, water heater, heating system, etc.) are turned on at a given time. Based on this information, it synchronizes the appliances to ensure the best energy efficiency, taking into account the pricing structure of the utility companies.

One appliance that has been subject to research for many years is the "intelligent refrigerator" (e.g., Nayak et al. 2011). It is named "intelligent" because it knows what is in it and is able to act and react based on this knowledge. Items entered into or removed from the refrigerator are automatically recorded by an RFID reader. Additional information about the products (e.g., expiration date, usage instructions) can be obtained via Internet from the product's homepage as mentioned above.

Using its "knowledge," the intelligent refrigerator is able to monitor the stock of the items inside and issue warnings when an expiration date is approaching. The idea is that the refrigerator will automatically place electronic replenishment orders with the supermarket whenever stock levels are below predefined thresholds.

In addition to inventory management, the intelligent refrigerator can automatically modify its power consumption to minimize energy bills, diagnose faults, and inform the service center what the problem is. It is worth noting that commercial products with these capabilities already exist (Economist 2011).

Outlook: An RFID-Enabled Milk Supply Chain To conclude this section with a preview of what may (or may not) be just down the road, we look at an example of this technology applied to tracking milk through an RFID-enabled supply chain. This example was presented by Ari Juels under the title "2030: A week in the life of a milk carton" (Juels 2006). It starts with Bessie, a happy cow, as illustrated in Fig. 11.18.

- April 30, 2030: RFID-tagged cow "Bessie" produces milk.
- April 30, 2030: The milk is transferred to an RFID-tagged tank. The cow's identity and milking time are recorded in the tank-tag database.
- May 1, 2030: The RFID portal on a truck records loading of refrigeration tanks. The truck also has active RFID (+ GPS) to track the geographic location and an RFID transponder to pay tolls.
- May 2, 2030: A chemical-treatment record for the milk barrel is written to the database. The record shows that compensatory sugars have been added to the milk, because Bessie's herd had consumed mustard grass.
- May 3, 2030: The milk is packaged in RFID-tagged cartons. A milk pedigree is recorded in the database associated with the carton tag.
- May 4, 2030: The RFID portal at the supermarket's loading dock records the arrival of the carton.
- May 5, 2030: A smart shelf records arrival of the carton in the customer area.
- May 5, 2030, 09:30: The smart shelf records removal of milk.
- May 5, 2030, 09:53: A point-of-sale terminal records a sale of milk (to Alice).
- May 5, 2030, 11:03: Alice's refrigerator records the arrival of milk.
- May 6, 2030, 14:05: Alice's refrigerator records removal of milk. It looks up the database-recorded pedigree and displays: "Woodstock, Vermont, grade A, light pasteurization, artisanal, USDA organic, breed: Jersey, genetic design #81726."
- May 6, 2030, 18:07: Alice's smart home warns the domestic robot that milk has been left out of the refrigerator for more than four hours.
- May 6, 2030, 21:09: Alice's refrigerator records the replacement of milk.
- May 7, 2030, 05:30: The domestic robot uses the RFID tag to locate milk in the refrigerator and refills a baby bottle.
- May 7, 2030, 23:57: The recycling center scans the RFID tag on the carton and directs the carton to the paper-brick recycling substation.

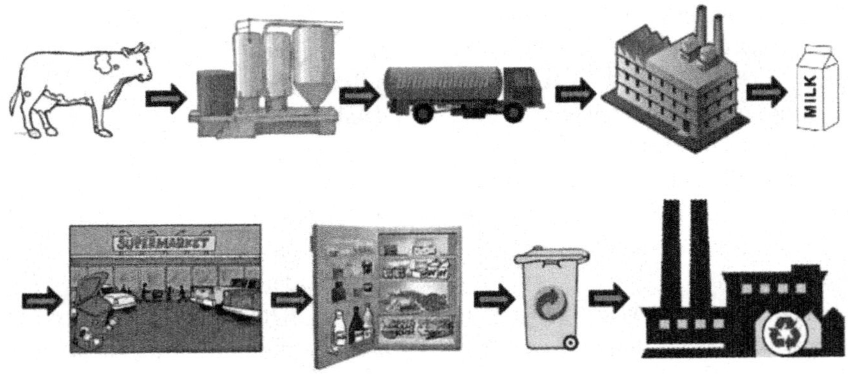

Fig. 11.18 RFID-enabled supply chain for milk (Juels 2006)

11.4.3 Business Benefits and Challenges

As indicated by the applications described above, RFID technology and the Internet of Things offer a high potential for improving business activities in general, and enterprise resource planning and supply chain management in particular. On the other hand, concerns about the technology and problems associated with it have been expressed by researchers and the general public. In this section, the benefits and challenges are discussed.

Benefits over the Product Life Cycle We start with the *benefits* that can be achieved over the life cycle of a product, touching on several areas of enterprise resource planning and supply chain management. The list of benefits presented below is based on a comprehensive overview by Ilie-Zudor and Kemény, who discussed the potential of RFID on the Internet of Things over the phases of a typical product life cycle (Ilie-Zudor and Kemény 2009). Figure 11.19 summarizes their findings.

Most benefits are at the level of tracking-based services, in particular tracking individual items and storing the tracking information in a database. The authors point out that more advanced item-level services are needed. When several companies are involved in a supply chain, item information has to be shared with the partners across company borders, especially if the same item identity needs to span several life-cycle stages (Ilie-Zudor and Kemény 2009, p. 217).

General Business Benefits Increased productivity and reduced costs are often attributed to RFID technology as the most important general business benefits, but they are not the only ones. Based on an analysis of business practices, Holloway identified eight major benefits (Holloway 2006):

1. *Improved productivity and cost avoidance:* Identifying items by RFID makes processes more efficient, because tasks such as receiving and putting away and picking and shipping goods require substantially less time and cost.
2. *Decreased cycle time, taking costs out:* Since processes moving goods through a supply chain are faster and more efficient, the need for large inventories is reduced.
3. *Reduced rework:* Since RFID scanning has a greater first-time-pass accuracy, fewer errors are generated and fewer retries are needed.
4. *Reduced business risk, better control of assets:* Assets can be located and controlled more easily. RFID-enabled data collection enhances the accuracy of record keeping and asset maintenance. Regulatory compliance can be achieved more effectively.
5. *Improved security:* Since information relating to an individual item can be validated, security is increased. This enables more effective access control and prevents shrinkage and

Legend:

Life-cycle phase
- **Application**
  - **Expected benefit**

Design
- Tracking product design documents
  - Better information on where design data is, how to access it, how to distribute it to all relevant parties, and how to update the data in all storage locations

Manufacturing
- Tracking in production
  - Better tracking of lead times, enabling complete lot tracking
  - Lower cost and shorter response time for replacements
  - Easier identification of components that cause failure
  - Improved picking and order accuracy
  - Ensured continuity in production and supply availability
  - Better and quicker management decisions due to accuracy and availability of information
  - Work-in-progress (WIP) tracking also possible for products undergoing treatment under special conditions
  - More competitive customer service by being able to give exact and timely information on the status of ordered products
- Quality control
  - Shorter production cycle thanks to more accurate management and tracing of WIP
  - Better quality control through incorrect-material alerts and control of mix materials
  - Better control of customer requirements
- Coping with customization
  - Composition of a product can be inspected during production, without significant delay
  - Customers receive valuable and timely information about the progress of their order
  - Easier to locate the components that caused a failure or unreliable functioning of a custom-built item

Transportation
- Distribution
  - Better asset and vehicle utilization
  - Better monitoring of container locations and transit times
  - Improved asset maintenance
  - More efficient merge-in-transit
- Material processing
  - Better management of unexpected volume fluctuations and destination changes
  - Increased data reliability
  - Improved loading and unloading processes
  - No line-of-sight needed
  - Fewer thefts
- Safety management
  - Better environment monitoring when transporting sensitive or hazardous goods
  - Improved quality of inspection and shorter inspection times
  - Better identification of damaged or contaminated containers

Storage
- Inventory management
  - Better control of WIP inventory locations, ensuring sufficient stock levels of critical items
  - More effective prevention of theft, obsolescence and losses
  - Fewer data entry errors
  - Pull-based requirements are enabled
- Warehousing: Picking
  - Improved information on inventory levels, higher precision
  - Increased order accuracy
  - Increased slot inventory and fewer misplaced items
  - Improved accuracy, ensuring that the correct goods are picked and staged in the right area
  - Goods do not need to be scanned
  - Less time needed to find items
  - Reduced material handling
- Warehousing: Receiving
  - Advance real-time notification of arrivals/delays
  - Higher accuracy of goods received due to elimination of human errors in checking, identification and storage in assigned bins
  - Reduced complexity of multiple stock-keeping units (SKUs)
  - More reliable advance shipping notices (ASNs)
  - Shorter dock-to-stock time

Fig. 11.19 (continued)

other losses. The ability to authenticate information helps to prevent counterfeiting and fraud.

6. *Improved utilization of resources:* Information obtained from the objects can be used to improve the planning of asset utilization. Likewise, business processes can be improved.
7. *Increased revenues:* RFID helps companies to avoid stock-outs. Through better item

- Warehousing: Shipping
    - Faster and more accurate loading
    - Improved accuracy, ensuring that the correct goods are loaded onto the assigned vehicle
    - Correct handover of goods from warehouse to carrier
    - Reduced congestion and customer claims
    - Direct loading from picking
    - Reduced operational expenditure to reconcile transfer and ownership
    - Automatic update of inventory management systems, automatic sending of ASNs
- Retailing: Inventory management
    - More accurate inventory levels and fewer out-of-stocks
    - Less labor needed in receiving due to enhanced visibility
    - Fewer counterfeit products
- Retailing: Shelf stock management
    - Fewer out-of-stock shelves, increased sales
    - No/fewer incorrect product locations, improved utilization of space
    - Refreshing products
- Retailing: Checkout
    - Increased checkout accuracy
    - No need for a line-of-sight
    - Fewer checkout staff due to self-check stations
    - Fewer invalid returns

Operation (product is in use)

- Recall campaigns
    - Easier identification of possible problem sources
    - Focused recall campaigns: product recall can be initiated on time and is limited to the smallest possible volume
- Resource management
    - Better use of reusable containers
    - Fewer reusable assets are lost
    - Less theft and obsolescence
    - Documented capability of containers

Maintenance and Repair

- Time-in-service management
    - Accurate service records
    - Staff is freed from paper work
    - Reduced time-in-service
    - Better after-sale service
- Warranty processing
    - Improved warranty processing by efficiently retrieving product information (authentication, warranty details, service history)
    - Better customer service

Decommissioning: Disposal or recycling

- Waste management
    - Decreased storage costs of parts
    - Focused, cost and time efficient disassembly
    - Reduced time-in-storage of dangerous waste
    - Reduced emissions

Fig. 11.19 RFID/IoT benefits in product life cycle (Ilie-Zudor and Kemény 2009, pp. 211–212)

availability, customers have more choice, avoiding lost sales and increasing revenues.

8. *Better exception management:* Information captured by RFID enables managers to be alerted when compensatory business decisions need to be taken.

In addition to these benefits, one more aspect is worth mentioning: data reliability. By *reliable data* we mean data that are unbiased. Fleisch calls this "trusted" (or "honest") data (Fleisch 2010, p. 17), meaning the data are not influenced by people's interests. This is the type of data captured with the help of RFID. It is created by machines. Employees and users cannot deliberately choose the time and place when and where the data are collected. Instead, this happens automatically as business processes are executed, for example, when an item on the shop floor is moved to the next machine, or when a shipment is received. Incoming goods data captured automatically by RFID readers are more trustworthy than data entered into a paper or electronic form.

Value Drivers of the Internet of Things Higher-level benefits derived from the Internet of Things can be observed by looking at the fundamental value drivers. Based on a study of about one hundred applications, Fleisch identified a number of value drivers including the following (Fleisch 2010, pp. 8–14):

- *Manual proximity trigger:* Smart things can share their identification number in a robust, fast, and convenient way when they are *manually* moved close to a proximity sensor (e.g., antenna, camera). As soon as the smart thing is close enough, a transaction is automatically triggered. This value driver is found in many applications, for example, checkout, access to buildings and skiing facilities, and payment procedures. Supermarket customers can check out themselves, decreasing labor cost for the company and increasing convenience for the customer.
- *Automatic proximity trigger:* Many smart things can trigger a transaction *automatically* when the distance between two things exceeds a threshold. Consider, for example, an RFID-tagged truck, a forklift, a pallet, a carton, a work-in-progress bin, or a consumer product. When the object leaves the area where it can be sensed, a transaction is initiated, such as a posting in accounting, notification of the warehouse manager, or ringing an alarm bell (when the customer leaves without paying). This leads to an increase in speed, accuracy, and convenience, reducing the cost of labor, process failures, and fraud. Productivity is enhanced as workers can be automatically supplied with work instructions, assembly plans, and other information they need for their current task.
- *Automatic sensor triggering:* Smart things that are capable of carrying data in addition to their identification number can be used to continuously collect sensor data, such as temperature, acceleration, localization, orientation, vibration, brightness, humidity, noise, smell, images, chemical composition, and life signals. A smart thing will sense its condition and environment and initiate actions using preprogrammed rules. (In "precision agriculture," a smart olive tree might continuously check the temperature, brightness, and humidity to optimally adjust its water supply.)
- *Automatic product security:* Based on the interplay between a smart thing and its "homepage" via the Internet of Things, a certain level of product-related security can be achieved. Typical applications include proof-of-origin, anti-counterfeiting, product pedigree, and access control.
- *Simple and direct user feedback:* Some smart things have simple mechanisms to give feedback to the humans who interact with them. An example is reassuring the user that a proximity trigger actually worked by producing an audio (e.g., beep) or visual signal (e.g., flashing LED) if a pallet was correctly identified by the RFID portal. When perishable goods are involved, a traffic-signal-like display may indicate the product's state in colors green, yellow, or red. In a production environment, smart assets can tell the operator where the material should be taken to next.
- *Rich user feedback:* More extensive feedback can be given when more computing power is available than what the "things" have themselves. Nowadays, this power is often provided by *smartphones*. These devices serve as gateways linking smart things with their homepages or other resources on the Internet. From these sources, information, and functionality augmenting the product can be obtained. Examples include additional information on the product (e.g., producer, dealer, product history, repair manual) as well as services such as on-the-spot price comparisons (what does the same product cost elsewhere?), political shopping advice (which country's labor produced this product?), product ratings (how did my friends like this?), and allergy and health warnings.

Automating Low-Level Management In the search for a paradigmatic goal of business informatics research, Mertens once formulated the goal of "reasonable full automation" of the enterprise (Mertens 1995, p. 48). By this he meant not only manufacturing automation and automated workflows but also a reasonable level of automating the company's management.

Being a low-level technology, RFID and the Internet of Things can definitely contribute to the automation of low-level management. On this level, many decisions are routine decisions. For example, purchase orders are placed when the inventory drops below a threshold. Actions are often based on controlling, that is, checking if the result of a task is as expected (or at least within tolerances). If this is not the case, some management action is required.

RFID technology helps the company to automate low-level management decisions and actions. Actual values obtained from RFID are compared with expected values, and deviations are detected early. Appropriate information systems react to real-world events directly, providing a basis for operational management by exception. Human managers are only called in for help when a tolerance limit is exceeded or an unknown state of affairs is recorded (Fleisch 2010, p. 21).

Challenges Facing the Internet of Things
When RFID technology was new, a major challenge was the *high cost* of the equipment. In particular, transponders were too expensive to be attached to millions of low-cost items sold by a supermarket, for example.

Transponder and tag prices have substantially decreased since then, but for many items they are still too high. Obviously, it makes little sense to put a 10-cent RFID tag on a 30-cent yogurt cup. Despite the potential business value, the cost ratio between the tag and the item is not reasonable.

Taking the cost into consideration, many of the before mentioned applications are still far from being realized. However, the use of RFID technology is undisputed today when more valuable items are involved.

Most challenges the Internet of Things is facing are societal and political issues. As with other new technologies, many people are concerned about their *privacy*. Masses of data are collected when everywhere smart products, transport means, and other equipment are RFID-tagged. Among these data are personal data, which are collected automatically and without the individual knowing that they are collected. Many people feel uncomfortable because they do not know where and by whom these data will be used in what way.

Related with this problem is the question of data ownership. Taking into account that items and their data are migrating (e.g., from the producer to the distributor to the supermarket to the household), this question is difficult to answer (Mattern and Flörkemeier 2010, p. 119). Equally difficult is the question of who has the power of disposition and who is liable for the data.

As with other advanced technologies, the IoT makes life easier (and business more effective), but the *dependence on technology* increases. Suppose a smart item only functions as intended when it is connected with its homepage. If the Internet connection fails, the item is "out of order." Likewise, software errors and malware may corrupt the item and perhaps lead to critical situations (Mattern and Flörkemeier 2010, p. 119).

Weapons and military equipment are also "things." The "smarter" these things are, the more they are susceptible to manipulation. In a *cyberwar*, opponents primarily seek to manipulate the other side's computers to make them fail or malfunction. When smart equipment is involved, it can also be manipulated and possibly controlled by the opponent.

Due to the many open questions to be answered in order to further advance the Internet of Things, a discussion on *IoT governance* has been started. Major protagonists are the United Nations' "Internet Governance Forum" (IGF—www.intgovforum.org) and a research initiative by the European Commission (called "Governance and Privacy Implications of the Internet of Things"). Both organizations state that the key issues under discussion are "whether the IoT needs a governance mechanisms and, if yes, how such a mechanism should be designed" (Euro-NF 2011).

Appendix: Data Models

ERP and SCM systems—and in fact most business information systems—are founded on databases. Therefore, data structures play an important role in the design and implementation of any ERP or SCM system.

A *data structure* defines data elements and how these elements are related with each other. On a higher level, the term also comprises the relationships between different data structures, which are then called data objects or data entities. Another term for this interpretation of "data structure" is "data model."

Data models are usually created before a database is implemented because data modeling—on a higher, nontechnical level of abstraction—is easier than directly creating the technical specifications needed for a database. When a data model is available, implementation of the database is largely straightforward.

Among the most common data models are the *entity-relationship model* and the *relational data model*. So-called *object-oriented data models* and *object models (class models)* have also been proposed, along with object-oriented programming, but they are not as common in data-intense environments such as ERP and SCM.

Entity-Relationship Model

The most common data model in the requirements stage—that is, the project stage in which the company's requirements for the new system are captured (Kurbel 2008, pp. 236–243)—is the *entity-relationship model (ERM)*. This model goes back to P.P. Chen (1976). It is a semi-graphical model that includes semantics and uses diagrams to visualize the relationships between data. Therefore, many people use the term *entity-relationship diagram (ERD)* as a synonym for entity-relationship model.

Although Chen's basic concepts were quite powerful, many real-life modeling situations proved to be more complex than what the original model was capable of describing. This is why many model extensions have been proposed over the years. Unfortunately, they are not standardized. Therefore, we will briefly summarize the modeling elements that are used in this book.

Basic concepts of the entity-relationship model include entities, relationships, and attributes.

An *entity* can be any object of the real world that is of interest to the modeler, for example, a product, a machine, or a customer. Entities can also represent abstract things, such as a quotation, an order, or a transportation lane.

Since a data model is usually created to describe general matters and relationships, and not specific objects and their relationships, we usually consider *entity types* (e.g., "supplier," material") rather than individual instances ("Gerber Inc.," "turbo charger"). In an ER diagram, entities or entity types are represented by rectangles.

A *relationship* connects two specific entities. On the level of entity types, the connections can also be regarded as types. In this case, we speak of a *relationship type*, meaning the type of relationship that exists between the two entity types involved (e.g., "provides"). Relationships and relationship types are represented by diamonds.

An *attribute* indicates a property of an entity or a relationship, for example, a name, a project number, or an address. Important attributes are

K.E. Kurbel, *Enterprise Resource Planning and Supply Chain Management*,
Progress in IS, DOI 10.1007/978-3-642-31573-2,

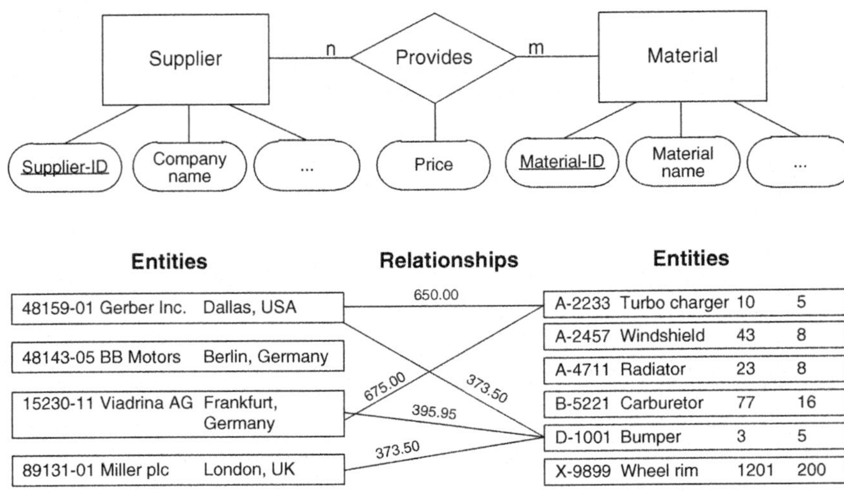

Fig. A.1 Entity-relationship diagram (example)

usually noted down inside ovals and connected with a rectangle or a diamond through a line.

Some attributes play a special role, as they are used to uniquely identify an entity or a relationship (e.g., "supplier-ID"). These attributes are called *key attributes* (or *keys*). In an ER diagram, they are usually underlined.

Figure A.1 illustrates the basic concepts of entity-relationship modeling with the help of a simple example. The upper part of the figure contains an ER diagram showing entity and relationship *types*. The lower part provides sample entities and how they are related. For example, the "Gerber Inc." entity of the "supplier" type is connected with the "turbo charger" entity of the "material" type through a particular relationship, which is characterized, among other things, by a price of 650.00 €.

Cardinalities (also called *complexities*) are used to specify the relationships between two entity types A and B more precisely. A cardinality indicates how many objects of type B an object of type A can be related with. Basic cardinalities are:

- *1:1 relationship:* An object of type A is related with exactly one object of type B and vice versa.
- *m:1 relationship:* An object of type A can be related with several objects of type B, while an object of type B can be related with only one object of type A.
- *1:n relationship:* An object of type B can be related with several objects of type A, while an object of type A can be related with only one object of type B.
- *m:n relationship:* An object of type A can be related with several objects of type B. An object of type B can be related with several objects of type A.

The relationship displayed in Fig. A.1 is an *m: n relationship*. This means that a particular supplier can provide several materials and a particular material can be obtained from more than one supplier. An assumption underlying the model is that the purchase prices have been negotiated with the suppliers, meaning that the same material can have different prices. For this reason, the price is an attribute of the relationship type and not of any of the entity types involved.

Different notations exist for representing cardinalities (and also, relationship types) in an ER diagram. The notation used in Fig. A.1 can be interpreted as follows: The number of individual relationships an entity of type A can have with entities of type B is noted down between the A rectangle and the diamond. Our example thus says that a particular supplier can be related with *n* materials, while *m* suppliers can provide a particular material.

If the company had the policy of purchasing each material exclusively from one of the supplier, the cardinality would have to be changed

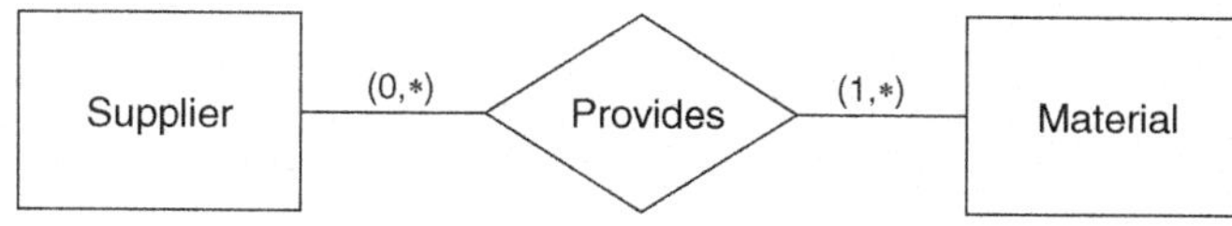

Fig. A.2 Min–max cardinalities (example)

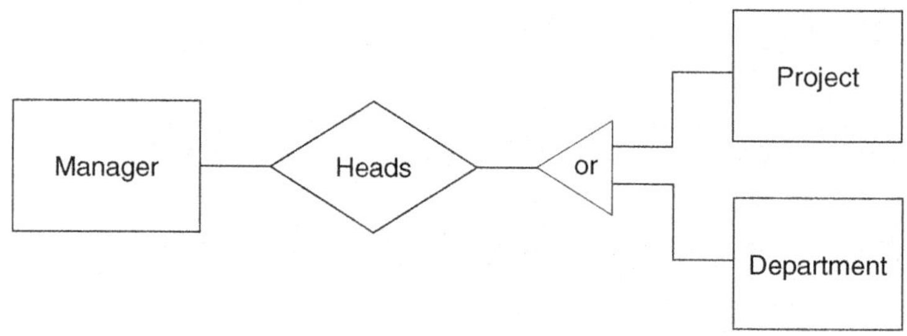

Fig. A.3 A logical connector (example)

from an *m:n* to an *m:1* cardinality. In this case, "price" is an attribute of "material," because it no longer depends on the relationship.

It is worth mentioning that in Chen's original work, cardinalities were noted down on the opposite sides. In the example of materials provided by one supplier only, "1" would be written between the diamond and the "supplier" entity type and "n" between the diamond and the "material" entity type. This notation is known as *look-across cardinality* (in contrast to *look-here cardinality* as used above).

Since it is a matter of convention, readers trying to understand ER diagrams should check which notation the author applied. This book uses the look-here cardinality type.

The simple cardinalities described so far are sufficient for sketching data structures during the initial stages of requirements engineering but are not precise enough for implementing a database. *Min–max cardinalities* provide a better way of expressing issues that would otherwise remain ambiguous. Consider, for example, the "provides" relationship above. What exactly does "m" mean? Does the relationship type allow, for example, that suppliers do not provide any material (i.e., does it include 0)?

In order to make things unambiguous, min–max cardinalities specify the precise minimum and maximum numbers of permissible relationships. In most cases, the inequalities

$$0 \leq \min \leq 1 \leq \max \leq^{*}$$

hold, with "*" standing for "many." Although min and max can be any integer numbers, depending on the context, typical min-max cardinalities are (0, 1), (0, *), (1, 1), and (1, *).

Suppose we want to model the case that a material stored in the database requires at least one supplier assigned to it. On the other hand, suppliers may be stored in the database even if they do not provide any material. This can be the case, for example, when a material has been discarded but the company wants to keep the supplier data in the database for the future. Then the cardinality on the "supplier" side is (0, *), and on the "material" side, it is (1, *), as shown in Fig. A.2.

Connectors are symbols connecting two or more entity types with a relationship type using logical operators ("and," "or," "xor"). In Fig. A.3, which models relationships between managers and the entities they are managing, a manager may be heading both a department and a project. If, however, the company wants their managers to be responsible *either* for a department *or* a project, but *not* for both, the "or" connector would have to be replaced by an "xor" connector.

Generalization means that similar types of entities are combined under a superordinate type. The opposite is *specialization*, meaning that a general entity type is split up into more specialized types. The reason for doing so is often to maintain the common attributes with the general entity type, while the attributes in which the subtypes differ are kept with the specialized types.

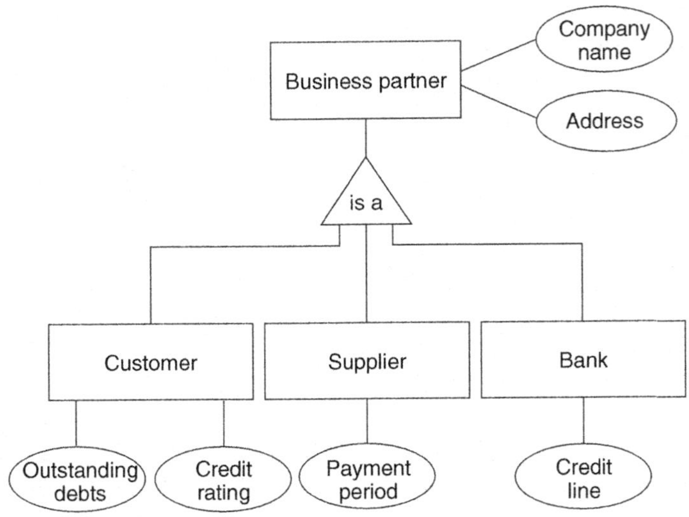

Fig. A.4 "Is a" relationship (example)

A common way of representing generalization and specialization is to use a particular relationship type called an *"is a" relation*. The meaning of this term is obviously that an object of any of the specialized types *is* also an object of the general type.

Figure A.4 illustrates generalization and specialization with the help of an example. The general type here is "business partner," while the specializations include "customer," "supplier," and "bank." Since all business partners have a name and an address, these common attributes are assigned to the "business partner" entity type. However, describing customers also requires different attributes than describing suppliers or banks. For example, outstanding debts and credit rating are meaningful attributes for a customer but not for a supplier or a bank. Regarding a supplier, the allowed payment period would be more useful, and regarding a bank, it would be the credit line.

In order to make the ERM in Fig. A.4 more accurate, logical connectors can be included. One possible ambiguity is that the model does not specify whether an entity can be both a customer and a supplier or whether a bank can also be a customer. With the help of logical connectors, these matters can be precisely defined. The extended example modeled in Fig. A.5 shows a case where a business partner can be a customer and also either a supplier or a bank at the same time. Note that the "is a" type of relationship has been written on the connecting line to avoid multiple triangles with different semantics.

It is worth mentioning that there are more ERM concepts than the ones described above. Among these are important concepts such as weak, strong, and dependent entity types and aggregation. Since these concepts have not been used in the ER diagrams of this book, they are not explained here.

Relational Data Model

The entity-relationship model is useful when nontechnical people are involved, because it provides a good overview and is easy to understand. ER modeling is common, for example, in requirements engineering when the relevant data structures have to be identified.

However, an ERM is not a model that can be directly implemented in a database management system (DBMS). The reason for this is that DBMSs organize their data structures according to different data models. The most common of these models is the *relational data model* (also known as *relational model*). Therefore, an entity-relationship model has to be mapped onto a relational model before it can be implemented.

The most fundamental notion of the relational data model is "relation." This is a mathematical

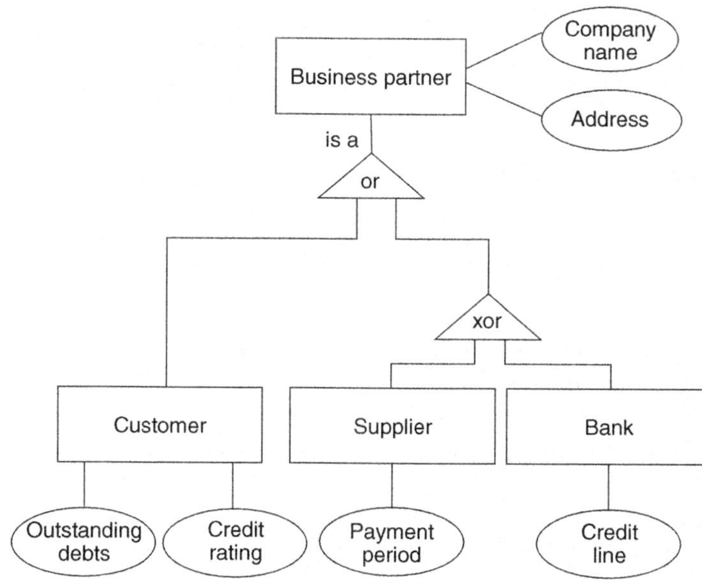

Fig. A.5 Generalization and specialization using connectors

term and not to be confused with the term "relationship" in the ER model.

To briefly explain the mathematical concept of a relation, consider an object that can be described by *n* different *attributes* A_j:

$$A_j = \{a_{ij} | i = 1, \ldots, m_j\} \ \forall j = 1, \ldots, n$$

m_j is the number of values attribute A_j can have. Attributes are the same as in the ER model (e.g., material-ID, material name, on stock, safety stock). Thus, the object can be represented as an *n-tuple* composed of entries a_{ij}, each one representing a value of one of the attributes A_j:

$$(a_{i1}, a_{i2}, \ldots, a_{in}).$$

Each attribute A_j has a *domain D*, which is the set of all possible values the attribute can take on:

$$D(A_j) = \{a_{ij}\}.$$

The *Cartesian product* over the domains of the attributes contains all possible combinations of attribute values, that is, all possible n-tuples:

$$D(A_1) \times D(A_2) \times \ldots \times D(A_n)$$

Translating this into real-life language, using the sample attributes mentioned above, the Cartesian product contains *all* combinations of supplier-IDs, company names, addresses, contacts, etc. However, a real supplier with a particular supplier-ID has only *one* address and only *one* contact (and not all possible ones).

Therefore, in a database we are not interested in all n-tuples but only in some, that is, in a subset R:

$$R(A_1, \ldots, A_n) \subseteq D(A_1) \times D(A_2) \times \ldots \times D(A_n)$$

The mathematical term for this subset is "relation." It is defined as follows:

An n-place *relation* (n-ary relation) over the domains $D(A_1), \ldots, D(A_n)$ is a subset of the *Cartesian product* $D(A_1) \times D(A_2) \times \ldots \times D(A_n)$.

Since the elements of a relation are tuples and a relation is a set, two properties immediately follow: Tuples are pairwise different (i.e., there are no duplicates), and there is no defined order of the tuples.

A common notation for relations is to write the relation's name, sometimes preceded by "R." (to indicate that it is a relation), followed by the attribute names. Key attributes are underlined, as in the entity-relationship model. For example, supplier and material relations might be defined as follows:

R.Supplier (<u>supplier-ID</u>, company name, address, contact,...)

R.Material (<u>material-ID</u>, material name, on stock, safety stock, ...)

Fig. A.6 "Material" table (relation)

Material			
Material-ID	Material Name	On Stock	Safety Stock
A-2233	Turbo charger	10	5
A-2457	Windshield	43	8
A-4711	Radiator	23	8
B-5221	Carburetor	77	16
D-1001	Bumper	3	5
X-9899	Wheel rim	1201	200

In *practice*, most people speak of "tables" instead of "relations" because the values of a relation are usually arranged and displayed in rows and columns. When the data items (i.e., the attribute values) of the entities in question are displayed and printed, the format is usually rectangular as illustrated in Fig. A.6.

Each *column* of the table contains specific values of one attribute. The name of this attribute is displayed as the column heading. Attributes are usually called *fields* or *columns*.

Each *row* represents one tuple, that is, one data object (entity). For example, the first row describes the material A-2233 (turbo charger) and the second row describes the material A-2457 (windshield). Practitioners usually speak of *rows* or *records* instead of tuples. All rows together make up the set of materials represented as a database *table*.

Mapping an ERM to a Relational Model

As mentioned above, the modeling effort usually starts with creating an entity relationship model of the problem domain. Later, this model has to be converted into a relational data model before it can be implemented in a database management system. Based on a number of mapping rules, the conversion is fairly straightforward.

1. *Mapping Entity Types*
   The general rule for mapping entity types is simple: Each entity type is mapped to one relation of the relational data model. The attributes of the entity type are adopted as attributes of the relation.
2. *Mapping Relationship Types*
   - An *m:n relationship* between two entity types A and B is mapped with the help of a connecting relation. This relation specifies through pairs "primary key of A—primary key of B" which tuple of A is connected with which tuple of B.
   - A *1:n relationship (m:1 relationship)* between two entity types A and B is mapped with the help of a foreign key attribute in A (B) that references a tuple in B (A). However, if the relationship type has been modeled to include attributes, the mapping has to be done in the same way as if it were an *m:n* relationship (see previous paragraph).
   - A *1:1 relationship* is mapped in such a way that foreign key attributes are included in the two entity types involved. This means that each tuple of A points to a tuple of B via a foreign key and vice versa.
3. *Mapping Generalization/Specialization*
   The general entity type and each specialization are mapped to separate relations. The relations representing the specialized entity types will use the same primary keys as the relation representing the general entity type.
   Example
   In order to illustrate the different mapping rules, we will refer to the example in Fig. A.1. This entity relationship model consists of two entity types and one relationship type. Since the relationship type is an m:n relationship, the resulting relational data model contains three relations:
   R.Supplier (supplier-ID, company name, address, contact, …)
   R.Material (material-ID, material name, on stock, safety stock, …)
   R.Provides (supplier-ID, material-ID, price,…)
   Figure A.7 shows these relations filled with sample data. The "provides" relation has five tuples because there are five specific connections

Fig. A.7 Supplier, material, and provides relations

Supplier

<u>Supplier-ID</u>	Company Name	Address
48159-01	Gerber Inc.	Dallas, USA
48143-05	BB Motors	Berlin, Germany
15230-11	Viadrina AG	Frankfurt, Germany
89131-01	Miller plc	London, UK

Material

<u>Material-ID</u>	Material Name	On Stock	Safety Stock
A-2233	Turbo charger	10	5
A-2457	Windshield	43	8
A-4711	Radiator	23	8
B-5221	Carburetor	77	16
D-1001	Bumper	3	5
X-9899	Wheel rim	1201	200

Provides

<u>Supplier-ID</u>	<u>Material-ID</u>	Price
48159-01	A-2233	650.00
48159-01	D-1001	373.50
15230-11	A-2233	675.00
15230-11	D-1001	395.95
89131-01	D-1001	373.50

between the four suppliers and the six materials, as already shown in Fig. A.1. For example, supplier 48159–01 (Gerber Inc.) provides material A-2233 (turbo charger) for 650.00 €. The same material is also provided by supplier 15230–11 (Viadrina AG) for 675.00 €.

References

Aarts EHL, Korst JHM (1989) Simulated annealing and Boltzmann machines—A stochastic approach to combinatorial optimization and neural computing. Wiley, Chichester, New York

Active Sensing (2009) Product lifecycle management (PLM); http://www.product-lifecycle-management.com/plm-glossary-N.htm (accessed Jan 23, 2013)

Adelsberger HH, Kanet JJ (1991) The Leitstand—a new tool for computer-integrated manufacturing. Production and Inventory Management J 32(1):43–48

Alavudeen A, Venkateshwaran N (2010) Computer integrated manufacturing. Prentice Hall, New Delhi

Ambler SW (2009) UML 2 Activity diagrams. http://www.agilemodeling.com/artifacts/activityDiagram.htm (accessed Mar 23, 2012)

Armbrust M, Fox A, Griffith R, et al. (2009) Above the clouds: A Berkeley view of cloud computing; EECS Department, University of California, Berkeley, Technical Report No. UCB/EECS-2009-28, February 10, 2009

Auto-ID Center, XPLANE.com (2002) How the EPC network will automate the supply chain. http://www.quintessenz.at/rfid-docs/www.autoidcenter.org/media/xplane/large/XPLANE-TheEPCNetwork-A.pdf (accessed Mar 23, 2012)

Auto-ID Center, XPLANE.com (2003) How efficient is your supply chain? http://www.rfidfactory.com/pdfs/XPLANE-TheEPCNetwork-B.pdf (accessed Mar 23, 2012)

Baily P, Farmer D, Crocker B, Jessup D, Jones D (2008) Procurement principles and management, 10th edn. Prentice Hall, Harlow, UK

Balla J, Layer F (2007) Production planning with SAP APO-PP/DS. Galileo, Bonn, Boston

Bareiss R (1989) Exemplar-based knowledge acquisition: a unified approach to concept representation, classification, and learning. Academic, San Diego

Behrenbeck K, Großpietsch J, Küpper J, Thonemann U (2003) Wie Hersteller und Handel kooperieren; Harvard Business Manager, September, pp. 39–47

Benz J, Höflinger M (2008) Logistikprozesse mit SAP, 2. Aufl. Vieweg+Teubner, Wiesbaden

BOC AG (2009) Supply Chain Management with ADOlog. BOC, Vienna. Available at http://www.boc-group.com/products/adolog/ (accessed Mar 23, 2012)

BOC AG (2012) Business Process Management with ADONIS; http://www.boc-group.com/adonis/ (accessed Mar 23, 2012)

Brehm N, Marx Gómez J (2007) Service-oriented development of federated ERP systems. In: Proceedings of the workshop on software engineering methods for service oriented architectures 2007 (on CD), Hannover, Germany

Brehm N, Marx Gómez J (2008) Federated ERP-systems on the basis of Web Services and P2P networks; Special Issue on "Service-Oriented Architecture and Firm Performance" of the International Journal of Information Technology and Management (IJITM) 2:28–42

Buyyaa R, Yeo CS, Venugopala S, Broberg J, Brandic I (2009) Cloud computing and emerging IT platforms: vision, hype, and reality for delivering computing as the 5th utility. Fut Gener Comput Syst 25:599–616

Chen PP (1976) The entity-relationship model – toward a unified view of data. ACM Trans Database Syst 1(1):9–36

Cheng F, Ettl M, Lin GY, Tonner M, Yao DD (2011) Designing flexible supply chain contracts with options. In: Kempf KG et al (eds) Planning production and inventories in the extended enterprise – a state of the art handbook, vol 2. Springer, New York, pp 207–229

Corsten H, Gössinger R (2008) Einführung in das Supply Chain Management, 2. Aufl. Oldenbourg, Munich, Vienna

Crnkovic I, Stafford J, Szyperski C (2011) Software components beyond programming – from routines to services. IEEE Software 28(3):22–26

Davenport TH (1993) Process innovation – reengineering work through information technology. Harvard Business School Press, Boston

DeMatteis JJ (1968) An economic lot sizing technique I – The part-period algorithm. IBM Syst J 7:30–38

Dickersbach JT (2009) Supply chain management with SAP APO – structures, modelling approaches and implementation of SAP SCM 2008, 3rd edn. Springer, Heidelberg

Dittrich J, Mertens P, Hau M, Hufgard A (2009a) Dispositions parameter von SAP R/3-PP, 5. Aufl. Vieweg +Teubner, Wiesbaden

Progress in IS, DOI 10.1007/978-3-642-31573-2,

Dittrich Y, Vaucouleur S, Giff S (2009b) ERP customization as software engineering: knowledge sharing and cooperation. IEEE Software 26(4):41–47

Economist (2011) D.T.: LG's new smart-fridge – One step closer to the home of the future. The Economist, April 22nd, 2011; http://www.economist.com/blogs/schumpeter/2011/04/lgs_new_smart-fridge (accessed Mar 23, 2012)

Euro-NF (2011) The Governance Dimension of the Internet of Things – EURO-NF & GOVPIMINT Workshop; Leipzig, Germany: March 24–25, 2011; http://www.medienstadt-leipzig.org/euronf/ (accessed Mar 23, 2012)

Factory Solutions GmbH (2012) AHP-Leitstand, Version 7.0, Product description. Available at http://www.factory-solutions.com/cms/upload/pdf/Product_AHP.pdf (accessed Mar 23, 2012)

Faisst W (2011a) Die nächste Generation der Unternehmens-Software am Beispiel von SAP Business ByDesign. Wirtschaftsinformatik und Management 4:24–30

Faisst W (2011b) SaaS, PaaS, cloud computing: the next generation of enterprise application software. Chapter 3: On-demand Solutions. Lecture at the University of Bamberg, Summer Term 2011, Powerpoint Presentation; Bamberg, Germany

Faisst W (2011c) SAP Commercial platform, Whitepaper Version 2.0; SAP AG, Walldorf, Germany

Fauser AG (2012) The JobDISPO Suite: Software for small and medium-sized enterprises; http://www.job-dispo.de/media/files/prospekte/en/JobDISPO_Suite_brochure_english.pdf (accessed Mar 23, 2012)

Ferdows K, Lewis MA, Machucha JAD (2004) Rapid-fire fulfillment. Harv Bus Rev 82(11):104–110

Finnegan D, Willcocks LP (2007) Implementing CRM: from technology to knowledge. Wiley, New York

Fitzgerald B (2006) The transformation of open source software. MIS Quarterly 30(3):587–598

Fleisch E (2010) What is the Internet of things? An Economic Perspective; Auto-ID Labs White Paper WP-BIZAPP-053; http://www.autoidlabs.org/uploads/media/AUTOIDLABS-WP-BIZAPP-53.pdf (accessed Mar 23, 2012)

Fleischmann B, Meyr H, Wagner M (2010) Advanced planning. In: [Stadtler 2010], pp 81–106

Forrester JW (1958) Industrial dynamics – a major break-through for decision makers. Harv Bus Rev July–August: 37–66

Forrester JW (1961) Industrial dynamics. MIT, Cambridge, MA

Gaddam B (2009) Capable to match (CTM) with SAP APO. Galileo Press, Bonn, Boston

Goldberg DE (1989) Genetic algorithms in search, optimization, and machine learning. Addison-Wesley, Reading, MA

Goo J, Kishore R, Rao HR, Nam K (2009) The role of service level agreements in relational management of information technology outsourcing: an empirical study. MIS Quarterly 33(1):119–145

Graupe D (2007) Principles of artificial neural networks, 2nd edn. World Scientific, Singapore

Gronau N (2009) Enterprise systems knowledge: a new way to detect changes in the ERP market in Central Europe. In: AMCIS 2009 Proceedings, Paper 203, http://aisel.aisnet.org/amcis2009/203 (accessed Mar 23, 2012)

Guillemin P, Friess P et al (2009) Internet of things – strategic research roadmap. European Commission, Brussels, http://ec.europa.eu/information_society/policy/rfid/documents/in_cerp.pdf (accessed Mar 23, 2012)

Hamady M, Leitz A (2009) Supplier collaboration with SAP SNC. Galileo Press, Boston

Hammer M (1990) Reengineering work: don't automate, obliterate. Harv Bus Rev 68:104–112

Hammer M, Champy J (1993) Reengineering the corporation – a manifesto for business revolution. Nicholas Brealey, London

Holloway S (2006) RFID: an introduction. http://msdn.microsoft.com/en-us/library/aa479355.aspx (accessed Mar 23, 2012)

Homer Computer Services (2007) Advanced planning system software selection guide; http://www.homercomputer.com.au/pdf/wapssamples.pdf (accessed Aug 16, 2007)

Hoppe M (2007) Sales and inventory planning with SAP APO. Galileo Press, Boston

Howson C (2008) Successful business intelligence – secrets to making BI a killer application. McGraw-Hill, New York

Hufgard A, Krüger S (2012) SAP business ByDesign. Galileo Press, Bonn

Hüllenkremer M (2003) Erfolgreiche Unternehmen arbeiten mit Produktkonfiguratoren. Industrie Management 19:37–40

Ilie-Zudor E, Kemény Z (2009) Potential of RFID Applications over a Product's life-cycle and relevance in an IOT context. In: Macchi M, Pinto R (eds) 11th International conference on the modern information technology in the innovation processes of the industrial enterprises. MITIP, Bergamo, Italy, pp 209–218

Inmon DW (2009) SAP NetWeaver and DW 2.0 – Comparing SAP's architecture evolution to the latest generation of data warehousing; Inmon Consulting Services 6/2009. Available at http://www.sap.com/platform/netweaver/components/businesswarehouse/index.epx (accessed Mar 23, 2012)

Joseph J (2009) Patterns for high availability, scalability, and computing power with windows Azure; MSDN magazine (2009) May; online available at http://msdn.microsoft.com/de-de/magazine/dd727504.aspx (accessed Mar 23, 2012)

Juels A (2006) RFID: A general overview; RSA Security Inc.; http://www.cs.umass.edu/~kevinfu/talks/rfid-tutorial/usenix-RFID-introduction.pdf (accessed Mar 23, 2012)

Kagermann H (2009) Von der Idee zur Innovation – Presentation at the Annual General Meeting of Shareholders, May 19, 2009; http://www.sap.com/corporate-en/investors/governance/meetings/index.epx (accessed Mar 23, 2012)

Kagermann H, Österle H (2006) Geschäftsmodelle 2010 – Wie CEOs Unternehmen transformieren. Frankfurter Allgemeine Buch, Frankfurt

Kallrath J, Maindl TI (2006) Real optimization with SAP APO. Springer, Berlin

Kandray DE (2010) Programmable automation. Industrial Press, New York

Kernler H (2000) PPS der 3. Generation – Grundlagen, Methoden, Anregungen, 3rd edn. Hüthig, Heidelberg

Khan A (2002) Implementing SAP with an ASAP methodology focus. iUniverse, Lincoln, NE

Khan KM, Malluhi Q (2010) Establishing trust in cloud computing. IT Professional 12(5):20–27

Kirkpatrick S, Gellat SD, Vecchi MP (1983) Optimization by simulated annealing. Science 220(5):671–680

Kletti J (2010) Manufacturing execution system – MES. Springer, Berlin

Knolmayer G (1985) Ein Vergleich von 30 "praxisnahen" Lagerhaltungsheuristiken. In: Ohse D et al (eds) Operations research proceedings 1984. Springer, Berlin, pp 223–230

Knolmayer G, Mertens P, Zeier A (2000) Supply Chain Management auf der Basis von SAP-Systemen. Springer, Berlin

Knolmayer G, Mertens P, Zeier A, Dickersbach JT (2009) Supply chain management based on SAP systems – architecture and planning processes. Springer, Berlin

Kuhn A, Hellingrath B (2002) Supply Chain Management – Optimierte Zusammenarbeit in der Wertschöpfungskette. Springer, Berlin

Kurbel K (1993) Production scheduling in a Leitstand system using a neural-net approach. In: Balagurusamy E, Sushila B (Eds.) Artificial intelligence technology – applications and management, Proceedings of the 4th international computing congress, Hyderabad, India, 1993, pp 297–305

Kurbel K (1998) A computational study of the effects of parameters on the performance of intelligent algorithms. In: Cantu FJ et al (eds) Application of advanced information technologies – Fourth World Congress on expert systems, Mexico City 1998, vol 1. Cognizant Communication, New York, pp 407–414

Kurbel K (2008) The making of information systems – software engineering and management in a globalized world. Springer, Berlin

Kurbel K, Meynert J (1989) Engpassorientierte Auftragsterminierung und Kapazitätsdisposition. In: Kurbel K et al (eds) Interaktive betriebswirtschaftliche Informations- und Steuerungssysteme. De Gruyter, Berlin, pp 69–87

Kurbel K, Ruppel A (1996) Integrating intelligent job-scheduling into a real-world production-scheduling system. J Intelligent Manufactur 7:373–377

Kurbel K, Dabkowski A, Jankowska AM (2003) A multi-tier architecture for mobile enterprise resource planning. In: Uhr W et al (eds) Wirtschaftsinformatik 2003/Band I – Medien, Märkte, Mobilität. Physica, Heidelberg, pp 75–93

Kurbel K, Schreber D, Ulrich B (2006) A Web services Façade for an open source ERP system. In: Proceedings of the 12th Americas conference on information systems, Acapulco, Mexico, August 4–6, 2006; ISBN 970-31-0621-8, pp 2547–2554

Kurbel K, et al. (Eds.)(2011): Enzyklopädie der Wirtschaftsinformatik, 6th edn. Oldenbourg, München. http://www.enzyklopaedie-der-wirtschaftsinformatik.de (accessed Oct 23, 2012)

Land AH, Doig AG (1960) An automatic method of solving discrete programming problems. Econometrica 28(3):497–520

Lawton G (2008) Developing software online with platform-as-a-service technology. Computer 41(6):13–15

Lee HL, Padmanabhan V, Whang S (1997a) The Bullwhip effect in supply chains. Sloan Manage Rev Spring: 93–102

Lee HL, Padmanabhan V, Whang S (1997b) Information distorsion in a supply chain – The Bullwhip effect. Manage Sci 43:546–557

Lewis S (2004) A basic introduction to RFID technology and its use in the supply chain, White Paper, 2004. http://www.idii.com/wp/LaranRFID.pdf (accessed Mar 23, 2012)

Loos P (2011) Kanban. In: [Kurbel 2012] (accessed Nov 30, 2012)

Magal SR, Word J (2009) Essentials of business processes and information systems. Wiley, Hoboken, NJ

Magal SR, Word J (2012) Integrated business processes with ERP systems. Wiley, Hoboken, NJ

Martin J (1989) Information engineering, Book I: Introduction. Prentice Hall, Englewood Cliffs, NJ

Matsui Y, Sato O (2002) An international comparison study on benefits of production information systems. Int J Operat Quantitat Manage 8(3):191–214

Mattern F, Flörkemeier C (2010) Vom Internet der Computer zum Internet der Dinge. Informatik Spektrum 33 (2):107–121

McCormack K, Wilkerson T, Marrow D, Davey M, Shah M, Yee D (2008) Managing risk in your organization with the SCOR methodology. Working Paper, June 2008. Available at http://supply-chain.org/f/Supply Chain Risk Project Report.pdf (accessed Mar 23, 2012)

McDermott J (1981) R1 – The formative years. AI Magazine 2(2):21–29

Mendling J (2007) Detection and prediction of errors in EPC business process models; Ph.D. Dissertation, Vienna University of Economics and Business Administration (WU Wien)

Mertens P (1995) Wirtschaftsinformatik – Von den Moden zum Trend. In: König W (ed) Wirtschaftsinformatik '95 – Wettbewerbsfähigkeit, Innovation. Wirtschaftlichkeit, Physica, Heidelberg, pp 25–64

Mertens P (2009) Integrierte Informationsverarbeitung 1 – Operative Systeme in der Industrie, 17. Aufl. Gabler, Wiesbaden

Meyr H, Wagner M, Rohde J (2010) Structure of advanced planning systems. In: [Stadtler 2010], pp 109–115

MPDV Mikrolab GmbH (2009) HYDRA – Machine data collection; Mosbach, Germany. Available at http://www.mpdv-usa.com/PDF-Files/HYDRA-MDE-Brochure_English.pdf (accessed Mar 23, 2012)

MPDV Mikrolab GmbH (2010) The quality management system HYDRA-CAQ; http://www2.mpdv.de/en/products/hydra_caq/default.htm (accessed Mar 23, 2012)

Murray M (2009) Discover logistics with SAP ERP. Galileo Press, Boston

Nahmias S (2008) Production and operations analysis, 6th edn. McGraw Hill, New York

National Intelligence Council (NIC) (2008) Disruptive civil technologies – Six technologies with potential impacts on US interests out to 2025. Conference Report CR 2008–07, April 2008; http://www.dni.gov/nic/confreports_disruptive_tech.html (accessed Mar 23, 2012)

Nayak S, Gangadhar G, Puttamadappa C (2011) Intelligent refrigerator with monitoring capability through Internet. Int J Comput Appl 2:65–68, Special Issue on "Wireless Information Networks & Business Information System"

Object Management Group (OMG) (2011a) Business Process Model and Notation (BPMN), Version 2.0; OMG Document Number: formal/2011-01-03, January 2011; http://www.omg.org/spec/BPMN/2.0 (accessed Mar 23, 2012)

Object Management Group (2011b) CORBA Basics; http://www.omg.org/gettingstarted/corbafaq.htm (accessed Mar 23, 2012)

Ohno T, Bodek N (1988) Toyota production system – Beyond large-scale production. Productivity, Portland

Presser M (Ed.) (2011) Inspiring the Internet of things; Alexandra Institute. Available at www.alexandra.dk/uk/services/ Publications/Documents/IoT_Comic_Book.pdf (accessed Mar 23, 2012)

Raymond ES (2000) The cathedral and the bazaar, Version 3.0, September 2000; http://www.catb.org/~esr/writings/cathedral-bazaar/cathedral-bazaar/cathedral-bazaar.ps (accessed Mar 23, 2012)

Riesbeck CK, Schank RC (1989) Inside case-based reasoning. Erlbaum, Hillsdale, NJ

Russell N, ter Hofstede AHM (2009) Surmounting BPM challenges: the YAWL Story. Comput Sci Res Develop 23(2):67–79

SAP Deutschland KG (2001) Supply chain event management mit mySAP Supply Chain Management. SAP AG, Walldorf

SAP Deutschland AG & Co. KG (2003) Plattform-Interoperabilität von SAP NetWeaver mit IBM WebSphere und Microsoft .NET, SAP White Paper. SAP AG, Walldorf

SAP AG (2006) SAP NetWeaver and enterprise services architecture – SAP solution in detail, SAP NetWeaver. SAP AG, Walldorf

SAP AG (2010) SAP event management: power and sophistication to manage your extended supply chain – SAP Solution in detail, SAP Supply Chain Management. SAP AG, Walldorf. Online available at http://www.sap.com/solutions/business-suite/scm/brochures/ (accessed Mar 11, 2012)

SAP AG (2012a) ERP software from SAP – a foundation to execute your business strategy. http://www.sap.com/solutions/business-suite/erp/ (accessed Mar 10, 2012)

SAP AG (2012b) SAP Documentation – SAP Library. http://help.sap.com/saphelp_ewm70/helpdata/en/, http://help.sap.com/saphelp_scm70/helpdata/en/, http://help.sap.com/saphelp_em70/helpdata/en/ (accessed Mar 12, 2012)

SAP AG (2012c) SAP NetWeaver – adaptive technology for the networked enterprise. http://www.sap.com/platform/netweaver/ (accessed Mar 12, 2012)

SAP AG (2012d) SAP supply chain management – Solution Map. http://www.sap.com/solutions/business-suite/scm/ (accessed Mar 15, 2012)

SAP Deutschland AG & Co. KG (2012e) SAP ERP Solution Map. http://www.sap.com/germany/solutions/business-suite/erp/businessmaps/ (accessed Mar 11, 2012)

SAP University Alliances (2011) SCM-IDES-Fallstudien v70—CPG3: SNP Planning (training material). SAP University Alliances EMEA, Walldorf, Germany

Schatz A, Egri P, Sauer M (2011) Open source ERP – Reasonable tools for manufacturing SMEs? Fraunhofer Institute for Manufacturing Engineering and Automation IPA 2011, Stuttgart, Germany. Online available at http://www.ipa.fraunhofer.de/fileadmin/www.ipa.fhg.de/pdf/Studien/OpenSource-ERP_Study_2011.pdf (accessed Mar 23, 2012)

Scheer A-W (1976) Produktionsplanung auf der Grundlage einer Datenbank des Fertigungsbereichs. Oldenbourg, München, Wien

Scheer A-W (1985) Computer: a challenge for business administration. Springer, Berlin

Scheer A-W (1994) CIM – Computer integrated manufacturing – towards the factory of the future, 3rd edn. Springer, Berlin

Scheer A-W (2000) ARIS: business process modeling, 3rd edn. Springer, Berlin

Silver B (2009) SAP Netweaver BPM White Paper; Bruce Silver Associates. Available at http://www.sap.com/platform/netweaver/brochures/index.epx (accessed Mar 23, 2012)

Singh K (1997) New trends in cell placement techniques as part of IC layout design methodologies. Ph.D. Thesis, Devi Ahilya University Indore, India, January 1997

Software AG (2012) ARIS Business Architect & Designer. http://www.softwareag.com/us/products/aris_platform/aris_design/business_architect/overview/default.asp (accessed Mar 23, 2012)

Stadtler H, Kilger C (eds) (2010) Supply chain management and advanced planning – concepts, models, software and case studies, 4th edn. Springer, Berlin

Stankov IE, Datsenka R, Kurbel K (2012) Service level agreement as an instrument to enhance trust in cloud computing – An analysis of infrastructure-as-a-service providers. proceedings of AMCIS 2012 – 18th Americas conference on information systems, Seattle, WA, Aug 9–11, 2012

Suh S-H, Kang S-K, Chung D-H, Stroud I (2010) Theory and design of CNC systems. Springer, London

Supply-Chain Council (2008) The SCOR Project Roadmap. In: Supply-Chain Council: executive overview, 2006, p 34; http://www.supply-chain.org/node/3946 (accessed Mar 23, 2012)

Supply-Chain Council (2010) Supply chain operations reference (SCOR) model – SCOR overview – Version 10.0. Supply Chain Council, Cypress, TX

Supply-Chain Council (2011) SCOR 10.0 overview, Executive presentation; http://supply-chain.org/f/15-%20SCOR%20Overview.pdf (accessed Mar 23, 2012)

Sweeney R (2010) Achieving service-oriented architecture: applying an enterprise architecture approach. Wiley, Hoboken, NJ

Takeda H (2006) The synchronized production system – going beyond just-in-time through Kaizen. Kogan Page, London, 2006

Theuer H, Klaukien M, Lass S (2010) Marktrecherche product lifecycle management system. Productivity Manage 15(2):33–36

Thonemann U (2010) Operations Management: Konzepte, Methoden und Anwendungen, 2. Aufl. Pearson, München

Trovarit AG (2012a) ERP-Matchmaker. http://www.erp-matchmaker.com/alle-softwareloesungen.html (accessed Mar 23, 2012)

Trovarit AG (2012b) IT-Matchmaker. http://www.trovarit.com/software-suchen/lastenheftvorlagen-erp.html (accessed Mar 23, 2012)

Vajna S, Weber C, Bley H, Zeman K (2009) CAx für Ingenieure – Eine praxisbezogene Einführung, 2. Aufl. Springer, Berlin

Verein Deutscher Ingenieure (2007) VDI-Richtlinien – Fertigungsmanagementsysteme – Manufacturing Execution Systems (MES), VDI 5600, ICS 35.240.50; Düsseldorf: Verein Deutscher Ingenieure e.V. 2007. Online available at http://www.vdi.de/uploads/tx_vdirili/pdf/1381197.pdf (accessed Mar 23, 2012)

Voluntary Interindustry Commerce Standards (VICS) Association (2004) Collaborative planning, forecasting and replenishment (CPFR) – An overview, 18 May 2004; http://www.vics.org/docs/committees/cpfr/CPFR_Overview_US-A4.pdf (accessed Mar 23, 2012)

vom Brocke J (2008) Total-Cost-of-Ownership von Anwendungssystemen. In: [Kurbel 2012] (accessed Nov 15, 2012)

Wiendahl H-P (1995) Load-oriented manufacturing control. Springer, Berlin

Wight OW (1984) Manufacturing resource planning: MRP II – unlocking America's productivity potential, Revised Edition. Wiley, New York

Winkler S (2006) An introduction to RFID. SearchSAP.com, Newton, MA; http://searchsap.techtarget.com/feature/An-Introduction-to-RFID (accessed Mar 23, 2012)

Wood DC (2007) SAP SCM – Applications and modeling for supply chain management (with BW Primer). Hoboken, NJ, Wiley

Wooldridge MJ (2009) An introduction to MultiAgent systems, 2nd edn. Wiley, Chichester, UK

World Wide Web Consortium (W3C) (2004) Web services glossary. http://www.w3.org/TR/2004/NOTE-ws-gloss-20040211/ (accessed April 11, 2012)

World Wide Web Consortium (W3C) (2006) Naming and addressing: URIs, URLs, ..., 27 Feb, 2006 http://www.w3.org/Addressing/ (accessed Mar 23, 2012)

Wu H, Cao L (2009) Community collaboration for ERP implementation. IEEE Software 26(4):48–55

Zangemeister C (1976) Nutzwertanalyse in der Systemtechnik, 4. Aufl. Wittemannsche Buchhandlung, München

Zimmermann G (1989) Neue Ansätze zur Strukturierung von PPS-Systemen. FB/IE 38(2):72–77

Index

K.E. Kurbel, *Enterprise Resource Planning and Supply Chain Management*, Progress in IS, DOI 10.1007/978-3-642-31573-2, © Springer-Verlag Berlin Heidelberg 2013

CPSIA information can be obtained at www.ICGtesting.com
Printed in the USA
LVOW03s0253311014

411370LV00005B/68/P